Mind,
Language and Reality

Philosophical Papers, Volume 2

Photo: Joseph Weizenbaum

Hilary Putnam has been Professor of Philosophy at Harvard University since 1965. He formerly held positions at Northwestern University, and Princeton University, and was Professor of the Philosophy of Science at M.I.T. from 1961 to 1965.

He was first trained in the philosophy of science by the late Hans Reichenbach, and in logic by W. V. Quine. He began serious research in mathematical logic as a result of encouragement and stimulation from the work of George Kreisel and Martin Davis. Since 1960 he has been particularly concerned with the philosophy of mathematics.

He has published articles in a wide range of philosophical, mathematical and scientific journals. His short introduction *Philosophy of Logic* was published by Harper and Row in 1971.

Mind, Language and Reality

Philosophical Papers, Volume 2

HILARY PUTNAM

Professor of Philosophy, Harvard University

CAMBRIDGE UNIVERSITY PRESS

CAMBRIDGE

LONDON · NEW YORK · MELBOURNE

Published by the Syndics of the Cambridge University Press
Bentley House, 200 Euston Road, London NW1 2DB
American Branch: 32 East 57th Street, New York, N.Y. 10022

© Cambridge University Press 1975

Library of Congress Catalogue Card Number: 75–8316

ISBN: 0 521 20668 5

First published 1975

Printed in the United States of America
by Halliday Lithograph Corporation
West Hanover, Massachusetts

Contents

To my Mother

Introduction: Philosophy of language and the rest of philosophy

For over a hundred years, one of the dominant tendencies in the philosophy of science has been verificationism: that is, the doctrine that to know the meaning of a scientific proposition (or of any proposition, according to most verificationists) is to know what would be evidence for that proposition. Historically, verificationism has been closely connected with positivism: that is, at least originally, the view that all that science really does is to describe regularities in human experience. Taken together, these views seem close to idealism. However, many twentieth-century verificationists have wanted to replace the reference to experience in the older formulations of these doctrines with a reference to 'observable things' and 'observable properties'. According to this more recent view, scientific statements about the color of flowers or the eating habits of bears are to be taken at face value as referring to flowers and bears; but scientific statements about such 'unobservables' as electrons are not to be taken as referring to electrons, but rather as referring to meter readings and the observable results of cloud chamber experiments. It is not surprising that philosophers who took this tack found themselves in a certain degree of sympathy with psychological behaviorism. Just as they wanted to 'reduce' statements about such unobservables as electrons to statements about 'public observables' such as meter readings, so they wanted to reduce statements about phenomena which, whatever their private status, were publicly unobservable, such as a person's sensations or emotions, to statements about such public observables as bodily behaviors.

At this point, they found themselves in a certain bind. On the one hand, the doctrine that talk about sensations or emotions is simply talk about a person's behavior is so implausible that almost no philosopher has been able to maintain it, or at least to maintain it for long. On the other hand, if the intuition behind recent verificationism is right, and to know the meaning of a statement is to know what would be *public* evidence for it, then it seems as if there has to be something right about behaviorism. And so philosophers tried to develop a philosophy to this effect – a philosophy that would say that 'naive behaviorism' was false but that nevertheless there was *some* kind of semantical or logical relation between statements about emotions and feelings and statements about behavior.

In my opinion, verificationism and behaviorism are fundamentally misguided doctrines. In the first volume of these collected papers I have tried to do a certain amount of philosophy of science from a nonverificationist and nonpositivist point of view, but without developing in detail a theory of meaning alternative to the positivists'. The papers in the present volume, while written over a number of years and betraying a number of changes of mind, have been largely concerned with the development of such a theory of meaning, a nonverificationist theory of meaning, and with the critique of verificationist philosophy of mind.

The defects of verificationism

One of the defects of verificationism that was early noticed by the more sophisticated verificationists themselves, and especially by Hans Reichenbach, was a certain distortion of the character of actual scientific methodology and inference. Naive verificationism would say that the statement 'There is current flowing in this wire' means 'The voltmeter needle is displaced', or something of that kind. That is, the relation between the so-called theoretical statement that current is flowing in the wire and the evidence for it is assimilated to the relation between 'John is a bachelor' and 'John is a man who has never been married'. Now the latter relation is itself not as simple a thing as it may seem at first blush (cf. the paper 'The analytic and the synthetic' in this volume), but it is roughly right that the relation is a *conventional*† one: 'John is a bachelor' is equated by some kind of conventional agreement with 'John is a man who has never been married'. But, as Reichenbach pointed out in *Experience and Prediction*, the relation between the theoretical statement and the evidence for it (say, 'There is current flowing in the wire' and 'The voltmeter needle is displaced') is a probabilistic inference within a theory. It is not that we equate the *sound-sequence* 'There is current flowing in this wire' with 'The voltmeter needle is displaced' by an act of conventional stipulation; it is rather that we accept a theory of electricity and of the structure of voltmeters from which it follows that, with a high probability, the voltmeter needle will be displaced if there is current flowing in the wire, and vice versa. To represent what are in fact probabilistic inferences within theories as logical equivalences is a serious distortion. To

† The conventionality of analytical sentences is well explicated, in my opinion, in Lewis (1969).

represent these inferences as purely conventional meaning equivalences is an even more serious distortion.

Some of the criticisms that I make of behaviorism in this volume really require little more than the critique of naive verificationism just alluded to. In particular, 'Dreaming and "depth grammar"', and 'Brains and behavior' represent criticisms of philosophical behaviorism from a nonverificationist standpoint; but those criticisms would be accepted, I believe, by a sophisticated verificationist like Reichenbach or Carnap.

But sophisticated verificationism found that it had escaped from one difficulty to land in another. If *meaning* is conflated or confounded with *evidence*, and what is evidence for a statement is a function of the total theory in which the statement occurs, then every significant change in theory becomes a change in the meaning of all the constituent words and statements of the theory. One of the early verificationists, Charles Peirce, anticipated this difficulty in the last century when he came to the conclusion that every change in a person's 'information' is a change in 'the meaning of his words'. But the distinction between the meaning of a man's words and what he believes about the facts, the distinction between disagreement in the meanings of words and disagreement about the facts, is precisely central to any concept of linguistic *meaning*. If we come to the conclusion that that distinction is untenable then, as Quine has long urged, we should abandon the notion of meaning altogether. With the exception of Quine, most verificationists have found this course unattractive. Thus they were caught in a serious dilemma – caught between their desire to continue talking about meaning in something like the traditional way, and their adherence to the network theory of meaning which taken seriously implies that nothing can be made of the notion of linguistic meaning.

For a realist, the situation is quite different. No matter how much our theory of electrical charge may change, there is one element in the meaning of the term 'electrical charge' that has not changed in the last two hundred years, according to a realist, and that is the reference. 'Electrical charge' *refers to the same magnitude* even if our theory of that magnitude has changed drastically. And we can identify that magnitude in a way that is independent of all but the most violent theory change by, for example, singling it out as the magnitude which is causally responsible for certain effects.

But the realist has his problems too. Traditionally realists thought that reference was determined by mental or Platonic entities, intensions. This doctrine of fixed 'meanings', either in the head or in the realm of abstract entities (and somehow connected to the head), determining reference once and for all, is open, interestingly enough, to some of the same objections that can be brought to bear against verificationism.

Thus, very recently realists have begun to redevelop their theory of meaning. Instead of seeing meanings as entities which determine reference, they now are beginning to see meanings as largely determined by reference, and reference as largely determined by causal connections. This sort of nonverificationist theory of meaning is presented briefly in 'Explanation and reference' and at more length in 'The meaning of "meaning"'.

I would not wish to give the impression that the only problem with verificationism is its inability to give a correct account of our customary notion of meaning, however. Truth and falsity are the most fundamental terms of rational criticism, and any adequate philosophy must give some account of these, or failing that, show that they can be dispensed with. In my opinion, verificationism has not succeeded in doing either. There is a sense in which Tarski's technical work in mathematical logic enables one to explicate the notion of truth in the context of a language with fixed meanings, and as long as there is no doubt that the terms of that language have clear reference. (Even in that context, one may question whether we have been given an account of what 'true' means, or simply a substitute for the word 'true' designed for that specific context.) But if the meaning of words is a function of the theory in which they occur, and changes as that theory changes, then if we limit ourselves to Tarski's methods, 'true' and 'false' can only be defined in the context of a particular theory. In particular, Tarskian semantics gives no explanation of the meanings of 'true' and 'false' when they are used to compare and criticize different theories, if meaning is really theory-dependent. But it is just the extra-theoretic notions of truth and falsity which are indispensible for rational criticism,† which is why they have always been taken as fundamental in the science of logic. In particular, a verificationist cannot explain why, if even the commonest scientific terms (e.g. 'voltage', 'density', 'pressure') have different meanings in the context of different theories, it should ever be justified to *conjoin* a proposition verified by one group of scientists and a proposition verified by a different group of scientists.‡ The simple fact that

---

† When I say that truth and falsity are the fundamental terms of rational criticism, I don't mean that we always are able to judge that a theory or doctrine is true or false; often we are lucky to be able to say that something is 'probably true' or 'approximately true'. But the semantics of probable truth and approximate truth presupposes the semantics of truth and falsity; these notions make no sense if truth and falsity make no sense.

‡ Suppose the first group of scientists are experts in paleontology, and they confirm a sentence S_1 in the context of Ph (basic physics) and Pa (paleontology), then the whole theory to which S_1 belongs is S_1 & *Ph* & *Pa*. Suppose a second group of scientists are experts on radioactivity, and they confirm a sentence S_2 in the context of *Ph* and *Ad*

the conjunction of true statements is true becomes replaced by the mysterious fact that scientists are in the habit of conjoining statements which use words with different meanings and somehow, nevertheless, manage to get successful results. (This and related criticisms of verificationism are put forward in two papers in the present volume, 'Explanation and reference' and 'Logical positivism and the philosophy of mind'. In an insightful unpublished essay titled 'Realism and Scientific Epistemology', Richard Boyd has argued that these defects of verificationism and positivism are symptomatic of a deeper defect; that even if verificationism could give a correct *description* of the practice of scientists, it lacks any ideas which would enable one to explain or understand why scientific practice *succeeds*.)

Philosophy of mind

Let us now leave the topic of verificationism, and ask the more general question 'How much can the philosophy of language tell us about the philosophy of mind?' (This question is discussed in general terms in 'Language and reality' and 'Logical positivism and the philosophy of mind'.) Certain facts lie more or less on the surface. It is conceivable that one could produce an imitation of a tree that would fool even a careful observer – say, a tree made of plastic, or better, of some new synthetic material that looked and felt like bark. Thus it is not a logically necessary truth (and probably not even a truth) that anything that a normal observer who is paying attention cannot distinguish from a tree is a tree. But anything that a normal person who is paying attention cannot distinguish from a pain – that is, anything that he or she cannot distinguish from a real honest-to-God pain – is necessarily a pain. If the term T is used in such a way that anything that a normal person who is paying attention cannot tell from a member of the extension of T *counts* as a member of the extension of T, then let us say that the term T has the *appearance-logic*. In this terminology, what has just been said may be restated thus: the term 'pain', like many other sensation terms, has the appearance-logic.

The fact that many sensation terms have the appearance-logic accounts, of course, for the 'incorrigibility' of certain sentences containing these terms, such as it is. (Oddly enough, this simple and metaphysically neutral explanation of 'incorrigibility' – that many sensation terms have the appearance-logic – appears to have been overlooked by

(advanced physical theory). So S_2 belongs to the theory S_2 & *Ph* &*Ad*. Since these are different theories, any term common to S_1 and S_2 must have *different meanings* in the two contexts, if meaning is theory-dependent. So concluding that S_1 & S_2 is true (in the context S_1 & S_2 & *Pa* &*Ph* & *Ad*) from the fact that S_1 and S_2 separately have been 'verified' would be a fallacy.

many philosophers.) Some philosophers of a materialist stamp have suggested that 'I have a pain in my arm' means that I am in the sort of state (i.e. the sort of physical state) that normally produces certain effects, or the sort of state that normally has certain causes, or the sort of state that normally has certain causes and certain effects. This theory cannot be right, for it would make the statement that I have a pain in my arm a *hypothesis*, and a rather risky one at that. Similarly 'I have a pain' cannot mean that I am in a state which obeys certain psychological laws, nor can it mean that I have certain behavior dispositions, for the same reason. Certain philosophers have suggested that the word 'pain' does not have the same meaning in 'I have a pain' and in 'You have a pain', in order to avoid this argument. But this far-fetched move appears to be totally unnecessary. I think that we should, rather, take seriously the idea that the word 'pain' is a *name*. It is the name of a sensation; it has a very important reporting use; it names the very sensation that that reporting use reports.

Of course there are many problems about the theory of reference in connection with names. (Saul Kripke has made a very important contribution to this topic in his 'Naming and Necessity'.) More needs to be done on the nature of names, and of reference, and of names of sensations in particular. But one thing is clear: if sensation terms are names, then that is no need to regard them as synonymous with or in any way logically connected to *descriptions*, whether those be descriptions in terms of brain states, or descriptions in terms of psychological theories, or descriptions in terms of behavior dispositions.

Against this, one hears the following line of argument, which goes back to the later Wittgenstein: sensation terms, say 'pain', are terms we learn from other people. Other people tell whether or not a speaker is using one of those words correctly on the basis of his behavior. But, now, the criteria that other speakers use to tell whether or not a speaker is using a word correctly are connected with the meaning of that word if anything is. So behavioral criteria *must* be connected with the meaning of such words as 'pain'.

It would be instructive to go through all the things that are wrong with this argument, but for the moment let me point out that there is a certain equivocation on the notion of a *criterion* here. A criterion may be either an abstract criterion (e.g. is the speaker using the word 'pain' to refer to *pain*?); or it may be an operational criterion, (e.g. does the speaker behave in such and such a way when he reports 'I have a pain'?). That the abstract criterion states a necessary condition for having a normal usage of the word pain I do not doubt; but without assuming the truth of some form of verificationism, I see no way to get from that harmless conclusion to the behaviorist conclusion that there is some logical relation between the statement that one is in pain and some particular behavior or behavior disposition. Of course, speakers must have some operational criteria or other to tell whether or not other speakers are using the language correctly. What is at issue is whether every change in such operational criteria has to be counted as a change in the meaning of words. In 'The meaning of "meaning"' I argue for a negative answer in the case of natural kind words; and I would similarly argue for a negative answer in the case of sensation words.

So far our conclusions are mainly negative. One cannot conclude from an examination of the meaning of psychological words that what they refer to are brain states, or that what they refer to are behavior dispositions, or that what they refer to are functional states, i.e. states characterized by psychological theories. No important theory of the nature of mind can either be confirmed or ruled out by an examination of the meanings of mental words.

Nevertheless I do argue for a particular theory of the nature of mental states in these papers. The theory for which I argue is a form of functionalism – not functionalism as a doctrine about the meanings of psychological words, but functionalism as a synthetic hypothesis about the nature of mental states.

According to functionalism, the behavior of, say, a computing machine is not explained by the physics and chemistry of the computing machine. It is explained by the machine's *program*. Of course, that program is realized in a particular physics and chemistry, and could, perhaps, be deduced from that physics and chemistry. But that does not make the program a physical or chemical property of the machine; it is an abstract property of the machine. Similarly, I believe that the psychological properties of human beings are not physical and chemical properties of human beings, although they may be realized by physical and chemical properties of human beings. Although any behavior of a computing machine that can be explained by the program of that computing machine can, in principle, be predicted on the basis of the physics and chemistry of the machine; the latter prediction may be highly unexplanatory. Understanding why the machine, say, computes the decimal expansion of π, may require reference to the abstract or functional properties of the machine, to the machine's program and not to its physical and chemical make up.

I was originally led to functionalism by a desire to defend materialism, but the considerations just mentioned seem to me to constitute a refutation of one kind of classical materialism, viz. reductionism. Although our psychological properties have their realization in our biological make up, psychology has, if my present view is right, an *autonomous* explanatory function. This change in my view is described in the paper 'Philosophy and our mental life'. (Having come this far I was pleasantly surprised to find that my view was substantially the same as Aristotle's, although stated a bit more precisely with the aid of the vocabulary of contemporary scientific methodology and cybernetics.)

I have said that my view is a synthetic hypothesis, not a contention about the meaning of mental words. While I am reasonably convinced that my view is the correct one, I should add that I am by no means certain that it is. Indeed, it would ill behoove anyone in the present state of our knowledge to be certain of any view on so central a mystery as the relation of our bodies and souls.

The *a priori* and the analytic–synthetic distinction

In 1951, Quine caused a commotion in the community of professional philosophers by publishing an attack on the venerable distinction between analytic and synthetic propositions. In their reply to Quine, Grice and Strawson advanced two arguments: (1) when there is so much agreement among the relevant speakers (in this case, professional philosophers) upon how to use a pair of terms with respect to an open class of sentences, then that pair of terms must mark *some* distinction; (2) Grice and Strawson argued (cf. Grice and Strawson, 1956) that the cases in which it appears that an analytic proposition was falsified can be explained away by contending that in each case the meaning of the words changed, and so the proposition that was at one time genuinely analytic was not the same proposition that was later falsified, although it was expressed by the very same sentence.

I agree with the first argument. There is an *obvious* difference (even if we have difficulty stating it) between, say, 'all bachelors are un-married', as a representative analytic sentence, and 'my hat is on the table', as a representative synthetic sentence. It seems impossible to say that so obvious a distinction doesn't really have *any* basis. But Grice and Strawson's second argument seemed to me to be far less successful. Consider the statement that one cannot return to the place from which one started by travelling in a straight line in space in a constant direction. If this statement was once analytic or *a priori* (in 1951, few philosophers of an analytic persuasion would have troubled to distinguish the two notions), and was later falsified by the discovery (let us say) that our world is Riemannian in the large, then the Grice–Strawson rescue move would consist in saying that some term, say, 'straight line' has changed its meaning in the course of the change from Euclidean to Riemannian cosmology. But even if 'straight line' has changed its 'connotations' – even if the theoretical aura surrounding the term is different – still this would not effect the *truth value* of the sentence unless the very reference of the term 'straight line' has changed, unless we are now referring to different paths in space as straight lines. But, having studied philosophy of physics and philosophy of geometry with Hans Reichenbach, I was not satisfied with this story at all. Whatever the nature of the conceptual revolution involved in the shift from Newtonian to relativistic cosmology may have been, it was not simply a matter of attaching the old labels, e.g. 'straight line', to new curves. What seemed *a priori* before the conceptual revolution was precisely that there *are* paths in space which behave in a Euclidean fashion; or, to drop reference to 'paths', what seemed *a priori* was precisely that there were infinitely many non-overlapping places (of, say, the size of an ordinary room) to get to. What turned out to be the case (or, rather, what will turn out to be the case if the universe in the large has compact spatial cross-sections), is precisely that there are only finitely many disjoint places (of the size of an ordinary room) in space to get to, travel as one will. Something literally *inconceivable* has turned out to be true; and it is not just a matter of attaching the old labels ('place', 'straight line') to different things.

To state the same point more abstractly: it often happens in a scientific revolution that something that was once taken to be an *a priori* truth is given up; and one cannot say that what has happened is simply that the words have been assigned to new referents, because, from the standpoint of the new theory, there are not and never were any objects which could plausibly have been the referents of the words in question. Nor can we say that the proposition in question used to mean that certain entities ('Euclidean straight lines', 'Euclidean places') *would* have certain properties if they existed, and that what has happened is that words ('straight line', 'place') which used to have no referents at all have now been assigned referents; for in the geometrical case there certainly were such entitites as *places the size of a room*, and what seemed necessary was that these *places* had the property of being infinite in number.

To put it another way, it seemed *a priori* that the terms 'path in space' and 'place the size of an ordinary room' had referents. To say that the existence propositions, 'There are places the size of an ordinary room' and 'There are paths in space', were *a posteriori* (in the old sense of the words), whereas the if-then proposition 'If anything is a place the size of a room, then there are infinitely many such places' is *a priori*, is utterly unmotivated, since these propositions did not differ in epistemological or methodological status prior to the conceptual revolution under discussion.

I was driven to the conclusion that there was such a thing as the overthrow of a proposition that was once *a priori* (or that once had the status of what we *call* an '*a priori*' truth). If it could be rational to give up claims as self evident as the geometrical propositions just mentioned, then, it seemed to me that there was no basis for maintaining that there are any *absolutely a priori* truths, any truths that a rational man is *forbidden* to even doubt. Grice and Strawson were wrong; the overthrow of '*a priori*' propositions is not a mere illusion that can be explained away as change in the meaning of words. Quine's attack on the analytic–synthetic distinction, reconstrued as an attack on the *a priori–a posteriori* distinction, seemed to me to be correct. At the same time, if by an analytic truth one means a statement which is reducible to something like principles of elementary logic via meaning relations that are in some sense conventional, then it still seemed to me that there were analytic truths. Empiricist philosophers had bloated the analytic–synthetic distinction by making it coextensive with the *a priori–a posteriori* distinction; the question of the existence of analytic truths, in the sense just mentioned, had to be separated from the question whether any truths, even truths of elementary logic, were *a priori*.

In 'The analytic and the synthetic' I undertook the double task of defending Quine's insight with the aid of examples from the history of physics and geometry, and of clarifying the nature of the analytic–synthetic distinction itself. The conclusions I reached in the course of writing that paper had a far-reaching impact on my later views in the philosophy of mathematics, geometry, and quantum mechanics, as the reader can see by glancing at the papers in the first volume of these collected papers.

Conventionalism

An issue which is closely connected to the issues surrounding the analytic–synthetic distinction, and its misuse by philosophers, is the issue of conventionalism. Just as some philosophers try to clear up some philosophical puzzles by contending that certain statements which appear to be statements of fact are *really* 'analytic', so some philosophers contend that certain statements which appear to be statements of fact are really 'up for grabs', i.e. their truth-value is a matter of convention. Applications of this idea to the philosophy of language and to the philosophy of geometry are criticized in 'The refutation of conventionalism'. It is of interest that conventionalism in the philosophy of space and time was originally motivated by a desire to give an account of the reference of scientific terms. Thus the critique of conventionalism naturally involves one in the very questions about reference that are taken up in the papers 'Explanation and reference' and 'The meaning of "meaning"'. (I also try to give an overview of relations between questions in the philosophy of language and questions in other parts of philosophy in the paper 'Language and reality'.)

I have not attempted in these papers to put forward any grand view of the nature of philosophy; nor do I have any such grand view to put forward if I would. It will be obvious that I do not agree with those who see philosophy as the history of 'howlers', and progress in philosophy as the debunking of howlers. It will also be obvious that I do not agree with those who see philosophy as the enterprise of putting forward *a priori* truths about the real world (since, for one thing, there are no *a priori* truths, in my view). I see philosophy as a field which has certain central questions, for example, the relation between thought and reality, and, to mention some questions about which I have *not* written, the relation between freedom and responsibility, and the nature of the good life. It seems obvious that in dealing with these questions philosophers have formulated rival research programs, that they have put forward general hypotheses, and that philosophers within each major research program have modified their hypotheses by trial and error, even if they sometimes refuse to admit that that is what they are doing. To that extent philosophy is a 'science'. To argue about whether philosophy is a science in any more serious sense seems to me to be hardly a useful occupation. The important thing is that in spite of the stereotypes of science and philosophy that have become blinkers inhibiting the view of laymen, scientists, and philosophers, science and philosophy are interdependent activities; philosophers have always found it essential to draw upon the scientific knowledge of the time, and scientists have always found it essential to do a certain amount of philosophy in their very scientific work, even if they denied that that was what they were doing. It does not seem to me important to decide whether science is philosophy or philosophy is science as long as one has a conception of both that makes both essential to a responsible view of the real world and of man's place in it.

Harvard University   H.P.
September 1974

I
Language and philosophy

In the present century philosophers have been extremely interested in language. To the layman this interest often seems curious, if not downright perverse. After all, there are so many aspects of reality that seem more *important* than questions about words and meanings: are not the nature of the cosmos, the foundations of knowledge, the present plight of mankind, all more fitting subjects for philosophical essays?

In part this attitude rests on a misconception of the nature of philosophy. Philosophy is often the starting point for what eventually turn out to be new consensuses in science and in human affairs; but the starting point is usually dry and technical. Bacon paved the way for all of modern empirical science by arguing that scientists should put their questions to nature, and not to the *a priori* intellect; but it was Newton and not Bacon who discovered the law of Universal Gravitation. Locke paved the way for the ideologues of the American revolution; but he did not make it. To be sure the plight of mankind may yet be improved (or made worse!) by a new consensus in morals or in politics arising out of philosophical ideas being published right now; but one must not expect technical philosophical books to bear their social significance on their sleeves (or dust jackets). If philosophers have become very interested in language in the past fifty years it is not because they have become *dis*interested in the Great Questions of philosophy, but precisely because they *are* still interested in the Great Questions and because they have come to believe that language holds the key to resolve (or in some way satisfactorily dispose of) the Great Questions.

In a way, the layman's impatience with philosophy is very understandable. The special sciences, such as physics, do not pretend to study matters which are immediately of interest to everyone. How many people have a natural and spontaneous interest in the rate at which freely falling bodies accelerate? The layman takes it for granted that physics should be a specialist subject, which is pursued partly because *some* people have a natural interest in these matters and partly because of its practical utility. (He often has very little conception of just how much inquiry goes on in Physics Departments purely for the satisfaction of someone's curiosity, with absolutely no likelihood of practical application.) But philosophy grows out of, or is popularly supposed to grow out of, concerns which are felt by every thinking man. It seems less intelligible, therefore, that it should so quickly become a specialist discipline (although it always has been – Aristophanes ridiculed Socrates for the technicality of the latter's interests!). Moreover, laymen are bored and disinterested by philosophy once it does become technical. Yet the culture requires that one profess an admiration for Philosophy, or at least for the Great Philosophers. It is natural, therefore, to say that one is bored, not with Philosophy, but with the current generation of philosophers. And so it has been said – in every generation, not just in this one – that the current generation of philosophers are no true philosophers at all, and that they have turned aside from the 'real' questions (whose discussion would, of course, interest one, and would never become technical).

This perennial tendency to criticize philosophy as 'too technical' is very much reinforced by the 'linguistic' character of contemporary philosophy. For language, as we remarked at the outset, is thought by the layman to be uninteresting in itself and irrelevant to the Great Questions.

We start, then, with a cultural situation. On the one side are the contemporary American and British philosophers, convinced, for the most part, of the overwhelming importance of the philosophical study of language. On the other side are the lay critics of philosophy – *Time* magazine, for example – convinced that such study is largely irrelevant, and that philosophy should return to the Great Questions (which, it is assumed, have been forgotten). Who is right?

As is usual with cultural situations, the answer seems to be that neither side is right. In this chapter, we will attempt to evaluate the success or failure of the attempt to bring semantical methods to bear on the Great Questions of philosophy. It will turn out, unless we are seriously mistaken, that the success claimed for these methods is exaggerated. Yet the lay criticism is misguided in two ways. First, the attempts, whether they have succeeded or failed, were not irrelevant to the basic problems of philosophy. Indeed, even if we have not discovered 'linguistic solutions' to those problems, we *have*, I contend, acquired a great deal of new knowledge about them. This will be discussed below. Secondly, even if the study of language is less relevant to philosophy than has been recently assumed, it is a topic of enormous scientific fascination in its own right, and philosophers have made a real contribution to at least an initial mapping of this topic.

But this is getting ahead of ourselves! Let us work up to the points just summarized in an orderly fashion, first seeing how it is that philosophers became involved with questions about language, then taking a look at what they have done with those questions, and only at the end making some overall evaluation.

Even the most cursory reading of the philosophers of the past will reveal that philosophers have always been interested in what have been called 'ideas' – our 'idea' of matter, our 'idea' of causality, our 'idea' of goodness, etc. Other philosophers have spoken of 'concepts' instead of ideas (e.g. Moore insists, in a famous book on ethics, that he is interested in the *concept* Good, and not in the *word*), and still others of 'properties'. Today it is often thought that these philosophers of the past were interested in the usage of words (and hence in linguistic rules, or norms, or anyway practices) without knowing it. Moreover, there is a certain plausibility to this view. What is it to have the concept 'chair', for example? It has often been thought that having such a concept is a simple matter of possessing some image (or the capacity to call up some image), but it is perceived today that this will not do. (This is largely because of the great forcefulness and convincingness of Wittgenstein's arguments against the conception of concepts as 'images', or, indeed, mental objects of any kind, in his book *Philosophical Investigations*.)

Why it will not do to identify concepts and images is a long story, but the basic ideas are not hard to indicate. Let us say that an organism possesses a *minimal concept* of a chair if it can recognize a chair when it sees one, and that it possesses a *full-blown concept* of a chair if it can employ the usual sentences containing the word *chair* in some natural language. (Instead of *chair* the word may, of course, be *fenêtre*, or *Fenster*, etc., depending upon the language, but we shall neglect this unless it becomes relevant.) Possessing the full-blown concept is possessing a very complicated (and presently very ill-understood) ability. It is easily seen that one might possess the capacity to have chair-images without having this ability. Very likely, a dog or a cat has chair-images from time to time; but a dog or a cat cannot speak a natural language.

Of course, this may be irrelevant. It may be, for example, that dogs and cats possess thought-forms which are just as complex and structured as English sentences. But this seems very unlikely. It seems very unlikely that a dog or a cat is capable, for example, of thinking 'if there had been a chair in the room, then the dinner would not have been delayed'. Moreover, a human being who *does* possess the ability to understand such sentences possesses much more than a set of images.

Consider the following mental experiment. Imagine a 'stream of consciousness' novel written in Japanese. Suppose that, without understanding a word of Japanese, you were to memorize a large portion of

3

this novel from hearing it played over and over on records. Suppose that, under the influence of a post-hypnotic suggestion, you were to 'mentally rehearse' this sequence of Japanese sentences, complete with appropriate pauses, intonations, emphasis, etc. If your behavior was not violently inappropriate to the content of what was passing through your mind, then it might be, in a certain sense, *as if* you were 'thinking in Japanese'. If other people could hear your 'inner speech', then they might be convinced that you were in fact thinking in Japanese. A native speaker of Japanese might, if he were telepathic, be absolutely certain that you were thinking in Japanese. It might be part of the post-hypnotic suggestion that you yourself should *feel* as if you understood the sentences passing through your mind, and be convinced that you thought in Japanese. Yet, clearly, you would not be thinking the propositions expressed by the sentences passing through your mind, since you would not *really* (whatever your 'sense of understanding') *understand* those sentences.

The understanding, then, does not reside in the words themselves, nor even in the appropriateness of the whole sequence of words and sentences. It lies, rather, in the fact that an *understanding* speaker can *do things* with the words and sentences he utters (or thinks in his head) *besides* just utter them. He can answer questions, for example (the man, in the example of the previous paragraph, who just memorized a lot of sentences in some language he did not understand, could not do this). Yet this is a bit disturbing. Questions are also sentences, after all, and so are answers to questions. To say that my understanding of the sentences I utter (or think in my head) consists in my ability to respond to questions (other sentences) with appropriate answers (further sentences), makes it sound as if language has nothing to do with the world: it is all a game played with sentences. Why, then, did I not rather say that understanding sentences is being able to point to whatever it is in the real world that corresponds to those sentences?

The reason is that, in the case of most sentences, there is not much to point to. I understand the sentence 'Julius Caesar was a great emperor', but what can I point to when I utter this sentence? Indeed, what can I point to when I say 'I had eggs for breakfast this morning?' (perhaps my stomach). It is quite true that understanding sentences does *involve* being able to use the right sentences in the right situations (if somebody said 'hello' when he was *departing*, we might suspect him of not knowing the meaning of this word); but mostly the 'situations' are defined by what had been *said* previously, and not by nonlinguistic facts. In short, it seems as if language is like a great balloon, anchored to the ground of nonlinguistic fact only by a number of widely scattered

4

and very thin (but all-important) ropes. If there were *no* 'interaction' between purely linguistic behavior and nonlinguistic events, then language would be just noise-making; but to determine whether someone understands language, we cannot in most cases compare his utterance with something nonlinguistic for appropriateness (or it would not settle the question of whether the man understood what he said, no matter how the comparison with nonlinguistic fact turned out, although it might settle the question of whether what he said was *true*); but we rather have to *converse* with the man, i.e. we have to see whether he was 'parroting', or whether he has the ability to use those sentences, and other related sentences, *selectively*, considering what has been said before.

We started out, however, to make the much more modest point that possessing the full-blown concept of a chair is *not* the same thing as possessing the 'image'. This is now clear, since we would not say of someone who could not produce the right answers to the right questions (even to such simple questions as 'what do people do with chairs?') that he had the full-blown concept, and possessing an *ability* is clearly a very different thing from possessing one image. (I do not mean that the operational procedure of asking questions and seeing if one gets linguistically appropriate responses is decisive for telling if someone has the full-blown concept. Someone might have the ability and fail to manifest it in the test situation for a variety of reasons, e.g. nervousness. But possession of the ability *is* at least a necessary condition for possession of the full-blown concept.)

We have also seen that possessing the full-blown concept is not a matter of possessing *further* images (say, images of the sentences, or even of whole discourses), since one could possess any system of images you please and not possess the *ability* to use sentences in situationally appropriate ways (considering both linguistic factors – what has been said before – and nonlinguisitc factors as determining 'situational appropriateness'). A man may have all the images you please, and still be completely at a loss when one says to him 'point to a chair', even if a lot of chairs are present. He may even have the image of what he is supposed to do, and still not know what he is supposed to do. For the image, if not accompanied by the *practice* of acting in certain ways, or the *ability* to act in the appropriate way, is just a *picture*, and acting in accordance with a picture is itself an ability that one may or may not have. (The man might picture himself pointing to a chair, but just for the sake of contemplating something logically possible: himself pointing to a chair just after someone has produced the – to him meaningless – sequence of sounds 'please point to a chair'.) He would still not know

5

that he was *supposed to point to a chair*, and he would still not *understand* 'point to a chair'.)

We have considered the ability to use certain sentences to be the criterion for possessing the full-blown concept, but this could easily be liberalized. We could allow symbolism consisting of elements which are not words in a natural language, for example, and we could allow such mental phenomena as images, and other types of internal events. What is essential is that these should have the same complexity, or be capable of having the same complexity, as sentences in a natural language. For, although a simple presentation – say, a blue flash – might serve a particular mathematician as the inner expression of the whole proof of the Prime Number Theorem, still, there would be no temptation to say this (and it would be ludicrously false to say this) if that mathematician could not 'unpack' his 'blue flash' into separate steps and logical connections. But, no matter what sort of inner phenomena we allow as possible *expressions* of thought, arguments exactly similar to the foregoing will indicate that it is not the phenomena themselves that constitute understanding, but rather the ability of the thinker to *employ* those phenomena, to produce the right phenomena in the right situations.

The foregoing is a very abbreviated version of Wittgenstein's argument in *Philosophical Investigations*. If it is correct, then the attempt to understand thought by what is called 'phenomenological' investigation (i.e. by introspection) is fundamentally misguided: for what the phenomenologists fail to see is that all they are doing is describing the inner *expression* of thought (which is an interesting and important task, to be sure); but that the *understanding* of that expression – one's understanding of one's own thoughts – is not an *occurrence* but an *ability*. Our earlier example of a man pretending to 'think in Japanese' (and deceiving a native Japanese telepath) already shows the futility of a phenomenological approach to the problem of *understanding*. For even if there is some introspectible quality which is present when and only when one *really* understands (this seems false on introspection, in fact); still that quality is only *correlated* with understanding, and it is still *logically* possible that the man fooling the Japanese telepath have that quality too and *still* not understand a word of Japanese.

On the other hand, consider the (logically possible) man who does not have any 'interior monologue' at all. He speaks perfectly good English, we will suppose, and if asked what his opinions are on a given subject, he will give them at length. But he never thinks (in words, images, etc.) when he is not speaking out loud; nor does anything 'go through his mind' when he speaks out loud, except that (of course) he hears his own voice speaking, and has the usual sense impressions from his surroundings, plus a general 'feeling of understanding'. Similarly, when he types a letter or goes to the store, etc., he is not having an internal 'stream of thought'; but his actions are intelligent and purposeful, and if anyone walks up and asks him 'what are you doing?' he will give perfectly coherent replies.

This man seems perfectly imaginable. No one would hesitate to say that he was conscious, understood language, disliked jazz (if he frequently expressed a strong aversion to jazz), etc., just because he did not think conscious thoughts except when speaking out loud.

What follows from all this is that (a) no set of mental events – images, or more 'abstract' mental happenings and qualities – *constitute* understanding; and (b) no set of mental events is *necessary* for understanding. In particular, *concepts cannot be identical with mental objects of any kind*. For, assuming that by a 'mental object' we understand something introspectible, we have just seen whatever it is, it may be imagined absent in a man who does understand the appropriate word (and hence has the full-blown concept), and present in a man who does not have the concept at all.

This is one of the most remarkable conclusions in the history of philosophy. For virtually no philosopher doubted, from the time of John Locke until roughly 1914, that, whatever concepts and ideas were, they were *clearly* mental objects of some kind. And no large-scale and comprehensive demolition job was done against this particularly widespread and influential philosophical misconception until Wittgenstein produced his *Philosophical Investigations* (which he finished in 1949, and which was not published until after his death, which occurred in 1951).

(We shall see later, however, that the turn away from Locke's 'way of Ideas', and from the concern with introspective psychology began long before the later Wittgenstein.)

Incidentally, even the minimal concept of a 'chair' cannot be an image. For an organism might conceivably have chair-images and not *discriminate* chairs (or even chair-images!). Indeed, something like this seems to happen in human infancy. To have even the minimal concept of *red*, for example, requires the formation of associations which are very difficult before the age of two. There is some evidence that the difficulty is physiological: that the association requires the use of paths connecting the tectum (the visual cortex) with other parts of the brain which are not fully mature until well past the age of two. On one theory, what this means is that the one-year-old child *sees* red (and may well have red images), but cannot *associate* to it. (This is discussed by Geschwind in a lengthy article in *Brain* published in 1965.) And,

7

conversely, someone who never has visual images (and there are many such people), may perfectly well possess the ability to discriminate red objects. Thus minimal concepts are no more 'mental objects' than are full-blown concepts.

The foregoing discussion may be reinforced by the following consideration. How do we in fact decide whether or not someone possesses a concept? We do not look inside his stream of consciousness to see if the word corresponding to the concept evokes a particular mental image or event of some kind. We rather observe (and put questions, if necessary) to see if he *knows how to use the word*. And even if I want to see if I myself have grasped some concept or other, I do much the same thing: I *put questions to myself*, and see if I can answer them. Finding out that you have the concept *chair* is not discovering that the word calls up an image in your head (or some other sort of mental event); it is simply discovering that you possess a certain complicated *ability*.

The case becomes even clearer when we consider what it is to find out that two people have the *same* concept. It does not matter if you think in images and I do not, or how different the phenomena called up in your mind and in mine by the word 'chair' may be: if we both agree that a chair is a portable seat for one with a back; if we both agree on the function of chairs, and on their normal appearance; if we agree on what to class as a chair and what to class as a nonchair; then in an important sense we have exactly the same concept of a chair. But having the same concept, in this sense, is not having the same mental presentation, but having the same set of linguistic and nonlinguistic abilities in a certain respect.

In sum, the traditional account suggests that finding out that someone has a concept is finding out that he has a particular mental presentation, and finding out that two people have the same concept is finding out that they have identical mental presentations. But this is *ludicrously* false; not because it fails to correspond to what we in fact *do*, but because it fails to correspond to what we in fact *mean*. Part of what is attractive about the Wittgensteinian account of conceptualization (which I am sketching here) is this: that whereas on the traditional account it is quite mysterious that one can ever discover that another person has a concept, on the Wittgensteinian account the mystery disappears. For, if discovering that someone has a concept is discovering that someone has a certain ability, then it is clear how we can discover that someone has this: we can discover that someone has a certain ability by seeing him exhibit that ability. (Of course, this wouldn't satisfy the sceptic. But then nothing would. That's the nature of scepticism.)

At this point one begins to feel serious doubts about Moore's sharp distinction, mentioned above, between the *concept* Good and the *word*. Moore writes as if there were an *object*, 'the concept Good', that one could pass about, inspect under a microscope, perhaps take to pieces (be careful not to break it!). The word, on this view, is only a convenient if accidental label for this object. Once we have had our attention called to the object, we can simply forget about the word and concentrate on the object. But what is this object? It seems as if all we in fact have is the word, or rather the ability to use a system of sentences. We decide whether or not someone has the concept Good by seeing whether or not he has this ability; we decide whether or not two people have the same concept of goodness by seeing whether or not their usages are in certain respects similar. Was not Moore *in fact* discussing the way we use the word, even if he thought he wasn't?

Considerations of this sort lead naturally to the idea that a great deal of philosophy should be *reconstrued* as about language, even if the authors in question did not *think* they were talking about language. (In particular, all of the traditional philosophy about 'ideas', 'concepts', etc., to which we alluded earlier.)

Of course, the objection is immediately voiced that concepts are not the same thing as words, and so talk about concepts *can't* be really about words. But this is a silly objection. What is it to know what concepts *are*? Clearly, if someone knows under what circumstances someone *has* a concept, and is able to distinguish that concept from all concepts which are not identical with it, then he knows what that concept is. (Some philosophers have supposed that even if I know how to verify arithmetical statements, e.g. 'there are two primes between two and seven', and how to use number words in such statements as 'there are two apples in my pocket'; 'this equation has three roots'; 'give me two and one-half quarts of milk'; still, I haven't the foggiest notion what numbers *are*. And they suppose that philosophy must answer this question. But *don't I, in fact* know what the number two is? It's the first even prime; it's the second number in the sequence 1, 2, . . . ; it's the number of hands I've got. If *that* doesn't count as knowing what the number two is, why should anything a philosopher dreams up count any more?) If you can tell when someone has the concept 'equilateral triangle', and you know that, e.g. 'equilateral triangle' is not at all the *same* concept as 'scalene triangle', then don't you know what the concept 'equilateral triangle' is?

Concepts aren't words (although having a concept is being able to use certain words, or certain symbols, or certain 'inner notation' with at least as much potential complexity as sequences of words or symbols). Neither are concepts abilities; although *having* a concept is, or at least

9

involves, having an ability. But this doesn't make concepts something mysterious.

What creates the appearance of mystery here is this. Many philosophers suppose that only certain kinds of things are *things* (sometimes the word 'entity', or the word 'object' is used instead of *thing*). For example, some philosophers suppose that only physical things are things, entities, objects, etc. It follows, for these philosophers, that *there are no such things* as concepts (or numbers, for that matter). Other philosophers use the words 'thing', 'entity', 'object', etc., to include concepts, properties, numbers, etc. For these philosophers, it is *trivial* that there are such things as concepts and numbers. Finally, some philosophers write as if it were an open question whether or not there are such entities as concepts and numbers. But how can this last view be correct? There is no clear and universally accepted notion of 'entity' to be appealed to here. Either the very explanation of the term resolves this question, or the question is hopelessly ill defined.

Discussing this question at length would, unfortunately, take us much too far afield. I should like, however, to suggest a view which I think provides a sane solution to the sort of problem just raised. This view, crudely put, is that different sets of statements (e.g. statements about people having or not having concepts versus statements about people having or not having the ability to employ certain sentences correctly; statements about numbers versus statements about classes of classes; etc.) may sometimes have the same cognitive content without being in any sense synonymous on a sentence-by-sentence basis. Even though we are very far from having any precise criterion for the 'sameness of cognitive content' of whole systems of statements, one can easily list cases in which it seems correct to say that two systems have the same cognitive content, and one can describe a number of the salient features of such cases. The most important feature is this: that there is some established procedure for passing back and forth between the two systems. This procedure must be such that it is immaterial, scientifically speaking, which system one adopts; all the purposes that can be served by the one way of speaking can equally well be served by the other.

Consider, for a moment, the example of numbers. Russell and White-head showed how to 'translate' all statements about numbers into statements about classes of classes. Some authors have argued that this proves that numbers *are* classes of classes (but this seems to be upset by the discovery of a plurality of equally workable but mutually incompatible 'translations'). Others have argued (on the grounds of 'simplicity' and 'economy') that we should 'dispense' with numbers and speak only of classes of classes. In its strong form, this last view holds that we have discovered that numbers do not exist; there are only classes of classes, at least for the purposes of number theory. Still others hold that there are both numbers and classes, and all we have discovered is an isomorphism. On the view that I am taking, all of these views are overly extreme. Let C be the language of classes (i.e. we can speak of physical objects, classes of physical objects, classes of classes of physical objects, ... but not of *numbers* in C). Let $C*N$ be the language of classes *and* numbers (i.e. in $C*N$ we can speak of everything we can speak of in C, and of numbers – construed as distinct objects, not reduced to classes). Then my view is that, although no sentence containing the term 'number' can be regarded as strictly synonymous with any sentence of C, still the whole system $C*N$ can, as a whole, be regarded as formulating the very same mathematical facts as C, even though C is more 'economical' in its choice of primitive vocabulary and $C*N$ more 'profligate'.

This view has two advantages. On the one hand, it follows from this view that the man on the street (or the mathematician on the street) is not making a *mistake* every time he says '*there is* a number such that . . .'; as he would be if numbers did literally not exist. (Nor is he speaking about particular classes of classes without knowing that he is; nor is he speaking vaguely of some classes or other without knowing which ones.) On the other hand, a mathematician who chooses to adopt the Russell–Whitehead 'translation', and speak only of classes of classes (i.e. he 'identifies numbers with' classes of classes) is not thereby open to the accusation that he has failed to describe the numbers, or the accusation that he has 'left numbers out', or the accusation that he has, by not *explicitly* speaking of 'numbers', given an *incomplete* statement of mathematical knowledge. For, if this view is correct, he *has* stated everything he wished to state about numbers, even though he never wrote down a single sentence about numbers. Arguing about which version of our mathematical knowledge is correct – the version we get if we formalize mathematics in the language C or the version we get if we formalize mathematics in the language $C*N$ – is like arguing whether a map based on Mercator's projection is 'correct', or whether, rather, it is the map of the very same geographical relations which we get if we use Polar projection which is 'correct'. *Both* are equally correct (or incorrect); in fact they are equivalent descriptions.

In the same way, consider the two languages: Language (A) in which we speak of 'concepts' as entities distinct from words, abilities, classes, numbers, physical things, etc.; and Language (B) in which we 'identify concepts with' classes of expressions. To give an example, in Language (B) 'the concept *chair*' is 'identified with' the class of all pairs (W, L)

such that W is a word (or, possibly, an expression consisting of more than one word) belonging to L, L is a language, and W is synonymous with *chair*. From the standpoint of Language (B) it may be said that 'concepts', if they exist at all, are merely *synonymy classes* of expressions (or ordered pairs (W, L)). Whereas we express the fact that someone 'has the concept Chair' in Language (A) by saying precisely that, we would express the same fact in Language (B) by saying that there are W, L such that W means *chair* (in L) and the person in question has mastered the use of W in L. And whereas we would express the fact that 'Chair and Table are different concepts' in Language (A) by saying precisely that, we would express the same fact in Language (B) by saying that 'chair' is not synonymous with 'table' in English.

[At this point we encounter a technical objection, due to Alonzo Church. This is that 'Chair and Table are different concepts' does not depend for its truth on the existence of the English language, or on any facts about that or any other language, whereas the proposed translation is an empirical statement about English. A full solution to this difficulty requires something like Frege's theory of 'sense' and 'denotation' – which is what Church urges. But that solution is quite compatible with identifying concepts with synonymy classes of expressions, although I doubt that Church would be happy with that identification. The idea, roughly is to 'translate' 'C_1 is not the same concept as C_2' by 'There is a pair (W, L) belonging to C_1 and a pair (W', L') belonging to C_2 such that W is not synonymous (in L) with W' (in L'). Next we say that in the context 'The concept Chair', the word 'Chair' names or denotes the synonymy class to which it belongs. (This does *not* mean that 'Chair' is *synonymous* with 'the class of pairs (W, L) such that W in L is synonymous with "chair" in English'.) Then 'The concept Chair is not the same concept as the concept Table' may be regarded as a sentence of Language (B), even though it contains the word 'concept' (since 'concepts' have been identified with synonymy classes, and are not the 'unreduced concepts' of Language (A). The logical point here is a very subtle one: that words may, in certain contexts, be said to name their synonymy class without being synonymous with phrases of the form 'the synonymy class of such and such a word of English'. The synonymy class must, so to speak, be thought of by its common property – the similarity in the use of all its elements – rather than by a description in terms of one element. Of course, the 'common property' – the similarity (or -ties) in the use of all the elements – is yet another entity with which the 'concept' could be 'identified'.]

The claim, again, would be that, although no sentence of Language

(*A*) may be exactly synonymous with any sentence of Language (*B*), still when we have described what concepts a man does or does not possess, what concepts are the same or different, etc., in both languages, we have, in the end, somehow conveyed exactly the same information. Cognitive synonymy of whole 'discourses' does not require any simple word by word or even sentence by sentence preservation of content. In this sense, then, anything that can be said about 'concepts' may equally well admit of a formulation in terms of statements about synonymy of expressions and ability to use expressions, notwithstanding the fact that anyone has the right, if he wishes to, to speak of concepts as 'entities' distinct from expressions, classes, etc.

In sum: say 'I am talking about the concept Good, and not about the word "good"' *if you like*. But whatever you end up telling us about 'the concept Good' will admit of restatement in the following forms: 'if someone is to mean *good* when he uses a word *W*, then he must (generally) use the word *W* (not use the word *W*) in the following ways...' For example, Moore's claim that it is a 'fallacy' to propose *any* 'naturalistic analysis' of Good comes to just this: that if anyone really uses a word *W* so that *W* is synonymous with *W'*, where *W'* is any one of the predicates that Moore regards as standing for 'a natural property', then he simply does not mean Good by *W* (i.e. *W* is not synonymous with 'good').

To repeat: the main question is not what concepts 'are'. The important locution is not 'a concept is (is not) a such-and such'. The important things that we say, when we employ the notion of a concept, is that someone has (does not have) such and such a concept, and that two concepts are the same (are different). Wittgenstein's analysis, crudely summarized before, does not say anything about what concepts 'are'. But it does say what it is to *have* a concept: to have a concept is (at least) to have a certain ability, the ability to use certain sentences. This is what makes Wittgenstein's discussion important, whereas all the discussion about whether or not concepts 'exist' is unimportant. And Wittgenstein's discussion is important not because the point is intrinsically difficult – it isn't – but because there was such a long tradition in the history of philosophy of thinking just the opposite, that concepts were something like images, and that having a concept was like having (or being able to call up) an image. (It will be noted that Wittgenstein's discussion, as we summarized it, says nothing about the other important locution mentioned – it does not say anything about the criterion for the sameness or difference of concepts. Whether any view on this point can be extracted from Wittgenstein's writing is extremely moot. Also, there is a third important thing that we sometimes say when we employ the notion of a concept, that I have deliberately neglected so far – that one concept includes or entails or implies another.)

So far, then, we have followed one reason for upgrading the importance of language in philosophy. Concepts and ideas were always thought important; language was thought unimportant, because it was considered to be merely a system of conventional signs for concepts and ideas (considered as mental entities of some kind, and quite independent of the signs used to express them). But today it seems doubtful that concepts and ideas can be thought of as mental *events* or *objects* (as opposed to *abilities*) and even more doubtful that they are independent of *all* signs (of course a concept is independent of any *particular* sign). But if having a concept is being able to use signs in particular ways, or if this is even a major part of the story, then all the attention that was traditionally accorded to matters of introspective psychology more properly belongs to the ways in which we use signs. Moreover, this has the advantage of being a public study, and more in the spirit of modern social science. If the way to find out what the concept Cause is, for example, is to introspect one's own images, etc., then we would hardly expect to get very reliable reports, let alone agreement. If analyzing the concept Cause is rather a matter of studying the way in which we use the word, and then abstracting from features which are 'accidental' (e.g. the particular *sound* of the word is accidental, which is just why one denies that the concept *is* the word), then the hope for reliable reports (or, at least, for a procedure for telling which reports are *not* reliable) is much greater. Again, the objection is made that this reduces philosophy to dull fact gathering. But all great theories have had to wait for at least some reliable data. Certainly Philosophy ought not to degenerate into mere linguistic *reporting*: but if lofty statements about the *concept* are ever to have any chance of being true, they ought to be based, one would think, on a careful study of how people do in fact employ the *word*.

There is, however, a very different line of thought which has also led to an upgrading of the importance of language, or at least of the study of the linguistic representation of beliefs by means of systems of sentences (possibly in some formalized logical or mathematical notation, rather than in natural language). Let us now turn to this second line of thought.

We may profitably begin once again with the concern of the British Empiricists with 'ideas' (conceived of, roughly, as images).

If one thinks of ideas as images, then one problem one gets oneself into is this: it seems just as possible to form an image of an image as an image of anything else. But how is an image of an image of a chair any different from an image of a chair?

This is, of course, an extremely naive question. It is so naive that it is difficult to say whether the naiveté is primarily philosophical or primarily psychological. Psychologically the naiveté consists in supposing that all mental presentations are *simply* images, and in neglecting the factors of 'set' to which Gestalt psychologists, among others, have now called our attention. When I form an image of an image of a chair, I do not form a different image in the sense of a different distribution of color-patches in visual space, but I *think* of it differently. I attend to my image differently, I have a different 'set'; and so the whole image 'feels' different. Indeed, if Gestalt psychologists are right, it *is* a different image, even though I cannot say that there is a different 'distribution of color patches in visual space'. The mistake (if Gestalt psychology is correct) lies, in fact, in the erroneous view that images are 'distributions of color patches' in the way in which photographs are distributions of color patches.

But if my thought of the chair is erroneously identified with my image of the chair, and my images of the chair is taken to be qualitatively identical with an image of an image of the chair, which is then erroneously identified with my idea of a visual image of the chair, one arrives at the astounding conclusion that there is absolutely no difference between the idea of a chair and the idea of an image of a chair. Indeed, on this way of thinking, to try to imagine a chair which is not a visual sense-datum (i.e. which is not the same thing as a subjective visual image of a chair) is to try to call up an image of a chair which is not (thought of as a distribution of color patches) identical (*as* a distribution of color patches) with any image of an image. Since this is impossible – no photograph of a chair can be distinguished from a sufficiently good *photograph of a photograph* of a chair – it follows that *we have no idea* of a chair which is *distinct from* our idea of a visual image of a chair (a 'chair-shaped sense-datum'); and so (with a little carelessness), that the idea of a chair which is something over and above a visual sense-datum (i.e. a purely 'phenomenal', or subjective thing) is either meaningless or self-contradictory.

It must surely have been something like the above line of thought that led Berkeley to just this very astounding conclusion. It is well known that Berkeley thought that reality is entirely 'mental'; that nothing exists except spirits (minds) and their ideas. What laymen often do not know is that Berkeley held the much more radical view that the opposing view – the common sense view that reality is *not* entirely mental, that material objects are *not* just our idea – was either meaningless or self-contradictory. In other words, Berkeley did not think that reality just happened to be mental; he did not think the other possibility was even conceivable. What we have just done is to trace one way in which one can arrive at this way of thinking if (1) one fails to see that concepts are *not* mental phenomena of the type of images; and (2) one subscribes to classical psychological atomism (i.e. the conception of, for example, visual images as agglomerations of little 'color patches' in 'visual space', rather than as whole 'Gestalts').

Of course, even if psychological atomism had been *right*, Berkeley would still have made a mistake. For even if an image of a chair is, in one way, identical with an image of an image of a chair, they are still different in being associated with different *concepts*. And, as we have seen, there are purely logical grounds (counting thought-experiments, such as our thought-experiment of fooling the Japanese telepath, as purely logical grounds) for denying that concepts are or could be merely images. But there is no denying that Berkeleyan idealism is much more plausible if one does accept psychological atomism.

It should not be thought that Berkeley was stupid, however. The fact that no one – no philosopher, no literary figure, no scientist (and members of all three professions thought about Berkeley's arguments) was able to clearly pinpoint Berkeley's mistakes until the twentieth century testifies adequately to the intrinsic difficulty of the conceptual issues raised by Berkeley. Only with the rise of a different theory of *meaning* (i.e. of what it is to have a concept of something) could one clearly see where the mistake lies. And this is a recent development.

What happened as long as the whole tradition of taking ideas (concepts) to be images, or, at any rate, mental presentations of *some* kind, was not challenged? Since philosophy is, by general consent, concerned (among other things) to study our ideas of, for example, *matter, cause, duty, good*, and since ideas were universally taken to be mental presentations of some sort, all philosophers, virtually without exception, took it to be their business to do introspective psychology. Even Reid, who came closest to delivering an adequate refutation of Berkeley, fails at this point: he sees the crucial issue to be that of refuting psychological atomism, instead of seeing the logical irrelevance of the whole psychological issue. But, as one spends more and more of one's time in attending to purely mental matters, it is naturally going to be harder and harder to refute the Idealist view that 'mental matters' are all there is. How, by simply attending to my own sensations, am I going to overcome the suggestion that minds and sensations are all there is? Thus, philosophy, until about the time of the first world war, dug itself deeper and deeper into an Idealist swamp, in spite of the valiant efforts of a few dissenters.

It is only by appreciating this historical fact – the immense strength and prestige of the philosophical movements that collectively made up Idealism at the end of the nineteenth century – that one can come to understand the reason for the 'linguistic turn' in philosophy, and the contribution that linguistic philosophers have made to the traditional problems of philosophy.

One way of breaking out of the Idealist swamp has been described in this chapter – to perform a Wittgensteinian analysis of the notion of a concept. But this was not the only way out, and it was the way that Wittgenstein took only late in his career. Another way out is better typified by the career of Carnap, although it was suggested by work of Bertrand Russell.

Briefly, what Carnap suggested (most notably in a highly technical book called *The Logical Syntax of Language*) was that such traditional philosophical problems as the one we have just mentioned might best be considered by looking at the theoretical relations between whole systems of sentences. An example may illustrate this. Consider, on the one hand, the position of the man who thinks that, in some sense, material objects are nothing but 'bundles of sensations', 'permanent possibilities of sensation' (Mill), or 'logical constructions out of sense-data' (Ayer). Traditionally, this would have been discussed by looking (introspectively) at our 'idea' of a material object and asserting that (on the basis of introspection) it was or was not the same 'idea' as the idea of a 'bundle of sensations'. Carnap would, rather, argue as follows: if there is anything to this point of view, then it must be that for each sentence about material objects there is a corresponding sentence about sense-data which expresses what the first sentence 'comes to' (on this view). For example, the sentence 'there is a book on the chair' might have as its 'translation' such a sentence as 'under such and such sensory conditions, there is a chair-shaped image in my visual field, and, under those conditions, there is a book-shaped image against the chair-shaped background, and if I move my eyes right the visual images are displaced to the left, and if I stretch out my hand until I appear to be touching the chair (chair-shaped image?) I have such and such tactile sensations, and . . .'. Let us call a sentence which speaks about sense-data (without assuming the existence of any physical objects) a *sense-datum sentence*. The above sentence 'under such and such sensory conditions etc.' would be an example of a sense-datum sentence, provided the 'sensory conditions' were specified without presupposing the existence of physical objects, and provided the notions of 'moving my eyes right' and 'stretching out my hand' were replaced by clauses to the effect that I should *seem* to myself to be doing those things. [Some Oxford philosophers, notably Austin and Strawson, have suggested that it is impossible to have a 'sense-datum language' because, allegedly, every sketch of such a language, or even of a single sense-datum sentence, contains terms which are parasitic on the notion of a material thing. This may be true; but I have here required, *not* that the concepts employed in a sense-datum sentence should be independent of the concepts employed in thing-sentences, but that the sentence as a whole should not presuppose the existence of physical things. If I say 'I see what looks to me to be a chair' then I may mean that I certainly see something, and it looks to me to be (but may not in fact be) a chair; or I may mean that I certainly have the visual experience of seeing a chair, but that experience may not in fact be the experience of seeing (correctly or incorrectly) any real material object (e.g. I may be hallucinating). In its second use (which may or may not be an 'ordinary' one – who cares?) the sentence still presupposes the *concepts* 'see', 'something', 'chair', and 'looking like', all of which are concepts whose primary application is to physical things (or whose primary application is in situations in which we believe there are physical things, to be more cautious); but it does not imply the existence of physical things. It is incorrect to argue, as Strawson does, that we could not learn these words if there were not physical things: the most that an argument about 'how we learn to use the words' could possibly show is that we could not learn to use these words if we did not *think* there were (and if there did not seem to be) physical things; and even that is not a logical necessity. Thus the sentence in question is a *sense-datum sentence* in my sense, when understood in the second of the two above ways, even if it is 'parasitic' on thing-concepts. (Why should not a phenomenalist grant that we have thing-*concepts* and that even the nature of direct experience is profoundly influenced by this?)]

Given this use of the term 'sense-datum sentence', and given the notion of a 'thing-sentence', we may then express Carnap's point as follows: if phenomenalism (i.e. the view that physical objects are 'bundles of sensations', or 'permanent possibilities of sensation', etc.) is right, then there must be a way of associating each thing-sentence S with a certain sense-datum sentence $T(S)$ which expresses the 'phenomenalistic content' of S. Whether S and $T(S)$ have the same 'meaning' will, of course, be disputed. But if the phenomenalist is to have even a *chance* of being right, then S and $T(S)$ should always have the same truth-value, or, as least, there should not be any situation in which it is clear (given our pre-philosophical notions of the meanings of S and $T(S)$) that S is true and $T(S)$ is false. For example, it would not be acceptable to say that 'there is a chair in front of me' means simply 'I have a chair-shaped visual sense-datum', since every philosopher who thinks that thing-sentences can be interpreted at all would grant that S can sometimes be true when $T(S)$ is false (e.g. I may have my eyes closed), and that S can be false when $T(S)$ is true (e.g. I may be hallucinating). Certainly, no scientist would take a phenomenalistic position seriously if it required him to believe that all sentences in science asserting the existence of unseen physical objects must henceforth be rejected as false, or that all sentences asserting the existence of hallucinations must be called false, and all visual experiences must be regarded as veridical. For the acceptance of such a philosophical position would require not reinterpreting, but simply scrapping science (and common sense) as we know it.

But, to continue with our exposition of Carnap, we now see that at least part of the traditional philosophical dispute about phenomenalism can be raised to a scientific level. For, if the phenomenalist cannot define a mapping T from thing-sentences to sense-datum sentences with the property that under no conceivable conditions is it the case that S is highly confirmed (highly disconfirmed) while $T(S)$ is highly disconfirmed (highly confirmed), then phenomenalism does not have to be taken seriously. On the other hand, if the phenomenalist does come up with a proposed mapping T, then we can look and see whether it is unproblematical that it preserves truth-value, or at least high (low) confirmation.

If we think about Carnap's treatment of this issue, then we quickly see that there are now *two* different forms of phenomenalism, where before there was only one. Namely,

(I) Ontological Phenomenalism: Material things *are* bundles of sensations.
(II) Linguistic Phenomenalism: Thing-sentences can be 'translated' into sense-datum sentences, by a 'translation' that preserves truth-value, according to the phenomenalist, and that even the realist must admit preserves high (low) confirmation.

Carnap's point is, then, that only if the phenomenalist asserts (II) as well as (I) does he assert anything testable, and if he asserts (II) then we can do research (of a conceptual rather than an experimental nature, to be sure, but still research of a scientific character) to determine whether or not any translation T can be found with the specified property. Thus was born a new discipline which has been called *logic of science*. Thus also perished phenomenalism! For, although Carnap (and many other philosophers) started out quite confident that (II) was true, thirty years of logical research have established, not that no mapping T with the desired properties exists (no one knows how to show this without looking at all possible mappings T, which is clearly unfeasible), but that all attempts to construct such a mapping are utter failures, and that none of the proposed approaches to the construction of such a mapping can work. Thus it appears overwhelmingly likely today that thing-language *cannot* be 'translated' into a sense-datum language in the sense of (II); and that, therefore, at least some thing-notions must be taken as 'primitive' in any language which is going to be adequate for science.

One result of reformulating the problem (I) by (II) (or exchanging (I) for (II)) has been remarked; Carnap started out as a phenomenalist (in the sense of (II)), and abandoned his phenomenalism, not as a result of a philosophical 'conversion', but as a result of hard scientific research. It is a striking fact that (II) is a formulation on whose falsity it has been possible to get widespread agreement, to the extent that I do not know of a single philosopher or logician of science who today believes (II) to be true, even though thirty years ago the consensus was, if anything, the other way around. In short, it has been possible (tentatively, to be sure) to get intersubjective agreement in philosophy on the falsity of an important philosophical thesis. The school to which Carnap belongs – the so-called Logical Empiricist school – has often been criticized for oversimplification and dogmatism. Oversimplification it has, indeed, been guilty of; but dogmatism seems a highly unfair accusation. I know of no group of philosophers who have been more willing to abandon their own cherished beliefs when careful logical analysis showed those beliefs to be untenable.

The importance of the Logical Empiricist contribution is often over-looked (or worse, deliberately played down) today because the real contribution has turned out to be entirely negative. Not a single one of the great positive theses of Logical Empiricism (that Meaning is Method of Verification; that metaphysical propositions are literally without sense; that Mathematics is True by Convention) has turned out to be correct. It detracts from the excitement of the fact that, by turning philosophical theses into linguistic ones in the fashion indicated by the pair (I)–(II), one can make philosophy more scientific, and settle the truth-value of philosophical propositions by hard scientific research, if the results one obtains are uniformly *negative*. But, while the sense of disappointment is, humanly speaking, all too understandable, and so is the desire to 'try something new', it still remains a great historical contribution to have shown us how to make philosophical propositions more precise. And if the propositions all turn out to be false – well, getting agreement on even that is surely an important progress.

Perhaps a better way of coming to appreciate the importance of Carnap's contribution is to ask ourselves if a positive case for a realistic attitude towards material objects could possibly be made out within the framework of such a 'linguistic' approach to philosophy. I say, a *positive* case, because one case that can be made out for realism is that the only precise alternative is the linguistic version of phenomenalism, and that version appears to be false. My question is whether the realist can say something for his view which is not of the form: the opposing view has such and such things wrong with it.

One positive argument which has been advanced for realism (for example, by Professor Donald Williams) is that the case for realism is an *inductive* one. The induction is not alleged to be of the form: most observed *A* have had the property *P*; so most *A* that will be observed in the future will have the property *P*; but to be an *explanatory induction*. That is, the induction has the form: the 'theory' that there are material objects explains and systematizes the phenomena we observe better than any proposed alternative theory. Therefore we are justified in accepting it, at least as long as no one proposes a simpler theory which has equally great explanatory power and which is incompatible with it.

One way in which one can test the clarifying power of the 'logical syntax' approach to philosophy is to try casting this argument into 'linguistic form'. I believe that doing this sheds light on some limitations of the argument, and also suggests how the argument might be improved.

First of all, if we are going to argue that 'thing theory' bears a certain relation, the relation of explanation (or at least the relation of being a possible explanation) to 'the phenomena we observe', we must decide upon what is to be understood by the expression 'the phenomena we observe'. Are the phenomena we observe sense-data (or sensations, etc.), or are they material things and events? It is clear that if we take the latter course, the course of saying that the phenomena explained by 'thing theory' are the existence and behavior of certain material things, then we will be begging the question. For we will be justifying belief in the existence of material things by saying: 'we all know that such and such material things do so and so. "Thing theory" is the best explanation of this'. But if we already know that such and such material things do so and so, then we already know *in some other way* that material objects exist, and no explanatory induction is needed.

Suppose, then, we take the course of saying that the phenomena to be explained are certain facts statable in a sense-datum language, say, that I have a chair-shaped sense-datum in my visual field. Does 'thing theory' indeed explain such facts?

It is clear that 'thing theory' does *not*, if 'thing theory' is taken to consist of the single sentence 'material objects exist'. For this one sentence is consistent with our having any experiences whatsoever. It is

even consistent with our having no experience of material objects at all!
(We might be disembodied spirits, and material objects might exist but
we might never experience them.) It seems that the one sentence
'material objects exist' is not an explanation of the truth of any sense-
datum statement at all, let alone a 'best explanation'.

More likely what is intended by proponents of the 'inductive argument' for realism is this: Consider the following argument:

(1) I am in a room which contains a chair and my eyes are focussed on
the chair.
There is normal illumination in the room.
I am conscious, and heeding my visual field.
Whenever I am in a room which . . . and there is normal illumination
. . . . and I am conscious and heeding my visual field, it is the case
that (or it is almost always the case that) there is a chair-shaped
sense-datum in my visual field.

(Conclusion) There is a chair-shaped sense-datum in my visual field.

This is a typical *explanatory argument*. The fact to be explained is the
conclusion. The argument shows that the conclusion is derivable from
the last premise, which is a widely accepted general proposition about
the perception of material objects, in conjunction with the other three
premises, which are 'auxiliary hypotheses' which I believe in this
particular case. Thus my whole *system* of beliefs about material things
(and about their relations to sense-experience) can be used to explain
(in accordance with a pattern of explanation widely exemplified in
scientific writings) an undoubted fact concerning my sense-experience.
Whether this Undoubted Fact is, in some sense, 'indubitable', and
whether it is really more 'basic' than facts about material things does
not even have to be discussed (which is one of the advantages of the
Inductivist position). All that is important is that it *is* a fact which the
opponent of realism – say, the subjective idealist – concedes, and hence
a fact which can be appealed to without question begging. (Similarly, in
any crucial experiment to choose between rival *scientific* theories, it is
not necessary that the observations appealed to should be 'epistemo-
logically basic', whatever that might mean, but only that they should
be conceded by both sides.) The ability of my total system of beliefs to
explain such facts, and to explain them simply and coherently, can, the
inductivist contends, be used without circularity or question-begging,
as an *inductive* argument for the correctness of the system as a whole,
not in every particular (which would be absurd), but in its main lines.
Doubtless many changes will be made in our system of knowledge in the

future; but that 'thing theory' will be replaced, not by a better *thing* theory, but by a 'no-thing theory', is enormously inductively unlikely. And if no 'no-thing theory' can be found which explains all the facts explained by 'thing theory', and explains them equally simply and coherently, then that itself is inductive indication that 'no-thing theory' is *false*, i.e. that material objects do exist.

A similar 'inductivist' argument has recently been employed by Paul Ziff in connection with the problem of other minds. Ziff writes:

No hypothesis that stands up under investigation, consideration, stands alone. One holds another, and if they prove tenable in time all transmute from hypothesis to fact, for a time anyway. (And that childish facts continually decay in time to discarded hypotheses should prove no cause for dismay.)

To the hypothesis that my mind and my brain stand in significant relation I conjoin the hypothesis that my mind and my brain stand in this relation not because the mind is mine but because of what minds and brains are. And to these hypotheses I (as many others do) conjoin the hypothesis that among the others that have minds other animals are to be counted. (Possibly man is the only conjectural beast but one can have a mind without being remarkably speculative.) But to say that horses, dogs, cats, cows, all have minds is not to deny that these beings may have qualitatively radically different experiences from men.

And to these hypotheses still others must of course be conjoined. What is in force and active here then is not a silly single hypothesis that there are other minds, this naively supposed to be somehow based on an unexplored analogy. Instead one is confronted with a complex conceptual scheme. The fact that there are other minds is an integral part of this scheme and presently essential to it.

And then Ziff adds, 'A conceptual scheme such as this, commodious enough to encompass rats and others, draws support from a multitude of observations and experiments'.

One difficulty is now obvious. The inductivist is no longer talking about a single hypothesis (indeed, Ziff, in his argument for the existence of other minds, stresses the fact that *many* hypotheses are involved). The claim is now that the explanatory power and mutual support of the whole system of accepted hypotheses somehow confirms, not every single proposition in the system, but the proposition that material objects exist (or that other minds, do, in Ziff's case), because this proposition 'is an integral part of this scheme and presently essential to it'.

I am in general sympathy with this line of thought. But let us see if we cannot make matters a little clearer.

First of all, is this kind of argument *really* a typical 'explanatory induction'? Suppose that instead of naively assuming that it is, we try first to list *differences* between the case for the existence of material objects, as the inductivist develops that case, and a typical explanatory induction in the empirical sciences.

A host of differences come to mind at once. We have already mentioned one of these differences. When two rival theories (e.g. the wave theory and the particle theory of light) are being tested, it is possible to discuss which one better explains 'the phenomena we observe' because the phenomena we observe are reported in an ordinary observational parlance that does not presuppose the truth of either one of the two theories at issue. If I say, e.g. that I have seen such and such shadows or such and such reflections, etc., then I am not presupposing the truth of either the classical wave theory of light of the classical particle theory of light. But the 'phenomena we observe' are, in practice, always reported in thing language, and hence in language that does presuppose the truth of thing theory. We have discussed one way of avoiding this difficulty, namely, to introduce a 'sense-datum language'. But it is important that no such language has ever *in fact* been constructed. I am not arguing that no such language *could* be constructed, or that it would be 'parasitic' on thing language in a way which would beg the question at issue if it were constructed (indeed, I just criticized such attempts on the part of Strawson and Austin). But it is one thing to say that we *might* have a 'sense-datum language', and another thing to say that we *do;* one thing to say that the existence of material objects *might* be established by an explanatory induction (if we went to the immense labour of constructing a sense-datum language first), and another thing to say that it *has been* so confirmed. As a *description* of what we in fact do, the account that we 'infer the existence of material objects from sense-datum statements by an explanatory induction' is just wildly unrealistic.

What I am saying is that the inductivist in fact makes the case for the existence of material objects look *weaker* than it is by overlooking an important part of that case. We don't have just a 'thing theory' – that is, a vast system of hypotheses, every one of which entails the existence of material things – but also a thing *language*, that is, a way of talking which *constantly* presupposes the existence of material things. And that language is not used only for explanation, but also for description. To be sure, a more guarded description than the one we usually give could be given without presupposing the existence of material things, if we had some reason to avoid that presupposition, for example, by using a sense-datum language. But the *utility for description* of thing language is surely part of our justification for accepting it.

In sum, this is one disparity between the case of 'inferring the existence of material objects', and the normal case of an explanatory induction in science: that the observation language used in science can be chosen to be neutral between two typical scientific theories, but can hardly be chosen to be neutral with respect to the existence of material objects. Avoiding locutions which presuppose the truth of either the wave or the particle theory of light is easy; but one cannot avoid locutions which presuppose the existence of material objects without departing from the ordinary way of describing the 'phenomena we observe' altogether. But let us put this point aside, for there is yet another important point about the actual methodology of science that inductivists typically overlook.

That point is that not all imaginable theories are regarded as worth testing. I can easily invent a story about a demon who is capable of doing all sorts of wonderful things. I can even make my 'demon theory' testable in various ways: for example, it might be a consequence of my 'theory' that the demon will appear if I rap on the table sixteen times while wearing a flour sack on my head. Yet I certainly am not going to rush out and procure a flour sack to put on my head so that I can test this theory.

Science, then, is not a matter of testing all the testable theories that we can think of. It is a matter of testing those theories that scientists regard as worth testing. If a scientist thinks that a theory is worth testing, he always has the right to test it, even if no other scientist thinks the theory has a chance. But if no one thinks that a theory is worth testing (like my 'demon theory') then it will never even be put into the field for testing.

Could this feature of the scientific method be eliminated? Suppose scientists were to test *all* the testable theories they could conceive of. What would happen?

It is easily seen, first, that the elimination of this feature of the scientific method is not feasible for beings constituted at all as we are (with our limitations of memory, time, etc.). The number of hypotheses we can think of with testable consequences is larger than the number of elementary particles in the milky way (even if we set a bound on the length of theories that we will consider). For example, let T_{16} be the demon theory just alluded to, let T_{17} be the theory modified to say that I must rap seventeen and not sixteen times, ..., $T\alpha_{100,099,977}$ be the theory modified to say that I must rap 100,099,977 times and not sixteen times, ... Even if I restrict myself to numbers containing not more than sixty digits, I can write down 10^{60} distinct theories of this kind, with distinct testable consequences. Science *must* proceed not by experimentally testing all imaginable theories (although scientists like to talk as if they did proceed in this way), but by rejecting all but a very small number of theories as *a priori* too implausible to be worth testing, and then testing only theories that at least one scientist regards as *a priori* plausible enough (given the philosophical background of his time, of which the operationalistically minded scientist pretends to be quite unconscious) to be worth testing.

Second, if this feature *could* be eliminated – if we could test all the testable consequences of all the theories (under a certain length, say) of which we are capable of thinking (except, of course, theories which cannot be tested except by *not* testing certain other theories!), still we would be no better off. For it is a truism of inductive logic that there are infinitely many distinct theories which agree with any finite set of observations. Even if all the balls drawn from an urn have been black, for example, the following theories will still all have had none but true testable consequences to date (assume today is 1 Jan. 1966): 'all balls drawn prior to 1 Jan. 1966 are black, and all balls that will be drawn thereafter are white', 'all balls drawn prior to 2 Jan. 1966 are black, and all balls that will be drawn thereafter are white', 'all balls drawn prior to 3 Jan. 1966 are black, and all balls that will be drawn thereafter are white', . . . as well as the preferred hypothesis 'all balls are black'. If I accept none of these theories as long as more than one theory in this set is left unrefuted, then I will never accept any theory at all. Yet, if at any point – say, 1 Jan. 1966 – I accept the theory that all balls in the urn are black, I do so not because all of the alternative theories have been refuted (this would be the case only if all the balls in the urn had been examined on 1 Jan. 1966, in which case I wouldn't need an *induction*), but because all of the alternatives that remain are *implausible*, or *ad hoc*, or something of that kind. In short, I will still have to prefer one theory over others not because the preferred theory has led to predictions or explanations that could not be derived from the rejected alternative theories, but on *a priori* grounds, or I will never make any inductions at all.

Sometimes it is said that what is involved is just *simplicity*. We choose the *simplest* theory compatible with the observational data. This use of the word 'simplicity' to cover all the *a priori* factors involved in induction makes it seem that we are not being so *a priori* after all, and also gives us a spurious sense of understanding what we really do not understand at all. Those who talk of simplicity are themselves *simpliste*. [To see this, just ask yourself how 'simplicity' is to be *measured*. Clearly the number of words used in the statement of a theory is no good guide to inductive plausibility – which is what people really mean by 'simplicity', I suspect – since a demon theory might well take fewer words to state than the General Theory of Relativity, notwithstanding the fact that any scientist would reject the demon theory as '*ad hoc*', etc. Some logicians have proposed a weighted count of (a) the number of predicates, and (b) the number of argument-places in each predicate. But again, there is no reason to suppose that such a measure would agree with the actual judgements of scientists, or would have anything to do with the rejection of certain theories as '*ad hoc*', etc. The fact is that we reject 'demon theories' not because they are long, contain too many many-place predicates, etc. – not, in short, because they are too *complicated* – but because no theory of that *type* has ever been successful in the past, and so we regard it as overwhelming unlikely that any such theory will be successful in the future. Moreover, the charge that a theory is '*ad hoc*' usually means that the evidence that the theory explains was known to the formulator of the theory before he formulated the theory, and so it is no 'accident' that the theory conforms to that evidence (and no confirmation of the theory, either). In short, it is not the *simplest*, but the most *probable* theory that gets chosen. But this remark is not a help, except in the sense of helping us to realize just how far we are from having a real theory of these matters. For (i) no real theory of the *probability of theories* exists today; and (ii) the probability of a theory, if it can ever be precisely measured, itself depends on a host of different factors.]

Given these remarks, it is easy to understand why all actually proposed systems of inductive logic of any real power come down to something like this: (i) Some kind of *a priori* ordering of hypotheses (called a 'simplicity ordering', although 'plausibility ordering' might be a better name in view of the foregoing) is presupposed; (ii) given a set S of actually proposed theories that scientists regard as worth testing (i.e. S consists of theories that are not 'too far out' in the simplicity ordering) one tests, if possible until only one 'survives', and then one accepts the survivor, if there is a survivor; (iii) as long as there is still more than one survivor, one accepts the 'simplest' survivor (i.e. the earliest theory in the simplicity ordering that is compatible with the data).

Some systems of inductive logic do not appear to have this form, at least at first blush. For example, Carnap simply introduces a probability metric over sentences, and then induction is just a matter of choosing the most 'probable' hypothesis on the evidence (i.e. the one with the highest 'probability' according to the metric). However, it can be shown that Carnap's system will lead to widely different probability values for the same hypothesis if the language is changed (i.e. the 'probability' is not just a function of the sentences themselves, but of the way they are written, or, more precisely, of what notions are taken as primitive). Thus the choice of a set of primitive predicates is, in a disguised way, a choice of a simplicity ordering of hypotheses.

In practice, it is not necessary that the simplicity ordering should be given by *rules*. But there must be *regularities* in what scientists regard as 'plausible' and 'implausible' hypotheses. If scientists could never come into agreement on this at all (in the social sciences it sometimes seems as if this is the case!), then whenever a scientist accepted a hypothesis, some other scientist would refuse to go along on the grounds that some theory that the first scientist regarded as 'too crazy to bother with' was still 'in the field'. In short, science is a procedure of (i) first coming to agree on a set of hypotheses that are *worth* testing (largely on the basis of intuitive judgements); and (ii) trying to rule out all by experiment, in the hope that exactly one 'survivor' will resist our efforts to rule it out. The net effect is that (i) we keep testing all the hypotheses that we take seriously; but (ii) at the same time we accept, at least tentatively, the theory that is compatible with the data and to which the highest 'plausibility' attaches according to the intuitive judgement of scientists. All induction seems, then, to be a matter of adjusting two demands: the demand that no theory be accepted unless stringent attempts have been made to test it, against the demand that the theory accepted should have as high a position as possible on an ordering that appears to be logically arbitrary, though methodologically very far from arbitrary indeed.

After this brief detour into the topic of inductive logic, let us return to the appraisal of the 'inductivist' argument for the existence of material objects. At this point, I think, a little discomfort ensues. We have just seen that genuine explanatory inductions in science involve stringent attempts to test the theory that we accept. Where are these stringent attempts that we have made to falsify the existence of material objects? Indeed, how should we go about trying to falsify the existence of material objects? And what alternative theories are in the field or ever were in the field?

The fundamental mistake that the inductivist makes is in having too simple a view of science. He writes as if empirical statements were all 'hypotheses', and as if 'hypotheses' had only two statuses, 'confirmed by experiment (or observation)' and 'not confirmed'. But there are many further possibilities, as should now be clear. First of all, an empirical proposition may be such that no alternative to it at all can be conceived at a given time. This was the case, for example, with the propositions of Euclidean geometry (interpreted as assertions about shortest paths in actual physical space), prior to the work of Lobachevsky, Gauss, Riemann, etc. In such a case, the proposition does not have the status of a 'hypothesis' (as long as no alternative can be conceived), but of a fact – indeed, of some kind of a necessary fact. Some would say that this is only a 'psychological' remark. But we have just seen that the line between psychology and methodology is not at all sharp (the actual 'simplicity ordering' unconsciously used by scientists is also a 'psychological' matter); and, furthermore, it is a legitimate methodological remark, in any case, that some theories can be overthrown by a specifiable observation (e.g. 'all crows are black' by a single accepted observation of a non-black crow), while other theories can only be overthrown by observation *plus* alternative theory (e.g. a system of geometry). Secondly, even if alternatives to a given empirical proposition are imaginable, if all of them are completely *silly*, in the actual judgment of scientists – if no scientist would go to the bother of testing one of these 'alternatives', any more than he would put a flour sack on his head and rap the table sixteen times – then that proposition has the status of *fact*, not hypothesis, and one *justifies* according it that status *not* by talking about an 'explanatory induction', but by challenging the person who *asks* for a justification to propose an alternative hypothesis that isn't too silly to bother with. Finally, an empirical proposition may have one status at one time and a different status at a later time. For example, Maxwell's equations were once the postulates of an empirical theory that could have been called a hypothesis, but today there is no alternative to them in the field; Euclidean geometry once had the status of necessary truth, while today those physicists who still think that space may be Euclidean (i.e. who reject General Relativity), are advancing a 'hypothesis'.

We see now what is so weird about the inductivist account of our reasons for believing in the existence of material objects. On that account, it is as if we always spoke sense-datum language, not thing language, and after thousands of years some brilliant scientist suggested the 'hypothesis' that there might be material objects. Various objections were proposed; alternative hypotheses were put forward; but after a series of crucial experiments, the 'survivor' was 'The Material Object Hypothesis'. So today the Material Object Hypothesis is 'well confirmed'.

We also see how to correct the distortions of this account while preserving the very important insight that is in this account – namely, that an answer to the sceptic *can* be given (unless the sceptic is also a sceptic with respect to the scientific method, and then it is at least well to smoke this out), and that that answer is, roughly, that the rationale for the acceptance of 'thing theory' has an important analogy to the rationale for the acceptance of certain propositions in empirical science. But it is important to get the analogy *right*. Our belief in the existence of material objects, insofar as it is not completely *sui generis* as, of course, it very largely is, is far more analogous to our acceptance of the *central* propositions of empirical science (e.g. 'space has three dimensions'), than it is to the acceptance of 'garden variety' empirical 'hypotheses'.

The analogy, in fact, extends to several distinct resemblances. Ordinary observation language presupposes both the existence of material objects and the three dimensionality of space; thus the 'observation reports' scientists actually make are not 'neutral' with respect to the theories being 'confirmed' when the existence of material objects or the three dimensionality of space are thought of as being these theories. Yet, if it were necessary for some reason one could make more guarded reports (e.g. in sense-datum language) which did not presuppose the existence of material objects, and one could find some way of couching ordinary observation reports which did not assume that space has only three dimensions. Alternative theories are just barely imaginable in both cases; but certainly no alternative has ever been seriously entertained (nor is there any reason now to entertain any such alternative), or even worked out in the detail that a scientist would require before he gave a theory serious consideration. If one were to consider seriously Descartes' suggestion that our sensations are caused by a 'demon', for example, one would want to know a good deal about the supposed nature and workings of demons. Neither theory has ever been 'tested', as a consequence, because the 'testing' of a theory demands in most cases (and certainly in this case) the existence of an alternative theory that has been elaborated to a certain stage. Thus it is incorrect to say that either the existence of material objects or the three dimensionality of space has been 'established': not because these propositions are 'not established', but because both 'established' and 'not established' assume that an inductive test has been carried out, and hence that an alternative theory has at some time been in the field. Rather, both the existence of material objects and the three dimensionality of space have the status of fact – not 'hypothesis', or 'theory', or 'established fact', but just fact *period*. And the answer to 'how do you know?' is *not* 'on the basis of such and such evidence', but just that no alternative theory has ever been in the field.

In sum, our acceptance of the proposition that there are material objects is both analogous and disanalogous to our acceptance of empirical theories on the basis of explanatory induction. It is disanalogous insofar as 'material objects exist' is, in the first instance, not a theory at all, but rather a logical consequence of a host of specific theories, hypotheses, laws, and plain ordinary empirical propositions. These have indeed (many of them) been established by explanatory induction; but in each case the alternatives were *not* theories which implied the *non*-existence of material objects, but alternative theories *about* material objects. It is also disanalogous insofar as it is 'built into' the language we use to make observation reports that material objects exist. It is analogous, however, in that *part* of the justification for the acceptance of the proposition that material objects exist is that to give up that proposition would require giving up all the theories, statements, etc., that imply it, and these later statements do have (many of them) the kind of explanatory role that the inductivist stresses. (Another part of the justification is the utility of thing language in *description*, as opposed to explanation.) It is also analogous in that many empirical theories are accepted today precisely for the two reasons that (a) they, or theories which presuppose them, provide intuitively plausible explanations of many phenomena; and (b) no alternative is today in the field. However, in the case of those empirical theories alternatives were *once* in the field; while in the case of the existence of material objects this is not so.

[Still another part of the problem, which it would lead us too far astray to go into here, has to do with the problem of so-called 'pseudo-hypotheses'. That is, what do we do if someone elaborates a hypothesis in all the detail one could require, but that hypothesis leads to exactly the same predictions as the normal 'thing theory'? E.g. suppose someone elaborates the hypothesis that there is a demon who causes us to have exactly the sensations that we would have if material objects really did exist, but that we are in fact all disembodied spirits, including the demon. One common move is to say that such hypotheses are 'meaning-less', but this is to invent an *ad hoc* conception of 'meaning' precisely for the purpose of rejecting such hypotheses, which is not satisfactory. Another move is to say that such hypotheses are *ad hoc*, parasitic on the 'normal' system, etc. But no criteria for '*ad hocness*', 'parasitism', 'complexity' etc., are really available today except the intuitive judg-ments of scientists. Perhaps this is the best that can be done: perhaps the scientific method just rests, beyond a certain point, on a *de facto* agreement as to what is 'plausible' and what is '*ad hoc*' (or just 'silly').]

Let us now compare this last discussion (of inductivist realism) with our earlier discussion of phenomenalism. In spite of the differences – in the one case one was making precise an idealistic metaphysics, in the hope that something in it might prove tenable, in the other case one is making precise a realistic metaphysics, for the sake of showing that something in *that* is tenable – there are strong methodological similarities. In both cases, an originally 'nonlinguistic' problem has been given a linguistic garb. In both cases, the linguistic garb depends upon a distinction between two 'languages', i.e. two grammatically closed sets of sentences: thing language, and some sort of 'sense-datum language'. In the first case, the attempt was to show that the relation between the two languages is one of translatability. In the second case, the focus was shifted from the languages to the 'theories', i.e. systems of sentences (or beliefs as represented by sentences) that we accept in the two languages, with the aim of showing that the relation between 'thing theory' and 'observation reports in sense-datum language' is one of *explanation* (going in the direction *from* thing theory *to* sense-datum statements) and *inductive support* (going in the direction *from* sense-datum statements *to* thing theory). Both claims turn out to be over-simplifications; but there is hardly a philosopher today who has studied both claims carefully who does not feel that the study has led to a deeper appreciation of the special role of thing theory and language, and to deep insights into the *traditional* problem of the existence of material objects.

2

The analytic and the synthetic*

The techniques employed by philosophers of physics are usually the very ones being employed by philosophers of a less specialized kind (especially empiricist philosophers) at the time. Thus Mill's philosophy of science largely reflects Hume's associationism; Reichenbach's philosophy of science reflects Viennese positivism with its conventionalism, its tendency to identify (or confuse) meaning and evidence, and its sharp dichotomy between 'the empirical facts' and 'the rules of the language'; and (coming up to the present time) Toulmin's philosophy of science is an attempt to give an account of what scientists do which is consonant with the linguistic philosophy of Wittgenstein. For this reason, errors in general philosophy can have a far-reaching effect on the philosophy of science. The confusion of meaning with evidence is one such error whose effects are well known: it is the contention of the present paper that overworking of the analytic–synthetic distinction is another root of what is most distorted in the writings of conventional philosophers of science.

The present paper is an attempt to give an account of the analytic–synthetic distinction both inside and outside of physical theory. It is hoped that the paper is sufficiently nontechnical to be followed by a reader whose background in science is not extensive; but it has been necessary to consider problems connected with physical science (particularly the definition of 'kinetic energy', and the conceptual problems connected with geometry) in order to bring out the features of the analytic–synthetic distinction that seem to me to be the most important.

In addition to the danger of overworking the analytic-synthetic distinction, there is the somewhat newer danger of denying its existence altogether. Although, as I shall argue below, this is a less serious error (from the point of view of the scientist or the philosopher interested in the conceptual problems presented by physical theory) than the customary overworking of the distinction, it is, nevertheless, an error. Thus the present paper fights on two fronts: it tries to 'defend' the distinction,

* First published in Herbert Feigl and Grover Maxwell (eds.), *Minnesota Studies in the Philosophy of Science*, III. University of Minnesota Press, Mpls. Copyright 1962 by the University of Minnesota.

while attacking its extensive abuse by philosophers. Fortunately, the two fronts are not too distant from each other; one reason that the analytic–synthetic distinction has seemed so difficult to defend recently is that it has become so bloated!

Replies to Quine

In the spring of 1951 Professor W. V. Quine published a paper entitled 'Two Dogmas of Empiricism' (Quine, 1951). This paper provoked a spate of replies, but most of the replies did not match the paper which stimulated them in originality or philosophic significance. Quine denied the existence of the analytic–synthetic distinction altogether. He challenged doctrines which had been dear to the hearts of a great many philosophers and (in spite of the title of his paper) not only philosophers in the empiricist camp. The replies to Quine have played mostly on a relatively small number of stereotyped themes. The tendency has been to 'refute' Quine by citing examples. Of course, the analytic–synthetic distinction rests on a certain number of classical examples. We would not have been tempted to draw it or to keep on drawing it for so long if we did not have a stock of familiar examples on which to fall back. But it is clear that the challenge raised by Quine cannot be met either by pointing to the traditional examples or by simply waving one's hand and saying how implausible it is that there should be no distinction at all when there seems to be such a clear one in at least some cases. I do not agree with Quine, as will be clear in the sequel. I am convinced that there is an analytic–synthetic distinction that we can correctly (if not very importantly) draw, and I am inclined to sympathize with those who cite the examples and who stress the implausibility, the tremendous implausibility, of Quine's thesis – the thesis that the distinction which certainly seems to exist does not in fact exist at all.

But to say that Quine is wrong is not in itself very fruitful or very interesting. The important question is How is he wrong? Faced with the battery of Quine's arguments, how can we defend the existence of any genuine analytic–synthetic distinction at all? Philosophers have the right to have intuitions and to believe things on faith; scientists often have no better warrant for many of their beliefs, at least not for a time. But if a philosopher really feels that Quine is wrong and has no statement to make other than the statement that Quine is wrong and that he feels this in his bones, then this is material to be included in that philosopher's autobiography; it does not belong in a technical journal under the pretense of being a reply to Quine. From this criticism I specifically exempt the article by P. F. Strawson and H. P. Grice (Strawson, 1956), who offer *theoretical* reasons for supposing that the analytic–synthetic distinction does in fact exist, even if they do not very satisfactorily delineate that distinction or shed much real light on its nature. Indeed, the argument used by them to the effect that *where there is agreement on the use of the expressions involved with respect to an open class, there must necessarily be some kind of distinction present,* seems to me correct and important. Perhaps this argument is the only one of any novelty to have appeared since Quine published his paper.

But important as it is to have a theoretical argument supporting the existence of the distinction in question (so that we do not have to appeal simply to 'intuition' and 'faith'), still the argument offered by Strawson and Grice does not go far toward clarifying the distinction, and this, after all, is Quine's challenge. In other words, we are in the position of *knowing* that there *is* an analytic–synthetic distinction but of not being able to make it very clear just what the nature of this distinction is.

Of course, in some cases it is not very important that we cannot make clear what the nature of a distinction is, but in the case of the analytic–synthetic distinction it seems that the nature of the distinction is far more important than the few trivial examples that are commonly cited, e.g. 'All bachelors are unmarried' (for the analytic side of the dichotomy) and 'There is a book on this table' (for the synthetic side). To repeat: philosophers who do not agree with Quine have found themselves in the last few years in this position: they know that there *is* an analytic–synthetic distinction but they are unable to give a satisfactory account of its nature.

It is, in the first place, no good to draw the distinction by saying that a man who rejects an analytic sentence is *said* not to understand the language or the relevant part of the language. For this is a comment on the use of the word 'understand' and, as such, not very helpful. There could be an analytic–synthetic distinction even in a language which did not use such words as 'analytic,' 'synthetic,' 'meaning,' and 'understanding.' We do not want, after all, to draw the analytic-synthetic distinction in terms of dispositions to use the words 'analytic' and 'synthetic' themselves, nor dispositions to use related expressions, e.g. 'have the same meaning' and 'does not understand what he is saying'. What is needed is something quite different: we should be able to indicate the nature and rationale of the analytic–synthetic distinction. What happens to a statement when it is analytic? What do people do with it? Or if one wishes to talk in terms of artificial languages: What point is there to having a separate class of statements called analytic statements? Why mark these off from all the others? What do you do with the statements so marked? It is only in this sort of terms that I think we can go beyond the level of saying, 'Of course there are analytic statements. I can give

35

you examples. If someone rejects one of these, we say he doesn't understand the language, etc.'. The real problem is not to describe the language game we play with words like 'meaning' and 'understanding' but to answer the deeper question, 'What is the point of the game?'

The analytic–synthetic distinction in philosophy

It should not be supposed that the axe I have to grind here is that Quine is wrong. That Quine is wrong I have no doubt. This is not a matter of philosophical argument: it seems to me there is as gross a distinction between 'All bachelors are unmarried' and 'There is a book on this table' as between any two things in the world, or, at any rate, between any two linguistic expressions in the world; and no matter how long I might fail in trying to clarify the distinction, I should not be persuaded that it does not exist. In fact, I do not understand what it would mean to say that a distinction between two things *that* different does not exist.

Thus I think that Quine is wrong. There are analytic statements: 'All bachelors are unmarried' is one of them. But in a deeper sense I think that Quine is right; far more right than his critics. I think that there is an analytic–synthetic distinction, but a rather trivial one. And I think that the analytic–synthetic distinction has been so radically overworked that it is less of a philosophic error, although it is an error, to maintain that there is no distinction at all than it is to employ the distinction in the way that it has been employed by some of the leading analytic philosophers of our generation. I think, in other words, that if one proceeds, as Quine does, on the assumption that there is no analytic–synthetic distinction at all, one would be right on far more philosophic issues and one will be led to far more philosophic insights than one will be if one accepts that heady concoction of ideas with which we are all too familiar: the idea that every statement is either analytic or synthetic, the idea that all logical truths are analytic, the idea that all analytic truth derives its necessity from 'linguistic convention'. I would even put the thesis to be defended here more strongly: ignore the analytic–synthetic distinction, and you will not be wrong in connection with any philosophic issues not having to do specifically with the distinction. Attempt to use it as a weapon in philosophical discussion, and you will consistently be wrong.

It is not, of course, an accident that one will consistently be wrong if one attempts to employ the analytic–synthetic distinction in philosophy. 'Bachelor' may be synonymous with 'unmarried man' but that cuts no philosophic ice. 'Chair' may be synonymous with 'movable seat for one with a back' but that bakes no philosophic bread and washes no philosophic windows. It is the belief that there are synonymies and analyticities of a deeper nature – synonymies and analyticities that cannot be discovered by the lexicographer or the linguist but only by the philosopher – that is incorrect.†

I don't happen to believe that there are such objects as 'sense data'; so I do not find 'sense-datum language' much more interesting than phlogiston language or leprechaun language. But even if sense data did exist and we granted the possibility of constructing sense-datum language, I do not think that the expression 'chair', although it is synonymous with 'movable seat for one with a back', is in the same way synonymous with any expression that one could in principle construct in the sense-datum language. This is an example of the type of 'hidden' synonymy or 'philosophic' synonymy that some philosophers have claimed to discover and that does not exist.

However, misuse of the analytic–synthetic distinction is not confined to translationists. I have seen it argued by a philosopher of a more contemporary strain that the hypothesis that the earth came into existence five minues ago (complete with 'memory traces', 'causal remains', etc.) is a *logically* absurd hypothesis. The argument was that the whole use of time words presupposes the existence of the past. If we grant the meaningfulness of this hypothesis, then, it is contended, we must grant the possibility that there is no past at all (the world might have come into existence at *this* instant). Thus, we have an example of a statement which uses time words, but which, if true, destroys the possibility of their use. This somewhat fuzzily described situation is alleged to be tantamount to the meaninglessness or self-contradictoriness of the hypothesis I described.

Now I agree that the hypothesis in question is more than empirically false. It *is* empirically false, if by empirically false one means simply that it is false about the world – the world did not come into existence at this instant nor did it come into existence five minutes ago. It is not empirically false if one means by 'empirically false statement' a statement which can be confuted by *isolated* experiments. But while it is important to recognize that this is not the sort of hypothesis that can be confuted by isolated experiment, it is not, I think, happy to maintain that the existence of a past is analytic, if one's paradigm for analyticity is the 'All bachelors are unmarried' kind of statement.‡ And I think that, while few philosophers would explicitly make the kind of mistake I have described,

---

† I do not wish to suggest that linguistic regularities, properly so called, are never of importance in philosophy, but only that analytic statements, properly so called, are not.

‡ To accept the hypothesis that the world came into existence five minutes ago does not make it necessary to give up any *particular* prediction. But I deny (a) that it 'makes no difference to prediction,' and (b) that 'it therefore (*sic!*) amounts to a change in our use of language.'

a great many philosophers tend to make it implicitly. The idea that every truth which is not empirical in the second of the senses I mentioned must be a 'rule of language' or that all necessity must be traced down to the obligation not to 'violate the rules of language' is a pernicious one, and Quine is profoundly right in rejecting it; the reasons he gives are, moreover, the right reasons. What I maintain is that there are no further rules of language beyond the garden variety of rules which a lexicographer or a grammarian might discover, and which only the philosopher can discover.

This is not to say that there are not some things which are very much *like* 'rules of language'. There is after all a place for *stipulation* in cognitive inquiry, and truth by stipulation has seemed to some the very model of analyticity. There is also the question of linguistic misuse. Under certain circumstances a man is said not merely to be in error but to be making linguistic mistakes – not to know the meaning of the very words he is employing. Philosophers have thought that by looking at such situations we could reconstruct a codex which might constitute the 'implicit rules' of natural language. For instance, they hold that, in many circumstances, to say of a man that he knows that p implies that he has, or had at some time, or can produce, or could produce at some time, evidence that p – and that such an implication is very much like the implication between being a bachelor and being unmarried. But, as I shall argue below, there are differences which it is absolutely vital to recognize. It is not that the statements I have mentioned fall into a third category. They fall into many different categories. Over and beyond the clear-cut rules of language, on the one side, and the clear-cut descriptive statements, on the other, are just an enormous number of statements which are not happily classified as either analytic or synthetic.

The case of stipulation is one in point. One must consider the role of the stipulation and whether the truth introduced by stipulation retains its conventional character or whether it later figures in inquiry on a par with other truths, without reference to the way in which it was introduced. We have to consider the question of the arbitrariness versus systematic import of our stipulations. There is one kind of wholly arbitrary stipulation which does indeed produce analytic statements, but we should not be led to infer that, therefore, every stipulation produces analytic statements. The Einstein stipulation that the constancy of the light velocity should be used to 'define' simultaneity in a reference system does not, Reichenbach to the contrary, generate an analytic truth of the same order as 'All bachelors are unmarried'. And even the case of *knowing* and *having* or *having had evidence* requires much treatment and involves special difficulties. I shall in the body of this paper try to draw some of the distinctions that I think need to be drawn. For the moment let me only say this: if one wants to have a model of language, it is far better to proceed on the idea that statements fall into three kinds – analytic, synthetic, and lots-of-other-things – than to proceed on the idea that, except for borderline fuzziness, every statement is either analytic or synthetic.

Of course many philosophers are aware that there are statements which are not happily classified as either analytic or synthetic. My point is not that there exist exceptional examples, but that there is a far larger class of such statements than is usually supposed. For example, to ask whether or not the principles of logic are analytic is to ask a bad question. Virtually all the *laws* of natural science are statements with respect to which it is not *happy* to ask the question 'Analytic or synthetic? It must be one or the other, mustn't it?' And with respect to the framework principles that are often discussed by philosophers, the existence of the past or the implication that some times exists between knowing and having had evidence, it is especially a mistake to classify these statements as 'rules of language' or 'true because of the logic of the concepts involved' or 'analytic' or 'L-true' or ... This is not to say that all these principles have the same nature or that they form a compact new class, e.g. framework principles (as if one were to take seriously the label I have been using). 'There is a past' is recognizably closer to the law of conservation of energy than 'If Jones knows that p, then he must have or have had evidence that p' (in the cases where the latter inference seems a necessary one); and 'If Jones knows that *p*, then he must have or have had evidence that *p*' is more like 'All bachelors are unmarried' than is 'There is a past'. But neither statement is of exactly the same kind as the law of conservation of energy, although that law too is a statement with respect to which it is not happy to say, 'Is it analytic or synthetic?' and neither statement is of exactly the same kind as 'All bachelors are unmarried'. What these statements reveal are different degrees of something like convention, and different kinds of systematic import. In the case of 'All bachelors are unmarried', we have the highest degree of linguistic convention and the minimum degree of systematic import. In the case of the statement 'There is a past', we have an overwhelming amount of systematic import – so much that we can barely conceive of a conceptual system which did not include the idea of a past. That is to say, such a conceptual system differs so greatly from our present conceptual system that the idea of ever making a transition from one to the other seems fantastic†. In the case of knowing without ever having any

† For example, we *could* accept the hypothesis that the world came into existence 1 January 1957, without changing the *meaning* of any word; but to do so would have

reason to believe, still other considerations are involved. We have to ask what we would say if people appeared to be able to answer questions truthfully about a certain subject matter although they had never had any acquaintance with that subject matter as far as we could detect. *Knowing* is something that we do not have much of a theory about. It makes little difference at *present* whether we say that such people would be correctly described as 'knowing' the answers to the various questions in the area in which they are able to act as an oracle, or whether we say that they have an 'uncanny facility at guessing the correct answer'; although, in the light of a more advanced theory, it might very well make a good deal of difference what we say. The concept of the past, on the other hand, and the concept of time, are deeply integrated into our physical theory, and any tampering with these concepts would involve a host of revisions if simple consistency is to be maintained. In the sequel I shall try to describe in somewhat more detail the diverse natures of the statements in that vast class with respect to which it is not happy to say 'analytic or synthetic'. But on the whole my story will resemble Quine's. That is to say, I believe that we have a conceptual system with centralities and priorities. I think the statements in that conceptual system – except for the *trivial* examples of analyticity, e.g. 'All bachelors are unmarried', 'All vixens are foxes' – fall on a continuum, a multi-dimensional continuum. More or less stipulation enters; more or less systematic import. But any one of these principles might be given up, farfetched though it may seem, and perhaps without altering the meaning of the constituent words. Of course, if we give up a principle that is analytic in the trivial sense ('All bachelors are unmarried'), then we have clearly changed the meaning of a word. But the revision of a sufficient number of principles, no one of which is by itself analytic in quite the way in which 'All bachelors are unmarried' is analytic, may also add up to what we should describe as a change in the meaning of a word. With Quine, I should like to stress the monolithic character of our conceptual system, the idea of our conceptual system as a massive alliance of beliefs which face the tribunal of experience collectively and not independently, the idea that 'when trouble strikes' revisions can, with a very few exceptions, come anywhere. I should like, with Quine, to stress the extent to which the meaning of an individual word is a function of its place in the network, and the impossibility of separating, in the actual use of a word, that part of the use which reflects the

a crippling effect on many sciences, and on much of ordinary life. (Think of the *ad hoc* hypotheses that would have to be invented to account for the 'creation'. And consider the role played by data concerning the past in, say, astronomy – not to mention ordinary human relations!)

'meaning' of the word and that part of the use which reflects deeply embedded collateral information.

Linguistic conventionalism

One more point will terminate this rather interminable set of preliminary remarks. The focus of this paper is the analytic–synthetic distinction, not because I think that distinction is of itself of overwhelming importance. In fact, I think it is of overwhelming unimportance. But I believe that the issues raised by Quine go to the very center of philosophy. I think that appreciating the diverse natures of logical truths, of physically necessary truths in the natural sciences, and of what I have for the moment lumped together under the title of framework principles – that clarifying the nature of these diverse kinds of statements is the most important work that a philosopher can do. Not because philosophy is necessarily about language, but because we must become clear about the roles played in our conceptual systems by these diverse kinds of truths before we can get an adequate global view of the world, of thought, of language, or of anything. In particular, I think we might begin to appreciate the real problems in the domain of formal science once we rid ourselves of the easy answer that formal truth is in some sense 'linguistic in origin'; and in any case I think that one's whole view of the world is deeply affected, if one is a philosopher, by one's view of what it is to have a view about the world. Someone who identifies conceptualization with linguistic activity and who identifies linguistic activity with response to observable situations in accordance with rules of language which are themselves no more than implicit conventions or implicit stipulations (in the ordinary unphilosophic sense of 'stipulation' and 'convention') will, it seems to me, have a deeply distorted conception of human knowledge and, indirectly, of some or all objects of human knowledge. We must not fall into the error of supposing that to master the total use of an expression is to master a repertoire of individual uses, that the individual uses are the product of something like implicit stipulation or implicit convention, and that the conventions and stipulations are arbitrary. (The notion of a nonarbitrary convention is of course an absurdity – conventions are used precisely to settle questions that are arbitrary.) For someone who uses language in the way that I have just described. there are observable phenomena at the macrolevel and there are conventional responses to these, and this is all of knowledge; one can, of course, say that 'there are atoms' and that 'science is able to tell us a great deal about atoms', but *this* turns out to be no more than making noises in response to macrostimuli *in accordance with arbitrary conventions*. I do not think that any philosopher explicitly maintains such a view of knowledge; and if he did it is clear that he would be a sort of mitigated phenomenalist. But I do think that a good many philosophers implicitly hold such a view, or fall into writing as if they held such a view, simply because they tend to think of use as a sum of individual uses and of linguistic use on the model suggested by the phrase 'rules of language'.

To sum up: I do not agree with Quine, that there is no analytic–synthetic distinction to be drawn at all. But I do believe that his emphasis on the monolithic character of our conceptual system and his negative emphasis on the *silliness* of regarding mathematics as consisting in some sense of 'rules of language', represent exceedingly important theoretical insights in philosophy. I think that what we have to do now is to settle the relatively trivial question concerning analytic statements properly so called ('All bachelors are unmarried'). We have to take a fresh look at the framework principles so much discussed by philosophers, disabusing ourselves of the idea that they are 'rules of language' in any literal or lexicographic sense; and above all, we have to take a fresh look at the nature of logical and mathematical truths. With Quine's contribution, we have to face two choices: We can ignore it and go on talking about the 'logic' of individual words. In that direction lies sterility and more, much more, of what we have already read. The other alternative is to face and explore the insight achieved by Quine, trying to reconcile the fact that Quine is overwhelmingly right in his critique of what other philosophers have *done* with the analytic–synthetic distinction with the fact that Quine is wrong in his literal thesis, namely, that the distinction itself does not exist *at all*. In the latter direction lies philosophic progress. For philosophic progress is nothing if it is not the discovery of new areas for dialectical exploration.

Analytic and nonanalytic statements

The 'kinetic energy definition'

As a step toward clarification of the analytic–synthetic distinction, I should like to contrast a paradigm case of analyticity – 'All bachelors are unmarried' – with an example which superficially resembles it: the statement that kinetic energy is equal to one half the product of mass and velocity squared, '$e = \frac{1}{2}mv^2$.' I think that if we can see the respect in which these two examples differ, we will have made important progress toward such a clarification.

Let us take the second statement first, '$e = \frac{1}{2}mv^2$'; this is the sort of statement that before relativistic physics one might well have called a 'definition of "kinetic energy"'. Yet, its history is unusual. Certainly, before Einstein, any physicist might have said, '"$e = \frac{1}{2}mv^2$"', that is just the definition of "kinetic energy". There is no more to it than that. The expression "kinetic energy" is, as it were, a sort of abbreviation for the longer expression "one-half the mass times the velocity squared"'.

If this were true, then the expression 'kinetic energy' would, of course, be in principle dispensable. One could simply use '$\frac{1}{2}mv^2$' wherever one had used 'kinetic energy.'

In the early years of the twentieth century, however, Albert Einstein developed a theory, a physical theory – but of an unusual sort. It is unusual because it contains words of a rather high degree of vagueness, at least in terms of what we usually suppose the laws of physics to be like. All this notwithstanding, the theory is, as we all well know, a precise and useful theory.

What I have in mind is Einstein's principle that all physical laws must be Lorentz-invariant. This is a rather vague principle, since it involves the general notion of a physical law. Yet in spite of its vagueness, or perhaps because of its vagueness, scientists have found it an extremely useful leading principle. Of course, Einstein contributed more than a leading principle. He actually proceeded to find Lorentz-invariant laws of nature; and the search for a Lorentz-invariant law of gravitation, in particular, produced the general theory of relativity.†

But it would be a mistake to think of the special theory of relativity as the sum of the special laws that Einstein produced. The *general* principle that all physical laws are Lorentz-invariant is certainly a legitimate part of the special theory of relativity, notwithstanding the fact that it is stated in what some purists might call 'the metalanguage'. And it is no good to say that 'a physical law' means 'any true physical statement': for so interpreted Einstein's principle would be empty. Any equation whatsoever can be made Lorentz-invariant by writing it in terms of suitable magnitudes. The principle that the laws of nature must be Lorentz-invariant is without content unless we suppose that the magnitudes to be contained in laws of nature must be in some sense real magnitudes– e.g. electricity, gravitation, magnetism – and that the equations expressing the laws must have certain characteristics of simplicity and plausibility. In practice, Einstein's principle is quite precise, in the only sense relevant to physical inquiry, notwithstanding the fact that it contains a vague term. The point is that the vagueness of the term 'physical law' does not affect the applications which the physicist makes of the principle. In practice, the physicist has no difficulty in recognizing laws or putative laws: any 'reasonable' equation proposed by a physicist in

† Of course, the general theory of relativity itself *replaces* the requirement of Lorentz-invariance with the requirement of covariance.

his right mind constitutes at least a putative law. Thus, the Einstein principle, although it might bother those logicians who are worried, and rightly worried, about the right distinction between a natural law and any true statement whatsoever, is one whose role in physical inquiry is clear-cut. It means simply that those equations considered by physicists as expressing possible laws of nature must, if they are to remain candidates for that role in the age of relativity, be Lorentz-invariant. Of course, the principle does not play only the purely negative role of ruling out what might otherwise be admissible scientific theories: the fact that laws of nature must be Lorentz-invariant has often been a valuable clue to fundamental new discoveries. The Einstein gravitation theory has already been mentioned; another famous example is Dirac's 'hole' theory, which led to the discovery of the positron.

Returning now to our account of the history of the 'energy definition': the principle just described led Einstein to change a great many physical laws. Some of the older laws, of course, survived: the Maxwell equations, for instance, turned out to be Lorentz-invariant as they stood. Some of the principles that Einstein revised would ordinarily be regarded as being of an empirical nature. The statements 'Moving clocks slow down' and 'One cannot exceed the velocity of light' are certainly statements which we should regard as synthetic. The interesting thing is that Einstein was to revise, and in an *exactly similar fashion*, principles that had traditionally been regarded as definitional in character. In particular Einstein, as we all know, changed the definition of 'kinetic energy'. That is to say, he replaced the law '$e = \frac{1}{2}mv^2$' by a more complicated law. If we expand the Einstein definition of energy as a power series, the first two terms are '$e = mc^2 + \frac{1}{2}mv^2 + \ldots$' We might, of course, reply that classically speaking '$\frac{1}{2}mv^2$' defines not 'energy' in general (e.g. 'potential energy') but only 'kinetic energy'; we might try to say that the energy that a body has because of its rest mass (this is represented by the term 'mc^2') should not be counted as part of its kinetic energy, as Einstein does. The point is that even the magnitude in the theory of relativity that corresponds to the classical kinetic energy of a particle, that is, its total kinetic energy minus the energy due to its rest mass, is not equal to $\frac{1}{2}mv^2$ except as a first approximation. If you take the total relativistic kinetic energy of a particle and subtract the energy due to its rest mass, you will obtain not only the leading term '$\frac{1}{2}mv^2$' but also terms in 'mv^4', etc.

It would clearly be a distortion of the situation to say that 'kinetic energy $= \frac{1}{2}mv^2$' was a definition, and that Einstein merely changed the definition. The paradigm that this account suggests is somewhat as follows: 'kinetic energy', before Einstein, was *arbitrarily* used to stand for '$\frac{1}{2}mv^2$'. After Einstein, 'kinetic energy' was *arbitrarily* used to stand for '$m + \frac{1}{2}mv^2 + \frac{3}{8}mv^4 + \text{—}$'† This account is, of course, incorrect.

What is striking is this: whatever the status of the 'energy definition' may have been before Einstein, in revising it, Einstein treated it as just another natural law. There was a whole set of pre-existing physical and mechanical laws which had to be tested for compatibility with the new body of theory. Some stood the test unchanged – others only with some revision. Among the equations that had to be revised (and formal considerations indicated a rather natural way of making the revision, one which was, moreover, borne out richly by experiments) was the equation '$e = \frac{1}{2}mv^2$'.

The moral of all this is not difficult to find. The 'energy definition' may have had a special status when it came into the body of accepted physical theory, although this is a question for the historian of science to answer. It may even, let us suppose, have originally been accepted on the basis of explicit stipulation to the effect that the phrase 'kinetic energy' was to be used in the sense of '$\frac{1}{2}mv^2$'. Indeed, there was some discussion between Newton and Leibniz on the question whether the term 'energy' should be applied to what we now do call 'energy' or what we call 'momentum'. Suppose, however, that a congress of scientists had been convened in, say, 1780 and had settled this controversy by legislating that the term 'kinetic energy' was to be used for $\frac{1}{2}mv^2$ and not for mv. Would this have made the principle '$e = \frac{1}{2}mv^2$' analytic? It would be true by stipulation, wouldn't it? It would be true by stipulation, yes, *but only in a context which is defined by the fact that the only alternative principle is '$e = mv$.'*

Quine has suggested that the distinction between truths by stipulation and truths by experiment is one which can be drawn only at the moving frontier of science. Conventionality is not 'a lingering trait' of the statements introduced as truths by stipulation. The principle '$e = \frac{1}{2}mv^2$' may have been introduced, at least in our fable, by stipulation; the Newtonian law of gravity may have been introduced on the basis of induction from the behavior of the known satellite system and the solar system (as Newton claimed); but in subsequent developments these two famous formulas were to figure on a par. Both were used in innumerable physical experiments until they were challenged by Einstein, without ever being regarded as themselves subject to test in the particular experiment. If a physicist makes a calculation and gets an empirically wrong answer, he does not suspect that the mathematical principles used in the calculation may have been wrong (assuming that those principles are themselves theorems of mathematics) nor does he suspect that the

† This formula assumes that the unit of time is chosen so that the speed of light = 1.

law '$f = ma$' may be wrong. Similarly, he did not frequently suspect before Einstein that the law '$e = \frac{1}{2}mv^2$' might be wrong or that the Newtonian gravitational law might be wrong. (Newton himself did, however, suspect the latter). These statements, then, have a kind of preferred status. They can be overthrown, but not by an isolated experiment. They can be overthrown only if someone incorporates principles incompatible with those statements in a successful conceptual system.

Principles of geometry

An analogy may be drawn with the case of geometry. No experiments – no experiments with light rays or tape measures or with anything else – could have overthrown the laws of Euclidean geometry before someone had worked out non-Euclidean geometry. That is to say it is inconceivable that a scientist living in the time of Hume might† have come to the conclusion that the laws of Euclidean geometry are false: 'I do not know what geometrical laws are true, but I know the laws of Euclidean geometry are false'. Principles as central to the conceptual system of science as laws of geometry are simply not abandoned in the face of experiment *alone*. They are abandoned because a rival *theory* is available.

On the other hand, before the development of non-Euclidean geometry by Riemann and Lobachevski, the best philosophic minds regarded the principles of geometry as virtually analytic. The human mind could not conceive their falsity. Hume would certainly not have been impressed by the claim that 'straight line' means 'path of a light ray', and that the meeting of two light rays mutually perpendicular to a third light ray could show, if it ever occurred, that Euclidean geometry is false. It would have been self-evident to Hume that such an experimental situation, if it ever occurred, would be correctly explained by supposing that the light rays travelled in a curved path in Euclidean space, and *not* by supposing that the light rays travelled in two straight lines which were indeed mutually perpendicular to a third straight line but which nevertheless met. Hume, had he employed the vocabulary of contemporary analytic philosophy, might even have said that this follows from the 'logic' of the words 'straight line'. It is a 'criterion', to use another popular word, for lines being straight that if two of them are perpendicular to a third the two do not meet. It may be another criterion that light travels in *approximately* straight lines; but only where this criterion does not conflict with the deeply seated meaning of the words

† This is not a historical remark. I mean that no scientist *ought* to have come to this conclusion at that time, no matter what experimental evidence might have been presented.

'straight line'. In short, the meaning of the words 'straight line' is such that light rays may sometimes be said not to travel in straight lines; but straight lines cannot be said to behave in such a way as to form a triangle the sum of whose angles is more than 180°. If he had used the jargon of another fashionable contemporary school of philosophy, Hume might have said that straight lines are 'theoretical constructs'. And that light ray paths constitute a 'partial interpretation' of geometrical theory but one that is only admissible on condition that it does not render any of the 'meaning postulates' of the geometrical theory false.

Of course Hume did not employ this jargon. But he employed what was for him an equivalent jargon: the jargon of conceiving, visualizing, mental imagery. One cannot form any image of straight lines that do not conform to the laws of Euclidean geometry. This, of course, was to be true because any image of lines not conforming to the axioms of Euclidean geometry is an image which is not *properly* called an image of *straight* lines at all. Hume did not put it that way, however. Rather he explained the alleged 'impossibility of imagining' straight lines not conformant to the laws of Euclidean geometry in terms of a theory of relations between our ideas.

Was Hume wrong? Reichenbach† suggested that 'straight line,' properly analyzed, means 'path of a light ray'; and with this 'analysis' accepted, it is clear that the principles of geometry always are and always were synthetic. They are and always were subject to experiment. Hume simply overlooked something which could *in principle*‡ have been seen even by the ancient Greeks. I think Reichbach is almost totally wrong. If the paradigm for an analytic sentence is 'All bachelors are unmarried' – and it is – then it is of course absurd to say that the principles of geometry are analytic. Indeed, we cannot any longer say that the principles of Euclidean geometry are analytic; because analytic sentences are true, and we no longer say that the principles of Euclidean geometry are

---

† Reichenbach actually claimed that there were various possible alternative 'coordinative definitions' of 'straight line'. However he contended that this one (and the ones physically equivalent to it) 'have the advantage of logical simplicity and require the least change in the results of science'. Moreover: 'The sciences have implicitly employed such a coordinative definition all the time, though not always consciously' – i.e. it renders the customary meaning of the term 'straight line,' (Reichenbach, 1956, p. 19).

‡ Reichenbach does not assert that the Greeks could (as a matter of psychological or historical possibility) have understood the 'true' character of geometric statements prior to the invention of non-Euclidean geometry: in fact, he denies this. But there is nothing in Reichenbach's analysis in Chap. I of *Space and Time* which *logically* presupposes a knowledge of non-Euclidean geometry. Thus, if Reichenbach is right, then the Greeks could *in principle* have 'realized' (a) that the question whether Euclidean geometry is correct for physical space presupposes the choice of a 'coordinative definition' and (b) that once the customary definition has been chosen, the question is an 'empirical' one.

47

true. But I want to suggest that before the work of nineteenth-century mathematicians, the principles of Euclidean geometry were as *close* to analytic as any nonanalytic statement ever gets. That is to say, that had the following status: no experiment that one could describe could possibly overthrow them, by itself.† Just plain experimental results, without any new theory to integrate them, would not have been accepted as sufficient grounds for rejecting Euclidean geometry by any rational scientist.‡ After the development of non-Euclidean geometry, the position was rather different, as physicists soon realized: give us a rival conceptual system, and some reason for accepting it, and we will consider abandoning the laws of Euclidean geometry.

When I say that the laws of Euclidean geometry were, before the development of non-Euclidean geometry, as analytic as any nonanalytic statements ever get, I mean to group them, in this respect, with many other principles: the law '$f = ma$' (force equals mass times acceleration), the principle that the world did not come into existence five minutes ago, the principle that one cannot know certain kinds of facts, e.g. fact about objects at a distance from one, unless one has or has had evidence. These principles play several different roles; but in one respect they are alike. They share the characteristic that no isolated experiment (I cannot think of a better phrase than 'isolated experiment' to contrast with 'rival theory') can overthrow them. On the other hand, most of these principles can be overthrown if there is good reason for overthrowing them, and such good reason would have to consist in the presentation of a whole rival theory embodying the denials of these principles, plus evidence of the success of such a rival theory. Any principle in our knowledge can be revised for theoretical reasons; although many principles resist refutation by isolated experimentation. There are indeed some principles (some philosophers of science call them 'low-level generalizations') which *can* be overthrown by isolated experiments, provided the experiments are repeated often enough and produce substantially the same results. But there are many, many principles – we might broadly classify them as 'framework principles' – which have the characteristic of being so central that they are employed as auxiliaries to make predictions in an overwhelming number of experiments, without themselves being jeopardized by any possible experimental results. This is the classical role of the laws of logic; but it is equally the role of certain physical

---

† As Mill very clearly states; see Mill, 1843, Chap. V, secs. 4, 5, 6. As Mill foresaw, 'There is probably no one proposition enunciated in this work for which a more unfavorable opinion is to be expected' (than, that is, his denial of the a priori character of geometrical propositions, notwithstanding the 'inconceivability' of their negations).

‡ This is not a historical remark.

principles, e.g. '$f = ma$,' and the principles we have been discussing: the laws of Euclidean geometry, and the law '$e = \frac{1}{2}mv^2$', at the time when those laws were still accepted.

I said that any principle in our knowledge can be revised for *theoretical* reasons. But this is not strictly correct. Any principle in our knowledge can be revised or abandoned for theoretical reasons unless it is *really* an analytic principle in the trivial sense in which 'All bachelors are unmarried' is an analytic principle. There are indeed analytic statements in science; and these are immune from revision, except the trivial kind of revision which arises from unintended and unexplained historical changes in the use of language. The point of the preceding discussion is that many principles which have been mistaken for analytic ones have actually a somewhat different role. There is all the difference in the world between a principle that can never be given up by a rational scientist and a principle which cannot be given up by rational scientists merely because of experiments, no matter how numerous or how consistent.

To summarize this discussion of geometry: I think that Hume was perfectly right in assigning to the principles of geometry the same status that he assigned to the principles of arithmetic. I think that in his time the principles of geometry *had* the same status as the principles of arithmetic. It is not that there is something – 'an operational definition' of 'straight line' – which Hume failed to apprehend. The idea that, had he been aware of the 'operational definition of straight line' on the one hand and of the 'reduction of mathematics to logic' on the other hand, Hume would have seen that geometry is not really so much like arithmetic after all, that geometry is synthetic and arithmetic analytic, seems a crude error. The principle that light travels in straight lines is not a definition of 'straight line': as such, it is hopeless since it contains the geometrical term 'travels'. The same objection arises if we say 'a straight line is defined as the path of a light ray'. In this case the definition of 'straight line' uses the topological term 'path.' The principle that light travels in a straight line is simply a law of optics, nothing more or less serious than that. What is often called 'interpreting mathematical geometry' is more aptly described as testing the conjunction of geometric theory and optical theory. The implicit standpoint of Hume was that if the conjunction should lead to false predictions, then the optical theories would have to be revised; the geometric theory was analytic. The Reichenbachian criticism is that the geometry was synthetic and the optical theory was analytic. Both were wrong. We test the conjunction of geometry and optics indeed, and if we get into trouble, then we can alter either the geometry or the optics, depending on the nature of the trouble. Before Einstein, geometrical principles had exactly the same status as analytic principles, or rather, they had exactly the same status as all the principles that philosophers mistakenly cite as analytic. After Einstein, especially after the general theory of relativity, they have exactly the same status as cosmological laws: this is because general relativity establishes a complex interdependence between the cosmology and the geometry of our universe.

Thus, we should not say that 'straight line' has changed its meaning: that Hume was talking about one thing and that Einstein was talking about a different thing when the term 'straight line' was employed. Rather, we should say that Hume (and Euclid) had certain beliefs about straight lines – not just about mental images of straight lines, but about straight lines in the space in which we live and move and have our being – which were, in fact, unknown to them, false. But we can say all this, and also say that the principles of geometry had, at the time Hume was writing, the same status as the laws of mathematics.

Law-cluster concepts

At this point, a case has been developed for the view that statements expressing the laws of mathematics and geometry and our earlier example '$e = \frac{1}{2}mv^2$' are not analytic, if by 'an analytic statement' one means a statement that a rational scientist can never give up. It remains to show that 'All bachelors are unmarried' *is* an analytic statement in that sense. This is not a trivial undertaking: for the 'shocking' part of Quine's thesis is that there are no analytic statements in this sense – that all of the statements in our conceptual system have the character that I have attributed variously to the laws of logic, the laws of the older geometry at the time when they were accepted, and certain physical principles. But before considering this question, there are certain possible objections against the account just given which must be faced. The objections I have in mind are two. (1) It may be argued, especially in connection with logical principles, that revision of these principles merely amounts to a change in the meaning of the constituent words. Thus, logical principles are not *really* given up; one merely changes one's language. (2) It may be held that the case of the principle '$e = \frac{1}{2}mv^2$' merely shows that we were able to 'change our definition of "kinetic energy"', and *not* that a principle which was at one time definitional or stipulative could be later abandoned for reasons not substantially different from the reasons given for abandoning certain principles which philosophers would classify as synthetic.

The first objection I have discussed in volume 1, chapter 9. The main point to be made is this: the logical words 'or', 'and', 'not' have a certain core meaning which is easily specifiable and which is *independent* of the principle of the excluded middle. Thus, in a certain sense the meaning does *not* change if we go over to three-valued logic or to intuitionist logic. Of course, if by saying that a change in the accepted logical principles is tantamount to a change in the meaning of the logical connective, what one has in mind is the fact that changing the accepted logical principles will affect the global use of the logical connectives, then the thesis is tautological and hardly arguable. But if the claim is that a change in the accepted logical principles would amount *merely* to redefining the logical connectives, then, in the case of intuitionist logic, this is demonstrably false. What is involved is the acceptance of a whole new network of inferences with profound systematic consequences; and it is a philosophical sin to say, even indirectly by one's choice of terminology, that this amounts to no more than stipulating new definitions for the logical connectives. A change in terminology never makes it impossible to draw inferences that could be validly drawn before; or if it does, it is only because certain words are missing, which can easily be supplied. But the adoption of intuitionist logic as opposed to 'classical' logic amounts to systematically forswearing certain classically valid inferences. Some of these inferences can be brought in again by redefinition. But others, inferences involving certain kinds of nonconstructive mathematical entities, are really forsworn in any form. To assimilate the change from one system of logic to another to the change that would be made if we were to use the noise 'bachelor' to stand for 'unmarried woman' instead of 'unmarried man' is assimilating a mountain to a molehill. There is a use of the term 'meaning' according to which any change in important beliefs may be said to change the 'meaning' of some of the constituent concepts. Only in this fuzzy sense may it be said that to change our accepted logical principles would be to change the 'meaning' of the logical connectives. And the claim that to change our logical system would be *merely* to change the meaning of the logical connectives is just false. With respect to the second objection, there are some similar remarks to be made. Once again, to speak of Einstein's contribution as a 'redefinition' of 'kinetic energy' is to assimilate what actually happened to a wholly false model.

Leibniz worried about the fact that statements containing a proper name as subject term seem never to be analytic. This seemed to be absurd, so he concluded that *all* such statements must be analytic – that is, that they must all follow from the nature of what they speak about. Mill took the different tack of denying that proper names connote; but this leaves it puzzling that they mean anything at all. Similarly, philosophers have wondered whether any statement containing the subject term 'man' is really analytic. Is it analytic that all men are rational? (We are no longer so happy with the Aristotelian idea that a necessary truth can have exceptions.) Is it analytic that all men are featherless? Aristotle thought not, thus displaying a commendable willingness to include our feathered friends, the Martians (if they exist), under the name 'man'. Suppose one makes a list of the attributes $P_1, P_2 \ldots$ that go to make up a normal man. One can raise successively the questions 'Could there be a man without P_1?' 'Could there be a man without P_2?' and so on. The answer in each case might be 'Yes', and yet it seems absurd that the word 'man' has no meaning at all. In order to resolve this sort of difficulty, philosophers have introduced the idea of what may be called a *cluster concept*. (Wittgenstein uses instead of the metaphor of a 'cluster', the metaphor of a rope with a great many strands, no one of which runs the length of the rope.) That is, we say that the meaning in such a case is given by a cluster of properties. To abandon a large number of these properties, or what is tantamount to the same thing, to radically change the extension of the term 'man', would be felt as an arbitrary change in its meaning. On the other hand, if most of the properties in the cluster are present in any single case, then under suitable circumstances we should be inclined to say that what we had to deal with was a man.

In analogy with the notion of a cluster concept, I should like to introduce the notion of a *law-cluster*. Law-cluster concepts are constituted not by a bundle of properties as are the typical general names like 'man' and 'crow', but by a cluster of laws which, as it were, determine the identity of the concept. The concept 'energy' is an excellent example of a law-cluster concept. It enters into a great many laws. It plays a great many roles, and these laws and inference roles constitute its meaning collectively, not individually. I want to suggest that most of the terms in highly developed science are law-cluster concepts, and that one should always be suspicious of the claim that a principle whose subject term is a law-cluster concept is analytic. The reason that it is difficult to have an analytic relationship between law-cluster concepts is that such a relationship would be one more law. But, in general, any one law can be abandoned without destroying the identity of the law-cluster concept involved, just as a man can be irrational from birth, or can have a growth of feathers all over his body, without ceasing to be a man.

Applying this to our example – 'kinetic energy' = 'kinetic' + 'energy' – the kinetic energy of a particle is literally the energy due to its motion. The extension of the term 'kinetic energy' has not changed. If it had, the extension of the term 'energy' would have to have changed.† But the

† Kinetic energy is only one of several kinds of energy, and can be transformed into

extension of the term 'energy' has not changed. The forms of energy and their behavior are the same as they always were, and they are what physicists talked about before and after Einstein. On the other hand, I want to suggest that the term 'energy' is not one of which it is *happy* to ask, What is its intension? The term 'intension' suggests the idea of a single defining character or a single defining law, and this is not the model on which concepts like energy are to be construed. In the case of a law-cluster term such as 'energy', any one law, even a law that was felt to be definitional or stipulative in character, can be abandoned, and we feel that the identity of the concept has, in a certain respect, remained.†

Thus, the conclusions of the present section still stand: A principle involving the term 'energy', a principle which was regarded as definitional, or as analytic, if you please, has been abandoned. And its abandonment cannot be explained always as mere 'redefinition' or as change in the meaning of 'kinetic energy', although one might say that the change in the status of the principle has *brought about* a change in the meaning of the term 'kinetic energy' in one rather fuzzy sense of 'meaning'.‡ It is important to see that the principle '$e = \frac{1}{2}mv^2$' might have been mistaken to have exactly the same nature as 'All bachelors are unmarried'. But 'All bachelors are unmarried' cannot be rejected unless we change the meaning of the word 'bachelor' and not even then unless we change it so radically as to change the *extension* of the term 'bachelor'. In the case of the terms 'energy' and 'kinetic energy', we want to say, or at any rate *I* want to say, that the meaning has not changed enough to affect 'what we are talking about'; yet a principle superficially very much like 'All bachelors are unmarried' has been abandoned. What makes the resemblance only superficial is the fact that if we are asked what the meaning of the term 'bachelor' is, we can *only* say that 'bachelor' means 'unmarried man', whereas if we are asked for the meaning of the term 'energy', we can do much more than give a definition. We can in fact show the way in which the use of the term 'energy' facilitates an enormous number of scientific explanations, and how it enters into an enormous bundle of laws.

other kinds (and vice versa). Thus an adequate physical theory cannot change the meaning of the term 'kinetic energy' without changing the meaning of the term 'energy', without giving up the idea that 'kinetic energy' is literally a kind of energy.

† Even the conservation law has sometimes been considered to be in doubt (in the development of quantum mechanics)! Yet it was the desire to preserve this law which led to the changes we have been discussing. In one context the law of the conservation of energy can thus serve to 'identify' energy, whereas in another it can be the Hamiltonian equations of particular systems that do this.

‡ The 'fuzziness' is evidenced by the fact that although one can say that 'kinetic energy' has a new meaning, one cannot say that 'kinetic' has a new meaning, or that 'energy' has a new meaning, or that 'kinetic energy' is an idiom.

The statement '$e = \frac{1}{2}mv^2$' is the sort of statement in physical theory that is currently called a 'definition'. That is to say, it can be taken as a definition, and many good authors did take it as a definition. Analyticity is often defined as 'truth by definition', yet we have just seen that '$e = \frac{1}{2}mv^2$' is not and was not analytic, if by an analytic statement one means a statement that no one can reject without forfeiting his claim to reasonableness.

At this point one may feel tempted to agree with Quine. If even 'definitions' turn out to be revisable in principle – and not in the trivial sense that arbitrary revision of our use of *noises* is always possible – then one might feel inclined to say that there is *no* statement which a rational man must hold immune from revision. I shall proceed to argue that this is wrong, but those who agree with me that this is wrong have often overlooked the fact that Quine can be wrong in his most 'shocking' thesis and still right about very important and very pervasive epistemological issues. To give a single example, I agree with Quine that in that context of argument which is defined by questions of necessity, factuality, of linguistic or nonlinguistic character, there is no significant distinction to be drawn between, say, the principle of the excluded middle and the principle that $f = ma$; and this is not to say that the law '$f = ma$' is analytic. (Of course we can imagine a physics based on $f = m^2a$, if we retain the identity of gravitational and inertial mass!) Nor is it to say that the laws of logic are 'synthetic', if the paradigm for a synthetic sentence is 'There is a book on this table'. But still there are truths that it could never be rational to give up, and 'All bachelors are unmarried' is one of them. This thesis will be elaborated in the following section.

The rationale of the analytic–synthetic distinction

The problem of justification

Let us consider first the question How could one draw the analytic–synthetic distinction as a formal distinction in connection with at least some hypothetical formalized languages? If the inventor of a formalized language singles out from all his postulates and rules a certain subset (e.g. 'L-postulates', 'meaning postulates', and 'logical axioms') and says that the designated statements, statements in the subset, are not to be given up, then these statements may be reasonably called 'analytic' in that language. In the context of formal reconstruction, then, this is the first model of analyticity that comes to mind. We draw an analytic distinction formally only in connection with formalized languages whose inventors list some statements and rules as 'meaning postulates'. That is, it is stipulated that to qualify as correctly using the language one must accept *those* statements and rules. There is nothing mysterious about this. A formal language has, after all, an inventor, and like any human being, he can give commands. Among the commands he can issue are ones to the effect that 'If you want to speak *my* language, then do thus and so'. If his commands have an escape clause, if he says, 'Accept these statements unless you get into trouble, and then make such and such revisions', then his language is hardly one with respect to which we can draw a formal analytic–synthetic distinction. But if he says that certain statements are 'to be accepted no matter what', then those statements in that language are true by stipulation, true by *his* stipulation, and that is all we mean when we say that they are 'analytic' (in this model).

Hempel has proposed an answer to this sort of move. His answer is this: if by an analytic statement one means one which is not to be given up, then in science there are no such statements. Of course, an individual might invent a language and rule that in that language certain statements are not to be given up; but this is of no philosophic interest whatsoever, unless the language constructed by this individual can plausibly be regarded as reconstructing some feature which actually exists in ordinary unreconstructed scientific activity.

This brings us to our second question: If an artificial language in which a formalized analytic–synthetic distinction can be drawn is one in which there are rules of the form 'Do not give up S under any circumstances', then what justification could there be for adopting such a language?

Certain philosophers have seen that the notion of a rule, in the sense of an *explicit* rule or explicit stipulation, is sufficiently clear to be worked with (Quine does not at all deny this), and they propose to define analytic statements as statements which are true by stipulation. Against this, there is Quine's remark that in the history of science a statement is often 'true by stipulation' at one moment, but later plays a role which is in no way different from the role played by statements which enter the body of accepted truths through more direct experimental inquiry. Stipulation, Quine says, is a trait of historical events, not a 'lingering trait' of the statements involved.

Philosophers who regard 'true by stipulation' as explicating analyticity and who take 'true by stipulation' in its literal sense, that is to say, who mean by 'stipulations' explicit stipulations, miss several points. In the first place, analytic statements in a natural language are not usually true by stipulation in anything but a metaphorical sense. 'True by stipulation' is the nature of analytic statements only in the model. And even if we confine ourselves to the model and ignore the existence of natural languages, there is still the question What is the point of the model? But this is the question: *Why* should we hold certain truths immune from revision?

Suppose we can show that if we were to adopt an 'official formalized language', it would be perfectly rational to incorporate into its construction certain conventions of the type described? Then I think we would have resolved the problem raised by Quine. Quine does not deny that some people may in fact hold some statements immune from revision; what he denies is that science does this, and his denial is not merely a descriptive denial: he doesn't think that science ought to do this. Thus the problem *really* raised by Quine is this: Once we have managed to make our own Quine's insight into the monolithic character of our conceptual system, how can we see why there should be any exceptions to this monolithic character? If science is characterized by interdependence of its principles and by the fact that revision may strike anywhere, then why should any principles be held immune from revision? The question at the moment is not What is the nature of the analytic–synthetic distinction? but rather Why ought there to be an analytic–synthetic distinction?

Rationale

The reply that I have to offer to the question of the rationale of the analytic–synthetic distinction, and of strict synonymy within a language, is this: first of all, the answer to the question Why should we have analytic statements (or strict synonymies†) in our language? is, in essence, Why not? or more precisely, It can't hurt. And, second, the answer to the derivative question How do you know it can't hurt? is that I use what I know. But it is obvious that both of these answers will need a little elaborating.

The first answer should, I think, be clear. There are obvious advantages to having strict synonyms in a language. Most important, there is the advantage of *brevity*. Also, there is the question of *intelligibility*. If some of the statements in a language are immune from revision and if some of the rules of a language are immune from revision, then linguistic usage with respect to the language as a whole is to a certain extent frozen. Now, whatever disadvantages this freezing may have, there is one respect in which a frozen language is very attractive. Different speakers of the same language can to a large extent understand each other better because they can predict in advance at least some of the uses of the other speaker.

Thus, I think we can see that if we are constructing a language, then there are some prima facie advantages to having 'fixed points' in that

† The close connection between synonymy and analyticity is pointed out by Quine (1951).

language. Hence the only real question is Why *not* have them? Quine, I believe, thinks that there is a reason why we should not have them. No matter what advantages in intelligibility and uniformity of usage might accrue, Quine is convinced that it would block the scientific enterprise to declare any statement immune from revision. And it may seem that I have provided Quine with more than sufficient ammunition. For instance, someone might have proposed, 'Let's make the statement "kinetic energy = $\frac{1}{2}mv^2$" analytic. It will help to stabilize scientific usage'. And accepting this proposal, which might have seemed innocuous enough, would not have been very happy. On my own account, we would have been mistaken had we decided to hold the statement 'kinetic energy = $\frac{1}{2}mv^2$' immune from revision. How can we be sure that we will not be similarly mistaken if we decide to hold *any* statement immune from revision?

In terms of the conceptual machinery developed above, the reason that we can safely decide to hold 'All bachelors are unmarried' immune from revision, while we could not have safely decided to hold 'kinetic energy = $\frac{1}{2}mv^2$' immune from revision, is that 'energy' is a law-cluster term, and 'bachelor' is not. This is not to say that there are no laws underlying our use of the term 'bachelor'; there are laws underlying our use of any words whatsoever. But it is to say that there are no exceptionless laws of the form 'All bachelors are . . . ' except 'All bachelors are unmarried', 'All bachelors are male', and consequences thereof. Thus, preserving the interchangeability of 'bachelor' and 'unmarried man' in all extensional contexts can never conflict with our desire to retain some other natural law of the form 'all bachelors are . . . '.

This cannot happen because bachelors are a kind of synthetic 'class'. They are not a 'natural kind' in Mill's sense. They are rather grouped together by ignoring all aspects except a single legal one. One is simply not going to find any laws, except complex statistical laws depending on sociological conditions, about such a class. Thus, it cannot 'hurt' if we decide always to preserve the law 'All bachelors are unmarried'. And that it cannot hurt is all the justification we need; the positive advantages are obvious.

As remarked, there may be *statistical* laws, dependent on sociological conditions, concerning bachelors. But these cannot be incompatible with 'All bachelors are unmarried men'. For the truth of a statistical law, unlike that of a deterministic law, is not affected by slight modifications in the extension of a concept. The law 'ninety-nine per cent of all As are Bs', if true, remains true if we change the extension of the concept A by including a few more objects or excluding a few objects. Thus, making *slight* changes in the extension of the term 'bachelor' would not affect any statistical law about bachelors, but by exactly the same token, neither would *refusing* to make such changes. And if the statistical law held true only provided we were willing to make a large change in the extension or putative extension of the term 'bachelor', then we would certainly reject the statistical law.

Let us consider one objection. I have maintained that there are no exceptionless laws containing the term 'bachelor'. But this statement is surely a guess on my part. Let us suppose that my 'guess' is wrong, and that there are exceptionless laws about bachelors. Let us suppose for instance that all bachelors share a special kind of neurosis universal among bachelors and unique to bachelors. Not to be too farfetched, let us call it 'sexual frustration'. Then the statement 'All bachelors suffer from sexual frustration, and only bachelors suffer from sexual frustration' would express a genuine law. This law could still not provide us with a *criterion* for distinguishing bachelors from nonbachelors, unless we were good at detecting this particular species of neurosis. It is alleged that some primitive peoples can in fact do this by smell; but let us make a somewhat more plausible assumption, in terms of contemporary mores. Let us suppose that we all mastered some form of super psychoanalysis; and let us suppose that we all became so 'insightful' that we should be able to tell in a moment's conversation whether someone suffered from the neurosis of 'sexual frustration' or not. Then this law would indeed constitute a criterion for bachelorhood, and a far more convenient criterion than the usual one. For one cannot employ the usual criterion without asking a man a somewhat personal question concerning his legal status; whereas, in our hypothetical situation, one would be able to determine by a quick examination of the man's conversation whether he was a bachelor or not, no matter what one conversed about. Under such circumstances, possession of the neurosis might well become the dominant criterion governing the use of the word. Then what should we say, if it turned out that a few people had the neurosis without being bachelors? Our previous stipulation that 'bachelor' is to be synonymous with 'unmarried man' might well appear inconvenient!

The point of this fable is as follows: even if we grant that 'bachelor' is not *now* a law-cluster term, how can we be *sure* that it will never become such a term? This leads to my second answer, and to a further remark, 'I use what I know'. It is logically possible that all bachelors should have a certain neurosis and that nobody else should have it; it is even possible that we should be able to detect this neurosis at sight. But, of course, there is no such neurosis. This I *know* in the way that I know most negative propositions. It is not that I have a criterion for as yet undiscovered neurosis, but simply that I have no good reason to suppose that there might be such a neurosis. And in many cases of this kind, *lack* of any good reason for supposing existence is itself the very best reason for supposing nonexistence.

In short, I regard my 'guess' that there are no exceptionless laws about bachelors as more than a guess. I think that in a reasonable sense we may say that this is something that we *know*. I shall not press this point. But *bachelor* is not now a law-cluster concept; I think we can say that, although it is *logically* possible that it might become a law-cluster concept, in fact it will not.

Let us summarize the position at this point: I have suggested that the statement 'All bachelors are unmarried' is a statement which we might render true by stipulation, in a hypothetical formalized language. I have argued that this stipulation is convenient, both because it provides us with one more 'fixed point' to help stabilize the use of our hypothetical language, and because it provides us with an expression which can be used instead of the somewhat cumbersome expression 'male adult human being who has never in his life been married'; and I have argued that we need not be afraid to accept these advantages, and to make these stipulations, because it can do no harm. It can do no harm because *bachelor* is not a law-cluster concept. Also it is not independently 'defined' by standard examples, which might only contingently be unmarried men. I have admitted that my knowledge (or 'state of pretty-sureness') that 'bachelor' will not become a law-cluster term is based upon what we might call, in a very broad sense, empirical argumentation. That *there are no exceptionless laws containing the term 'bachelor'* is empirical in the sense of being a fact about the world; although it is not empirical in the sense of being subject to confrontation with isolated experiments. More precisely: it occupies the anomalous position of being falsifiable by isolated experiments (since isolated experiments could verify an empirical generalization which *would* constitute a 'law about all bachelors'); but it could not be verified by isolated experiments. One cannot examine a random sample of *laws*, and verify that they are not-about-bachelors. But the statement is empirical, at least in the first sense, and it is 'synthetic' to the extent that it is revisable in principle. So my position is this: a 'synthetic' statement, a statement which could be revised in principle, may serve as a warrant for the decision that another statement should not be revised, no matter what. One may safely hold certain statements immune from revision; but *this* statement is itself subject to certain risks.

But there is no real paradox here at all. To say that an intention is to do something permanently is not the same as saying that the intention is permanent. To marry a woman is to legally declare an intention to remain wedded to her for life; although the bride and groom know perfectly well that there exists such an institution as divorce, and that they may avail themselves of it. The existence of divorce does not change the fact that the legal and declared intention of the person getting married is to be wedded for life. And this is the further remark that I wish to make in connection with my second answer. It is perfectly rational to make stipulations to the effect that certain statements are never to be given up, and those stipulations remain stipulations to that effect, notwithstanding the fact that under certain circumstances the stipulations *themselves* might be given up.

All of this may sound like a bit of sophistry, if one forgets that we are still in the context of formalized languages. Thus, if one has in mind 'implicit stipulations' and natural language, one might feel tempted to say: 'What is the difference between having a stipulation to the effect that every statement can be revised, and having a stipulation to the effect that certain statements are never to be revised, if the latter stipulations are themselves always subject to revision?' But in connection with formalized languages, there is all the difference in the world. The rule 'Let every statement be subject to revision' is not sufficiently precise to be a formal rule. It would have to be supplemented by further rules determining what revisions to make, and in what order. And there is all the difference in the world between making a decision in accordance with a pre-established plan, and making the decision by 'getting together' and doing whatever seems most cogent in the light of the circumstances at the moment and the standards or codes we see accepted at the moment. The first case would arise in connection with a language in which Quine's ideas concerning priorities and centralities had been formalized – a language in which any statement may be given up and in which there are rules telling one which statement to give up first and under what circumstances. Such a language could in principle be constructed. But compare the case of a scientist who is in difficulties, and who resolves his difficulties by using a predetermined rule, with the following case: we imagine that we have a formalized language in which 'All bachelors are unmarried' is a 'meaning postulate'. We further imagine, as in our 'fable', that all bachelors suffer from a neurosis and that only bachelors suffer from that particular neurosis. Also we suppose that the neurosis is detectable at sight and that it is used as the dominant criterion. Then it is discovered that one person or a very few people have the neurosis although they are married. The question might then arise as to which would be more convenient: to preserve 'All bachelors are unmarried' or to get together and modify the rules of the language. Contrast the procedure which would be employed if the latter alternative were the one adopted, with the procedure of settling the question in accordance with a predetermined plan. There would be, let us say, a convention at which some would argue that it is better to preserve the rules that were agreed upon for the language, and to give up the psychological law that had been thought to hold without exception; there might be others who would argue that the new use of the term 'bachelor' was so standard that it would be simpler to grace the new use with the hallmark of legality and to change the rules of the language. In short, the question would be settled by informal argument.

Thus, at the level of formalized languages, there *is* a difference, and a rather radical difference between these different systems: a formal language which can be described as having rules to the effect that every statement may be revised, and a formal language having rules to the effect that certain statements are never to be revised – notwithstanding the fact that, even if one employs a formal language of the second kind, one retains the option of later altering or abandoning it. And even if one uses a system of the first kind, a 'holistic' system of the sort Quine seems to envisage, there is still the possibility that one might find it desirable to revise the rules determining the nature and order of revisions, when they are to be made – the centralities and priorities of this system. And the same difference mirrors itself in the difference between those questions which one settles in accordance with the antecedently established rules and those questions which one settles by informal argument when they arise.

In short: if we think in terms of people using formalized languages, then we have to distinguish between the things that are done inside the language in accordance with whatever rules and regulations may have been previously decided upon and published, and the informal argumentation and discussion that takes place outside of the language, and which perhaps leads to a decision, in its turn to be duly formalized, to alter the language. This distinction is not the same as the analytic–synthetic distinction, but it is deeply relevant to it. If we use the model of people employing formalized languages, then we have to imagine those people as deciding upon and declaring certain rules. And it is perfectly rational in human life to make a rule that something is always to be done; and the rule is no less a rule that something is always to be done on account of the fact that the rule itself may someday be abandoned.

There are a host of examples: for instance, it is a rule of etiquette that one is not to address a person to whom one has never been introduced by his first name (with a few exceptions). The rule may someday be changed. But that does not change the fact that the present rule is to the effect that this is to be done under *all* circumstances. In the same way, a rational man may perfectly well adopt a rule that certain statements are *never* to be given up: he does not forfeit his right to be called reasonable on account of what he does, and he can give plenty of good reasons in support of his action.

The analytic–synthetic distinction in natural language

The formal language model

The foregoing discussion is characterized by an air of fictionality. But this does not obliterate its relevance to Quine's difficulties. Quine does not deny that there may be some statements which some individuals will never give up. His real contention is that there are no statements which *science* holds immune from revision. And this is not a descriptive judgment; judgments by philosophers containing the word 'science' almost never are. What Quine really means is that he cannot see why science ought to hold any statements immune from revision. And this is the sort of difficulty that one may well resolve by telling an appropriate fable.

Still we are left with the problem of drawing an analytic–synthetic distinction in natural language; and this is a difficult problem. Part of the answer is clear. We commonly use formalized objects to serve as models for unformalized objects. We talk about a game whose rules have never been written down in terms of a model of a game whose rules have been agreed upon and codified, and we talk about natural languages in terms of models of formal languages; and, if a formal language means a 'language whose rules are written down', then we have been doing this for a long time, and not just since the invention of symbolic logic. The concept of a rule of language is commonly used by linguists in describing even the unwritten languages of primitive peoples, just as the concept of a rule of social behavior is used by anthropologists. Such reference is sometimes heavily disguised by current jargon, but is nevertheless present. For instance, if a linguist says: 'The pluralizing morphophoneme —*s* has the zero allophone after the morpheme *sheep*', what he is saying is that it is a rule of English that the plural of 'sheep' is 'sheep' and not 'sheeps.' And his way of saying this is not so cumbersome either: he would not really write the sentence I just quoted, but would embed the information it contains in an extremely compact morphophoneme table.

Thus I think that we may say that the concept *rule of language*, as applied to natural language, is an 'almost full-grown' theoretical concept. Linguists, sent out to describe a jungle language, describe the language on the model of a formal language. The elements of the *model* are the expressions and rules of a formal language, that is, a language whose rules are explicitly written down. The corresponding elements in the real world are the expressions of a natural language and certain of the dispositions of the users of that language. The model is not only a useful descriptive device, but has genuinely explanatory power. The distinction at present very loosely specified, between a rule of language and a *mere* habit of the speakers of the language is an essential one. Speakers of English (except very small speakers of English) rarely use the word 'sheeps'. Speakers of English rarely use the word 'otiose'. But someone who uses the word 'sheeps' is said to be speaking incorrectly; whereas someone who uses the word 'otiose' is only using a rare word. That we behave differently in the two cases is explained, and it is a genuine explanation, by saying that it is a rule of English that one is to use 'sheep' as the plural of 'sheep', and it is not a rule of English that one is not to use the word 'otiose'; it is just that most people do not know *what* the rule for using the word 'otiose' is at all, and hence do not employ it.

But all this will not suffice. True, we have a model of natural language according to which a natural language has 'rules', and a model with some explanatory and predictive value, but what we badly need to know are the respects in which the model is exact, and the respects in which the model is misleading. For example, in many circumstances it is extremely convenient to talk about electron currents on the model of water flowing through a pipe; but physical scientists know very well in which respects this model holds exactly and in which respects it is extremely misleading. The same can hardly be said in the case just described – the case wherein we employ a formal language as a model for a natural language. The difficulty I have in mind is not the difficulty of determining what the rules of natural language are. The art of describing a natural language in terms of this kind of model is one that is relatively well developed; and linguists are aware that the correspondence between this kind of model and a given natural language is not unique: there are alternative 'equally valid descriptions'. The dispositions of speakers of a natural language are *not* rules of a formal language, the latter are only used to represent them in a certain technique of representation; and the difficulty lies in being sure that other elements of the model, e.g. the sharp analytic–synthetic distinction, correspond to anything at all in reality.

To give only one example: I argued above, and it was a central part of the argument, that there is a clear-cut difference between solving a problem by relying on a pre-established rule, and solving it by methods construed on the spot. But one might wonder whether the distinction is so sharp if the pre-established rule is only an *implicit* rule to begin with. It is clear that there is a difference between stipulations allowing for revisions and stipulations prohibiting revisions, but themselves always subject to informal revision. But is it so clear that there is such a distinction if the stipulations are themselves informal and 'implicit'? In view of this difficulty, and other related difficulties, it seems to me that we must look at natural language directly, and try to draw the analytic–synthetic distinction without relying on the formal language model, if we are to be sure that it exists at all.

The nature of the distinction in natural language

The statements which satisfy the criteria presented below are a *fundamental subset* of the totality of analytic statements in the natural language. They are the so-called 'analytic definitions', e.g. 'Someone is a bachelor if and only if he is an unmarried man'. Other statements may be classified as 'analytic', although they do *not* satisfy the criteria, because they are consequences of statements which *do* satisfy the criteria. The older philosophers recognized a related though different distinction by referring to 'intuitive' and 'demonstrative' truths. The distinction had a point: there is a difference, even in our formal model, between those statements whose truth follows from *direct* stipulation and statements whose truth follows from the fact that they are *consequences* of statements true by direct stipulation. The latter statements involve not only arbitrary stipulation but also logic.

Nevertheless, the term 'intuitive' has bad connotations. And because of these bad connotations, philosophers have been led not to reformulate the distinction between intuitive and demonstrative truths but to abandon it. So today the fashion is to lump together the analytic statements which would traditionally have been classified as intuitive with all their consequences, and to use the word 'analytic' for the whole class. *The criteria to be presented do not, however, apply equally well to the whole class, or even to all the 'intuitive' analytic truths, but to a fundamental subset. This fundamental subset is, roughtly speaking, the set of analytic definitions*, or less roughly, it is the set of analytic definitions which are also 'intuitive' and not 'demonstrative'.

In short, I shall present criteria which are intended to show what is unique or different about certain analytic statements. Such criteria do not constitute a definition but one might obtain a definition, of a rough and ready sort, from them: an analytic statement is a statement which satisfies the criteria to be presented, or a consequence of such statements, or a statement which comes pretty close to satisfying the criteria, or a consequence of such statements. The last clause in this 'definition' is designed to allow for the fact that there are some 'borderline' cases of analyticity, e.g. 'Red is a color'. However, it is not a very important point that the analytic–synthetic distinction *is* afflicted with 'borderline fuzziness'. The trouble with the analytic–synthetic distinction *construed as a dichotomy* is far more radical than mere 'borderline fuzziness'. Yet, there are borderline cases, and the reason for their existence is that the analytic–synthetic distinction is tied to a certain model of natural language and correspondence between the model and the natural language is not unique. To say that it is not unique is not, however, to say that it is arbitrary. Some statements in natural language really are analytic; others may be *construed* as analytic; still others really are synthetic; others *may be construed* as synthetic; still other statements belong to still other categories or may be construed as belonging to still other categories.

The following are the criteria in question:

(1) The statement has the form: 'Something (Someone) is an *A* if and only if it (he, she) is a *B*', where *A* is a single word.†

(2) The statement holds without exception, and provides us with a *criterion* for something's being the sort of thing to which the term *A* applies.

(3) The criterion is the only one that is generally accepted and employed in connection with the term.

(4) The term *A* is not a 'law-cluster' word.

Criterion (1) itself is surely insufficient to separate analytic definitions from natural laws in all cases. Thus let us examine criteria (2), (3), and (4). A statement of the form 'Something is an *A* if and only if it is a *B*' provides a criterion for something's being a thing to which the term *A* applies if people can and do determine whether or not something is an *A* by *first* finding out whether or not it is a *B*. For instance, the only generally accepted method for determining whether or not someone is a bachelor, other than putting the question itself, is to find out whether or not the person is married and whether or not he is an adult male. There are of course independent tests for both marital status (consult suitable records) and masculinity.

One objection must be faced at the outset: it might be argued that these criteria are circular in a vicious way, since knowing that the two statements, (a) 'Someone is a bachelor if and only if he is an unmarried man' and (b) 'Someone is a bachelor if and only if he is an unwed man', provide the same criterion for the application of the term 'bachelor' is the same thing as knowing that 'unmarried' and 'unwed' are *synonyms*.

† The requirement that *A* be a single word reflects the principle that the meaning of a whole utterance is a function of the meanings of the individual words and grammatical forms that make it up. This requirement should actually be more complicated to take care of words which consist of more than one morpheme and of idioms, but these complications will not be considered here. We can now give another reason why 'Kinetic energy $= \frac{1}{2}mv^2$' was never an analytic statement: its truth did not follow from the meanings of the words 'kinetic' and 'energy.' On the other hand, it would be absurd to maintain that, during its tenure of office, it was an 'empirical statement' in the usual sense (subject to experimental test, etc.).

For the present purposes, however, identity of criteria can be construed behavioristically: criteria (say, X and Y) correspond to the same way of ascertaining that a term A applies if subjects who are instructed to use criterion X do the same thing† as subjects who are instructed to use criterion Y. Thus, if I were instructed to ascertain whether or not Jones is unmarried, I would probably go up to Jones and ask 'Are you married?' – and answer 'No' to the original question if Jones' answer was 'Yes', and vice versa. On any such occasion, I could truthfully say that I 'would have done the same thing' if I had been instructed to ascertain whether Jones was 'unwed' instead of whether Jones was 'unmarried'. Thus, in my idiolect,‡ 'being an unmarried man' and 'being an unwed man' are not two criteria for someone's being a bachelor, but one.

But let us consider a somewhat different type of objection. On what basis are we to rule out the statement 'Someone is a bachelor if and only if he is either an unmarried man or a unicorn' as nonanalytic?§ Here three grounds are relevant: (a) the statement is a linguistically 'odd'‖ one, and is not clearly true; (b) the statement would not be generally accepted; (c) people do not ascertain that someone is a bachelor by first finding out that he is either an unmarried man *or* a unicorn. To take these in turn: (a) The English 'or' and 'if and only if' are not synonymous with the truth functions 'v' and '$\equiv$' of formal logic. Thus it is not even clear that the quoted statement is an intelligible English statement, let alone true. (b) Even if we grant truth, it would not be generally accepted. Many persons would reject it, and others, who might not actually reject it, might decline to accept it (e.g. they might query its intelligibility or express puzzlement). (c) People (other than formal logicians) would certainly deny that they ascertain that someone is a bachelor by first

† The use of expression 'do the same thing' here will undoubtedly raise questions in the minds of certain readers. It should be noted that what is meant is not total identity of behavior (whatever that might be) but the absence of relevant and statistically significant regularities running through the behavior of the one group of subjects and not of the other. Separation of 'relevant' from 'irrelevant' regularities does not seem difficult in practice, however difficult it might be to 'mechanize' our 'intuitions' in these matters.

‡ An 'idiolect' is the speech of a single speaker.

§ The difficulty here is that the class of bachelors = the sum of the class of bachelors and the class of unicorns (the latter being the null class). What has to be shown is that the so-called 'intensional' difference between the two terms 'unmarried man' and 'unmarried man or unicorn' is reflected by our criteria, at least in connection with the definition of bachelor.

‖ The quoted sentence is even *ungrammatical*, using the term in the sense of Noam Chomsky (1957); for its transformational history involves the ungrammatical sentence 'Someone is a unicorn'. To change the example: 'Someone is a bachelor if and only if he is either an unmarried man or eleven feet tall' is grammatical, but pretty clearly *false*, given the counterfactual force of the ordinary 'if and only if'.

finding out that he is *either* unmarried *or* a unicorn. In fine, the quoted statement does not provide a criterion for someone's being a bachelor, in the sense in which 'criterion' is being used here; and it is not a generally accepted criterion for someone's being a bachelor.

Since a good deal of the present discussion depends upon the way in which the word 'criterion' is being used, I should like to emphasize two points. Although sufficient conditions, necessary conditions, etc., are sometimes called 'criteria' (e.g. the above 'criteria' for analyticity), the sense of 'criterion' in which an analytic definition provides a criterion for something's being the sort of thing to which a term applies is a very strong one: (a) the 'criteria' I am speaking of are necessary *and* sufficient conditions for something's being an A; and (b) by means of them people *can and do determine* that something is an A. For instance, there are various things that we might call *indications* of bachelorhood: being young, high spirited, living alone. Using these, one can often *tell* that someone is a bachelor without falling back on the criterion; but the only *criterion* (satisfying (a) and (b)) by means of which one can *determine* that someone is a bachelor is the one which is provided by the analytic definition.

Returning now to our main concern, what is the relevance of the four criteria for analyticity? Someone imbued with the view that an analytic statement is *simply* one which is true by the rules of the language, i.e. one who insists on stating the distinction in terms of a model, instead of discussing the relevance of the model to that vast disorderly mass of human behavior that makes up a natural language, may be wholly dissatisfied with what has been said. I can imagine someone objecting: 'What you are saying is that the difference between an analytic principle and a natural law consists in the accidental fact that no laws happen to be known containing the subject term of the analytical principle'. This is almost what I am saying. But the emphasis is wrong; and in any case the thing is not so implausible once one has grasped the *rationale* of analyticity.

In the first place it is not just that there do not *happen* to be any *known* principles concerning bachelors other than the principle that someone is a bachelor if and only if he is an unmarried man: it is reasonable to suppose that there do not exist any exceptionless (as opposed to statistical) scientific laws to be discovered about bachelors.† And even if there

---

† It has occurred to me that someone might argue that 'all bachelors have mass' is an example of an exceptionless 'law about bachelors'. Even if this were granted, the objection is not serious. In the first place, in deciding whether or not a word is a 'law-cluster' word, what we have to consider are not all the laws (including the unknown ones) containing the word, but only those statements which are accepted as laws and which contain the word. It does not even matter if some of these are false: if a word

were an exceptionless law about bachelors, it is extremely unlikely that it would have the form 'Someone is a bachelor if and only if . . . ' – i.e. that it would provide a *criterion* for someone's being a bachelor.

But still we have to face the questions (1) Why is the exceptionless principle that provides the criterion governing a *one-criterion* concept analytic? (2) What happens if, contrary to our well-founded beliefs and expectations, a large number of exceptionless laws of high systematic import containing the subject term are someday discovered? The second question has already been discussed. If 'bachelor' ever becomes a 'law-cluster' word, then we shall simply have to admit that the linguistic character of the word has changed. The word 'atom' is an example of a word which was once a 'one-criterion' word and which has become a 'law-cluster' word (so that the sentence 'Atoms are indivisible', which was once used to make an analytic statement, would today express a false proposition).

But to consider the first question: Why is a statement which satisfies the criteria analytic? Well, in the first place, *such a statement is certainly not a synthetic statement in the usual sense;* it cannot be confuted by isolated experiments, or, what amounts to the same thing, it cannot be verified by 'induction' in the sense of induction by simple enumeration. To verify or confute a statement of the form 'Something is an *A* if and only if it is a *B*' in this way requires that we have *independent* criteria for being an *A* and for being a *B*. Moreover, since the subject concept is not a law-cluster concept, the statement has little or no systematic import. In short, there could hardly be *theoretical* grounds for accepting or rejecting it. It is for these reasons that such statements might plausibly be regarded as constituting the arbitrary fixed points in our natural language.

There they are, the analytic statements: unverifiable in any practical sense, unrefutable in any practical sense, yet we do seem to have them. This must always seem a mystery to one who does not realize the significance of the fact that in any rational way of life there must be certain arbitrary elements. They are 'true by virtue of the rules of the language'; they are 'true by stipulation'; they are 'true by implicit convention'. Yet all these expressions are after all nothing but metaphors: true statements, but couched in metaphor nonetheless. What is the reality behind the metaphor? The reality is that they are true because they are accepted as

appears in a large number of statements (of sufficient importance, interconnectedness, and systematic import) which are accepted as laws, then in the language of that time it is a 'law-cluster' word. And second, if a statement would be accepted as true, but is regarded as so unimportant that it is not stated as a law in a single scientific paper or text, then it can certainly be disregarded in determining whether or not a word is a 'law-cluster' word.

true, and because this acceptance is quite arbitrary in the sense that the acceptance of the statements has no systematic consequences beyond those described in the previous section, e.g. that of allowing us to use pairs of expressions interchangeably.

Finally, the question as to whether it is *rational* to accept as true statements satisfying the four criteria is answered in the affirmative. This is the question as to whether all these statements may reasonably be taken as true in a 'sensible' rational reconstruction of our actual language. To discuss this point in detail would involve repeating the argument of the preceding section, since this is just the problem which was treated in that section.

Does the fact that everyone accepts a statement make it rational to go on believing it? The answer is that it *does*, if it can be *shown* that it would be reasonable to render the statement immune from revision by stipulation, *if* we were to formalize our language.

In short, analytic statements are statements which we all accept and for which we do not give reasons. This is what we mean when we say that they are true by 'implicit convention'. The problem is then to distinguish them from other statements that we accept, and do not give reasons for, in particular from the statements that we *un*reasonably accept. To resolve this difficulty, we have to point out some of the crucial distinguishing features of analytic statements (e.g. the fact that the subject concept is not a law-cluster concept), and we have to connect these features with what, in the preceding section, was called the 'rationale' of the analytic–synthetic distinction. Having done this, we can see that the acceptance of analytic statements is *rational*, even though there are no reasons (in the sense of 'evidence') in connection with them.

3

Do true assertions correspond to reality?*

In this paper I want to explore the question: whether any sense can be made of the traditional view that a true assertion is one that corresponds to reality. Two opinions seem to be widespread: (a) that some sense *can* be made of the view, and that some sense *is* made of it (as much as can be hoped for) by Tarski's 'Semantical Conception of Truth'; (b) that the view collapses as soon as one asks searching questions about the nature of the alleged 'correspondence'. I shall try to show that both of these opinions are incorrect.

Tarski's conception of truth

According to Tarski, an adequate definition of 'true as a sentence of English' should have the feature that from it follows:

> 'Snow is white' is true as a sentence of English if and only if snow is white.

> 'Grass is green' is true as a sentence of English if and only if grass is green.

Tarski claims that this is a formalization of the 'correspondence theory of truth'. But is it?

Assume for the moment that Tarski's Criterion of Adequacy (roughly described above) is correct. Even so, it seems to refer to purely *inter-linguistic* aspects of the usage of 'true'. This can be seen, for example, by observing that if the meta-language, say, ML, is only partially interpreted, we might still be able to certify a definition of 'true as a sentence of L' to be 'adequate' by checking that Tarski's Criterion of Adequacy was conformed to (all biconditionals of the form '$S*$ is true as a sentence of $L \equiv S$' are theorems of ML, where S is an arbitrary sentence of L and $S*$ is the name – or Gödel number – of S), even though the extra-logical constants of L are totally uninterpreted. In this case the conclusion seems unavoidable that what we are being told is

---

* This paper was read at Oxford, sometime during the winter of 1960. I don't recall the occasion, but Michael Dummett was the commentator (and strongly disagreed).

not that a sentence is true if and only if it bears some specifiable relation to extra-linguistic facts, but simply that we must *define* 'true' (if we *want* an explicit definition, say for metamathematical reasons) so that 'true' will be *eliminable* in certain contexts. For example, if 'the Snark was a Boojum' is a sentence of the object language under consideration, we must define 'true' (I omit the explicit reference to the object language, henceforth) so that it follows that:

'The Snark was a Boojum' is true if and only if the Snark was a Boojum.

But what does this tell us? If it tells us anything (and a strong case can be made out for the view that it doesn't), what it does is to convey the information that the sentences on the left and right of the 'if and only if' are somehow equivalent: that, e.g. anyone who accepts the one is committed to accepting the other. This may be an important fact, if it is a fact, about the usage of 'true', but it is hardly the sort of fact that the correspondence theorist thought that he was pointing out.

Notice also that Tarski's theory gives no indication as to how we might construe the remark (often made by philosophers) that certain assertions (or sentences having the grammatical form of assertions) are neither true nor false. (A correspondence theorist would presumably say that neither they nor their negations bear the appropriate relation C to suitable extra-linguistic facts.) Indeed, Tarski's theory does not even enable us to construe the remark 'What he said is true', in the case in which the person referred to spoke in a language which is not a sub-language of the metalanguage *we* 'speak'. E.g. it offers no model for the situation which arises when someone makes an assertion in French, and someone later says in English that the assertion was *true*. And, of course, a still worse case arises (for the theory) if someone makes an assertion in a language which is not sentence-by-sentence *translatable* into our 'metalanguage'.

These remarks are enough to show, I believe, that whatever Tarski's theory may do, it does not provide a relation C (of correspondence) such that a true sentence (in whichever language) is just one that stands in the relation C to certain extra-linguistic facts (or even linguistic facts, in the case of assertions which are *about* language). Nor does it imply or assume that such a relation C exists. But I believe it to be undeniable (as a remark in the history of philosophy) that correspondence theorists *were* (a) asserting that such a relation exists; and (b) sometimes (e.g. Russell) trying to say what the relation is, or at least what sort of relation it is. All of this is compatible with the idea that Tarski has successfully analyzed the meaning of 'true'. And strictly speaking, there is no reason for me in this paper to go into the question whether Tarski is right or wrong in the claims he makes for the philosophical significance of the work on Truth (its technical significance is, I believe, beyond dispute). But it may be of interest to point out, in passing, that it is quite wrong to say that the Criterion of Adequacy provides us with an insight into the meaning of 'true in L' (for arbitrary L), even if it does not provide us with a definition of 'true in L' (where 'L' is a *variable* over formal languages, not a constant). It seems, in fact, that we should all be a great deal better off if Tarski had (a) shown how to construct 'truth-definitions' for formalized languages (this was his technical contribution, and it could have been easily done in ten pages): (b) *mentioned* the derivability of the biconditionals of the form 'S is true in $L \equiv S$' as a *check* on the adequacy of such truth-definitions in meta-mathematical work; (c) made no philosophical claims whatsoever. Instead he made the following assertions, all of which are false:

(1) That 'true in L' cannot be defined or even taken as primitive in L itself, without contradiction ('semantically closed languages are inconsistent').

(2) (As a consequent of (1)) All natural languages are inconsistent (because they are 'semantically closed').

(3) (The remark mentioned above) That the Criterion of Adequacy clarifies the notion 'true in L' (for arbitrary constant L), although it does not yield a definition of 'true in L' for variable L. (Moreover: this is a 'best possible' result, since any S in which one *could* define 'true in L', where the range of the variable L included S, would be 'semantically closed' and hence inconsistent.)

The first claim is false because it takes the hierarchy of meta-languages (analogue of the theory of types) as the only way of avoiding the semantical paradoxes. But there are (at least) two ways of avoiding the semantical paradoxes, just as there are (at least) two ways of avoiding the set theoretical paradoxes. In the case of set theory, we can either adopt the theory of types, or deny that every well-formed condition defines a set. Similarly, in the case of the semantical paradoxes, we can either stratify into a hierarchy of metalanguages, or we can deny that every closed well-formed formula is a 'statement' (is either true or false). As far as I know, the second way of avoiding the semantical paradoxes has never been formalized, but such a formalization would not appear to be difficult. (The system of 'type-free logic' constructed by Ackermann and investigated by Schütte would appear to be a natural vehicle for such a formalization, since the idea that some sentences are not 'statements' – do not satisfy *tertium non datur* – is already built into the system. In fact, in Ackermann's system it *is* possible to define a set of all true sentences within the system itself, in a straightforward way, and no paradox results – only a proof that a certain 'self-referring sentence' does not satisfy *tertium non datur*.)

The second claim is false not only because it rests upon the first claim (this only shows that it is ungrounded), but because only *theories* (systems of assertions) are inconsistent, and natural languages, e.g. English, are not theories. Someone speaking English may assert that there is a set of all those sets that do not contain themselves, or that all grammatical English declarative sentences are either true or false, but 'English' does not assert these things!

The third claim is false if understood in the sense intended: that the Criterion of Adequacy (i) does not presuppose the notion of truth (or immediately related notions, such as 'naming'); (ii) is materially sufficient (when L is a sublanguage of ML); and (iii) resolves the perennial philosophical disputes about 'truth'. For suppose ML is *incorrect* (ML is, of course, a *theory*, not a language – otherwise the notion of a *theorem* of ML makes no sense – but notice how corrupting Tarski's terminology is!). Then the biconditionals ('S^* is true in $L \equiv S$') may all be theorems of ML even though some of them are *false*. In this case, the definition of 'true' would satisfy Tarski's Criterion of Adequacy even though it was extensionally incorrect! So either (ii) is false, or we must strengthen the Criterion by requiring that all axioms of ML be *true* – in which case (i) becomes false. However (i) is false also for other (no less important) reasons: the Criterion of Adequacy presupposes the semantical notion of *naming* (S^* must *name* S and not, e.g. the negation of S) and the semantical notion of a *biconditional* (a connective with a certain *truth-table*). Note that none of this militates against the more modest remark, that Tarski might have made, that the derivability (in ML) of all biconditionals of the form 'S^* is true in $L \equiv S$' is a useful *check* on the correctness of one's formal definition of 'true in L'. Why shouldn't a 'useful check' rely on one's preanalytic notion of a correct set of axioms, or of a truth-table?

A restatement of the traditional view

To begin with, I propose to seek a statement of the traditional view which is (a) still in traditional language (and thus something to be clarified rather than a clarification of something); but (b) somewhat more precise than the formulations we have hitherto mentioned. To motivate the discussion, let us start with the question: what does *understanding* a sentence (as opposed to knowing whether it is true or false) involve? On the traditional view, it would seem that understanding a sentence must involve something like this: knowing in which *possible* worlds the sentence *would* be true. This suggests: there must be a natural 'correspondence' between sentences in a language, on the one hand, and *sets* of possible worlds on the other. Following Carnap, let us call the set of possible worlds corresponding to a sentence S the *range* of S. Then the relation between the actual world and any true sentence S is just this – 'belonging to the range of'.

This suggests a strategy, which we shall follow in this paper. Instead of trying to characterize directly the alleged relation ('correspondence') between true sentences and 'facts' (or 'the actual world'), we shall try to characterize the relation between *grammatical* sentences and their ranges. Even this relation we shall not try to explicitly define: I do not see any direct way to *define* a suitable mapping from arbitrary sentences in an arbitrary language onto sets of possible worlds, without triviality. Rather we shall suppose that the thesis is this:

(1) that there exists a unique *natural* mapping of sentences onto sets of possible worlds; and that the set corresponding to a true sentence always contains, and the set corresponding to a false sentence never contains, the actual world.

– and what we shall attempt is a characterization, in terms of systematic and operational conditions conjointly, of the relevant kind of 'naturalness'. To put it another way: if someone asks, 'What is the function f that maps an arbitrary sentence of a language L onto its range (onto the 'right' set of possible worlds)?', our answer will be that the 'definition' of f will be of the form: 'The unique function f satisfying such and such conditions' – where the conditions will refer not just to the sentence in question, but to the grammatical structure of the whole language to which the sentences belongs, and to the behavior of speakers in connection with all of the sentences of the language. Two remarks close the present section of this paper:

(A)

(1) is the, so to speak, 'semi-traditional' view that we promised to formulate at the beginning of this section. (1) is, as we said it would be, something in need of a clarification rather than a clarification of something: we have just pointed out the problem of characterizing 'natural' (in '*natural* mapping'), and it is too obvious to need mentioning that 'possible world' will need to be made more precise. Our reason for regarding (1) as a good starting point (rather than some other view) is that it seems obvious that (i) the relation, if there is one, between linguistic and nonlinguistic entities that the correspondence theorist is concerned with is almost certainly one whose definition will have to be

indirect in the sense just indicated. Attempts to define such a relation in a *simple* way (e.g. Russell's attempt to take 'imaging' or 'picturing' as the relation) have notoriously failed. (ii) If, however, systematic considerations are to enter (we are to try to define relations or mappings over whole languages, rather than sentence-by-sentence), then it seems best to start with a relation (like the relation between a sentence and its range) defined over all *grammatical* sentences, and not just over *true* sentences. The reason is, of course, that the grammatical sentences are a *generated* set: they are built up from finitely many sentences (called 'kernel' sentences by linguists) by means of recursive rules, whereas the true sentences certainly do not have any easily describable structure, regarded as a set. And it is much more likely that an inductively generated set will have *natural* isomorphisms and homomorphisms onto other sets than an amorphous set.

(B)

It might be argued that 'sets of possible worlds' are not really *extralinguistic* entities at all. This might be said for either of two reasons: (a) because one thinks that 'possible worlds' are *linguistic* entities (e.g. one may want to identify them with consistent sets of sentences, possibly infinite sets); (b) because one feels squeamish about 'sets'. Qualm (b) I shall not deal with. The present paper is not nominalistic at all, not because I am unsympathetic to nominalism, but because the whole question of a correspondence theory cannot 'get off the ground' if we deny that there are such things as sets, relations, correspondences, at all. It seems interesting to see how far we can get with a correspondence theory if we are willing to be 'platonistic': since that is our project, 'platonistic' we shall be. Difficulty (a) seems better deferred until we come to the notion 'possible world'. For the time being let us operate as if 'possible worlds' were something clear, and were clearly something non-linguistic, wisecracks about 'blackberries' notwithstanding.

Natural and 'unnatural' languages

So far, I have allowed myself to follow Tarski in speaking of *sentences* as true or false. This way of speaking is sometimes objected to on the ground that a mere pattern of sounds (or of ink marks) cannot be either true or false in any intelligible sense; but this takes the notion of a 'sentence' somewhat too narrowly. A sentence, in one perfectly good usage, is at least a sequence of sounds *associated with a particular language* (which provides, among other things, a grammatical analysis and a set of semantical regularities associated with that sentence). The same sequence of sounds may, in this sense, be sometimes a sentence of English and sometimes a sentence of Friesian. (Note that the above objection to calling sentences 'true' or 'false' would also be an objection to asking, e.g. what the third *word* of a sentence is: we should always have to say 'what is the third word of this sentence in English', rather than 'what is the third word of this sentence'.) A better objection is that statement-making is only one of the acts that can be performed with a sentence. To call a sentence 'true' when it is used, e.g. to ask a question, seems extremely misleading. (Although we *might* say that the sentence 'the train is late' is true, if the train *is* late, even if it is uttered with an intonation contour which indicates that the speaker is using the sentence to ask 'is the train late?'. We could say that the speaker said something which was in fact true, not with the intention of asserting it, but with the intention of finding out if it was true.) But if a sentence can be used to make only one statement (variations in emphasis which do not affect truth-value aside), and that statement has a clear truth-value, it seems a perfectly understandable way of speaking to 'transfer' the truth value to the sentence. Two further objections arise, one good and the other bad. The bad objection is that 'it is really *statements* (as opposed to sentences) that are true or false'. If this isn't just a way of saying: 'we don't ordinarily speak of *sentences* as true or false', it becomes some kind of metaphysics of 'propositions' (only re-baptized 'statements' to make them respectable). I like Austin's healthy-minded way of putting it: 'the statement is a "logical construction" out of the makings of statements'. The good objection is that, although in a formalized language it does no harm to speak of sentences as true or false, in a natural language we should have to speak of sentence *tokens* as true or false (since tokens of the same type are frequently used to make in-equivalent statements) rather than sentence *types*, and this is so inconvenient that it is preferable to stick to the customary parlance of 'assertion', 'what was said', 'statement', etc. – although all of these things could be identified, if a need for formalization arose, with suitable equivalence-classes of sentence-tokens or discourse-tokens.

This brings us to the general issue of the difference between natural and formalized languages. For the purpose of this paper, we shall adopt the following fiction: we shall pretend that all natural languages have the same grammar, and that, moreover, that grammar is the grammar of an interpreted first order formal system. We shall also assume that a given 'well formed formula' of a natural language (or rather 'unnatural language', as we shall say to emphasize the fiction) can be used to make only one statement. This will permit us to go on talking of *sentences* as true or false instead of explicitly introducing equivalence-classes of sentence tokens. We could do without this idealization: it would not be as difficult to dispense with it as one might suppose. Nevertheless, our presentation is materially simplified by keeping it for the time being.

What is a 'natural' mapping?

In one way of thinking it, (1) is certainly false. Namely, suppose one interprets (1) as meaning: 'for any plausible concept of "natural", there is only one "natural" mapping of sentences onto sets of possible worlds (the same for all concepts of "natural")'. Then no one would suppose that (1), so interpreted, was true. Rather, (1) must be interpreted as a 'promissory note'; that is, as meaning: 'there is only one mapping of sentences onto sets of possible worlds satisfying the following conditions ... (followed by a list of conditions)'; where the conditions listed must be 'natural' ones from a certain standpoint, and must not be such as to trivialize the remainder of the assertion (1).

Our task, then is to find such conditions.

The first conditions we impose will be systematic ones, of which the following are typical: the range of $\sim S$ must be the complement of the range of S, the range of a disjunction must be the union of the ranges of the disjuncts, the range of a conjunction must be the intersection of the ranges of the conjuncts, existential quantifications must be treated as (possibly infinite) disjunctions (in a certain sense), and universal quantifications as (possibly infinite) conjunctions. A mapping satisfying these (and suitable other conditions of the same kind) will be called a *compositional* mapping. Compositional mappings have the feature that their (value) for a complex sentence is a simple function of their value for related simple sentences. (For a natural, as opposed to an 'unnatural', language the concept of a compositional mapping should be so defined that the range of a complex sentence should depend on the ranges of sentences of the kinds occurring in the 'derivational history' of the complex sentence. The above conditions on disjunctions, conjunctions, and quantifications are – for formalized languages – special cases of this principle.)

Let us ask: why do we require that the range of a disjunction *should* be the union of the range of the disjuncts? Viewing L-speakers from 'outside' (where L is a language over which we are defining a mapping), the obvious corresponding fact about their behavior is this: when they accept either component, they accept a disjunction, and when they reject both components, they reject the disjunction. The rule: *let the range of the disjunction be the union of the ranges of the disjuncts* is in obvious agreement with this behavioral observation. The *nature* of the agreement is, however, interesting. What the intuitive 'agreement' depends upon here is the fact that we are seeking a range-definition that *preserves inferential connections* (including incompatibility relations). That is, if speakers obviously recognize some sort of inferential connection between A and B (e.g. if someone says A, then he evokes 'bizarreness reactions' if he immediately dissents from B), we assume that (i) they believe that the inference $A \therefore B$ preserves 'truth' (the range of A is included in the range of B); and (ii) as far as possible, we try to 'interpret' their language so that inferences that they *believe* to be truth-preserving *are* in fact truth-preserving. Of course, some inferences may not be this 'strong' (the range of A may not be included in the range of B) – e.g. they may infer B from A because they have the unstated 'background knowledge' C, and the range of the conjunction $A \& C$ is included in the range of B. Also, some accepted inferential connections may just be *wrong*. But notice that if we did not have this charitable attitude towards L-speakers – if we were not inclined to believe that they are (i) *trying* to say what is 'true', and (ii) at least some of the time (in everyday cases, at least *most* of the time) succeeding – their linguistic and extra-linguistic behavior could not 'agree' or 'disagree' with any range-assignment, or any translation into another language!

The next condition we shall impose on our mappings is this: choose a compositional mapping which (in addition to preserving as many inferential connections as possible) *makes as many of the things L-speakers say 'true' as possible*. (Here a sentence is 'true' under a mapping if the set of possible worlds onto which it is mapped by the mapping includes the actual world.) This is a very strong principle of 'charity' – possibly too strong. Note, however, that it does not call for *absolute* charity. We try to 'construe' utterances of L (assign ranges) so that they come out true as often as possible; but we don't expect to succeed in all cases. Moreover, we are strongly restricted: the requirement that the mapping must be compositional implies that the set of 'true' sentences must be consistent in first order predicate logic, and the principle of preserving inferential connections (which, I believe, should be given a higher priority than the present principle) may easily conflict with the present principle ('assume that they're right'). If the last requirement turns out to be too strong (i.e. if 'as often as possible' turns out to be 'not very often'), we might try to weaken it.

The problem with which we are dealing is obviously analogous to the problem of *translation* (and our remarks have been influenced by Quine's remarks on the latter problem in *Word and Object*): assigning ranges to sentences is, in a sense, 'interpreting' them; and our systematic and operational constraints are just the systematic and operational constraints on any interpretation – scheme – that is, any systematic scheme for interpreting an arbitrary sentence of L. One serious difficulty of principle now arises. Suppose all the things L-speakers say *are* 'true' (under some mapping), and we find such a mapping. Even if we require the mapping to be compositional, this mapping will *never* be unique by a theorem of logic known as the Lowenheim theorem. This asserts the existence of an interpretation over the universe of natural numbers for any finite set of sentences that we can interpret at all. Roughly speaking, this means that if L-speakers are consistent, then no matter what they are *really* talking about, they can be reinterpreted as talking number-theory! And we can easily show that there will be other, equally unintended interpretations. In short, the previous requirement may be both too strong and too weak! No matter how we interpret the predicates of L (assigning ranges to *atomic* sentences is, in a sense, interpreting predicates, and thereby fixing the ranges of arbitrary sentences, because of the compositional nature of the mapping), we may be unable to make more than a fraction of L- speakers' utterances 'true' (if they are very inconsistent); and the ones we do make 'true' will also be made 'true' by other – in fact, by infinitely many other – mappings.

This last problem (of unintended interpretations guaranteed by the Lowenheim theorem) does not arise in the case of ordinary interpretation schemes, however, simply because such schemes are based, not upon the totality of L-speakers' utterances, but upon some small subset (a 'corpus' as linguists call it), and the interpretation constructed from the corpus is then inductively testable against independent samples. This ensures, in practice, that only *simple* interpretation schemes (as simple as is consonant with the data) will be considered. This suggests that we should introduce some way of measuring the simplicity of our mappings. This problem will not be gone into here. However, it does seem likely that unintended interpretations could be ruled out by imposing suitable requirements of simplicity upon the compositional mappings we are willing to accept.

It may be, also, that the idea: 'try to interpret their utterances so that they're true' is fundamentally misguided.† In this case, we would probably have to do two things: (1) restrict this last condition to a subset of observational utterances (Quine discusses the problem of identifying 'observational' utterances in an arbitrary language in *Word*

---

† Actually, the Principle of Charity on which I rely here does now seem misguided to me in the form in which it is stated in this paper. If the line I take in 'Language and reality' is right, then the constraints on a 'natural' mapping are much more complicated than I make out in the present paper.

and Object), and (2) for the remaining utterances, adopt a policy of trying to interpret them so that they are *coherent*, in a suitable sense (this is discussed in my paper *Meaning and Dreaming*) rather than 'true'. Later in this paper I shall return to the relation between the 'interpretation' problem (assigning ranges) and the 'translation' problem.

'Possible worlds'

The difficulty with the notion of a 'possible world' is not that there is no way of making it precise – there are many ways in the literature, e.g. models, state-descriptions, etc. – but that there are too many ways, and none of them seems to be any good for present purposes. The main difficulty is in getting a set of possible worlds which will be *complete*. If we are willing to settle for a kind of empirical completeness, then a notion can be constructed, however, along the following lines:

We consider physical magnitudes, e.g. mass, charge, defined over all points in space–time. (We shall assume an infinite Euclidean world, and ignore quantum mechanics, for the sake of simplicity.) Such magnitudes (or their densities) may be thought of as functions of quadruplets of real numbers (the coordinates of space–time points). As values they may take scalars, or vectors, or even tensors; but for the sake of simplicity, again, we shall assume that all physical magnitudes have real values. A list of physical magnitudes, including *mass*, may be called 'physically complete', if there are differential equations permitting the extrapolation of all trajectories of particles from a knowledge of these magnitudes and their derivatives at one time. (A 'particle' is, for present purposes, just a world-line along which the magnitude *mass* has a non-zero value.) (In classical physics the list *mass*, *charge* would have been thought to be 'physically complete' in this sense. Quantum mechanics has added new magnitudes, or 'degrees of freedom', however – e.g. spin, strangeness, lepton number. Also, in quantum mechanics the requirement involving extrapolation of trajectories would have to be applied 'before quantization' to make sense.)

By a *valuation over $M_1, \ldots$' M_n* (where $M_1, \ldots$' M_n are physical magnitudes), let us understand any n-tuplet of functions of space–time points (quadruplets of real numbers). We impose the restriction that if M_1 has a restricted range (e.g. *mass* takes on only non-negative values, *spin* takes on only half-integral values) then f_i (the i-th function in the n-tuplet) should have a correspondingly restricted range. The crucial problem will be to define the notion of a *correct* valuation without using 'true' or any of its synonyms. This is accomplished as indicated by the following example (for *fixed* $M_1, \ldots, M_n$; it can also be accomplished for variable $M_1, \ldots, M_n$ and n, but then set-theoretic devices have to be employed):

(2) V is a correct valuation over *mass*, *charge* if and only if there is a function f_1 and a function f_2 such that V is the ordered pair $f_1; f_2$ and for all x, y, z, t the mass-density at the space–time point x, y, z, t is $f_1(x, y, z, t)$ and the electric charge density at x, y, z, t is $f_2(x, y, z, t)$.

Then there is a unique correct valuation over *mass*, *charge* (or, more generally, over $M_1, \ldots, M_n$) and in fact it is just the ordered pair mass, charge! (Identifying a physical magnitude with the corresponding function.) Our proposal, assuming some list of physical magnitudes to be empirically complete (say, *mass*, *charge*) is to identify 'the actual world' with the correct valuation over those magnitudes.† Assuming *mass*, *charge* to be an empirically complete list, (1) would now become the following highly non-trivial assertion:

(3) There is, for any given language L, a unique compositional mapping onto sets of valuations over *mass*, *charge* which is (a) 'simple' (in a suitable sense); (b) preserves most inferential connections, and (c) makes a maximum number of utterances by L-speakers 'true'. (Maps them onto a set which contains the correct valuation over *mass*, *charge*.) Moreover, a sentence of L is true if and only if it is 'true' under this mapping.

The philosophically interesting point is that, although (3) could certainly be false, it could also certainly be true. If it were true (or something like it were true), it would not give us the linguistic meaning of 'true' as a word in English. Thus, it would not support the claims of the correspondence theory as a semantical analysis of 'true'. But it would provide an interesting *synthetic* sense in which, *in fact*, the true sentences were just the ones which bore a certain nontrivial relation to the actual world. For the assertion that there is a unique mapping of the kind described in (3) and that S (a given sentence) is mapped by that mapping onto a pair $f_1; f_2$ which is extensionally identical with the pair

† This way of representing possible worlds may seem to presuppose that all properties are physical properties, i.e. Materialism. Actually, it does not. It only presupposes that whatever non-physical properties there may be are not 'supervenient', i.e. metaphysically *independent* of physical properties. For example, on my view psychological properties are functional, not physical. But the functional properties of a thing are metaphysically determined by its physical properties. So the range of a full sentence of a psychological predicate P (a sentence of the form $P(a)$) can be represented in the way indicated in the text, even though the property P is not a physical property. Secondly, it is in no way essential to my view that the basic parameters employed all be *physical* parameters. The view depends on its being *somehow* possible to parametrize possible worlds; the use of physical parameters is not essential to the view, only convenient.

mass, charge, would be a nontrivial assertion about S which would be true exactly when S was true. Moreover, it (this assertion) would depend for its truth on both the 'facts of the world' (the way mass and charge are distributed at space–time points) and upon the grammar of L and the way L-speakers actually and potentially behave with respect to sentences of L. In this sense, it would assert the existence of a 'relation between S and extra-linguistic (and linguistic) facts'. Perhaps the main way in which the (traditional) correspondence view would be false, on this account, would be in having left out the parenthetical 'and linguistic' – it is very important that a true sentence is *not* one which bears a certain relation to extra-linguistic facts, but one which bears a certain relation to extra-linguistic facts *and to the rest of the language.* (The 'correspondence' is triadic rather than diadic.)

Of course, there *could* be other nontrivial relations between true sentences and 'the world'. For instance, it might be true that all true sentences and no false ones are uttered at some time (past, present, or future) by a red-haired person (but it isn't). However, (a) we don't have any plausible candidates for such other relations; and (b) such an *accidental* relation would be quite different from the relation asserted by (3). (3) does not give us the meaning of 'true', but it might give us the nature of truth.

Some objections

In the case of a natural language (as opposed to an 'unnatural' one) ranges will have to be defined over equivalence-classes of sentence-tokens, instead of over sentence-types. Moreover, this will have to be done in such a way that the range of a token frequently depends upon the context of utterance. But all this occasions no particular difficulty of principle. For the sake of an example, consider the sentence 'Here is a chair'. Presumably we will best conform to our third principle (maximizing 'truth') by letting the range of a token of this type be the set of possible worlds in which a chair is in an appropriate relation to the speaker at the time and place of utterance, or rather the corresponding set of valuations over *mass, charge.* This much is unproblematical.

But then the objection arises that we have, in effect, *defined* a 'chair' in terms of theoretical notions, and that such a definition, if correct, is only empirically so. Since all of our ranges will rest upon such empirical identifications (of the 'water is H_2O' type), *analyticity* relations will be badly distorted. In particular, a sentence may well have universal range without being analytic and empty range without being a self-contradiction.

The best answer to this objection is 'so what?'. I have argued elsewhere that one does not have analytic sentences of the paradigmatic 'a bachelor is a never-been-married man' type in connection with *theoretical* terms, and that it is on the quite special linguistic character of the words 'bachelor', 'pediatrician', 'spinster' that the familiar analytic truths involving these words rests. If this is right, then it is plausible that Carnap's attempts to use the notion of 'range' to distinguish analytic from synthetic sentences quite generally (including in theoretical language) should fail. But we have not been trying to define *analytic* but rather to characterize *true*, which is quite a different problem. Roughly, our standpoint is that the notion of range can be a useful tool in semantical analysis, but that the use of the notion does not depend upon the rule that one must never use collateral information ('water is H_2O') in setting up ranges. (Cf. Quine's remarks on the related problem of 'radical translation' (Quine, 1960).)

Again, it may be asked how we would set up ranges not for empirical statements but for statements of pure mathematics. The answer is that for quite a lot of pure mathematics there is no trouble. We are, after all, assuming an actual nondenumerable infinity of space–time points, and given so rich an 'ontology' there is no difficulty in accommodating all of classical analysis. Indeed, inductive rules can easily be given which assign a range to arbitrary statements of set theory, provided one is willing to use set theory in the definition of 'compositional mapping'. Of course, these ranges are all either empty or universal; but the requirement that 'range' must be inductively defined makes this a technical problem nonetheless, though not an insuperable one.

Relations to Tarski's work

Our proposal above has a certain relation to Tarski's work – not to the Criterion of Adequacy, but rather to the notion of a formalized 'truth definition'. This may be seen as follows: instead of functions f_1, f_2 we could use infinite conjunctive sets of sentences of the form $f_1(r_1) = r_2$, $f_2(r_1) = r_2$, where r_1 and r_2 are real numbers given by infinite decimal expansions. (These 'sentences' would then be denumerably infinite; and a valuation would be a nondenumerably infinite set of infinite sentences.) If we think of a 'valuation' in this new sense, then we see that (2) above is essentially a 'truth-definition' in Tarski's sense – for a conjunctive set in a certain notation. Thus our proposal is somewhat akin to the following idea: first define truth (by means of a 'truth-definition' in Tarski's sense) for a certain 'universal language' U, and then define 'S is true in L' (for arbitrary L) to mean: there is an S' such that S'' is the translation of S into U and S' is true in U.

The objection which would usually be made is that such a universal language U is impossible for the following reason: if every language is translatable into U, then in particular MU (the meta-language in which 'true in U' is defined) is translatable into U. Hence 'true in U' is expressible in U. So U is 'semantically closed'. Hence U is inconsistent. [This is nonsense. Let U contain a primitive predicate Stat(n) such that Stat(n) means that the formula with the Gödel number n is a *statement* (where the notion of a statement is taken as primitive, as the notion of a set is in axiomatic set theory.) Call a definition of 'true in U' *adequate* if the following are all theorems *of* U *itself*: Stat($n*$) $\supset \cdot$ $n*$ is true in $U \equiv S_n$; where S_n is a sentence of U and $n*$ is its Gödel number. Then an adequate definition of 'true in U' (in this sense) can perfectly well exist in U itself. All one can prove (using the familiar diagonal arguments) is that a certain sentence of U is not a statement.]

However, there are nonformal objections to the idea just put forward which seem more decisive. Given what we know about languages, the idea of a language into which any other language is translatable *sentence-by-sentence* seems unconvincing – especially if U is required to be a formalized language. We have avoided this difficulty essentially by liberalizing the notion of 'translation' in two directions: allowing the free use of empirical information in the 'translation', and allowing the use of *sets* of 'expressions' (which are themselves infinite conjunctions) as 'translations'. Similar, but less extreme, liberalizations might be enough to permit the carrying through of the program of defining 'true in L' in terms of 'true in U' for some fixed U. This U would, it seems, have to possess some property of empirical completeness analogous to the empirical completeness property required of our list of physical magnitudes $M_1, M_2, \ldots M_n$.

Concluding unscientific postscript

Coming back to natural languages, it is enough to remark that the notion of range is easily modified to handle vague, ambiguous, etc., sentences. Also, it is obvious that it will be convenient to leave the notion of range *undefined* for many sentences – even declarative sentences. Far from being a disadvantage, this is a virtue of the approach – because it means we can make sense of the notion that some sentences are 'neither true nor false', which was one of our objectives.

84

4
Some issues in the theory of grammar*

Introduction

Although this symposium is devoted to problems in the field of mathematical linguistics (a peculiar field, in that some of its leading experts doubt its existence), in my paper I am not going to attempt to prove any theorems or state any results. Rather, I shall take advantage of my privilege as a philosopher and devote myself to a survey of work done by others in the area and to a discussion of issues raised by linguists concerning the work done in this area. There are, in addition to the difficult technical problems, whose existence everyone acknowledges, also very serious conceptual difficulties, as is shown by the fact that Chomsky's book *Syntactic Structures*, which is regarded by some as a foundation-stone for this kind of activity, has been described by no less an authority than Roman Jakobson as an *argumentum a contrario* (Jakobson, 1959), showing the impossibility of the whole enterprise.

What I want to do first is to provide, so to speak, a conceptual setting for the kind of work that Chomsky is doing. I believe that the conceptual setting I will provide is one that will be acceptable to Chomsky himself – but this, of course, is not vital. The interpretations of a scientific theory most acceptable to the scientist himself may often be the least tenable ones, and so we shall worry about finding an interpretation or conceptual setting, for the theory of grammars which seems to us to be correct, not necessarily one which some particular linguist will ratify.

In particular, I propose to connect the theory of grammars with a program in linguistics initiated by Paul Ziff and presented by him in his book, *Semantic Analysis* (1960). Ziff is concerned of course not only, or even primarily, with questions of grammar, but with questions of meaning. Even if most linguists, however, are not yet primarily or very deeply concerned with semantical questions, it seems to me fairly obvious that at some not very distant date, linguistics must begin to deal

* Reprinted with permission of the publisher, The American Mathematical Society, from *Proceedings of Symposia in Applied Mathematics*. Copyright © 1961, Volume 12, pp. 25 to 42.

with these questions much more extensively than it is doing today, and that programs in grammar are to be judged to some extent at least, by the way in which they fit into reasonable programs for linguistic investigation as a whole – that means, in the long run, into programs for investigating not only grammatical but also semantical aspects of natural languages.

I. On understanding deviant utterances

The main concept with which Ziff works is the concept of a *deviant* sentence (or, as he prefers to say, 'deviant utterance'). By a deviant sentence, he means any sentence which deviates from any linguistic regularity whatsoever, where by a linguistic regularity we may understand either an inductively certifiable generalization concerning the observable behavior of informants, or a projection introduced by the linguist for reasons of systematic simplicity, that is to say an idealization of some sort. I shall assume here that some degree of idealization is inevitable in linguistic work, and I shall also assume that the question of how much idealization is legitimate is one that has no general answer. What one has to answer in a specific case is whether the idealizations made by a particular linguist in a particular context were or were not too severe.

Now, the regularities from which a deviant sentence deviates may be sometimes grammatical regularities or sometimes semantical regularities. The sentence 'She goed home.' we would all presumably classify as deviant, and presumably there would be no hesitation in classifying the deviation as a deviation at the level of grammar. The sentence 'The star by which seafarers normally steer is graceful.' is also deviant, but at a more subtle level. What is deviant about this sentence is that the word 'graceful' ordinarily has to do with form and motion, and a star does not have form or motion. This kind of deviation is obviously at the level of semantics.

Two things should be noticed at once: first, some linguists believe that they can do without any notion of linguistic deviation, but this is a mistake. If one recognizes linguistic regularities at all, then one must recognize actual or possible deviations from those regularities. Now then, a grammar of a language is nothing but a statement of certain supposed linguistic regularities. Anyone who writes a grammar of any natural language is therefore automatically classifying certain sentences as nondeviant, and by implication, certain others as deviant. Secondly, some linguists claim that any sentence, which could under any circumstances, no matter how farfetched, be 'passed' by an informant, is nondeviant. This may be a nice theoretical position, although I shall argue against it in a moment; but it should be observed, that even if it were the correct theoretical position, it is a position that no linguist actually conforms to in practice. I am quite sure that the very linguists who claim that any sentence that an informant might conceivably use is nondeviant, will in writing a grammar of any language whatsoever automatically rule out, by implication at least, many sentences that informants might employ. For example, Joseph Applegate once reported to me an amusing conversation with another linguist who had somewhat rashly claimed that an English speaker would under no circumstances understand a sentence in which the verb 'sneezed' was used as a transitive verb. Within a very few minutes in the same conversation he had succeeded in tricking the other linguist into herself using the somewhat 'exotic' sentence 'Pepper doesn't sneeze me.' Now then, this is extremely amusing, and it does establish a point: namely, that no matter how deviant a sentence may be it is extremely unwise to say that there are no circumstances under which a speaker of the language might produce or a hearer of the language might construe it. But this example should not be taken as making the quite different point that the sentence 'Pepper does not sneeze me.' is nondeviant. I shall argue this below. For the moment I only make the weaker claim that even if a linguist when arguing linguistic theory claims that, for instance, 'Pepper does not sneeze me.' is nondeviant; when *writing* a grammar of English, he is very likely to inadvertently contradict his own philosophy of linguistics by ruling out this very sentence. He may not rule it out explicitly by calling it ungrammatical; in fact, he may not use the term 'ungrammatical' at all. But that does not matter. If he gives rules for producing grammatical sentences of English and these rules have the feature that they would never produce the sentence just mentioned, then we may obviously say that he has ruled out the sentence just mentioned by implication. It is clear, in fact that the only way in which one could avoid ruling out any sentences of the form exhibited by 'Pepper does not sneeze me.' as deviant, would be by writing a grammar of English in which every verb was allowed to be used as a transitive verb. And even if one did that, it wouldn't help! For presumably, unless the grammar is the one-sentence grammar which says 'Any finite sequence of English words is a sentence.', then there must be *some* finite sequences of English words which, by implication at least, are ruled out as deviant and I will here and now guarantee to find situations under which informants would produce some of these sentences and hearers would understand some of them. In short, if someone says, 'Why isn't this a reasonable program for linguistic theory: to write a grammar of, say, English which predicts

87

all and only those sentences which English speakers might conceivably use or English hearers might conceivably understand?', the answer is two-fold. First, that a grammar in this sense would not resemble any grammar ever written by any linguist (and I include linguists who claim that the program just alluded to is *their* program) and secondly, that the program would either be trivial or impossible of execution. It would be trivial of execution if one took the standpoint that for any finite sequence of English words not exceeding a certain length there are some circumstances under which that sequence might be employed; then one gets the one-sentence grammar alluded to before. In fact, one can write a single one-sentence grammar for all natural languages at once on this view! If one, however, interprets more narrowly the notion of a sentence that an English speaker might use or an English hearer might understand, then, I think two things are going to happen: namely, some degree of arbitrariness is going to creep in (e.g. one linguist will count 'Pepper does not sneeze me.' as a sentence that an English speaker might use, and another will reject it), and secondly, arbitrariness or no arbitrariness, no one will succeed in carrying out the task. This prediction is not as daring as it might seem, for it takes only a moment's reflection to see that the program we have just been criticizing is the program of doing wholly without idealizations in linguistic theory; and no science, whether it be a life science or a physical science, has ever managed to take a single step without the very liberal use of idealizations. Even those linguists, and they are fortunately few, who have an exaggerated confidence in the powers of such statistical techniques as multiple-factor analysis, forget that multiple-factor analysis is itself one of the most ingenious idealizations ever introduced into the empirical sciences.

Let me assume, then, that our objective is going to be to set down some system of linguistic regularities characterizing some aspects of a particular natural language, and that we are going to be willing, indeed eager to idealize and 'oversimplify' to some extent. To put it another way, we will be worried about the criticism that someone has produced a better description of the same language than we have, but not worried about the criticism that our description is not ideal in the impossible sense of conforming exactly to the exact behavior of every hearer and speaker.

There are now two questions which face us corresponding to the two classes we have distinguished: deviant and nondeviant. These are, what to say about the nondeviant sentences, and what to say about the deviant sentences. The former problem is the problem of showing how the nondeviant sentences are built up, what their composition is, how their meaning is determined by their composition, et cetera. This is the problem which, at the grammatical level, occupies Chomsky in his *Syntactic Structures*, and which occupies Ziff at the semantical level in *Semantic Analysis*.

Important and seemingly insuperable as this problem is, I wish to neglect it here and to focus attention on a different problem, namely the problem of what to say about the deviant sentences. One thing we might do, of course, is to say nothing about them. We might take the standpoint that to call a sentence deviant is to say 'Let's forget about it. Linguistic theory does not have to deal with this'. But if this were our standpoint then I would be inclined to sympathize with all the linguists who dislike such notions as 'deviant', 'ungrammatical', and so forth. Shutting one's eyes to the very empirical facts one is supposed to be trying to account for is not good scientific practice; and this is presumably what the people who make the unrealistic proposal that we should count every sentence ever heard as nondeviant, have in mind. Indeed, as Ziff repeatedly emphasizes, since a great deal of the discourse most commonly used and especially the discourse of greatest conceptual importance, discourse of innovators in every field – in science, in politics, in moral life, in philosophy – consists of deviant sentences, to reject the problem of accounting for the use and the understanding of deviant sentences is to reject one of the most interesting problems in linguistics. Thus, Ziff proposes as a program for linguistics, not merely to provide a description of the nondeviant sentences of a language, but to go on, using that description as a base, and try to account for the various kinds of deviancy in terms of meaning, function, structure, and so forth. This program is only stated as a program in *Semantic Analysis*, which focusses attention mainly on nondeviant sentences; however, Ziff, since the completion of *Semantic Analysis*, has been working extensively on a theory of the way in which we understand deviant utterances.

The details of this theory need not concern us here, but I will give one or two very simple examples in order to illustrate what is meant by accounting for the way in which we understand deviant sentences, and to show the role played by the notion of a deviant sentence in the account. The first example is the Dylan Thomas line. 'A grief ago I saw him there.' Clearly, 'grief' is being used figuratively here. But what exactly does it mean to say that a word is being used figuratively? A plausible account might be along somewhat the following lines: The hearer, on hearing the sentence, 'A grief ago I saw him there.', immediately recognizes that the sentence he has just heard is deviant. He then proceeds to find a similar sentence which is nondeviant from which the given sentence may be, in some sense or other, derived. One such sentence would be, 'A moment ago I saw him there.'; another would be,

'A year ago I saw him there'; another would be, 'An age ago I saw him there'; and so forth. Notice that the substitution of a single word for the word 'grief' is capable of turning the sentence, 'A grief ago I saw him there.' into a nondeviant sentence; and notice, moreover, that all the words that we have so far substituted in order to regularize this sentence have this semantical feature in common: that they are measures of time. This accords with the natural, informal explanation of the line: namely, 'Grief is being used as if it were a measure of time.' Notice what we have done here: although we call the sentence 'A grief ago I saw him there.' a deviant sentence, this does not mean that it is in any sense a bad sentence, or that Dylan Thomas ought not to have used it. The term 'deviant' is obviously a technical term which has an explanatory, and not a valuational, function. Calling the sentence deviant is also not to say that it is a freak, that it is something that transcends all possibility of linguistic explanation. On the contrary, calling it deviant is an essential part of the explanation.

'But then,' the reader may object, 'if you are going to recognize this sentence as a "good" sentence, if you are going to try to account for it, why call it deviant at all? Why not just modify your grammar so that the word "grief" can occur in any position in which a measure of time can occur?' This proposal, however, leads us right back to the blind alley of rejecting all idealizations. A more reasonable proposal is this: We first rather stringently, perhaps over-stringently rule out all but certain privileged uses of the word 'grief' as deviant. We then frame a definition of the word 'grief' which covers the remaining nondeviant uses. Notice that this is possible precisely because we have been so stringent in what we are willing to accept as non-deviant uses. The lenient standpoint which counts all possible uses on a par has as one of its many disadvantages that it makes the framing of ordinary dictionary definitions either impossible or untestable. The framing of an adequate dictionary definition of the word 'grief' is impossible if the definition is supposed to account for all uses of the word 'grief', and all uses count as equally good. Try to think of a definition of the word 'grief' that would be reasonable in a dictionary and that would fit the use of 'grief' both as a mood or feeling and as 'a measure of time'. On the other hand, if we retain the usual dictionary definitions and also count all uses on a par, but simply say that a definition need not agree with the uses of the word of which the definition is a definition – then it becomes wholly unclear what the function of a definition is, or how one definition might be said to be correct and another might be said to be incorrect. All of these matters have been taken up at much more length in the book by Ziff I have mentioned, and I will not discuss them further here.

Moreover, it will be noticed that the program of first accounting for the regularities which are represented by a distinguished set of non-deviant uses, and then trying to account for a much wider set of deviant uses by regarding these as in some sense derived from the nondeviant uses, fits the ancient and intuitive distinction between literal and figurative uses of a word.

Finally, and this is the most important point, notice that the recommendation that we draw no distinction between the use of 'grief' in the sentence, 'A grief ago I saw him there.', and the sentence, 'She was in a state of grief.' – while it sounds ever so much more lenient and non-discriminatory than the Ziffian approach – in fact, gives one not the slightest hint of a procedure for explaining the Dylan Thomas line in question. On the other hand, the discriminatory procedure of beginning with the idea that the sentence is deviant actually gives us a method not of rejecting the sentence but of understanding it. Namely, we have the procedure (this, of course, is a procedure only for a very simple class of deviant sentences) of trying to find a nondeviant sentence from which the deviant sentence in question may be derived by a one-word substitution and then of seeing the meaning associated with the whole class of relevant one-word substitutions. This was the technique we used above, and, of course, this particular sentence is a very good one for this particular technique.

Classifying a sentence as deviant can often be the most useful first step in analyzing it in terms of what it deviates from, and how and why. Following Fodor,† we might go further and, for example, introduce the notion of standard deviations from standardness, uniform mechanisms for producing and understanding whole classes of deviant sentences, e.g. irony.

In the present connection, I should like to take up an argument of Jakobson's against Chomsky's work. Jakobson contends‡ that certain sentences that are ruled out by Chomsky's description of English, for example, 'Ideas are green.', are perfectly regular, nondeviant sentences. His view is that the sentence, 'Ideas are green.' is simply a false sentence. Now then, one should never call a sentence ungrammatical or even deviant at a semantical level if the only thing wrong with it is that it happens to be false. But I think that there is something decidedly wrong with the view that such sentences as 'Ideas are green.', or 'Virtue swims.', are *merely* 'false'.

I don't want to go into this issue at length, simply because it has been discussed for so many years by so many philosophers; but let me, as it

† In *Some uses of 'use'*, Princeton Doctoral Dissertation, 1960.
‡ (Jakobson, 1959)

were, allude to some of the results of the philosophic debate. In the first place, philosophers have found it useful to distinguish between a sentence-type or sentence on the one hand, and the various acts that could be performed with sentences of that type on the other, e.g. statement-making. As soon as one draws this distinction one is inclined to be unhappy with the notion of a *false sentence*. If a sentence had the feature that every token of the type could be used to make one and only one statement, and that statement had a clear truth-value – if it was always truth or always falsity – then one might understand the locution 'This sentence is false.' as short for 'The statement that one would be making, if one employed a token of this type in order to make a statement, would be false.' But the fact is that there are very few, perhaps no, sentences in English which can be used to make one and only one statement.

Moreover, I think the sentence 'Ideas are green.' is clearly *not* such a sentence. If one uttered the sentence 'Ideas are green.' one would probably be taken not to be making a statement at all, but to be doing something else – for instance, telling a joke, interrupting a conversation, et cetera. Try it and see! Linguists and philosophers are too prone *not* to make such simple experiments as this one. But I am quite serious. Try to use the sentence 'Ideas are green.' to make a statement, and see what reaction you get from your hearers. You may, in your own opinion, succeed in using the sentence 'Ideas are green.' to make a statement, but I doubt whether you will be taken as having made a statement by the people who listen to you. Giggles, rather than dissent, are likely to be the reaction you will face; and giggles, be it remembered, are the normal reaction when it is believed that someone, when uttering a sentence in a statement-making tone of voice has not made a statement and has not really in fact intended to make a statement.

But suppose we grant that, in some farfetched circumstances perhaps, the sentence 'Ideas are green.' might be employed to make a statement. Jakobson says that the statement would be a false one – but how does he know? Presumably he thinks that there is only one statement that the sentence 'Ideas are green.' could plausibly be used to make, and that the statement is clearly false; but I would think, and many philosophers would agree with me that (a) there is no statement that the sentence 'Ideas are green.' could plausibly be used to make, and (b) there are a number of statements that the sentence 'Ideas are green.' could implausibly be used to make, and, of the latter, some are probably true and some are probably false.

Note that it would do no good to say in an authoritative tone of voice that when one says the sentence 'Ideas are green.' is false, one is assuming of course, that the sentence 'Ideas are green.' is being used to make one particular statement, namely the statement *that ideas are green.* For saying, with no contextual clue to help the hearer out, 'When I say "ideas are green", I *mean* ideas are green', is not saying what you mean at all. If someone says, 'Well just consider the context of philosophic discussion. Suppose one asserted as an abstract truth, "Ideas are green", he would have made a false statement, wouldn't he?' My position is that he wouldn't have made any statement that I understand at all.

But I don't wish to rest my case on the sentence–statement distinction just alluded to. Let me assume for the sake of argument that Jakobson is right; that there is, considered in the abstract, such a statement as the statement that ideas are green, and that this statement is clearly false. Does it follow that when we reject the sentence 'Ideas are green.' as deviant, we are rejecting it *merely* because it's 'false'? Not at all! For suppose that my necktie is not green and consider the two sentences 'Ideas are green.' and 'My necktie is green.' Both are 'false', but it is quite clear that the two sentences must be 'false' in different ways. Traditional philosophers distinguished the two kinds of 'falsity' as *a priori* falsity and *a posteriori* falsity. That is, 'My necktie is green.' is contingently false; on the other hand, the 'statement' 'Ideas are green.' must, if it has a truth value at all, be *a priori* false. This distinction is, however, all we need to justify calling the sentence 'Ideas are green.' a deviant sentence, for as soon as we have the distinction between *a priori* and contingent falsity, we can ask, 'What is the characteristic of the nouns *N*, such that "*N*'s are green." is not *a priori* false or nonsense?' The characteristic would presumably be that these are the so-called concrete nouns. This might be rendered by saying that the phrase 'are green' 'takes' a concrete subject; and saying that the sentence 'Ideas are green.' deviates from a linguistic regularity by employing with the phrase 'are green' a subject that the phrase does not 'take'.

Thus the sentences 'Ideas are green.', 'Virtue swims.', 'Golf plays John.', and so forth deviate from stable linguistic regularities, at least at the level of semantics. Moreover, this is so independently of whether one regards them as 'false' or not. Showing that they are deviant may involve methodological problems; but these problems (of justifying a description of a language) arise even at the level of grammar.

II. The line between grammar and semantics

So far, the only question we have considered is the question whether a sentence is deviant or nondeviant. Given that a sentence is deviant, we have not raised the further question whether it should be called grammatical or ungrammatical. But this question can no longer be postponed;

for the job of a grammar is not to rule out all deviant sentences – e.g. a grammar should not rule out the sentence 'The star by which seafarers normally steer is graceful.' – but to rule out only those deviant sentences whose deviancy is in some sense grammatical deviancy. But how are we to tell whether a given case of deviancy is grammatical or semantical?

A position that I have heard linguists put forward is that there are two sharply different kinds of deviancy, grammatical deviancy and semantical deviancy, and that very little is grammatically deviant. That is to say, most of the sentences we have been calling deviant are deviant, but deviant for reasons that should be called semantical and not grammatical.

A few examples may make the dispute clear. These linguists would for example reject the category 'animate noun' as a permissible grammatical category, although they would of course admit it as a potential semantical category. Now, suppose a Frenchman says, referring to a table, 'She is red', or, to put more of the context into the sentence itself, suppose he says, 'George gave me a table and I saw at once that she was red and had four legs.' Chomsky would say that this sentence is ungrammatical because the pronoun 'she' does not agree with the inanimate noun 'table'. These linguists, on the other hand, would maintain that the sentence in question is grammatical, simply because they have no basis for calling it ungrammatical. One wonders how they would deal with such languages as German and French, where questions of gender have long been regarded as grammatical questions: Would they proceed the same way, or would they have one policy for English and another for French, and if so, on what basis? Their position, as I gather it, is that it is only features that are arbitrary, that have nothing to do with meaning, that are properly called grammatical. However, I agree with Jakobson and with Boas, that there do not appear to be any arbitrary features in a language in the sense indicated. For example, if one says that it is arbitrary that we say 'She is here.' and not 'Is she here.', the obvious answer is that while it may be arbitrary in some absolute sense, in the context of English it is not arbitrary; we use one when we want to make a statement and the other when we want to ask a question. Notice that if we agree that the categories 'abstract' and 'concrete' should be prohibited in grammar, then on exactly the same grounds we should prohibit 'masculine' and 'feminine' on the one hand, and 'indicative' and 'interrogative' on the other.

There is, of course, an absolute sense which one has a vague feeling for but which one has difficulty putting into words, in which one is tempted to say that word-order in English is arbitrary; that is to say, the conventions determining *which* word-order is declarative and which is interrogative could conceivably have been reversed without, as far as we can see, impairing the functional efficiency of the language. The trouble is that in this absolute sense, if it can be made sense of at all, semantical features are just as arbitrary as syntactical ones. Any word might, after all, have meant something different from what it does mean.

Without prolonging this dispute any further, let us just say this: that adding a category to our grammar has mainly the function of enabling us to state more regularities. If these regularities seem to pertain to a very small class of sentences we will in general be unhappy at calling them grammatical regularities; if they pertain to a great many sentences, or to the use of important morpheme classes, e.g. the pronouns or the articles, then it will seem more conventional to call them grammatical regularities. On this view, exactly where we should draw the line between semantics and grammar is a matter of convenience, and not a genuine theoretical question at all.

III. Independence of meaning

An issue that we can hardly bypass, if only because it has generated so much controversy, is the issue between those who assert and those who deny that grammar can be done 'independently of meaning'. Among American linguists, Zellig Harris was the first I know of to emphasize this claim. On the other hand, Jakobson claims in the article alluded to above that Chomsky's monograph is a 'magnificent *argumentum a contrario*' on this very point, and speaks optimistically of a pending 'hierarchy of grammatical meanings'.

As a preliminary to taking a look at this vexed question, let me consider a somewhat parallel (if irrelevant-sounding) question: 'Can one discover a man's occupation without seeing him at work?' The answer is obviously 'yes' – one can, for example, put the question 'What do you do for a living?' But even if this is ruled out as 'cheating', the answer is not necessarily 'no'. Sherlock Holmes, as we all know, could discover an enormous number of things about someone – not just his occupation – from the most irrelevant seeming clues. So the proper answer to the above question is (roughly): 'It depends on how good a detective you are'.

Coming to language: it is apparent that the question 'Can one discover the phonemes (morphemes, form-classes, etc.) of a language without learning the language (learning the meaning of any form, learning that any two forms are synonymous)?' is quite parallel to the occupation question, and it seems evident (to me, at least) that the immediate answer is the same: 'It depends on how good a detective you are'.

95

Thus, some linguists apparently maintain (at least when they are arguing this question) that one cannot discover the phonemes of a language without learning the meanings of the forms in that language (or at least learning that certain pairs are pairs of nonsynonymous expressions). I am sure that these very same linguists, however, would not be surprised (provided the statement were not connected with this 'controversy') to hear that some linguist had inferred the phonemes of a language X from the way the X-speaker spoke English (*a fortiori*, without learning X). One would, of course, regard this as an amazing *tour de force*, but not as impossible in principle. But if someone could conceivably do this as a *tour de force*, why might he not do it repeatedly, and even train graduate students in the art. (Cf. the accomplishments of Pike in establishing rapid comprehension of portions of an alien language. These would count as an individual *tour de force* – except that Pike has repeated the 'trick' on many occasions, and has taught it to some of his students.) Finally, why might one not even 'mechanize' such a trick, by reducing it to, say, a standardized test of some kind that could be administered by a properly trained clerk (or a machine)?

Again, if there is nothing inconceivable in the idea of someone's inferring the phonemes of a language from the way the speaker of that language speaks a different language, why might not a list of nonsense syllables take the place of the different language? I am not saying that any of these procedures is practicable today or will ever be practicable, but only that no issue of principle is involved. Every linguist believes that phonemics have an 'obligatory' character, and that the phonemics of one's native language influence the way one speaks (in the overwhelming majority of cases) even when one is speaking a different language, reciting (or making up) nonsense syllables, etc. But then how on earth could it be impossible in principle to discover the phonemes of an alien language except in one way?

Viewed in this light, Harris's methods do not appear so surprising. Harris discovers the phonemes of a language in roughly the following way: the linguist recites a sequence of expressions, e.g. 'cat, cat, cad, cab, cab, cad', and the informant describes what he heard. If the informant says: 'you said A twice and then B and then C twice and then B' (where A, B, C in the above example would be cat, cad, cab as pronounced by the informant, or approximations thereto) then one would conclude (tentatively, of course!) that b, c, t were allophones of different phonemes in the alien tongue. On the other hand, if the informant says: 'you said A three times and then B twice and then A again' (where A is cad or cat or something intermediate, and B is cab) then one would be pretty sure that b, d were allophones of different phonemes and *d*, *t* were allophones of the same phoneme in the alien language. (Harris would normally use expressions in the alien language itself in this test, but the test might conceivably 'work' with nonsense syllables, in which case one would have the possibility envisaged in the preceding paragraphs.)

Coming to morpheme boundaries, Harris again uses 'structural' methods, instead of relying on such notions as 'shortest meaningful unit'. I will not describe these methods in detail, but they depend roughly on the counting of 'exclusions' – that is, sounds that cannot occur immediately after certain initial segments of sentences, e.g. all sounds except '*t*' are excluded after the initial segment 'Isn't that a daguerreo-'. These exclusions are exclusions 'going from left to right'. Similarly one can count exclusions 'going from right to left' – that is, sounds that cannot occur immediately before certain terminal segments of sentences (e.g. '*h*' is excluded immediately before '-ing'). Then (Harris finds) morpheme boundaries can be identified as local minima in the number of exclusions which are minima counting both from left to right and from right to left. This test not only does not 'depend on meaning', but seems more successful than any test that *does* 'depend on meaning' that I know of.

But why should all of this evoke argument among linguists? I don't mean, why should Harris' methods in particular evoke argument (anybody's methods naturally evoke argument, in any science) – perhaps these particular methods don't work; I mean, why should there be argument that methods of this kind *can't* work in principle? Why couldn't there be a linguistic counter-part of Sherlock Holmes?

I suppose what is bothering Harris' opponents is this: the notions 'phoneme' and 'morpheme' have been conventionally defined in terms of semantical notions; hence any method of discovering what the phonemes/morphemes of a language are must utilize semantical information. But this is a *non sequitur*! (Just as it would be a *non sequitur* to conclude from the definition of 'occupation' as the way a man makes his living, that one cannot *discover* a man's occupation unless he is engaged in working.) Language is doubtless learned when its various parts are performing their various semantical functions; but once one has learned the segmentation of one's language into parts, one may 'give away' this segmentation in other apparently irrelevant contexts, just as one may give away anything else one knows.

Of course, I should not like to give the impression that I believe Harris to have found a procedure whereby one cannot fail (in principle) to discover the phonemes or morphemes of a natural language. Harris and his opponents both seem to think that linguistics can provide uniform discovery procedures. I agree with Chomsky that whether one uses 'semantical information' about a language or not, the objective of a uniform procedure for discovering the correct description is as utopian in linguistics as in any other natural science. And that is yet another reason for finding the pseudo-issue of 'independence of meaning' not very interesting; it depends too fundamentally on the misconception that the task of linguistic theory is to eliminate the theorist altogether, not just to provide him with useful tools (tests, procedures, etc.).

IV. The autonomy of grammar

An issue closely related to the one discussed in the preceding section is this: Is it possible to define the fundamental concepts of grammar, e.g. 'morpheme' 'phoneme' in nonsemantical terms? Although this issue *is* closely related to the one discussed in the preceding section, it is important to realize that two distinct issues are involved. In the preceding section we were discussing the feasibility of discovery procedures in linguistics which do not require any semantical information, as input. In this section we are discussing the way in which certain fundamental concepts in linguistics should be defined. Unfortunately, a great deal of confusion seems to be rife in linguistic circles as to the difference between these two issues.

Chomsky seems inclined to the view that the fundamental concepts of structural linguistics can be defined without employing any semantical notions, and this is perhaps what he means when he speaks of the autonomy of grammar. On the other hand, it should be realized that even if Chomsky is wrong, his work cannot possibly be taken as an *argumentum a contrario* against the thesis of the autonomy of grammar, simply because Chomsky does not, in fact, define the fundamental concepts of structural linguistics at all. He takes them as primitive or undefined notions in his entire work. Indeed, it is just this that makes Jakobson's attack on Chomsky so puzzling. Many of Jakobson's criticisms are to the effect that certain sentences are being ruled out by Chomsky as ungrammatical merely because they are false or somehow absurd on the basis of their meaning. But this would seem to indicate, not that Chomsky is placing too little reliance on meaning but too much reliance on meaning. If anything, the charge should then be that Chomsky's work is an *argumentum a contrario* against the possibility of basing a grammar on certain fundamental semantical notions, e.g. truth and falsity. Certainly it is not an *argumentum a contrario* against the thesis that there exist non-semantical discovery procedures in linguistics, because Chomsky refrains from talking about discovery procedures at all, except a pessimism (which I share) with respect to the possibility of finding useful uniform discovery procedures, whether or not one uses semantical information; and, as just remarked, Chomsky does not define the fundamental notions 'phoneme', 'morpheme', 'noun', 'verb', etc. at all; rather, he models his grammar exclusively on a hypothetico-deductive system in which certain terms are taken as 'primitives'. But Chomsky's work aside, we are left with the question of just how, if at all, to define such notions as 'phoneme' and 'morpheme'.

Before saying something about this question, however, let us first consider what might be meant by the distinction between semantical and syntactical notions, as applied to a natural language. I wish to suggest that we might take the fundamental syntactical notion to be the notion of structural identity. We might say that two sequences of phones in a natural language are structurally identical if a speaker of the language counts them as the same expression and otherwise structurally non-identical. Of course, this raises a number of problems: it is not crystal clear what it means to say that a speaker of a natural language counts two phone sequences as the same expression, apart from contexts in which we have available a bilingual informant who is willing to make explicit metalinguistic statements, at least of a very simple kind ('You said the same word twice!'), and a linguist who is willing to rely on such explicit metalinguistic statements. If we ask for characterization of what it means to say that an informant counts two phone sequences as the same, where the informant is a speaker of only one language x, and the characterization is to be wholly behavioral, and not to refer to dispositions to make certain kinds of explicit metalinguistic statements about x, then we shall probably not be able at present to say very much. Moreover, even if we succeed in thinking of a number of things that we might call 'symptoms' of the disposition to count two phone sequences as the same expression, it would still be a mistake to think that one could arrive at an explicit definition of this disposition in terms of such symptoms. I will not go into this last point any further, since to do so would take us afield into the familiar controversy for and against operationalism. Instead I will just remark that here we are reminded that linguistics is after all a social science and that its fundamental concepts have the same kind of dispositional and human character as do the fundamental concepts of any other social science.

Another less serious problem that we must face is this: What if someone says that the relation of structural identity, as defined above, is a semantical notion and that therefore syntax, as the study of the properties of phone sequence that are invariant under this relation, is a branch of semantics? This problem is not serious because it is obviously purely

99

verbal. Of course, one can 'prove' that syntax is not autonomous by defining the terms 'syntax' and 'semantics' so that syntax becomes *by definition* a part of semantics. But no useful object is thereby gained. I would propose, guided admittedly by the usual practice in formal languages, to take as the fundamental notions of semantics the notions of truth and synonymy; and my thesis is that the relation of structural identity of expressions is more basic than the notions of semantics in two senses: the latter notions seem to presuppose the former notion; and the notion of structural identity is, I believe, not definable in terms of the semantical notions referred to.

Assuming that the notion of structural identity and non-identity is an acceptable one, however, we are part of the way to the notion of a phoneme. Namely, the notion of a contrasting pair may now be defined. Two structurally nonidentical phone sequences A and A' are a contrasting pair, if A is identical with A' except A' contains one occurrence of a phone P', where A has one occurrence of a phone P. In this case we shall say that P and P' are verifiably nonequivalent phones. Now then, if the complementary relation, the relation of *not* being verifiably nonequivalent phones, were only an equivalence relation, we should have the full notion of a phoneme. Namely, the phonemes would be just the equivalence classes generated by this equivalence relation. Unfortunately, and this is what makes the notion of a phoneme a somewhat difficult one, although it is obviously based on the relation of not being verifiably nonequivalent phones, the relation which holds between two phones if and only if they are allophones of the same phoneme *is* to be an equivalence relation. What one does in practice is to seek the biggest relation which *is* an equivalence relation and whose complement includes the relation of verifiable nonequivalence alluded to above. But in general there is no unique such biggest relation, and thus there is some degree of arbitrariness in the classification of the phones of a language into separate phonemes. What this goes to show, however, is not that the notion of a phoneme is fundamentally a semantical one, but that it is to some extent a defective one; or to put it better, that it should be relativized not just to a language but to a particular description of a language.

To sum up: the classification of phones into phonemes is a somewhat artificial classification which is based on deliberately ignoring the fact that the complement of the verifiable nonequivalence relation is not an equivalence relation. But this classification, artificial though it may be, is by our lights a purely structural matter. Phonemics, then, is autonomous in Chomsky's sense. When we come to the notion of a morpheme, however, it is more difficult to know what to say. Speaking for myself, I should say that I have never seen a satisfactory definition of this concept in either semantical or nonsemantical terms. Also, I am not satisfied with Chomsky's idea of taking the concept as primitive. The trouble with modeling linguistic theory on the notion of a hypothetico-deductive system is that the model does not seem a particularly reasonable one. A hypothetico-deductive system is a reasonable model for a physical theory in which one is inferring unobservable entities from observable entities. But I don't think that Chomsky wants to say that morphemes are inferred entities, and if he does want to say this, then *I* want to say that I find myself very unclear as to the alleged nature of these inferred entities and as to the nature of the supposed inference to their existence. Sometimes Chomsky writes as if he held both the view that a hypothetico-deductive system is a reasonable model for a physical theory and the view that the primitive terms in such a system need not be supposed to refer to anything. On this view, scientific theories are, so to speak, merely computational devices. I don't know whether I do Chomsky an injustice or not in ascribing this view to him. But I do know that I do not find it an acceptable philosophy of science for physics, and I should be extremely suspicious of the view that it was an acceptable philosophy of science for any one of the social sciences, including linguistics.

Another possible way out would be this: we might say that the morphemes of a language, relative to a particular grammar, are the shortest phone sequences which are assigned to phrase-structure categories in that grammar. Besides bringing in a host of new undefined terms, e.g. phrase-structure categories, this proposal would have the drawback of relativizing the notion of morpheme to a grammar. This relativization goes against the very deep-seated intuitive feeling that a language does have natural building blocks, no matter how difficult it may be to make this concept of the natural building-block precise, and that the morphemes are they.

Yet another proposal, which is extracted not so much from Chomsky's work as from discussions with Chomsky, might be to first relativize the notion of a morpheme to a grammar, in the way just proposed, and then to say that the 'real' morphemes in a language are to be identified with the morphemes according to a simplest grammar of that language. This last proposal seems to have two objectionable features: first, that it is by no means clear that there is such a thing as a well defined simplest grammar of a natural language, and secondly that if there is such a thing, then there may be two simplest grammars *A* and *B* which do not segment the language into building-blocks in the same way. If this last eventuality – the possibility of two non-isomorphic simplest descriptions of a natural language – is not really a possibility, then the reason it is not really a possibility must be that a natural language really has a set of fundamental building-blocks in some sense which has nothing to do with descriptions of that language. But then we should try to make that sense clear, and not go the long way around via talk about all possible theories and via employment of the catch-all term 'simplicity'.

I am not recommending that we abandon the concept 'morpheme'; I think the vague characterization of the morphemes as the smallest units that belong to phrase-structure categories is enough to go on for the time being. On the other hand, further attempts to provide a foundation for the notion are clearly in order. To put it bluntly, I feel that there are a great many things here that are presently not *understood*, and that it will take more insight into language structure as a whole before we are able to say in precisely what sense a language has natural building-blocks.

V. The grammatical sentences of a language are a recursive set

In this section I should like to present evidence of several kinds for the view that the grammatical sentences of a natural language, under a mild idealization, form a recursive set. The following facts seem to me to point in this direction:

(1) The self-containedness of language. By the self-containedness of language, I mean the fact that speakers can presumably classify sentences as acceptable or unacceptable, deviant or nondeviant, et cetera, without reliance on extra-linguistic contexts. There are of course exceptions to this rule, but I am more impressed by the multiplicity of non-exceptions. I imagine, for example, that if I were on any number of occasions presented with a *list* of sentences and asked to say which ones I thought were grammatical and which ones I thought were ungrammatical, I would on each occasion and without any information on the supposed context of use of the individual sentence classify 'Mary goed home!' as an ungrammatical sentence, and 'Mary went home!' as a grammatical sentence. This act of classifying sentences as grammatical or ungrammatical seems to be one I can perform given no input except the sentences themselves. In short, it seems that in doing this job of classifying I am implicitly relying on something like an effective procedure.

In this connection, I am of course relying on certain very general hypotheses as to the character of the human brain. To be specific, I would suggest that there are many considerations which point to the idea that a Turing machine plus random elements is a reasonable model for the human brain. Now, although the idea that random elements are a part of the human brain is important in the life sciences in a great many contexts, the present context is one in which the role of the random elements should be left out, at least for purposes of idealization. Even if it is true, that given a list of sentences to classify as grammatical or ungrammatical, my behavior would be to a tiny extent random, e.g. one time in a hundred I might classify 'Mary goed home' as grammatical instead of as ungrammatical, this is a fact which we wish to leave out in our idealization. In other words, we wish to pretend that the classifier, if he will classify a sentence as grammatical on one occasion, will classify it as grammatical on any occasion. With this idealization in force, it seems to me that we are in effect committed (at least if we have the overall mechanistic view of the brain that I do) to viewing the classifier as simply a Turing machine.

Even if the classifier is a Turing machine, however, it does not follow that the set of grammatical sentences is recursive. This only follows if the classifier is a Turing machine without input; or more precisely, without input other than the individual sentence that he is classifying. That the individual sentence that he is classifying may be regarded as the sole relevant input, amounts, however, to saying just that if a sentence is counted as grammatical, then it will be counted as grammatical even if presented on a different occasion, and even if different sentences have been previously presented, and this seems, if not exactly true of actual classifiers, at least a reasonable idealization. This, of course, is just what I mean by the self-containedness of language.

(2) A second argument supporting the view that the classification of sentences as grammatical and nongrammatical is something effective or mechanical (and hence that the set of grammatical sentences is recursive, at least if we assume Church's thesis) is the usability of nonsense sentences. As Chomsky has pointed out, one can perfectly well ask a classifier to look through a list of nonsense sentences and to say which ones are grammatical and which ones are ungrammatical. Here again it seems to be very much the case that the relevant input is simply the sentence being classified and that, moreover, the features of the sentence being classified that are relevant are almost certainly purely structural. Jakobson has pointed out that so-called grammatical nonsense sentences can often be construed, but I feel that we may neglect this in the present context. Even if it is true that after some minutes of reflection I can succeed in construing the sentence 'Colorless green ideas sleep furiously.', I feel very certain that I do not tell that it is grammatical by first construing it in the manner suggested in Jakobson's paper.

(3) A third consideration supporting the view that the classification of sentences into grammatical and ungrammatical is a machine-like

affair is the teachability of grammar and the relative independence of intelligence level of this skill. Even a person of very low-grade intelligence normally learns both to speak his particular dialect grammatically and to recognize deviations from grammaticalness. It is important, of course, in connection with this point, not to confuse the grammar of the particular dialect with 'grammar' in the high-school sense, that is to say the grammar of the prestige dialect. I am well aware that people belonging to lower-income groups often speak 'ungrammatically' (that is to say, they speak their own dialect perfectly grammatically, but speaking their own dialect is what is usually called 'speaking ungrammatically'). My point is that a moron whose parents happen to speak the prestige dialect may have serious vocabulary deficiencies but he rarely has grammar deficiencies. He too learns to speak the prestige dialect, and to feel that there is something wrong with sentences that deviate from the grammatical regularities of the prestige dialect, even if he does not have the extremely complicated skill (parsing) which is required to say what is wrong. But an ability of this kind, which can be acquired by practically anyone or which can be utilized by practically anyone independently of intelligence level, is almost certainly quasi-mechanical in character.

I am willing to grant that no one of the considerations cited above is by itself decisive; but it seems to me that the collection of these facts – the self-containedness of language, the usability of nonsense sentences, and the relative universality of grammar intuitions within a dialect group, taken together support the model of the classifier as a Turing machine who is processing each new sentence with which he is provided according to some mechanical program. To accept this idealization, however, is just to accept the following model of grammar; that the grammatical sentences under consideration are a recursive set.

Accepting this idealization makes it legitimate to seek recursive function-theoretic structures which could serve as models for grammars. In Chomsky's book *Syntactic Structures* a number of such models are examined and found too narrow. In particular, a widely used model, phrase-structure grammar, is found by Chomsky to be over-restrictive since it rules out certain extremely convenient types of rules. For example, the following very simple rule, which would seem to be a legitimate kind of linguistic rule, is not a phrase-structure rule. If S_1 and S_2 are grammatical sentences, and S_1 differs from S_2 only in that x appears in S_1 where y appears in S_2, and x and y are constituents of the same type in S_1 and S_2, respectively, then S_3 is a sentence, where S_3 is the result of replacing x by x *and* y in S_1.

To make an analogy with formal languages, we may say that phrase-structure grammars employ rules that correspond to axiom schemata in, say, the propositional calculus. On the other hand, a transformational rule like the familiar rule that 'any formula of the form $(x) A \supset A'$ is to be an axiom, provided A' is like A except for containing free y wherever A has free x' already goes beyond the bounds of phrase-structure grammar. And Chomsky is, in effect, proposing that structural grammars may legitimately use rules that are modeled on the last-cited rule, and not just on axiom schemata.

I find the examples that Chomsky gives of transformations in English extremely convincing. (I mean his examples of permissible kinds of linguistic rules. There may be empirical objections to certain of them as statements about English.) However, Chomsky's general characterization of a transformational grammar is much too wide. It is easy to show that any recursively enumerable set of sentences could be generated by a transformational grammar in Chomsky's sense. Since, however, the whole motive for seeking transformational grammars was to reflect the character of natural languages and since the fundamental insight, if it is an insight, on which transformational grammars are based is the insight that the set of sentences in a natural language is a recursive set, then transformational grammars should be characterized in such a way that this feature is 'built in'.

In short, I think Chomsky has convincingly set the problem for theory of grammars – namely, the problem of delimiting a class of transformational grammars which is wide enough to include all the grammars we will ever want to write as grammars of natural languages, but not so wide as to include any grammar for a non-recursive language (that is, for a language in which the set of grammatical sentences is not recursive). This problem appears, however, to be extremely difficult. In closing I shall make a few remarks about the direction in which one might seek for a solution.

VI. The problem of characterizing transformational grammars

The transformations employed by Chomsky in *Syntactic Structures* mostly have the property that the product is longer than the datum.

(1) It might be possible, without altering the resultant set of 'terminal strings' (grammatical sentences yielded by the grammar) to rewrite the grammar so as to use *only* rules with this property (let us call them 'cut-free' rules). Then (as is easily verified) the set of terminal strings would always be recursive.

The above suggestion (1) seems unattractive, however, since using only cut-free rules, even if it can be done (and it is not known whether or not it can be) involves *complicating* the statement of the grammar, and the main argument for admitting 'transformations' in the first place was the resultant simplification.

(2) One might impose two restrictions on all grammars for natural languages: (a) that not more than n_1 words may be deleted in a deletion-transformation; and (b) that not more than n_2 deletion-transformations may occur in the derivation of a terminal string, where n_1, n_2 are constants depending on the language. However, the second restriction seems *ad hoc* and unattractive. (The first restriction can usually be met in a natural way, e.g. by confining deletions to cases of the form 'preposition + pronoun.') It seems to me that it would be quite natural and important to seek to prove a theorem of the form: *Whenever one can derive σ in L* (where σ is a variable over terminal strings and L is some language), *one can find a* derivation (of the same string σ) *which does not use more than n_2 deletions* (where n_2 may depend on L); but this is quite different from making a restriction on the number of deletions part of the definition of a derivation. However, there is no hope of proving a theorem of this kind for all L's which possess a transformational grammar, unless one first has a suitable definition of 'transformational grammar'. This, then, is a significant (and probably very difficult) open question: to define 'transformational grammar' in a way which is (i) wide enough for all linguistic purposes; (ii) free of 'artificial' clauses like the one restricting the number of uses of deletion in a derivation; and (iii) such that a 'cut-elimination' theorem will be forthcoming about all L's with a transformational grammar. Unfortunately, I have no idea how to solve this problem.

5

The 'innateness hypothesis' and explanatory models in linguistics*

I. The innateness hypothesis

The 'innateness hypothesis' (henceforth, the 'IH') is a daring – or apparently daring; it may be meaningless, in which case it is not daring – hypothesis proposed by Noam Chomsky. I owe a debt of gratitude to Chomsky for having repeatedly exposed me to the IH; I have relied heavily in what follows on oral communications from him; and I beg his pardon in advance if I mis-state the IH in any detail, or misrepresent any of the arguments for it. In addition to relying upon oral communications from Chomsky, I have also relied upon Chomsky's paper 'Explanatory models in linguistics' (Chomsky, 1962), in which the IH plays a considerable role.

To begin, then, the IH is the hypothesis that the human brain is 'programmed' at birth in some quite *specific* and *structured* aspects of human natural language. The details of this programming are spelled out in some detail in 'Explanatory models in linguistics'. We should assume that the speaker has 'built in'† a function which assigns weights to the grammars G_1, G_2, G_3, ... in a certain class Σ of transformational grammars. Σ is not the class of all *possible* transformational grammars; rather all the members of Σ have some quite strong similarities. These similarities appear as 'linguistic universals' – i.e. as characteristics of *all* human natural languages. If intelligent nonterrestrial life – say, Martians – exists, and if the 'Martians' speak a language whose grammar does not belong to the subclass Σ of the class of all transformational grammars, then, I have heard Chomsky maintain, humans (except possibly

---

* First published in *Synthese*, 17 (1967) 12–22.
† What 'built in' means is highly unclear in this context. The weighting function by itself determines only the relative ease with which various grammars can be learned by a human being. If a grammar G_1 can be learned more easily than a grammar G_2, then doubtless this is 'innate' in the sense of being a fact about human learning *potential*, as opposed to a fact about what has been learned. But this sort of fact is what learning theory tries to account for; *not* the explanation being sought. It should be noticed that Chomsky has never offered even a schematic account of the sort of device that is supposed to be present in the brain, and that is supposed to do the job of selecting the highest weighted grammar compatible with the data. But only a description, or at least a theory, of such a device could properly be called an innateness *hypothesis* at all.

for a few geniuses or linguistic experts) would be unable to learn Martian; a human child brought up by Martians would fail to acquire language; and Martians would, conversely, experience similar difficulties with human tongues. (Possible difficulties in *pronunciation* are not at issue here, and may be assumed *not* to exist for the purpose of this argument.) As examples of the similarities that all grammars of the subclass Σ are thought to possess (above the level of phonetics), we may mention the *active–passive* distinction, the existence of a *nonphrase-structure* portion of the grammar, the presence of such major categories as *concrete noun, verb taking an abstract subject,* etc. The project of delimiting the class Σ may also be described as the project of defining a *normal form for grammars.* Conversely, according to Chomsky, any nontrivial normal form for grammars, such that correct and perspicuous grammars of all human languages can and should be written in that normal form, 'constitutes, in effect, a hypothesis concerning the innate intellectual equipment of the child' (Chomsky, 1962 p. 550).

Given such a high *restricted* class Σ of grammars (high restricted in the sense that grammars not in the class are perfectly conceivable, not more 'complicated' in any absolute sense than grammars in the class, and may well be employed by nonhuman speakers, if such there be), the performance of the human child in learning his native language may be understood as follows, according to Chomsky. He may be thought of as operating on the following 'inputs' (Chomsky, 1962 pp. 530–1): a list of utterances, containing both grammatical and ungrammatical sentences, a list of corrections, which enable him to classify the input utterances *as* grammatical or ungrammatical; and some information concerning which utterances count as *repetitions* of earlier utterances. Simplifying slightly, we may say that, on this model, the child is supplied with a list of grammatical sentence *types* and a list of ungrammatical sentence *types.* He then 'selects' the grammar in Σ compatible with this information to which his weighting function assigns the highest weight. On this scheme, the general *form* of grammar is not learned from experience, but is 'innate', and the 'plausibility ordering' of grammars compatible with given data of the kinds mentioned is likewise 'innate'.

So much for a statement of the IH. If I have left the IH vague at many points, I believe that this is no accident – for the IH seems to me to be *essentially* and *irreparably* vague – but this much of a statement may serve to indicate *what* belief it is that I stigmatize as irreparably vague.

A couple of remarks may suffice to give some idea of the role that IH is supposed to play in linguistics. Linguistics relies heavily, according to

Chomsky, upon 'intuitions' of grammaticality. But *what* is an intuition of 'grammaticality' an intuition *of*? According to Chomsky, the sort of theory-construction programmatically outlined above is what is needed to give this question the only answer it can have or deserves to have. Presumably, then, to 'intuit' (or assert, or conjecture, etc.) that a sentence is grammatical is to 'intuit' (or assert, or conjecture, etc.) that the sentence is generated by the highest-valued G_i in the class Σ which is such that it generates all the grammatical sentence types with which we have been supplied by the 'input' and none of the ungrammatical sentence types listed in the 'input'.†

Chomsky also says that the G_i which receives the highest value must do *more* than agree with 'intuitions' of grammaticality; it must account for certain ambiguities, for example.‡ At the same time, unfortunately, he lists no semantic information in the input, and he conjectures (Chomsky, 1962, p. 531, n. 5) that a child needs semantic information only to 'provide motivation for language learning', and not to arrive at the *formal* grammar of its language. Apparently, then, the fact that a grammar which agrees with a sufficient amount of 'input' must be in the class Σ to be 'selected' by the child is what rules out grammars that generate all and only the grammatical sentences of a given natural language, but fail to correctly 'predict'§ ambiguities (cf. *ibid.*, p. 533).

In addition to making clear what it *is* to be grammatical, Chomsky believes that the IH confronts the linguist with the following tasks: to *define* the normal form for grammars described above, and to *define* the weighting function. In *Syntactic Structures* Chomsky, indeed, gives this as an objective for linguistic theory: to give an *effective* procedure for choosing between rival grammars.

Lastly, the IH is supposed to justify the claim that what the linguist provides is 'a hypothesis about the innate intellectual equipment that a child brings to bear in language learning' (*ibid.*, p. 530). Of course, even if language is *wholly* learned, it is still true that linguistics 'characterizes the linguistic abilities of the mature speaker', and that a grammar 'could properly be called an explanatory model of the linguistic intuition of the native speaker' (*ibid.*, p. 533). However, one could with equal truth say that a driver's manual 'characterizes the car-driving abilities of the

† I doubt that the child really is told which sentences it hears or utters are *ungrammatical*. At most it is told which are *deviant* – but it may not be told which are deviant for *syntactical* and which for *semantical* reasons.

‡ Many of these – e.g. the alleged 'ambiguity' in 'the shooting of the elephants was heard' – *require coaching to detect*. The claim that grammar 'explains the ability to recognize ambiguities' thus lacks the impressiveness that Chomsky believes it to have. I am grateful to Paul Ziff and Stephen Leeds for calling this point to my attention.

§ A grammar 'predicts' an ambiguity, in Chomsky's formalism, whenever it assigns two or more structural descriptions to the same sentence.

mature driver' and that a calculus text provides 'an explanatory model of the calculus-intuitions of the mathematician'. Clearly, it is the idea that *these* abilities and *these* intuitions are close to the human *essence*, so to speak, that gives linguistics its 'sex appeal', for Chomsky at least.

II. The supposed evidence for the IH

A number of empirical facts and alleged empirical facts have been advanced to support the IH. Since limitations of space make it impossible to describe all of them here, a few examples will have to suffice.

(a) The *ease* of the child's original language learning. 'A young child is able to gain perfect mastery of a language with incomparably greater ease [*than an adult* – H.P.] and without any explicit instruction. Mere exposure to the language, and for a remarkably short period, seems to be all that the normal child requires to develop the competence of the native speaker' (*ibid.*, p. 529).

(b) The fact that reinforcement, 'in any interesting sense', seems to be unnecessary for language learning. Some children have apparently even learned to speak without *talking*†, and then displayed this ability at a relatively late age to startled adults who had given them up for mutes.

(c) The ability to 'develop the competence of the native speaker' has been said not to depend on the intelligence level. Even quite low IQs 'internalize' the grammar of their native language.

(d) The 'linguistic universals' mentioned in the previous section are allegedly accounted for by the IH.

(e) Lastly, of course, there is the 'argument' that runs '*what else* could account for language learning?' The task is so incredibly complex (analogous to learning, at least implicitly, a complicated physical theory, it is said), that it would be miraculous if even one tenth of the human race accomplished it without 'innate' assistance. (This is like Marx's 'proof' of the Labour Theory of Value in *Capital*, vol. III, which runs, in essence, '*What else* could account for the fact that commodities have different value *except* the fact that the labor-content is different?'.)

III. Criticism of the alleged evidence

A. The irrelevance of linguistic universals

1. Not surprising on any theory

Let us consider just how surprising the 'linguistic universals' cited above really are. Let us assume for the purpose a community of Martians whose 'innate intellectual equipment' may be supposed to be as different

---

† Macaulay's *first* words, it is said, were: 'Thank you, Madam, the agony has somewhat abated' (to a lady who had spilled hot tea on him).

from the human as is compatible with their being able to speak a language at all. What could we expect to find in their language?

If the Martians' brains are not vastly richer than ours in complexity, then they, like us, will find it possible to employ a practically infinite set of expressions only if those expressions possess a 'grammar' – i.e. if they are built up by recursive rules from a limited stock of basic forms. Those basic forms need not be built up out of a *short* list of phonemes – the Martians might have vastly greater memory capacity than we do – but if Martians, like humans, find rote learning difficult, it will not be surprising if they too have *short* lists of phonemes in their languages.

Are the foregoing reflections arguments *for* or *against* the IH? I find it difficult to tell. If belief in 'innate intellectual equipment' is *just* that, then how *could* the IH be false? How could something with *no* innate intellectual equipment *learn* anything? *To be sure*, human 'innate intellectual equipment' is relevant to language learning; if this means that such parameters as memory span and memory capacity play a crucial role. But what rank Behaviorist is supposed to have ever denied *this*? On the other hand, that a particular mighty arbitrary set Σ of grammars is 'built in' to the brain of *both* Martians and Humans is *not* a hypothesis we would have to invoke to account for *these* basic similarities.

But for what similarities above the level of phonetics, where constitutional factors play a large role for obvious reasons, *would* the IH have to be invoked *save* in the trivial sense that memory capacity, intelligence, needs, interests, etc., are all relevant to language learning, and all depend, in part, on the biological makeup of the organism? If Martians are such strange creatures that they have no interest in physical objects, for example, their language will contain no concrete nouns; but would not this be *more*, not *less* surprising, on any *reasonable* view, than their having an interest in physical objects? (Would it be surprising if Martian contained devices for forming truth-functions and for quantification?)

Two more detailed points are relevant here. Chomsky has pointed out that no natural language has a phrase structure grammar. But this too is not surprising. The sentence 'John and Jim came home quickly' is not generated by a phrase-structure rule, in Chomsky's formalization of English grammar. But the sentence 'John came home quickly and Jim came home quickly' *is* generated by a phrase-structure rule in the grammar of mathematical logic, and Chomsky's famous 'and-transformation' is just an abbreviation rule. Again, the sentence 'That was the lady I saw you with last night' is not generated by a phrase-structure rule in English. or at least not in Chomsky's description of English, But the sentence 'That is $\imath x$ (x is a lady and I saw you with x last night)' is generated by a phrase-structure rule in the grammar of mathematical logic. And again the idiomatic English sentence *can* be obtained from its phrase-structure counterpart by a simple rule of abbreviation. Is it really surprising, does it really point to anything more interesting than *general intelligence*, that these operations which break the bounds of phrase-structure grammar appear in every natural language?†

Again, it may appear startling at first blush that such categories as noun, verb, adverb, etc. have 'universal' application. But, as Curry has pointed out, it is easy to multiply 'facts' here. If a language contains nouns – that is, a phrase-structure category which contains the proper names – it contains noun phrases, that is, phrases which occupy the environments of nouns. If it contains noun phrases it contains verb phrases – phrases which when combined with a noun phrase by a suitable construction yield sentences. If it contains verb phrases, it contains adverb phrases – phrases which, when combined with a verb phrase yield a verb phrase. Similarly, adjective phrases, etc., can be defined in terms of the *two* basic categories 'noun' and 'sentence'. Thus the existence of nouns is all that has to be explained. And this reduces to explaining two facts: (1) The fact that all natural languages have a large phrase-structure portion in their grammar, in the sense just illustrated, in spite of the effect of what Chomsky calls 'transformations'. (2) The fact that all natural languages contain proper names. But (1) is not surprising in view of the fact that phrase-structure rules are extremely simple algorithms. Perhaps Chomsky would reply that 'simplicity' is subjective here, but this is just not so. The fact is that all the natural measures of complexity of an algorithm – size of the machine table, length of computations, time, and space required for the computation – lead to the same result here, quite independently of the detailed structure of the computing machine employed. Is it surprising that algorithms which are 'simplest' for virtually any computing system we can conceive of are also simplest for naturally evolved 'computing systems'? And (2) – the fact that all natural languages contain proper names – is not surprising in view of the utility of such names, and the difficulty of always finding a definite description which will suffice instead.

† Another example of a transformation is the 'active–passive' transformation (cf. *Syntactic Structures*). But (a) the presence of this, if it *is* a part of the grammar, is not surprising – why should not there be a systematic way of expressing the *converse* of a relation? – and (b) the argument for the existence of such a 'transformation' at all is extremely slim. It is contended that a grammar which 'defines' active and passive forms separately (this can be done by even a phrase-structure grammer) fails to represent something that every speaker knows, namely, that active and passive forms are *related*. But why must every *relation* be mirrored by *syntax*? Every 'speaker' of the canonical languages of mathematical logic is aware that each sentence $(x) (Fx \supset Gx)$ is related to a sentence $(x) (\overline{G}x \supset \overline{F}x)$; yet the definition of 'well formed formula' fails to mirror 'what every speaker knows' in this respect, and is not inadequate on that account.

Once again, 'innate' factors are relevant *to be sure* – if choosing *simple* algorithms as the basis of the grammar is 'innate', and if the need for identifying persons rests on something innate – but what Behaviorist would or should be surprised? Human brains are computing systems and subject to some of the constraints that effect all computing systems; human beings have a natural interest in one another. If *that* is 'innateness', well and good!

2. *Linguistic universals could be accounted for, even if surprising, without invoking the IH*

Suppose that language-using human beings evolved *independently* in two or more places. Then, if Chomsky were *right*, there should be two or more *types* of human beings descended from the two or more original populations, and normal children of each type should fail to learn the languages spoken by the other types. Since we do not observe this, since there is only *one* class Σ built into *all* human brains, we have to conclude (if the IH is true) that language-using is an evolutionary 'leap' that occurred only *once*. But in that case, it is overwhelmingly likely that all human languages are descended from a single original language, and that the existence today of what are called 'unrelated' languages is accounted for by the great lapse of time and by countless historical changes. This is, indeed, likely even if the IH is false, since the human race itself is now generally believed to have resulted from a single evolutionary 'leap', and since the human population was extremely small and concentrated for millennia, and only gradually spread from Asia to other continents. Thus, even if language-using was learned or invented rather than 'built in', or even if only some general dispositions in the direction of language-using are 'built in',† it is likely that some one group of humans first developed language as we know it, and then spread this through conquest or imitation to the rest of the human population. Indeed, we do know that this is just how *alphabetic* writing spread. In any case, I repeat, this hypothesis – a single origin for human language – is certainly *required* by the IH, but much weaker than the IH.

But just this *consequence* of the IH is, in fact, enough to account for 'linguistic universals'! For, if all human languages are descended from a common parent, then just such highly useful features of the common parent as the presence of some kind of quantifiers, proper names, nouns, and verbs, etc., would be expected to survive. Random variation may, indeed, alter many things; but that it should fail to strip language of

---

† It is very difficult to account for such phenomena as the spontaneous babbling of infants without *this* much 'innateness'. But this is not to say that a class Σ and a function f are 'built in', as required by the IH.

proper names, or common nouns, or quantifiers, is not *so* surprising as to require the IH.

B. *The 'ease' of language learning is not clear*

Let us consider somewhat closely the 'ease' with which children do learn their native language. A typical 'mature' college student seriously studying a foreign language spends three hours a week in lectures. In fourteen weeks of term he is thus exposed to forty-two hours of the language. In four years he may pick up over 300 hours of the language, very little of which is actual listening to native informants. By contrast, direct method teachers estimate that 300 hours of direct-method teaching will enable one to converse fluently in a foreign language. Certainly 600 hours – say, 300 hours of direct-method teaching and 300 hours of reading – will enable any adult to speak and read a foreign language with ease, and to use an incomparably larger vocabulary than a young child.

It will be objected that the adult does not acquire a perfect accent. So what? The adult has been speaking one way all of his life, and has a huge set of habits to unlearn. What can equally well be accounted for by learning theory should not be cited as evidence for the IH.

Now the child by the time it is four or five years old has been exposed to *vastly* more than 600 hours of direct-method instruction. Moreover, even if 'reinforcement' is not necessary, most children are consciously and repeatedly reinforced by adults in a host of ways – e.g. the constant repetition of simple one-word sentences ('cup', 'doggie') in the presence of babies. Indeed, any foreign adult living with the child for those years would have an incomparably better grasp of the language than the child does. The child indeed has a better accent. Also, the child's grammatical mistakes, which are numerous, arise not from carrying over previous language habits, but from not having fully acquired the first set. But it seems to me that this 'evidence' for the IH stands the facts on their head.

C. *Reinforcement another issue*

As Chomsky is aware, the evidence is today slim that *any* learning requires reinforcement 'in any interesting sense'. Capablanca, for example, learned to play chess by simply watching adults play. This is comparable to Macaulay's achievement in learning language without speaking. Nongeniuses normally do require practice both to speak correctly and to play chess. Yet probably anyone *could* learn to speak *or to* play chess without practice if muffled, in the first case, or not allowed to play, in the second case, with sufficiently prolonged observation.

D. Independence of intelligence level an artifact

Every child learns to speak the native language

What does this mean? If it means that children do not make serious grammatical blunders, even by the standards of descriptive as opposed to prescriptive grammar, this is just not true for the young child. By nine or ten years of age this has ceased to happen, perhaps (I speak as a parent), but nine or ten years is enough time to become pretty darn good at *anything*. What is more serious is what 'grammar' *means* here. It does not include mastery of vocabulary, in which even many adults are deficient, nor ability to understand *complex* constructions, in which many adults are *also* deficient. It means purely and simply the ability to learn what every *normal* adult learns. Every normal adult learns what every normal adult learns. What this 'argument' reduces to is 'Wow! How complicated a skill every normal adult learns. What else could it be but *innate*'. Like the preceding argument, it reduces to the 'What Else?' argument.

But what of the 'What Else?' argument? Just how impressed should we be by the failure of current learning theories to account for complex learning processes such as those involved in the learning of language? If Innateness were a *general* solution, perhaps we should be impressed. But the I.H. *cannot*, by its very nature, *be* generalized to handle all complex learning processes. Consider the following puzzle (called 'jump'):

```
            *   *   *
            *   *   *
    *   *   *   *   *   *   *
    *   *   *   ●   *   *   *
    *   *   *   *   *   *   *
            *   *   *
            *   *   *
```

To begin with, all the holes but the center one are filled. The object of the game is to remove all the pegs but one by 'jumping' (as in checkers) and to end with the one remaining peg in the center. A clever person can get the solution in perhaps eight or ten hours of experimentation. A not so clever person can get a 'near-solution' – two pegs left – in the same time. No program exists, to my knowledge, that would enable a computer to solve even the 'near solution' problem without running out of both time and space, even though the machine can spend the equivalent of many human lifetimes in experimentation. When we come to the discovery of even the simplest mathematical theorem the situation is even more striking. The theorems of mathematics, the solutions to puzzles, etc., cannot on *any* theory be *individually* 'innate'; what must be 'innate' are heuristics, i.e. learning strategies. In the absence of any knowledge of what *general multipurpose learning strategies* might even look like, the assertion that such strategies (which absolutely must exist and be employed by all humans) cannot account for this or that learning process, that the answer or an answer schema must be 'innate', is utterly unfounded.

I will be told, of course, that *everyone* learns his native language (as well as everyone does), and that not everyone solves puzzles or proves theorems. But everyone does learn pattern recognition, automobile driving, etc., and everyone in fact can solve many problems that no computer can solve. In conversation Chomsky has repeatedly used precisely such skills as these to support the idea that humans have an 'innate conceptual space'. Well and good, if true. *But that is no help. Let a complete seventeenth century Oxford University education be innate if you like*; still the solution to 'jump' was not innate; the Prime Number Theorem was not innate; and so on. *Invoking 'Innateness' only postpones the problem of learning; it does not solve it.* Until we understand the strategies which make general learning possible – and vague talk of 'classes of hypotheses' – and 'weighting functions' is utterly useless here – no discussion of the *limits* of learning can even begin.

6

How not to talk about meaning*

Comments on J. J. C. Smart

Professor Smart is not only a philosopher whose work has stimulated us and provoked controversy among us; he speaks to us as a representative of Australian philosophy – of a philosophy which has ties to both British and American philosophy, as well as a distinctive flavor of its own. He is a kind of philosophical Ambassador – and would that all Ambassadors were as well liked! On the present occasion he speaks to us not of his own philosophical work, unfortunately, but rather gives his impressions of the scene here. And, being a good philosophical diplomat, his impressions are friendly ones. But even giving friendly impressions of his host country can land an Ambassador in hot water. So it is not surprising, even if it is regrettable, that I, as a native of this particular philosophical jungle, should feel compelled to rebuff compliments so nicely turned, and should sadly retort that what he praises as the beauties of our philosophical landscape seem to me to be merely weeds.

The views that Smart reports *in extenso* are the views of Paul Feyerabend. Smart also has a few words to say about some related views of Wilfrid Sellars. In my comment, I shall concentrate on Feyerabend's view, with which I am better acquainted than the papers by Sellars; and I shall rely not only on Smart's account of those views, but on the paper (Feyerabend, 1962) in *Minnesota Studies in the Philosophy of Science* to which Smart refers. Until otherwise indicated, all references to Feyerabend will be to this paper.

Reduction

The first part of Smart's paper (roughly, the first seven paragraphs) deals with an issue which is subsidiary to the main one, and which I should like to discuss first. This is the question: whether *reduction* (of one scientific theory or discipline to another, e.g. geometrical optics to electromagnetic field theory) is best conceived of as *deduction* of the reduced theory from the reducing theory, with the aid of biconditionals

---

* First published in R. Cohen and M. Wartofsky (eds.) *Boston Studies in the Philosophy of Science*, Volume II: In Honor of Philipp Frank (New York, Humanities Press Inc., 1965).

expressing 'coordinating definitions', or as mere *replacement*. Is the older theory *deduced* from the newer theory, or is it merely superseded by it? My comments on this issue will be two: one historical and one philosophical.

The historical remark is that Feyerabend and Smart are unaware of the literature. The Nagel view (reduction by means of biconditionals) was criticized along these lines and in detail by Kemeny and Oppenheim in 1956. Moreover, Oppenheim and I, writing in the same series as Feyerabend but one volume earlier (*Minnesota Studies in the Philosophy of Science*, vol. II) had summarized the Kemeny–Oppenheim view. These proprietary questions are not of much importance, to be sure, but it is necessary to keep the literature straight.

The philosophical remark is that the Nagel view does not appear to me to be *so* seriously false. Smart himself expresses some doubts, in this section of his paper, on the substantive character of this particular dispute.

The issue comes down to this: according to Smart, Nagel might 'save' his position by saying that it is the *approximate* truth of the reduced theory (say, again, optics) that is deduced from the reducing theory (say, electromagnetic field theory). But, Smart seems to suggest, this would not *really* save Nagel, for Feyerabend would have a (presumably effective) rejoinder: 'Perhaps Feyerabend would say that truth cannot be approximate but only predictive value can be: that the old theory is useful he will not deny, but he could still claim that this is more a matter for engineers than for natural philosophers'.

I must now object that this rejoinder is not effective at all. It is perfectly clear what it means to say that a theory is approximately true, as it is clear what it means to say that an equation is approximately correct: it means that the relationships postulated by the theory hold not exactly, but with a certain specifiable degree of error. In short, it means that the theory is not true, but that a certain *logical consequence* of the theory, obtained, for example, by replacing 'equals' with 'equals plus or minus delta' *is* true.† Such a logical consequence may be called an *approximation theory*. Let us now ask:

† This replacement is only given for the sake of an example. Other possible replacements would be (a) the replacement of 'equals' by 'equals with probability greater than .90' and (b) the replacement of 'equals' by 'equals in circumstances of kind C'. Of course, all of these kinds of replacements (and still other kinds) may be made simultaneously. The result in each case is a *weakening* of the original theory, in the logical sense of 'weakening' – i.e. the resulting theory is always a *logical consequence* of the original theory. The term 'approximation theory' introduced in the text may naturally be extended to cover all these kinds of replacements. I contend that scientific knowledge *is* cumulative, notwithstanding the fact that scientific postulates are usually false as stated, in the sense that, even if a good scientific theory is not *exactly*

(1) Suppose O (the theory of geometrical optics) is not deducible from E (electromagnetic field theory) with the aid of bridge laws, but a suitable approximation theory O' is so deducible. How much of a change is this in Nagel's view? *Answer.* No Change. Nagel himself is quite aware that the *unchanged* reduced theory O is *inconsistent* with the reducing theory E.

(2) *Can* the concept 'light ray' be introduced into E in such a way that a suitable O' turns out to be correct? *Answer.* Yes. (Define a 'light ray' as a normal to the wave front.)

In view of (1) and (2), I no longer see what the fuss is about. Feyerabend's failure to see such obvious points seems, at first blush, perverse. Later, however, we shall see that this is no accidental or localized failure of vision on Feyerabend's part; it is his whole strategy to minimize and deny the extent to which science is the *cumulative* acquisition of knowledge about Nature, in order to enhance the plausibility of his own curious view, which is that the best we can hope for (indeed, all it makes sense to hope for) is to arrive, not at correct explanations of phenomena, but at alternative explanations by means of false theories. That we must learn to aim at a plurality of theories, rather than at a single correct explanation, and that we must expect that all of these theories will later turn out to be false, and will be superseded by new batteries of false theories, with no 'convergence' to what Feyerabend scornfully calls 'One True Theory', is the central contention of Feyerabend's papers. (This might surprise the reader who has only Smart's account of Feyerabend's view, however; for Smart reports only those of Feyerabend's views which he finds especially sympathetic or interesting.)

Incidentally, Kemeny and Oppenheim, unlike Feyerabend, did recognize 'reduction by means of biconditionals' (Nagelian reduction) as an important special type of reduction.

Meaning and common sense

The most interesting part of Feyerabend's view, as reported by Smart, rests on the identification of the *meaning* of a term with a certain accepted *theory* containing the term. In order to make this view apply to terms in ordinary language, Feyerabend holds that our common sense conceptual scheme is a false theory. It should be emphasized that this identification of meaning with theory is implicit rather than explicit in Feyerabend's

correct, a reasonable approximation theory usually is correct, and will eventually become a permanent part of our 'background knowledge'. Indeed, if scientific knowledge were not cumulative in even this sense, it is hard to see why it would be of any theoretical (as opposed to engineering) interest.

paper. Feyerabend does not *say* that the meaning of a term is a theory. What he does is to slide from the term 'meaning' to some such locution as 'accepted usage' (which is harmless enough, in one sense of 'accepted usage') and then cite empirical beliefs containing the term as examples of the accepted usage. This occurs again and again in the paper. For example, the 'manner' in which the terms 'up-down' (strictly speaking, $\alpha\nu\alpha$ and $\kappa\alpha\tau\alpha$) were 'used' by Thales is supposed to show that 'cosmological assumptions' were 'implicit in the common idiom' p. 85). (These 'cosmological assumptions', as stated by Feyerabend, involve anachronistically the Newtonian concept of a 'force'.) Feyerabend has simply *confused* 'usage', in the linguistic sense, with *occurrence*; and his whole argument rests upon this crude mistake.

It should be clear how the different parts of the Feyerabendian doctrine hang together, once this identification is accepted. Feyerabend's main contention, as he is interpreted and presented by Smart, is that if the same term occurs in two different theories T_1 and T_2, it cannot be supposed to have the same meaning. For Feyerabend this is virtually a tautology: 'difference in theory implies difference in meaning' only says that 'difference in theory implies difference in theory'. Feyerabend himself puts it that 'meanings are not invariant with respect to the process of explanation', i.e. the fact explained contains terms which change their meaning when the statement in question is deduced from a theory.

The most radical suggestion Feyerabend is led to make (pp. 90–1) is that since (on Feyerabend's view of 'meaning') the meaning of ordinary language psychological terms (e.g. 'sensation', 'pain') is a theory, and the theory may be false, we do not have to worry about 'linguistic' objections to materialism,† 'which have, I hope, been shown to be completely irrelevant'. 'The mental connotations of mental terms may be spurious'.

Since Feyerabend does not distinguish between conceptually necessary propositions (which rest, according to him, upon empirical theories) and empirical propositions, the assertion that, for example, *if I assert that I am in pain, and I am clear on what I am asserting, and I am sincere, then I must be in pain,* would be for him an assertion which future

---

† By 'materialism' I mean here the doctrine that pain, anger, etc., *are* neurophysiological states (or events). I have argued in [Chapter 29 of this volume] that this doctrine is incorrect (on 'linguistic' grounds, which Feyerabend would surely regard as 'irrelevant'). I do not reject 'materialism' in the wider sense – the view that a whole human being is simply a physical-chemical system with a certain cybernetical organization. Indeed, I think that in the wider sense materialism is correct. And I would agree with Feyerabend in rejecting 'linguistic' arguments against materialism in the wider sense. But I don't know of any such arguments that are worthy of serious consideration.

empirical theory might just as well refute as any other. I am aware that there are difficulties both in establishing the character of the analytic–synthetic distinction, and in the contention that the italicized statement is analytic; but surely Feyerabend's short way with 'linguistic' arguments is just *too* short!

If we reject Feyerabend's view of 'meaning' (as we must, if we want to talk about meaning, in the customary sense, at all), then we may perfectly well say that even if *some* common sense beliefs about pain *are false*, still it is certainly not false that there *are* pains – not in some Pickwickian sense of 'pain', but in the customary sense. And if statements about pain are conceptually necessary (i.e. necessary by virtue of the rules of the language, assuming that these do *not* essentially presuppose a 'false theory'), then any definition of pain, materialistic or otherwise, must be compatible with these.

In his turn, Feyerabend must either (a) abandon the analytic–synthetic distinction altogether; but then he has no business using the term 'meaning' at all! or (b) claim that the *rules of English* (not just some common sense empirical beliefs) in connection with 'pain' essentially presuppose a false theory. In this latter case, he must say what the theory is, and show both that it *is* empirical† and that it *is* presupposed. This, however, would involve discussing just the linguistic issues which he intended to prove to be irrelevant.

The Feyerabend–Smart examples

Let us notice just how unconvincing, from a linguistic point of view, are the examples cited by Feyerabend and Smart. According to Feyerabend, we do not mean by the word 'temperature' what Galileo meant (i.e. what Galileo meant by the synonymous Italian word). The reason Feyerabend gives is that we have abandoned the proposition that 'the temperature shown by a thermometer is not dependent upon the chemical composition of the fluid used', which Feyerabend takes to be constitutive of the Galilean concept. If this was, indeed, 'built into' Galileo's concept of temperature, then Galileo would not have been able to understand the denial of this statement. This is, of course, absurd. What Galileo meant was that intrinsic property of the body which the thermometer measures, and not the result of the measurement. And

† Feyerabend appears to suggest that the false theory in question is that pains, etc., are *mental*. Now then, it is plausible that it is a semantical consequence of the rules of English (or, more simply, that it is analytic), that, say *anger is a mental state*. But why is this a (false) *empirical theory*? Why isn't it a tautology, which simply illustrates how we use the locution 'mental state?'

Galileo could *understand* the statement that measured temperature does not exactly correspond to true temperature, and that measured temperature depends to some extent on the fluid used, just as well as you or I can, independently of our degree of physical sophistication.

Nor are the other examples more convincing. If it was constitutive of the meaning of 'down' that the earth would fall down if not supported (or that the people at the antipodes would), and that down is always the same direction, then the ancients could not have speculated that the earth is an unsupported sphere (and the antipodeans do not fall off). For we cannot speculate that 'some bachelors may really be married', since we have built being unmarried into the concept of bachelorhood; and no more can one speculate that an unsupported object may not fall down, or that down may not always be the same direction, if the contrary is linguistically required. But there is not the slightest evidence that 'an unsupported object will fall down' was ever linguistically required, in any sense. And there is no evidence that 'down is always the same direction' was ever linguistically required. There have always been fairy tales in which unsupported objects did not fall down; and native speakers – even small children – have shown no difficulty in *understanding* these tales. And there have been spherical earth theories for millenia. It is precisely because Feyerabend is wrong that one can explain such theories to anyone, even to a child, in quite ordinary English.

Some of Smart's examples are even less convincing. That 'chimney pot' has changed its meaning as a result of modern physics is obviously false.

The misuse of the term 'meaning' by philosophers

It is evident that Feyerabend is misusing the term 'meaning.' He is not alone in such misuse: in the last thirty years, misusing the term 'meaning' has been one of the most common, if least successful, ways of 'establishing' philosophical propositions. But how did this distressing state of affairs come to be?

The blame must be placed squarely upon the Logical Positivists. The 'Verifiability Theory of Meaning' ('the meaning of a sentence is its method of verification') was, from the first, nothing but a persuasive redefinition. If to call metaphysical propositions 'meaningless' were only to assert that these propositions are empirically untestable, it would be harmless (the metaphysicians always *said* that their assertions were neither empirically testable nor tautologies); but, of course, it is not harmless, because the Positivist hopes that we will accept his redefinition of the term 'meaning,' *while retaining the pejorative connotations of being 'meaningless' in the customary (linguistic) sense, i.e. being literally without sense.* Since, for example, theses which are literally without sense cannot be debated or discussed, anyone who says that metaphysical philosophy is 'meaningless' feels free to reject it *in toto* without constructing arguments against it. If 'God exists' is meaningless, then Hume's careful examination of the arguments for and against in the *Dialogues on Natural Religion* was unnecessary; indeed, how could there *be* arguments for and against a *meaningless sentence?*

The stock Positivist reply, that the Verifiability Theory of Meaning is an 'explication', and that an explication need not exactly agree with the 'pre-analytical use' of the explicandum is disingenuous. 'Method of verification' is *not* an explication of the concept of meaning which is employed in linguistic theory and in everyday life, and it was not (as we have just seen) really intended to serve as such. In order to accomplish its purpose (ruling out metaphysics, normative ethics, theology, etc.), it was precisely necessary that the Verifiability Theory of Meaning should *fail* to explicate the customary conception of 'meaning'.

One of the most widely discussed objections to the Verifiability Theory of Meaning in its original form ('the meaning of a sentence is its method of verification') is due to Quine. This is the objection that it is not an isolated *sentence* that has a method of verification, but a whole *theory*. It is large groups of sentences, not single sentences, that figure in the construction of empirical tests. We may regard the test, indeed, as the test of one single sentence S when the *other* sentences $S_1, S_2, \ldots, S_n$ involved in the context are not (practically) subject to doubt; but still, the test is not a 'test of S' just by virtue of the meaning of S, but by virtue of the meaning of S together with the meaning of $S_1, S_2, \ldots, S_n$, and the fact that $S_1, S_2, \ldots, S_n$ are regarded as empirically true.

The Logical Positivists have reacted to this difficulty in two different ways. Some have adopted Quine's suggestion, and abandoned the notions of sameness of meaning and change of meaning altogether. On this view, there is such a thing as being meaning*ful* (and the criterion is incorporability in an empirical theory) and questions of verification enter indirectly in determining whether or not a word or sentence is meaningful; but there is no sense at all to the question, whether two words have the same meaning, or whether a word has changed its meaning. We can, of course, ask if two words have the same *extension;* but this is just a factual question, to be decided by ordinary scientific procedures. (What ordinary scientific procedures are to be used to tell if all bachelors are unmarried or not, is a somewhat embarrassing question for this view; the somewhat vague answer given seems to be that such statements are 'justified by their place in a whole system'.)

The other approach, taken by Carnap, is as follows: questions of verification (existence of testable consequences) enter into determining whether or not a set of sentences is an empirical theory. The role of terms in the formulation of empirical theories is what renders them meaningful (as in the preceding approach). Thus, again, questions of verifiability enter indirectly into questions of meaningfulness; but not into questions of *sameness* or *difference* of meaning. These concern the *synonymy class* to which a word belongs, and are settled by consulting the semantical rules of the language. Thus, in effect, Carnap operates with *two* conceptions of meaning; he employs the customary (linguistic) conception when *synonymy* is at issue; he employs the Verifiability Theory of Meaning, in its present much modified form, when the question 'is a term in the language at all?' is at issue.

Feyerabend expressed considerable opposition to Logical Positivism, especially in its current form. Yet his misuse of the term 'meaning' seems to have been influenced by the Verifiability Theory of Meaning. Thus, at one point he argues that Galileo meant by temperature 'what a thermometer measures', which has some germ of truth, but he takes the term 'measures' in a queer sense, which amounts to making Galileo an instrumentalist;† and at another point, he uses Nagel's premise, that the 'procedures' of phenomenological thermodynamics fix the meaning of the term 'temperature'. Whether I am correct in conjecturing that it is Positivism that has seduced Feyerabend into playing fast and loose with the term 'meaning' or not, the fact remaining that Feyerabend cannot escape the very difficulties that have bedevilled the Positivists (or, rather, he could not escape them if he ever attempted to subject his own usage of the term 'meaning' in philosophy to some kind of responsible analysis and elaboration).

To see that this is the case, it suffices to recall that for Feyerabend the meaning of a term depends on a whole *theory* containing the term. Thus, he cannot escape being involved in the following questions: *Which* theories are constitutive of the meanings of terms? Since a theory contains many different terms, how do we tell which *terms* it determines the meaning of? What changes in theory, or, more broadly, empirical belief do *not* affect the meaning of terms? No answer to these questions

† What Feyerabend asserts is that the thermometer 'measures' not temperature, but a complicated function of many physical variables (including temperature). What he means, of course, is that the *exact reading* depends upon such a complicated function of many variables. On this usage of 'measures,' every measuring instrument is *perfect;* only we sometimes make mistakes about what is *measured.* And to attribute to Galileo the view 'temperature is what the thermometer measures', where 'measures' is taken in *this* sense is just to turn Galileo into an extreme operationalist. Needless to say, this is an unreasonable use of the word 'measures': and it is unreasonable to say, as Feyerabend does, that we do not today believe that thermometers measure temperature.

is even suggested in Feyerabend's paper; and these are just the difficulties that have forced the proponents of the Verifiability Theory of Meaning to restrict the Verifiability Theory to questions of *significance*, and to look elsewhere (if anywhere) for an understanding of *synonymy*.

One might, of course, take the radical line that *any* change in theory is a change in the meaning of terms. (Which terms? All of them? Even the logical connectives? Why not?) But I expect Feyerabend would not want to take this line. For to say that *any* change in our empirical beliefs about Xs is a change in the meaning of the term X† would be to *abandon* the distinction between questions of meaning and questions of fact. To say that the semantical rules of English cannot at all be distinguished from the empirical beliefs of English speakers would just be to throw the notion of a semantical rule of English overboard.

What is curious is that Feyerabend does *not* follow this course. Indeed, many of his purposes would have been better served had he chosen to follow Quine in repudiating the theory of meaning altogether. He wishes to show that linguistic philosophy is irrelevant and misguided; clearly, if it all rests on a mistaken notion, that there are such thing as *rules of language*, then it is badly misguided. (So is the whole science of linguistics; an objection which Quine has attempted to turn, in *Word and Object*, by allowing some purpose to constructing linguistic descriptions of natural language, and some operational and theoretical constraints to be satisfied by such descriptions.) He wishes to show that it is not a valid objection to 'pain is an event in the brain', that to say this is merely to change the meaning of 'pain'. If 'change of meaning' is itself a *meaningless* notion, his work is done for him. He wishes to show that false theories are presupposed by ordinary language; if no distinction is to be drawn between 'ordinary language' and 'common sense' (i.e. the everyday beliefs of most speakers), then this is just to say that most people believe many false things, and who has ever doubted *this*?

However, all appearance of sensation would have vanished, had Feyerabend followed this course. For the 'sensation' here depends on sliding back and forth between a noncustomary conception of meaning and the customary conception. Consider, for example, the assertion that excites Smart; that even the term 'chimney pot' has changed its meaning, since we have abandoned the common sense view of the composition of chimney pots. If the 'meaning' *is* the common sense view, then this is a tautology: 'we have changed our view, so we have changed our view'. It is only by sliding from the fact that the 'meaning'

---

† The second occurrence of 'X' in the sentence in the text should be in quasi-quotes (Quine's 'corners') to avoid a mention-use mistake. I have ignored such logical niceties in the present chapter.

in the Feyerabendian sense (if, indeed, there is one) has changed to the assertion that the meaning *in the customary sense* has changed that a 'sensation' results!

Finally, one of Feyerabend's main conclusions – the one with which Smart's entire paper is, in a sense, concerned – simply does not follow without this 'slide'. This conclusion is that, since ordinary language presupposes false theories, we may have to *discard ordinary language*. It is no surprise that we may have to change many of our common sense beliefs; we may have to say different things *in* ordinary English, French, German, etc.; these beliefs are the 'meaning'; only by supposing that they are also the 'meaning' in the customary sense can one obtain the conclusion that we may have to discard everyday English, French, German, etc., altogether. Here Quine and Feyerabend would, of course, part company. If the 'ordinary usage' of a term X depends on the false proposition that all X are P, then Quine would recommend that we start saying instead what is true, namely 'some X are not P', and not that we necessarily drop the term X. If 'common sense' is false, let us find out what is true. Many technical terms may have to be introduced; but that ordinary non-technical language cannot be used to say what is true, that it is somehow *essentially infected with falsity* is a conclusion that Quine would reject as he rejects 'essentialism' in general. Indeed, Feyerabend's views are an unholy mixture of Quine's refusal to separate meaning from empirical theory and just the essentialism that Quine attacks.

What meaning is

I have repeatedly spoken of the 'customary sense' of the word 'meaning'. What is this customary sense?

In one sense, we all know well enough what 'meaning ' means. Thus what is wanted here is not a *synonym* for the word 'meaning' (e.g. 'significance'), but a conceptual analysis. Attempted conceptual analyses of the concept of meaning have sometimes taken the form of investigations into the foundations of linguistic theory (cf. the important book by Paul Ziff), and sometimes the form of formal models. I shall attempt nothing so ambitious here. What I say will, I hope, be acceptable to all philosophers of language who do not, like Quine, reject the theory of meaning altogether.

The theory of meaning depends upon the idea that a natural language has *rules*. (Ziff objects to the term 'rule', but his 'state regularities' and 'state projections' *are* 'rules' as *I* shall use the term.) These rules are sometimes syntactical and sometimes not. The syntactical rules determine what phones are allophones of what phonemes in a language; what sequences of phonemes are morphemes (more strictly, allomorphs of morphemes); and what sequences of morphemes are well-formed sentences. The nonsyntactical rules distinguish linguistically *regular* from linguistically *deviant* uses of sentences. To call a married man a 'bachelor', or to refer to a geometrical point as 'graceful' is to violate semantical rules of English.

To discover the different sorts of nonsyntactical rules that there are, to succeed in stating them perspicuously, is the main task of semantic theory. Thus I shall not commit myself here, beyond giving a few examples, on the form and content of the semantical rules of a natural language. Even at the present early stage, however, certain things seem clear. It is generally agreed that a speaker's knowledge of the rules of his native language is implicit and not explicit; only the very sophisticated speaker can verbalize even (some of) the *syntactical* rules of his native language. The unconscious and obligatory character of linguistic rules has long been noted. The 'meaning' of a word is a function of the rules governing its employment. These determine among other things, which locutions are synonymous (coextensive by linguistic stipulation), which locutions have more than one meaning (are governed by alternative batteries of rules), which sentences are analytic on which readings, etc.

The unconscious character of linguistic rules is important in understanding what happens when someone asks for the 'meaning' of a word. What the inquirer wishes to gain is a knowledge of the rules governing the employment of the word – so that *he* will be able to employ it too. But he does not wish for an explicit statement of these rules, but for the kind of implicit knowledge that I alluded to above. Thus it is the respondent's task, in such a situation, to say something from which the inquirer, employing his considerable (implicit) linguistic knowledge, can 'pick up' the information he wishes – 'information' which neither the inquirer nor the respondent can verbalize, and 'pick up' by a process which *no one* today understands.

It is this that accounts for the hodgepodge of things that get counted as answers to the question 'what is the meaning of such-and-such a word?' Traditional dictionary definitions, for example, contain a fantastic mixture of empirical and linguistic information. Nevertheless, they succeed often enough in enabling speakers to acquire the usage of words they did not previously understand.

Suppose, for example, that one asks a typical native speaker of English for the meaning of the word 'gold'. He is likely to give one a mass of empirical information about gold (that it is precious, normally yellow, incorruptible, etc.), in addition to the essential linguistic information that 'gold' is the name of a metal. Yet, if gold became as 'cheap as dirt', or began to rust, or turned green, the meaning of the *word* 'gold' would not change. Only if we stopped using 'gold' as the name of a metal, or used it to name a different metal, would the primary meaning change. (I say 'the primary meaning', because the *connotations* of 'gold' *do* depend on the facts that gold is normally yellow, precious, etc.).

One should notice, also, that one may know the meaning of the word 'gold' without knowing *how to tell* whether or not a given thing is gold. (Of course, someone must be able to *identify* gold; otherwise the word couldn't be used as the name of a real metal; but it isn't true that only those people who can identify gold know the meaning of the word, or even that they know *more* of the meaning of the word. They simply know *more about gold*.)

Similarly with Feyerabend's example of the word 'temperature'. As long as we continue to use the word 'temperature' to refer to the same physical magnitude, we will not say that the 'meaning' of the word has changed, even if we revise our beliefs many times about the exact laws obeyed by that magnitude, and no matter how sophisticated our instruments for measuring temperature may become. However, one 'theory' *is* essential to the meaning of the word 'temperature' – that the magnitude we identify as 'temperature', and quantify by means of thermometers, or however, is the magnitude whose greater and lower intensities are measured by the human sensorium as *warmer* and *colder* respectively. This does *not* mean that the human sensorium is never fooled, but that when it is not fooled, when the differences in felt warmness are accounted for by a difference in some property of the object rather than of the subject, it is generally a difference in 'temperature' that is responsible. The use of the word 'temperature' rests upon the empirical fact that there exists a single physical magnitude (in fact, molecular energy) which is normally responsible for differences in 'felt warmness', because it is *analytic* that 'if X has a higher temperature than Y, then X is warmer than Y' – i.e. the words 'temperature' and 'warmer' are semantically linked – and because the functioning of the human sensorium underlies the 'stimulus meaning'† of the word 'warmer'. The word 'temperature' is 'theory loaded'; and, fortunately, the theory is correct.

I asserted in a preceding section that Galileo used the word (or, rather, the corresponding word in Italian) to refer to the physical magnitude we call 'temperature' today. But what reason is there to say this? One reason, of course, is that all scientists accept the well known reduction of phenomenological thermodynamics to statistical mechanics (identifying 'temperature' with mean kinetic energy of the molecules). This is a 'reduction' in the Nagelian sense – reduction by means of

† The term 'stimulus meaning' comes from Quine, 1960.

biconditionals – and it leads to the deduction of a very good approximation theory to phenomenological thermodynamics from statistical mechanics. Accepting the reduction is precisely accepting that phenomenological thermodynamics and statistical mechanics (with the added postulate 'temperature is average molecular kinetic energy') are theories of 'temperature' *in the same sense*, as Nagel correctly points out.

Two points of a more 'linguistic' character are also relevant to this example:

(1) On the basis of *linguistic intuition*, it seems clearly linguistically regular to say that Galileo was measuring and theorizing about the magnitude we call 'temperature' in English, but that we have somewhat different beliefs concerning it than he did. The fact that native speakers have certain intuitions of regularity does not *prove* anything, of course, but it *is* part of the data available to the linguist. When he goes counter to strong and widespread linguistic intuitions, he must have a good reason to give.

Feyerabend, as might be expected from his general position, rejects this kind of appeal to linguistic intuition. For him the 'linguistic intuitions' of native speakers simply reflect the false theories that they have deeply internalized; and conformity to linguistic intuitions is thus a sign of conformity of false theories, and is hence *undesirable* (cf. Feyerabend, 1963). But there is a confusion here. Linguists and philosophers of language rely on linguistic intuition, as well as on methodological considerations (e.g. simplicity of the overall descriptions of the syntax and semantics of the language), in order to discover a correct semantic characterization of a word X. In saying that such-and-such is a correct semantic characterization of a word X, they do not thereby commit themselves to the existence of Xs, much less to the correctness of whatever empirical beliefs may be entailed in calling something an X. If the use of a word X *does* presuppose some false empirical theory or other, then this is just what we would hope to find out by this procedure. If we reject linguistic intuitions to begin with as somehow 'dirty' (essentially infected with falsity), then we will never discover the semantic characterization of any word, and hence never discover if such theses as those of Feyerabend – that most words presuppose false empirical theories; that various terms have changed their meaning; that meanings are not invariant under the processes of reduction and explanation – are true or false.

(2) Given two semantic descriptions of part or all of a language, even if they are approximately equal in simplicity and factual adequacy, there is always a strong *methodological* reason to prefer the one that postulates fewer meaning changes. Namely, the fact that two uses conform to the

same lexical characterization (have such-and-such features in common) is a fact about the language; whereas the fact that they can be given two separate 'entries' is trivial – the meaning of any word can be 'split up' under as many entries as one pleases. Thus one will not discover the semantic structure of the language unless one conforms to the maxim 'differences of meaning are not to be postulated without necessity'. (Ziff calls this 'Occam's eraser'.)

Thus we see again that given the operational and methodological constraints appropriate to linguistic theory, it is unreasonable to say that such words as 'temperature' change their meanings whenever we change our theory concerning the corresponding magnitudes. We have just given two examples of the kinds of constraints that are accepted by semantic theorists. Quine has expressed considerable scepticism that such constraints single out a *unique* semantic description of a natural language. However, this does not trouble us in the present context.†
Our difficulty today is not that we are confronted with a plurality of 'equally valid descriptions' of English, and do not know how to choose (or if it makes sense to choose at all), but that no one has constructed even *one* wholly adequate description of English. And certainly it is not the case that *every* description is adequate (as Quine admits, in *Word and Object*).

The customary sense of the word 'meaning' may be somewhat vague; but the great interest in semantic theory among linguists, as well as among philosophers of language, and the developing integration of semantic and syntactic studies in linguistics, affords hope that it may be clarified, and perhaps supplemented by a battery of more technical notions. We are well on our way to knowing a responsible and theoretically fruitful way of talking about 'sameness of meaning' and 'change of meaning' in the linguistic sense. Smart offers the suggestion, in defense of Feyerabend, that Feyerabend may be talking about 'meaning' *in some other sense*. But what *exactly* is the other sense? What constraints are there upon this other way of talking about 'meaning'? In another

† Incidentally, the constraints allowed by Quine are clearly much too weak. For example, on the formal side, Quine requires only that a translation scheme be general recursive. This allows wildly irregular mappings as 'correct'. In practice something approximating to word-by-word substitution is always used, at least as a first approximation. On the operational side, Quine rejects conformity to the linguistic intuitions of native speakers as a constraint, on the grounds that this constraint begs the philosophical questions. (Where did these 'linguistic intuitions' come from, if not from an implicit theory of the language, Quine asks. And what were the constraints upon this implicit theory?) But this seems puristic. Quine is right, that the *foundations* of linguistic theory cannot be permanently rested upon appeals to linguistic intuition (as they are for example, by Chomsky and his followers); but this does not mean that we cannot rely upon such appeals at all. Fortunately, we can proceed with sciences whose conceptual foundations are far from being in order!

paper, Feyerabend says in one place that it is '(empirical) meaning' that does not remain invariant. The only existing theory of 'empirical meaning' is the Verifiability Theory of Meaning, and, as we have seen in its present form the theory affords only a criterion of empirical meaning*fulness*, and no criterion of empirical *synonymy* (sameness of 'empirical meaning'). I cannot join Smart in hailing it as a great discovery that terms are constantly changing their meaning in some completely unspecified sense of the word 'meaning'; nor can I accept the argument that, since ordinary language presupposes false theories in some completely unexplained way, ordinary language may have to be discarded.

7
Review of *The concept of a person**

It is strikingly apparent that the twentieth century has been a golden
one for the sort of philosophy that is logically and empirically oriented.
Merely to list the names of the analytical philosophers who have
achieved greatness or near-greatness in this century is to provide
impressive evidence of this: Russell and Wittgenstein (who stand on a
level by themselves); G. E. Moore (whose influence Keynes described so
well in the lovely memoir 'My Early Beliefs'); F. P. Ramsey (also
memorialized by Keynes); Carnap and Reichenbach; John Austin; and
– to take the risk of mentioning some philosophers in mid-career – W.
V. Quine and Nelson Goodman. The writings of these men have illuminated field after field of philosophy: ethics (Moore); mathematical
philosophy (Russell, Wittgenstein, Quine); epistemology and philosophy
of science (all of the figures mentioned). The nature of moral valuation;
of natural laws; of mathematical necessity; the nature of language and
its relation to reality; of truth and meaning; of common sense knowledge
and of scientific knowledge; and above all, the nature of philosophy
itself, have been the subject of essays and books as brilliant, as full
of insights and surprises (including surprising mistakes, naturally) as
any produced in the entire history of philosophy. If any further evidence
were needed of the healthy state of philosophy today, it would be provided by the hordes of intellectuals who complain that philosophy is
overly 'technical', that it has 'abdicated' from any concern with 'real'
problems etc. For such complaints have always occurred precisely when
philosophy was significant and vital! Aristophanes found Socrates silly
and technical; Berkeley was thought ridiculous by lay opinion until
Hume and Kant appreciated the significance of the challenge he posed;
Hume and Kant in their turn were ridiculed and misunderstood (Kant
by no less a figure than Goethe, who saw in Kant a good intellect
prostituting itself in the service of the Church). The sad fact is that good
philosophy is and always has been *hard*, and that it is easier to learn the
names of a few philosophers than it is to read their books. Those who
find philosophy overly 'technical' today would no more have found the

* This review was not published nor was it solicited by any journal. I wrote it in the
1960s as a reaction to reading A. J. Ayer's book, and then put it away in a drawer.

time or the inclination to follow Socrates' long chains of argument, or to read one of the *Critiques*, in an earlier day.

If philosophy at its best has always been hard and frequently technical, it is all the more pleasant to encounter from time to time a philosopher who can express philosophical ideas so clearly that they become accessible to a wider audience. Such a philosopher is Alfred Jules Ayer. His famous *Language, Truth, and Logic* made widely accessible the ideas of the Logical Positivists (Carnap and Reichenbach); while his subsequent books have traced his gradual evolution to a more independent position, and, at the same time, shown how an intelligent philosopher wrestles with the traditional problems of the Theory of Knowledge in the current epoch. The present book seems to me to be far below the level of Ayer's best work; but even so it is interesting as a document in an ongoing philosophical fight.

The fight concerns the vogue of so-called 'ordinary language philosophy' (which Ayer vigorously opposes) and especially the views of the later Wittgenstein (who changed his position markedly in the mid-thirties). Ayer's case against this position is set out in the first three essays in this volume, and ripostes against it occur in virtually all of the other six essays. The first essay ('Philosophy and Language') states the case most completely. This essay was Ayer's inaugural address as Wykeham Professor of Logic at Oxford. I shall focus attention on this essay in what follows.

Ayer's case against Ordinary Language philosophy rests upon his exposition of it. Indeed, his case, *is* the exposition of the position he is attacking; if his description of Ordinary Language philosophy is accurate, then attack is hardly necessary; the position hardly stands up long enough to be pushed down. In this respect Ayer's attack is like Gellner's attack in *Words and Things;* however, it must be emphasized that Ayer's *tone*, unlike Gellner's, is fair-minded throughout.

As Ayer describes it, there is little to Ordinary Language philosophy beyond the appeal to 'what we ordinarily say' (the so-called 'Paradigm Case Argument'). We 'ordinarily say' in certain circumstances, 'there is a chair in the room'. *Therefore*, it is *true* in certain circumstances that there is a chair in some room or other. Therefore chairs exist. But 'material object' is just a philosophical place-holder for some more specific noun such as 'chair'. Thus if chairs exist, so do material objects (chairs are necessarily material objects). So the traditional problem, 'do material objects *really* exist?' is solved in the affirmative, and moreover solved by a trivial observation concerning the linguistic behavior of English speakers.

Ayer's reply is the obvious one: what we 'ordinarily say' is not always *true.* But this point hardly needs making. Is there really such a school as 'ordinary language philosophy', and is it really as silly as all this?

That Ayer himself feels some discomfort about this is indicated by section IV of 'Philosophy and Language', in which he recognizes that Wittgenstein, in particular, does a great deal which hardly fits the description just given. Indeed, section IV hardly seems integrated with the rest of this essay: only the barest hint of the suggestion that Wittgenstein and Ryle *thought* they were describing 'our verbal habits' whereas they were really doing something much more traditionally philosophical is advanced, and only this suggestion seems to connect the account of the work of Wittgenstein and Ryle given in this section with the account given in the preceding section.

In point of fact, most philosophers who are acquainted with the figures that Ayer is attacking would say that (1) there is, perhaps, a 'school', but not any single *position* that could be called 'ordinary language philosophy' (Ayer's favored term is 'linguistic philosophy'). The two main figures that one might think of as 'ordinary language philosophers' were Wittgenstein and Austin (whom Ayer never mentions by name, although there is an unmistakeable hostile reference in the form of a grossly distorted account of Austin's views on page 16). Ryle, whom Ayer does frequently discuss, is an important philosopher, but to my knowledge he has not had followers in the way in which Wittgenstein and Austin have had and still have a following. Of course, many younger philosophers have been influenced by *both* Wittgenstein and Austin; and contemporaries of Wittgenstein and Austin developed somewhat similar ways of philosophizing at about the same time, although it would be risky and possibly unjust to say who influenced whom. But, as a rough schematization, 'ordinary language philosophers' are the people who have been influenced by Wittgenstein, or by Austin, or who philosophize similarly to one or the other. And since Wittgenstein and Austin had *very little* in common besides an interest in ordinary language – since their views, both on the nature of philosophy and on its relation to the study of language, were entirely incompatible – roughly as incompatible as Protagoras and Aristotle – I find myself entirely mystified by people who think that 'ordinary language philosophy' is a *position*. (2) Wittgenstein did not employ *arguments*, in the traditional philosophical sense, at all (least of all arguments to 'prove' that 'material objects exist', or that 'our wills are free') and Austin regarded the so-called 'Paradigm Case Argument' as a simple example of the fallacy of Begging the Question (which it is). So if there *were* a *position* of 'ordinary language philosophy' or 'linguisitic philosophy', its central tenet *couldn't* be the 'Paradigm Case Argument'.

134

Wittgenstein and Austin, in fact, were two highly original and highly independent philosophers, each of whom contributed radical new ideas to philosophy – ideas which have not yet been definitively assessed, and the discussion of which will continue for years to come. In the case of Wittgenstein, one might speak of a *functional conception of language*, and also of a *therapeutic conception of philosophy*. Wittgenstein believed that the concepts of *reference* and *truth* were not really of much use in philosophy, and that one should ask, not 'what do our words refer to?' (as if that could be separated from the language we employ), but 'how do we *use* our words?'– what *functions* they have in human activity, and how those functions change, overlap, are taught and learned, is in the center of the investigation. To know the 'use' of a descriptive word includes knowing the criteria for its application, if it is governed by criteria, but also includes familiarity with an entire set of human institutions involving the word. All the sentences in the language – including religious sentences, metaphysical sentences, ethical sentences – that people actually employ have 'uses' in Wittgenstein's sense, even if they do not have a 'method of verification' in the Logical Positivist sense. Thus Ayer's claim that 'ask for the use' means 'ask for the method of verification' is as gross an error as one could make in this connection.

The various families of word-uses that we discover in language are not wholly arbitrary, on Wittgenstein's view, but neither are they 'forced' by the subject-matter in the way in which a traditional philosopher might suppose. Rather Man is the Measure for Wittgenstein: our concepts reflect human nature in a particular cultural setting, and the human contribution is discerned by Wittgenstein even where one might think it most absent – in the concepts and assertions of pure mathematics.

Traditional philosophers, on Wittgenstein's view, are men in the grip of a 'picture'. For example, there is the picture of mathematics as the description of a platonic heaven of 'mathematical objects'. Or again, there is the picture of perception as 'directly seeing one's own sense data' (as if material objects could only be 'inferred' and not *seen*, because – on this picture – they are hidden *behind* one's own sense data). The task of philosophy – Wittgensteinian philosophy – is to break the hold of these pictures by providing a *perspicuous representation* of the way in which we use our language (e.g. how we really speak of numbers in mathematics, or of sensations and seeing in ordinary language). The very emphasis which Wittgenstein places on the notion of a *perspicuous representation* contradicts Ayer's suggestion that Wittgenstein thought it was sufficient to just 'look at the facts without preconceptions'. Oddly enough, after attacking the idea that there is such a thing as a 'neutral record of facts' on page 21, Ayer criticizes Wittgenstein's account of his own procedure by urging (1) that looking at our uses of philosophically important terms is not separable from looking at non-linguistic facts, which Wittgenstein himself emphasized, and then concludes that all Wittgenstein is really doing is (2) trying to 'see the facts for what they are' (as if the language, so to speak, dropped out).

In the case of Austin, the whole atmosphere is different. Radical suggestions concerning the dependence of truth (even in pure mathematics) on human nature are absent. The idea of philosophy as a purely therapeutic activity which yields no knowledge properly so called, but only liberates us from confusion and enables us to see things 'perspicuously', is likewise absent. Rather Austin is radical in a quite different direction: the radical suggestion is that philosophy may, after all, become a cooperative enterprise in which cumulative and verified knowledge is possible! This suggestion is coupled with great caution. Philosophers have not come to agreement in the past thousands of years, in Austin's view, not because such agreement is impossible (as is now generally believed), but because they have leaped prematurely to the level of generalization and theory construction. It is as if physicists had not bothered to perform any experiments before setting out to construct a complete system of cosmology and elementary particle mechanics. Austin's sole agreement with Wittgenstein is in the critique of traditional philosophy: traditional philosophers *have* been in the grip of false theories (Austin would, I believe, have been displeased with Wittgenstein's trick of referring to these as 'pictures', thereby suggesting that no theoretical content is involved, or indeed possible). They have *not* bothered to look closely either at the way language works or at the nonlinguistic facts. But the remedy is not a 'perspicuous representation' of an essentially nonscientific kind, but rather a new kind of *science of language*. Whether this science would make philosophy unnecessary altogether, or only provide the solid bedrock of observation on which philosophy could finally get properly going, is not altogether clear from Austin's writing. In the opinion of a number of philosophers, Austin made an important and substantial contribution to the creation of the kind of philosophical science of language that he had in mind before his premature death in 1960.

In closing this account, I cannot resist considering one problem to which Ayer repeatedly alludes: the alleged 'ordinary language' treatment of 'freedom of the will'. According to Ayer, 'it is agreed that the extent to which (people) are responsible is the measure of the extent to which they are free' (page 16, in a paragraph which could hardly apply to anyone but Austin). Then, Ayer says, (unspecified) ordinary language philosophers argue that since there are expressions such as 'couldn't help himself' which we can learn to use *correctly*, there must be circumstances in which we are, and circumstances in which we are not *responsible. Therefore*, we are free.

Now let us note what Austin actually says on these matters (in a *Plea for Excuses*):

There is much to be said for the view that, philosophical tradition apart, Responsibility would be a better candidate for the role here ascribed to Freedom. If ordinary language is to be our guide, it is to evade responsibility, or full responsibility, that we most often make excuses, and I have used the word myself in this way above. But in fact 'responsibility' too seems not really apt in all cases ... It may be, then, that at least two key terms, Freedom and Responsibility, are needed: the relation between them is not clear, and it may be hoped that the investigation of excuses will contribute towards its clarification [So much for 'it is agreed'!]

And on the alleged assumption that what we 'ordinarily say' is always true (Austin refers to this alleged assumption by the phrase 'the Last Word'), Austin writes:

Then, for the Last Word. Certainly ordinary language has no claim to be the last word, if there is such a thing. It embodies, indeed, something better than the metaphysics of the Stone Age, namely, as was said, the inherited experience and acumen of many generations of men. But then that acumen has been concentrated primarily upon the practical purposes of life. If a distinction works well for practical purposes in ordinary life (no mean feat, for even ordinary life is full of hard cases), then there is sure to be something in it, it will not mark nothing: yet this is likely enough not to be the best way of arranging things if our interests are more extensive or intellectual than the ordinary. And again, that experience has been derived only from the sources available to ordinary men through most of civilized history; it has not been fed from the resources of the microscope and its successors. And it must be added, too, that superstition and error and fantasy of all kinds do become incorporated in ordinary language and even sometimes stand up to the survival test (only, when they do, why should we not detect it?). Certainly, then, ordinary language is *not* the last word: in principle it can everywhere be supplemented and improved upon and superseded. Only remember, it is the *first* word.

In closing, I want to emphasize again that at no point do I suspect Ayer of *intentional* unfairness to the philosophers he is criticizing. The difficulty, it seems to me, is that although for certain purposes it *may* be useful to use such rubrics as 'linguistic philosophy', 'ordinary language philosophy', to group certain philosophers together for study, say, usefulness of these rubrics ceases when the context is one of *attack*. For the philosophers so grouped simply do not agree on sufficiently many doctrines or ideas for *one* attack to demolish all of them (if they can be demolished at all). Without committing myself to the rightness or wrongness of either Wittgenstein or Austin, I hope that I have succeeded in suggesting that these philosophers have far more intellectual and personal power than one could ever gather from such a description as the one Ayer gives.

8

Is semantics possible?*†

In the last decade enormous progress seems to have been made in the syntactic theory of natural languages, largely as a result of the work of linguists influenced by Noam Chomsky and Zellig Harris. Comparable progress seems *not* to have been made in the semantic theory of natural languages, and perhaps it is time to ask why this should be the case. Why is the theory of meaning so *hard*?

The meaning of common nouns

To get some idea of the difficulties, let us look at some of the problems that come up in connection with general names. General names are of many kinds. Some, like *bachelor*, admit of an explicit definition straight off ('man who has never been married'); but the overwhelming majority do not. Some are derived by transformations from verbal forms, e.g. *hunter = one who hunts*. An important class, philosophically as well as linguistically, is the class of general names associated with *natural kinds* – that is, with classes of things that we regard as of explanatory importance; classes whose normal distinguishing characteristics are 'held together' or even explained by deep-lying mechanisms. *Gold, lemon, tiger, acid*, are examples of such nouns. I want to begin this paper by suggesting that (1) *traditional* theories of meaning radically falsify the properties of such words; (2) logicians like Carnap do little more than formalize these traditional theories, inadequacies and all; (3) such semantic theories as that produced by Jerrold Katz and his co-workers likewise share all the defects of the traditional theory. In Austin's happy phrase, what we have been given by philosophers, logicians, and 'semantic theorists' alike, is a 'myth-eaten description'.

* Reprinted from H. Kiefer and M. Munitz (eds.) *Languages, Belief and Metaphysics*, Volume I of *Contemporary Philosophic Thought: The International Philosophy Year Conferences at Brockport* by permission of the State University of New York Press. Copyright © 1970 by State University of New York.

† While responsibility for the views expressed here is, of course, solely mine, they doubtless reflect the influence of two men who have profoundly affected my attitude towards the problems of language: Paul Ziff and Richard Boyd. I owe them both a debt of gratitude for their insight, their infectious enthusiasm, and for many happy hours of philosophical conversation.

In the traditional view, the meaning of, say 'lemon', is given by specifying a conjunction of *properties*. For each of these properties, the statement 'lemons have the property P' is an analytic truth; and if $P_1, P_2, \ldots, P_n$ are all the properties in the conjunction, then 'anything with all of the properties $P_1, \ldots, P_n$ is a lemon' is likewise an analytic truth.

In one sense, this is trivially correct. If we are allowed to invent unanalyzable properties *ad hoc*, then we can find a single property – not even a conjunction – the possession of which is a necessary and sufficient condition for being a lemon, or being gold, or whatever. Namely, we just postulate *the property of being a lemon*, or *the property of being gold*, or whatever may be needed. If we require that the properties $P_1, P_2, \ldots, P_n$ *not* be of this *ad hoc* character, however, then the situation is very different. Indeed, with any natural understanding of the term 'property', it is just *false* that to say that something belongs to a natural kind is just to ascribe to it a conjunction of properties.

To see why it is false, let us look at the term 'lemon'. The supposed 'defining characteristics' of lemons are: yellow color, tart taste, a certain kind of peel, etc. Why is the term 'lemon' *not* definable by simply conjoining these 'defining characteristics'?

The most obvious difficulty is that a natural kind may have *abnormal members*. A green lemon is still a lemon – even if, owing to some abnormality, it *never* turns yellow. A three-legged tiger is still a tiger. Gold in the gaseous state is still gold. It is only normal lemons that are yellow, tart, etc.; only normal tigers that are four-legged; only gold under normal conditions that is hard, white or yellow, etc.

To meet this difficulty, let us try the following definition: X is a *lemon = df*; X belongs to a natural kind whose normal members have yellow peel, tart taste, etc.

There is, of course, a problem with the 'etc.' There is also a problem with 'tart taste' – shouldn't it be *lemon* taste? But let us waive these difficulties, at least for the time being. Let us instead focus on the two notions that have come up with this attempted definition: the notions *natural kind* and *normal member*.

A natural kind *term* (so shift attention, for the moment, from natural kinds to their preferred designations) is a term that plays a special kind of role. If I describe something as a *lemon*, or as an *acid*, I indicate that it is likely to have certain characteristics (yellow peel, or sour taste in dilute water solution, as the case may be); but I also indicate that the presence of those characteristics, if they are present, is likely to be accounted for by some 'essential nature' which the thing shares with other members of the natural kind. What the essential nature is is not a matter of language analysis but of scientific theory construction; today we would say it was chromosome structure, in the case of lemons, and being a proton-donor, in the case of acids. Thus it is tempting to say that a natural kind term is simply a term that plays a certain kind of role in scientific or pre-scientific theory: the role, roughly, of pointing to common 'essential features' or 'mechanisms' beyond and below the obvious 'distinguishing characteristics'. But this is vague, and likely to remain so. Meta-science is today in its infancy: and terms like 'natural kind', and 'normal member', are in the same boat as the more familiar meta-scientific terms 'theory' and 'explanation', as far as resisting a speedy and definitive analysis is concerned.

Even if we *could* define 'natural kind' – say, 'a natural kind is a class which is the extension of a term P which plays such-and-such a methodological role in some well-confirmed theory' – the definition would obviously embody a theory of the world, at least in part. It is not *analytic* that natural kinds are classes which play certain kinds of roles in theories; what *really* distinguishes the classes we count as natural kinds is itself a matter of (high level and very abstract) scientific investigation and not just meaning analysis.

That the proposed definition of 'lemon' uses terms which themselves resist definition is not a fatal objection however. Let us pause to note, therefore, that if it is correct (and we shall soon show that even it is radically oversimplified), then the traditional idea of the force of general terms is badly mistaken. To say that something is a lemon is, on the above definition, to say that it belongs to a natural kind whose normal members have certain properties; but not to say that it necessarily has those properties itself. There are no *analytic* truths of the form *every lemon has* P. What has happened is this: the traditional theory has taken an account which is correct for the 'one-criterion' concepts (i.e. for such concepts as 'bachelor' and 'vixen'), and made it a general account of the meaning of general names. A theory which correctly describes the behavior of perhaps three hundred words has been asserted to correctly describe the behavior of the tens of thousands of general names.

It is also important to note the following: if the above definition is correct, then knowledge of the properties that a thing has (in any natural and non 'ad hoc' sense of property) is not enough to determine, in any mechanical or algorithmic way, whether or not it is a lemon (or an acid, or whatever). For even if I have a description in, say, the language of particle physics, of what are in fact the chromosomal properties of a fruit, I may not be able to tell that it is a lemon because I have not developed the theory according to which (1) those physical-chemical characteristics are the chromosomal structure-features (I may not even have the notion 'chromosome', and (2) I may not have discovered that chromosomal structure is the *essential* property of lemons. Meaning does not determine extension, in the sense that given the meaning and a list of all the 'properties' of a thing (in any particular sense of 'property') one can simply *read off* whether the thing is a lemon (or acid, or whatever). Even given the meaning, whether something is a lemon or not, is, or at least sometimes is, or at least may sometimes be, a matter of what is the best conceptual scheme, the best theory, the best scheme of 'natural kinds'. (This is, of course, one reason for the failure of phenomenalistic translation schemes.)

These consequences of the proposed definition are, I believe, correct, even though the proposed definition is itself still badly oversimplified. Is it a necessary truth that the 'normal' lemons, as we think of them (the tart yellow ones) are really normal members of their species? Is it logically impossible that we should have mistaken what are really very atypical lemons (perhaps diseased ones) for normal lemons? On the above definition, if there is no natural kind whose normal members are yellow, tart, etc., then even these tart, yellow, thick-peeled fruits that I make lemonade from are *not literally lemons*. But this is absurd. It is clear that they are lemons, although it is not analytic that they are *normal* lemons. Moreover, if the color of lemons changed – say, as the result of some gases getting into the earth's atmosphere and reacting with pigment in the peel of lemons – we would not say that lemons had ceased to exist, although a natural kind whose normal members were *yellow* and had the other characteristics of lemons *would* have ceased to exist. Thus the above definition is correct to the extent that what it says *isn't* analytic indeed isn't; but it is incorrect in that what would be analytic if it were correct isn't. We have loosened up the logic of the natural kind terms, in comparison with the 'conjunction of properties' model; but we have still not loosened it up enough.

Two cases have just been considered: (1) the normal members of the natural kind in question may not really be the ones we *think* are normal; (2) the characteristics of the natural kind may change with time, possibly due to a change in the conditions, without the 'essence' changing so much that we want to stop using the same word. In the first case (normal lemons are blue, but we haven't seen any normal lemons), our theory of the natural kind is false; but at least there is a natural kind about which we have a false theory, and that is why we can still apply the term. In the second case, our theory was at least once true; but it has ceased to be true, although the natural kind has not ceased to exist, which is why we can still apply the term.

Let us attempt to cover both these kinds of cases by modifying our definition as follows:

X is a *lemon* = *df* X belongs to a natural kind whose . . . (as before) OR X belongs to a natural kind whose normal members used to . . . (as before) OR X belongs to a natural kind whose normal members were formerly believed to, or are now incorrectly believed to . . . (as before).

Nontechnically, the trouble with this 'definition' is that it is slightly crazy. Even if we waive the requirement of sanity (and, indeed, it is all too customary in philosophy to waive any such requirement), it still doesn't work. Suppose, for example, that some tens of thousands of years ago lemons were unknown, but a few atypical oranges were known. Suppose these atypical oranges had exactly the properties of peel, color, etc., that lemons have: indeed, we may suppose that only a biologist could tell that they were really queer oranges and not normal lemons. Suppose that the people living at that time took them to be normal members of a species, and thus thought that oranges have exactly the properties that lemons in fact do have. Then all now existing oranges would be lemons, according to the above definition, since they belong to a species (a natural kind) of which it was once believed that the normal members have the characteristics of yellow peel, lemon taste, etc.

Rather than try to complicate the definition still further, in the fashion of system-building philosophers, let us simply observe what has gone wrong. It is true – and this is what the new definition tries to reflect – that one possible use of a natural kind term is the following: to refer to a thing which belongs to a natural kind which does *not* fit the 'theory' associated with the natural kind term, but which was believed to fit that theory (and, in fact, to be *the* natural kind which fit the theory) when the theory had not yet been falsified. Even if cats turn out to be robots remotely controlled from Mars we will still call them 'cats'; even if it turns out that the stripes on tigers are painted on to deceive us, we will still call them 'tigers'; even if normal lemons are blue (we have been buying and raising very atypical lemons, but don't know it), they are still lemons (and so are the yellow ones.) Not only will we still *call* them 'cats', they are cats; not only will we still call them 'tigers', they are tigers; not only will we still call them 'lemons', they are lemons. But the fact that a term has several possible uses does not make it a disjunctive term; the mistake is in trying to represent the complex behavior of a natural kind word in something as simple as an analytic definition.

To say that an analytic definition is too simple a means of representation is not to say that no representation is possible. Indeed, a very simple representation is possible, namely:

lemon: natural kind word   associated characteristics:
yellow peel, tart taste, etc.

To fill this out, a lot more should be said about the linguistic behavior of natural kind words: but no more need be said about *lemon*.

Katz's theory of meaning

Carnap's view of meaning in natural language is this: we divide up logical space into 'logically possible worlds'. (That this may be highly language-relative, and that it may presuppose the very analytic–synthetic distinction he hopes to find by his quasi-operational procedure are objections he does not discuss.) The informant is asked whether or not he would say that something is the case in each logically possible world: the assumption being that (1) each logically possible world can be described clearly enough for the informant to tell; and (2) that the informant can say that the sentence in question is *true/false/not clearly either* just on the basis of the description of the logically possible world and the meaning (or 'intension') he assigns to the sentence in question. The latter assumption is false, as we have just seen, for just the reason that the traditional theory of meaning is false: even if I know the 'logically possible world' you have in mind, deciding whether or not something is, for example, a lemon, may require deciding what the best *theory* is; and this is not something to be determined by asking an informant yes/no questions in a rented office. This is not to say that 'lemon' has no meaning, of course: it is to say that meaning is not *that* simply connected with extension, even with 'extension in logically possible worlds'.

Carnap is not my main stalking-horse, however. The theory I want to focus on is the 'semantic theory' recently propounded by Jerrold Katz and his co-workers. In main outlines this theory is as follows:

(1) Each word has its meaning characterized by a string of 'semantic markers'.

(2) These markers stand for 'concepts' ('concepts' are themselves brain processes in Katz's philosophy of language; but I shall ignore this *jeu d'esprit* here). Examples of such concepts are: *unmarried, animate, seal*.

144

(3) Each such concept (concept for which a semantic marker is introduced) is a 'linguistic universal', and stands for an *innate* notion – one in some sense-or-other 'built into' the human brain.

(4) There are recursive rules – and this is the 'scientific' core of Katz's 'semantic theory' – whereby the 'readings' of whole sentences (these being likewise strings of markers) are derived from the meanings of the individual words and the deep structure (in the sense of transformational grammar) of the sentence.

(5) The scheme as a whole is said to be justified in what is said to be the manner of a scientific theory – by its ability to explain such things as our intuitions that certain sentences have more than one meaning, or the certain sentences are queer.

(6) Analyticity relations are also supposed to be able to be read off from the theory: for example, from the fact that the markers associated with 'unmarried' occur in connection with 'bachelor', one can see that 'all bachelors are unmarried' is analytic; and from the fact that the markers associated with 'animal' occur in connection with 'cat', one can see (allegedly) that 'all cats are animals' is analytic.

There are internal inconsistencies in this scheme which are apparent at once. For example, 'seal' is given as an example of a 'linguistic universal' (at least, 'seal' occurs as part of the 'distinguisher' in one reading for 'bachelor' – the variant reading: *young male fur seal*, in one of Katz's examples); but in no theory of human evolution is contact with seals universal. Indeed, even contact with *clothing*, or with *furniture*, or with *agriculture* is by no means universal. Thus we must take it that Katz means that whenever such terms occur they could be further analyzed into concepts which really are so primitive that a case could be made for their universality. Needless to say, this program has never been carried out, and he himself constantly ignores it in giving examples. But the point of greatest interest to us is that this scheme is an unsophisticated translation into 'mathematical' language of precisely the traditional theory that it has been our concern to criticize! Indeed, as far as general names are concerned, the only change is that whereas in the traditional account each general name was associated with a list of properties, in Katz's account each general name is associated with a list of *concepts*. It follows that each counterexample to the traditional theory is at once a counterexample also to Katz's theory. For example, if Katz lists the concept 'yellow' under the noun 'lemon', then he will be committed to 'all lemons are yellow'; if he lists the concept 'striped' under the noun 'tiger', then he will be committed to the analyticity of 'all tigers are striped'; and so on. Indeed, although Katz denies that his 'semantic markers' are themselves *words*, it is clear that they can be regarded as a kind of artificial language. Therefore, what Katz is saying is that:

(1) A mechanical scheme can be given for translating any natural language into this artificial 'marker language' (and this scheme is just what Katz's 'semantic theory' is).

(2) The string of markers associated with a word has exactly the meaning of the word.

If (1) and (2) were true, we would at once deduce that there exists a possible language – a 'marker language' – with the property that every word that human beings have invented or could invent has an analytic definition in that language. But this is something that we have every reason to disbelieve! In fact: (1) We have just seen that if our account of 'natural kind' words is correct, then none of these words has an analytic definition. In particular, a natural kind word will be analytically translatable into marker language only in the special case in which a marker happens to have been introduced with its exact meaning. (2) There are many words for which we haven't the foggiest notion what an analytic definition would even look like. What would an analytic definition of 'mammoth' look like? (Would Katz say that it is analytic that mammoths are extinct? Or that they have a certain kind of molar? These are the items mentioned in the dictionary!) To say that a word is the name of an extinct species of elephant is to exactly communicate the use of that word; but it certainly isn't an analytic definition (i.e. an analytically necessary and sufficient condition). (3) *Theoretical terms* in science have no analytic definitions, for reasons familiar to every reader of recent philosophy of science; yet these are surely items (and not atypical items) in the vocabulary of natural languages.

We have now seen, I believe, one reason for the recent lack of progress in semantic theory: you may dress up traditional mistakes in modern dress by talking of 'recursive rules' and 'linguistic universals', but they remain the traditional mistakes. The problem in semantic theory is to get away from the picture of the meaning of a word as something like a *list of concepts*; not to formalize that misguided picture.

Quine's pessimism

Quine has long expressed a profound pessimism about the very possibility of such a subject as 'semantic theory'. Certainly we cannot assume that *there is* a scientific subject to be constructed here just because ordinary people have occasion to use the word 'meaning' from time to time; that would be like concluding that there must be a scientific subject to be constructed which will deal with 'causation' just because ordinary people have occasion to use the word 'cause' from time to time. In one sense, *all* of science is a theory of causation; but not in the sense that it uses the word *cause*. Similarly, any successful and developed theory of language-use will in one sense be a theory of meaning; but not necessarily in the sense that it will employ any such notion as the 'meaning ' of a word or of an utterance. Elementary as this point is, it seems to be constantly overlooked in the social sciences, and people seem constantly to expect that psychology, for example, must talk of 'dislike', 'attraction', 'belief', etc., simply because ordinary men use these words in psychological description.

Quine's pessimism cannot, then, be simply dismissed; and as far as the utility of the traditional notion of 'meaning' is concerned, Quine may well turn out to be right. But we are still left with the task of trying to say what are the real problems in the area of language-use, and of trying to erect a conceptual framework within which we can begin to try to solve them.

Let us return to our example of the natural kind words. It is a fact, and one whose importance to this subject I want to bring out, that the use of words can be taught. If someone does not know the meaning of 'lemon', I can somehow convey it to him. I am going to suggest that in this simple phenomenon lies the problem, and hence the *raison d'être*, of 'semantic theory'.

How do I convey the meaning of the word 'lemon'? Very likely, I show the man a lemon. Very well, let us change the example. How do I convey the meaning of the word 'tiger'? *I tell him what a tiger is.*

It is easy to see that Quine's own theoretical scheme (in *Word and Object*) will not handle this case very well. Quine's basic notion is the notion of *stimulus meaning* (roughly this is the set of nerve-ending stimulations which will 'prompt assent' to *tiger*). But: (1) it is very unlikely that I convey exactly the stimulus-meaning that 'tiger' has in my idiolect; and (2) in any case I don't convey it directly, i.e. by describing it. In fact, I couldn't describe it. Quine also works with the idea of *accepted sentences*; thus he might try to handle this case somewhat as follows: 'the hearer in your example already shares a great deal of language with you; otherwise you couldn't tell him what a tiger is. When you "tell him what a tiger is", you simply tell him certain sentences that you accept. Once he knows what sentences you accept, naturally he is able to use the word, at least observation words.'

Let us, however, refine this last counter somewhat. If conveying the meaning of the word 'tiger' involved conveying the totality of accepted scientific theory about tigers, or even the totality of what I believe about tigers, then it would be an impossible task. It is true that when I tell someone what a tiger is I 'simply tell him certain sentences' – though not necessarily sentences I *accept*, except as descriptions of linguistically stereotypical tigers. But the point is, *which* sentences?

In the special case of such words as 'tiger' and 'lemon', we proposed an answer earlier in this paper. The answer runs as follows: there is somehow associated with the word 'tiger' a *theory*; not the actual theory we believe about tigers, which is very complex, but an oversimplified theory which describes a, so to speak, tiger *stereotype*. It describes, in the language we used earlier, a *normal member* of the natural kind. It is not necessary that we believe this theory, though in the case of 'tiger' we do. But it is necessary that we be aware that *this* theory is associated with the word: if our stereotype of a tiger ever changes, then the word 'tiger' will have changed its meaning. If, to change the example, lemons all turn blue, the word 'lemon' will not immediately change its meaning. When I first say, with surprise, 'lemons have all turned blue', lemon will still mean what it means now – which is to say that 'lemon' will still be associated with the stereotype *yellow lemon*, even though I will use the word to deny that lemons (even normal lemons) are in fact yellow. I can refer to a natural kind by a term which is 'loaded' with a theory which is known not to be any longer true of that natural kind, just because it will be clear to everyone that what I intend is to refer to *that* kind, and not to assert the theory. But, of course, if lemons really did turn blue (and stayed that way) then in time 'lemon' would come to have a meaning with the following representation:

lemon: natural kind word   associated   characteristics:
                               blue peel, tart taste, etc.

Then 'lemon' would have changed its meaning.

To sum this up: there are a few facts about 'lemon' or 'tiger' (I shall refer to them as *core facts*) such that one can convey the use of 'lemon' or 'tiger' by simply conveying those facts. More precisely, one cannot convey the approximate use *unless* one gets the core facts across.

Let me emphasize that this has the status of an empirical hypothesis. The hypothesis is that there are, in connection with almost any word (not just 'natural kind' words), certain core facts such that (1) one cannot convey the normal use of the word (to the satisfaction of native speakers) without conveying those core facts, and (2) in the case of many words and many speakers, conveying those core facts is sufficient to convey at least an approximation to the normal use. In the case of a natural kind word, the core facts are that a normal member of the kind has certain characteristics, or that this idea is at least the stereotype associated with the word.

If this hypothesis is false, then I think that Quine's pessimism is probably justified. But if this hypothesis is right, then I think it is clear what the problem of the theory of meaning is, regardless of whether or not one chooses to call it 'theory of *meaning*': the question is to explore and explain this empirical phenomenon. Questions which naturally arise are: what different kinds of words are associated with what different kinds of core facts? and by what mechanism does it happen that just conveying a small set of core facts brings it about that the hearer is able to imitate the normal use of a word?

Wittgensteinians, whose fondness for the expression 'form of life' appears to be directly proportional to its degree of preposterousness in a given context, say that acquiring the customary use of such a word as 'tiger' is coming to share a form of life. What they miss, or at any rate fail to emphasize, is that while the acquired disposition may be sufficiently complex and sufficiently interlinked with other complex dispositions to warrant special mention (though hardly the overblown phrase 'form of life'), what *triggers* the disposition is often highly discrete – e.g. a simple lexical definition frequently succeeds in conveying a pretty good idea of how a word is used. To be sure, as Wittgenstein emphasizes, this is only possible because we have a shared human nature, and because we have shared an acculturation process – there has to be a great deal of stage-setting before one can read a lexical definition and guess how a word is used. But in the process of 'debunking' this fact – the fact that something as simple as a lexical definition *can* convey the use of a word – they forget to be impressed by it. To be sure there is a great deal of stage-setting, but it is rarely stage-setting specifically designed to enable one to learn the use of *this* word. The fact that one *can* acquire the use of an indefinite number of new words, and on the basis of simple 'statements of what they mean', is an amazing fact: it is *the* fact, I repeat, on which semantic theory rests.

Sometimes it is said that the key problem in semantics is: how do we come to understand a new sentence? I would suggest that this is a far simpler (though not unimportant) problem. How logical words, for example, can be used to build up complex sentences out of simpler ones is easy to describe, at least in principle (of course, natural language analogues of logical words are far less tidy than the logical words of the mathematical logician), and it is also easy to say how the truth-conditions, etc., of the complex sentences are related to the truth-conditions of the sentences from which they were derived. This much *is* a matter of finding a structure of recursive rules with a suitable relation to the transformational grammar of the language in question. I would suggest that the question, How do we come to understand a new *word*? has far more to do with the whole phenomenon of giving definitions and writing dictionaries than the former question. And it is this phenomenon – the phenomenon of writing (and needing) dictionaries – that gives rise to the whole idea of 'semantic theory'.

Kinds of core facts

Let us now look a little more closely at the kind of information that one conveys when one conveys the meaning of a word. I have said that in the case of a 'natural kind' word one conveys the associated *stereotype*: the associated idea of the characteristics of a normal member of the kind. But this is not, in general, enough; one must also convey the extension, one must indicate *which* kind the stereotype is supposed to 'fit'.

From the point of view of any traditional meaning theory, be it Plato's or Frege's or Carnap's or Katz's, this is just nonsense. How can I 'convey' the extension of, say 'tiger'? Am I supposed to give you all the tigers in the world (heaven forfend!). I can convey the extension of a term only by giving a description of that extension; and then that description must be a 'part of the meaning', or else my definition will not be a meaning-statement at all. To say: 'I gave him certain conditions associated with the word, *and* I gave him the extension' (as if that weren't just giving *further* conditions) can only be nonsense.

The mistake of the traditional theorist lies in his attachment to the word 'meaning'. If giving the meaning is *giving* the *meaning*, then it is giving a definite thing; but giving the meaning isn't, as we shall see in a moment, giving some one definite thing. To drop the word 'meaning', which is here extremely misleading: there is no *one* set of facts which has to be conveyed to convey the normal use of a word; and taking account of this requires a complication in our notion of 'core facts'.

That the same stereotype might be associated with different kinds seems odd if the kind word one has in mind is 'tiger'; but change the example to, say, 'aluminum' and it will not seem odd at all. About all *I* know about aluminum is that it is a light metal, that it makes durable pots and pans, and that it doesn't appear to rust (although it does occasionally discolor). For all I know, every one of these characteristics may also fit molybdenum.

Suppose now that a colony of English-speaking Earthlings is leaving in a spaceship for a distant planet. When they arrive on their distant planet, they discover that no one remembers the atomic weight (or any other defining characteristic) of aluminum, nor the atomic weight (or other characteristic) of molybdenum. There is some aluminum in the spacecraft, and some molybdenum. Let us suppose that they guess which is which, and they guess wrong. Henceforth, they use 'aluminum' as the name for molybdenum, and 'molybdenum' as the name for aluminum. It is clear that 'aluminum' has a different meaning in this community than in ours: in fact, it means *molybdenum*. Yet how can this be? Didn't they possess the normal 'linguistic competence'? Didn't they all 'know the meaning of the word "aluminum"'?

Let us duck this question for a moment. If I want to make sure that the word 'aluminum' will continue to be used in what counts as a 'normal' way by the colonists in my example, it will suffice to give them some test for aluminum (or just to give them a carefully labelled sample, and let them discover a test, if they are clever enough). Once they know how to *tell* aluminum from other metals, they will go on using the word with the correct extension as well as the correct 'intension' (i.e. the correct stereotype). But notice: it does not matter *which* test we give the colonists. The test isn't part of the meaning; but that there be some test or other (or something, e.g. a sample, from which one might be derived), is necessary to preservation of 'the normal usage'. Meaning indeed determines extension; but only because extension (fixed by *some* test or other) is, in some cases, 'part of the meaning'.

There are two further refinements here: if we give them a test, they mustn't make it part of the stereotype – that would be a change of meaning. (Thus it's better if they don't all *know* the test; as long as only experts do, and the average speaker 'asks an expert' in case of doubt, the criteria mentioned in the test can't infect the stereotype.) Asking an expert is enough of a test for the normal speaker; that's why we don't give a test in an ordinary context.

We can now modify our account of the 'core facts' in the case of a natural kind word as follows: (1) The core facts are the stereotype *and the extension*. (2) Nothing normally need be said about the extension, however, since the hearer knows that he can always consult an expert if any question comes up. (3) In special cases – such as the case of colonists – there may be danger that the word will get attached to the wrong natural kind, even though the right stereotype is associated with it. In such cases, one must give some way of getting the extension right, but no one *particular* way is necessary.

In the case of 'lemon' or 'tiger' a similar problem comes up. It is logically possible (although empirically unlikely, perhaps) that a species of fruit biologically unrelated to lemons might be indistinguishable from lemons in taste and appearance. In such a case, there would be two possibilities: (1) to call them *lemons*, and thus let 'lemon' be a word for any one of a number of natural kinds; or (2) to say that they are not lemons (which is what, I suspect, biologists would decide to do). In the latter case, the problems are exactly the same as with *aluminum*: to be sure one has the 'normal usage' or 'customary meaning' or whatever, one has to be sure one has the right extension.

The problem: that giving the extension is part of giving the meaning arises also in the case of names of sensible qualities, e.g. colors. Here, however, it is normal to give the extension by giving a sample, so that the person learning the word learns to recognize the quality in the normal way. Frequently it has been regarded a defect of *dictionaries* that they are 'cluttered up' with color samples, and with stray pieces of empirical information (e.g. the atomic weight of aluminum), not sharply distinguished from 'purely linguistic' information. The burden of the present discussion is that this is no defect at all, but essential to the function of conveying the core facts in each case.

Still other kinds of words may be mentioned in passing. In the case of 'one-criterion' words (words which possess an analytical necessary and sufficient condition) it is obvious why the core fact is just the analytical necessary and sufficient condition, e.g. 'man who has never been married', in the case of 'bachelor'). In the case of 'cluster' words (e.g. the name of a disease which is known not to have any one underlying cause), it is obvious why the core facts are just the typical symptoms or elements of the cluster; and so on. Given the *function* of a kind of word, it is not difficult to explain why certain facts function as core facts for conveying the use of words of that kind.

The possibility of semantics

Why, then, is semantics so hard? In terms of the foregoing, I want to suggest that semantics is a typical social science. The sloppiness, the lack of precise theories and laws, the lack of mathematical rigor, are all characteristic of the social sciences today. A general and precise theory which answers the questions (1) why do words have the different sorts of functions they do? and (2) exactly how does conveying core facts enable one to learn the use of a word? is not to be expected until one has a general and precise model of a language-user; and that is still a long way off. But the fact that Utopia is a long way off does not mean that daily life should come to a screeching halt. There is plenty for us to investigate, in our sloppy and impressionistic fashion, and there are plenty of real results to be obtained. The first step is to free ourselves from the oversimplifications foisted upon us by the tradition, and to see where the real problems lie. I hope this paper has been a contribution to that first step.

9

The refutation of conventionalism*

I shall discuss conventionalism in Quine's writings on the topic of radical translation, and in the writings of Reichenbach and Grünbaum on the nature of geometry.

Let me say at the outset that Quine and Reichenbach are the two philosophers who have had the greatest influence on my own philosophical work. If Quine's ideas have not had the full influence they deserve, it may be in part because of the intensely paradoxical nature of the doctrines put forward – or seemingly put forward – in *Word and Object*. The doctrines of *Word and Object* – in particular the impossibility of radical translation – look wrong to many philosophers. Since these doctrines are thought by Quine himself to follow from the doctrines put forward in 'Two dogmas of empiricism', they cast doubt on 'Two dogmas' itself. My contention here will be that the impossibility of radical translation does not follow from the critique of the analytic-synthetic distinction. I believe that Quine is right in his critique of the analytic-synthetic distinction, but wrong in his argument for the impossibility of radical translation. By showing that one does not have to accept Quine's arguments for the impossibility of radical translation, I hope, therefore, to clarify just what it is in Quine's work that is true and important.

Similarly, I think that Reichenbach understood the importance of non-Euclidean geometry for epistemology as it has not been understood by philosophers in general to the present day. I think that he understood the issues surrounding the verifiability theory of meaning in his book *Experience and Prediction* far more deeply than they have been generally understood, and I think his writings on the philosophical foundations of induction clarify the nature of the problems in an unparalleled way, even if Reichenbach's particular solutions cannot be accepted. In Reichenbach's case too, it is a peculiar kind of conventionalism that seems to flow from his work that has led philosophers to downgrade him or even to dismiss him as just a 'positivist'. Again, I

* First published in M. Munitz (ed.) *Semantics and Meaning* (New York, 1975). Reprinted by permission of New York University Press.

think this conventionalism need not, in fact, follow from Reichenbach's work, and does not follow from the best of his work, and that separating the wheat from the chaff in Reichenbach's work may enable his work too to achieve the philosophical influence that it so richly deserves.

One last preliminary remark: in one respect the situation is more complicated with respect to the views of both of these men than the preceding remarks would indicate. With respect to Quine, the situation is so confused that one perhaps should distinguish between *two* Quines – $Quine_1$ and $Quine_2$. $Quine_1$ is the Quine who everybody thinks wrote *Word and Object*. That is to say the Quine whose supposed proof of the impossibility of radical translation, of the impossibility of there being a unique correct translation between radically different and unrelated languages is discussed in journal article after journal article and the topic of at least fifty per cent of graduate student conversation nowadays. $Quine_2$ is the far more subtle and guarded Quine who defended his formulations in *Word and Object* recently at the Conference on Philosophy of Language at Storrs. In the light of what Quine said at Storrs, I am inclined to think that *Word and Object* may have been widely misinterpreted. At any rate, Quine seems to think that *Word and Object* has been widely misinterpreted, although he was charitable enough to take some of the blame himself for his own formulations. In what follows, then, I shall be criticizing the views of $Quine_1$, even if $Quine_1$ is a cultural figment, not to be identified with the Willard Van Orman Quine who teaches philosophy at Harvard. It is the views of $Quine_1$ that are generally attributed to Willard Van Orman Quine, and it is worthwhile showing what is wrong with those views. If I can have the help of $Quine_2$ – of Willard Van Orman Quine himself – in refuting the views of $Quine_1$, then so much the better.

There is a similar problem with respect to the work of Reichenbach. The arguments for the conventionality of geometry that are widely attributed to Reichenbach do not, in fact, appear in the writings of Reichenbach. They appear rather in the writings of Adolf Grünbaum. The conclusions that Reichenbach himself draws from his analysis of the status of geometry in the last pages of *Philosophy of Space and Time* are not only different from Grünbaum's, they are quite incompatible with Grünbaum's. Thus here too we have to distinguish between two Reichenbachs: $Reichenbach_1$, alias Adolf Grünbaum, and $Reichenbach_2$, alias Hans Reichenbach. In what follows, it will be the views of $Reichenbach_1$, that is, Adolf Grünbaum, that I shall be concerned to refute. At the end of this essay I will say something about the views of both $Quine_2$ and $Reichenbach_2$.

The strategy of this paper

The strategy of this paper is to try and show that a single argument underlies the work of both Grünbaum and Quine$_1$. That this is even something that could be true is not evident on the surface. At first blush, Grünbaum's writings on the Philosophy of Space and Time, like those of Hans Reichenbach, appear to be full of extremely substantive and topic-specific considerations. The arguments seem to depend on facts about space. Similarly, Quine's writings on radical translation are imbedded in the context of linguistic theory, or at least in the context of philosophical discussion of linguistic theory. There is a great deal of talk about linguistic questions, such as the nature of grammaticality, the nature of language, psychology of language learning, etc. All of these considerations appear to be topic-specific to linguistics and philosophy of language. But topic-specificity can be an illusion. One of the accomplishments of the axiomatic method in mathematics has been to bring out a sense in which the same proof may occur in what look like totally different areas of mathematics. Once we see the structure of a mathematical argument, we may often see that the conclusion depended on very little that was specific to one mathematical domain as opposed to another. I am going to argue here that here is a general *conventionalist ploy* which appears in many many different areas of philosophy, and that the conclusions of Quine and Grünbaum do not in fact depend on any specific facts about space or about geometry, but are simply instances of this same conventionalist ploy. I shall also argue that the ploy is fallacious, and that the conclusions to which it leads should be viewed as suspect in every area of philosophy.

Reichenbach and Grünbaum on space and time

Reichenbach used to begin his lectures on the Philosophy of Space and Time in a way which already brought an air of paradox to the subject. He would take two objects of markedly different size, say an ash tray and a table, situated in different parts of the room, and ask the students 'How do you know that one is bigger than the other?'

The students would propose various ways of establishing this, and Reichenbach would criticize each of these proposed tests. For example, a student might suggest that one could simply *measure* the ash tray and *measure* the table, and thus verify that the ash tray is smaller than the table. Then, Reichenbach would ask the student, 'How do we know that the measuring rod stays the same length when transported?' Or, someone might say that we can simply *see* that the table is larger than the ash tray, but then Reichenbach would point out that sight is reliable only if light travels in straight lines. Perhaps light travels in curved paths in such a way that the table, although the same size as the ash tray, or even smaller than the ash tray, does not look smaller than the ash tray. Or someone might propose, again, to bring the ash tray over to the table. When we set the ash tray down on the table, we see that the ash tray is clearly smaller than the table. This assumes the stipulation that if one object coincides with any proper part of another, then the first object is smaller than the second.

Granting this as a definition, or partial definition, of 'smaller than' in the case of objects which are together, i.e. actually touching in an appropriate way, then we have only established that the ash tray is smaller than the table when the ash tray is actually touching the table. How do we know that the ash tray is smaller than the table when the ash tray and the table are separated?

The question reduces to the question 'How do we know that the ash tray doesn't change size when transported?' which is just the question we had about the measuring rod. It might be objected that when I move the measuring rod or the ash tray around the room, say, I carry them around the room in my hand, I do not feel the ash tray or the measuring rod get larger or smaller. But perhaps my hand gets larger or smaller, and that is why I don't feel a difference!

One might try to rule out this whole line of questioning on some *a priori* philosophical ground or other, e.g. 'the series of questions has to come to an end'. But it is necessary to be careful here. The series of questions Reichenbach is asking is formally just the same as the series of questions that Einstein asked about 'How do we ever know that two events at a distance happened simultaneously?' It cannot be in principle illegitimate to ask such questions or even to push them back and back as Einstein and Reichenbach did. And the Einstein example shows that this kind of epistemological questioning can have great value, at least in exposing hidden presuppositions of everyday discourse, and perhaps, as Einstein and Reichenbach thought, in exposing definitional elements in what we mistakenly take to be purely factual statements as well. Reichenbach's conclusion, from his own line of questioning, was that the statement that the measuring rod stays the same length when transported cannot be *proved* without vicious circularity. And he proposed that this statement or some such statement must be regarded as a *definitional element* in geometrical theory. We naively think that it is a matter of fact that watches run at the same rate when transported, and that measuring rods stay the same length when transported. Neither statement can be maintained to be true without qualification in a relativistic world, as Einstein showed, and in a Newtonian world, or in a world in which all objects are transported at the same rate relative to some fixed inertial system, the two statements can be maintained to be true only in the sense of being adopted as a definition, according to Reichenbach and according to Einstein, at least on Reichenbach's reading of Einstein.

At this point let me leave the views of Reichensbach$_2$ – that is, Reichenbach, and move to the views of Reichenbach$_1$ – that is, Grünbaum. The conclusion that Grünbaum draws from the situation just described is the following:

There are certain axioms that any concept of distance, that is to say any *metric*, has to satisfy. For example, *for any point* x *in the space, the distance from* x *to* x *is zero*; *for any points* x *and* y *in the space, the distance from* x *to* y *equals the distance from* y *to* x; *for any three points in the space* x, y, z, *the distance from* x *to* y *plus the distance from* y *to* z *is greater than or equal to the distance from* x *to* z; *distance is always a non-negative number*; *the distance from* x *to* y *is zero if and only if* x *is identical with* y. But any continuous space that can be metricized at all, i.e. over which it is possible to define a concept of distance satisfying these and similar axioms, can be metricized in infinitely many different ways.

Now, let S be a space which is homeomorphic to Euclidean space, and let M_1 and M_2 be metrics such that S is Euclidean relative to M_1 and S is Lobachevskian relative to M_2. Grünbaum's conclusion, based largely although not exclusively on Reichenbach's discussion, is that there is no fact of the matter as to whether S is Euclidean or Lobachevskian or neither. The choice of a metric is a matter of convention. The space S cannot 'intrinsically' have metric M_1 rather than M_2, or M_2 rather than M_1. If we adopt a convention according to which M_1 is the metric for the space S, then the statement 'S is Euclidean' will be true. If we adopt a convention according to which M_2 is the metric for the space S, then the statement 'S is Lobachevskian' will be true.

Let me emphasize that Grünbaum is *not* saying that any two metrics will lead to equally simple physical laws, or that any two metrics are such that it would be *feasible* to use either one in everyday determinations of distance. It is possible that the world be such that if we use the metric M_1, then the laws of nature would assume, let us say, a Newtonian form. If we then went over to a metric M_2, according to which the space is Lobachevskian, the laws of nature would become incredibly complicated. It is even likely that everyday questions about distance, e.g. 'What is the distance from my house to my car?' could not be feasibly answered if we went over to the metric M_2. Nevertheless, Grünbaum insists, this does not show that the metric M_2 is somehow not the true metric of the space S, or that in some sense the metric M_1 *is* the true metric of the space S.

Secondly, it should be emphasized that Grünbaum is not just talking about space in the sense of ordinary three-dimensional space. Although most of his examples are drawn from this case, he means his remarks to apply just as well to the question of the metricization of space–time. In a relativistic world, there is indeed a sense in which the choice of the metric for just three dimensional space is relative. But the choice of a metric for space–time – that is, the choice of a g_{ik} tensor – is not ordinarily regarded as a matter of convention. But Grünbaum has emphasized that in his view this is a matter of convention just as the choice of a metric for space in a Newtonian world is, in his view, a matter of convention.

Since the gravitational field is identified with the g_{ik} tensor by Einstein, it follows that there is, in Grünbaum's view, no fact of the matter as to which is the correct equation for the gravitational field. The choice of a nonstandard g_{ik} tensor would lead to an immensely complicated form for the law of gravitation. Very likely, space–time distance could not practically be computed using such a tensor, i.e. it would be totally unfeasible to use it in practice. Nevertheless, in Grünbaum's view, there would be no sense in which our space–time objectively did not have such a nonstandard g_{ik} tensor, and there is no sense in which our space–time objectively does have the standard g_{ik} tensor.†

† My criticisms of Grünbaum's views are presented at length in Putnam (1963). Grünbaum replies to these criticisms in Grünbaum (1968) chapter III. I have not previously replied to Grünbaum's rejoinder, because I felt that, although it clears up some misunderstandings (e.g. the status, in Grünbaum's view, of the law $F = ma$), it does not answer the main criticisms made in my paper. But, for the purpose of the present paper, let me consider Grünbaum's treatment of the question of the conventionality of the space–time metric in the GTR (General Theory of Relativity) in his reply to my paper. This is a clear consequence of Grünbaum's view: *any* continuous space can be metricized in more than one way, and for *any* continuous space, the choice of a metric is a matter of convention (according to Grünbaum). Since the 4-space of general relativity is a continuous space, the conventionality of *its* metric is an immediate consequence of his thesis. Moreover, this consequence is explicitly drawn by Grünbaum himself: 'what does impress me, in concert with Riemann and Clifford, is that *after* the term "congruent" is already preempted to mean extensional equality, there is nothing in the nature of the continuous physical manifolds which would require us to *ascribe congruence*, i.e. *spatial* or *spatiotemporal equality*, to certain disjoint intervals as opposed to others.' (Grünbaum, 1968, p. 226). I argued in my paper that this consequence is unacceptable, for reasons similar to those given in the present paper.

Grünbaum's reply was to reiterate that the choice of a metric is a matter of convention ('descriptive simplicity'), while accusing me of saddling him with the view that it is not *simpler* to use the standard g_{ik} tensor: 'Nothing in this [Grünbaum's conception] precludes the use of the criterion of *descriptive simplicity* and *convenience* to employ a particular kind of metrization, and thereby to select a unique class of classes of congruent intervals to the exclusion of others in certain theoretical contexts.' (Putnam, 1963, p. 219, italics mine.) Yet on p. 209 Grünbaum has written: 'It is now

Radical translation

Chapter 2 of Quine's *Word and Object* contains what may well be the most fascinating and the most discussed philosophical argument since Kant's Transcendental Deduction of the Categories. On one page, Quine – evidently Quine$_1$ – writes 'There can be no doubt that rival systems of analytical hypotheses can fit the totality of dispositions to speech behavior as well, and still specify mutually incompatible translations of countless sentences insusceptible of independent control.' But a bit of explanation is in order.

Quine is talking here about the following context. A linguist is trying to translate an alien language into his home language. The two languages are supposed not to be cognate. Also the two linguistic communities are supposed to have a minimum of shared culture. In particular, there is no standard translation from the alien language into the home language. The alien language is often thought of by Quine as a primitive language, a 'jungle' language, which is being translated for the first time. A translation manual is called by Quine an analytical hypothesis. Constructing a translation manual in such a context is undertaking the enterprise Quine calls *radical translation*.

Quine's procedure will be reviewed only very sketchily here. What Quine does is to assume that we can somehow identify *assent* and *dissent* in an alien language. *Modulo* this assumption, he argues that we can at least riskily identify *truth functions* in an alien language. We can distinguish *occasion sentences*, sentences such as 'This is a chair' to which some stimulations prompt assent, and other stimulations prompt dissent, and distinguish them from *standing sentences* – sentences such as 'Australia is in the Southern Hemisphere'. Standing sentences have the property that speakers, once they have been prompted to assent to them or dissent from them, continue to assent to them or dissent from them without further immediate stimulation from the environment.

Quine's central theoretical notion in this chapter is the notion of

plain that nothing about my claim that the insight contained in Riemann's doctrine has substantial relevance to the GTR requires that there be alternative *space–time* congruences *in addition to* the undeniably present alternative time congruences and alternative space congruences. And, as will become clear in the sequel, Riemann's conception accommodates the GTR's unique space–time congruences as well as the alternative congruences of time and space.' In fact, what 'becomes clear in the sequel' is that 'Riemann's insight' *does* require that there be 'alternative space–time congruences', but that one choice of a metric may be 'descriptively simpler'. Thus, on p. 217 Grünbaum states explicitly: 'If the term "transport" is suitably generalized so as to pertain as well to the extrinsic metric standards applied to intervals of time and of space–time respectively, then this claim of conventionality holds not only for time but also *mutatis mutandis* for the *space–time continuum* of *punctual events*!' (emphasis in the original).

stimulus meaning. The stimulus meaning of a sentence is identified by Quine with the set of stimulations of a native speaker's nerve endings which would *prompt assent* to the sentence in question. Two sentences have the same stimulus meaning for a speaker if the same stimulations would prompt assent to each of the two sentences. A sentence is *stimulus analytic* for a speaker if he assents to it under all possible conditions of stimulation, *stimulus contradictory* if he dissents from it under all possible conditions of stimulation.

Our previous definition of the occasion sentence may be restated in terms of the notion of stimulus meaning. Thus: a sentence is an occasion sentence if a speaker assents to it or dissents from it just in case a stimulation in its stimulus meaning (respectively, the stimulus meaning of its negation), is presented within a certain time interval, the modulus of stimulation. Quine ingeniously proposes to define the *observation sentences* as those sentences which are (1) occasion sentences and (2) possess *intersubjective stimulus meaning*. In other words, *a sentence is an observation sentence just in case it is an occasion sentence and it has the same stimulus meaning for every speaker of the linguistic community*.

We may now say just what an *analytical hypothesis* is in a more technical way. An analytical hypothesis is a general recursive function whose domain is the set of all sentences of the alien language, and whose range is a subset, possibly a proper subset, of the set of all sentences of the home language, and which has the following properties. (1) if a is an observation sentence of the alien language, then $f(a)$ is an observation sentence of the home language, and $f(a)$ has the same stimulus meaning for speakers of the home language as a does for speakers of the alien language. (2) f commutes with truth functions, that is to say, $f(a \lor b)$ equals $f(a) \lor f(b)$, etc. (3) if a is a stimulus analytic (respectively, stimulus contradictory) sentence of the alien language, then $f(a)$ is a stimulus analytic (respectively, stimulus contradictory) sentence of the home language. If the linguist is bilingual, then condition (1) can be strengthened to condition (1'): if a is an occasion sentence of the alien language, then $f(a)$ is an occasion sentence of the home language, and the stimulus meaning of a for the linguist is the same as the stimulus meaning of $f(a)$ for the linguist. These are, in my paraphrase, Quine's conditions (1)–(4), (1')–(4) of chapter 2.

The thrust of chapter 2 is as follows: first Quine says in the sentence quoted above that it is possible to have 'rival' analytical hypotheses which 'fit the totality of speech behavior to perfection' and which 'still specify mutually incompatible translations of countless sentences insusceptible of independent control'. Now let f_1 and f_2 be two such rival analytical hypotheses. Then Quine's view is that there is no 'fact of the matter' as to whether the translations provided by f_1 are the correct translations from the alien language into the home language, or whether the translations provided by f_2 are the correct translations from the alien language into the home language. There is no such thing as correct translation in any absolute sense. The notion of correct translation has to be relativized to an analytical hypothesis. The translations provided by f_1 are the correct translation relative to f_1, tautologically. And similarly the translations provided by f_2 are the correct translations relative to f_2, tautologically. Although Quine does not put it that way, he might have summed this up, or at any rate Quine_1 might well have summed this up by saying that *the choice of an analytical hypothesis is a matter of convention.*

The conventionalist ploy

What is the common structure to the argument of Grünbaum and the argument of Quine_1? Each argument falls into the following normal form: a set of conditions is given which (partly) specifies the extension of a notion. In the case of geometry, these conditions are the axioms which must be satisfied by a metric. In the case of radical translation, these conditions are Quine's conditions (1)–(4) or (1')–(4) plus the condition that the function f, that is, the translation manual, be general recursive. Secondly, a claim is made that the conditions given *exhaust* the content of the notion being analyzed. Grünbaum emphasizes again and again† that any notion of distance that satisfies the axioms for a metric is equally entitled to be termed *distance*, and equally entitled in a particular case, to be termed the distance from an object x or point x to an object or point y.

In *Word and Object*, it is *not* claimed that conditions (1)–(4) 'cover all

† E.g. Grünbaum writes, (Grünbaum, 1968, pp. 248–9): 'Putnam is insensitive to the fact that whereas the meaning of "congruent" has been changed with respect to the *extension* of the term [when we go over to a different metric – H.P.], its meaning has not changed at all with respect to designating a spatial equality relation!... According to [the classical] account, the intension of a term determines its extension uniquely. But the fact that "being spatially congruent" means sustaining the relation of spatial equality does not suffice at all to determine its extension uniquely in the class of spatial intervals. In the face of the classical account, this nonuniqueness prompted me to refrain from saying that the relation of spatial equality is the "intension" of "spatially congruent"; by the same token, I refrained from saying that the latter term has the same intension in the context of a nonstandard metric as when used with a standard metric. But since the use of "spatially congruent" in conjunction with *any one* of the metrics $ds^2 = g_{ik}dx^i dx^k$ does mean sustaining the spatial equality relation, I shall refer to this fact by saying that "congruent" has the same "nonclassical intension" in any of these uses.'

available evidence'. For as Quine remarks, the linguist can go bilingual, and thus avail himself of (1')–(4) instead of (1)–(4) as constraints on an analytical hypothesis. But (1')–(4) are supposed (by Quine₁, anyway) to exhaust all the possible evidence for an analytical hypothesis. This seems to be implicit in the statement on page 71 'Even our bilingual, when he brings off translations not allowed for under (1')–(3), must do so essentially by the method of analytical hypotheses, however unconscious'. It looks implicit again on page 72 when Quine₁ writes 'and yet countless native sentences, admitting no independent check, not falling under (1')–(3), may be expected to receive radically unlike and incompatible English renderings under the two systems'. (Note the identification of 'admitting no independent check' and 'not falling under (1')–(3)'. And the claim that (1')–(4) (or (1')–(3), since (4) has been dropped as superfluous) are all the 'independent checks' there are, seems to be made implicitly once more on page 74 when Quine, in the process of listing causes of 'failure to appreciate the point' writes 'A fifth cause is that linguists adhere to implicit supplementary canons that help to limit their choice of analytical hypotheses. For example, if a question were to arise of equating a short locution of "rabbit" and a long one to "rabbit part" or vice versa, they would favor the former course, arguing that the more conspicuously segreted wholes are likelier to bear the simple terms. Such an implicit canon is all very well, *unless mistaken for a substantive law of speech behavior.*') (Our italics)

Once a set of constraints has been postulated as determining the content of the notion in question – the notion of *distance* or of *metric*, in the case of geometry; the notion of *analytical hypothesis*, or more coloquially *translation*, in the case of linguistics – a proof is given that the constraints in question do not determine the extension of the notion in question. There can be two or more different metrics which assign different distances to the same intervals, and which satisfy the axioms for a metric; there can be rival analytical hypotheses which specify incompatible translations and which conform to (1')–(3), or (1')–(4).

As a final step, the claim is advanced that whenever there are incompatible objects that satisfy the constraints given, then there is no fact of the matter as to which of the objects is the correct one. There is no fact of the matter as to which of the two metrics is the correct one provided they both agree with the topology of the space in question; there is no fact of the matter as to which of the two analytical hypotheses is the correct one as long as they both conform to (1')–(3), or (1')–(4).

The structure of the argument shows what is wrong with the argument, I think. *Conventionalism is at bottom a form of essentialism.* It is not usually identified as essentialism because it is a favorite of reductionist philosophers, and we think of reductionist philosophers as anti-essentialists, and anti-reductionist philosophers as essentialists. Nevertheless, it *is* a form of essentialism, even if it is not one with which Plato or Aristotle would have been happy.

What the conventionalist does is to claim that certain constraints *exhaust the meaning* of the notion he is analyzing. He claims to intuit not just that the constraints in question – the axioms for a metric or Quine's conditions $(1')$–(3) or $(1')$–(4) – are *part* of the meaning of the notion of a metric or of the notion of an analytical hypothesis, but that *any further condition* that one might suggest *would definitely not be part of the meaning* of the notion in question, and also *would not be a 'substantive law'* about the notion in question (since a 'substantive law' would presuppose that the extension of the notion in question had somehow been fixed, and the conventionalist intuits that there is nothing to fix it beyond the conditions that he lists). Once we recognize that this is the structure of the conventionalist argument we can also detect it in many other areas of philosophy.

Consider *emotivism* in ethics, by way of example. The emotivist claims that ethical sentences typically have some emotive force. He intuits that a certain standard emotive force is part of the meaning of ethical sentences. It is part of the meaning of 'That was a good thing you did' when uttered in a moral context that the speaker feels approval, or that the speaker is performing an act of 'Commending' or something of that kind. Notice, however, that even if this is right, typical emotivist conclusions – e.g. that ethical sentences lack truth value – do not follow from this. Emotivism derives its punch from a further claim – the claim that the emotive force of ethical sentences *exhausts their content*. The emotivist claims to intuit not only that ethical sentences have a certain emotive meaning, but that any descriptive component that might be proposed is *not* part of their meaning.

This is hardly an empirical claim. It may well be that actions satisfying certain descriptions, e.g. *torturing small children just for the fun of it*, are universally despised and condemned. *Even so*, the emotivist insists that it would be a *mistake* to regard it as part of the meaning of an ethical sentence to the effect that a certain action is good or permissible or not wrong. That it does not satisfy one of those descriptions is *simply not part of the content* of the ethical sentences in question, even if the factual claim that *the act commended does not satisfy any one of those descriptions* is universally understood to be conversationally implicated by the ethical sentence. No descriptive component is or could be part of the meaning of an ethical sentence. Also, an ethical sentence could not, just as a matter of fact, have a descriptive truth condition. For to say that it has certain truth conditions, as a fact and not as a matter of its meaning, would presuppose that its extension has somehow been fixed, and there is nothing to fix the extension of an ethical term other than its meaning, and its emotive meaning exhausts its meaning.

We see now why conventionalism is not usually recognized as essentialism. It is not usually recognized as essentialism because it is *negative* essentialism. Essentialism is usually criticized because the essentialist *intuits too much*. He claims to see that *too many* properties are part of a concept. The negative essentialist, the conventionalist, intuits not that a great many strong properties are part of a concept, but that only a few *could be* part of a concept. But he still makes an essentialist claim.

The refutation of conventionalism

Once we understand the structure of the conventionalist argument, we also perceive the difficulty in which the conventionalist lands himself. In one respect, it is a triviality that language is conventional. It is a triviality that we might have meant something other than we do by the noises that we use. The noise 'pot' could have meant what is in fact meant by the word 'dog', and the word 'dog' could have meant what is in fact meant by the word 'fish'.

Let us call this kind of conventionality TSC (Trivial Semantic Conventionality). Grünbaum emphasizes that he does not intend the thesis of the conventionality of the choice of a metric to be an instance of TSC. The thesis that there is no fact of the matter as to whether *distance* is *distance as defined by the metric M_1 or distance as defined by the metric M_2*, is not to be interpreted as meaning that the word 'distance' might have been assigned to a different magnitude, as, for example, 'pressure' might have been assigned to *temperature*, and 'temperature' might have been assigned to *pressure*. The thesis is rather that, even *given* what we mean by 'distance', there is no fact of the matter as to which is the true distance. And certainly $Quine_1$ does not think he is telling us that 'translation' might have meant, e.g. *postage stamp*. The question is just this: *can* the conventionalist successfully defend the thesis that the choice of a metric or the choice of a translation manual is a matter of convention, and *not* have this thesis be either false or truistic, that is, be either false or an instance of TSC? In my opinion he cannot. The conventionalist fails precisely because of an insight of Quine's. That is the insight that *meaning*, in the sense of reference, is a function of theory,† and that the enterprise of trying to list the statements containing a term which are true by virtue of its meaning, let alone to give a list of statements which *exhausts* its meaning, is a futile one. If Quine is right in this, and I think he is, then there is no reason, given the problem that Reichenbach so brilliantly sets before us, why we have to opt for a conventionalist solution. Reichenbach convincingly shows that reference is not, so to speak, an act of God. We cannot suppose that the term 'distance' intrinsically refers to one physical magnitude rather than another. But its reference need not be fixed by a convention. It can be fixed by *coherence*.

Let us try to formulate total science in such a way as to maximize internal and external coherence. By *internal coherence* I mean such matters as simplicity, and agreement with intuition. By external coherence, I mean agreement with experimental checks. Grünbaum certainly has not *proved* that there are two such formulations of total science leading to two different metrics for physical space–time. And Quine$_1$ certainly has not *proved* that there are two distinct analytical hypotheses both in agreement with a maximally simple and intuitive psychology, linguistic theory, etc.

Thus, consider the following case: Suppose metric M_1 is one which

† This insight must not be confused with Feyerabend's position, that a term cannot have the same reference in substantially different theories ('incommensurability'). Thus, let T_1 and T_2 be two theories containing the word 'eau'. T_1 and T_2 may be *very* different theories; yet the best translation of 'eau' into *our* language may well be 'water' in both cases. If we accept the statement that water is H_2O, then we will say that

'eau' in T_1 refers to H_2O

and also that

'eau' in T_2 refers to H_2O

even if this contradicts T_1 or T_2. Theory *helps* to determine translation; but translation does not have to make *all* of a theory come out *true*. Thus change of theory does not always imply change of extension. (I agree with Quine that to ask when a change in theory is a change in *intension* is a bad question.)

Moreover, in translating a term, we may take into account not just the theory of the speaker, but the theory of other speakers to whom the speaker is causally linked. Thus, this kind of 'theory dependence' of reference is not incompatible with the sort of causal theory of reference for magnitude terms suggested in chapter 11 in this volume.

Coming to the geometry case: suppose Oscar accepts just the atomic statements about 'distance' that we accept about $f(x,y,z,t,x',y',z',t')$, where x,y,z,t and x',y',z',t' are the coordinates of the points, and f satisfies the axioms for a metric. Suppose also, that Oscar accepts $f = ma$, that he postulates strange forces acting on measuring rods in order to preserve the statement that 'distance $= f(x,y,z,t,x',y',z',t')$', etc. Finally, suppose that Oscar is 'bilingual' relative to us, and he *tells* us that when he says 'distance' he means distance, that his theory is *right* and ours is *wrong*, etc. In this case we will decide that Charity begins at home, and choose homophonic translation. We will say that Oscar's word 'distance' refers to distance in *our* sense, and that Oscar's theory is just false.

If asked, 'How do you know it's false?' (given that Oscar's theory doesn't imply any false predictions), we will point to the fact that Oscar's theory assumes *improbably* leads to a Newtonian physics for the entire world. Suppose that metric M_2 leads to a physics according to which all objects are contracting towards the center of a certain sphere at a uniform rate. This contraction is undetectable because, according to the physics based on the metric M_2, measuring rods themselved are contracting at the same rate. The universal contraction affects all measuring rods in the same way. A measuring rod made of jelly is deformed by the *universal force* that we postulate to account for the contraction to exactly the same extent as a measuring rod made of steel, not withstanding its much lower resistance to deformation. The laws of the physics based on the metric M_2 are infinitely more complicated than the laws of the physics based upon the metric M_1. The fundamental principles of the physics based on the metric M_2 – the existence of universal forces, and the universal contraction towards the center of the sphere – are totally counter-intuitive; and distances according to the metric M_2 cannot be computed in practice, and are totally unusable in practice.

According to Grünbaum, there is no fact of the matter as to which is the true geometry plus physics – the conjunction of the metric M_1 with the physics based upon the metric M_1, or the conjunction of the metric M_2 with the physics based upon M_2. If, however, coherence can determine *reference*, then why should we not say that in a world one of whose admissible descriptions is the metric M_1 and the physics based upon the metric M_1, the distance according to the metric M_1 is what we

complicated mechanisms. In short, speaking from the perspective of *our* theory, we will say that Oscar is wrong and our theory is *truer*, not just *descriptively simpler* – i.e. there is a 'fact of the matter', and simplicity is here one indicator of *truth*.

On the other hand, if Oscar himself regards the difference between us as 'semantic', if he doesn't postulate any strange forces – if he just talks as we would if our present language were changed in the one respect that 'distance' *meant* '$f(x,y,z,t,x', y', z', t')$'– then we will obey the Principle of Charity, and translate Oscar's word 'distance' as '$f(x,y,z,t,x',y',z',t')$'. In this case, we will say that the difference between Oscar's theory and ours is one of descriptive simplicity. (It is also an instance of Trivial Semantic Conventionality).

Quine's position (i.e. Quine$_2$'s position) is that there is no sharp line between case 1 and case 2. Relative to one analytical hypothesis, ('*distance*' means '$f(x,y,z,t,x',y', z',t')$') the choice between Oscar's theory and our theory in the second case is a matter of descriptive simplicity; relative to another analytical hypothesis ('*distance*' *means* '*distance*') the choice is one between falsity and truth. But there *may not be* any grounds for choosing between these analytical hypotheses – no 'fact of the matter as to whether or not there is a fact of the matter'. Quine$_1$'s position, on the other hand, is that there are *always* these two possibilities, and hence there is *never* a fact of the matter as to whether a choice is one of descriptive simplicity or falsity versus truth (or falsity versus *different* falsity). Grünbaum's position is that the choice is *always* one of descriptive simplicity. My position is that sometimes one analytical hypothesis is correct, and the choice is one of descriptive simplicity; sometimes the other is correct, and the choice is one of truth versus falsity (or of factual content versus different factual content, to put it more precisely); and sometimes the choice is arbitrary.

mean by distance, i.e. that it is to *this* magnitude that we are referring when we used the word 'distance'?†

If we take this line, then we will say that forces, according to the physics corresponding to the metric M_1, are what we mean by 'force' – i.e. that it is to these that we are referring when we use the word 'force'. We will also say that there are no universal forces causing our measuring rods to contract in an undetectible way, and that it is simply not the case that all the objects in the world are contracting towards the center of a sphere.

The point that we could use the metric M_2 and the physics corresponding to the metric M_2 will then be an instance of trivial semantic conventionality (TSC). It is not that there are universal forces, or even that there is no fact of the matter as to whether or not there are universal forces. It is simply that by 'force' we could have meant something else – something of no conceivable interest, in fact – and that by 'distance' we could have meant something else, and that there is a certain correlation between the, let us call it 'shmorce', and the, let us call it, 'shmistance' between the end points of a body. That there is a correlation between

---

† Suppose, for example, we modify the example in the previous note by letting Oscar's theory be methodologically preferable to ours, rather than methodologically inferior. Then, instead of translating 'distance' by '$f(x,y,z,t,x',y',z',t')$', we would do better to use homophonic translation and, in addition, to *adopt Oscar's theory*. In this case we will say that (1) the magnitude Oscar calls 'distance' is the one we did and do call 'distance'; and (2) Oscar has *discovered* the fundamental physical law that distance $= f(x,y,z,t,x',y',z',t')$, and our theory was in some respects mistaken. On this account, the *reference* of 'distance' has not changed; only our *beliefs* about it have changed.

Grünbaum's position in Grünbaum (1968) p. 367 is that even if it were the case that the reference of 'distance' is fixed by what we described in Putnam (1963) as constraints on the form of physical theory as a whole (and not by a stipulation that the length of the measuring rod be constant after the correction for the action of differential forces) – even if, in our present terminology, the reference is fixed by external and internal coherence – the choice of those constraints (standards of coherence) as the determinant of the congruences in the space is itself conventional. The choice of a metric would *still* be *conventional* even if there is no one specifiable sentence that expresses the *convention*. Conventionality follows, according to Grünbaum, from the fact that the metric is not 'built in' to the space.

To say this implies that the choice of a metric is a matter of 'descriptive simplicity', or is 'conventional', is to assert that there is a fundamental difference between (1) a choice of a 'metric' which violates one of the usual axioms, say the triangle inequality. (Actually, the *space–time* metrics used in relativity theory violate *two* axioms – they have the property that the distance from x to y can be 0 even when $x \neq y$.) And (2) a metric which preserves the usual axioms, but violates some *other* obvious property of distance – say, one according to which my left little finger is bigger than my house (when I am outside my house) and my right little finger is smaller than a microbe. This is just to insist that the axioms for a metric are *essential* in a way that the other obvious properties – or the standards of coherence – are not, which is what we are criticizing.

the *shmorce* acting on a body and the *shmistance* between its end points is not a very interesting fact. It is only by relabelling 'shmorce' *force* and relabelling 'shmistance' *distance* that we can make it *appear* to be an interesting fact. When we use the word 'distance' we are customarily referring to distance, i.e. to a certain physical magnitude, even if it is not fixed by any *convention* which physical magnitude it is that we are referring to.

This case may be contrasted to the relativistic case. In the relativistic case, there are a number of different definitions of distance which lead to equally simple laws of nature. Thus in the relativistic case there really is a relativity of the *spatial metric*, and the choice of any one of the admissible spatial metrics may be described, somewhat unhappily in our opinion, as a matter of 'convention'. But, as far as we know, the choice of any nonstandard *space–time* metric would lead to infinite complications in the form of the laws of nature, and to an unusable concept of space–time distance. Thus, as far as we know, the metric of space–time is not relative to anything. There is no interesting sense in which we can speak of a conventional 'choice' of a metric for space–time in a general or special relativistic universe.

Radical translation

I wish now to discuss Quine's position as it would be developed in detail by $Quine_1$ in strict analogy to Grünbaum's development of Reichenbach's position. I should emphasize that the position I shall develop for $Quine_1$ in this section is not a position which the actual Quine – $Quine_2$ – in fact accepts. Nevertheless, I think it will have value to develop and criticize it.

Although Quine is especially interested in radical translation, the considerations in *Word and Object* are meant to apply also to translation between familiar languages, and even to English–English translation. It is just that the nature of the problem and of the solution is supposed to be clearer in the case of radical translation. I shall, therefore, in this section develop two translation manuals for the English–English case. The first is just homophonic translations, that is, the identity function. The second translation is more complicated. Let us pick two standing sentences which are neither stimulus analytic nor stimulus contradictory, say 'The distance from the earth to the sun is 93 million miles', and 'There are no rivers on Mars'. We define the function f as follows:

1. f ('The distance from the earth to the sun is 93 million miles') = 'There are no rivers on Mars'.

2. f ('There are no rivers on Mars') = 'The distance from the earth to the sun is 93 million miles'.
3. If S is any other non-truth functional sentence (i.e. any sentence which has no *immediate* truth functional constituents except itself), then $f(S) = S$.
4. f commutes with truth functions.

It is clear from this definition that f is a general recursive function. Moreover f is the identity on every occasion sentence. Also f preserves stimulus analyticity, and f commutes with truth functions. Thus f satisfies Quine's conditions $(1')$–(4). According to Quine$_1$, there is, therefore, no fact of the matter as to whether the correct translation of the sentence 'The distance from the earth to the sun is 93 million miles' is the one given by the identity function, that is, 'The distance from the earth to the sun is 93 million miles', or the correct translation is the one given by f, that is 'There are no rivers on Mars'.

Imagine now that a speaker reasons out loud as follows: 'The distance from the earth to the sun is 93 million miles; light travels 186 000 miles a second; that is the reason it takes 8 minutes for light from the sun to reach the earth.'

If we accept the analytical hypothesis, f, then we have to interpret this speaker as reasoning as follows: 'there are no rivers on Mars; the speed of light is 186 000 miles per second; that is the reason it takes 8 minutes for light from the sun to reach the earth.' If we take the speaker, call him Oscar, to be speaking sincerely, then we have to attribute to him a very strange psychology. Since he does not say anything which we can translate as *explaining a reason for thinking* that there is a connection between the nonexistence of rivers on Mars, and the fact that it takes 8 minutes for light from the sun to reach the earth, we have to suppose that Oscar *just believes* that there is a connection between the nonexistence of rivers on Mars and the one-way trip time for light travelling from the sun to the earth, and that no explanation can be given of how Oscar *comes to believe this*, and no *route* can be provided *to this belief* which would make it plausible to us that a human being in our own culture could have such a belief. Quine$_1$, of course, maintains that just as there is no fact of the matter as to whether Oscar means *the distance from the sun to the earth is 93 million miles*, or means *there are no rivers on Mars*, so there is likewise no fact of the matter as to whether standard psychological theory or the highly nonstandard psychological theory which attributes such a strange and unexplained inferential connection to Oscar is correct. The underdetermination of translation by conditions $(1')$–(4) becomes an *underdetermination of psychology, sociology, anthropology, etc. by all conceivable empirical data.*

It is instructive to try to meet Quine$_1$'s arguments in various ways and to see why the counter arguments fail, or at least why they fail to convince Quine$_1$. Thus, suppose we argue as follows. It is a striking fact that any two human cultures can intercommunicate. In Quine's terminology, what this fact comes to is that it has proved possible, even in the case of the most different languages and cultures, to construct an analytical hypothesis which is actually usable, and on the basis of which actual communication can and does take place. This is, of course, an empirical fact. It is logically possible that we should someday find a 'jungle' language such that any analytical hypothesis at all that met Quine's $(1')$–(4) would be so hideously complex as to be unlearnable, or would involve attributing to the 'jungle' speakers inferential connections as weird as those that f requires us to attribute to Oscar, or both. One plausible explanation of the universal inter-communicability of all human cultures is that there are at least some facts about human psychology which are universal, i.e. independent of culture. It is not that people in another culture cannot have crazy beliefs – there are plenty of people in our own culture who have what any one of us would count as crazy beliefs. It is rather that in all or at least a great number of cases, when one person has what another would count as a crazy belief, it turns out to be possible to specify a *route* to that belief, a way in which the person got to that belief, which renders it as least partly intelligible to the other, that a human being might come to such a belief. If this assumption is true as a substantive statistical law, then the fact that accepting the analytical hypothesis f requires us to assume that Oscar violates this law, whereas accepting the homophonic analytical hypothesis does not, would count as *evidence* in favor of homophonic translation.

Quine$_1$ would not be convinced by this argument because he would say that there is simply no fact of the matter as to whether the analytical hypotheses that we customarily accept are correct, and the proposed psychological generalization is correct, or whether noncustomary analytical hypotheses are correct, and the proposed psychological generalization is false.

Another argument we might try is the following. Suppose that future psychology and neurophysiology disclose that there are brain processes and brain units of both physiological and functional significance, such that, if we accept one system of analytical hypotheses relating to various languages, then there turn out to be deep similarities between the linguistic processing that goes on in the case of speakers of different languages at the brain level; whereas if we adopt nonstandard analytical hypotheses, then we cannot even correlate the various linguistic processes of *producing sentences, understanding sentences, parsing sentences, making inferences in explicit linguistic form,* with anything that goes on in terms of these or any other natural brain processes and units. Would this not be evidence for the correctness of the standard system of analytical hypotheses relating the various languages? Once again, Quine$_1$ would answer 'No, there is simply no fact of the matter as to whether the supposed psychological laws are correct or not, be they stated in mentalese or Turing machine-ese.'

It will be seen that the position of our hypothetical Quine$_1$ is exactly parallel to Grünbaum's, and that the same objection applies to it. If the adoption of one system of analytical hypotheses rather than another permits a great simplification of such sciences as neurophysiology, psychology, anthropology, etc., then why should we not say that what we mean by 'translation' is *translation according to the manuals that have this property?* Why should we not maintain that to say of Oscar that when he says 'The sun is 93 million miles from the earth', he means 'There are no rivers on Mars', is simply to change the meaning of 'means' in an uninteresting way? This objection is even stronger against Quine$_1$ than against Grünbaum. For, it should be remembered, it is generally believed that Quine$_1$ is the Quine who wrote 'Two dogmas of empiricism'. Since 'Two dogmas of empiricism' explicitly rejects the analytic-synthetic distinction, and Quine has from 'Truth by Convention' on expressed scepticism about the notion of a convention, then he should feel highly uncomfortable at being caught in what is after all an essentialist maneuver. His position, after all, does not differ much, if at all, from saying that $(1')$–(4) are *Meaning Postulates* for the notion of 'translation', and that they are all the Meaning Postulates that there are for the notion of 'translation'. One would think that the Quine who wrote 'Two dogmas of empiricism' would feel much more comfortable with what we have called a coherence account of reference than with the idea that reference is fixed (or left undetermined) by a finite set of meaning postulates.

Reichenbach on geometry

It may shed some light on these problems to review Reichenbach's own solution to the problem that he posed, in *Philosophy of Space and Time.* Reichenbach saw that the term 'distance' corresponds to a magnitude. He also saw that it is the task of philosophy to say something about the nature of this correspondence. If a word corresponds to one thing rather than another, then it must be something humans do or specify that controls this. It is the task of philosophy, in Reichenbach's view, to say just what it is that we do or specify that controls the reference of such terms as 'distance'.

There is a superficial similarity to the thought of the later Wittgenstein here. Wittgenstein too saw that meaning is a function of human practice. Indeed, he saw this far more completely than any philosopher before him. But the similarity is only superficial. For Wittgenstein, when he came to see the extent to which meaning is a function of human practice, somehow also came to the conclusion – the erroneous conclusion, in my opinion – that talk about human practice obviated talk of correspondence or reference altogether. Reichenbach's perspective is the more correct one. There is a correspondence between words and things or words and magnitudes, and it is a function of human practice. A central task of philosophy is to spell out the nature of this function.

It is interesting that Reichenbach presents his solution to the problem in the form of a series of successive approximations. The first approximation – the, so to speak, first order approximation to a solution – is to say that we specify a metric implicitly by specifying that a rigid measuring rod is to stay the same length when transported. That is to say, the length of the measuring rod is to *count as* the same even when the measuring rod is in different places. But to *literally* make a *particular* measuring rod the standard of congruence would involve insuperable difficulties. Reichenbach illustrates these difficulties charmingly by means of the following example. Suppose we were to create a standard of time congruence by specifying that the interval between the king's successive heartbeats is to *count as* the same. Then the laws of nature would assume a very strange form. For example, it would become a law of nature that whenever the king runs upstairs, then all natural processes slow down! It is therefore necessary to allow for what Reichenbach calls the *interposition of theories*. We specify, not that the measuring rod remains the same length when transported, but that the *theoretically corrected length of the measuring rod* is to remain the same.

At first blush, this involves us in a dangerous circularity. Correcting the length of the measuring rod for the action upon it of various forces requires a theory. The theory required is one that has the notion of 'distance', or some similar notion, as a primitive. But 'distance' is to acquire a 'meaning', i.e. a specified reference, by way of the very coordinating definition that we are in the process of setting up. Thus it seems as if the constraint – that the length of the measuring rod, after correction for the action upon it of all the various forces postulated by a correct physical theory, should remain the same on transportation – is so weak as to leave *distance* still wholly indeterminate.

Reichenbach solves this problem by saying that what we have to do is impose *further* constraints upon the *form* of physical theory. The constraint that he chooses is the constraint that universal forces vanish, i.e. that there be no forces with the properties that (1) the total deformation they produce upon any body is the same, independently of the internal resistance to deformation of that body; (2) the forces are permanently associated with regions of space; (3) the forces have no sources and no shields – they cannot be turned off or modified by moving their sources away or by putting shields around the objects affected.

In a later work, Reichenbach explains the same line of thinking in the following way. Choose any metric compatible with the topology of space–time. Then a true physics based upon that metric is a system of physical laws which correctly predict the *trajectories* of all the particles, when the trajectories are described in terms of that metric. If M is a metric, and P is a system of physics such that in some possible world P is the true system of physics based upon the metric M, then we call $M + P$ an admissible 'geometry plus physics'. Now, let $M + P$ be any admissible geometry plus physics, and let M' be any metric which can be obtained from M by a homeomorphic mapping. Let P' be a system of physics based upon M' with the property that the two systems $M + P$ and $M' + P'$ lead to exactly the same predictions – not just the same predictions with respect to *observation sentences*, but the same predictions with respect to *possible trajectories*. That is to say that if we take the trajectories predicted by $M + P$ and 'translate' them into the language of the metric M', then those trajectories are exactly the trajectories predicted by $M' + P'$. In this case, Reichenbach speaks of the two systems of geometry plus physics, the systems $M + P$ and $M' + P'$, as *equivalent descriptions*. The set of all $M' + P'$ equivalent to a given $M + P$ is called the *equivalence class* of $M + P$. If an equivalence class has a member which satisfies the constraint described above, the constraint that universal forces vanish, then that member is called the *normal* member of the equivalence class. Reichenbach's position was that there is *one and only one true equivalence class* of geometries plus physicses – that is, there is one and only one equivalence class such that the pairs $M + P$ in that equivalence class give correct predictions with respect to the possible trajectories of bodies in our world. If someone proposes an $M + P$ which belongs to any other equivalence class, then he is presenting a false theory. Which equivalence class is the equivalence class of true geometries plus physicses, is not in any sense a matter of convention. On the other hand, the choice of a geometry plus physics *from the true equivalence class* is a matter of convention; the usual convention is to *choose the normal member*.

It will be seen that the notion of a *definition* undergoes successive widening in Reichenbach's successive approximations to the definition of the metric. Even the first stipulation, the stipulation that the transported rod stays the same length, is not a definition in the technical logical sense of an explicit definition. It does not provide a nonmetrical *substitute* for metrical notions; it does not provide a way of eliminating metrical notions where they occur in science. What it does is to fix the reference of metrical notions by specifying a standard of congruence. It was for this reason that Reichenbach referred to this type of definition as a *coordinating definition*. But with the introduction of the element of 'interposition of theories', and especially when it comes to pass that the work of fixing the reference of geometrical notions is mainly done by a stipulation on the *form* of geometry plus physics *as a whole* – the stipulation that universal forces vanish – the term 'definition' becomes wholly inappropriate.

Perhaps not wholly. For there is a tradition, even in mathematical logic, whereby a condition which has a unique solution is sometimes referred to as an 'implicit definition'. If Reichenbach were right, if the condition that physical theory include the statement that universal forces vanish uniquely determined the metric, then this stipulation might be termed an *implicit definition* of the metric. Reichenbach's position might then be stated simply thus: the metric is implicitly defined by the condition that universal forces vanish, together with the condition that $f = ma$, which requires that all deformations in bodies be ascribed to forces.

Unfortunately, Reichenbach is wrong. As a matter of mathematical fact, the condition that universal forces vanish does not single out a unique geometry plus physics (see Appendix). In fact any metric that agrees with the topology of a space at all is compatible with some 'true' system of geometry plus physics according to which universal forces vanish. But this fact need not be fatal for Reichenbach's enterprise. I do not think that Reichenbach would have been terribly disturbed by the fact that the constraint that universal forces vanish is not a sufficient constraint. If we have to add the further constraints that the geometry plus physics as a whole have additional formal properties – say, that they preserve various intuitive requirements, where these requirements can be preserved without cost, and that they be maximally simple in some sense of simple which is connected with feasibility and utility in scientific practice, then why should we not add these constraints in the very same spirit that led Reichenbach to speak of the 'interposition of theories'? (Note, by the way, that Reichenbach was writing of the 'interposition of theories' in the very same year that Bridgeman published *The Logic of Modern Physics* – a book notable for totally ignoring the interposition of theories.) If we adopt this suggestion, then we can no longer speak of the metric as having an *implicit* definition; for our constraint on scientific theory no longer has the form of a *sentence*. But why should we retain the doctrine that reference is fixed by stipulating *sentences*?

Reichenbach should not have been bothered by the remark that the conventionality of the choice of the metric for physical space is merely an instance of TSC. In the final pages of *Philosophy of Space and Time*, he himself points out that his analysis of the metricization of space–time is meant to apply, *mutatis mutandis*, to such cases as temperature, pressure, etc. – that is, to all physical magnitudes. Grünbaum, on the other hand, insists that his doctrine is a doctrine of the *intrinsic metrical amorphousness* of space–time, that it applies to distance but it does not apply to pressure. Pressure, according to Grünbaum, has an *intrinsic* metric, whereas space–time does not.

The reason that Reichenbach should not have been bothered by our charge of TSC is simply this: he would have said that of course the choice of a metric is the choice of a 'meaning', i.e. a reference, for the word 'distance'. But, he would have said, the whole philosophical problem is to say *how* we go about choosing a reference for the term 'distance'. TSC simply says that any term that refers at all could have referred to something different. That is true. The philosopher's job is to explain *how* terms can refer to something at all. Reichenbach was a philosopher pioneering in the very difficult and unexplored terrain of the theory of reference of scientific terms.

In one important respect Reichenbach was mistaken, however. Seduced by Einstein's own fallacious analysis of his own special theory of relativity – an analysis that Einstein later seems to retract – Reichenbach *identified* the problem of specifying the mechanism of reference for magnitude terms with the problem of separating definitional and empirical elements in scientific theory. For Reichenbach, the analytic-synthetic distinction was essential. The whole job of the philosopher reduced to the job of deciding which sentences in scientific theory are *really* analytic, appearances to the contrary, and which ones are really synthetic. But he was led to this conception of the philosopher's job precisely because he identified the problem of separating analytic and synthetic, or definitional and empirical, elements in science, with the problem of explaining the mechanism of reference of scientific terms. Reichenbach, writing twenty years before the discussion at Harvard that eventuated in Quine's 'Two dogmas of empiricism', could not have foreseen that it would be possible to provide an answer – what we have called a 'coherence account' – to the question of reference of scientific terms which not only did not presuppose the analytic–synthetic distinction, but which was in spirit fundamentally hostile to that distinction. I suggest that we retain Reichenbach's concern with explicating reference while giving up the analytic–synthetic distinction. I suggest that we agree with Reichenbach that the 'choice' of a metric is an instance of TSC, while not losing interest in the question of just how it is that the reference of the term 'distance' is fixed.

Causal theory of reference

In a couple of these papers, I have suggested that we extend Kripke's causal theory of reference from proper names to natural kind words and physical magnitude terms in science.† I will not review the details here. But suffice it to say that I do not claim that a physical magnitude term can only be introduced by a causal description. But I do claim that a customary way of introducing physical magnitude terms is via a causal description, that is, a description of the form 'By x I mean the magnitude that is responsible for such and such effects.' For example, Benjamin Franklin might well have given a causal description of electricity by telling us that electricity obeyed an equation of continuity, and that it collected in clouds, and that when it reached a certain concentration, some of it flowed from the cloud to the earth, and that this sudden flow of a large quantity of electricity took the form of what we recognize as lightning. The reader may wonder why I have not hitherto appealed to a causal theory of reference in order to answer the conventionalist. Since the distance between space–time points is no longer something which enters into physical laws neither as an effect nor a cause, since space is no longer a mere arena in which physical processes take place, but an agent and an actor in the physical drama, and an actor which is itself affected by the physical drama, why should we not specify the reference of the term distance, or of the technical term the g_{ik} tensor, by specifying certain *causal* properties of distance or of the g_{ik} tensor?

The reason why this answer would not meet the conventionalist criticism, at least by itself, is that the conventionalist is fully prepared to be a conventionalist about causes and effects *too*. If we choose a nonstandard geometry plus physics, then we will choose a nonstandard account both of the phenomena and of their causes. It is necessary, thus, at some point to argue that the reference of *cause* and

---

† See chapter 11 in this volume for a causal theory of reference in connection with magnitude terms, and chapter 12 for a discussion of natural kind words and the general problem of meaning and reference.

effect is not up for grabs to the extent that the conventionalist thinks. There is no such effect as the universal contraction of all objects towards the center of a certain sphere, and there are no such causes as universal forces. The coherence account, far from being incompatible with the causal account of reference, is a necessary part of the story.

Enter Quine$_2$

The position of Quine$_1$ may be explained in the following way: let (5) be some plausible constraint that one might think of adding to Quine's constraints (1)–(4) or (1′)–(4) in order to obtain unique or more unique translation. Such a constraint might be the constraint Quine himself suggests, that we ask that expressions which are short in English, or whatever the home language may be, correspond to short expressions in the alien language; or it might be the constraint we suggested above, that the translation manual be compatible with certain psychological or neuropsychological hypotheses; or it might be a more subtle constraint on the structure of the translation manual itself. (Geoffrey Hellman, in a recent Harvard dissertation, has explored a number of such constraints. Some of Hellman's constraints may well rule out such examples as the notorious *gavagai*.) The position of Quine$_1$ with respect to such a constraint (5) would be that it in no way reduces the indeterminacy of translation. For even if (5) had the property that there was in every case a *unique* translation satisfying constraints (1)–(5), still there is no fact of the matter as to whether (5) is a correct constraint, and hence no fact of the matter as to whether a translation satisfying (1)–(5) is correct versus a translation satisfying (1)–(4) and violating (5). Translations violating (1)–(4) are objectively wrong; they go against the *evidence*. But (1)–(4), or rather (1′)–(4), are all the objective constraints there are. This is the position that we criticized above as involving the same conventionalist ploy as Grünbaum's position on the conventionalism of the metric of physical space–time, in a relativistic world, or of the metric of space in a Newtonian world.

At the Storrs Conference on the Philosophy of Language, however, Quine admitted that *Word and Object* was widely interpreted in this way, but explicitly repudiated this interpretation as unrepresentative of his intentions and his actual philosophical views. His view as he expressed it is not that there is no fact of the matter as to whether an added constraint (5) would be objectively correct or not, but that there is 'no fact of the matter as to whether or not there is a fact of the matter'.

This is not just an *aperçu* on Quine's part. In fact, Quine is here taking a position which is far more consonant with the position of his other writings than is the position of Quine$_1$. Quine is a realist. That is, he believes that the sentences of physical science have a truth value, and that that truth value depends upon the external world, not just upon human language or human sensation or human convention, etc. But, like any sensible realist, Quine believes that human convention plays *some* part in the determination of the truth values of sentences of physical theory. Where he differs from, say Reichenbach, is in holding that it is futile to try to distinguish the contributions of human convention and objective fact, sentence by sentence. Human convention and objective fact both contribute; but there are no sentences which are true just by virtue of objective fact, and no sentences which are true just by virtue of human convention.

The position of Quine$_1$ goes against this because it maintains that $(1')$–(4) are, as it were, meaning conventions. They stipulate the meaning of 'translation'. A fifth constraint could not be a substantive law since it is underdetermined by $(1')$–(4); therefore it could at best amount to an arbitrary stipulation to redefine the notion of 'translation'. The position of the real Quine, Quine$_2$, is that it is a bad question to ask whether the adoption of a fifth constraint would express the discovery of a substantive law or the adoption of a new meaning for 'translation'. 'Is that a statement of fact or a meaning-stipulation?' is as bad a question in linguistic theory as it is in physical theory, in Quine's view. Quine's real view thus allows that we may have further constraints over and above $(1')$–(4). It allows that such constraints may be well motivated, motivated by just the considerations of agreement with intuition ('conservativism'), agreement with experimental evidence, fertility, coherence with the rest of science, etc. that are operative in the growth and development of physical theory. At the Storrs Conference, Quine went on to say that it was his belief that even the discovery/stipulation of such further constraints on radical translation as might prove well motivated would still not determine a unique translation. There would still be, he expects, some indeterminacy of translation.

Note, then, that in Quine's view the indeterminacy of translation is a hypothesis, not something of which Quine claims to have a logical or mathematical proof.

The importance of the indeterminacy of translation

Quine believes that there is not a shred of scientific evidence for the existence of 'propositions' as irreducible, nonbehaviorally linked, nonphysical entities, and I certainly agree with him on this. What there are, in Quine's view, are isomorphisms between languages. When we say that a sentence in a language L_1 has the same meaning as a sentence in a language L_2, no reference to irreducible propositions is needed to explain what we mean. What we mean is simply that there is an isomorphism – more precisely, a behavior-preserving mapping – of one language onto the other that sends one of the two sentences onto the other.

If this is a reasonable account of sameness of meaning, and *prima facie* it certainly seems to be, then at first blush it would seem that propositions could be restored, at least as logical constructions out of linguistic behavior. Let us simply say that two sentences express the same proposition just in case one is a translation of the other. The trouble with this proposal is that it assumes that for any two languages, if there is an isomorphism between them at all, then there is a unique isomorphism between them. This is precisely the thesis that is challenged by the hypothesis of the indeterminacy of translation. Quine's examples show that it is quite conceivable that there are two or more isomorphisms between two different languages, and that a sentence which is mapped onto a sentence S_1 by one of those isomorphisms may be mapped onto a different, even an incompatible, sentence S_2 under the other of those isomorphisms. If there are many isomorphisms between any two languages, then the notion of *sameness of meaning* has to be relativized to the isomorphism that we pick.

Even if talk of 'propositions' is not meant metaphysically, it is still a very bad idea at this stage in our knowledge. For it begs just the question which is raised by the hypothesis of the indeterminacy of translation: the question whether or not isomorphism between different languages is unique, or almost unique. It should be noted that the importance of the hypothesis of the indeterminacy of translation in this respect does not depend upon the hypothesis being *true*. Recognizing that *we do not know* what constraints upon translation would determine a unique translation, if there are any reasonable constraints that would do this, and recognizing, further, that it may be that no reasonable constraints upon translation would determine *unique* translations, is enough. It is enough that the hypothesis of the indeterminacy of translation *might* be true; it is not necessary that it should be true.

Underdetermination of theories

Quine's reasons for believing that there will turn out to be some indeterminacy of translation, even if additional constraints upon translation prove to be justified, are basically two. He argues for the indeterminacy of translation first from the general underdetermination of scientific theories by true observation sentences, and second from ontological relativity. We shall consider the argument from ontological relativity in the next section. Let us take a look now at the under-determination of scientific theories.

The topic of the underdetermination of scientific theories is such a large topic that we cannot undertake to really discuss it here. What we can do is very briefly consider its relevance to the topics of this paper. Our standpoint is, briefly, that it is quite unclear to what extent scientific theories are underdetermined by what, and what to make of the fact that they are underdetermined if they are.

Thus, a physicist would be likely to regard two theories as equivalent descriptions if no physically possible experiment could ever decide between them. Some scientific realists would question the justifiability of even this weak requirement, the requirement of the physical possibility of a crucial experiment. But it is important to note that when Quine says that scientific theory is underdetermined by the totality of all possible observations, he does not mean what the physicist means. He does not mean that there are two theories such that no physically possible experiment *could* decide between them, and such that both are equally acceptable on the basis of such canons as simplicity, etc. When Quine speaks of the totality of all *possible observations*, he means the totality of all *true observation sentences*, i.e. of the totality of all *ordered pairs consisting of an observation sentence and a point in space–time at which that observation sentence could have been truly uttered*, whether or not someone was present at that point in space–time to truly utter it. He does not count counterfactual observation sentences, e.g. 'This match would have lit if it had been struck', and *a fortiori*, he does not count sentences about what the outcomes of various experiments which were not performed *would have been* if those experiments had been performed.

To make the point clear: two theories are observationally inequivalent, by Quine's criterion, if one implies an observation sentence and the other implies the negation of that observation sentence. E.g. if one implies 'There is a red apple at the point in space–time with coordinates *xyzt*', and the other implies that 'There is no red apple at the point in space–time with coordinates *xyzt*'. Two observationally complete theories, i.e. two theories which settle the truth value of all observation sentences, and which agree in their assignment of truth values to all observation sentences, are observationally equivalent, by Quine's criterion. In particular, they are still observationally equivalent even if one of them implies that *if* a certain amount of energy *had been* employed in making a certain measurement, say, the measurement of the position of a certain particle, it would have been found in a region r, and the other implies that *if* that amount of energy had been employed and the measurement had been made, then the particle *would have been* found *outside* the region *r*. Of course if the measurement was made, then the statement of the result of the measurement is an observation sentence, and if the two theories disagree in the truth value they assign to that observation sentence, they are observationally inequivalent. But if we suppose that no human being ever employs the amount of energy required in making an experiment simply as a matter of sociological fact, and that therefore the experiment is never performed, then the two theories are *not* inequivalent. It seems to me that here Quine's criterion differs from that which is accepted by physicists. The fact that people never get around to performing certain experiments, or that people never have available enough energy to perform certain experiments, etc., does not mean that two such theories become equivalent. As long as the theories imply different predictions about what *would* have happened *if* the experiments *had* been performed, then they are inequivalent, as most physicists understand the matter.

What this shows is that even if there should be observationally equivalent theories in Quine's sense, which in addition to being equivalent were equally simple, etc., i.e. which would come out as equally good on all of the usual methodological canons, still it would not follow that there was no fact of the matter as to which of the two theories was right. The step from the underdetermination of scientific theories by the totality of true observation sentences, if it is a fact, to there being no fact of the matter as to which theory is right, is not an obvious step at all.

Sometimes Quine seems to assume that the Verifiability Theory is correct provided that the unit of meaning is taken to be scientific theory as a whole, and not the individual sentence. I am not myself persuaded that this is right; but even if we accept this, it does not follow that there is no fact of the matter as to which of two observationally equivalent theories, by Quine's criterion, is correct. For many Verificationists have counted counterfactual verification as part of empirical meaning. That is, it is customary even for Verificationists to count two theories as differing in empirical meaning in the case discussed above. Nelson Goodman has urged that the counterfactual conditionals are meaningless unless we can somehow succeed in construing counterfactual talk as highly derived talk about actual events. In Goodman's view, talk about what the outcomes would have been of experiments using higher energies than will ever be available to human beings, is meaningless unless it can be translated into talk about things that actually do happen. Perhaps it would follow that there is no fact of the matter as to which of two observationally equivalent descriptions is the true theory, if we assume *both* the holistic version of verificationism *and* Nelson Goodman's stand with respect to counterfactual conditionals. For our present purposes it is enough to remark that there is no clear route from '(observationally) equivalent descriptions' to 'no fact of the matter' unless we are willing to assume such difficult and problematical philosophical doctrines as the holistic version of verificationism and the rejection of counterfactual conditionals, or at least, the rejection of realism with respect to counterfactual conditionals.

Quine's position is that one can only say whether two theories are compatible or incompatible once we have fixed a background theory *and* a translation of each theory into the language of one's background theory. If they come out incompatible on that translation, then (relative to that translation) they *are* incompatible. Since we speak from the point of view of our background theory, we say there *is* a fact of the matter as to which is true – even if the two theories be observationally equivalent in the sense just discussed. Thus Quine does not believe that there is any step, in general, from the fact that the choice between theories is underdetermined, in his sense, to there being 'no fact of the matter'.

In the special case of indeterminacy of translation, however, these difficulties can be sidestepped. For if we agree that meanings, insofar as they are legitimate scientific entities at all, must be functions of isomorphisms between languages and linguistic behaviors, then evidence that there is no unique isomorphism satisfying whatever are the appropriate constraints is *ipso facto* evidence that there are no unique meanings. If many isomorphisms satisfy the optimal constraints, whatever they may be, then asking which of the isomorphisms translates sentences *preserving meaning*, i.e. which of the isomorphisms is *the correct translation*, is, in effect, asking which of the isomorphisms satisfies the Great Constraint in the Sky. The answer is that there is no Great Constraint in the Sky, and hence there is no fact of the matter as to which of the optimal isomorphisms satisfies it. In general, I am inclined to think that this is a reasonable line to take.

In the case of the indeterminacy of translation, what Quine is reminding us of is this: not any sentential function is an implicit definition. For a sentential function to be an implicit definition it is necessary that it should have a unique solution. That is, there must be one thing satisfying it, and only one thing satisfying it. When we specify an object by saying that that object is the object satisfying certain constraints, then in the absence of any proof that there is only one object satisfying those constraints, we are not justified in assuming uniqueness. The general underdetermination of scientific theories by observational facts is clear only when the constraints upon scientific theory are very weak. If the only constraints are those of deductive consistency, then the point is trivial. Once some kind of strong coherence is added as an additional constraint, then the extent of underdetermination becomes quite problematical. (It is also quite problematical why we should require, pending argument, consistency with all true observation sentences, and not, say, consistency with all true sentences about the actual and possible trajectories of particles.) This appeal to the underdetermination of scientific theories by observational facts can strengthen the case for the indeterminacy of translation only by reminding us of the logical point just made. The constraints that it may be justifiable to place upon analytical hypotheses are not just facts about correct translation manuals; they define what it is to be a correct translation manual. Pending proof, we cannot assume that such a set of constraints has a unique solution.

Ontological relativity

The other argument that Quine offers for the indeterminacy of translation is the fact of ontological relativity. According to the doctrine of ontological relativity, there exist thoroughly intertranslatable theories which do not even agree on ontology, that is, on what objects there are.

Let T and T' be two such theories. Then if the speakers of the 'jungle' language utter sentences which may be correctly translated (according to some translation manual) by the sentences of T, then by composing that translation manual with the translation of T into T', we could equally well translate the jungle speakers as holding the theory T'. If T and T' are formally incompatible, then this gives us an example of the indeterminacy of translation. The indeterminacy of translation follows from the relativity of ontology.

There is no doubt that this ingenious argument strongly moves Quine. I should like to raise some doubts about the argument here, however. In the first place, what are the considerations that lead Quine to the doctrine of the relativity of ontology? One consideration is a formal trick. Suppose, for example, we assign numbers to all the objects in the world in some effective way. For example, we might pick some particular particle, say Oscar, and assign it the number 1. The object nearest to Oscar, if there is an object nearest to Oscar, is then assigned the number 2. If more than one object has the distance r from Oscar where r is the closest any other object gets to Oscar, then among the particles with the distance r from Oscar we pick the one with the smallest Θ, (thinking of Oscar as the center of a system of polar co-ordinates), and assign that object the number 2. If there are two or more particles which both have the distance r from Oscar and the angle Θ, then we pick the one with the least ρ and assign it the number 2. Continuing in this fashion, we can assign an integer to every particle in the entire universe, assuming that there are only a countable number of particles in the universe. The method has been explained only for particles existing at one time; however, it can easily be extended to a four dimensional universe.

Now, suppose we have defined a 'proxy function' in this way, that is a function mapping particles onto integers. Any physical thing, that is, any thing consisting of a finite number of particles, can then be identified with a finite set of integers. If we Gödel number finite sets of integers, which is easy to do, then we can represent both particles and finite collections of particles by means of integers. Then any theory which quantifies over physical things (over particles and finite collections of particles) can be replaced by a theory which quantifies over integers. It suffices to replace any predicate of physical things e.g. 'is red', by the corresponding predicate of integers. The notion of 'corresponding predicate' can be explained by means of an example: if the given predicate is 'is red', then the corresponding predicate is 'is the number which is assigned to an object which is red'. Thus the sentence 'Oscar is red' goes over into the sentence 'The number 1 is the number of an object which is red'. If T is a theory which quantifies over physical objects, and T' is the corresponding theory which quantifies over integers, then there is no doubt that T and T' are thoroughly inter-translatable, if T' has been constructed in the way just outlined. There is also no doubt that T and T' have a different ontology, if we accept Quine's criterion of ontological commitment. But Quine's criterion does not seem plausible to me in this case. It seems to me that a theory may presuppose objects as much through the predicates it employs as through the objects it quantifies over; and that, intuitively, T' in the above example has an ontology of material objects just as much as T does. Once again, a consideration offered in support of the indeterminacy of translation proves to be itself a difficult and problematical philosophical doctrine.

Quine also appeals to examples from the history of science, notably the notorious wave-particle duality. Let us take a somewhat better example than the wave-particle case: the case of a Newtonian world and the following two presentations of Newtonian theory: action at a distance theory, quantifying only over particles, and field theory, quantifying over particles and fields. These two theories do intuitively have different ontologies. Intuitively the former says that the world consists of particles; the latter says that the world consists of particles *and fields*. And there is also no doubt that these two theories are thoroughly intertranslatable as long as we assume Newtonian physics. Thus, as long as we adopt only Quine's original constraints on radical translation, only the constraints $(1')$–(4), then the step from the translatability of these two theories to a possible indeterminacy of translation seems sound. But the fact is that while these two theories are thoroughly intertranslatable, they are also notationally and mathematically quite different. A physicist doing his calculations in the style of field theory writes down different expressions than a physicist doing his calculations in the style of action at a distance theory. Thus, if we add to the constraints $(1')$–(4) the further constraint that Quine himself mentions, the constraint that we choose analytical hypotheses that preserve length of expression, i.e. that send short expressions in the target language onto short expressions in the home language, then it seems as if we *could* say that the calculations done by the 'jungle' physicist should be translated by the calculations of the action at a distance theorist, or by the calculations of the field theorist, whichever the case might be. The fact is that the step from examples of ontological relativity, even if they be bona fide, to indeterminacy of translation is a valid step only for Quine$_1$.

Summary

We have examined some of the considerations that lead Quine to the hypothesis of the indeterminacy of translation. Two of these considerations – the underdetermination of scientific theory by observational fact, and the existence of ontological relativity, seem to us quite problematical. We cannot see any sure step from these considerations to the indeterminacy of translation, but neither can we see any proof of the *determinacy* of translation. Quine is right: how much indeterminacy of translation there is, if there is indeterminacy of translation, is surely an empirical question. Like all empirical questions, it involves elements of discovery and elements of stipulation; and to ask whether any particular sentence, that we may adopt as linguistic theory and translation theory develop, is a meaning stipulation or a substantive law will be futile. But our purpose here has not been to discover if there is indeterminacy of translation, but rather to refute the argument of Quine$_1$ and the allied argument of Grünbaum. Once that argument is recognized to be an instance of the general conventionalist ploy, and that ploy is recognized as having no validity, then the way is clear for the consideration of the substantive questions raised by Reichenbach and Quine: how is the reference of scientific terms fixed? and to what extent is reference determinate?

Appendix

In Putnam (1968) I sketched a proof of the following theorem:

THEOREM. Let P be a system of physics (based on a suitable system of coordinates) and E be a system of geometry. Then the world described by E plus P can be redescribed in terms of an arbitrarily chosen metric g_{ik} (compatible with the given topology) *without postulating 'universal forces'*, i.e. forces permanently associated with a spatial region and producing the same deformations (over and above the deformations produced by the usual forces) independently of the composition of the body acted upon. In fact, according to the new description g_{ik} plus P' (which has exactly the same factual content as E plus P):

(1) All deformations are ascribed to three sources: the electromagnetic forces, the gravitational forces, and gravitational-electromagnetic interactions.

(2) All three types of forces are dependent upon the composition of the body acted upon.

(3) If there are small deformations constantly taking place in solid bodies according to E plus P (as there are, owing to the atomic constitution of matter), then no matter what geometry may be selected, the new g_{ik} can be so chosen that the deformations according to g_{ik} plus P' will be of the same order of magnitude. Moreover, it will be impossible to transform them away by going back to E plus P.

(4) If it is possible to construct rods held together by only gravitational forces or only electromagnetic forces, then (in the absence of the other type of field) the interactional forces of the third type (postulated by P') will vanish.

(5) If there are already 'third type forces' according to E plus P, then the situation will be thoroughly symmetrical, in the sense that (i) going from the old metric to g_{ik} involves postulating additional deformations (relative to the description given in E plus P) which are the same for all bodies, and (ii) going from g_{ik} back to E plus P involves postulating additional deformations which are also the same for all bodies, *relative to the description given in g_{ik} plus P'*; and the same number and kind of fundamental forces are postulated by both P and P'.

I now give a much simpler proof. (The proof will be longer, because I will be more detailed.) Afterwards, I will discuss Grünbaum's criticism of the original proof.

Proof: Let *E plus P* be based on a metric g_{ik}. Let g'_{ik} be an arbitrarily chosen metric compatible with the given topology. We replace the original notion of distance (given by g_{ik}), wherever it occurs in physical laws by the appropriate function of the coordinates. The second law of motion is now destroyed, since it now reads

$$F = m\ddot{\mathbf{x}}$$

and $\ddot{\mathbf{x}}$ (the second derivative of the position vector) is no longer 'acceleration', owing to the arbitrary character of the coordinate system as viewed from the new g_{ik} tensor. (We assume the new g_{ik} is compatible with the original topology.) But we can restore the second law by construing 'force' in the old laws as not force at all, but some other quantity – say 'phorce' (*P*). Then the above law is rewritten as

$$P = m\ddot{\mathbf{x}}$$

and the law $F = ma$ is reintroduced as a definition of 'force'. (Here a must be defined in terms of the new g_{ik} tensor.) The difficulty is that so far we have only defined *total resultant force*. To obtain a resolution into component forces, we proceed as follows: Let A and B be two arbitrary *logically possible* differential forces (whether physically actual or not). For example, A might be electromagnetic force, on the assumption that Maxwell's Laws are strictly true (in the metric g_{ik}), whether they are in reality or not, and B might be gravitational force, on the assumption that Newton's Law (or some relativistic law, if one prefers) is true (in the metric g_{ik}), whether it is in reality or not. Without loss of generality, we assume $A + B \neq F$. Determine C from the equation $A + B + C = F$. If C is differential, we are through: we just set $E = A, G = B, I = C$, and the theorem follows. If C is universal, we express the differential force B as the sum of two differential forces B_1 and B_2 ($B = B_1 + B_2$); this can always be done. Moreover, if B is Newton's Law of Gravity or some relativistic law, B_1 can be chosen to be approximately B; hence, approximately Newton's law or the relativistic law. Then $A + B + C = F$, and $B = B_1 + B_2$; so $A + B_1 + (B_2 + C) = F$. Since B_2 is differential and C is universal, $(B_2 + C)$ is differential. So we just set $E = A, G = B_1, I = (B_2 + C)$, q.e.d.

Our original proof was unnecessarily complicated because we determined E and G in the metric g'_{ik} and transformed to find them in the metric g_{ik}, instead of just working with the metric g_{ik} and the total resultant force F. Our description of the procedure was as follows:

'Now set the gravitational field equal to zero, determine the total 'phorce' that would now be acting on B, and determine from this the total force that would be acting on B. Call this E (electromagnetic force). Similarly, set the electromagnetic field equal to zero, and obtain the total force that would be acting on B. Call this G (gravitational force). Finally define I (interactional force) from the equation $F = E + G + I$.'

In Grünbaum (1968) chapter III, Grünbaum gives both a 'counterexample' to the theorem and a criticism of the proof. But the 'counterexample' is a counterexample to what Grünbaum takes me to have meant by some statements in the proof; not an example to show the theorem is *false*. (If I wished to imitate Grünbaum's style in Grünbaum (1968), I would now accuse Grünbaum of 'shocking ignorance' and of not knowing the meaning of 'counterexample'.) So all we have is a criticism of my proof (of which the relevant part is 'b' pp. 363–4). The criticism of my proof is based on the assumption that when I wrote 'set the gravitational field equal to zero' I must have intended *either* the original physics P to be used (in which case a host of objections arise, depending on the character of P) or the new physics P' to be used, in which case one has to already know P' to construct it. What I had in mind was neither of these alternatives. When I wrote 'determine the total "phorce" that would now be acting on B', I meant determine the total 'phorce' that would be acting *using any convenient system of physics* (whether it agrees with P or not). (For example, one can just assume that if the gravitational field is zero, then the 'phorce' that would be acting on B would strictly obey Maxwell's laws, in the metric g'_{ik}, if one wishes. Similarly, one can assume that if the electromagnetic field is zero, then the 'phorce' that would be acting on B would obey Newton's Law of Gravity, if one wishes.) Then E, G, and I are well defined.

Grünbaum's other criticism (p. 364) is that I do not prove that E, G, and I will be differential (although it should have been clear that it is only by sheer chance that any one of them will be universal). This criticism is correct, and I have supplied details above.

Note that part (3) of the theorem holds because even if a space is, say, Euclidean relative to g'_{ik} and we wish to be Lobachevskian relative to g_{ik}, this is compatible with the distance between two events being almost the same in the two metrics at usual distances. (I.e. the two metrics can almost agree at non-astronomical distances.) In particular, the disagreements can be made small relative to molecular vibrations or even relative to the Compton wave-length of an electron – so there is no possibility of an *operational* definition of 'rigid measuring rod' deciding between g_{ik} and g'_{ik}. And, since the total force F is always differential (since different objects have different internal forces and vibrations), total deformation cannot be transformed away.

To verify part (4), we have to put additional constraints on the forces

A and B (or B_1), which is no problem, since these are arbitrary differential forces. Namely, let A and B never both vanish, and let neither A nor B vanish in the case of the great majority of physical objects (this is in agreement with both classical and contemporary physics). Then, instead of setting $E = A$, $G = B$, $I = C$, define E, G, I at each space–time point p as follows:

If $A \neq 0$, $B \neq 0$ at p, set $E = A$, $G = B$, $I = C$ at p.
If $A = 0$ at p, set $E = 0$, $G = B + C$, $I = 0$ at p.
If $B = 0$ at p, set $E = A + C$, $G = 0$, $I = 0$ at p.

(If it is necessary to split B into B_1, B_2, put instead:

If $A \neq 0$, $B_1 \neq 0$ at p, set $E = A$, $G = B_1$, $I = B_2 + C$ at p.
If $A = 0$ at p, set $E = 0$, $G = B_1 + B_2 + C$, $I = 0$ at p.
If $B_1 = 0$ at p, set $E = A + B_2 + C$, $G = 0$, $I = 0$ at p.)

Then E, G, and I are still differential, because for most bodies $E = A$, $G = B$, $I = C$, and these are differential forces; and I vanishes whenever E or G does. Part (4) of the theorem was really unnecessary, since E and G never vanish *globally*, and there is no reason why the local I-forces should depend only on local E and G forces.

Part (5) summarizes the import of the whole theorem.

Discussion

In the above theorem we have not discussed the notion of a 'rod'. The reason is that, although Grünbaum and Reichenbach take 'the rod corrected for differential forces' as the standard of congruence, such an object – an object that *would* stay rigid if all differential forces vanished – cannot, in general, exist in a geometry of variable curvature. If there is a 'bump' in the space, then a rod which is large relative to the 'bump' *must* change shape as it moves through the bump even if all differential forces (except the 'tidal' force due to the curvature itself) vanish. And it makes no sense to 'correct' for *tidal* forces. These are represented by vectors in tangent space, and unless we construe the tangent space as a real embedding space, we cannot say what the object would do if these were set equal to zero. (If we *do* construe the tangent space as an embedding space, then (1) the object won't even stay in the original space, if the tidal forces are set equal to zero; and (2) what it will do will depend on *how* the embedding is done; not just on the intrinsic geometry of the original space itself.) For these reasons, it is customary to understand a 'rod' as a *small* object in dealing with curved space – small relative to a local Euclidean (or Lorentzian, in the space–time case) frame, in the sense that, given the accuracy of the measurements in question, 'tidal' effects can be ignored. (Cf. Misner, 1973, pp. 393–9.)

We have followed Reichenbach in *separating* space and time, and discussed only the problem of remetricizing *space*. Earman has remarked to us that it is a defect of Reichenbach's book that he discusses space and time separately, and only discusses *space–time* at the end. Following a suggestion of Earman's (but not holding him responsible for the present discussion) we now generalize the above theorem to the case of space–time. In this case the equation $F = ma$ becomes

$$m \left(\frac{d^2 x^i}{d\tau^2} + g' \underset{jk}{\overset{i}{\Gamma}} \frac{dx^j}{d\tau} \frac{dx^k}{d\tau} \right) = F \text{ (total force)} \tag{1}$$

(assuming that if the metric is g', then the connection is the unique symmetric one g' compatible with g').

In order to preserve the form of this law and predict the same particle orbits the advocate of g has to add on a rather complicated additional force *relative to the description given by g'*

$$F_A = F(1 - \phi^2) + m \frac{dx}{d\tau'} \frac{d\phi}{d\tau'} \frac{1}{\phi} + m \left(g' \underset{jk}{\overset{i}{\Gamma}} - g \underset{jk}{\overset{i}{\Gamma}} \right) \frac{dx^j}{d\tau'} \frac{dx^k}{d\tau'}, \text{ where } g = \phi^2 g' \tag{2}$$

(We assume g and g' are conformally equivalent: otherwise, as Earman points out the change in metric will result in causal propagation outside the null cone). The total force is now $F' = F + F_A$, and the equation of motion is

$$m \left(\frac{d^2 x^i}{d\tau'^2} + g \underset{jk}{\overset{i}{\Gamma}} \frac{dx^j}{d\tau'} \frac{dx^k}{d\tau'} \right) = F' \text{ (total force)} \tag{3}$$

The new total force F' is always differential, and it can be split into parts E, G, I such that all three parts are differential and E satisfies Maxwell's Laws (locally),† G satisfies your favorite gravitational equation (locally)† and I depends on *both* masses and charges (an 'interactional' force), but is not universal.

The equation (3) implies that a system consisting of two free particles whose world lines are *parallel* geodesics in a local Lorentz frame (parallelism is only defined *locally*) will be 'rigid', since (3) implies that in the absence of forces, particles follow geodesics of the metric g and not g'. Of course, what types of 'rods' will actually be *possible* will depend on the physics and the metric g' as Misner, *et al.* remark:

---

† Apart from singularities, of course.

One need not – and indeed must not! – postulate that proper length is measured by a certain type of rod (e.g. platinum meter-stick), or that proper time is measured by a certain type of clock (e.g. hydrogen-maser clock). Rather one must ask the laws of physics themselves what types of rods and clocks will do the job. Put differently, one *defines an 'ideal' rod or clock* to be one which measures proper length as given by $ds = (g'_{\alpha\beta}dx^\alpha \ dx^\beta)^{1/2}$ or proper time as given by $d\tau = -(g_{\alpha\beta}dx^\alpha dx^\beta)^{1/2}$ (Misner, Thorne, Wheeler, 1973, p. 393).

10

Reply to Gerald Massey*

Let me say that I admire the vigor of Professor Massey's reply. Let me also say that all the references to Grünbaum in my paper were references to Grünbaum's pre-1970 publications, in particular to his reply to me. Pre-1970 Grünbaum is no figment of my imagination. Pre-1970 Grünbaum indicated in many places that he was using the expression 'convention' in a perfectly standard philosophical sense; for example he equated the statement that the choice of a metric is 'conventional' with the statement that the choice is just a matter of descriptive simplicity. 'Descriptive simplicity' is a term introduced by Reichenbach for those choices in science which do not affect the truth value of what is said, i.e. for those choices which are conventional in a perfectly standard philosophical sense of conventional. Massey sometimes seems to suggest that one cannot infer from the fact that something is 'convention laden' in Grünbaum's sense that it is conventional in the sense of any other philosopher. Also, as Massey himself recognizes, pre-1970 Grünbaum did hold that the term 'relation of spatial equality' has an 'intension' which fails to determine the extension of 'relation of equality' in the case of continuous physical spaces and space–time.

Now the question is: to what extent is the position of post-1970 Grünbaum a substantial improvement on the pre-1970 position? Professor Grünbaum's post-1970 position is certainly more complicated than his pre-1970 position. One notion used by Professor Grünbaum, both early and late, and which I did not discuss in my paper, is the notion of a metric being *intrinsic*. In what follows I am going to replace the word 'intrinsic' by 'boojum' in order to remind you that I regard this notion as a meaningless one as it is employed by Professor Grünbaum.† But if you are more fortunate than I in being able to understand the notion of an intrinsic metric, then you can simply replace the word 'boojum' where it occurs by the word 'intrinsic'. What Grünbaum

* This is my reply to Gerald Massey's comment on 'The refutation of conventionalism' at the St Louis meeting of the American Philosophical Association on 26 April 1974. The paper of Grünbaum's referred to in the text is Grünbaum (1970).

† In the discussion following this paper, Professor Massey remarked that he also finds the notion of an intrinsic metric to be a 'boojum' notion.

insists, both pre-and post-1970, is that if a space happens to possess a nontrivial boojum metric and that nontrivial boojum metric is unique, then 'relation of spatial equality' means relation of spatial equality *which agrees with the unique nontrivial boojum metric.*† What Grünbaum also insists both pre-and post-1970 is that if a space has no boojum metric, and has, as is generally the case, a plurality of alternative non-boojum ('extrinsic') metrics, then the choice of any one of those metrics to be the relation of spatial equality is conventional, or as he now says, convention-laden.

There are three significant differences between the pre-1970 Grünbaum position and the post-1970 Grünbaum position: whereas pre-1970 Grünbaum regarded it as an *a priori* truth that a continuous physical space has no boojum metric, post-1970 Grünbaum regards this as an empirical hypothesis. Since I don't regard this as a meaningful hypothesis, needless to say I don't agree that it is empirical, but I won't discuss this point. Secondly, the criteria for a manifold's possessing a boojum metric are spelled out in some (unintelligible) detail. Thirdly, what Massey calls 'the intuitive semantics' of the pre-1970 position is given up and in its place something comes in that I find interesting, and to a certain extent, congenial. This is the idea that scientific terms have what Massey calls a *normative force* (although I think that way of putting it may be misleading). When we say that the distance from x to y is such and such, we are not (on a post-1970 account) just saying that the distance from x to y is such and such according to this, that, or the other conventionally chosen metric; we may also be *prescribing* that that metric *ought* to be chosen. Here, of course, the 'ought' is not a *moral* ought; the 'ought' simply means that given the aims and procedures of science, given what features we are actually interested in, regard as important, etc., this particular choice is the optimal one.

What I find congenial about this is the following. I think that *in general* in science when we introduce a term we understand that that term is to refer not to whatever meets certain constraints that we can explicitly state at the time, but to whatever *optimally* meets those constraints. In a recent paper‡ I illustrate this in connection with common, natural kind terms. But it is misleading to say that a term used in this way is used *prescriptively*. I would rather say that the term is used *descriptively* to refer to whatever optimally meets the constraints in question, and that we philosophers of science are the ones who prescribe when *we* say that this is the way in which scientific terms are used and

---

† Professor Massey disassociated himself from this position of Grünbaum's in the discussion.

‡ Chapter 12 in this volume.

ought to be used. Philosophy of science, to borrow a phrase from Richard Boyd, is normative description of science. It is not that in the general theory of relativity, for example, the expression 'space–time distance' is used prescriptively, in the sense that the scientist is constantly saying 'you ought to use the metric of general relativity theory'. It is rather that the expression 'space–time distance' refers to space–time distance according to the metric that in fact one ought to use in that context. If this is what Massey means by saying that the use of the expression is *prescriptive*, then I would say that being used 'prescriptively' in a case in which it is clear which reference is optimal is to have an objective reference; that 'space–time distance' refers to space–time distance according to the metric appropriate to the context. However, Grünbaum qualifies this idea in his 1970 paper, by insisting that 'it is the job of a metric to render the intrinsic [i.e. boojum – H.P.] facts'.

Now let me try to clarify what is at issue by means of an example. Imagine a philosopher, I'll call him McX, who wishes to deny that it is an instance of TSC that 'pot' refers to pots and not to radios. He argues as follows: 'There are not just two possibilities but three (in fact, infinitely many, but I'll just stick to three). It is the job of the word "pot" to *render the unicornish facts*.' ('I used to say, it was part of the intension,' says McX, 'but I've given up that intuitive semantic talk.') 'So "pot" would refer to unicorns *if unicorns existed*. Unfortunately there are no unicorns: so it is a matter of convention that we pick pots rather than radios for the *semantically pre-empted word* "pot" to refer to.'

McX's ground for denying that the conventionality of the choice of an extension for 'pot' is an instance of TSC is that even after 'pot' is 'preempted' by being assigned the job of rendering the unicornish facts, it is still open what 'pot' shall refer to if *there are no unicorns*. So our statement that the choice of an extension for 'pot' is conventional ('I now say, convention-laden' remarks McX) has empirical content – it implies the empirical fact that there are no unicorns. Indeed, even *given* the fact that there are no unicorns, it is still only an *empirical hypothesis* that there are no unicornish facts which *determine* that 'pot' refers to pots – perhaps, says McX, pots have some special unicornish properties that we don't know about. 'The convention-laden status of the reference of "pot" can never be more than an empirical hypothesis.'

It is clear why we would not be convinced by McX that the assignment of 'pot' to pots rather than radios is *not* an instance of TSC. We would not agree that it is the 'job' (what I called the 'essence') of the word 'pot' to 'render the unicornish facts'. So, although we would certainly agree that it is an empirical fact that unicorns do not exist (and perhaps an empirical fact that pots and other things don't have uni-cornish properties), we would not agree that *that* is what anyone would rightfully understand by 'the assignment of "pot" to pots rather than radios is conventional'.

But these are just my grounds for rejecting the Grünbaum position. Granting for the sake of argument that the notion of an 'intrinsic' metric does make sense, and granting for the sake of argument that physical space–time has no intrinsic metric, I see *no* basis for saying that the 'job' of 'relation of spatial equality' as applied to congruence relations for physical space or space–time is to 'render the intrinsic facts', if *there are not and never were any intrinsic facts to render*. Grünbaum says that the following statement: 'The assignment of the *semantically preempted* word "congruent" to a particular "extrinsic" relation in the GTR is convention-laden' is not an instance of TSC because it implies that there is no (unique, nontrivial) 'intrinsic' metric for physical space or space–time. But it *can't* imply that, in any reasonable sense of 'convention-laden', unless it is part of the *essence* of 'congruent' that it *would* refer to the 'intrinsic' metric if there were one, and also it can't imply that unless it is *not equally* part of the *essence* of 'congruent' that it would refer to the optimal 'extrinsic' metric if there is one (and there is no 'intrinsic' metric). Massey seems to say that 'convention-laden' means by stipulation 'there is no intrinsic metric'; but this is clearly wrong. In short, I think the Conventionalist Ploy is still present, though in a disguised form.

II

Explanation and reference*

I. General significance of the topic

In this paper I try to contrast realist theories of meaning with what may
be called 'idealist' theories of meaning. But a word of explanation is
clearly in order.

There is no Marxist 'theory of meaning' but there are a series of
remarks on the correspondence between concepts and things, on concepts, and on the impossibility of *a priori* knowledge in the writings of
Engels (cf. Engels, 1959) which clearly bear on problems of meaning and
reference. In particular, there is a passage† in which Engels makes the
point that a concept may contain elements which are not correct.
A contemporary scientific characterization of fish would include,
Engels says, such properties as life under water and breathing through
gills; yet lungfish and other anomalous species which lack these properties are classified as fish for scientific purposes. And Engels argues, I
think correctly, that to stick to the letter of the 'definition' in applying
the concept *fish* would be bad science. In short, Engels contends that:

(1) Our scientific conception (I would say 'stereotype') of a fish
includes the property 'breathing through gills', but

(2) 'All fish breath through gills' is not true! (and, *a fortiori*, not
analytic).

I do not wish to ascribe to Engels an anachronistic sophistication
about contemporary logical issues, but without doing this it is fair to say
on the basis of this argument that Engels *rejects* the model according to
which such a concept as *fish* provides anything like analytically necessary
and sufficient conditions for membership in a natural kind. Two further
points are of importance: (1) The fact that the concept 'natural kind *all*
of whose members live under water, breath through gills, etc.' does not

---

* First published in G. Pearce and P. Maynard (eds.) *Conceptual Change* (Dordrecht-
Reidel 1973) 199–221.
† In a letter written to Conrad Schmidt in 1895; cf. Marx (1942), pp. 527–30. My
agreement is with Engels' realism, not his 'dialectical materialism'.

strictly fit the natural kind Fish does not mean that the concept does not *correspond* to the natural kind Fish. As Engels puts it, the concept is not exactly correct (as a description of the corresponding natural kind) but that does not make it a *fiction*. (2) The concept is continually changing as a result of the impact of scientific discoveries, but that does not mean that it ceases to correspond to the same natural kind (which is itself, of course, also changing). Again, without attributing to Engels a sophisticated theory of meaning and reference, it is fair, I think, to restate the essential gist of these two points in the following way: concepts which are not strictly true of anything may yet refer to something; and concepts in different theories may refer to the same thing. Of these two points, the second is obvious for most realists; with a few possible exceptions (e.g. Paul Feyerabend), realists have held that there are successive scientific theories about the *same* things: about heat, about electricity, about electrons, and so forth; and this involves treating such terms as 'electricity' as *trans-theoretical* terms, as Dudley Shapere has called them (cf. Shapere, 1969), i.e. as terms that have the same reference in different theories. The first point is more controversial; the idea that concepts provide necessary and sufficient conditions for class membership has often been attacked but, nonetheless, constantly reappears. Without it, however, the other point is moot. Bohr assumed in 1911 that there are (at every time) numbers p and q such that the (one dimensional) position of a particle is q and the (one dimensional) momentum is p; if this was part of the meaning of 'particle' for Bohr, and in addition, 'part of the meaning' means 'necessary condition for membership in the extension of the term', then electrons are *not* particles in Bohr's sense, and, indeed, there are *no* particles 'in Bohr's sense'. (And no 'electrons' in Bohr's sense of 'electron', etc.) None of the terms in Bohr's 1911 theory referred! It follows on this account that we cannot say that present electron theory is a better theory of the same particles that Bohr was referring to. I take it that this is the line of thinking that Paul Feyerabend represents. On an account like Shapere's, however, Bohr would have been referring to electrons when he used the word 'electron', notwithstanding the fact that some of his beliefs about electrons were mistaken, and *we* are referring to those same particles notwithstanding the fact that some of our beliefs – even beliefs included in our scientific 'definition' of the term 'electron' – may very likely turn out to be equally mistaken. This seems right to me. The main technical contribution of this paper will be a sketch of a theory of meaning which supports Shapere's insights.

An 'idealist' theory of meaning, as I am using the term, might go like this (in its simplest form): the meaning of such a sentence as 'electrons exist' is a function of certain *predictions* that can be derived from it (in a pure idealist theory, these would have to be predictions about *sensations*); these predictions are clearly a function of the *theory* in which the sentence occurs; thus 'electrons exist' has no meaning apart from this, that or the other theory, and it has a different meaning in different theories.

The question of 'reference' is a harder one for an idealist: the essence of idealism is to view scientific theories and concepts as instruments for predicting sensations and not as representatives of real things and magnitudes. But a sophisticated idealist is likely to say that the question of reference is 'trivial':† if one has a scientific language L containing the term 'electron', then one can certainly construct a metalanguage ML over it *à la* Tarski, and define 'reference' in such a way that '"electron" refers to electrons' is a trivial theorem. But if different scientific theories T_1 and T_2 are associated with different formal languages L_1 and L_2 (as they must be if the words have different meanings in T_1 and T_2), then they will be associated with different *meta*-languages ML_1 and ML_2. In ML_1 we can say '"electron" refers to electrons', meaning that 'electron' in the sense of T_1 refers to electrons *in the sense of T_1*, and in ML_2 we can say '"electron" refers to electrons' meaning that 'electron' in the sense of T_2 refers to electrons *in the sense of T_2*; but there is no ML in which we can even express the statement that 'electron' refers to the same entities in T_1 and T_2 – or, at least, no prescription for constructing such an ML has been provided by Positivist philosophers of science. In short, just as the idealist regards 'electron' as *theory dependent,* so does he regard the semantical notions of reference and truth as theory dependent; just as the realist regards 'electron' as *trans-theoretical,* so does he regard truth and reference as trans-theoretical.

II. The meaning of physical magnitude terms

A. A causal account of meaning

My purpose here is to sketch an account of the meaning of physical magnitude terms (e.g. 'temperature', 'electrical charge'); not an account of meaning in general, although I will try to indicate similarities between what is said here about these terms and what Kripke has said about proper names and what I have said elsewhere about natural kind words. (Kripke's work has come to me second hand; even so, I owe him a large debt for suggesting the idea of causal chains as the mechanism of reference.)

On a traditional view, any term has an intension and an extension.

† See, for example, the discussion by Hempel (1965), pp. 217–18. A contrasting view is sketched in chapter 13, volume 1 of these papers.

'Knowing the meaning' is having knowledge of the intension; what it is to 'know' an intension (construed, usually, as an abstract entity of some kind) is never explained. The extension of the color term 'red', for example, is the class of red things; the intension, according to Carnap, is the property Red. Carnap spoke of 'grasping' the intension of terms; what it would be to 'grasp' the property Red was never explained; probably Carnap would have equated it with knowing how to verify sentences of the form 'x is red', but this comes from his theory of knowledge, not his writings on semantics. In any case, understanding words is a matter of having knowledge. Full linguistic competence in connection with a word may require more knowledge than just the intension; for example, syntactical knowledge, knowledge of cooccurrence regularities, etc.; but linguistic competence, like understanding, is a matter of *knowledge* – not necessarily explicit knowledge – knowledge in the wide sense, implicit as well as explicit, 'knowing how' as well as 'knowing that', skills and abilities as well as facts, but all *knowledge* none the less.

According to the theory I shall present this is fundamentally wrong. Linguistic competence and understanding are not just *knowledge*. To have linguistic competence in connection with a term it is not sufficient, in general, to have the full battery of usual linguistic knowledge and skills; one must, in addition, be in the right sort of relationship to certain distinguished situations (normally, though not necessarily, situations in which the *referent* of the term is present). It is for this reason that this sort of theory is called a 'causal theory' of meaning.

Coming to physical magnitude terms, what every user of the term 'electricity' knows is that electricity is a magnitude of some sort – and, in fact, not even that: electricity was thought at one time to possibly be a sort of substance, and so was heat. At any rate, speakers know that 'electricity' and 'heat' are putative physical *quantities* – capable of more and less, and capable of location. (I do not think that even these statements are *analytic*, but I think they have a kind of *linguistic* association with the terms in question.) In a developed semantic theory one might introduce a special semantic marker, e.g. 'physical quantity', for terms of this sort. I cannot, however, think of anything that *every* user of the term 'electricity' *has* to know except that electricity is (associated with the notion of being) a physical magnitude of some sort, and, possibly, that 'electricity' (or electrical charge or charges) is capable of flow or motion. Benjamin Franklin knew that 'electricity' was manifested in the form of sparks and lightning bolts; someone else might know about currents and electromagnets; someone else might know about atoms consisting of positively and negatively charged particles. They could all use the term 'electricity' without there being a discernible 'intension' that they all share. I want to suggest that what they do have in common is this: that each of them is connected by a certain kind of causal chain to a situation in which a *description* of electricity is given, and generally a *causal* description – that is, one which singles out electricity as *the* physical magnitude *responsible* for certain effects in a certain way.

Thus, suppose I were standing next to Ben Franklin as he performed his famous experiment. Suppose he told me that 'electricity' is a physical quantity which behaves in certain respects like a liquid (if he were a mathematician he might say 'obeys an equation of continuity'); that it collects in clouds, and then, when a critical point of some kind is reached, a large quantity flows from the cloud to the earth in the form of a lightning bolt; that it runs along (or perhaps 'through') his metal kite string; etc. He would have given me an *approximately correct definite description* of a physical magnitude. I could now use the term 'electricity' myself. Let us call this event – my acquiring the ability to use the term 'electricity' in this way – an *introducing event*. It is clear that each of my later uses will be causally connected to this introducing event, as long as those uses exemplify the ability I acquired in that introducing event. Even if I use the term so often that I forgot when I first learned it, the intention to refer to the same magnitude that I referred to in the past by using the word links my present use to those earlier uses, and indeed the word's being in my present vocabulary at all is a causal product of earlier events – ultimately of the introducing event. If I teach the word to someone else by telling him that the word 'electricity' is the name of a physical magnitude, and by telling him certain facts about it which do not constitute a causal description – e.g. I might tell him that like charges repel and unlike charges attract, and that atoms consist of a nucleus with one kind of charge surrounded by satellite electrons with the opposite kind of charge – even if the facts I tell him do not constitute a definite description of any kind, let alone a causal description – still, the word's being in his vocabulary will be causally linked to its being in my vocabulary, and hence, ultimately, to an introducing event.

I said before that different speakers use the word 'electricity' without there being a discernible 'intension' that they all share. If an 'intension' is anything like a necessary and sufficient condition, then I think that this is right. But it does not follow that there are no ideas about electricity which are in some way linguistically associated with the word. Just as the idea that tigers are striped is linguistically associated with the word 'tiger', so it seems that some idea that 'electricity' (i.e. electric charge or charges) is capable of flow or motion *is* linguistically associated with 'electricity'. And perhaps this is all – apart from being a physical magnitude or quantity in the sense described before – that is linguistically associated with the word.

Now then, if anyone knows that 'electricity' is the name of a physical quantity, and his use of the word is connected by the sort of causal chain I described before to an introducing event in which the causal description given was, in fact, a causal description of electricity, then we have a clear basis for saying that he uses the word to refer to electricity. Even if the causal description failed to describe electricity, if there is good reason to treat it as a mis-description *of electricity* (rather than as a description of nothing at all) – for example, if electricity was described as the physical magnitude with such-and-such properties which is responsible for such-and-such effects, where in fact electricity is responsible for the effects in question, and the speaker intended to refer to the magnitude responsible for those effects, but mistakenly added the incorrect information 'electricity has such-and-such properties' because he mistakenly thought that the magnitude responsible for those effects had those further properties – we still have a basis for saying that both the original speaker and the persons to whom he teaches the word use the word to refer to electricity.

If a number of speakers use the word 'electricity' to refer to electricity, and, in addition, they have the standard sorts of associations with the word – that it refers to a magnitude which can move or flow – then, I suggest, the question of whether it has 'the same meaning' in their various idiolects simply does not arise. If a word is linguistically associated with a necessary and sufficient condition in the way that 'bachelor' is, then that sort of question *can* arise; but it does not arise, for example, in the case of proper names, and it does not arise, for a similar reason, in the case of physical magnitude terms. Thus if you know that 'Quine' is a name and I know that 'Quine' is a name and, in addition, we both refer to the same person when we use the word (even if the causal chains linking us to the referent are quite different) then the question of whether 'Quine' has the same meaning in my idiolect and in yours does not arise. More precisely: if the referent is the same, and we both associate the same minimal linguistic information with the word 'Quine', namely that it is a person's name, then the word is treated as the same word whether it occurs in your idiolect or in mine. Similarly, 'electricity' is the same word in Ben Franklin's idiolect and in mine. Of course, if you had wrong linguistic ideas about the name 'Quine' – for example, if you thought 'Quine' was a female name (not just that Quine was a woman, but that the name was restricted to females) – then there would be a difference in meaning.

This account stresses causal descriptions because physical magnitudes are invariably discovered through their effects, and so the natural way to first single out a physical magnitude is as the magnitude responsible for certain effects. Of course, the words 'responsible', 'causes', etc., do not literally have to occur in the description: *spin*, for example, was introduced by describing it as a physical magnitude having half-integral values characteristic of certain elementary particles, and giving a *law* connecting it with magnitudes previously introduced; I intend the notion of a causal description to include this case. And it is not a 'necessary truth' that the description introducing a new physical magnitude should involve a notion of cause or law; but I am not trying in this paper to state 'necessary truths'.

Once the term 'electricity' has been introduced into someone's vocabulary (or into his 'idiolect', as the dialect of a single speaker is called) whether by an introducing event, or by his learning the word from someone who learned it via an introducing event, or by his learning the word from someone linked by a chain of such transmissions to an introducing event, the referent in that person's idiolect is also fixed, even if no knowledge that that person has fixed it. And once the referent is fixed, one can use the word to formulate any number of theories about that referent (and even to formulate theoretical definitions of that referent which may be correct or incorrect scientific characterizations of that referent), without the word's being in any sense a different word in different theories. Thus the account just given fullfils the desideratum with which we started – it makes such terms as 'electricity' trans-theoretical. The 'operational criteria' you can give for the presence of electricity will depend strongly on what theory you accept; but, without the illicit identification of meaning with operational criteria, it does not follow at all that *meaning* depends on the theory you accept.

The possibility of formulating definite descriptions (or even misdescriptions) of physical magnitudes depends upon the availability in our language of such 'broad spectrum' notions as *physical magnitude* and *causes*; that these play a crucial role in the introduction of physical magnitude terms was argued in chapter 13, volume 1. In that paper, however, I did not distinguish between *defining* what I then called theoretical terms and *introducing* them. Of course, if we have available a language in which we can formulate descriptions of the referents of our various physical magnitude terms, then we can consider the various theories that we have containing those terms as so many different systems of sentences in that one language. To the extent that we can do this, we can treat the notions of reference and truth appropriate to that language as trans-theoretical notions also.

B. *Kripke's theory of proper names*

I have already acknowledged a heavy indebtedness to Kripke's (unpublished) work on proper names. Since I have heard mainly secondhand reports of that work, I shall not attempt to describe it here in any great detail. But, as it has come down to me, the key idea is that a person may use a proper name to refer to a thing or person X even though he has *no* true beliefs about X. For example, suppose someone asks me who Quine is, and I falsely tell him that Quine was a Roman emperor. If he believes me, and if he goes on to use the word 'Quine' with the intention of referring to the person to whom *I* refer as Quine, then he will say such things as 'Quine was a Roman emperor' – and he will be referring to a contemporary logician. Of course, he still has some true beliefs about Quine (beyond the belief that Quine is or was a person); for example, that Quine is or was named 'Quine'; but Kripke has more elaborate examples to show that even this is not always the case. On Kripke's view, the essential thing is this: that the use of a proper name to refer involves the existence of a causal chain of a certain kind connecting the user of the name (and the particular event of his using the name) to the bearer of the name.

Now then, I do not feel that one should be quite as liberal as Kripke is with respect to the causal chains one allows. I do not see much point, for example, in saying that someone is referring to Quine when he uses the name 'Quine' if he thinks that 'Quine' was a Roman emperor, and that is all he 'knows' about Quine; unless one has *some* beliefs about the bearer of the name which are true or approximately true, then it is at best idle to consider that the name refers to that bearer in one's idiolect. But what seems right about Kripke's account is that the knowledge an individual user of a language has need not at all fix the reference of the proper names in that individual's idiolect; the reference is fixed by the fact that that individual is causally linked to other individuals who were in a position to pick out the bearer of the name, or of some names from which the name descended. Indeed, what is important about Kripke's theory is not that the use of proper names is 'causal' – what is not? – but that the use of proper names is *collective*. Anyone who uses a proper name to refer is, in a sense, a member of a collective which had 'contact' with the bearer of the name: if it is surprising that a particular member of the collective need not have had such contact, and need not even have any good idea of the bearer of the name, it is only surprising because we think of language as private property.

The relationship of this theory of Kripke's to the above theory of physical magnitude terms should be obvious. Indeed, one might say that physical magnitude terms *are* proper names: they are proper names of *magnitudes* not *things* – however, this would be wrong, I think, since some physical magnitude terms (e.g. 'heat') are linguistically associated with rather rich information about the referent. The important thing about proper names is that it would be ridiculous to think that having linguistic competence can be equated in their case with knowledge of a necessary and sufficient condition – thus one is led to search for something other than the knowledge of the speaker which fixes the referent in their case.

It will be noted that I required a causal chain from the use of the physical magnitude term back to an introducing event – not back to an event in which the physical magnitude played a significant role. The reason is that, although no one in practice is going to be in a position to give a definite description of a physical magnitude unless he is causally connected to such an event, the nature of *that* causal chain seems not to matter. As long as one is in a position to give a definite description (or even a misdescription), one is in a position to introduce the term; and the chain from there on is something about which much more definite statements can be made. (In my opinion, it would be good to make a similar modification in Kripke's theory of proper names.)

C. Natural kind words

In chapter 8 of this volume I presented an account of natural kind words (e.g. 'lemon') which has some relation to the present account of physical magnitude terms. I suggested that anyone who has linguistic competence in connection with 'lemon' satisfies three conditions: (1) He has implicit knowledge of such facts as the fact that 'lemon' is a concrete noun, that it is the 'name of a fruit', etc. – information given by classifying the word under certain natural syntactic and semantic 'markers'. I criticized Jerrold Katz for the view that natural systems of semantic markers can enable us to give the exact meaning of each term (or of *any* natural kind term); but *some* of the information associated with a word can naturally be represented by classifying the word under such familiar headings as 'noun', 'concrete', etc. (2) He associates the word with a certain 'stereotype' – yellow color, tart taste, thick peel, etc. (3) He uses the word to *refer* to a certain natural kind – say, a natural kind of fruit whose most essential feature, from a biologist's point of view, might be a certain kind of DNA.

Two points were most important in the argument of that paper. The first was that the properties mentioned in the stereotype (and, I would add, the properties indicated by the semantic markers) are not being analytically predicated of each member of the extension, or, indeed, of any members of the extension. It is not analytic that all tigers have stripes, nor that some tigers have stripes; it is not analytic that all lemons are yellow, nor that some lemons are yellow; it is not even analytic that tigers are animals or that lemons are fruits. The stereotype is *associated* with the word; it is not a necessary and sufficient condition for membership in the corresponding class, nor even for being a normal member of the corresponding class. Engels' example of the word 'fish' fits right in here: what Engels was pointing out was precisely that the stereotype associated with the term 'fish' even in scientific, as opposed to lay, usage is not a necessary and sufficient condition. The second point was that speakers must be referring to a particular natural kind for us to treat them as using the same word 'lemon', or 'aluminum', or whatever. The weakness of that paper, apart from being very poorly organized and presented, is that nothing positive is said about the conditions under which a speaker who uses a word (say 'aluminum' or 'elm tree') is referring to one set of things rather than another. Clearly, the speaker who uses the word 'aluminum' need not be able to tell aluminum from molybdenum, and the speaker who use the term 'elm tree' cannot tell elm trees from beech trees if he happens to be me. But then what does determine the reference of the terms 'aluminum', and 'molybdenum' in my idiolect? In the previous papers, I suggested that the reference is fixed by a test known to experts; it now seems to me that this is just a special case of my use being causally connected to an introducing event. For natural kind words too, then, linguistic competence is a matter of knowledge plus causal connection to introducing events (and ultimately to members of the natural kind itself). And this is so far the same reason as in the case of physical magnitude terms; namely, that the use of a natural kind word involves in many cases membership in a 'collective' which has contact with the natural kind, which knows of tests for membership in the natural kind, etc., only as a collective. The idea that linguistic competence in connection with a natural kind word involves more than just having the right extension or reference (where this is now explained via a causal account), but also associating the right stereotype seems to me to carry over to physical magnitude words. Natural kind words can be associated with 'strong' stereotypes (stereotypes that give a strong picture of a stereotypical member – even to the point of enabling one to tell, in most cases, if something belongs to the natural kind), as in the case of 'lemon' or 'tiger', or with 'weak' stereotypes (stereotypes that give no idea of what a sufficient condition for membership in the class would be), as in the case of 'molybdenum' or (unless I am a very atypical speaker) 'elm'. Similarly, it seems to me that the physical magnitude term 'temperature' is associated with a very strong stereotype, and 'electricity' with a weak one.

D. Objections and questions

It is obvious that the account presented here must face certain hard questions. Without attempting to think of all of them myself, I should like to list a few that may help to launch discussion.

(1) One question that must be faced by all causal theories of meaning is how to make more precise the notion of a causal chain of the appropriate kind. How precisely can we describe the sorts of causal chains that must exist from one use of a word to a later use of the same word if we are to say that the referent or referents are the same in the two cases? And how much of a defect in these sorts of theories is it if one cannot be more precise on this point?

(2) It may seem counterintuitive that a natural kind word such as 'horse' is sharply distinguished from a term for a fictitious or nonexistent natural kind such as 'unicorn', and that a physical magnitude term such as 'electricity' is sharply distinguished from a term for a fictitious or nonexistent physical magnitude or substance such as 'phlogiston'. Indeed, I myself believe that if unicorns were found to exist and people began to discover facts about them, give nonobvious definite descriptions or approximately correct descriptions of the class of unicorns, etc., then the linguistic character of the word 'unicorn' would change; and similarly with 'phlogiston'; but this is certain to be controversial.

(3) Some people will argue that definitions of such terms as 'electricity' (or, more precisely, 'charge') are crucial in the exact sciences, and further that such definitions should be regarded as *meaning stipulations*. I agree with the first part of this – that definitions are important in science, provided one remembers what Quine has pointed out, that 'definition' is relative to a particular text or presentation, and that there is no such thing, in general, as the definition of a term 'in physics' or 'in biology' – only the definition in X, Y, or Z's presentation or axiomatization. I disagree with the last part – that 'definitions' in science are meaning stipulations – but, again, this is certain to be controversial.

(4) Finally, there will be objections to my use of causal notions, from Humeans who expect them to be reduced away, and to my use of the term 'physical magnitude' from extensionalists and nominalists. Here I can only plead guilty to the belief that talk about what causes what, or what the laws of nature are, or what would happen if other things happened is *not* highly derived talk about mere regularities, and to the

belief that the real world requires for its description not only reference to things but reference to physical magnitudes (cf. chapter 19, volume 1 of these papers) – in a sense of 'physical magnitude' in which physical magnitudes exist contingently, not as a matter of logical necessity, and in which magnitudes can be synthetically identical (e.g. temperature is the same magnitude as mean molecular kinetic energy).

III. Why positivistic theory of science is wrong

My contention in this paper is not that what is wrong with positivist theory of science is positivist theory of meaning. What is wrong with positivist theory of science is that it is based on an idealist or idealist-tending world view, and that that view does not correspond to reality. However, the idealist element in contemporary positivism enters precisely through the theory of meaning; thus part of any realist critique of positivism has to include at least a sketch of rival theory. In the present section, I want to turn from the task of sketching such a rival theory, which was just completed, to the task of showing that positivistic theory of explanation broadly construed – that is, positivist theory of scientific theory – does not correspond to reality any better than the older and less sophisticated idealist theories to which it is historically the successor.

Let us for a moment review some of those older theories. The oldest theory is Bishop Berkeley's. Here one already meets what might be called the *adequacy claim*: that is, the claim that a convinced Berkelian is *entitled* to accept standard scientific theory and practice, that Berkeley can give an account of the scientific method which would justify this. Indeed, I have heard philosophers argue that acceptance of Berkeley's metaphysics would not make any difference to the scientific theories one would accept. Here one already meets an important ambiguity. One can be claiming that a Berkelian can make the move of 'accepting' scientific theory in some sense other than accepting it as true or approximately-true: say, accepting it as a useful prediction heuristic. If this is what one means, then the claim is trivial. To be sure, Berkeley can 'accept' Newtonian physics in the Pickwickian sense of 'accept' as a useful scheme for making predictions. But Berkeley, to do him justice, was interested in much more: what he claimed was that an idealist could *reinterpret* (only he would not consider it *re*-interpretation, but rather *correct* interpretation) the notion of object so as to square both the layman's and the scientist's talk of objects with the idealist claim that reality consists of minds and their sensations ('spirits' and their 'ideas').

The difference between the two claims is the difference between accepting the idea that social practice is the test of truth and rejecting it, between accepting the idea that the overwhelming success of scientific theory offers some reason for accepting that theory as true or approximately-true, and claiming that success in practice is *no* indication of truth. Machian positivism fails for the same reason that Berkelian idealism does: although Mach makes the claim that his construction of the world out of sensations ('Empfindungen') is compatible with lay and scientific object-talk, no demonstration at all is given that this is so. The first philosopher to both precisely state and to undertake the task of *translating* thing-language into phenomenalistic language was Carnap (in *Logische Aufbau der Welt*). And what does Carnap do? He devotes the entire book to *preliminaries*, to 'reconstructions' *within* sensationalistic language (i.e. reductions of some sensation-concepts to others, not of thing-concepts to sensation-concepts), and then in the last chapter gives a sketch of the relation of thing-language to sensation-language which is *not* a translation, and which, indeed, amounts to no more than the old claim that we pick the thing-theory that is 'simplest' and most useful. In short, no demonstration is given at all that the positivist is entitled to quantify over (or refer to) material things.

It is with the failure of the phenomenalist translation enterprise, that is, with the failure to find *any* interpretation of object-concepts under which the prima facie incompatibility between an idealist world-view and a materialist world-view, between a world consisting of 'spirits and their ideas', or of 'Empfindungen', or of total experience-slices in one 'specious present', and a world consisting of fields and particles, simply *disappears* – it is with this failure that contemporary positivistic philosophy of science begins. Basically, two moves were made by the positivists after the failure of phenomenalist translation. The first was to give up construing scientific theories as systems of statements each of which had to have an intelligible interpretation (intelligible from the standpoint of what was taken as 'completely understood' or 'fully interpreted'), and to construe them rather as mere calculi, whose objective was to give successful predictions and otherwise to be as 'simple' as possible. 'Scientific theories are partially interpreted calculi' (chapter 13, volume 1 of these papers). The second move was to shift from phenomenalist language to 'observable thing language' as one's reduction-base – i.e. to say that one was seeking an interpretation or 'partial interpretation' of physical theory in 'observable thing language', not in 'sensationalistic language'.

The second move may make it appear questionable whether positivism is still correctly characterized as an 'idealist' tendency – i.e. as a tendency which regards or tends to regard the 'hard facts' as just facts about actual and potential *experiences*, and all other talk as somehow just highly derived talk about actual and potential experiences. I, myself, think this characterization *is* still fundamentally correct despite the shift to 'observable thing predicates' for two reasons: (1) The cut between observable things and 'theoretical entities' was historically introduced as a substitute for the thing/sensation dichotomy. Indeed, the reduction of 'theoretical entities' to 'observable things and qualities' would hardly seem to be a natural problem to someone who did not have in the back of his head the older problem of reduction to *sensations*. The reduction of things to sensations is both a historically motivated problem and one which rests upon the sharpness of the distinction between a material thing and a sensation (of course, even this sharpness is partly an illusion, in a materialist view – substitute 'material process' for 'material thing'!), as well as the supposed 'certainty' one has concerning one's own sensations. But the reduction of electrons to tables and chairs, or, more generally, of 'unobservable' things to 'observable' things is not historically motivated, the distinction is not sharp (Grover Maxwell asked years ago if a dust note is something 'given' when it is just big enough to see and a 'construct' when it is just too small to see – can the distinction between data and construct be a matter of size?), and one is not supposed to have certainty concerning observable things. (2) The positivists themselves frequently say that one could carry their analysis back down to the level of sensations, and that stopping with 'observable thing predicates' is a matter of *convenience*.†

In the remainder of this section I want to show that the first move – construing scientific theories as partially interpreted calculi – does not solve the adequacy problem at all. The positivist today is no more entitled than Berkeley was to accept scientific theory and practice – that is, his own story leads to no reason to think either that scientific theory is true, or that scientific practice tends to discover truth. In a sense, this is immediate. The positivist does not claim that scientific theory is 'true' in any trans-theoretic sense of 'true'; the only trans-theoretic notions he has are of the order of 'leads to successful prediction' and 'is simple'. Like the Berkelian, he has to fall back on the position that scientific theory is *useful* rather than true or approximately-true. But he does try to provide some account of the acceptability of scientific theories, even some account of their 'interpretation'. And he wants to maintain that in some sense the principle on which realist philosophy of science rests – that social practice is the test of truth, that the success of scientific theories is reason to think they are true or approximately-true –

† E.g. Carnap says this on p. 63 in Carnap (1956).

is right. What I want to show is that the notion of 'truth' that the positivist can give us is not the one on which scientific practice is based.

A. Truth

When a realistically minded scientist – that is to say, a scientist *whose practice* is realistic, not one whose official 'philosophy of science' is realistic – accepts a theory, he accepts it as true (or probably true, or approximately-true, or probably approximately-true). Since he also accepts *logic*† he knows that certain moves *preserve truth*. For example, if he accepts a theory T_1 as true and he accepts a theory T_2 as true, then he knows that T_1 & T_2 – the *conjunction* of T_1 and T_2 – is also true, by logic, and so he accepts T_1 & T_2. If we talk about probability, we have to say that if T_1 is very highly probably true and T_2 is very highly probably true, then the conjunction T_1 & T_2 is also highly probable (though not *as* highly as the conjuncts separately), provided that T_1 is not negatively relevant to T_2 – i.e. provided that T_2 is not only highly probable on the evidence, but also no less probable on the added assumption of T_1 (this is a judgement that must be made on the basis of what T_1 *says* and of background knowledge, of course). If we talk about approximate-truth, then we have to say that the approximations probably involved in T_1 and T_2 need to be compatible for us to pass from the approximate-truth of T_1 and T_2 to the approximate-truth of their conjunction. None of these matters is at all deep, from a realist point of view. But even if we confine ourselves to the simplest case, the case in which we can neglect the chances of error and the presence of approximations, and treat the acceptance of T_1 and T_2 as simply the acceptance of them as true, I want to suggest that the move from this acceptance to the acceptance of the conjunction is one to which one is not entitled on positivist philosophy of science. One of the simplest moves that scientists daily make, a move they make as a matter of propositional logic, a move which is central if scientific inquiry is to have any *cumulative* character at all, is totally *arbitrary* if positivist philosophy of science is right.

The difficulty is very simple. Acceptance of T_1, for a positivist, means acceptance of the calculus T_1 as leading to successful predictions (i.e. all *observation sentences* which are theorems of T_1 are true; not all *sentences* which are theorems of T_1 are 'true' in any fixed trans-theoretic sense). Similarly, the acceptance of T_2 means the acceptance of T_2 as leading to successful predictions. But from the fact that T_1 leads to successful predictions and the fact that T_2 leads to successful predictions it does not follow at all that the conjunction T_1 & T_2 leads to successful predic-

† The role of logic in empirical science is discussed in Putnam (1971) and in chapter 10, volume 1 of these papers.

tions. The difficulty, in a nutshell, is that the predicate which plays the *role* of truth – the predicate 'leads to successful predictions' – does not have the *properties* of truth. The positivist may teach in his philosophy seminar that acceptance of a scientific theory is acceptance of it as 'simple and leading to true predictions', and then go out and do science (or his students may go out and do science) by verifying theories T_1 and T_2, conjoining theories which have been previously verified, etc. – but then there is just as great a discrepancy between what he teaches in his philosophy seminar and his *practice* as there was between Berkeley's teaching that the world consisted of spirits and their ideas and continuing in practice to daily rely on the material object conceptual system.

Nor does it help to bring in 'simplicity'. It is not obvious that the conjunction of simple theories is simple; and even if simplicity is preserved, the conjunction of simple theories which separately lead to no false predictions may even be *inconsistent* (examples are easy to construct). More sophisticated moves have indeed been made. Thus, for Carnap truth of a theory is the same as truth of its 'Ramsey sentence' (for details see Hempel, 1965). But exactly the same objection applies: 'truth of the Ramsey sentence' does not have the properties of truth: if T_1 has a true Ramsey sentence and T_2 has a true Ramsey sentence it does not at all follow that the conjunction does.

(For those readers familiar with Carnap's use of the Hilbert epsilon-symbol, it may be pointed out that the difficulty comes out in very sharp form in Carnap's symbolization of his interpretations of individual theoretical terms. Thus let $T_1(P)$, $T_2(P)$ be two theories containing exactly one theoretical term P. On Carnap's own symbolization of his view, what P means in T_1 is $\varepsilon P T_1(P)$; what P means in T_2 is $\varepsilon P T_2(P)$; and what P means in $T_1 \& T_2$ is $\varepsilon P[T_1(P) \& T_2(P)]$; this makes it explicit that P has different meanings in T_1 and T_2 and *yet a third meaning* in their conjunction.)

B. Simplicity

It is easy to construct a 'theory' in the positivist sense (a calculus containing some observation terms) which leads to no false predictions but which no scientist would dream of accepting. This is usually handled by saying that scientists only choose 'simple' theories. Also, a simple theory may mess up science as a whole: so it is said that scientists are trying to maximize the simplicity of 'total science'. 'Theory' means, then, 'formalization of total science, or of some piece which is independent of the rest of total science'. Unfortunately, no one has ever written down or ever will write down a 'theory' in this sense. The fact is, that positivist philosophy of science depends on a constant slide between giving the impression that one is talking about 'theories' in the customary sense – Newton's theory, Maxwell's theory, Darwin's theory, Mendel's theory – and saying, at key points of difficulty such as the one just alluded to, that one is *really* talking about a 'formalization of total science', or some such thing.

The difficulty with the rule 'choose the simplest theory compatible with the evidence' is that it is probably not *right*, or would probably not be right, even if one *could* formalize 'total science' (at a given time). Scientists are not trying to maximize some formal property of 'simplicity'; they are trying to maximize *truth* (or improve their approximation to truth, or increase the amount of approximate-truth they know without decreasing the goodness of the approximation, and so forth).

Of course, a realist might accept the rule 'choose the simplest hypothesis', if it could be shown that the simplest hypothesis is always the most *probable* on the basis of the rest of his knowledge. But this is not so on any usual measure of simplicity. For example, suppose I know just three points on interstate highway 40, and those three points lie on a straight line. Suppose also that the statement 'IS 40 is straight' is logically consistent with my total knowledge. Then accepting 'IS 40 is straight' would, on the usual simplicity metrics, be accepting the simplest hypothesis. Yet I would not in fact accept 'IS 40 is straight', nor would anyone with our background knowledge. Given that every other interstate highway has curves, and given the enormous length of IS 40 and the enormous impracticality of making a straight highway across the entire United States, it is overwhelmingly probable that IS 40 is *not* straight.

Can we not say that my *total* 'knowledge' is less simple if I accept 'IS 40 is straight'? Not, it seems to me, on the basis of any criterion of *simplicity* that I know of. What is obviously involved here is not *simplicity* but plausibility: what introducing the word 'simplicity' does is make it look as if a calculation which is in fact the calculation of the probability of a state of affairs is in reality just a calculation of a formal property (such as number of argument places, number of primitive symbols, length and number of the axioms, perhaps shape of the curves mentioned) of an uninterpreted or semi-interpreted *calculus*, even if the property of being the most probable hypothesis on background knowledge could be *represented* syntactically, omitting to mention that the representing property was the syntactic representation of a *probability measure*, and pretending that it was *just* a formal property (like having simple axioms), would be a way of disguising rather than revealing what was going on.

C. Confirmation

Indeed, positivist philosophers of science have made attempts at formalizing the logic of confirmation. These attempts are interesting (though so far unsuccessful) researches on *any* philosophy of science. But not only do they have nothing to do with positivist theory of meaning; they are in fact *incompatible* with it. Thus when they write about meaning, positivists tell us that 'theoretical terms' have different meanings in different theories; when they formalize confirmation theory, they invariably treat theories as systems of sentences in *one* language, and assume that all semantical concepts are *trans*-theoretic. Thus the positivists are engaged in formalizing *realistic* confirmation theory: not the confirmation theory (if there is one!) to which their own theory of meaning should lead.

What is going on here should be evident from Carnap's work on the foundations of mathematics. Carnap has a consistent tendency to *identify* concepts with their syntactic representations: thus, mathematical truth with theoremhood (after the discovery of Gödel's theorem, he either allowed 'nonconstructive rules of proof', or simply assumed set theory, and took 'logical consequence' rather than derivability as the basic notion, although this trivialized the 'analysis' of mathematical truth). In the same way he would have liked to identify a state of affairs having a probability of, say, 0.9, with the corresponding sentence's having a c-value of 0.9 (where 'c' would be a syntactically defined measure on sentences in a formalized language). Even if Carnap had found a successful 'c-function', the fact is that it would have been successful because it corresponded to a reasonable probability measure over some collection of states of affairs; but this is just what Carnap's positivism did not allow him to say.

D. Auxiliary hypotheses

Sometimes, as we mentioned, the positivists make it explicit that the 'theories' to which their theory of science applies are 'formalizations of total science', and not theories in the usual sense; but their readers do, I think, tend to come away with the impression that their model *is* a model of a scientific theory in the usual sense – especially, a physical theory. Believing this involves believing that a physical theory is a calculus, or could easily be formalized as a calculus, and that its predictions are *self-contained* – that they are deduced from the explicitly stated assumptions of the theory itself. This leads to a comparison with social sciences which is derogatory to the social sciences – for the classic social science theories are clearly *not* self-contained in this sense. In short, the positivist attitude tends to be that social science is science only when and to the extent that it apes *physics*. And this for the reason that the mathematical model of a scientific theory provided by the positivists is thought to clearly fit *physical* theories.

But, in fact, it fits physical theories very badly, and this for the reason that even physical theories in the usual sense – e.g. Newton's Theory of Universal Gravitation, Maxwell's theory – lead to no predictions at all without a host of auxiliary assumptions, and moreover without auxiliary assumptions that are not at all law-like, but that are, in fact, assumptions about boundary conditions and initial conditions in the case of particular systems. Thus, if the claim that the term 'gravitation', for example, had a meaning which depended on the theory were true, and the theory included such auxiliary assumptions as that 'space is a hard vacuum', and 'there is no tenth planet in the solar system', then it would follow that discovery that space is *not* a hard vacuum or even that there is a tenth planet would change the meaning of 'gravitation'. I think one has to be pretty idealistic in one's intuitions to find this at all plausible! It is not so implausible that knowledge of the meaning of the term 'gravitation' involves some knowledge of the theory (although I think that this is wrong: the stereotype associated with 'gravitation' is not nearly as strong as a particular theory of gravitation), and this is probably what most readers think of when they encounter the claim that physical magnitude terms (usually called 'theoretical terms' to prejudge just the issue this paper discusses) are 'theory loaded'; but the actual meaning-dependence required by positivist meaning theory would be a dependence not just on the *laws* of the theory, but on the particular auxiliary assumptions – for, if these are not counted as part of the theory, then the whole theory-prediction scheme collapses at the outset.

Finally, neglect of the role that auxiliary assumptions actually play in science leads to a wholly incorrect idea of how a scientific theory is confirmed. Newton's theory of gravitation was not confirmed by checking predictions derived from it plus some set of auxiliary statements fixed in advance; rather the auxiliary assumptions had to be continually modified and expanded in the history of Celestial Mechanics. That scientific problems as often have the form of finding auxiliary hypotheses as they do of finding and checking predictions is something that has been too much neglected in philosophy of science;† this neglect is largely the result of the acceptance of the positivist model and its uncritical application to actual physical theories.

† I discuss this in chapter 16, volume 1 of these papers.

12

The meaning of 'meaning'*

Language is the first broad area of human cognitive capacity for which we are beginning to obtain a description which is not exaggeratedly oversimplified. Thanks to the work of contemporary transformational linguists,† a very subtle description of at least some human languages is in the process of being constructed. Some features of these languages appear to be *universal*. Where such features turn out to be 'species-specific' – 'not explicable on some general grounds of functional utility or simplicity that would apply to arbitrary systems that serve the functions of language' – they may shed some light on the structure of mind. While it is extremely difficult to say to what extent the structure so illuminated will turn out to be a universal structure of *language*, as opposed to a universal structure of innate general learning strategies,‡ the very fact that this discussion can take place is testimony to the richness and generality of the descriptive material that linguists are beginning to provide, and also testimony to the depth of the analysis, insofar as the features that appear to be candidates for 'species-specific' features of language are in no sense surface or phenomenological features of language, but lie at the level of deep structure.

The most serious drawback to all of this analysis, as far as a philosopher is concerned, is that it does not concern the meaning of words. Analysis of the deep structure of linguistic forms gives us an incomparably more powerful description of the *syntax* of natural languages than we have ever had before. But the dimension of language associated with the word 'meaning' is, in spite of the usual spate of heroic if misguided attempts, as much in the dark as it ever was.

In this essay, I want to explore why this should be so. In my opinion, the reason that so-called semantics is in so much worse condition than syntactic theory is that the *prescientific* concept on which semantics is

* First published in K. Gunderson (ed.) *Language, Mind and Knowledge*, Minnesota Studies in the Philosophy of Science, VII (University of Minnesota Press, Mpls.) © 1975 University of Minnesota.

† The contributors to this area are now too numerous to be listed: the pioneers were, of course, Zellig Harris and Noam Chomsky.

‡ For a discussion of this question see Putnam (1967) and N. Chomsky (1971), especially chapter 1.

based – the prescientific concept of *meaning* – is itself in much worse shape than the prescientific concept of syntax. As usual in philosophy, skeptical doubts about the concept do not at all help one in clarifying or improving the situation any more than dogmatic assertions by conservative philosophers that all's really well in this best of all possible worlds. The reason that the prescientific concept of meaning is in bad shape is not clarified by some general skeptical or nominalistic argument to the effect that meanings don't exist. Indeed, the upshot of our discussion will be that meanings don't exist in quite the way we tend to think they do. But electrons don't exist in quite the way Bohr thought they did, either. There is all the distance in the world between this assertion and the assertion that meanings (or electrons) 'don't exist'.

I am going to talk almost entirely about the meaning of words rather than about the meaning of sentences because I feel that our concept of word-meaning is more defective than our concept of sentence-meaning. But I will comment briefly on the arguments of philosophers such as Donald Davidson who insist that the concept of word-meaning *must* be secondary and that study of sentence-meaning must be primary. Since I regard the traditional theories about meaning as myth-eaten (notice that the topic of 'meaning' is the one topic discussed in philosophy in which there is literally nothing but 'theory' – literally nothing that can be labelled or even ridiculed as the 'common sense view'), it will be necessary for me to discuss and try to disentangle a number of topics concerning which the received view is, in my opinion, wrong. The reader will give me the greatest aid in the task of trying to make these matters clear if he will kindly assume that *nothing* is clear in advance.

Meaning and extension

Since the Middle Ages at least, writers on the theory of meaning have purported to discover an ambiguity in the ordinary concept of meaning, and have introduced a pair of terms – *extension* and *intension*, or *Sinn* and *Bedeutung*, or whatever – to disambiguate the notion. The *extension* of a term, in customary logical parlance, is simply the set of things the term is true of. Thus, 'rabbit', in its most common English sense, is true of all and only rabbits, so the extension of 'rabbit' is precisely the set of rabbits. Even this notion – and it is the *least* problematical notion in this cloudy subject – has its problems, however. Apart from problems it inherits from its parent notion of *truth*, the foregoing example of 'rabbit' *in its most common English sense* illustrates one such problem: strictly speaking, it is not a term, but an ordered pair consisting of a term and a 'sense' (or an occasion of use, or something else that distinguishes a term in one sense from the same term used in a different sense) that has an extension. Another problem is this: a 'set', in the mathematical sense, is a 'yes–no' object; any given object either definitely belongs to S or definitely does not belong to S, if S is a set. But words in a natural language are not generally 'yes–no': there are things of which the description 'tree' is clearly true and things of which the description 'tree' is clearly false, to be sure, but there are a host of borderline cases. Worse, the line between the clear cases and the borderline cases is itself fuzzy. Thus the idealization involved in the notion of *extension* – the idealization involved in supposing that there is such a thing as the set of things of which the term 'tree' is true – is actually very severe.

Recently some mathematicians have investigated the notion of a *fuzzy set* – that is, of an object to which other things belong or do not belong with a given probability or to a given degree, rather than belong 'yes–no'. If one really wanted to formalize the notion of extension as applied to terms in a natural language, it would be necessary to employ 'fuzzy sets' or something similar rather than sets in the classical sense.

The problem of a word's having more than one sense is standardly handled by treating each of the senses as a different word (or rather, by treating the word as if it carried invisible subscripts, thus: 'rabbit$_1$' – animal of a certain kind; 'rabbit$_2$' – coward; and as if 'rabbit$_1$' and 'rabbit$_2$' or whatever were different words entirely). This again involves two very severe idealizations (at least two, that is): supposing that words have discretely many senses, and supposing that the entire repertoire of senses is fixed once and for all. Paul Ziff has recently investigated the extent to which both of these suppositions distort the actual situation in natural language;† nevertheless, we will continue to make these idealizations here.

Now consider the compound terms 'creature with a heart' and 'creature with a kidney'. Assuming that every creature with a heart possesses a kidney and vice versa, the extension of these two terms is exactly the same. But they obviously differ in meaning. Supposing that there is a sense of 'meaning' in which meaning = extension, there must be another sense of 'meaning' in which the meaning of a term is not its extension but something else, say the 'concept' associated with the term. Let us call this 'something else' the *intension* of the term. The concept of a creature with a heart is clearly a different concept from the concept of a creature with a kidney. Thus the two terms have different intension. When we say they have different 'meaning', meaning = intension.

† This is discussed by Ziff (1972) especially chapter VIII.

Intension and extension

Something like the preceding paragraph appears in every standard exposition of the notions 'intension' and 'extension'. But it is not at all satisfactory. Why it is not satisfactory is, in a sense, the burden of this entire essay. But some points can be made at the very outset: first of all, what evidence is there that 'extension' *is* a sense of the word 'meaning'? The canonical explanation of the notions 'intension' and 'extension' is very much like 'in one sense "meaning" means *extension* and in the other sense "meaning" means *meaning*'. The fact is that while the notion of 'extension' is made quite precise, relative to the fundamental logical notion of *truth* (and under the severe idealizations remarked above), the notion of intension is made no more precise than the vague (and, as we shall see, misleading) notion 'concept'. It is as if someone explained the notion 'probability' by saying: 'in one sense "probability" means frequency, and in the other sense it means *propensity*'. 'Probability' *never* means 'frequency', and 'propensity' is at least as unclear as 'probability'.

Unclear as it is, the traditional doctrine that the notion 'meaning' possesses the extension/intension ambiguity has certain typical consequences. Most traditional philosophers thought of concepts as something *mental*. Thus the doctrine that the meaning of a term (the meaning 'in the sense of intension', that is) is a concept carried the implication that meanings are mental entities. Frege and more recently Carnap and his followers, however, rebelled against this 'psychologism', as they termed it. Feeling that meanings are *public* property – that the *same* meaning can be 'grasped' by more than one person and by persons at different times – they identified concepts (and hence 'intensions' or meanings) with abstract entities rather than mental entities. However, 'grasping' these abstract entities was still an individual psychological act. None of these philosophers doubted that understanding a word (knowing its intension) was just a matter of being in a certain psychological state (somewhat in the way in which knowing how to factor numbers in one's head is just a matter of being in a certain very complex psychological state).

Secondly, the timeworn example of the two terms 'creature with a kidney' and 'creature with a heart' does show that two terms can have the same extension and yet differ in intension. But it was taken to be obvious that the reverse is impossible: two terms cannot differ in extension and have the same intension. Interestingly, no argument for this impossibility was ever offered. Probably it reflects the tradition of the ancient and medieval philosophers who assumed that the concept

corresponding to a term was just a conjunction of predicates, and hence that the concept corresponding to a term must *always* provide a necessary and sufficient condition for falling into the extension of the term.†
For philosophers like Carnap, who accepted the verifiability theory of meaning, the concept corresponding to a term provided (in the ideal case, where the term had 'complete meaning') a *criterion* for belonging to the extension (not just in the sense of 'necessary and sufficient condition', but in the strong sense of *way of recognizing* if a given thing falls into the extension or not). Thus these positivistic philosophers were perfectly happy to retain the traditional view on this point. So theory of meaning came to rest on two unchallenged assumptions:

(I) That knowing the meaning of a term is just a matter of being in a certain psychological state (in the sense of 'psychological state', in which states of memory and psychological dispositions are 'psychological states'; no one thought that knowing the meaning of a word was a continuous state of consciousness, of course).

(II) That the meaning of a term (in the sense of 'intension') determines its extension (in the sense that sameness of intension entails sameness of extension).

I shall argue that these two assumptions are not jointly satisfied by *any* notion, let alone any notion of meaning. The traditional concept of meaning is a concept which rests on a false theory.

'Psychological state' and methodological solipsism

In order to show this, we need first to clarify the traditional notion of a psychological state. In one sense a state is simply a two-place predicate whose arguments are an individual and a time. In this sense, *being five feet tall, being in pain, knowing the alphabet*, and even *being a thousand miles from Paris* are all states. (Note that the *time* is usually left implicit

† This tradition grew up because *the* term whose analysis provoked all the discussion in medieval philosophy was the term 'God', and the term 'God' was thought to be defined through the conjunction of the terms 'Good', 'Powerful', 'Omniscient', etc. – the so called 'Perfections'. There was a problem, however, because God was supposed to be a Unity, and Unity was thought to exclude His essence being complex in *any* way – i.e. 'God' was defined through a conjunction of terms, but God (without quotes) could not be the logical product of properties, nor could He be the unique thing exemplifying the logical product of two or more *distinct* properties, because even this highly abstract kind of 'complexity' was held to be incompatible with His perfection of Unity. This is a theological paradox with which Jewish, Arabic, and Christian theologians wrestled for centuries (e.g. the doctrine of the Negation of Privation in Maimonides and Aquinas). It is amusing that theories of contemporary interest, such as conceptualism and nominalism, were first proposed as solutions to the problem of predication in the case of God. It is also amusing that the favorite model of definition in all of this theology – the conjunction-of-properties model – should survive, at least through its consequences, in philosophy of language until the present day.

or 'contextual'; the full form of an atomic sentence of these predicates would be '*x is five feet tall at time t*', '*x is in pain at time* t', etc.) In science, however, it is customary to restrict the term state to properties which are defined in terms of the parameters of the individual which are fundamental from the point of view of the given science. Thus, being five feet tall is a state (from the point of view of physics); being in pain is a state (from the point of view of mentalistic psychology, at least); knowing the alphabet might be a state (from the point of view of cognitive psychology), although it is hard to say; but being a thousand miles from Paris would *not* naturally be called a *state*. In one sense, a psychological state is simply a state which is studied or described by psychology. In this sense it may be trivially true that, say *knowing the meaning of the word 'water'* is a 'psychological state' (viewed from the standpoint of cognitive psychology). But this is not the sense of psychological state that is at issue in the above assumption (1).

When traditional philosophers talked about psychological states (or 'mental' states), they made an assumption which we may call the assumption of methodological solipsism. This assumption is the assumption that no psychological state, properly so called, presupposes the existence of any individual other than the subject to whom that state is ascribed. (In fact, the assumption was that no psychological state presupposes the existence of the subject's *body* even: if *P* is a psychological state, properly so called, then it must be logically possible for a 'disembodied mind' to be in *P*.) This assumption is pretty explicit in Descartes, but it is implicit in just about the whole of traditional philosophical psychology. Making this assumption is, of course, adopting a *restrictive program* – a program which deliberately limits the scope and nature of psychology to fit certain mentalistic preconceptions or, in some cases, to fit an idealistic reconstruction of knowledge and the world. Just *how* restrictive the program is, however, often goes unnoticed. Such common or garden variety psychological states as *being jealous* have to be reconstructed, for example, if the assumption of methodological solipsism is retained. For, in its ordinary use, *x is jealous of y* entails that *y* exists, and *x is jealous of y's regard for z* entails that both *y* and *z* exist (as well as *x*, of course). Thus *being jealous* and *being jealous of someone's regard for someone else* are not psychological states permitted by the assumption of methodological solipsism. (We shall call them 'psychological states in the wide sense' and refer to the states which are permitted by methodological solipsism as 'psychological states in the narrow sense'.) The reconstruction required by methodological solipsism would be to reconstrue *jealousy* so that I can be jealous of my own hallucinations, or of figments of my imagination, etc. Only if we assume that psychological states in the narrow sense have a significant degree of causal closure (so that restricting ourselves to psychological states in the narrow sense will facilitate the statement of psychological *laws*) is there any point in engaging in this reconstruction, or in making the assumption of methodological solipsism. But the three centuries of failure of mentalistic psychology is tremendous evidence against this procedure, in my opinion.

Be that as it may, we can now state more precisely what we claimed at the end of the preceding section. Let A and B be any two terms which differ in extension. By assumption (II) they must differ in meaning (in the sense of 'intension'). By assumption (I), *knowing the meaning of A* and *knowing the meaning of B* are psychological states *in the narrow sense* – for this is how we shall construe assumption (I). *But these psychological states must determine the extension of the terms A and B just as much as the meanings ('intensions') do.*

To see this, let us try assuming the opposite. Of course, there cannot be two terms A and B such that *knowing the meaning of A* is the same state as *knowing the meaning of B* even though A and B have different extensions. For *knowing the meaning of A* isn't just 'grasping the intension' of A, whatever that may come to; it is also knowing that the 'intension' that one has 'grasped' *is* the intension of A. (Thus, someone who knows the meaning of 'wheel' presumably 'grasps the intension' of its German synonym *Rad*; but if he doesn't know that the 'intension' in question is the intension of *Rad* he isn't said to 'know the meaning of *Rad*'.) If A and B are different terms, then *knowing the meaning of A* is a different state from *knowing the meaning of B* whether the meanings of A and B be themselves the same or different. But by the same argument, if I_1 and I_2 are different *intensions* and A is a term, then *knowing that I_1 is the meaning of A* is a different psychological state from *knowing that I_2 is the meaning of A*. Thus, there cannot be two different logically possible worlds L_1 and L_2 such that, say, Oscar is in the *same* psychological state (in the narrow sense) in L_1 and in L_2 (in all respects), but in L_1 Oscar understands A as having the meaning I_1 and in L_2 Oscar understands A as having the meaning I_2. (For, if there were, then in L_1 Oscar would be in the psychological state *knowing that I_1 is the meaning of A* and in L_2 Oscar would be in the psychological state *knowing that I_2 is the meaning of A*, and these are different and even – assuming that A has just *one* meaning for Oscar in each world – incompatible psychological states in the narrow sense.)

In short, if S is the sort of psychological state we have been discussing – a psychological state of the form *knowing that I is the meaning of A*, where I is an 'intension' and A is a term – then the *same* necessary and sufficient condition for falling into the extension of A 'works' in *every* logically possible world in which the speaker is in the psychological state S. For the state S *determines* the intension I, and by assumption (II) the intension amounts to a necessary and sufficient condition for membership in the *extension*.

If our interpretation of the traditional doctrine of intension and extension is fair to Frege and Carnap, then the whole psychologism/Platonism issue appears somewhat a tempest in a teapot, as far as meaning-theory is concerned. (Of course, it is a very important issue as far as general philosophy of mathematics is concerned.) For even if meanings are 'Platonic' entities rather than 'mental' entities on the Frege–Carnap view, 'grasping' those entities is presumably a psychological state (in the narrow sense). Moreover, the psychological state uniquely determines the 'Platonic' entity. So whether one takes the 'Platonic' entity or the psychological state as the 'meaning' would appear to be somewhat a matter of convention. And taking the psychological state to be the meaning would hardly have the consequence that Frege feared, that meanings would cease to be public. For psychological states are 'public' in the sense that different people (and even people in different epochs) can be in the *same* psychological state. Indeed, Frege's argument against psychologism is only an argument against identifying concepts with mental particulars, not with mental entities in general.

The 'public' character of psychological states entails, in particular, that if Oscar and Elmer understand a word A differently, then they must be in *different* psychological states. For the state of *knowing the intension of* A *to be, say,* I is the *same* state whether Oscar or Elmer be in it. Thus two speakers cannot be in the same psychological state in all respects and understand the term A differently; the psychological state of the speaker determines the intension (and hence, by assumption (II), the extension) of A.

It is this last consequence of the joint assumptions (I), (II) that we claim to be false. We claim that it is possible for two speakers to be in exactly the *same* psychological state (in the narrow sense), even though the extension of the term A in the idiolect of the one is different from the extension of the term A in the idiolect of the other. Extension is *not* determined by psychological state.

This will be shown in detail in later sections. If this is right, then there are two courses open to one who wants to rescue at least one of the traditional assumptions; to give up the idea that psychological state (in the narrow sense) determines *intension*, or to give up the idea that intension determines extension. We shall consider these alternatives later.

Are meanings in the head?

That psychological state does not determine extension will now be shown with the aid of a little science-fiction. For the purpose of the following science-fiction examples, we shall suppose that somewhere in the galaxy there is a planet we shall call Twin Earth. Twin Earth is very much like Earth; in fact, people on Twin Earth even speak *English*. In fact, apart from the differences we shall specify in our science-fiction examples, the reader may suppose that Twin Earth is *exactly* like Earth. He may even suppose that he has a *Doppelgänger* – an identical copy – on Twin Earth, if he wishes, although my stories will not depend on this.

Although some of the people on Twin Earth (say, the ones who call themselves 'Americans' and the ones who call themselves 'Canadians' and the ones who call themselves 'Englishmen', etc.) speak English, there are, not surprisingly, a few tiny differences which we will now describe between the dialects of English spoken on Twin Earth and Standard English. These differences themselves depend on some of the peculiarities of Twin Earth.

One of the peculiarities of Twin Earth is that the liquid called 'water' is not H_2O but a different liquid whose chemical formula is very long and complicated. 1 shall abbreviate this chemical formula simply as XYZ. I shall suppose that XYZ is indistinguishable from water at normal temperatures and pressures. In particular, it tastes like water and it quenches thirst like water. Also, I shall suppose that the oceans and lakes and seas of Twin Earth contain XYZ and not water, that it rains XYZ on Twin Earth and not water, etc.

If a spaceship from Earth ever visits Twin Earth, then the supposition at first will be that 'water' has the same meaning on Earth and on Twin Earth. This supposition will be corrected when it is discovered that 'water' on Twin Earth is XYZ, and the Earthian spaceship will report somewhat as follows:

'On Twin Earth the word "water" means XYZ.'

(It is this sort of use of the word 'means' which accounts for the doctrine that extension is one sense of 'meaning', by the way. But note that although 'means' does mean something like *has as extension* in this example, one would *not* say

'On Twin Earth the meaning of the word "water" is XYZ.'

unless, possibly, the fact that 'water is XYZ' was known to every adult speaker of English on Twin Earth. We can account for this in terms of the theory of meaning we develop below; for the moment we just remark that although the verb 'means' sometimes means 'has as extension', the nominalization 'meaning' *never* means 'extension'.)

Symmetrically, if a spaceship from Twin Earth ever visits Earth, then the supposition at first will be that the word 'water' has the same meaning on Twin Earth and on Earth. This supposition will be corrected when it is discovered that 'water' on Earth is H_2O, and the Twin Earthian spaceship will report:

'On Earth† the word "water" means H_2O.'

Note that there is no problem about the extension of the term 'water'. The word simply has two different meanings (as we say): in the sense in which it is used on Twin Earth, the sense of water$_{TE}$, what *we* call 'water' simply isn't water; while in the sense in which it is used on Earth, the sense of water$_E$, what the Twin Earthians call 'water' simply isn't water. The extension of 'water' in the sense of water$_E$ is the set of all wholes consisting of H_2O molecules, or something like that; the extension of water in the sense of water $_{TE}$ is the set of all wholes consisting of XYZ molecules, or something like that.

Now let us roll the time back to about 1750. At that time chemistry was not developed on either Earth or Twin Earth. The typical Earthian speaker of English did not know water consisted of hydrogen and oxygen, and the typical Twin Earthian speaker of English did not know 'water' consisted of XYZ. Let Oscar$_1$ be such a typical Earthian English speaker, and let Oscar$_2$ be his counterpart on Twin Earth. You may suppose that there is no belief that Oscar$_1$ had about water that Oscar$_2$ did not have about 'water'. If you like, you may even suppose that Oscar$_1$ and Oscar$_2$ were exact duplicates in appearance, feelings, thoughts, interior monologue, etc. Yet the extension of the term 'water' was just as much H_2O on Earth in 1750 as in 1950; and the extension of the term 'water' was just as much XYZ on Twin Earth in 1750 as in 1950. Oscar$_1$ and Oscar$_2$ understood the term 'water' differently in 1750 *although they were in the same psychological state*, and although, given the state of science at the time, it would have taken their scientific communities about fifty years to discover that they understood the term 'water' differently. Thus the extension of the term 'water' (and, in fact, its 'meaning' in the intuitive preanalytical usage of that term) is *not* a function of the psychological state of the speaker by itself.

But, it might be objected, why should we accept it that the term 'water' has the same extension in 1750 and in 1950 (on both Earths)? The logic of natural-kind terms like 'water' is a complicated matter,

† Or rather, they will report: 'On Twin Earth (*the Twin Earthian name for Terra* – H.P.) the word "water" means H_2O.'

but the following is a sketch of an answer. Suppose I point to a glass of water and say 'this liquid is called water' (or 'this is called water', if the marker 'liquid' is clear from the context). My 'ostensive definition' of water has the following empirical presupposition: that the body of liquid I am pointing to bears a certain sameness relation (say, *x is the same liquid as y*, or *x is the same$_L$ as y*) to most of the stuff I and other speakers in my linguistic community have on other occasions called 'water'. If this presupposition is false because, say, I am without knowing it pointing to a glass of gin and not a glass of water, then I do not intend my ostensive definition to be accepted. Thus the ostensive definition conveys what might be called a defeasible necessary and sufficient condition: the necessary and sufficient condition for being water is bearing the relation same$_L$ to the stuff in the glass; but this is the necessary and sufficient condition only if the empirical presupposition is satisfied. If it is not satisfied, then one of a series of, so to speak, 'fallback' conditions becomes activated.

The key point is that the relation same$_L$ is a *theoretical* relation: whether something is or is not the same liquid as *this* may take an indeterminate amount of scientific investigation to determine. Moreover, even if a 'definite' answer has been obtained either through scientific investigation or through the application of some 'common sense' test, the answer is *defeasible*: future investigation might reverse even the most 'certain' example. Thus, the fact that an English speaker in 1750 might have called XYZ 'water', while he or his successors would not have called XYZ water in 1800 or 1850 does not mean that the 'meaning' of 'water' changed for the average speaker in the interval. In 1750 or in 1850 or in 1950 one might have pointed to, say, the liquid in Lake Michigan as an example of 'water'. What changed was that in 1750 we would have mistakenly thought that XYZ bore the relation same$_L$ to the liquid in Lake Michigan, while in 1800 or 1850 we would have known that it did not (I am ignoring the fact that the liquid in Lake Michigan was only dubiously water in 1950, of course).

Let us now modify our science-fiction story. I do not know whether one can make pots and pans out of molybdenum; and if one can make them out of molybdenum, I don't know whether they could be distinguished easily from aluminum pots and pans. (I don't know any of this even though I have acquired the word 'molybdenum'.) So I shall suppose that molybdenum pots and pans *can't* be distinguished from aluminum pots and pans save by an expert. (To emphasize the point, I repeat that this could be true for all I know, and *a fortiori* it could be true for all I know by virtue of 'knowing the meaning' of the words *aluminum* and *molybdenum*.) We will now suppose that molybdenum is as common on Twin Earth as aluminum is on Earth, and that aluminum is as rare on Twin Earth as molybdenum is on Earth. In particular, we shall assume that 'aluminum' pots and pans are made of molybdenum on Twin Earth. Finally, we shall assume that the words 'aluminum' and 'molybdenum' are *switched* on Twin Earth: 'aluminum' is the name of *molybdenum* and 'molybdenum' is the name of *aluminum*.

This example shares some features with the previous one. If a spaceship from Earth visited Twin Earth, the visitors from Earth probably would not suspect that the 'aluminum' pots and pans on Twin Earth were not made of aluminum, especially when the Twin Earthians *said* they were. But there is one important difference between the two cases. An Earthian metallurgist could tell very easily that 'aluminum' was molybdenum, and a Twin Earthian metallurgist could tell equally easily that aluminum was 'molybdenum'. (The shudder quotes in the preceding sentence indicate Twin Earthian usages.) Whereas in 1750 no one on either Earth or Twin Earth could have distinguished water from 'water', the confusion of aluminum with 'aluminum' involves only a part of the linguistic communities involved.

The example makes the same point as the preceding one. If Oscar$_1$ and Oscar$_2$ are standard speakers of Earthian English and Twin Earthian English respectively, and neither is chemically or metallurgically sophisticated, then there may be no difference at all in their psychological state when they use the word 'aluminum'; nevertheless we have to say that 'aluminum' has the extension *aluminum* in the idiolect of Oscar$_1$ and the extension *molybdenum* in the idiolect of Oscar$_2$. (Also we have to say that Oscar$_1$ and Oscar$_2$ mean different things by 'aluminum', that 'aluminum' has a different meaning on Earth than it does on Twin Earth, etc.) Again we see that the psychological state of the speaker does *not* determine the extension (*or* the 'meaning', speaking preanalytically) of the word.

Before discussing this example further, let me introduce a *non*-science-fiction example. Suppose you are like me and cannot tell an elm from a beech tree. We still say that the extension of 'elm' in my idiolect is the same as the extension of 'elm' in anyone else's, viz., the set of all elm trees, and that the set of all beech trees is the extension of 'beech' in *both* of our idiolects. Thus 'elm' in my idiolect has a different extension from 'beech' in your idiolect (as it should). Is it really credible that this difference in extension is brought about by some difference in our *concepts*? My *concept* of an elm tree is exactly the same as my concept of a beech tree (I blush to confess). (This shows that the identification of meaning 'in the sense of intension' with *concept* cannot be correct, by the way.) If someone heroically attempts to maintain that the difference between the extension of 'elm' and the extension of 'beech' in *my* idiolect is explained by a difference in my psychological state, then we can always refute him by constructing a 'Twin Earth' example – just let the words 'elm' and 'beech' be switched on Twin Earth (the way 'aluminum' and 'molybdenum' were in the previous example). Moreover, I suppose I have a *Doppelgänger* on Twin Earth who is molecule for molecule 'identical' with me (in the sense in which two neckties can be 'identical'). If you are a dualist, then also suppose my *Doppelgänger* thinks the same verbalized thoughts I do, has the same sense data, the same dispositions, etc. It is absurd to think *his* psychological state is one bit different from mine: yet he 'means' *beech* when he says 'elm' and *I* 'mean' *elm* when I say elm. Cut the pie any way you like, 'meanings' just ain't in the *head*!

A socio-linguistic hypothesis

The last two examples depend upon a fact about language that seems, surprisingly, never to have been pointed out: that there is *division of linguistic labor*. We could hardly use such words as 'elm' and 'aluminum' if no one possessed a way of recognizing elm trees and aluminum metal; but not everyone to whom the distinction is important has to be able to make the distinction. Let us shift the example: consider *gold*. Gold is important for many reasons: it is a precious metal, it is a monetary metal, it has symbolic value (it is important to most people that the 'gold' wedding ring they wear *really* consist of gold and not just *look* gold), etc. Consider our community as a 'factory': in this 'factory' some people have the 'job' of *wearing gold wedding rings*, other people have the 'job' of *selling gold wedding rings*, still other people have the 'job' of *telling whether or not something is really gold*. It is not at all necessary or efficient that everyone who wears a gold ring (or a gold cufflink, etc.), or discusses the 'gold standard', etc., engage in buying and selling gold. Nor is it necessary or efficient that everyone who buys and sells gold be able to tell whether or not something is really gold in a society where this form of dishonesty is uncommon (selling fake gold) and in which one can easily consult an expert in case of doubt. And it is *certainly* not necessary or efficient that everyone who has occasion to buy or wear gold be able to tell with any reliability whether or not something is really gold.

The foregoing facts are just examples of mundane division of labor (in a wide sense). But they engender a division of linguistic labor: everyone to whom gold is important for any reason has to *acquire* the word 'gold'; but he does not have to acquire the *method of recognizing* if something is or is not gold. He can rely on a special subclass of speakers. The features that are generally thought to be present in connection with a general name – necessary and sufficient conditions for membership in the extension, ways of recognizing if something is in the extension ('criteria'), etc. – are all present in the linguistic community *considered as a collective body;* but that collective body divides the 'labor' of knowing and employing these various parts of the 'meaning' of 'gold'.

This division of linguistic labor rests upon and presupposes the division of *non*linguistic labor, of course. If only the people who know how to tell if some metal is really gold or not have any reason to have the word 'gold' in their vocabulary, then the word 'gold' will be as the word 'water' was in 1750 with respect to that subclass of speakers, and the other speakers just won't acquire it at all. And some words do not exhibit any division of linguistic labor: 'chair', for example. But with the increase of division of labor in the society and the rise of science, more and more words begin to exhibit this kind of division of labor. 'Water', for example, did not exhibit it at all prior to the rise of chemistry. Today it is obviously necessary for every speaker to be able to recognize water (reliably under normal conditions), and probably every adult speaker even knows the necessary and sufficient condition 'water is H_2O', but only a few adult speakers could distinguish water from liquids which superficially resembled water. In case of doubt, other speakers would rely on the judgement of these 'expert' speakers. Thus the way of recognizing possessed by these 'expert' speakers is also, through them, possessed by the collective linguistic body, even though it is not possessed by each individual member of the body, and in this way the most recherché fact about water may become part of the *social* meaning of the word while being unknown to almost all speakers who acquire the word.

It seems to me that this phenomenon of division of linguistic labor is one which it will be very important for sociolinguistics to investigate. In connection with it, I should like to propose the following hypothesis:

HYPOTHESIS OF THE UNIVERSALITY OF THE DIVISION OF LINGUISTIC LABOR: Every linguistic community exemplifies the sort of division of linguistic labor just described: that is, possesses at least some terms whose associated 'criteria' are known only to a subset of the speakers who acquire the terms, and whose use by the other speakers depends upon a structured cooperation between them and the speakers in the relevant subsets.

It would be of interest, in particular, to discover if extremely primitive peoples were sometimes exceptions to this hypothesis (which would indicate that the division of linguistic labor is a product of social evolution), or if even they exhibit it. In the latter case, one might conjecture that division of labor, including linguistic labor, is a fundamental trait of our species.

It is easy to see how this phenomenon accounts for some of the examples given above of the failure of the assumptions (1), (2). Whenever a term is subject to the division of linguistic labor, the 'average' speaker who acquires it does not acquire anything that fixes its extension. In particular, his individual psychological state *certainly* does not fix its extension; it is only the sociolinguistic state of the collective linguistic body to which the speaker belongs that fixes the extension.

We may summarize this discussion by pointing out that there are two sorts of tools in the world: there are tools like a hammer or a screwdriver which can be used by one person; and there are tools like a steamship which require the cooperative activity of a number of persons to use. Words have been thought of too much on the model of the first sort of tool.

Indexicality and rigidity†

The first of our science-fiction examples – 'water' on Earth and on Twin Earth in 1750 – does not involve division of linguistic labor, or at least does not involve it in the same way the examples of 'aluminum' and 'elm' do. There were not (in our story, anyway) any 'experts' on water on Earth in 1750, nor any experts on 'water' on Twin Earth. (The example *can* be construed as involving division of labor *across time*, however. I shall not develop this method of treating the example here.) The example *does* involve things which are of fundamental importance to the theory of reference and also to the theory of necessary truth, which we shall now discuss.

There are two obvious ways of telling someone what one means by a natural-kind term such as 'water' or 'tiger' or 'lemon'. One can give him a so-called ostensive definition – 'this (liquid) is water'; 'this (animal) is a tiger'; 'this (fruit) is a lemon'; where the parentheses are meant to indicate that the 'markers' *liquid, animal, fruit,* may be either explicit or implicit. Or one can give him a *description*. In the latter case the description one gives typically consists of one or more markers

---

† The substance of this section was presented at a series of lectures I gave at the University of Washington (Summer Institute in Philosophy) in 1968, and at a lecture at the University of Minnesota.

together with a *stereotype* (see chapter 8 in this volume) – a standardized description of features of the kind that are typical, or 'normal', or at any rate stereotypical. The central features of the stereotype generally are *criteria* – features which in normal situations constitute ways of recognizing if a thing belongs to the kind or, at least, necessary conditions (or probabilistic necessary conditions) for membership in the kind. Not all criteria used by the linguistic community as a collective body are included in the stereotype, and in some cases the stereotypes may be quite weak. Thus (unless I am a very atypical speaker), the stereotype of an elm is just that of a common deciduous tree. These features are indeed necessary conditions for membership in the kind (I mean 'necessary' in a loose sense; I don't think 'elm trees are deciduous' is *analytic*), but they fall far short of constituting a way of recognizing elms. On the other hand, the stereotype of a tiger does enable one to recognize tigers (unless they are albino, or some other atypical circumstance is present), and the stereotype of a lemon generally enables one to recognize lemons. In the extreme case, the stereotype may be *just* the marker: the stereotype of molybdenum might be *just* that molybdenum is a *metal*. Let us consider both of these ways of introducing a term into someone's vocabulary.

Suppose I point to a glass of liquid and say '*this* is water', in order to teach someone the word 'water'. We have already described some of the empirical presuppositions of this act, and the way in which this kind of meaning-explanation is defeasible. Let us now try to clarify further how it is supposed to be taken.

In what follows, we shall take the notion of 'possible world' as primitive. We do this because we feel that in several senses the notion makes sense and is scientifically important even if it needs to be made more precise. We shall assume further that in at least some cases it is possible to speak of the same individual as existing in more than one possible world.† Our discussion leans heavily on the work of Saul Kripke, although the conclusions were obtained independently.

Let W_1 and W_2 be two possible worlds in which I exist and in which this glass exists and in which I am giving a meaning explanation by pointing to this glass and saying 'this is water'. (We do *not* assume that the *liquid* in the glass is the same in both worlds.) Let us suppose that in W_1 the glass is full of H_2O and in W_2 the glass is full of XYZ. We shall also suppose that W_1 is the *actual* world and that XYZ is the stuff typically called 'water' in the world W_2 (so that the relation between English speakers in W_1 and English speakers in W_2 is exactly the same

† This assumption is not actually needed in what follows. What *is* needed is that the same *natural kind* can exist in more than one possible world.

as the relation between English speakers on Earth and English speakers on Twin Earth). Then there are two theories one might have concerning the meaning of 'water'.

(1) One might hold that 'water' was *world-relative* but *constant* in meaning (i.e. the word has a *constant relative meaning*). In this theory, 'water' *means the same* in W_1 and W_2; it's just that water is H_2O in W_1 and water is XYZ in W_2.

(2) One might hold that water is H_2O in all worlds (the stuff called 'water' in W_2 isn't water), but 'water' doesn't have the same meaning in W_1 and W_2.

If what was said before about the Twin Earth case was correct, then (2) is clearly the correct theory. When I say '*this* (liquid) is water', the 'this' is, so to speak, a *de re* 'this' – i.e. the force of my explanation is that 'water' is whatever bears a certain equivalence relation (the relation we called 'same$_L$' above) to the piece of liquid referred to as 'this' *in the actual world*.

We might symbolize the difference between the two theories as a 'scope' difference in the following way. In theory (1), the following is true:

(1') (For every world W) (For every x in W) (x is water $\equiv x$ bears same$_L$ to the entity referred to as 'this' in W)

while on theory (2):

(2') (For every world W) (For every x in W) (x is water $\equiv x$ bears same$_L$ to the entity referred to as 'this' *in the actual world W_1*).

(I call this a 'scope' difference because in (1') 'the entity referred to as "this"' is within the scope of 'For every world W' – as the qualifying phrase 'in W' makes explicit, whereas in (2') 'the entity referred to as "this"' means 'the entity referred to as "this" *in the actual world*', and has thus a reference *independent* of the bound variable 'W'.)

Kripke calls a designator 'rigid' (in a given sentence) if (in that sentence) it refers to the same individual in every possible world in which the designator designates. If we extend the notion of rigidity to substance names, then we may express Kripke's theory and mine by saying that the term 'water' is *rigid*.

The rigidity of the term 'water' follows from the fact that when I give the ostensive definition '*this* (liquid) is water' I intend (2') and not (1').

We may also say, following Kripke, that when I give the ostensive definition '*this* (liquid) is water', the demonstrative 'this' is *rigid*.

What Kripke was the first to observe is that this theory of the meaning (or 'use', or whatever) of the word 'water' (and other natural-kind terms as well) has startling consequences for the theory of necessary truth.

To explain this, let me introduce the notion of a *cross-world relation*. A two-term relation R will be called *cross-world* when it is understood in such a way that its extension is a set of ordered pairs of individuals *not all in the same possible world*. For example, it is easy to understand the relation *same height as* as a cross-world relation: just understand it so that, e.g. if x is an individual in a world W_1 who is five feet tall (in W_1) and y is an individual in W_2 who is five feet tall (in W_2), then the ordered pair x, y belongs to the extension of *same height as*. (Since an individual may have different heights in different possible worlds in which that same individual exists, strictly speaking it is not the ordered pair x, y that constitutes an element of the extension of *same height as*, but rather the ordered pair x-*in-world-*W_1, y-*in-world-*W_2.)

Similarly, we can understand the relation $same_L$ (same liquid as) as a cross-world relation by understanding it so that a liquid in world W_1 which has the same important physical properties (in W_1) that a liquid in W_2 possesses (in W_2) bears $same_L$ to the latter liquid.

Then the theory we have been presenting may be summarized by saying that an entity x, in an arbitrary possible world, is *water* if and only if it bears the relation $same_L$ (construed as a cross-world relation) to the stuff *we* call 'water' in the *actual* world.

Suppose, now, that I have not yet discovered what the important physical properties of water are (in the actual world) – i.e. I don't yet know that water is H_2O. I may have ways of *recognizing* water that are successful (of course, I may make a small number of mistakes that I won't be able to detect until a later stage in our scientific development) but not know the microstructure of water. If I agree that a liquid with the superficial properties of 'water' but a different microstructure *isn't really water*, then my ways of recognizing water (my 'operational definition', so to speak) cannot be regarded as an analytical specification of *what it is to be* water. Rather, the operational definition, like the ostensive one, is simply a way of pointing out a standard – pointing out the stuff *in the actual world* such that for x to be water, in *any* world, is for x to bear the relation $same_L$ to the *normal* members of the class of *local* entities that satisfy the operational definition. 'Water' on Twin Earth is not water, even if it satisfies the operational definition, because it doesn't bear $same_L$ to the *local* stuff that satisfies the operational definition, and local stuff that satisfies the operational definition but has a microstructure different from rest of the local stuff that satisfies the operational definition isn't water either, because it doesn't bear $same_L$ to the *normal* examples of the local 'water'.

Suppose, now, that I discover the microstructure of water – that water is H_2O. At this point I will be able to say that the stuff on Twin Earth that I earlier *mistook* for water isn't really water. In the same way, if you describe not another planet in the actual universe, but another possible universe in which there is stuff with the chemical formula XYZ which passes the 'operational test' for *water*, we shall have to say that that stuff isn't water but merely XYZ. You will not have described a possible world in which 'water is XYZ', but merely a possible world in which there are lakes of XYZ, people drink XYZ (and not water), or whatever. In fact, once we have discovered the nature of water, nothing counts as a possible world in which water doesn't have that nature. Once we have discovered that water (in the actual world) is H_2O, *nothing counts as a possible world in which water isn't H_2O*. In particular, if a 'logically possible' statement is one that holds in some 'logically possible world', *it isn't logically possible that water isn't H_2O*.

On the other hand, we can perfectly well imagine having experiences that would convince us (and that would make it rational to believe that) water *isn't* H_2O. In that sense, it is conceivable that water isn't H_2O. It is conceivable but it isn't logically possible! Conceivability is no proof of logical possibility.

Kripke refers to statements which are rationally unrevisable (assuming there are such) as *epistemically necessary*. Statements which are true in all possible worlds he refers to simply as necessary (or sometimes as 'metaphysically necessary'). In this terminology, the point just made can be restated as: a statement can be (metaphysically) necessary and epistemically contingent. Human intuition has no privileged access to metaphysical necessity.

Since Kant there has been a big split between philosophers who thought that all necessary truths were analytic and philosophers who thought that some necessary truths were synthetic *a priori*. But none of these philosophers thought that a (metaphysically) necessary truth could fail to be *a priori*: the Kantian tradition was as guilty as the empiricist tradition of equating metaphysical and epistemic necessity. In this sense Kripke's challenge to received doctrine goes far beyond the usual empiricism/Kantianism oscillation.

In this paper our interest is in theory of meaning, however, and not in theory of necessary truth. Points closely related to Kripke's have been made in terms of the notion of *indexicality*.† Words like 'now', 'this',

---

† These points were made in my 1968 lectures at the University of Washington and the University of Minnesota.

'here', have long been recognized to be *indexical,* or *token-reflexive* –
i.e. to have an extension which varied from context to context or token
to token. For these words no one has ever suggested the traditional
theory that 'intension determines extension'. To take our Twin Earth
example: if I have a *Doppelgänger* on Twin Earth, then when I think
'I have a headache', *he* thinks 'I have a headache'. But the extension of
the particular token of 'I' in his verbalized thought is himself (or his
unit class, to be precise), while the extension of the token of 'I' in *my*
verbalized thought is *me* (or my unit class, to be precise). So the same
word, 'I', has two different extensions in two different idiolects; but it
does not follow that the concept I have of myself is in any way
different from the concept my *Doppelgänger* has of himself.

Now then, we have maintained that indexicality extends beyond the
obviously indexical words and morphemes (e.g. the tenses of verbs).
Our theory can be summarized as saying that words like 'water' have
an unnoticed indexical component: 'water' is stuff that bears a certain
similarity relation to the water *around here.* Water at another time or
in another place or even in another possible world has to bear the relation same$_L$ to *our* 'water' *in order to be water.* Thus the theory that
(1) words have 'intensions', which are something like concepts associated with the words by speakers; and that (2) intension determines
extension – cannot be true of natural-kind words like 'water' for the
same reason the theory cannot be true of obviously indexical words
like 'I'.

The theory that natural-kind words like 'water' are indexical leaves
it open, however, whether to say that 'water' in the Twin Earth dialect
of English has the same *meaning* as 'water' in the Earth dialect and a
different extension (which is what we normally say about 'I' in different
idiolects), thereby giving up the doctrine that 'meaning (intension)
determines extension'; or to say, as we have chosen to do, that difference
is extension is *ipso facto* a difference in meaning for natural-kind words,
thereby giving up the doctrine that meanings are concepts, or, indeed,
mental entities of *any* kind.

It should be clear, however, that Kripke's doctrine that natural-kind
words are rigid designators and our doctrine that they are indexical are
but two ways of making the same point. We heartily endorse what
Kripke says when he writes:

Let us suppose that we do fix the reference of a name by a description. Even
if we do so, we do not then make the name synonymous with the description,
but instead we use the name rigidly to refer to the object so named, even in
talking about counterfactual situations where the thing named would not
satisfy the description in question. Now, this is what I think is in fact true for

those cases of naming where the reference is fixed by description. But, in fact, I also think, contrary to most recent theorists, that the reference of names is rarely or almost never fixed by means of description. And by this I do not just mean what Searle says: 'It's not a single description, but rather a cluster, a family of properties that fixes the reference.' I mean that properties in this sense are not used at all. (Kripke, 1972, p. 157)

Let's be realistic

I wish now to contrast my view with one which is popular, at least among students (it appears to arise spontaneously). For this discussion, let us take as our example of a natural-kind word the word *gold*. We will not distinguish between 'gold' and the cognate words in Greek, Latin etc. And we will focus on 'gold' in the sense of gold in the solid state. With this understood, we maintain: 'gold' has not changed its *extension* (or not changed it significantly) in two thousand years. Our methods of *identifying* gold have grown incredibly sophisticated. But the extension of χρυσός in Archimedes' dialect of Greek is the same as the extension of *gold* in my dialect of English.

It is possible (and let us suppose it to be the case) that just as there were pieces of metal which could not have been determined *not* to be gold prior to Archimedes, so there were or are pieces of metal which could not have been determined *not* to be gold in Archimedes' day, but which we can distinguish from gold quite easily with modern techniques. Let X be such a piece of metal. Clearly X does not lie in the extension of 'gold' in standard English; my view is that it did not lie in the extension of χρυσός in Attic Greek, either, although an ancient Greek would have *mistaken* X for gold (or, rather, χρυσός).

The alternative view is that 'gold' *means* whatever satisfies the *contemporary* 'operational definition' of *gold*. 'Gold' a hundred years ago meant whatever satisfied the 'operational definition' of *gold* in use a hundred years ago; 'gold' now means whatever satisfies the operational definition of *gold* in use in 1973; and χρυσός meant whatever satisfied the operational definition of χρυσός in use *then*.

One common motive for adopting this point of view is a certain skepticism about *truth*. In the view I am advocating, when Archimedes asserted that something was gold (χρυσός) he was not just saying that it had the superficial characteristics of gold (in exceptional cases, something may belong to a natural kind and *not* have the superficial characteristics of a member of that natural kind, in fact); he was saying that it had the same general *hidden structure* (the same 'essence', so to speak) as any normal piece of local gold. Archimedes would have said that our hypothetical piece of metal X was gold, but he would have been *wrong*. But *who's to say* he would have been wrong?

The obvious answer is: *we are* (using the best theory available today). For most people either the question (*who's to say?*) has bite, and our answer has no bite, or our answer has bite and the question has no bite. Why is this?

The reason, I believe, is that people tend either to be strongly anti-realistic or strongly realistic in their intuitions. To a strongly anti-realistic intuition it makes little sense to say that what is in the extension of Archimedes' term χρυσός is to be determined using *our* theory. For the antirealist does not see our theory and Archimedes' theory as two approximately correct descriptions of some fixed realm of theory-independent entities, and he tends to be skeptical about the idea of 'convergence' in science – he does not think our theory is a *better* description of the *same* entities that Archimedes was describing. But if our theory is *just* our theory, then to use *it* in deciding whether or not X lies in the extension of χρυσός is just as arbitrary as using Neanderthal theory to decide whether or not X lies in the extension of χρυσός. The only theory that it is *not* arbitrary to use is the one the speaker himself subscribes to.

The trouble is that for a strong antirealist *truth* makes no sense except as an intra-theoretic notion (see the preceding chapter for a discussion of this point). The antirealist can use truth intra-theoretically in the sense of a 'redundancy theory'; but he does not have the notions of truth and reference available *extra-theoretically*. But *extension is tied to the notion of truth*. The extension of a term is just what the term is *true of*. Rather than try to retain the notion of extension via an awkward operationalism, the antirealist should reject the notion of extension as he does the notion of truth (in any extra-theoretic sense). Like Dewey, for example, he can fall back on a notion of 'warranted assertibility' instead of truth (relativized to the scientific method, if he thinks there is a *fixed* scientific method, or to the best methods available at the time, if he agrees with Dewey that the scientific method itself evolves). Then he can say that 'X is gold (χρυσός)' was warrantedly assertible in Archimedes' time and is not warrantedly assertible today (indeed, this is a *minimal* claim, in the sense that it represents the minimum that the realist and the antirealist can agree on); but the assertion that X was in the extension of χρυσός will be rejected as meaningless, like the assertion that 'X is gold (χρυσός)' was *true*.

It is well known that narrow operationalism cannot successfully account for the actual use of scientific or common-sense terms. Loosened versions of operationalism, like Carnap's version of Ramsey's theory, agree with, if they do not account for, actual scientific use (mainly because the loosened versions agree with any possible use!), but at the expense of making the communicability of scientific results a *miracle*. It is beyond question that scientists use terms as if the associated criteria were not *necessary and sufficient conditions*, but rather *approximately* correct characterizations of some world of theory-independent entities, and that they talk as if later theories in a mature science were, in general, *better* descriptions of the *same* entities that earlier theories referred to. In my opinion the hypothesis that this is *right* is the only hypothesis that can account for the communicability of scientific results, the closure of acceptable scientific theories under first-order logic, and many other features of the scientific method.† But it is not my task to argue this here. My point is that if we are to use the notions of truth and extension in an extra-theoretic way (i.e. to regard those notions as defined for statements couched in the languages of theories other than our own), then we should accept the realist perspective to which those notions belong. The doubt about whether *we* can say that X does not lie in the extension of 'gold' as *Jones* used it is the *same* doubt as the doubt whether it makes sense to think of Jones's statement that 'X is gold' as *true or false* (and not just 'warrantedly assertible for Jones and not warrantedly assertible for us'). To square the notion of truth, which is essentially a realist notion, with one's antirealist prejudices by adopting an untenable theory of meaning is no progress.

A second motive for adopting an extreme operationalist account is a dislike of unverifiable hypotheses. At first blush it may seem as if we are saying that 'X is gold ($\chi\rho\upsilon\sigma\grave{o}s$)' was false in Archimedes' time although Archimedes could not *in principle* have known that it was false. But this is not exactly the situation. The fact is that there are a host of situations that *we* can describe (using the very theory that tells us that X isn't gold) in which X would have behaved quite unlike the rest of the stuff Archimedes classified as gold. Perhaps X would have separated into two different metals when melted, or would have had different conductivity properties, or would have vaporized at a different temperature, or whatever. If we had performed the experiments with Archimedes watching, he might not have known the theory, but he would have been able to check the empirical regularity that 'X behaves differently from the rest of the stuff I classify as $\chi\rho\upsilon\sigma\grave{o}s$ in several respects'. Eventually he would have concluded that 'X may not be gold'.

The point is that even if something satisfies the criteria used at a

† For an illuminating discussion of just these points, see R. Boyd's *Realism and Scientific Epistemology* (unpublished: Xerox draft circulated by author, Cornell Dept. of Philosophy).

given time to identify gold (i.e., to recognize if something is gold), it may behave differently in one or more situations from the rest of the stuff that satisfies the criteria. This may not *prove* that it isn't gold, but it puts the hypothesis that it may not be gold in the running , even in the absence of theory. If, now, we had gone on to inform Archimedes that gold had such and such a molecular structure (except for X), and that X behaved differently because it had a different molecular structure, is there any doubt that he would have agreed with us that X isn't gold? In any case, to worry because things may be *true* (at a given time) that can't be *verified* (at that time) seems to me ridiculous. In any reasonable view there are surely things that are true and can't be verified at *any* time. For example, suppose there are infinitely many binary stars. *Must* we be able to verify this, even *in principle*? (See chapter 22 in this volume, and chapters 17 and 18, volume 1.)

So far we have dealt with *metaphysical* reasons for rejecting our account. But someone might disagree with us about the empirical facts concerning the intentions of speakers. This would be the case if, for instance, someone thought that Archimedes (in the *Gedankenexperiment* described above) would have said: 'it doesn't matter if X *does* act differently from other pieces of gold; X is a piece of gold, because X has such-and-such properties and that's all it takes to be gold'. While, indeed, we cannot be certain that natural-kind words in ancient Greek had the properties of the corresponding words in present-day English, there cannot be any serious doubt concerning the properties of the latter. If we put philosophical prejudices aside, then I believe that we know perfectly well that no operational definition does provide a necessary and sufficient condition for the application of any such word. We may give an 'operational definition', or a cluster of properties, or whatever, but the intention is never to 'make the name *synonymous* with the description'. Rather 'we use the name *rigidly*' to refer to whatever things share the *nature* that things satisfying the description normally possess.

Other senses

What we have analyzed so far is the predominant sense of natural-kind words (or, rather, the predominant *extension*). But natural-kind words typically possess a number of senses. (Ziff has even suggested that they possess a *continuum* of senses.)

Part of this can be explained on the basis of our theory. To be water, for example, is to bear the relation same$_L$ to certain things. But what is the relation same$_L$?

x bears the relation same$_L$ to y just in case (1) x and y are both liquids, and (2) x and y agree in important physical properties. The term 'liquid' is itself a natural-kind term that I shall not try to analyze here. The term 'property' is a broad-spectrum term that we have analyzed in previous papers. What I want to focus on now is the notion of *importance*. Importance is an interest-relative notion. Normally the 'important' properties of a liquid or solid, etc., are the ones that are *structurally* important: the ones that specify what the liquid or solid, etc., is ultimately made out of – elementary particles, or hydrogen and oxygen, or earth, air, fire, water, or whatever – and how they are arranged or combined to produce the superficial characteristics. From this point of view the characteristic of a typical bit of water is consisting of H_2O. But it may or may not be important that there are impurities; thus, in one context 'water' may mean *chemically pure water*, while in another it may mean the stuff in Lake Michigan. And a speaker may sometimes refer to XYZ as water if one is *using* it as water. Again, normally it is important that water is in the liquid state; but sometimes it is unimportant, and one may refer to a single H_2O molecule as water, or to water vapor as water ('water in the air').

Even senses that are so far out that they have to be regarded as a bit 'deviant' may bear a definite relation to the core sense. For example, I might say 'did you see the lemon', meaning the *plastic* lemon. A less deviant case is this: we discover 'tigers' on Mars. That is, they look just like tigers, but they have a silicon-based chemistry instead of a carbon-based chemistry. (A remarkable example of parallel evolution!) Are Martian 'tigers' tigers? It depends on the context.

In the case of this theory, as in the case of any theory that is orthogonal to the way people have thought about something previously, misunderstandings are certain to arise. One which has already arisen is the following: a critic has maintained that the *predominant* sense of, say, 'lemon' is the one in which anything with (a sufficient number of) the superficial characteristics of a lemon is a lemon. The same critic has suggested that having the hidden structure – the genetic code – of a lemon is necessary to being a lemon only when 'lemon' is used as a term of *science*. Both of these contentions seem to me to rest on a misunderstanding, or, perhaps, a pair of complementary misunderstandings.

The sense in which literally *anything* with the superficial characteristics of a lemon is necessarily a lemon, far from being the dominant one, is extremely deviant. In that sense something would be a lemon if it looked and tasted like a lemon, even if it had a silicon-based chemistry, for example, or even if an electron-microscope revealed it to be a *machine*. (Even if we include growing 'like a lemon' in the superficial

239

characteristics, this does not exclude the silicon lemon, if there are 'lemon' trees on Mars. It doesn't even exclude the machine-lemon; maybe the tree is a machine too!)

At the same time the sense in which to be a lemon something has to have the genetic code of a lemon is *not* the same as the technical sense (if there is one, which I doubt). The technical sense, I take it, would be one in which 'lemon' was *synonymous* with a description which *specified* the genetic code. But when we said (to change the example) that to be *water* something has to be H_2O we did not mean, as we made clear, that the *speaker* has to *know* this. It is only by confusing *metaphysical* necessity with *epistemological* necessity that one can conclude that, if the (metaphysically necessary) truth-condition for being water is being H_2O, then 'water' must be synonymous with H_2O – in which case it is certainly a term of science. And similarly, even though the predominant sense of 'lemon' is one in which to be a lemon something has to have the genetic code of a lemon (I believe), it does not follow that 'lemon' is synonymous with a description which specifies the genetic code explicitly or otherwise.

The mistake of thinking that there is an important sense of 'lemon' (perhaps the predominant one) in which to have the superficial characteristics of a lemon is at least *sufficient* for being a lemon is more plausible if among the superficial characteristics one includes *being cross-fertile with lemons*. But the characteristic of being cross-fertile with lemons presupposes the notion of being a lemon. Thus, even if one can obtain a sufficient condition in *this* way, to take this as inconsistent with the characterization offered here is question-begging. Moreover the characterization in terms of *lemon*-presupposing 'superficial characteristics' (like being cross-fertile with *lemons*) gives no truth-condition which would enable us to decide which objects in other possible worlds (or which objects a million years ago, or which objects a million light years from here) are lemons. (In addition, I don't think this characterization, question-begging as it is, is *correct*, even as a sufficient condition. I think one could invent cases in which something which was not a lemon was cross-fertile with lemons and looked like a lemon, etc.)

Again, one might try to rule out the case of the machine-lemon (lemon-machine?) which 'grows' on a machine-tree (tree-machine?) by saying that 'growing' is not really *growing*. That is right; but it's right because *grow* is a natural-kind *verb*, and precisely the sort of account we have been presenting applies to *it*.

Another misunderstanding that should be avoided is the following: to take the account we have developed as implying that the members of the extension of a natural-kind word necessarily *have* a common hidden structure. It could have turned out that the bits of liquid we call 'water' had *no* important common physical characteristics *except* the superficial ones. In that case the necessary and sufficient condition for being 'water' would have been possession of sufficiently many of the superficial characteristics.

Incidentally, the last statement does not imply that water could have failed to have a hidden structure (or that water could have been anything but H_2O). When we say that it could have *turned out* that water had no hidden structure what we mean is that a liquid with no hidden structure (i.e. many bits of different liquids, with nothing in common *except* superficial characteristics) could have looked like water, tasted like water, and have filled the lakes, etc., that are actually full of water. In short, we could have been in the same epistemological situation with respect to a liquid with no hidden structure as we were actually with respect to water at one time. Compare Kripke on the 'lectern made of ice' (Kripke, 1972).

There are, in fact, almost continuously many cases. Some diseases, for example, have turned out to have no hidden structure (the only thing the paradigm cases have in common is a cluster of symptoms), while others have turned out to have a common hidden structure in the sense of an etiology (e.g. tuberculosis). Sometimes we still don't know; there is a controversy still raging about the case of multiple sclerosis.

An interesting case is the case of *jade*. Although the Chinese do not recognize a difference, the term 'jade' applies to two minerals: jadeite and nephrite. Chemically, there is a marked difference. Jadeite is a combination of sodium and aluminum. Nephrite is made of calcium, magnesium, and iron. These two quite different microstructures produce the same unique textural qualities!

Coming back to the Twin Earth example, for a moment; if H_2O and XYZ had both been plentiful on Earth, then we would have had a case similar to the jadeite/nephrite case: it would have been correct to say that there were *two kinds of 'water'*. And instead of saying that 'the stuff on Twin Earth turned out not to really be water', we would have to say 'it turned out to be the XYZ *kind of water*'.

To sum up: if there is a hidden structure, then generally it determines what it is to be a member of the natural kind, not only in the actual world, but in all possible worlds. Put another way, it determines what we can and cannot counterfactually suppose about the natural kind ('water could have all been vapor?' yes/'water could have been XYZ' no). But the local water, or whatever, may have two or more hidden structures – or so many that 'hidden structure' becomes irrelevant, and superficial characteristics become the decisive ones.

Other words

So far we have only used natural-kind words as examples; but the points we have made apply to many other kinds of words as well. They apply to the great majority of all nouns, and to other parts of speech as well.

Let us consider for a moment the names of artifacts – words like 'pencil', 'chair', 'bottle', etc. The traditional view is that these words are certainly defined by conjunctions, or possibly clusters, of properties. Anything with all of the properties in the conjunction (or sufficiently many of the properties in the cluster, on the cluster model) is necessarily a *pencil, chair, bottle,* or whatever. In addition, some of the properties in the cluster (on the cluster model) are usually held to be *necessary* (on the conjunction-of-properties model, *all* of the properties in the conjunction are necessary). *Being an artifact* is supposedly necessary, and belonging to a kind with a certain standard purpose – e.g. 'pencils are artifacts', and 'pencils are standardly intended to be written with' are supposed to be necessary. Finally, this sort of necessity is held to be *epistemic* necessity – in fact, analyticity.

Let us once again engage in science fiction. This time we use an example devised by Rogers Albritton. Imagine that we someday discover that *pencils are organisms*. We cut them open and examine them under the electron microscope, and we see the almost invisible tracery of nerves and other organs. We spy upon them, and we see them spawn, and we see the offspring grow into full-grown pencils. We discover that these organisms are not imitating other (artifactual) pencils – there are not and never were any pencils except these organisms. It is strange, to be sure, that there is *lettering* on many of these organisms – e.g. BONDED *Grants* DELUXE made in U.S.A. No. 2. – perhaps they are intelligent organisms, and this is their form of camouflage. (We also have to explain why no one ever attempted to manufacture pencils, etc., but this is clearly a possible world, in some sense.)

If this is conceivable, and I agree with Albritton that it is, then it is epistemically possible that *pencils could turn out to be organisms*. It follows that *pencils are artifacts* is not epistemically necessary in the strongest sense and, *a fortiori*, not analytic.

Let us be careful, however. Have we shown that there is a possible world in which pencils are organisms? I think not. What we have shown is that there is a possible world in which certain organisms are the *epistemic counterparts* of pencils (the phrase is Kripke's). To return to the device of Twin Earth: imagine this time that pencils on Earth are just what we think they are, artifacts manufactured to be written with, while 'pencils' on Twin Earth are organisms à la Albritton. Imagine, further, that this is totally unsuspected by the Twin Earthians – they have exactly the beliefs about 'pencils' that we have about pencils. When we discovered this, we would not say: 'some pencils are organisms'. We would be far more likely to say: 'the things on Twin Earth that pass for pencils aren't really pencils. They're really a species of organism'.

Suppose now the situation to be as in Albritton's example both on Earth and on Twin Earth. Then we would say 'pencils are organisms'. Thus, whether the 'pencil-organisms' on Twin Earth (or in another possible universe) are really *pencils* or not is a function of whether or not the *local* pencils are organisms or not. If the local pencils are just what we think they are, then a possible world in which there are pencil-organisms is *not* a possible world in which *pencils are organisms*; there are *no* possible worlds in which pencils are organisms in this case (which is, of course, the actual one). That pencils are artifacts *is* necessary in the sense of true in all possible worlds – metaphysically necessary. But it doesn't follow that it's epistemically necessary.

It follows that 'pencil' is not *synonymous* with any description – not even loosely synonymous with a *loose* description. When we use the word 'pencil', we intend to refer to whatever has the same *nature* as the normal examples of the local pencils in the actual world. 'Pencil' is just as *indexical* as 'water' or 'gold'.

In a way, the case of pencils turning out to be organisms is complementary to the case we discussed some years ago (see my chapter 15, volume 1) of cats turning out to be robots (remotely controlled from Mars). In Katz (forthcoming), Katz argues that we misdescribed this case: that the case should rather be described as its *turning out that there are no cats in this world*. Katz admits that we might *say* 'Cats have turned out not to be animals, but robots'; but he argues that this is a semantically deviant sentence which is glossed as 'the things I am referring to as "cats" have turned out not to be animals, but robots'. Katz's theory is bad linguistics, however. First of all, the explanation of how it is we can *say* 'Cats are robots' is simply an all-purpose explanation of how we can say *anything*. More important, Katz's theory predicts that 'Cats are robots' is *deviant*, while 'There are no cats in the world' is nondeviant, in fact standard, in the case described. Now then, I don't deny that there *is* a case in which 'There are not (and never were) any cats in the world' would be standard: we might (speaking epistemically) discover that we have been suffering from a collective hallucination. ('Cats' are like pink elephants.) But in the case I described, 'Cats have turned out to be robots remotely controlled from Mars' is surely nondeviant, and 'There are no cats in the world' is highly deviant.

Incidentally, Katz's account is not only bad linguistics; it is also bad as a rational reconstruction. The reason we *don't* use 'cat' as synonymous with a description is surely that we know enough about cats to know that they do have a hidden structure, and it is good scientific methodology to use the name to refer rigidly to the things that possess that hidden structure, and not to whatever happens to satisfy some description. Of course, if we *knew* the hidden structure we could frame a description in terms of *it*; but we don't at this point. In this sense the use of natural-kind words reflects an important fact about our relation to the world: we know that there are kinds of things with common hidden structure, but we don't yet have the knowledge to describe all those hidden structures.

Katz's view has more plausibility in the 'pencil' case than in the 'cat' case, however. We think we *know* a necessary and sufficient condition for being a *pencil*, albeit a vague one. So it is possible to make 'pencil' synonymous with a loose description. We *might* say, in the case that 'pencils turned out to be organisms' *either* 'Pencils have turned out to be organisms' *or* 'There are no pencils in the world' – i.e. we might use 'pencil' either as a natural-kind word or as a 'one-criterion' word.†

On the other hand, we might doubt that there *are* any true one-criterion words in natural language, apart from stipulative contexts. Couldn't it turn out that pediatricians aren't doctors but Martian spies? Answer 'yes', and you have abandoned the synonymy of 'pediatrician' and 'doctor specializing in the care of children'. It seems that there is a strong tendency for words which are introduced as 'one-criterion' words to develop a 'natural kind' sense, with all the concomitant rigidity and indexicality. In the case of artifact-names, this natural-kind sense seems to be the predominant one.

(There is a joke about a patient who is on the verge of being discharged from an insane asylum. The doctors have been questioning him for some time, and he has been giving perfectly sane responses. They decide to let him leave, and at the end of the interview one of the doctors inquires casually, 'What do you want to be when you get out?' 'A teakettle'. The joke would not be intelligible if it were literally inconceivable that a person could be a teakettle.)

There are, however, words which retain an almost pure one-criterion character. These are words whose meaning derives from a transformation: *hunter = one who hunts*.

Not only does the account given here apply to most nouns, but it also applies to other parts of speech. Verbs like 'grow', adjectives like 'red', etc., all have indexical features. On the other hand, some syncategore-

---

† The idea of a 'one-criterion' word, and a theory of analyticity based on this notion, appears in chapter 2 in this volume.

matic words seem to have more of a one-criterion character. 'Whole', for example, can be explained thus: *The army surrounded the town* could be true even if the *A* division did not take part. *The whole army surrounded the town* means every part of the army (of the relevant kind, e.g. the *A* Division) took part in the action signified by the verb.†

Meaning

Let us now see where we are with respect to the notion of meaning. We have now seen that the extension of a term is not fixed by a concept that the individual speaker has in his head, and this is true both because extension is, in general, determined *socially* – there is division of linguistic labor as much as of 'real' labor – and because extension is, in part, determined *indexically*. The extension of our terms depends upon the actual nature of the particular things that serve as paradigms,‡ and this actual nature is not, in general, fully known to the speaker. Traditional semantic theory leaves out only two contributions to the determination of extension – the contribution of society and the contribution of the real world!

We saw at the outset that meaning cannot be identified with extension. Yet it cannot be identified with 'intension' either, if intension is something like an individual speaker's *concept*. What are we to do?

There are two plausible routes that we might take. One route would be to retain the identification of meaning with concept and pay the price of giving up the idea that meaning determines extension. If we followed this route, we might say that 'water' has the same *meaning* on Earth and on Twin Earth, but a different *extension*. (Not just a different *local* extension but a different *global* extension. The *XYZ* on Twin Earth isn't in the extension of the tokens of 'water' that I utter, but it is in the extension of the tokens of 'water' that my *Doppelgänger* utters, and this isn't just because Twin Earth is far away from me, since molecules of H_2O are in the extension of the tokens of 'water' that I utter no matter how far away from me they are in space and time. Also, what I can counterfactually suppose water to be is different from what my *Dopelgänger* can counterfactually suppose 'water' to be.) While this is the correct route to take for an *absolutely* indexical word like 'I', it seems incorrect for the words we have been discussing. Consider 'elm' and 'beech', for example. If these are 'switched' on Twin Earth, then surely we would *not* say that 'elm' has the same meaning on Earth and Twin

† This example comes from an analysis by Anthony Kroch (in his M.I.T. doctoral dissertation, 1974, Department of Linguistics).

‡ I *don't* have in mind the Flewish notion of 'paradigm' in which any paradigm of a *K* is *necessarily* a *K* (in reality).

Earth, even if my *Doppelgänger's* stereotype of a beech (or an 'elm', as he calls it) is identical with my stereotype of an elm. Rather, we would say that 'elm' in my *Doppelgänger's* idiolect means *beech*. For this reason, it seems preferable to take a different route and identify 'meaning' with an ordered pair (or possibly an ordered *n-tuple*) of entities, *one of which is the extension*. (The other components of the, so to speak, 'meaning vector' will be specified later). Doing this makes it trivially true that *meaning determines extension* (i.e. difference in extension is *ipso facto* difference in meaning), but totally abandons the idea that if there is a difference in the meaning my *Doppelgänger* and I assign to a word, then there *must* be some difference in our concepts (or in our psychological state). Following this route, we can say that my *Doppelgänger* and I *mean something different* when we say 'elm', but this will not be an assertion about our psychological states. All this means is that the tokens of the word he utters have a different extension than the tokens of the word I utter; but this difference in extension is not a reflection of any difference in our individual linguistic competence considered in isolation.

If this is correct, and I think it is, then the traditional problem of meaning splits into two problems. The first problem is to account for the *determination of extension*. Since, in many cases, extension is determined socially and not individually, owing to the division of linguistic labor, I believe that this problem is properly a problem for sociolinguistics. Solving it would involve spelling out in detail exactly how the division of linguistic labor works. The so-called 'causal theory of reference', introduced by Kripke for proper names and extended by us to natural-kind words and physical-magnitude terms (in the preceding chapter), falls into this province. For the fact that, in many contexts, we assign to the tokens of a name that I utter whatever referent we assign to the tokens of the same name uttered by the person from whom I acquired the name (so that the reference is transmitted from speaker to speaker, starting from the speakers who were present at the 'naming ceremony', even though no fixed *description* is transmitted) is simply a special case of social cooperation in the determination of reference.

The other problem is to describe *individual competence*. Extension may be determined socially, in many cases, but we don't assign the standard extension to the tokens of a word *W* uttered by Jones *no matter how* Jones uses *W*. Jones has to have some particular ideas and skills in connection with *W* in order to play his part in the linguistic division of labor. Once we give up the idea that individual competence has to be so strong as to actually determine extension, we can begin to study it in a fresh frame of mind.

In this connection it is instructive to observe that nouns like 'tiger' or 'water' are very different from proper names. One can use the proper name 'Sanders' correctly without knowing anything about the referent except that he is called 'Sanders' – and even that may not be correct. ('Once upon a time, a very long time ago now, about last Friday, Winnie-the-Pooh lived in a forest all by himself under the name of Sanders.') But one cannot use the word tiger correctly, save *per accidens*, without knowing a good deal about tigers, or at least about a certain conception of tigers. In this sense concepts *do* have a lot to do with meaning.

Just as the study of the first problem is properly a topic in socio-linguistics, so the study of the second problem is properly a topic in psycholinguistics. To this topic we now turn.

Stereotypes and communication

Suppose a speaker knows that 'tiger' has a set of physical objects as its extension, but no more. If he possesses normal linguistic competence in other respects, then he could use 'tiger' in *some* sentences: for example, 'tigers have mass', 'tigers take up space', 'give me a tiger', 'is that a tiger?', etc. Moreover, the *socially determined* extension of 'tiger' in these sentences would be the standard one, i.e. the set of tigers. Yet we would not count such a speaker as 'knowing the meaning' of the word *tiger*. Why not?

Before attempting to answer this question, let us reformulate it a bit. We shall speak of someone as having *acquired* the word 'tiger' if he is able to use it in such a way that (1) his use passes muster (i.e. people don't say of him such things as 'he doesn't know what a tiger *is*', 'he doesn't know the meaning of the word "tiger"', etc.); and (2) his total way of being situated in the world and in his linguistic community is such that the socially determined extension of the word 'tiger' in his idiolect is the set of tigers. Clause (1) means, roughly, that speakers like the one hypothesized in the preceding paragraph don't count as having acquired the word 'tiger' (or whichever). We might speak of them, in some cases, as having *partially acquired* the word; but let us defer this for the moment. Clause (2) means that speakers on Twin Earth who have the same linguistic habits as we do, count as having acquired the word 'tiger' only if the extension of 'tiger' in their idiolect is the set of tigers. The burden of the preceding sections of this paper is that it does *not* follow that the extension of 'tiger' in Twin Earth dialect (or idiolects) is the set of tigers merely because their linguistic habits are the same as ours: the nature of Twin Earth 'tigers' is also relevant. (If Twin Earth organisms have a silicon chemistry, for example, then their 'tigers' aren't really tigers, even if they look like tigers, although the linguistic habits of the lay Twin Earth speaker exactly correspond to those of Earth speakers.) Thus clause (2) means that in this case we have decided to say that Twin Earth speakers have not acquired our word 'tiger' (although they have acquired another word with the same spelling and pronunciation).

Our reason for introducing this way of speaking is that the question 'does he know the meaning of the word "tiger"?' is biassed in favor of the theory that acquiring a word is coming to possess a thing called its 'meaning'. Identify this thing with a concept, and we are back at the theory that a sufficient condition for acquiring a word is associating it with the right concept (or, more generally, being in the right psychological state with respect to it) – the very theory we have spent all this time refuting. So, henceforth, we will 'acquire' words, rather than 'learn their meaning'.

We can now reformulate the question with which this section began. The use of the speaker we described does not pass muster, although it is not such as to cause us to assign a nonstandard extension to the word 'tiger' in his idiolect. Why doesn't it pass muster?

Suppose our hypothetical speaker points to a snowball and asks, 'is that a tiger?'. Clearly there isn't much point in talking tigers with *him*. Significant communication requires that people know something of what they are talking about. To be sure, we hear people 'communicating' every day who clearly know nothing of what they are talking about; but the sense in which the man who points to a snowball and asks 'is that a tiger?' doesn't know anything about tigers is so far beyond the sense in which the man who thinks that Vancouver is going to win the Stanley Cup, or that the Vietnam War was fought to help the South Vietnamese, doesn't know what he is talking about as to boggle the mind. The problem of people who think that Vancouver is going to win the Stanley Cup, or that the Vietnam war was fought to help the South Vietnamese, is one that obviously cannot be remedied by the adoption of linguistic conventions; but not knowing what one is talking about in the second, mind-boggling sense can be and is prevented, near enough, by our conventions of language. What I contend is that speakers are *required* to know something about (stereotypical) tigers in order to count as having acquired the word 'tiger'; something about elm trees (or anyway, about the stereotype thereof) to count as having acquired the word 'elm'; etc.

This idea should not seem too surprising. After all, we do not permit people to drive on the highways without first passing some tests to determine that they have a *minimum* level of competence; and we do not dine with people who have not learned to use a knife and fork. The linguistic community too has its minimum standards, with respect both to syntax and to 'semantics'.

The nature of the required minimum level of competence depends heavily upon both the culture and the topic, however. In our culture speakers are required to know what tigers look like (if they acquire the word 'tiger', and this is virtually obligatory); they are not required to know the fine details (such as leaf shape) of what an elm tree looks like. English speakers are *required by their linguistic community* to be able to tell tigers from leopards; they are not required to be able to tell elm trees from beech trees.

This could easily have been different. Imagine an Indian tribe, call it the Cheroquoi, who have words, say *uhaba'* and *wa'arabi* for elm trees and beech trees respectively, and who make it *obligatory* to know the difference. A Cheroquoi who could not recognize an elm would be said not to know what an *uhaba'* is, not to know the meaning of the word *uhaba'* (perhaps, not to know the word, or not to *have* the word); just as an English speaker who had no idea that tigers are striped would be said not to know what a tiger is, not to know the meaning of the word 'tiger' (of course, if he at least knows that tigers are large felines we might say he knows part of the meaning, or partially knows the meaning), etc. Then the translation of *uhaba'* as 'elm' and *wa'arabi* as 'beech' would, in our view, be only *approximately* correct. In this sense there is a real difficulty with radical translation,† but this is not the abstract difficulty that Quine is talking about.‡

What stereotypes are

I introduced the notion of a 'stereotype' in my lectures at the University of Washington and at the Minnesota Center for the Philosophy of Science in 1968. The subsequently published 'Is semantics possible?' (chapter 8 in this volume) follows up the argumentation, and in the present essay I want to introduce the notion again and to answer some questions that have been asked about it.

In ordinary parlance a 'stereotype' is a conventional (frequently malicious) idea (which may be wildly inaccurate) of what an X looks like or acts like or is. Obviously, I am trading on some features of the ordinary parlance. I am not concerned with malicious stereotypes (save where the language itself is malicious); but I am concerned with conventional ideas, which may be inaccurate. I am suggesting that just such

† The term is due to Quine (in *Word and Object*): it signifies translation without clues either from shared culture or cognates.

‡ For a discussion of the supposed impossibility of uniquely correct radical translation see chapter 9 in this volume.

a conventional idea is associated with 'tiger', with 'gold', etc., and, moreover, that this is the sole element of truth in the 'concept' theory.

In this view someone who knows what 'tiger' means (or, as we have decided to say instead, has acquired the word 'tiger') is *required* to know that *stereotypical* tigers are striped. More precisely, there is *one* stereotype of tigers (he may have others) which is required by the linguistic community as such; he is required to have this stereotype, and to know (implicitly) that it is obligatory. This stereotype must include the feature of stripes if his acquisition is to count as successful.

The fact that a feature (e.g. stripes) is included in the stereotype associated with a word X does not mean that it is an analytic truth that all Xs have that feature, nor that most Xs have that feature, nor that all normal Xs have that feature, nor that some Xs have that feature.† Three-legged tigers and albino tigers are not logically contradictory entities. Discovering that our stereotype has been based on nonnormal or unrepresentative members of a natural kind is not discovering a logical contradiction. If tigers lost their stripes they would not thereby cease to be tigers, nor would butterflies necessarily cease to be butterflies if they lost their wings.

(Strictly speaking, the situation is more complicated than this. It is possible to give a word like 'butterfly' a sense in which butterflies would cease to be butterflies if they lost their wings – through mutation, say. Thus one can find *a* sense of 'butterfly' in which it is analytic that 'butterflies have wings'. But the most important sense of the term, I believe, is the one in which the wingless butterflies would still be butterflies.)

At this point the reader may wonder what the value to the linguistic community of having stereotypes is, if the 'information' contained in the stereotype is not necessarily correct. But this is not really such a mystery. Most stereotypes do in fact capture features possessed by paradigmatic members of the class in question. Even where stereotypes go wrong, the way in which they go wrong sheds light on the contribution normally made by stereotypes to communication. The stereotype of gold, for example, contains the feature *yellow* even though chemically pure gold is nearly white. But the gold we see in jewelry is typically yellow (due to the presence of copper), so the presence of this feature in the stereotype is even useful in lay contexts. The stereotype associated with *witch* is more seriously wrong, at least if taken with existential import. Believing (with existential import) that witches enter into pacts with Satan, that they cause sickness and death, etc., facilitates communication only in the sense of facilitating communication internal to witch-

† This is argued in chapter 8.

theory. It does not facilitate communication in any situation in which what is needed is more agreement with the world than agreement with the theory of other speakers. (Strictly speaking, I am speaking of the stereotype as it existed in New England three hundred years ago; today that witches aren't *real* is itself part of the stereotype, and the baneful effects of witch-theory are thereby neutralized.) But the fact that our language has *some* stereotypes which impede rather than facilitate our dealings with the world and each other only points to the fact that we aren't infallible beings, and how could we be? The fact is that we could hardly communicate successfully if most of our stereotypes weren't pretty accurate as far as they go.

The 'operational meaning' of stereotypes

A trickier question is this: how far is the notion of stereotype 'operationally definable'. Here it is necessary to be extremely careful. Attempts in the physical sciences to *literally* specify operational definitions for terms have notoriously failed; and there is no reason the attempt should succeed in linguistics when it failed in physics. Sometimes Quine's arguments against the possibility of a theory of meaning seem to reduce to the demand for operational definitions in linguistics; when this is the case the arguments should be ignored. But it frequently happens that terms do have operational definitions not in the actual world but in idealized circumstances. Giving these 'operational definitions' has heuristic value, as idealization frequently does. It is only when we mistake operational definition for more than convenient idealization that it becomes harmful. Thus we may ask: what is the 'operational meaning' of the statement that a word has such and such a stereotype, without supposing that the answer to this question counts as a theoretical account of what it is to be a stereotype.

The theoretical account of what it is to be a stereotype proceeds in terms of the notion of *linguistic obligation*; a notion which we believe to be fundamental to linguistics and which we shall not attempt to explicate here. What it means to say that being striped is part of the (linguistic) stereotype of 'tiger' is that it is *obligatory* to acquire the information that stereotypical tigers are striped if one acquires 'tiger', in the same sense of 'obligatory' in which it is obligatory to indicate whether one is speaking of lions in the singular or lions in the plural when one speaks of lions in English. To describe an idealized experimental test of this hypothesis is not difficult. Let us introduce a person whom we may call the linguist's *confederate*. The confederate will be (or pretend to be) an adult whose command of English is generally excellent, but who for some reason (raised in an alien culture? brought up in a monastery?) has totally failed to acquire the word 'tiger'. The confederate will say the word 'tiger' or, better yet, point to it (as if he wasn't sure how to pronounce it), and ask 'what does this word mean?' or 'what is this?' or some such question. Ignoring all the things that go wrong with experiments in practice, what our hypothesis implies is that informants should typically tell the confederate that tigers are, *inter alia*, striped.

Instead of relying on confederates, one might expect the linguist to study children learning English. But children learning their native language aren't taught it nearly as much as philosophers suppose; they learn it but they aren't taught it, as Chomsky has emphasized. Still, children do sometimes ask such questions as 'what is a tiger?' and our hypothesis implies that in these cases too informants should tell them, *inter alia*, that tigers are striped. But one problem is that the informants are likely to be parents, and there are the vagaries of parental time, temper, and attention to be allowed for.

It would be easy to specify a large number of additional 'operational' implications of our hypothesis, but to do so would have no particular value. The fact is that we are fully competent speakers of English ourselves, with a devil of a good sense of what our linguistic obligations are. Pretending that we are in the position of Martians with respect to English is not the route to methodological clarity; it was, after all, only when the operational approach was abandoned that transformational linguistics blossomed into a handsome science.

Thus if anyone were to ask me for the meaning of 'tiger', I know perfectly well what I would tell him. I would tell him that tigers were feline, something about their size, that they are yellow with black stripes, that they (sometimes) live in the jungle, and are fierce. Other things I might tell him too, depending on the context and his reason for asking; but the above items, save possibly for the bit about the jungle, I would regard it as *obligatory* to convey. I don't have to experiment to know that this is what I regard it as obligatory to convey, and I am sure that approximately this is what other speakers regard it as obligatory to convey too. Of course, there is some variation from idiolect to idiolect; the feature of having stripes (apart from figure–ground relations, e.g. are they black stripes on a yellow ground, which is the way I see them, or yellow stripes on a black ground?) would be found in all normal idiolects, but some speakers might regard the information that tigers (stereotypically) inhabit jungles as obligatory, while others might not. Alternatively, some features of the stereotype (big–cat–hood, stripes) might be regarded as obligatory, and others as *optional*, on the model of certain syntactical features. But we shall not pursue this possibility here.

Quine's 'Two dogmas' revisited

In 'Two dogmas of empiricism' Quine launched a powerful and salutory attack on the currently fashionable analytic–synthetic distinction. The distinction had grown to be a veritable philosophical man-eater: analytic *equalling* necessary *equalling* unrevisable in principle *equalling* whatever truth the individual philosopher wished to explain away. But Quine's attack itself went too far in certain respects; some limited class of analytic sentences can be saved, we feel (see chapter 2). More importantly, the attack was later construed, both by Quine himself and by others, as implicating the whole notion of meaning in the downfall of the analytic–synthetic distinction. While we have made it clear that we agree that the traditional notion of meaning has serious troubles, our project in this paper is constructive, not destructive. We come to revise the notion of meaning, not to bury it. So it will be useful to see how Quine's arguments fare against our revision.

Quine's arguments against the notion of analyticity can basically be reduced to the following: that no behavioral significance can be attached to the notion. His argument (again simplifying somewhat) was that there were, basically, only two candidates for a behavioral index of analyticity, and both are totally unsatisfactory, although for different reasons. The first behavioral index is *centrality*: many contemporary philosophers call a sentence analytic if, in effect some community (say, Oxford dons) holds it immune from revision. But, Quine persuasively argues, maximum immunity from revision is no exclusive prerogative of analytic sentences. Sentences expressing fundamental laws of physics (e.g. the conservation of energy) may well enjoy maximum behavioral immunity from revision, although it would hardly be customary or plausible to classify them as analytic. Quine does not, however, rely on the mere implausibility of classifying all statements that we are highly reluctant to give up as analytic; he points out that 'immunity from revision' is, in the actual history of science, a *matter of degree*. There is no such thing, in the actual practice of rational science, as *absolute* immunity from revision. Thus to identify analyticity with immunity from revision would alter the notion in two fundamental ways: analyticity would become a matter of degree, and there would be no such thing as an absolutely analytic sentence. This would be such a departure from the classical Carnap-Ayer-*et al.* notion of analyticity that Quine feels that if *this* is what we mean to talk about, then it would be less misleading to introduce a different term altogether, say, *centrality*.

The second behavioral index is *being called 'analytic'*. In effect, some philosophers take the hallmark of analyticity to be that trained informants (say, Oxford dons) *call* the sentence analytic. Variants of this index are: that the sentence be deducible from the sentences in a finite list at the top of which someone who bears the ancestral of the graduate-student relation to Carnap has printed the words 'Meaning Postulate'; that the sentence be obtainable from a theorem of logic by substituting synonyms for synonyms. The last of these variants looks promising, but Quine launches against it the question, 'what is the criterion of synonymy?'. One possible criterion might be that words W_1 and W_2 are synonymous if and only if the biconditional (x) (x is in the extension of $W_1 \equiv x$ is in the extension of W_2) is *analytic*; but this leads us right back in a circle. Another might be that words W_1 and W_2 are synonymous if and only if trained informants *call* them synonymous; but this is just our second index in a slightly revised form. A promising line is that words W_1 and W_2 are synonymous if and only if W_1 and W_2 are interchangeable (i.e. the words can be switched) *salva veritate* in all contexts of a suitable class. But Quine convincingly shows that this proposal too leads us around in a circle. Thus the second index reduces to this: a sentence is analytic if either it or some expression, or sequence of ordered pairs of expressions, or set of expressions, related to the sentence in certain specified ways, lies in a class to all the members of which trained informants apply a certain *noise*: either the *noise* ANALYTIC, or the *noise* MEANING POSTULATE, or the *noise* SYNONYMOUS. Ultimately, this proposal leaves 'analytic', etc., *unexplicated noises*.

Although Quine does not discuss this explicitly, it is clear that taking the intersection of the two unsatisfactory behavioral indexes would be no more satisfactory; explicating the analyticity of a sentence as consisting in centrality *plus* being called ANALYTIC is just saying that the analytic sentences are a subclass of the central sentences without in any way telling us wherein the exceptionality of the subclass consists. In effect, Quine's conclusion is that analyticity is either centrality misconceived or it is nothing.

In spite of Quine's forceful argument, many philosophers have gone on abusing the notion of analyticity, often confusing it with a supposed highest degree of centrality. Confronted with Quine's alternatives, they have elected to identify analyticity with centrality, and to pay the price – the price of classifying such obviously synthetic-looking sentences as 'space has three dimensions' as analytic, and the price of undertaking to maintain the view that there is, after all, such a thing as absolute unrevisability in science in spite of the impressive evidence to the contrary. But this line can be blasted by coupling Quine's argument with an important argument of Reichenbach's.

Reichenbach (Reichenbach, 1965, p. 31) showed that there exists a *set* of principles each of which Kant would have regarded as synthetic *a priori*, but whose conjunction is incompatible with the principles of special relativity and general covariance. (These include normal induction, the continuity of space, and the Euclidean character of space.) A Kantian can consistently hold on to Euclidean geometry come what may; but then experience may force him to give up normal induction or the continuity of space. Or he may hold on to normal induction and the continuity of space come what may; but then experience may force him to give up Euclidean geometry (this happens in the case that physical space is not even homeomorphic to any Euclidean space). In his article in Schilpp (1951) Reichenbach gives essentially the same argument in a slightly different form.

Applied to our present context, what this shows is that there are principles such that philosophers fond of the overblown notion of analyticity, and in particular philosophers who identify analyticity with (maximum) unrevisability, would classify then as analytic, but whose conjunction has testable empirical consequences. Thus either the identification of analyticity with centrality must be given up once and for all, or one must give up the idea that analyticity is closed under conjunction, or one must swallow the unhappy consequence that an analytic sentence can have testable empirical consequences (and hence that an *analytic* sentence might turn out to be *empirically false*).

It is no accident, by the way, that the sentences that Kant would have classified as synthetic *a priori* would be classified by these latter-day empiricists as analytic; their purpose in bloating the notion of analyticity was precisely to dissolve Kant's problem by identifying *a prioricity* with analyticity and then identifying analyticity in turn with truth by convention. (This last step has also been devastingly criticized by Quine, but discussion of it would take us away from our topic.)

Other philosophers have tried to answer Quine by distinguishing between *sentences* and *statements*: all *sentences* are revisable, they agree, but some *statements* are not. Revising a sentence is not changing our mind about the statement formerly expressed by that sentence just in case the sentence (meaning the syntactical object together with its meaning) after the revision is, in fact, not synonymous with the sentence prior to the revision, i.e. just in case the revision is a case of meaning change and not change of theory. But (1) this reduces at once to the proposal to explicate analyticity in terms of synonymy; and (2) if there is one thing that Quine has decisively contributed to philosophy, it is the realization that meaning change and theory change cannot be sharply separated. We do not agree with Quine that meaning change cannot be defined at all, but it does not follow that the dichotomy 'meaning change *or* theory change' is tenable. Discovering that we live in a non-Euclidean world *might* change the meaning of 'straight line' (this would happen in the – somewhat unlikely – event that something like the parallels postulate was part of the stereotype of straightness); but it would not be a *mere* change of meaning. In particular it would not be a change of *extension*: thus it would not be right to say that the parallels postulate was 'true in the former sense of the words'. From the fact that giving up a sentence *S* would involve meaning change, it does not follow that *S* is *true*. Meanings may not fit the world; and meaning change can be forced by empirical discoveries.

Although we are not, in this paper, trying to explicate a notion of analyticity, we are trying to explicate a notion that might seem closely related, the notion of meaning. Thus it might seem that Quine's arguments would also go against our attempt. Let us check this out.

In our view there is a perfectly good sense in which being striped is part of the meaning of 'tiger'. But it does not follow, in our view, that 'tigers are striped' is analytic. If a mutation occurred, all tigers might be albinos. Communication presupposes that I have a stereotype of tigers which includes stripes, and that you have a stereotype of tigers which includes stripes, and that I know that your stereotype includes stripes, and that you know that my stereotype includes stripes, and that you know that I know...(and so on, à la Grice, forever). But it does not presuppose that any particular stereotype be *correct*, or that the majority of our stereotypes remain correct forever. Linguistic obligatoriness is not supposed to be an index of unrevisability or even of truth; thus we can hold that 'tigers are striped' is part of the meaning of 'tiger' without being trapped in the problems of analyticity.

Thus Quine's arguments against identifying analyticity with centrality are not arguments against identifying a feature's being 'part of the meaning' of *X* with its being obligatorily included in the stereotype of *X*. What of Quine's 'noise' argument?

Of course, evidence concerning what people *say*, including explicit metalinguistic remarks, is important in 'semantics' as it is in syntax. Thus, if a speaker points to a *clam* and asks 'is that a tiger?' people are likely to guffaw. (When they stop laughing) they might say 'he doesn't know the meaning of "tiger"', or 'he doesn't know what tigers are'. Such comments can be helpful to the linguist. But we are not *defining* the stereotype in terms of such comments. To say that being 'big-cat-like' is part of the meaning of tiger is not merely to say that application of 'tiger' to something which is not big-cat-like (and also not a tiger) would provoke certain *noises*. It is to say that speakers acquire the information that 'tigers are (stereotypically) big-cat-like' as they acquire the word 'tiger' and that they feel an obligation to guarantee that those to whom they teach the use of the word do likewise. Information about the minimum skills required for entry into the linguistic community is significant information; no circularity of the kind Quine criticized appears here.

Radical translation

What our theory does not do, by itself at any rate, is solve Quine's problem of 'radical translation' (i.e. translation from an alien language/culture). We cannot translate our hypothetical Cheroquoi into English by matching stereotypes, just because finding out what the stereotype of, say, *wa'arabi* is involves translating Cheroquoi utterances. On the other hand, the constraint that each word in Cheroquoi should match its image in English under the translation-function as far as stereotype is concerned (or approximately match, since in many cases exact matching may not be attainable), places a severe *constraint* on the translation-function. Once we have succeeded in translating the basic vocabulary of Cheroquoi, we can start to elicit stereotypes, and these will serve both to constrain future translations and to check the internal correctness of the piece of the translation-function already constructed.

Even where we can determine stereotypes (relative, say, to a tentative translation of 'basic vocabulary'), these do not suffice, in general, to determine a unique translation. Thus the German words *Ulme* and *Buche* have the same stereotype as elm; but *Ulme* means 'elm' while *Buche* means 'beech'. In the case of German, the fact that *Ulme* and 'elm' are cognates could point to the correct translation (although this is far from foolproof – in general, cognate words are not synonymous); but in the case of Greek we have no such clue as to which of the two words ὀξύα, πτελέα means *elm* and which *beech*; we would just have to find a Greek who could tell elms from beeches (or *oxya* from *ptelea*). What this illustrates is that it may not be the *typical* speakers' dispositions to assent and dissent that the linguist must seek to discover; because of the division of linguistic labor, it is frequently necessary for the linguist to assess who are the experts with respect to *oxya*, or *wa'arabi*, or *gavagai*, or whatever, before he can make a guess at the socially determined extension of a word. Then this socially determined extension *and* the stereotype of the *typical* speaker, inexpert though he is, will *both* function as constraints upon the translation-function. Discovery that the stereotype of *oxya* is wildly different from the stereotype of 'elm' would disqualify the translation of *oxya* by 'elm' in all save the most extensional contexts; but the discovery that the *extension* of *oxya* is not even approximately the class of elms would wipe out the translation altogether, in all contexts.

It will be noted that we have already enlarged the totality of facts counted as evidence for a translation-function beyond the ascetic base that Quine allows in *Word and Object*. For example, the fact that speakers say such-and-such when the linguist's 'confederate' points to the word *oxya* and asks 'what does this mean?' or 'what is this?' or whatever is not allowed by Quine (as something the linguist can 'know') on the ground that this sort of 'knowledge' presupposes already having translated the query 'what does this word mean?'. However, if Quine is willing to assume that one can *somehow* guess at the words which signify *assent* and *dissent* in the alien language, it does not seem at all unreasonable to suppose that one can somehow convey to a native speaker that one does not understand a word. It is not necessary that one discover a locution in the alien language which literally means 'what does this word mean?' (as opposed to: 'I don't understand this word', or 'this word is unfamiliar to me' or 'I am puzzled by this word', etc.). Perhaps just saying the word *oxya*, or whatever, with a tone of puzzlement would suffice. Why should *puzzlement* be less accessible to the linguist than *assent*?

Also, we are taking advantage of the fact that segmentation into *words* has turned out to be linguistically universal (and there even exist tests for word and morpheme segmentation which are independent of meaning). Clearly, there is no motivated reason for allowing the linguist to utter whole sentences and look for assent and dissent, while refusing to allow him to utter words and morphemes in a tone of puzzlement.

I repeat, the claim is not being advanced that enlarging the evidence base in this way solves the problem of radical translation. What it does is add further constraints on the class of admissible candidates for a correct translation. What I believe is that enlarging the class of constraints can determine a unique translation, or as unique a translation as we are able to get in practice. But constraints that go beyond linguistic theory proper will have to be used, in my opinion; there will also have to be constraints on what sorts of beliefs (and connections between beliefs, and connections of beliefs to the culture and the world) we can reasonably impute to people. Discussion of these matters will be deferred to another paper.

A critique of Davidsonian semantic theory

In a series of publications, Donald Davidson has put forward the interesting suggestion that a semantic theory of a natural language might be modelled on what mathematical logicians call a *truth definition* for a formalized language. Stripped of technicalities, what this suggestion comes down to is that one might have a set of rules specifying (1) for each word, under what conditions that word is true of something (for words for which the concept of an extension makes sense; all other words are to be treated as syncategorematic); (2) for sentences longer than a single word, a rule is given specifying the conditions under which the sentence is true as a function of the way it is built up out of shorter sentences (counting words as if they were one-word sentences, e.g. 'snow' as 'that's snow'). The choice of one-word sentences as the starting point is my interpretation of what Davidson intends; in any case, he means one to start with a *finite* stock of *short* sentences for which truth conditions are to be laid down *directly*. The intention of (2) is not that there should be a rule for each sentence not handled under (1), since this would require an infinite number of rules, but that there should be a rule for each sentence *type*. For example, in a formalized language one of the rules of kind (2) might be: if S is (S_1 & S_2) for some sentences S_1, S_2, then S is true if and only if S_1, S_2, are both true.

It will be noticed that, in the example just given, the truth condition specified for sentences of the sentence type (S_1 & S_2) performs the job of specifying the meaning of '&'. More precisely, it specifies the meaning of the structure (——— & ———). This is the sense in which a truth definition can be a theory of meaning. Davidson's contention is that the *entire* theory of meaning for a natural language can be given in this form.

There is no doubt that rules of the type illustrated can give the meaning of some words and structures. The question is, what reason is there to think that the meaning of most words can be given in this way, let alone all?

The obvious difficulty is this: for many words, an extensionally correct truth definition can be given which is in no sense a theory of the meaning of the word. For example, consider '*Water*' *is true of* x *if and only if* x *is* H_2O. This is an extensionally correct truth definition for 'water' (strictly speaking, it is not a truth definition but a 'truth of' definition – i.e. a *satisfaction*-in-the-sense-of-Tarski definition, but we will not bother with such niceties here). At least it is extensionally correct if we ignore the problem that water with impurities is also called 'water', etc. Now, suppose most speakers don't *know* that water is H_2O. Then this formula in no way tells us anything about the *meaning* of 'water'. It might be of interest to a chemist, but it doesn't count as a theory of the meaning of the term 'water'. Or, it counts as a theory of the *extension* of the term 'water', but Davidson is promising us more than just that.

Davidson is quite well aware of this difficulty. His answer (in conversation, anyway) is that we need to develop a theory of *translation*.
This he, like Quine, considers to be the real problem. Relativized to such
a theory (relativitized to what we admittedly don't yet have), the theory
comes down to this: we want a system of truth definitions which is
simultaneously a system of translations (or approximate translations, if
perfect translation is unobtainable). If we had a theory which specified
what it is to be a good translation, then we could rule out the above truth
definition for 'water' as uninteresting on the grounds that x *is* H_2O is
not an acceptable translation or even near-translation of x *is water* (in
a prescientific community), even if water $= H_2O$ happens to be true.

This comes perilously close to saying that a theory of meaning is a
truth definition plus a theory of meaning. (If we had ham and eggs we'd
have ham and eggs – *if* we had ham and *if* we had eggs.) But this story
suffers from worse than promissoriness, as we shall see.

A second contention of Davidson's is that the theory of translation
that we don't yet have is necessarily a theory whose basic units are
sentences and not *words* on the grounds that our *evidence* in linguistics
necessarily consists of assent and dissent from sentences. Words can be
handled, Davidson contends, by treating them as sentences ('water' as
'that's water', etc.).

How does this ambitious project of constructing a theory of meaning
in the form of a truth definition constrained by a theory of translation
tested by 'the only evidence we have', speakers' dispositions to use
sentences, fare according to the view we are putting forward here?

Our answer is that the theory cannot succeed in principle. In special
cases, such as the word 'and' in its truth-functional sense, a truth
definition (strictly speaking, a clause in what logicians call a 'truth
definition' – the sum total of all the clauses is the inductive definition
of 'truth' for the particular language) can give the meaning of the word
or structure because the stereotype associated with the word (if one
wants to speak of a stereotype in the case of a word like 'and') is so
strong as to actually constitute a necessary and sufficient condition. If
all words were like 'and' and 'bachelor' the program could succeed.
And Davidson certainly made an important contribution in pointing
out that linguistics has to deal with inductively specified truth conditions. But in the great majority of words, the requirements of a theory
of truth and the requirements of a theory of meaning are mutually
incompatible, at least in the English–English case. But the English–
English case – the case in which we try to provide a significant theory
of the meaning of English words which is itself couched in English – is
surely the basic one.

The problem is that in general the only expressions which are both coextensive with X and have roughly the same stereotype as X are expressions containing X itself. If we rule out such truth definitions (strictly speaking, clauses, but I shall continue using 'truth definition' both for individual clauses and for the whole system of clauses, for simplicity) as

'X is water' is true if and only if X *is water*

on the grounds that they don't say anything about the meaning of the word 'water', and we rule out such truth definitions as

'X is water' is true if and only if X *is* H_2O

on the grounds that what they say is wrong as a description of the *meaning* of the word 'water', then we shall be left with nothing.

The problem is that we want

W *is true of* x *if and only if* ——

to satisfy the conditions that (1) the clause be extensionally correct (where —— is to be thought of as a condition containing 'x', e.g. 'x is H_2O'); (2) that —— be a *translation* of W – on our theory, this would mean that the stereotype associated with W is approximately the same as the stereotype associated with ——; (3) that —— not contain W itself, or syntactic variants of W. If we take W to be, for example, the word 'elm', then there is absolutely no way to fulfill all three conditions simultaneously. Any condition of the above form that does not contain 'elm' and that is extensionally correct will contain a —— that is absolutely terrible as a *translation* of 'elm'.

Even where the language contains two exact synonyms, the situation is little better. Thus

'Heather' is true of x *if and only if* x *is gorse*

is true, and so is

'Gorse' is true of x *if and only if* x *is heather*

– *this* is a *theory* of the *meaning* of 'gorse' and 'heather'?

Notice that the condition (3) is precisely what logicians do *not* impose on *their* truth definitions.

'Snow is white' is true if and only if snow is white

is the paradigm of a truth definition in the logician's sense. But logicians are trying to give the extension of 'true' with respect to a particular language, not the meaning of 'snow is white'. Tarski would have gone so far as to claim he was giving the *meaning* (and not just the extension) of 'true'; but he would never have claimed he was saying *anything* about the meaning of 'snow is white'.

It may be that what Davidson really thinks is that theory of meaning, in any serious sense of the term, is impossible, and that all that is possible is to construct translation-functions. If so, he might well think that the only 'theory of meaning' possible for English is one that says '"elm" is true of x if and only if x is an elm', '"water" is true of x if and only if x is water', etc., and only rarely something enlightening like 'S_1 & S_2 is true if and only if S_1, S_2 are both true'. But if Davidson's 'theory' is just Quinine skepticism under the disguise of a positive contribution to the study of meaning, then it is a bitter pill to swallow.

The contention that the only evidence available to the linguist is speakers' dispositions with respect to whole sentences is, furthermore, vacuous on one interpretation, and plainly false on the interpretation on which it is not vacuous. If dispositions to say certain things *when queried about individual words or morphemes or syntactic structures* are included in the notion of dispositions to use sentences, then the restriction to dispositions to use sentences seems to rule out nothing whatsoever. On the non-vacuous interpretation, what Davidson is saying is that the linguist cannot have access to such data as what informants (including the linguist himself) say when asked the meaning of a word or morpheme or syntactic structure. No reason has ever been given why the linguist cannot have access to such data, and it is plain that actual linguists place heavy reliance on informants' testimony about such matters, in the case of an alien language, and upon their own intuitions as native speakers, when they are studying their native languages. In particular, when we are trying to translate a whole sentence, there is no reason why we should not be guided by our knowledge of the syntactic and semantic properties of the constituents of that sentence, including the deep structure. As we have seen, there are procedures for gaining information about individual constituents. It is noteworthy that the procedure that Quine and Davidson claim is the only *possible* one – going from whole sentences to individual words – is the *opposite* of the procedure upon which every success ever attained in the study of natural language has been based.

Critique of California semantics

I wish now to consider an approach to semantic theory pioneered by the late Rudolf Carnap. Since I do not wish to be embroiled in textual questions, I will not attribute the particular form of the view I am going to describe to any particular philosopher but will simply refer to it as 'California semantics'.

We assume the notion of a *possible world*. Let f be a function defined on the 'space' of all possible worlds whose value $f(x)$ at any possible world x is always a subset of the set of entities in x. Then f is called an *intension*. A term T has meaning for a speaker X if X associates T with an intension f_T. The term T is *true of* an entity e in a possible world x if and only if e belongs to the set $f(x)$. Instead of using the term 'associated', Carnap himself tended to speak of 'grasping' intensions; but, clearly, what was intended was not just that X 'grasp' the intension f, but that he grasp *that f* is the intension *of T* – i.e. that he *associate f* with T in some way.

Clearly this picture of what it is to understand a term disagrees with the story we tell in this paper. The reply of a California semanticist would be that California sementics is a description of an *ideal* language; that actual language is *vague*. In other words, a term T in actual language does not have a single precise intension; it has a set – possibly a fuzzy set – of intensions. Nevertheless, the first step in the direction of describing natural language is surely to study the idealization in which each term T has exactly one intension.

(In his book *Meaning and Necessity*, Carnap employs a superficially different formulation: an intension is simply a *property*. An entity e belongs to the extension of a term T just in case e has whichever property is the intension of T. The later formulation in terms of functions f as described above avoids taking the notion of *property* as primitive.)

The first difficulty with this position is the use of the totally unexplained notion of *grasping* an intension (or, in our reformulation of the position, *associating* an intension with a term). Identifying intensions with set-theoretic entities f provides a 'concrete' realization of the notion of intension in the current mathematical style (relative to the notions of possible world and set), but at the cost of making it very difficult to see how anyone could have an intension in his mind, or what it is to think about one or 'grasp' one or 'associate' one with anything. It will not do to say that thinking of an intension is using a word or functional substitute for a word (e.g. the analogue of a word in 'brain code', if, as seems likely, the brain 'computes' in a 'code' that has analogies to and possibly borrowings from language; or a thought form such as a picture or a private symbol, in cases where such are employed in thinking) which *refers* to the intension in question, since *reference* (i.e. being in the extension of a term) has just been defined in terms of *intension*. Although the characterization of what it is to think of an abstract entity such as a function or a property is certainly correct, in

the present context it is patently circular. But no noncircular characterization of this fundamental notion of the theory has ever been provided.

This difficulty is related to a general difficulty in the philosophy of
mathematics pointed out by Paul Benacerraf (Benacerraf, 1973).
Benacerraf has remarked that philosophies of mathematics tend to fall
between two stools: either they account for what mathematical objects
are and for the necessity of mathematical truth and fail to account for
the fact that people can *learn* mathematics, can *refer to* mathematical
objects, etc., or else they account for the latter facts and fail to account
for the former. California semantics accounts for what intensions *are*,
but provides no account that is not completely circular of how it is that
we can 'grasp' them, associate them with terms, think about them,
refer to them, etc.

Carnap may not have noticed this difficulty because of his Verificationism. In his early years Carnap thought of understanding a term as
possessing the *ability to verify* whether or not any given entity falls in
the extension of the term. In terms of intensions: 'grasping' an intension
would amount, then, to possessing the ability to verify if an entity e in
any possible world x belongs to $f(x)$ or not. Later Carnap modified this
view, recognizing that, as Quine puts it, sentences face the tribunal of
experience collectively and not individually. There is no such thing as
the way of verifying that a term T is true of an entity, in general, independent of the context of a particular set of theories, auxiliary hypotheses, etc. Perhaps Carnap would have maintained that something like
the earlier theory was correct for a limited class of terms, the so-called
'observation terms'. Our own view is that the verifiability theory of
meaning is false both in its central idea and for observation terms, but
we shall not try to discuss this here. At any rate, if one is *not* a verificationist, then it is hard to see California semantics as a theory at
all, since the notion of *grasping* an intension has been left totally
unexplained.

Second, if we assume that 'grasping an intension' (associating an
intension with a term T) is supposed to be a *psychological state* (in the
narrow sense), then California semantics is committed to both principles
(1) and (2) that we criticized in the first part of this paper. It must hold
that the psychological state of the speaker determines the intension of
his terms which in turn determines the extension of his terms. It would
follow that if two human beings are in the same total psychological
state, then they necessarily assign the same extension to every term they
employ. As we have seen, this is totally wrong for natural language. The
reason this is wrong, as we saw above, is in part that extension is determined socially, not by individual competence alone. Thus California

semantics is committed to treating language as something private – to totally ignoring the linguistic division of labor. The extension of each term is viewed by this school as totally determined by something in the head of the individual speaker all by himself. A second reason this is wrong, as we also saw, is that most terms are *rigid*. In California semantics every term is treated as, in effect, a *description*. The *indexical* component in meaning – the fact that our terms refer to things which are similar, in certain ways, to things that we designate *rigidly*, to *these* things, to the stuff we call 'water', or whatever, *here* – is ignored.

But what of the defense that it is not actual language that the California semanticist is concerned with, but an idealization in which we 'ignore vagueness', and that terms in natural language may be thought of as associated with a set of intensions rather than with a single well-defined intension?

The answer is that an *indexical* word cannot be represented as a vague family of non-indexical words. The word 'I', to take the extreme case, is *indexical* but not *vague*. 'I' is not synonymous with a *description*; neither is it synonymous with a fuzzy set of descriptions. Similarly, if we are right, 'water' is synonymous neither with a description nor with a fuzzy set of descriptions (intensions).

Similarly, a word whose extension is fixed socially and not individually is not the same thing as a word whose extension is *vaguely* fixed individually. The reason my individual 'grasp' of 'elm tree' does not fix the extension of elm is not that the word is vague – if the problem were simple vagueness, then the fact that my concepts do not distinguish elms from beeches would imply that elms are beeches, as I use the term, or, anyway, borderline cases of beeches, and that beeches are elms, or borderline cases of elms. The reason is rather that the extension of 'elm tree' in my dialect is not fixed by what the average speaker 'grasps' or doesn't 'grasp' at all; it is fixed by the community, including the experts, through a complex cooperative process. A language which exemplifies the division of linguistic labor cannot be approximated successfully by a language which has vague terms and no linguistic division of labor. Cooperation isn't vagueness.

But, one might reply, couldn't one replace our actual language by a language in which (1) terms were replaced by coextensive terms which were *not* indexical (e.g. 'water' by 'H_2O', assuming 'H_2O' is not indexical); and (2) we eliminated the division of linguistic labor by making every speaker an expert on every topic?

We shall answer this question in the negative; but suppose, for a moment, the answer were 'yes'. What significance would this have? The 'ideal' language would in no sense be similar to our actual language;

nor would the difference be a matter of 'the vagueness of natural language'.

In fact, however, one can't carry out the replacement, for the very good reason that *all* natural-kind words and physical-magnitude words are indexical in the way we have described, 'hydrogen', and hence 'H_2O', just as much as 'water'. Perhaps 'sense data' terms are not indexical (apart from terms for the self), if such there be; but 'yellow' as a *thing* predicate is indexical for the same reason as 'tiger'; even if something *looks* yellow it may not *be* yellow. And it doesn't help to say that things that look yellow in normal circumstances (to normal perceivers) are yellow; 'normal' here has precisely the feature we called indexicality. There is simply no reason to believe that the project of reducing our language to nonindexical language could be carried out in principle.

The elimination of the division of linguistic labor might, I suppose, be carried out 'in principle'. But, if the division of linguistic labor is, as I conjectured, a linguistic universal, what interest is there in the possible existence of a language which lacks a constitutive feature of *human* language? A world in which every one is an expert on every topic is a world in which social laws are almost unimaginably different from what they now are. What is the *motivation* for taking such a world and such a language as the model for the analysis of *human* language?

Incidentally, philosophers who work in the tradition of California semantics have recently begun to modify the scheme to overcome just these defects. Thus it has been suggested that an intension might be a function whose arguments are not just possible worlds but, perhaps, a possible world, a speaker, and a nonlinguistic context of utterance. This would permit the representation of some kinds of indexicality and some kinds of division of linguistic labor in the model. As David Lewis develops these ideas, 'water', for example, would have the same *intension* (same function) on Earth and on Twin Earth, but a different extension. (In effect, Lewis retains assumption (1) from the discussion in the first part of this paper and gives up (2); we chose to give up (1) and retain (2).) There is no reason why the formal models developed by Carnap and his followers should not prove valuable when so modified. Our interest here has been not in the utility of the mathematical formalism but in the philosophy of language underlying the earlier versions of the view.

Semantic markers

If the approach suggested here is correct, then there is a great deal of scientific work to be done in (1) finding out what sorts of items can

appear in stereotypes; (2) working out a convenient system for representing stereotypes; etc. This work is not work that can be done by philosophical discussion, however. It is rather the province of linguistics
and psycholinguistics. One idea that can, I believe, be of value is the
idea of a *semantic marker*. The idea comes from the work of J. Katz and
J. A. Fodor; we shall modify it somewhat here.

Consider the stereotype of 'tiger' for a moment. This includes such
features as being an animal; being big-cat-like; having black stripes on
a yellow ground (yellow stripes on a black ground?); etc. Now, there
is something very special about the feature *animal*. In terms of
Quine's notion of *centrality* or *unrevisability*, it is qualitatively different
from the others listed. It is not impossible to imagine that tigers might
not be animals (they might be robots). But spelling this out, they must
always have been robots; we don't want to tell a story about the tigers
being *replaced* by robots, because then the robots wouldn't be tigers. Or,
if they weren't always robots, they must have *become* robots, which is
even harder to imagine. If tigers are and always were robots, these
robots mustn't be too 'intelligent', or else we may not have a case in
which tigers aren't animals – we may, rather, have described a case in
which some robots are animals. Best make them 'other directed' robots
– say, have an operator on Mars controlling each motion remotely.
Spelling this out, I repeat, is difficult, and it is curiously hard to think
of the case to begin with, which is why it is easy to make the mistake of
thinking that it is 'logically impossible' for a tiger *not* to be an animal.
On the other hand, there is no difficulty in imagining an individual
tiger that is not striped; it might be an albino. Nor is it difficult to imagine
an individual tiger that doesn't look like a big cat: it might be horribly
deformed. We can even imagine the whole species losing its stripes or
becoming horribly deformed. But tigers ceasing to be animals? Great
difficulty again!

Notice that we are not making the mistake that Quine rightly criticized, of attributing an absolute unrevisability to such statements as
'tigers are animals', 'tigers couldn't change from animals into something
else and still be tigers'. Indeed, we can describe farfetched cases in
which these statements would be given up. But we maintain that it is
qualitatively harder to revise 'all tigers are animals' than 'all tigers have
stripes' – indeed, the latter statement is not even true.

Not only do such features as 'animal', 'living thing', 'artifact', 'day
of the week', 'period of time', attach with enormous centrality to the
words 'tiger', 'clam', 'chair', 'Tuesday', 'hour'; but they also form
part of a widely used and important *system of classification*. The centrality guarantees that items classified under these headings virtually

never have to be *re*classified; thus these headings are the natural ones to use as category-indicators in a host of contexts. It seems to me reasonable that, just as in syntax we use such markers as 'noun', 'adjective', and, more narrowly, 'concrete noun', 'verb taking a person as subject and an abstract object', etc., to classify words, so in semantics these category-indicators should be used as markers.

It is interesting that when Katz and Fodor originally introduced the idea of a semantic marker, they did not propose to exhaust the meaning – what we call the stereotype – by a list of such markers. Rather, the markers were restricted to just the category-indicators of high centrality, which is what we propose. The remaining features were simply listed as a 'distinguisher'. Their scheme is not easily comparable with ours, because they wanted the semantic markers *plus* the distinguisher to always give a necessary and sufficient condition for membership in the extension of the term. Since the whole thing – markers and distinguisher – were supposed to represent what every speaker implicitly knows, they were committed to the idea that every speaker implicitly knows of a necessary and sufficient condition for membership in the extension of 'gold', 'aluminum', 'elm' – which, as we have pointed out, is not the case. Later Katz went further and demanded that *all* the features constitute an *analytically* necessary and sufficient condition for membership in the extension. At this point he dropped the distinction between markers and distinguishers; if all the features have, so to speak, the infinite degree of centrality, why call some 'markers' and some 'distinguishers'? From our point of view, their original distinction between 'markers' and 'distinguisher' was sound – provided one drop the idea that the distinguisher provides (together with the markers) a necessary and sufficient condition, and the idea that any of this is a theory of *analyticity*. We suggest that the idea of a semantic marker is an important contribution, when taken as suggested here.

The meaning of 'meaning'

We may now summarize what has been said in the form of a proposal concerning how one might reconstruct the notion of 'meaning'. Our proposal is not the only one that might be advanced on the basis of these ideas, but it may serve to encapsulate some of the major points. In addition, I feel that it recovers as much of ordinary usage in common sense talk and in linguistics as one is likely to be able to conveniently preserve. Since, in my view something like the assumptions (I) and (II) listed in the first part of this paper are deeply embedded in ordinary meaning talk, and these assumptions are jointly inconsistent with the facts, no reconstruction is going to be without some counter-intuitive consequences.

Briefly, my proposal is to define 'meaning' not by picking out an object which will be identified with the meaning (although that might be done in the usual set-theoretic style if one insists), but by specifying a normal form (or, rather, a *type* of normal form) for the description of meaning. If we know what a 'normal form description' of the meaning of a word should be, then, as far as I am concerned, we know what meaning *is* in any scientifically interesting sense.

My proposal is that the normal form description of the meaning of a word should be a finite sequence, or 'vector', whose components should certainly include the following (it might be desirable to have other types of components as well): (1) the syntactic markers that apply to the word, e.g. 'noun'; (2) the semantic markers that apply to the word, e.g. 'animal', 'period of time'; (3) a description of the additional features of the stereotype, if any; (4) a description of the extension.

The following convention is a part of this proposal: the components of the vector all represent a hypothesis about the individual speaker's competence, *except the extension*. Thus the normal form description for 'water' might be, in part:

SYNTACTIC MARKERS	SEMANTIC MARKERS	STEREOTYPE	EXTENSION
mass noun, concrete;	*natural kind;*	*colorless;*	H_2O
	liquid;	*transparent;*	*(give or*
		tasteless;	*take*
		thirst-quenching;	*impurities)*
		etc.	

– this does *not* mean that knowledge of the fact that water is H_2O is being imputed to the individual speaker or even to the society. It means that (*we* say) the extension of the term 'water' as *they* (the speakers in question) use it is *in fact* H_2O. The objection 'who are *we* to say what the extension of *their* term is in fact' has been discussed above. Note that this is fundamentally an objection to the notion of *truth*, and that extension is a relative of truth and inherits the family problems.

Let us call two descriptions *equivalent* if they are the same except for the description of the extension, and the two descriptions are coextensive. Then, if the set variously described in the two descriptions is, *in fact*, the extension of the word in question, and the other components in the description are correct characterizations of the various aspects of competence they represent, *both* descriptions count as correct. Equivalent descriptions are both correct or both incorrect. This is another way of making the point that, although we have to use a *description* of the extension to *give* the extension, we think of the component in question as being the *extension* (the *set*), not the description of the extension.

In particular the representation of the words 'water' in Earth dialect and 'water' in Twin Earth dialect would be the same except that in the last column the normal form description of the Twin Earth word 'water' would have XYZ and not H_2O. This means, in view of what has just been said, that we are ascribing the *same* linguistic competence to the typical Earthian/Twin Earthian speaker, but a different extension to the word, nonetheless.

This proposal means that we keep assumption (II) of our early discussion. Meaning determines extension – by construction, so to speak. But (I) is given up; the psychological state of the individual speaker does not determine 'what he means'.

In most contexts this will agree with the way we speak, I believe. But one paradox: suppose Oscar is a German–English bilingual. In our view, in his total collection of dialects, the words 'beech' and *Buche* are *exact synonyms*. The normal form descriptions of their meanings would be identical. But he might very well not know that they are synonyms! A speaker can have two synonyms in his vocabulary and not know that they are synonyms!

It is instructive to see how the failure of the apparently obvious 'if S_1 and S_2 are synonyms and Oscar understands both S_1 and S_2 then Oscar knows that S_1 and S_2 are synonyms' is related to the falsity of (I), in our analysis. Notice that if we had chosen to omit the extension as a component of the 'meaning-vector', which is David Lewis's proposal as I understand it, then we would have the paradox that 'elm' and 'beech' have the *same meaning* but different extensions!

On just about any materialist theory, believing a proposition is likely to involve processing some *representation* of that proposition, be it a sentence in a language, a piece of 'brain code', a thought form, or whatever. Materialists, and not only materialists, are reluctant to think that one can believe propositions *neat*. But even materialists tend to believe that, if one believes a proposition, *which* representation one employs is (pardon the pun) immaterial. If S_1 and S_2 are both representations that are *available* to me, then if I believe the proposition expressed by S_1 under the representation S_1, I must also believe it under the representation S_2 – at least, I must do this if I have any claim to rationality. But, as we have just seen, this isn't right. Oscar may well believe that *this* is a 'beech' (it has a sign on it that says 'beech'), but not believe or disbelieve that this is a '*Buche*'. It is not just that belief is a process involving representations; he believes the proposition (if one

270

wants to introduce 'propositions' at all) under one representation and not under another.

The amazing thing about the theory of meaning is how long the subject has been in the grip of philosophical misconceptions, and how strong these misconceptions are. Meaning has been identified with a necessary and sufficient condition by philosopher after philosopher. In the empiricist tradition, it has been identified with method of verification, again by philosopher after philosopher. Nor have these misconceptions had the virtue of exclusiveness; not a few philosophers have held that meaning = method of verification = necessary and sufficient condition.

On the other side, it is amazing how weak the grip of the facts has been. After all, what have been pointed out in this essay are little more than home truths about the way we use words and how much (or rather, how little) we actually know when we use them. My own reflection on these matters began after I published a paper in which I confidently maintained that the meaning of a word was 'a battery of semantical rules', (chapter 6 in this volume) and then began to wonder how the meaning of the common word 'gold' could be accounted for in this way. And it is not that philosophers had never considered such examples: Locke, for example, uses this word as an example and is not troubled by the idea that its meaning is a necessary and sufficient condition!

If there is a reason for both learned and lay opinion having gone so far astray with respect to a topic which deals, after all, with matters which are in everyone's experience, matters concerning which we all have more data than we know what to do with, matters concerning which we have, if we shed preconceptions, pretty clear intuitions, it must be connected to the fact that the grotesquely mistaken views of language which are and always have been current reflect two specific and very central philosophical tendencies: the tendency to treat cognition as a purely *individual* matter and the tendency to ignore the *world*, insofar as it consists of more than the individual's 'observations'. Ignoring the division of linguistic labor is ignoring the social dimension of cognition; ignoring what we have called the *indexicality* of most words is ignoring the contribution of the environment. Traditional philosophy of language, like much traditional philosophy, leaves out other people and the world; a better philosophy and a better science of language must encompass both.

13
Language and reality*

About a century ago, Charles Sanders Peirce asserted that the meaning of an 'intellectual conception' is identical with the 'sum' of its 'practical consequences' (cf. Peirce, 1958). And he thought this idea sufficiently important that he made it the primary maxim of the philosophy he called Pragmatism. This is nothing but an early statement of the Verifiability Theory of Meaning. And Pragmatism was the first philosophy dedicated to the proposition that theory of meaning can solve or dissolve the traditional problems of philosophy.

Today the Verifiability Theory of Meaning has been pretty well abandoned, not, alas!, because the fundamental intuition behind it has been universally conceded to be erroneous, but simply because there are formidable *technical* objections to the doctrine. The fundamental intuition behind the doctrine has two closely related components. One component is the Open Question Argument: *what more* does the expression mean, if it means more than that we will have certain experiences? The other component is the argument, often found in nineteenth century literature (and still occasionally found today) that to believe in things that are not *concepts* (or at least mental entities) is to believe in things that are inconceivable.†

The reply to the Open Question argument is that the Verificationist philosopher is here speaking *as if* he had succeeded in the enterprise of translating our commonplace talk of things into a sensationalistic vernacular. We should not demand of him that he preserve *meaning* when translating each sentence of thing talk into a sentence of sensation talk; for that would be to beg the question at issue. But at least he must preserve deductive and inductive relations. If Verificationists *could* translate thing talk,‡ preserving deductive and inductive relations, then

---

* This was delivered as a Machette lecture at Princeton, 22 May 1974.

† E.g. Peirce says, 'But if it be asked, whether some realities do not exist, which are entirely independent of thought; I would in turn ask, what is meant by such an expression and what can be meant by it. What idea can be attached to that of which there is no idea? For if there be an idea of such a reality, it is the object of that idea of which we are speaking, and which is not independent of thought.' (Peirce, 1958, 7, paragraph 345, 1873)

‡ Or if non-phenomenalist Verificationists could translate 'theoretical' talk into 'observation language'.

they would be in an impressive position. And they might well ask, for any given sentence of thing language: in what does its supposed 'surplus meaning' (as compared with its sensationalistic translation) consist, and why should we care about this alleged 'surplus meaning'? But they can only confront or confound us in this way when they have their translation at hand. Lacking a successful translation, asking *what more* a thing sentence means than its (unspecified and, for all we know, nonexistent) phenomenalist translation is empty rhetoric.

The reply to the second of the two arguments is that something is conceivable if it is *represented* by a concept, it does not have to *be* a concept to be conceivable. No contradiction ensues if one believes that some things are not concepts and proceeds to talk about them. One is not thereby pretending to conceive the inconceivable; but only to conceptualize the nonmental. The genesis of this argument appears to be in Berkeley's assumption that only *like* can represent *like*, where *likeness* is identified with phenomenal similarity. In this day of familiarity with abstract structure and with many novel and unintuitive methods of representing data, Berkeley's assumption lacks credibility. Yet this argument, weird as it is, leaves us with a major unsolved problem: to say something positive about the way in which concepts represent entities which are not concepts. That this may ultimately be a scientific problem is no reason for philosophers to neglect it; determining at least some of the *possible* answers to problems of importance to *Weltanschauung* is, after all, the primary task of philosophy.

Against the fundamental intuition of Verificationism and phenomenalism (for all Verificationism is phenomenalism at heart), there is the contrary intuition of realism: that human experience is only a part of reality, reality is not part or whole of human experience. I shall not defend or dwell upon this intuition here, but what I say will certainly reflect it.

As the Verifiability Theory of Meaning was wrong, so was Peirce's second claim. Philosophy of Language cannot solve the traditional problems of philosophy by showing them to be psuedo-problems. At this Wittgenstein was no more successful than Carnap, and Carnap no more successful than Peirce, the enormous differences between these three philosophers notwithstanding.

This does not mean that Philosophy of Language, and more generally meta-philosophy, can contribute nothing to the improvement of philosophical practice. If sweeping maxims connecting meaning with 'effects as might have practical bearing', or with 'method of verification', or with 'use', do little in philosophy, maxims of less scope can accomplish much if judiciously applied. Here are two examples.

My first maxim is *The Principle of Benefit of Doubt* (I would call it the Principle of Charity, but that name has been preempted by N. L. Wilson for a Principle which is, in fact, incompatible with the view I present here). In order to explain it, I need a little stage setting.

Many terms are first introduced into language with the aid of descriptions, or at least descriptions are implicit in the context. Thus a scientist may say 'I think there is a particle which is responsible for such-and-such effects. I shall call it a *quark*.' Or a painter may say 'I call *this* shade cadmium yellow', meaning the color of a certain spot. Or a parent may name 'this child' Mary Jane. I agree with Kripke that such 'dubbing ceremonies' do not engender *synonymies*. 'Quark' is not *synonymous* with 'particle responsible for such and such effects' (and 'Mary Jane' is certainly not synonymous with 'this child'. Rather, the description picks out the particle, color, child, or whatever the dubber intends to refer to. But such statements as 'Quarks might not have been responsible for those effects if conditions had been different', 'The spot I am pointing to might have been colored other than cadmium yellow', 'The contextually definite child in the situation in which the birth certificate was filled out might not have been Mary Jane' all make sense and are even true, as they would not be if dubbing the thing satisfying a description D by a term T were the same thing as stipulating that T and D are synonymous expressions (cf. chapter 12 in this volume, and Kripke, 1972b).

Secondly, there is, in connection with many terms, a *linguistic division of labor*. What I refer to as an 'elm' is, with my consent and that of my linguistic community, what people who can distinguish elms from other trees refer to as an elm. This point supplements the previous point: the 'expert', whose usage determines what many other people are referring to when they use a term T may be (but is not necessarily) the person who originally introduced the term. In such a case, a person is in the extension of 'Mary Jane' as used by me just in case it is in the extension of 'Mary Jane' as used by the dubber *and* I am linked to the dubber by a chain of transmission of the appropriate kind.

This 'historical' theory of denotation is popular nowadays, and many refinements have been suggested in connection with it. The important thing, or so it seems to me, is *not* that the original 'dubber' is *necessarily* an expert (we may no longer care about the original use of the term) but that my denotation may be, by general consent, the denotation assigned by persons distant from me in space and even in time, but linked to me by relations of cooperation. Moreover, in giving up my right to be the authority on the denotation of my own words, I give up, often, the ability to give *any* satisfactory description of my own denotations. I can refer to elms as well as the next man; but I probably couldn't tell an elm from a beech if my life depended on it.

To complete the stage setting, imagine now that there is something the original dubber, or the relevant expert, intends to dub with his term *T*, but through ignorance or inadvertance he singles it out by a misdescription. This is not very likely if the entity in question is a person; but it is exceedingly likely in the case of terms of theoretical science. If I describe a quark as 'the particle responsible for such-and-such effects', almost certainly it is going to turn out that *no* particle is responsible for *exactly* the effects I specified; but that does not mean that there aren't quarks.

The Principle of Benefit of Doubt is simply the principle that we should give the dubber, or the relevant expert, if the person at the other end of the chain of transmissions or cooperations isn't the original dubber, the benefit of the doubt in such cases by assuming he would accept reasonable modifications of his description. Like all methodological principles it is partly a descriptive principle; I assume that we all wish the benefit of the doubt to be accorded to us when *we* are the dubbers and the experts – thus the principle describes intentions which actually exist and are for the most part honored in the linguistic community – and it is a *normative* principle; we *should* honor it, for otherwise stable reference to theoretical entities would almost surely be impossible.

To give an example: there is nothing in the world which *exactly* fits Bohr's description of an electron. But there are particles which *approximately* fit Bohr's description: they have the right charge, the right mass, and, most important, they are responsible for key *effects* for which Bohr thought 'electrons' were responsible; for example, electric current (in a wire) is flow of these particles. The Principle of Reasonable Doubt dictates that we treat Bohr and other experts as referring to *these* particles when they introduced and when they now use the term 'electron'.

Of course, this is not an absolute rule. The experts may intend something to the contrary; but then we would no longer be according them *reasonable* doubt.

N. L. Wilson's Principle of Charity (Wilson, 1959, 521–39) is that we should assign the designatum that makes the largest possible number of the speaker's beliefs true. While Charity leads to the same result as Reasonable Doubt in the case of Bohr, the two principles are in considerable conflict as far as basics are concerned. First, Wilson applies his principle also to counterfactual designation (designation in other possible worlds). Thus, suppose that if conditions were different electrons would lose their charge, become twice as heavy, and no longer constitute ordinary electric currents, and that some other particles would take on most of the properties that electrons have. Then these other particles would *be* electrons, according to Wilson's account. This seems to me plainly false. Assuming gen-identity were preserved (that is, the possibility of tracing world-lines), electrons would still be electrons even if the conditions were such that almost all of their 'distinctive' properties were different. To modify an example used by Wilson himself; suppose that Julius Caesar was originally a fictional character (the historians have made a dreadful mistake), but that Pompey founded the Roman Empire and crossed the Rubicon and invented the 'Julian' calendar. Let Smith be a man who only 'knows' that Caesar founded the Roman Empire, crossed the Rubicon, and invented the 'Julian' calendar. Then most of Smith's beliefs about 'Caesar' become true if we assign the designatum Pompey. So, in Wilson's view, Smith is referring to Pompey whenever he says 'Caesar'.

Of course, this is wrong in a 'historical' account of the use of proper names. Smith is referring to no actual person when he uses the name 'Caesar'; like the rest of us, he mistakenly believes that the other end of the chain of transmissions of the name Caesar has properties it doesn't actually have. Descriptively Wilson's theory is wrong. We would not consider someone who had heard of a Quine (other than Willard Van Orman Quine) and mistakenly thought that *that* Quine was a logician, to be referring to Willard Van Orman Quine just because such a designatum-assignment was most charitable. And normatively it seems bad to me because it rules out a great deal of *intratheoretically sensible* counterfactual talk. (It is not surprising that Wilson deduces a form of Verificationism – he calls it 'a species of Absolute Idealism' – from his principle.)

By contrast, the Principle of Benefit of Doubt only applies to actual situations. To apply it to counterfactual situations would be to miss the distinction between what *we* mean by our terms, even in speaking of non-actual situations, and what we *would mean* if those were the actual situations. It misses what Kripke calls the 'rigidity' of some of the terms we use in discussing non-actual situations.

The second defect of the Principle of Charity is that it is too egalitarian. What makes *my* beliefs about elm trees true is of no importance in determining the denotation of 'elm', because I am an elm-ignoramus; and what makes a layman's beliefs about electrons true may be of no importance for determining the denotation of 'electron', *even in his idiolect*, if he happens to be an electron-ignoramus (cf. the preceding chapter).

The third defect of the Principle of Charity is one which requires a gloss on our Principle of Benefit of Doubt, if it is not to suffer the same defect. This is that the Principle is too *numerological*. Truths range from important to utterly trivial, and there are many dimensions of importance, depending upon the context. Just *counting* beliefs made true and beliefs made false by a designation assignment with no sort of *weighting* for importance can never be good policy.

Consider the Bohr case again. Suppose there are some particles which have virtually all the properties Bohr thought electrons have – call them 'shmelectrons'. But suppose that 'Shmelectrons' exists only in the other half of this universe. Shmelectrons satisfy the laws Bohr thought electrons satisfied; electrons and electricity do not. Shmelectrons are even responsible for currents – shmelectric currents; these can be used to light shmelectric lights and power shmelectric toasters, etc. Shmelectricity, let us suppose, obeys Maxwell's laws, etc. Still there are no shmelectrons *here*; the particular phenomena Bohr was interested in are explained by the behavior of *electrons*, not *shmelectrons* (we suppose).

Now, in this case we could 'modify Bohr's description' (of electrons) in such a way that it would become a correct description of shmelectrons. Indeed, if we applied Wilson's Principle of Charity, we should be obliged to do this. But this would be a mistake. Bohr was not referring to shmelectrons; he was referring to electrons. And what this shows is the primacy of phenomena; Bohr intended the atomic theory to explain certain phenomena he and other scientists had observed, *phenomena-for-us*. And any modification of Bohr's description that is to be reasonable given these intentions must preserve at least some of the structure of these explanations.

My second maxim requires less stage-setting. I have already spoken of the linguistic division of labor. There is also, in connection with many terms, a *contribution of the environment*. This is obvious in the case of the obviously indexical; 'you' has a reference which depends on the environment of the speaker, different 'yous' in different environments. But there is also a subtler contribution of the environment in the case of natural kind words; water is stuff that has the same microstructure as most of the paradigm water; and paradigm water is *paradigm-for-us*, is water in *our* environment. On another possible world or another planet a word might be associated with much the same stereotype and much the same criteria as our term 'water', but it might designate XYZ and not H_2O. At least this could happen in a prescientific era. And it would not follow that XYZ *was* water; it would only follow that XYZ could *look like* water, *taste like* water, etc. What 'water' refers to depends on *the actual nature of the paradigms*, not just on what is in our heads.

The Principle of Reasonable Ignorance is simply that a speaker may 'have' a word, in the sense of possessing normal ability to use it in discourse, and not know the mechanism of reference of that term, explicitly or even implicitly. 'Knowing the meaning' of a word in the sense of being able to use it is implicitly knowing *something*; but it isn't knowing nearly as much as philosophers tend to assume. I can know the meaning of the word 'gold' without knowing, explicitly or implicitly, the criteria for being gold (contrary to John Locke), and without having any very clear idea at all just *how* the word is tied to whatever it is tied to. Our two principles complement one another nicely. The Principle of Benefit of Doubt forbids us to assume that dubbers and other experts are factually omniscient; the Principle of Reasonable Ignorance forbids us to assume that any speakers are philosophically omniscient (even unconsciously).

Applications

The second Principle seems to be especially often violated in Philosophy of Mind. I shall discuss some examples.

My own view is that psychological predicates correspond to *functional* properties of human beings and other sentient beings. The presence of these properties *explains* the clustering of what some have called the 'symptoms' and 'criteria' of the various psychological states and conditions. Be this as it may, the Principle of Reasonable Ignorance tells us that we need not postulate that speakers *know* (implicitly or explicitly) that psychological predicates correspond to functional states, nor need they *know* (implicitly or explicitly) a functional characterization of the particular state to which a predicate corresponds.

This is connected with the 'contribution of the environment' – in this case the speaker's own inner nature being (malapropistically) the 'environment'. The speaker has a certain nature. This is not very much known to him. He is able to make a reporting use of words like 'pain'. He uses 'pain' to denote whatever state is in *fact* the state his pain-reports bespeak. But he need not know *what* that state is, in the sense of being able to characterize it. If he has the reporting use of pain and the ability to conceive of others as feeling pain and to use the sentences to express what he is conceiving, then this is certainly *sufficient* to say that he has acquired the concept of pain: yet absolutely nothing about the metaphysical nature of pain need be known to the speaker (cf. chapter 22 in this volume).

If this is right, then a great deal of contemporary philosophy of mind must be wrong. For example, it has been suggested that 'I see a yellow spot', uttered as a sensation-report (i.e. in the sense that I have the visual impression of a yellow spot) means 'what is going on in me is the same process that goes on when I see a yellow spot', where this last 'see' means 'actually perceive'. Such a theory makes all sensation reports *hypotheses* (and rather risky ones, at that) (assuming the notion 'same process' is sufficiently clear, when used without specification, to mean anything at all). In particular, if it turned out that 'seeing a yellow spot' in the sense of having the visual impression of a yellow spot, and 'seeing a yellow spot' in the sense of actually perceiving a yellow spot were totally *dissimilar* processes physiologically, then a materialist would have to conclude that *we never really see yellow spots* (in the visual impression sense) – i.e. all visual impression reports are *false*. This seems absurd. How have some otherwise perceptive philosophers been driven to so strange a conclusion?

First, these philosophers arrived at the extremely sound idea that psychological terms (and many other terms as well) are best thought of as denoting *conditions* or *causes* which explain the familiar symptoms and 'criteria', not the presence of the symptoms or criteria. Secondly, being materialists, they took these conditions or causes to be *physical states* – neurological states, or at any rate, physiological states of the body. This, I believe was a mistake; as Aristotle saw, psychological predicates describe our *form*, not our *matter*. But this is not my topic here. Lastly, having proposed their account of what visual impressions *are*, they felt required to say what visual impression reports *mean*, and here they failed. But their failure is instructive. What happened is that these philosophers felt that the mechanism of reference must be implicitly known to the speakers of the language. This is just the assumption that the Principle of Reasonable Ignorance counsels us against making.

Still other philosophers of mind, again of a materialist stripe, have proposed that 'I am in pain' or 'I see a yellow spot' are synonymous with sentences of the form 'I am in the physical state which satisfies such and such a functional characterization'. Clearly, if these philosophers are right, anyone who reports a pain, or seeing a yellow spot is, once again, asserting a *hypotheses* (and again a risky one). Even if it be true that pain, or a particular visual impression, is identical with a physical state, rather than, as I believe, with a functional state, there is no reason except dubious philosophy of language to assume that the speaker implicitly knows even a functional characterization of the state in question. Again, the Principle of Reasonable Ignorance would have enabled the philosopher to avoid his error.

Finally, there are philosophers of a Logical Behaviorist stripe who argue

279

that 'you have a pain' or 'you see a yellow spot' are equivalent to, or at least entail (sometimes in a specially invented sense of 'entail') assertions about behavior-dispositions. To avoid having to say that the corresponding *first person* reports are hypotheses, they sometimes treat them as, in effect, *grunts* – mere *symptoms* of the conditions they bespeak, rather than assertions with the obvious referential semantics. But this still leaves them with the necessity to maintain that anyone who has the concept of pain, or the concept of a yellow spotish sense impression, *necessarily* knows a great deal about behavior dispositions, at least implicitly. This seems plainly false. Suppose someone totally paralyzed were brought up never seeing anyone in pain. He is taught the word by being hurt ('Now your finger hurts', 'Now I will make your left ear hurt'); through the direct control of his nervous system. Is there any reason to doubt that he could learn and use the words 'hurt', 'pain', etc.? Yet if asked: 'What do people normally do when they are in pain?' 'What normally causes people to have pain?' he might truthfully reply, 'I haven't the slightest idea'. No doubt a stubborn Logical Behaviorist could deny that such a person *really* has the concept of pain; but this is just saving his theory by throwing out the data. Or, he could maintain that the relevant behavior dispositions are *linguistic ones*. But then, what of the child who has just learned pain talk? Does he *know*, even implicity, *general* facts about the linguistic behavior dispositions of speakers? Or does he only *really* know what 'pain' means when he learns how people generally *talk*? Again, there is no need for any of these maneuvers once we accept the Principle of Reasonable Ignorance. Hypothesize what you like about these psychological predicates: that they stand for functional states, soul states, body states, behavior dispositions – but don't pretend any of this is what speakers *mean*. The moral is: you wouldn't believe how *little* speakers 'mean'.

While my examples have all been selected from the Philosophy of Mind, the Principle of Reasonable Ignorance applies to other areas of philosophy as well. To moral philosophy, obviously (the problem as Plato saw, is the Unity of the Virtues – what goodness *is*; not what 'good' means), and to philosophy of the natural sciences. The assumption that everyone who has acquired the term 'water' or the term 'voltage' knows a necessary and sufficient condition for being water or for having a particular voltage has had a powerful and deleterious effect on the philosophy of science.†

† As Kuhn points out in Kuhn, 1974. E.g. Kuhn says, 'The distinction between a theoretical and a basic vocabulary will not do in its present form because many theoretical terms can be shown to attach to nature in the same way, whatever it may be, as basic terms. But I am in addition concerned to inquire how "direct attachment" may work, whether of a theoretical or basic vocabulary. In the process I attack the

I shall give two examples of the philosophical application of the Principle of Benefit of Doubt. It will be noted that the Principle of Benefit of Doubt, together with its 'stage setting' always works in conjunction with the Principle of Reasonable Ignorance.

The first example is on the question of 'commensurability' of theories. First of all, as Scheffler has pointed out (Scheffler, 1967), theories do not need to enjoy common 'meanings' to be comparable: it is enough (assuming standard referential semantics) that there be sufficiently many terms with the same *reference*. Since the Principle of Benefit of Doubt is precisely a procedure for *preserving reference across theory change*, it allows us to say that even radically different theories can be compared within the framework of deductive logic and referential semantics. We do not have to agree with Sir Karl Popper or with Paul Feyerabend that there is an incompatibility between accepting the existence of radical paradigm change in science and accepting the idea of a growth of objective knowledge (of course, Popper and Feyerabend, while agreeing on the incompatibility, differ on whether to reject radical paradigm change or growth of objective knowledge). We can have our paradigm shifts *and* our objective knowledge too.

My final example requires correcting the account I gave in 'The analytic and the synthetic'. In that paper I characterized such terms as 'man' and 'swan' as *cluster terms* – that is, 'man' was supposed to be synonymous with 'entity possessing sufficiently many of the following properties: – – – – (list)'; and I characterized 'kinetic energy' as a '*law cluster term*' – that is, as synonymous with 'magnitude satisfying sufficiently many of the following laws to a sufficiently good approximation: – – – – (list)'. Both of these accounts now seem incorrect. I present a different account of natural kind words, such as 'man' and 'water', consonant with the causal/social outlook sketched above in the preceding chapter; the beginnings of a similar account for theoretical magnitude terms is sketched in another paper (chapter II in this volume). Two aspects of that account should be evident from what has been said here: knowledge of *laws* cannot be attributed to individual speakers who happen to have acquired 'energy' or 'voltage' or 'electron'; thus, even

often implicit assumption that anyone who knows how to use a basic term correctly has access, conscious or unconscious, to a set of criteria which define that term or provide necessary and sufficient conditions governing its application. For that mode of attachment-by-criteria I am also here using the term "correspondence rule", and that does violate normal usage. My excuse for the extension is my belief that explicit reliance on correspondence rules and implicit reliance on criteria introduce the same procedure and misdirect attention in the same ways. Both make the deployment of language seem more a matter of convention than it is. As a result they disguise the extent to which a man who acquires either an everyday or scientific language simultaneously learns things about nature which are not themselves embodied in verbal generalizations.'

if the 'law cluster' theory were right as an account of the *social determination of reference*, it could not be correct as an account of what every speaker implicitly 'means'. My account violated the Principle of Reasonable Ignorance. And, secondly, a theoretical magnitude term, or particle term, etc., can keep fixed denotation even though we change our minds about the laws it obeys. This point *was* made in 'The analytic and the synthetic' (it was crucial to my account of 'energy' and 'straight line'); but the Principle of Benefit of Doubt clarifies the reason that this is so.

My final example is the vexed question of the conventionality of the choice of a metric. Adolf Grünbaum and I have discussed this question through the years, and have by no means come to agreement. But there has been some convergence in our views, and I think this is explained by our acceptance of the idea that the metric (for space–time) is fixed by *laws* and not by 'correspondence rules' (cf. Grünbaum, 1973). Of course, 'fixed by laws' does not mean *implicitly defined by laws* in any of the familiar senses in which 'implicit definition' is used in technical logic. The Principle of Benefit of Doubt implies that we can change our minds about the laws, and we do not *have* to say that we have changed the denotation of our terms. Thus, if there is a metric that is *optimal* for physical space–time, and we gradually come to laws which are better and better approximations to a true description of the manifold under that metric, we can say that we are *discovering* more and more facts about the metric of space–time (Grünbaum would say: about the extrinsically unique nontrivial metric of space–time, if I understand his present position alright); and we do not have to say we are progressively *inventing* a metric, or stipulating a *succession* of metrics, or anything like that. Of course, there are still big areas of disagreement. Grünbaum feels that the unique nontrivial 'extrinsic' metric is still 'convention-laden', and I do not accept this. And I do not accept Grünbaum's 'intrinsic/ extrinsic' distinction. But the point is that Grünbaum and I have been able to come to a substantial measure of agreement by agreeing to reject a certain philosophy of language. Again we see that while the two Principles I have propounded are much less grand than the Pragmatic Maxim or the Verifiability Theory of Meaning, they can be useful in many different areas of philosophy.

Words and the world

So far I have spoken of matters we are beginning to understand, thanks to the progress in philosophy of language beginning with Quine's *Two dogmas of empiricism*. (Incidentally, both the Principle of Benefit of Doubt and the Principle of Reasonable Ignorance seem to me highly consonant with Quine's general approach. In particular, I suspect that my Principle of Benefit of Doubt is likely to be his Principle of Charity, his citation of Wilson notwithstanding.) Let me now plunge recklessly into territory that is less well mapped.

Both our Principles presuppose the notion of reference. (Our talk of 'fitting Bohr's description' was just disguised talk of *reference* in the logician's sense: what 'fits' a description is what the description 'refers to', that is, what the description is *true of*.) Reference is a relation between words and the world; this is just a fancy way of saying that the extension of the relation 'refers to' is a class of ordered pairs of terms and things. The pair $\langle$'lemon', $\alpha\rangle$ is in the class which is the extension of the reference relation for English† just in case α is a lemon; the pair $\langle$'Rad', $\beta\rangle$ is in the class which is the extension of the reference relation for German† just in case β is a wheel; and so on. Any relation which (when restricted to a particular language†) maps words onto things is a *words–world relation*. Reference is a words–world relation; but so is its complement (or rather, the restriction of its complement to the domain of words, the converse domain being unrestricted); the pair $\langle$'lemon', the Eiffel Tower$\rangle$ lies in the complement of the reference relation. And there are many other words–world relations. Thus, just saying that reference is a words–world relation is saying practically nothing about it.

But unless we can say something informative about this relation, our entire philosophy of language rests comfortably in cloud-cuckoo-land. The Principle of Benefit of Doubt belongs to a methodology for saying what speakers *refer to*; if we don't know what *referring to* is, we may assert that Bohr was referring to electrons when he used the word 'electron' or deny that he was; since it is unclear just *what* relation between Bohr's word 'electron' and the particles in question is being affirmed or denied, a methodology for such affirmations and denials is a methodology for a science which, however valuable and important its results, still rests upon unclear notions.

Many philosophers believe that Tarski's work makes the notion of reference (and the related notion of truth) perfectly precise. I do not share this view. Hartry Field has pointed out that 'truth-definitions' and 'reference-definitions' of the sort used in technical logic do *not* clarify the notions of reference and truth (Field, 1972).

Some Tarskians argue that Tarski's criterion of adequacy ('Convention *T*') (see Tarski, 1951, p. 166) makes the notions of truth and

† Strictly speaking, reference is a triadic relation between a symbol, an entity and a language; but when the third argument is held constant we speak of the 'reference relation for L', where L is the language in question.

reference clear, not the formalized truth-definition themselves. But 'Convention T' employs the notions of *naming* a sentence and of *following from*; notions intimately related to and as much in need of clarification as truth and reference themselves.

Nor does Sellars' analysis (cf. Sellars, 1967 and 1962) of 'designation' help us either. Sellars proposes that

(1) 'Rad' in German designates wheel.

This means that 'Rad' has the *role* in German that 'wheel' has in English. To avoid Church's objection – that (1) is not a statement about the English word 'wheel' – Sellars introduces a special device he calls 'dot quotation' (cf. Sellars, 1963 and 1964) (related, in a way, to Frege's 'oblique sense'). A word in dot quotes denotes its own linguistic role. Thus ·wheel· and ·Rad· are both names for a certain role (the same role, in fact). It is important that '·wheel·' is not synonymous with a *description* of that role (e.g. 'the role of "wheel"'); it is rather a name of that role.

Then Sellars' analysis is that (1) means

(2) 'Rad' in German has the role ·wheel·.

On this analysis the extension of *designates* is a class of ordered pairs of a word and a role, not a class of ordered pairs of a word and a thing. Sellars' 'designation' is not a words–world relation but a words–role relation. This soes not trouble Sellars, because fundamentally he does not think of 'designation' as a relation at all (as a Nominalist, he does not construe the statement that 'Rad' has a certain role as really presupposing the existence of 'roles', as abstract entities, at all). But it means that Sellars' view sheds no light on the problem of reference.

Primitive reference

Imagine a race of creatures – perhaps higher animals – who are just beginning to evolve pre-speech behaviors. They notice middle-sized material objects of various kinds, and occasionally they need to call one another's attention to various of these objects. One especially clever creature develops the habit of *pointing with his finger* at an object and saying a noise which sounds like 'Lewkthis'. Other members of the tribe imitate this (after recent observations of chimpanzee behavior both in the wild and in experimental situations, this is not so implausible); and soon the creatures develop a full set of what I shall call *Grician intentions* (cf. Grice, 1957, 1968, 1969); that is intentions to call attention to an object by pointing and uttering 'lewkthis'; the intention being to do this partly by recognition of this very intention. (It may be questioned by some whether nonspeaking animals can *consciously cooperate*, which is what is at issue in ascribing these Grician intentions; I shall take the stance that the answer is 'yes'.) Clearly these creatures do not yet have a *language*; but they do have a primitive sort of *reference*. I shall refer to 'lewkthis' as a *demonstrative* for these creatures; and when one of these creatures points at an object and says 'lewkthis' with the Grician intention of getting another member of the tribe to pay attention to that object, I shall say that he has *demonstratively referred* to that object.

Imagine that we absent ourselves from the tribe for a few centuries and go into suspended animation. After being revived we go back to see what has happened to the tribe. We find that their linguistic or pre-linguistic behavior has become much more complex. They now utter not only 'lewkthis', but also strange to say, 'Pee-wun-this', 'Pee-too-this', ..., 'Pee-sevunteen-this'. After some investigation we discover that what is happening is the following: there are seventeen properties $P_1 \ldots P_{17}$ which are easily discriminated by these creatures. More precisely, there are seventeen conditions $C_1 \ldots C_{17}$ which are states of the creatures themselves, such that if a creature looks at a middle-sized material object then he is normally caused to go into condition C_1 or into a condition $\bar{C}_1$ incompatible with C_1 (and similarly with $C_2 \ldots C_{17}$). Moreover, the presence or absence of property P_i is what determines whether he is caused to go into condition C_i or condition $\bar{C}_i$. The chain of causation which connects the occurrence of property P_i (or the absence of P_i) with the occurrence of the condition C_i (or $\bar{C}_i$) in the creature is one which *we*, in our advanced state of knowledge, can describe as a standard mode of visual perception. (For simplicity I am ignoring all senses except vision; obviously the account could be complicated to get a closer approach to realism.)

Finally, the creature utters 'Pee-wun-this' when the object he demonstratively refers to as 'this' (a shortened form of 'lewkthis') produces in him the condition C_1 (and similarly with the other sixteen forms). Moreover, he has Grician intentions with respect to 'Pee-wun-this', etc.; he intends his hearer to behave towards the object demonstratively referred to by the token of 'this' and to have expectations towards that object which are appropriate in that tribe towards Pee-wunnish objects. Clearly, this is still not a language, or at least not a complete language; but it is getting more *like* a language. I shall refer to 'Pee-wun', etc., as *predicates* for these creatures, and I shall say that these predicates refer to whatever has the properties $P_1, P_2 \ldots P_{17}$, respectively.

Notice that our theory is so far a 'causal' theory of reference: the creatures demonstratively refer to objects they are connected to by causal chains of a certain kind (the description of which, even for such simple creatures, would involve at least the psychology of perception, of attention, and of cooperative behavior); and they refer by means of predicates only to objects which have properties that they are capable of perceiving (so that they are causally connected to at least some members of the extension of these predicates). Incidentally, although their mode of linguistic behavior is much more complicated than it was a few hundred years before, it is not clear that the psychological theory required to describe it would have to be substantially more complicated than that required to describe so simple a matter as the use of 'lewkthis'.

So far our speakers only utter 'Pee-wun-this' when they themselves have observed the 'this' in question and it has been perceived to have P_1; but the model could be complicated by letting them say 'Pee-wun-this' demonstratively referring to an object such that they themselves cannot tell, for one reason or another, whether it has P_1, but which is such that they have been *told* by another speaker that it has P_1. Thus we extend the concept of *communication* in this hypothetical community. Again, we could complicate the model by introducing past, present, and future tenses; or even duration terms (*last year, yesterday, five months ago*, etc.) Let me emphasize that I am not, repeat *not*, trying to give *necessary and sufficient conditions* for reference, even primitive reference. I am trying to describe a fairly understandable situation in which we can *employ* a primitive notion of reference.

Semantic ascent

There is nothing in principle to prevent our tribe from some day coming to employ the very notion of reference (call it 'reference$_1$') *we* have been employing in describing their transactions with the world. Thus, if Uk-ook says 'Pee-wun-this', pointing to an apple, Ab-sum might remark 'Uk-ook reefur this' – pointing to the same 'this'. And this use might have tensed forms: 'Uk-ook reefurud this yestiday', for example.

To avoid semantic paradoxes we assume that referring to something with the aid of the semantic predicate 'reefur' does not count as 'reefurring'. Most likely, the problem simply would not be noticed, however.

Quantifiers

Coming back to our tribe after a few thousand more years, we may imagine they have added quantifiers and truth-functions to their repertoire. At this point we would not hesitate to call their system of communication a *language*. Also, it is obvious how we would extend the notion of reference to cover quantificational and truth functional idioms;

at least it is obvious since Tarski. (As Hartry Field pointed out, this is something of philosophical interest that Tarski accomplished: showing how to reduce reference to something akin to what I have been calling primitive reference.) But we must notice that each extension of the notion of reference seems to have altered the notion. Demonstratives used in the presence of the thing they demonstratively refer to have one sort of causal connection with their referent; predicates, of the simple sort so far envisaged, need not have any causal connection with each referent – that is, the act of uttering a token of the predicate need not causally involve every member of the extension – but normal acts of uttering a token of the predicate in an atomic sentence of the predicate in the present or past tense will involve a causal connection with some member of the extension, although the connection may not be a perceptual one (a speaker may have learned from a 'chain' of other speakers that something has or had a property, and not from his own experience). But once we introduce quantifiers, all *specifiable* connection between referring to an X and being causally connected with an X appears to be lost. If this is the case, we may wonder why we still use the term 'refer' when we extend the notion to quantified expressions. I shall return to this question shortly.

Proper names

Up to this point we have not introduced proper names into our model, although we have used them ourselves in referring to the hypothetical members of the tribe. If we wanted to mimic the 'historical' theory of proper names sketched in the first part of this paper, we might do so as follows: let the notion of reference as so far developed for the language including quantifiers but not yet including proper names be 'reference$_2$'. Let us suppose the notion of 'reefurring' used by the speakers has been extended to signify referring$_2$. Then when a speaker uses the name 'Ab-ook' we suppose that he has the following Grician intentions:

(1) If the discourse is ordinary discourse (i.e. about what is actually the case) then the speaker who utters a sentence $F(Ab\text{-}ook)$ intends to produce the belief that $F(D)$ where D is the following description: 'the creature referred$_2$ to by whatever description the introducer† of the name "Ab-ook" intended to be used for this purpose' (or rather, D is the translation of this description into the language of the tribe).

(2) If the discussion is about what would be the case in a hypothetical situation (and note that even philosophers who object to counterfactuals

---

† In my view, the 'introducer' need not be the person who *first* 'dubbed' Ab-ook, nor need the causal chain go through the *first* person the hearer learned the name "Ab-ook" from. The 'causal chain' is a chain of cooperations connecting the hearer to the relevant experts, as determined by the society.

admit that we sometimes use language in this way, and that language used in this way need not explicitly contain counterfactuals), then the name *Ab-ook* is replaceable in the given discourse by any description D' such that the creature referred to as Ab-ook by the introducer of the name – that is, the creature referred$_2$ to by whatever description the introducer intended to be used for this purpose and for the purpose of (1) – *would* satisfy D' in the hypothetical situation.

Let 'reference$_3$' be reference as extended to the language including proper names. Explaining the use of proper names involves explaining the structure of a 'chain of transmissions', and doing this involves use of the notion 'reference$_2$' in the manner just indicated. But it does not require the use of 'reference$_3$' itself; thus the use of 'intentions to refer' in the statement of the causal theory of proper names is not a vicious circularity.

Properties

If we add quantifiers over properties (see chapter 19, volume 1) to the language (thinking of properties as physically or metaphysically real nonmental and nonlinguistic entities like the color blue, or temperature, or kinetic energy, and not as mere *concepts*, as some philosophers unfortunately use the term), then we can introduce descriptions of theoretical entities into the language. In my opinion, theoretical terms are related to these descriptions much as proper names are related to ordinary thing or person descriptions. But for our present purposes, the key problem is the one we already noted in the case of individual quanti-fication: what does the notion of reference as extended to the language with, say, quantifiers over properties have in common with, say, 'reference$_3$'? – that is, reference as employed in speaking about the speakers of a language with tenses, proper names, individual variables and quantifiers, truth functions, and *relatively observable predicates* (that is, the *primitive* predicates of the language were supposed to be close to perception; using individual quantifiers and tenses the speakers could, of course, talk about many unobservable things). The problem is not *how* to extend the notion of reference once quantifiers over properties are admitted; standard *second order* referential semantics tells us how to do that; the problem, again, is one of *motivation*. Don't our successive notions of 'reference' just have a 'family resemblance' and no core meaning?

Motivating 'reference'

To answer the question, what *motivates* the successive extensions of the notion of reference that we have introduced into our oversimplified model (for all that this fairy tale of pre-linguistic 'creatures' was intended to do was to present and successively complicate a model for some aspects of reference), we might usefully stop and ask ourselves: how did we identify certain idioms as *quantifiers* over properties (or even over individuals) to begin with? Certainly patterns of deductive inference could carry us part of the way. But even if one infers $(Ex)P(x)$ from $P(a)$ and $P(a)$ from $(x)P(x)$ (for arbitrary terms and – in the case of individuals – demonstratives a) it still does not follow that (Ex) and (x) must be the standard quantifiers. They might be quantifiers, but over entities other than we think; or they might have a range smaller or larger than the domain we think, for example. It seems to me that only if we know something about the *inductive* inferences, that is the nondeductive inferences, that speakers accept can we have good grounds for any assignment of a domain. The clearest case is the case in which speakers use procedures for accepting and rejecting sentences of the forms $(Ex)P(x)$, $(EP)F(P)$, $(x)P(x)$, and $(P)F(P)$ which are, by our lights, *good* procedures *if the variables do range over individuals and properties as we take them to.*

Davidson has remarked that in translation we seek to make the translatees 'believers of truths, seekers of beauty, and lovers of the good'. This is rhetorical exaggeration, of course; but the fact is that we do apply Benefit of Doubt to individuals and communities (although caution is in order; Wilson's Principle of Charity goes beyond prudence, as we saw). Although I would not dream of trying to give a necessary and sufficient condition for idioms to be quantifiers over properties or over things, it seems to me that the clearest case is that of a community whose inductive procedures are reasonably sound procedures *if* the idioms *are* quantifiers. In this sense, the inductive logic of a community cannot be separated from its linguistic competence (cf. chapter 15 in this volume).

But if this is how we *identify* the quantifiers, at least in the 'paradigm case', then the answer to the question of motivation is near at hand. The concepts of reference we have constructed and (by implication) of truth have the following property: reference and truth are so construed that, at least in the 'paradigm case', at least for important classes of sentences, at least if things go as they should, sentences will tend to be accepted in the long run if and only if they are *true*, and predicates will be applied to things if and only if those things have the properties *corresponding* to those predicates. It makes no sense to say that language maps the world unless we have some parametrization of 'the world' in mind; what a reference concept does, at least in the ideal case, is to specify a parametrization of the world and correlate it to a parametrization of a language in such a way that accepted sentences tend in the long run to correlate to states of affairs (in the sense of the parametrization) that actually obtain.

This in no way contradicts Wittgenstein's insight that mere isomorphism between a set of things and a set of possible states of affairs does not make those things *symbols*; something is only a symbol if it is part of a system which has appropriate functions. But to stress function is not incompatible, as some have thought, including possibly the later Wittgenstein himself, with stressing *correspondence*. A picture theory of meaning is not totally wrong; just one-sided, just as a 'use' theory of meaning is not totally wrong but just one-sided.

The view of reference sketched here is consonant with Boyd's principles that *Terms in a mature scientific theory typically refer*; *Laws of a mature scientific theory are typically approximately true* (Boyd, 1973). Conversely, Boyd's principles are just what we need to justify our claim that in the paradigm case accepted sentences convergently mirror the truth. Of course, Boyd's principles are empirical claims about science; like Boyd, I feel that they explain the success of science better than any alternative hypothesis and that their implicit acceptance by scientists explains much that is normative in scientific practice (which is why acceptance of the 'null hypothesis' of instrumentalism is not a good alternative to empirical realism). Of the principles in the first part of this paper, the Principle of Benefit of Doubt is especially closely tied to Boyd's principles. However, I do not believe that the account of reference presented here is limited to the institution of science. I would apply a generally causal account of reference also to moral terms and terms from many other areas of life.

As language develops, the causal and noncausal links between bits of language and aspects of the world become more complex and more various. To look for any one uniform link between word or thought and object of word or thought is to look for the occult; but to see our evolving and expanding notion of reference as just a proliferating family is to miss the essence of the relation between language and reality. The essence of the relation is that language and thought do asymptotically correspond to reality, to some extent at least. A theory of reference is a theory of the correspondence in question.

Peirce and his Positivist and Therapeutic successors thought that good philosophy of language could clear up all the traditional problems of philosophy. I would be repeating their mistake from a different standpoint if I claimed that the realistic account of reference was the Philosopher's Stone (or even the Universal Solvent). I do not claim this. But I do claim that it makes sense, and that the truly best therapy is a sensible theory of the world.

14
Philosophy and our mental life*

The question which troubles laymen, and which has long troubled philosophers, even if it is somewhat disguised by today's analytic style of writing philosophy, is this: are we made of matter or soul-stuff? To put it as bluntly as possible, are we just material beings, or are we 'something more'? In this paper, I will argue as strongly as possible that this whole question rests on false assumptions. My purpose is not to dismiss the question, however, so much as to speak to the real concern which is behind the question. The real concern is, I believe, with the autonomy of our mental life.

People are worried that we may be debunked, that our behavior may be exposed as really explained by something mechanical. Not, to be sure, mechanical in the old sense of cogs and pulleys, but in the newer sense of electricity and magnetism and quantum chemistry and so forth. In this paper, part of what I want to do is to argue that this can't happen. Mentality is a real and autonomous feature of our world.

But even more important, at least in my feeling, is the fact that this whole question has nothing to do with our substance. Strange as it may seem to common sense and to sophisticated intuition alike, the question of the autonomy of our mental life does not hinge on and has nothing to do with that all too popular, all too old question about matter or soul-stuff. We could be made of Swiss cheese and it wouldn't matter.

Failure to see this, stubborn insistence on formulating the question as *matter or soul*, utterly prevents progress on these questions. Conversely, once we see that our substance is not the issue, I do not see how we can help but make progress.

The concept which is key to unravelling the mysteries in the philosophy of mind, I think, is the concept of *functional isomorphism*. Two systems are functionally isomorphic if *there is a correspondence between the states of one and the states of the other that preserves functional relations.*

* This paper was presented as a part of a Foerster symposium on 'Computers and the Mind' at the University of California (Berkeley) in October, 1973. I am indebted to Alan Garfinkel for comments on earlier versions of this paper.

To start with computing machine examples, if the functional relations are just sequence relations, e.g. *state* A *is always followed by state* B, then, for *F* to be a functional isomorphism, it must be the case that state *A* is followed by state *B* in system 1 if and only if state *F(A)* is followed by state *F(B)* in system 2. If the functional relations are, say, data or print-out relations, e.g. *when print π is printed on the tape, system 1 goes into state A,* these must be preserved. *When print π is printed on the tape, system 2 goes into state F(A),* if *F* is a functional isomorphism between system 1 and system 2. More generally, if *T* is a correct theory of the functioning of system 1, at the functional or psychological level, then an isomorphism between system 1 and system 2 must map each property and relation defined in system 2 in such a way that *T* comes out true when all references to system 1 are replaced by references to system 2, and all property and relation symbols in *T* are reinterpreted according to the mapping.

The difficulty with the notion of functional isomorphism is that it *presupposes the notion of a thing's being a functional or psychological description.* It is for this reason that, in various papers on this subject, I introduced and explained the notion in terms of Turing machines. And I felt constrained, therefore, to defend the thesis that *we* are Turing machines. Turing machines come, so to speak, with a normal form for their functional description, the so-called machine table – a standard style of program. But it does not seem fatally sloppy to me, although it is sloppy, if we apply the notion of functional isomorphism to systems for which we have no detailed idea at present what the normal form description would look like – systems like ourselves. The point is that even if we don't have any idea what a comprehensive psychological theory would look like, I claim that we know enough (and here analogies from computing machines, economic systems, games and so forth are helpful) to point out illuminating differences between any possible psychological theory of a human being, or even a functional description of a computing machine or an economic system, and a physical or chemical description. Indeed, Dennett and Fodor have done a great deal along these lines in recent books.

This brings me back to the question of *copper, cheese, or soul.* One point we can make immediately as soon as we have the basic concept of functional isomorphism is this: two systems can have quite different constitutions and be functionally isomorphic. For example, a computer made of electrical components can be isomorphic to one made of cogs and wheels. In other words, for each state in the first computer there is a corresponding state in the other, and, as we said before, the sequential relations are the same – if state *S* is followed by state *B* in the case of the electronic computer, state A would be followed by state B in the case of the computer made of cogs and wheels, and it doesn't matter at all that the *physical realizations* of those states are totally different. So a computer made of electrical components can be isomorphic to one made of cogs and wheels or to human clerks using paper and pencil. A computer made of one sort of wire, say copper wire, or one sort of relay, etc. will be in a different physical and chemical state when it computes than a computer made of a different sort of wire and relay. But the functional description may be the same.

We can extend this point still further. Assume that one thesis of materialism (I shall call it the 'first thesis') is correct, and we are, as wholes, just material systems obeying physical laws. Then the second thesis of classical materialism cannot be correct – namely, our mental states, e.g. *thinking about next summer's vacation*, cannot be *identical* with any physical or chemical states. For it is clear from what we already know about computers etc., that whatever the program of the brain may be, it must be physically possible, though not necessarily feasible, to produce something with that same program but quite a different physical and chemical constitution. Then to identify the state in question with its physical or chemical realization would be quite absurd, given that that realization is in a sense quite accidental, from the point of view of psychology, anyway (which is the relevant science).† It is as if we met Martians and discovered that they were in all functional respects isomorphic to us, but we refused to admit that they could feel pain because their C fibers were different.

Now, imagine two possible universes, perhaps 'parallel worlds', in the science fiction sense, in one of which people have good old fashioned souls, operating through pineal glands, perhaps, and in the other of which they have complicated brains. And suppose that the souls in the soul world are functionally isomorphic to the brains in the brain world. Is there any more sense to attaching importance to this difference than to the difference between copper wires and some other wires in the computer? Does it matter that the soul people have, so to speak, immaterial brains, and that the brain people have material souls? What matters is the common structure, the theory T of which we are, alas, in deep ignorance, and not the hardware, be it ever so ethereal.

† Even if it were not physically possible to realize human psychology in a creature made of anything but the usual protoplasm, DNA, etc., it would still not be correct to say that psychological states are identical with their physical realizations. For, as will be argued below, such an identification has no *explanatory* value *in psychology*. On this point, compare Fodor, 1968.

One may raise various objections to what I have said. I shall try to reply to some of them.

One might, for example, say that if the souls of the soul people are isomorphic to the brains of the brain people, then their souls must be automata-like, and that's not the sort of soul we are interested in. 'All your argument really shows is that there is no need to distinguish between a brain and an automaton-like soul.' But what precisely does that objection come to?

I think there are two ways of understanding it. It might come to the claim that the notion of functional organization or functional isomorphism only makes sense for automata. But that is totally false. Sloppy as our notions are at present, we at least know this much, as Jerry Fodor has emphasized: we know that the notion of functional organization applies to anything to which the notion of a psychological theory applies. I explained the most general notion of functional isomorphism by saying that two systems are functionally isomorphic if there is an isomorphism that makes both of them models for the same psychological theory. (That is stronger than just saying that they are both models for the same psychological theory – they are isomorphic realizations of the same abstract structure.) To say that real old fashioned souls would not be in the domain of definition of the concept of functional organization or of the concept of functional isomorphisms would be to take the position that whatever we mean by the soul, it is something for which there can be no theory. That seems pure obscurantism. I will assume, henceforth, that it is not built into the notion of mind or soul or whatever that it is unintelligible or that there couldn't be a theory of it.

Secondly, someone might say more seriously that even if there is a theory of the soul or mind, the soul, at least in the full, rich old fashioned sense, is supposed to have powers that no mechanical system could have. In the latter part of this chapter I shall consider this claim.

If it is built into one's notions of the soul that the soul can do things that violate the laws of physics, then I admit I am stumped. There cannot be a soul which is isomorphic to a brain, if the soul can read the future clairvoyantly, in a way that is not in any way explainable by physical law. On the other hand, if one is interested in more modest forms of magic like telepathy, it seems to me that there is no reason in principle why we couldn't construct a device which would project subvocalized thoughts from one brain to another. As to reincarnation, if we are, as I am urging, a certain kind of functional structure (my identity is, as it were, my functional structure), there seems to be in principle no reason why that could not be reproduced after a thousand years or a million years or a billion years. Resurrection: as you know, Christians believe in resurrection in the flesh, which completely bypasses the need for an immaterial vehicle. So even if one is interested in those questions (and they are not my concern in this paper, although I am concerned to speak to people who have those concerns), even then one doesn't need an immaterial brain or soul-stuff.

So if I am right, and the question of matter or soul-stuff is really irrelevant to any question of philosophical or religious significance, why so much attention to it, why so much heat? The crux of the matter seems to be that both the Diderots of this world and the Descartes of this world have agreed that if we are matter, then there is a physical explanation for how we behave, disappointing or exciting. I think the traditional dualist says *'wouldn't it be terrible if we turned out to be just matter, for then there is a physical explanation for everything we do'*. And the traditional materialist says *'if we are just matter, then there is a physical explanation for everything we do. Isn't that exciting!'* (It is like the distinction between the optimist and the pessimist: an optimist is a person who says 'this is the best of all possible worlds'; and a pessimist is a person who says 'you're right'.)†

I think they are both wrong. I think Diderot and Descartes were both wrong in assuming that if we are matter, or our souls are material, then there is a physical explanation for our behavior.

Let me try to illustrate what I mean by a very simple analogy. Suppose we have a very simple physical system – a board in which there are two holes, a circle one inch in diameter and a square one inch high, and a cubical peg one-sixteenth of an inch less than one inch high. We have the following very simple fact to explain: *the peg passes through the square hole, and it does not pass through the round hole.*

In explanation of this, one might attempt the following. One might say that the peg is, after all, a cloud or, better, a rigid lattice of atoms. One might even attempt to give a description of that lattice, compute its electrical potential energy, worry about why it does not collapse, produce some quantum mechanics to explain why it is stable, etc. The board is also a lattice of atoms. I will call the peg 'system *A*', and the holes 'region 1' and 'region 2'. One could compute all possible trajectories of system *A* (there are, by the way, very serious questions about these computations, their effectiveness, feasibility, and so on, but let us assume this), and perhaps one could deduce from just the laws of particle mechanics or quantum electrodynamics that system *A* never passes through region 1, but that there is at least one trajectory which enables

† Joke Credit: Joseph Weizenbaum.

it to pass through region 2. Is this an explanation of the fact that the peg passes through the square hole and not the round hole?

Very often we are told that if something is made of matter, its behavior must have a physical explanation. And the argument is that if it is made of matter (and we make a lot of assumptions), then there should be a deduction of its behavior from its material structure. *What makes you call this deduction an explanation?*

On the other hand, if you are not 'hipped' on the idea that *the* explanation must be at the level of the ultimate constituents, and that in fact the explanation might have the property that *the ultimate constituents don't matter*, that *only the higher level structure matters*, then there is a very simple explanation here. The explanation is that the board is rigid, the peg is rigid, and as a matter of geometrical fact, the round hole is smaller than the peg, the square hole is bigger than the cross-section of the peg. The peg passes through the hole that is large enough to take its cross-section, and does not pass through the hole that is too small to take its cross-section. That is a correct explanation whether the peg consists of molecules, or continuous rigid substance, or whatever. (If one wanted to amplify the explanation, one might point out the geometrical fact that a square one inch high is bigger than a circle one inch across.)

Now, one can say that in this explanation certain *relevant structural features of the situation* are brought out. The geometrical features are brought out. It is *relevant* that a square one inch high is bigger than a circle one inch around. And the relationship between the size and shape of the peg and the size and shape of the holes is *relevant*. It is *relevant* that both the board and the peg are *rigid* under transportation. And nothing else is relevant. The same explanation will go in any world (whatever the microstructure) in which those *higher level structural features* are present. In that sense *this explanation is autonomous.*

People have argued that I am wrong to say that the microstructural deduction is not an explanation. I think that in terms of the *purposes for which we use the notion of explanation*, it is not an explanation. If you want to, let us say that the deduction *is* an explanation, it is just a terrible explanation, and why look for terrible explanations when good ones are available?

Goodness is not a subjective matter. Even if one agrees with the positivists who saddled us with the notion of explanation as deduction from laws, one of the things we do in science is to look for laws. Explanation is superior not just subjectively, but *methodologically*, in terms of facilitating the aims of scientific inquiry, if it brings out relevant laws. An explanation is superior if it is more general.

Just taking those two features, and there are many many more one could think of, compare the explanation at the higher level of this phenomenon with the atomic explanation. The explanation at the higher level brings out the relevant geometrical relationships. The lower level explanation conceals those laws. Also notice that the higher level explanation applies to a much more interesting class of systems (of course that has to do with what we are interested in).

The fact is that we are much more interested in generalizing to other structures which are rigid and have various geometrical relations, than we are in generalizing to *the next peg that has exactly this molecular structure*, for the very good reason that there is not going to *be* a next peg that has exactly this molecular structure. So in terms of real life disciplines, real life ways of slicing up scientific problems, the higher level explanation is far more general, which is why it is *explanatory*.

We were only able to deduce a statement which is lawful at the *higher* level, that the peg goes through the hole which is larger than the cross-section of the peg. When we try to deduce the possible trajectories of 'system *A*' from statements about the individual atoms, we use premises which are totally accidental – this atom is here, this carbon atom is there, and so forth. And that is one reason that it is very misleading to talk about a reduction of a science like economics to the level of the elementary particles making up the players of the economic game. In fact, their motions – buying this, selling that, arriving at an equilibrium price – these motions cannot be deduced from just the equations of motion. Otherwise they would be *physically necessitated*, not *economically necessitated*, to arrive at an equilibrium price. They play that game because they are particular systems with particular boundary conditions which are totally accidental from the point of view of physics. This means that the derivation of the laws of economics from *just* the laws of physics is *in principle* impossible. The derivation of the laws of economics from the laws of physics and *accidental statements about which particles were where when* by a Laplacian supermind might be in principle possible, but why want it? A few chapters of, e.g. von Neumann, will tell one far more about regularities at the level of economic structure than such a deduction ever could.

The conclusion I want to draw from this is that we do have the kind of autonomy that we are looking for in the mental realm. Whatever our mental functioning may be, there seems to be no serious reason to believe that it is *explainable* by our physics and chemistry. And what we are interested in is not: given that we consist of such and such particles, could someone have predicted that we would have this mental functioning? because such a prediction is not *explanatory*, however great a feat it may be. What we are interested in is: can we say at this autonomous level that since we have this sort of structure, this sort of program, it follows that we will be able to learn this, we will tend to like that, and so on? These are the problems of mental life – the description of this autonomous level of mental functioning – and that is what is to be discovered.

In previous papers, I have argued for the hypothesis that (1) a whole human being is a Turing machine, and (2) that psychological states of a human being are Turing machine states or disjunctions of Turing machine states. In this section I want to argue that this point of view was essentially wrong, and that I was too much in the grip of the reductionist outlook.

Let me begin with a technical difficulty. A *state* of a Turing machine is described in such a way that a Turing machine can be in exactly one state at a time. Moreover, memory and learning are not represented in the Turing machine model as acquisition of new states, but as acquisition of new information printed on the machine's tape. Thus, if human beings have any states at all which resemble Turing machine states, those states must (1) be states the human can be in at any time, independently of learning and memory; and (2) be *total* instantaneous states of the human being – states which determine, together with learning and memory, what the next state will be, as well as totally specifying the present condition of the human being ('totally' from the standpoint of psychological theory, that means).

These characteristics establish that *no* psychological state in any customary sense can be a Turing machine state. Take a particular kind of pain to be a 'psychological state'. If I *am* a Turing machine, then my present 'state' must determine not only whether or not I am having that particular kind of pain, but also whether or not I am about to say 'three', whether or not I am hearing a shrill whine, etc. So the psychological state in question (the pain) is not the same as my 'state' in the sense of *machine state*, although it is possible (so far) that my machine state *determines* my psychological state. Moreover, *no* psychological theory would pretend that having a pain of a particular kind, being about to say 'three', or hearing a shrill whine, etc., all belong to *one* psychological state, although there could well be a machine state characterized by the fact that I was in it only when simultaneously having that pain, being about to say 'three', hearing a shrill whine, etc. So, even if I am a Turing machine, my machine states are *not* the same as my psychological states. My description *qua* Turing machine (machine table) and my description *qua* human being (*via* a psychological theory) are descriptions at two totally different levels of organization.

So far it is still possible that a psychological state is a large disjunction (practically speaking, an almost infinite disjunction) of machine states, although no *single* machine state is a psychological state. But this is very unlikely when we move away from states like 'pain' (which are almost *biological*) to states like 'jealousy' or 'love' or 'competitiveness'. Being jealous is certainly not an *instantaneous* state, and it depends on a great deal of information and on many learned facts and habits. But Turing machine states are instantaneous and are independent of learning and memory. That is, learning and memory may cause a Turing machine to go into a state, but the identity of the state does not depend on learning and memory, whereas, no matter what state I am in, identifying that state as 'being jealous of X's regard for Y' involves specifying that I have learned that X and Y are persons and a good deal about social relations among persons. Thus jealousy can neither be a machine state nor a disjunction of machine states.

One might attempt to modify the theory by saying that being jealous = either being in State A and having tape c_1 *or* being in State A and having tape c_2 *or*...being in State B and having tape d_1 *or* being in State B and having tape d_2...being in State Z and having tape y_1...*or* being in State Z and having tape y_n – i.e. define a psychological state as disjunction, the individual disjuncts being not Turing machine states, as before, but conjunctions of a machine state and a tape (i.e. a total description of the content of the memory bank). Besides the fact that such a description would be literally infinite, the theory is now without content, for the original purpose was to use the machine table as a model of a psychological theory, whereas it is now clear that the machine table description, although different from the description at the elementary particle level, is as removed from the description *via* a psychological theory as the physico-chemical description is.

What is the importance of machines in the philosophy of mind? I think that machines have both a positive and a negative importance. The positive importance of machines was that it was in connection with machines, computing machines in particular, that the notion of functional organization first appeared. Machines forced us to distinguish between an abstract structure and its concrete realization. Not that that distinction came into the world for the first time with machines. But in the case of computing machines, we could not avoid rubbing our noses against the fact that what we had to count as to all intents and purposes the same structure could be realized in a bewildering variety of different ways; that the important properties were not physical-chemical. That the machines made us catch on to the idea of functional organization is extremely important. The negative importance of machines, however, is that they tempt us to oversimplification. The notion of functional organization became clear to us through systems with a very restricted, very specific functional organization. So the temptation is present to assume that we must have that restricted and specific kind of functional organization.

Now I want to consider an example – an example which may seem remote from what we have been talking about, but which may help. This is not an example from the philosophy of mind at all. Consider the following fact. The earth does not go around the sun in a circle, as was once believed, it goes around the sun in an ellipse, with the sun at one of the foci, not in the center of the ellipse. Yet one statement which would hold true if the orbit was a circle and the sun was at the centre still holds true, surprisingly. That is the following statement: the radius vector from the sun to the earth sweeps out equal areas in equal times. If the orbit were a circle, and the earth were moving with a constant velocity, that would be trivial. But the orbit is not a circle. Also the velocity is not constant – when the earth is farthest away from the sun, it is going most slowly, when it is closest to the sun, it is going fastest. The earth is speeding up and slowing down. But the earth's radius vector sweeps out equal areas in equal times.† Newton deduced that law in his *Principia*, and his deduction shows that the only thing on which that law depends is that the force acting on the earth is in the direction of the sun. That is absolutely the only fact one needs to deduce that law. Mathematically it is equivalent to that law.‡ That is all well and good when the gravitational law is that every body attracts every other body according to an inverse square law, because then there is always a force on the earth in the direction of the sun. If we assume that we can neglect all the other bodies, that their influence is slight, then that is all we need, and we can use Newton's proof, or a more modern, simpler proof.

But today we have very complicated laws of gravitation. First of all, we say what is really going is that the world lines of freely falling bodies in space–time are geodesics. And the geometry is determined by the mass-energy tensor, and the ankle bone is connected to the leg bone, etc. So, one might ask, how would a modern relativity theorist explain

† This is one of Kepler's Laws.
‡ Provided that the two bodies – the sun and the earth – are the whole universe. If there are other forces, then, of course, Kepler's law cannot be *exactly* correct.

Kepler's law? He would explain it very simply. *Kepler's laws are true because Newton's laws are approximately true.* And, in fact, an attempt to replace that argument by a deduction of Kepler's laws from the field equations would be regarded as almost as ridiculous (but not quite) as trying to deduce that the peg will go through one hole and not the other from the positions and velocities of the individual atoms.

I want to draw the philosophical conclusion that Newton's laws *have a kind of reality in our world* even though they are not *true*. The point is that it will be necessary to appeal to Newton's laws in order to explain Kepler's laws. Methodologically, I can make that claim at least plausible. One remark – due to Alan Garfinkel – is that *a good explanation is invariant under small perturbations of the assumptions.* One problem with deducing Kepler's laws from the gravitational field equations is that if we do it, tomorrow the gravitational field equations are likely to be different. Whereas the explanation which consists in showing that whichever equation we have implies Newton's equation to a first approximation is invariant under even moderate perturbations, quite big perturbations, of the assumptions. One might say that every explanation of Kepler's laws 'passes through' Newton's laws.

Let me come back to the philosophy of mind, now. If we assume a thorough atomic structure of matter, quantization and so forth, then, at first blush, it looks as if *continuities* cannot be relevant to our brain functioning. Mustn't it all be discrete? Physics says that the deepest level is discrete.

There are two problems with this argument. One is that there are continuities even in quantum mechanics, as well as discontinuities. But ignore that, suppose quantum mechanics were a thoroughly discrete theory.

The other problem is that if that were a good argument, it would be an argument against the utilizability of the model of air as a continuous liquid, which is the model on which aeroplane wings are constructed, at least if they are to fly at anything less than supersonic speeds. There are two points: one is that a discontinuous structure, a discrete structure, can approximate a continuous structure. The discontinuities may be irrelevant, just as in the case of the peg and the board. The fact that the peg and the board are not continuous solids is irrelevant. One can say that the peg and the board only approximate perfectly rigid continuous solids. But if the error in the approximation is irrelevant to the level of description, so what? It is not just that discrete systems can approximate continuous systems; the fact is that the system may behave in the way it does *because* a continuous system would behave in such and such a way, and the system approximates a continuous system.

This is not a Newtonian world. Tough. Kepler's law comes out true because the sun–earth system approximates a Newtonian system. And the error in the approximation is quite irrelevant at that level.

This analogy is not perfect because physicists are interested in laws to which the error in the approximation is relevant. It seems to me that in the psychological case the analogy is even better, that continuous models (for example, Hull's model for rote learning which used a a continuous potential) could perfectly well be correct, whatever the ultimate structure of the brain is. We cannot deduce that a digital model has to be the correct model from the fact that ultimately there are neurons. The brain may work the way it does because it approximates some system whose laws are best conceptualized in terms of continuous mathematics. What is more, the errors in that approximation may be irrelevant at the level of psychology.

What I have said about *continuity* goes as well for many other things. Let us come back to the question of the soul people and the brain people, and the isomorphism between the souls in one world and the brains in the other. One objection was, if there is a functional isomorphism between souls and brains, wouldn't the souls have to be rather simple? The answer is no. Because brains can be essentially infinitely complex. A system with as many degrees of freedom as the brain can imitate to within the accuracy relevant to psychological theory any structure one can hope to describe. It might be, so to speak, that the ultimate physics of the soul will be quite different from the ultimate physics of the brain, but that at the level we are interested in, the level of functional organization, the same description might go for both. And also that that description might be formally incompatible with the actual physics of the brain, in the way that the description of the air flowing around an aeroplane wing as a continuous incompressible liquid is *formally incompatible with the actual structure of the air*.

Let me close by saying that these examples support the idea that our substance, what we are made of, places almost no first order restrictions on our form. And that what we are really interested in, as Aristotle saw,† is form and not matter. *What is our intellectual form?* is the question, not what the matter is. And whatever our substance may be, soul-stuff, or matter or Swiss cheese, it is not going to place any interesting first order restrictions on the answer to this question. It may, of course, place interesting higher order restrictions. Small effects may have

---

† E.g. Aristotle says: '...we can wholly dismiss as unnecessary the question whether the soul and the body are one: it is as meaningless to ask whether the wax and the shape given to it by the stamp are one, or generally the matter of a thing and that of which it is the matter.' (See *De Anima*, 412 a6–b9.)

to be explained in terms of the actual physics of the brain. But when we are not even at the level of an *idealized* description of the functional organization of the brain, to talk about the importance of small perturbations seems decidedly premature. My conclusion is that we have what we always wanted – an autonomous mental life. And we need no mysteries, no ghostly agents, no *élan vital* to have it.

15
Dreaming and 'depth grammar'*

Introduction

1. In this paper I wish to examine certain general doctrines having to do with language which are employed by Norman Malcolm in his book *Dreaming* (Malcolm, 1959). I say 'employed', not 'stated', because Malcolm never does fully state these doctrines. Yet his arguments turn not on the linguistic properties of individual words, but on these almost formal principles, involving such notions as 'concept', 'sense', 'logical independence', 'stipulation', 'giving a use', 'being unverifiable in principle', 'criterion', 'indication' and 'inference'.

His arguments are also of interest in that they can be read as simple versions of some famous arguments of Wittgenstein's as he is interpreted by Malcolm. If this interpretation of Malcolm's is faithful to what Wittgenstein had in mind, then these famous arguments are bad arguments and prove nothing. But this relation to Wittgenstein's philosophy may, in the present years, be a further reason for finding Malcolm's book interesting to discuss.

2. The following quotations will serve to indicate the flavor of the relevant parts of Malcolm's book:

(i) There are *two concepts of sleep*, because there are two methods of verification: 'With adults and older children there are two criteria of behaviour and testimony; with animals and human infants there is only the one criterion of behaviour. The concept of sleep is not exactly the same in the two cases' (p. 23).

(ii) 'Asleep' applied to a sleep-walker is a 'new use': 'To say that a man who is walking is "asleep" is a new use of the expression' (p. 27).

(iii) 'Asleep' applied to someone having a violent nightmare is an 'extended use':

To say that a sleep walker, a person in a hypnotic trance,† and someone having a violent nightmare is 'asleep', is to make a natural extension of the

* First published in R. Butler (ed.) *Analytical Philosophy First Series* (Oxford, 1962). Reprinted by permission of Basil Blackwell & Mott.
† Note the juxtaposition!

use of that word beyond its primary use. It is not surprising that an expression used to *name a certain phenomenon* should come to be applied to other phenomena that resemble it more or less (p. 28—*italics mine*).

(iv) On alleged inductive inferences with unverifiable conclusions:

If it were established, for example, that whenever a person makes a judgment the electrical output of a certain region of his brain rises and falls in some characteristic way, the occurrence of this electrical phenomenon in a sleeping person would not provide *any probability* that the sleeper was making a judgment. The imagined correlation would, of necessity, have been established only for the case of people who were awake, since the *criteria* for saying some person made a judgment could not be fulfilled when he was asleep. The attempt to extend the inductive reasoning to the case of sleeping persons would yield a conclusion that was *logically incapable of confirmation*. It would be impossible to know if this conclusion was true or false (p. 43—*italics mine*).

(v) One cannot ask whether *criteria* are good or not:

One may think to overcome these difficulties by allowing that the *descriptions* that people give of their private states provide a determination of what those states are and whether they are the same. But if one takes this line (which is correct) one cannot then permit a question to be raised as to whether those descriptions are in error or not – for this would be to fall back into the original difficulty. One must treat the descriptions as the *criterion* of what the inner occurrences are (p. 55).

(vi) We may say that dreams and waking impressions are two different things: but not – two logically independent things (p. 60).

(vii) Scientists who try to tell what people are dreaming by studying eye movements during sleep are making *stipulations*; are introducing a new concept that *remotely* resembles the old one; their discoveries *do not pertain to dreaming* (!); and their concept *is not a concept of dreaming at all*. The scientists are in a 'muddle' (p. 78), and their uses spring from confusion:

Without an adequate realization of what they are doing, Dement and Kleitman are proposing a new concept . . . [p. 80].
We ought to consider the consequences of these *stipulations* and ask ourselves whether it is appropriate to call this *creation* a concept of dreaming [p. 10 – *final italics Malcolm's*].
Considering the radical conceptual changes that the adoption of a physiological criterion would entail, it is evident that a new concept would have been created that only remotely resembled the old one. To use the name 'dreaming' for the new concept would spring from confusion and result in confusion. All of this can be avoided by holding firmly to waking testimony as the sole criterion of dreaming [p. 81].

3. The following points in Malcolm's view are especially important for our discussion: criteria are ways of settling a question with certainty (p. 60); their connection with a concept is logical, not empirical; they are related to the way we teach and learn the use of an expression; if they are all fulfilled we have a 'paradigmatic case'; it is nonsense to speak of an inductive inference unless the sentence used to express the alleged conclusion of the inference is one whose application is governed by *criteria*. Thus, language is criterion-governed; learning and teaching a language is, in large part, learning and teaching conformity to criteria.

Malcolm's views on criteria (like Reichenbach's on 'co-ordinative definitions' (Reichenbach, 1958)) are supported not by general or special considerations drawn from linguistic theory, but by *sceptical* arguments. The Malcolm of 1959 believes, like the Reichenbach of 1930, that *only* by answering the question 'How do you know?' by saying in certain cases 'It's a *criterion*' (or 'It's a *co-ordinative definition*') can we avoid the supposedly bottomless pit of scepticism. The motto of these philosophers might be: 'If there were no analytic-synthetic distinction, it would be necessary to invent one.'

Here I use 'analytic-synthetic' to refer not to the 'surface' distinction between, say, 'All pediatricians are doctors' and 'My hat is on the table', but to the idea of 'depth grammar' which provides a 'fact-convention' dichotomy on a level inaccessible to ordinary lexicographic investigations. The lexicographer would undoubtedly perceive the logical (or semantical) connection between being a pediatrician and being a doctor, but he would miss the *allegedly* 'logical' character of the connection between dreams and waking impressions. I have argued in chapter 2 in this volume that this 'depth grammar' kind of analyticity (or 'logical dependence') does not exist: however, the present paper will be independent of that discussion.

4. Truth is important; but so is importance. Why is it important to show that Malcolm is wrong? Malcolm's is the sharpest statement of Verificationism in the 1950s. If Malcolm is right, then the 'naive' way of understanding our language and our knowledge is wrong.

Thus, in Malcolm's view, it is impossible to refer to a thing (or kind of thing) if in no case do we have better than *indications* of its presence or absence. If this it right, then for everything in the world we can presently name there is at least one case in which we can *settle with certainty* whether it is present or absent. But, on the 'naive' view – i.e. in the view of present scientific theory, taken more or less literally, more or less without philosophical interpretation – there are many things for whose presence or absence we never have better than probabilistic indicators. So, if Malcolm is right, either we cannot refer to these things, or the theory is wrong, or the naive way of understanding it is. This is what makes Malcolm's view an interesting one: if it is right, we must either know a devil of a lot less than we think or a devil of a lot more.

On having 'indications' and no 'criterion'

1. Malcolm speaks of 'senselessness, in the sense of impossibility of verification' (p. 83). Elsewhere (p. 44) he uses 'unintelligible' as a synonym for 'senseless' in this sense. But *is* this a sense of 'senseless'?

When is an utterance unintelligible? Some, perhaps all, strongly a-grammatical utterances have this property: e.g. Chomsky's 'Furiously sleep ideas green colourless.'(Chomsky, 1957, p. 15). The same words in the reverse order, 'Colourless green ideas sleep furiously.', are still unintelligible, but not so strongly so. For instance, one can propose ways of construing them, as Roman Jakobson did (Jakobson, 1959). And the utterance is still not fully grammatical, for the verb 'sleep' takes a concrete subject, and 'ideas' is a pluralized abstract noun. Carnap's examples of 'grammatical nonsense sentences', e.g. 'The stone is thinking about Vienna.', suffer from the same defects: they are neither fully grammatical nor fully nonsense.

Suppose we take a fully grammatical nonsense sentence, e.g. 'Dead linguists smoke buildings.' Perhaps this too is not fully unintelligible. Let us mark this down: to the extent that a sentence is fully grammatical, in the sense of obeying *all* the regularities in a transformational grammar, possibly it has *some* sense. Grammar may be a part of sense.

Henceforth let us make this strong restriction on the discussion: we will consider only fully grammatical sentences. What can we associate with such a sentence's being more or less intelligible?

The following comes to mind: an intelligible utterance is one a native speaker can paraphrase.†

The connection between grammar and sense begins to become clear. I can paraphrase any grammatical sentence, although not always word by word, because I know the meanings of the words *and* the forms of composition. If there are no forms of composition, then I can still paraphrase word by word, but how can I know if I am preserving (or transforming in an equivalent way, e.g. from active to passive) the grammatical structure?

But 'paraphrase' can be taken in different ways. I might set out to paraphrase the sentence about dead linguists considered 'in the abstract,' thus: 'Linguists who are no longer alive smoke edifices.' (Note the role played by my grammatical knowledge: 'who are no longer alive' *follows*

† I am indebted for this suggestion to Mr J. A. Fodor.

the noun, whereas what it replaced preceded; and 'edifices' must occupy the *same* place to be a 'direct object'.)

But suppose someone *uttered* the 'dead linguists' sentence (say, as a line in a 'totally unintelligible' modern poem). Suppose I am asked, 'What does he mean, "Dead linguists smoke buildings"?' Very likely, I *cannot* paraphrase.

This suggests: an utterance is unintelligible in a context if (to the degree that) a native speaker cannot paraphrase it in that context (as opposed to 'in the abstract').

A second, very different sort of condition associated with intelligibility is this: if an utterance is intelligible a native speaker (an imaginative one) should be able to think of discourses in which it would naturally occur. ('Discourse' is a linguist's term for a series of utterances.) Of course, a number of restrictions must be imposed: the utterances must be 'used' and not 'mentioned' in the discourse; the discourse must not be one in which linguistic regularities are regularly violated,† etc. Roughly, but only very roughly speaking, the discourse must be an 'ordinary' one: more precisely, it must be the kind of discourse from which a linguist might project the basic compositional structure of the language (cf. Ziff, 1960). Let us assume that this kind of discourse is what we would mean here and now by a 'discourse' anyway.

Note the difference between the two conditions we have associated with intelligibility: the first rests on the fact that native speakers have an ability to make certain kinds of explicit metalinguistic statements about their language, while the second rests upon the ability of sophisticated speakers to think of actual linguistically coherent and situationally appropriate discourses. Of course, one speaker may be able to imagine a case in which one would employ an utterance U while a less imaginative speaker might fail; and even given a context, one speaker may be able to make a paraphrase while another may not, either because he 'doesn't understand' the utterance in question or because he 'can't think of a different way of saying it'. But the two conditions seem to be sufficient (if not necessary): if almost any speaker (in the relevant group) can think of discourses in which a sentence could occur without any kind of linguistic or situational inappropriateness, and can paraphrase it readily in those discourses, then it is clearly an intelligible sentence (for that group). None of this shows that Malcolm is *wrong* in maintaining that a declarative sentence, uttered with the evident purpose of asserting something, is used unintelligibly if there is no way in which we could

† Philosophers' and linguists' discourses are hopeless for the description of a language for just this reason – which is not to say that there is no point at which linguistic theory has to take account of them.

(in some cases, if not always the one at hand) *settle with certainty* whether what was said was true or false; but note that none of this gives the slightest reason to think that Malcolm is right, either. Linguistic intelligibility appears to depend on matters quite other than what we can or cannot 'settle with certainty': e.g. on grammar, on ability to occur in coherent and appropriate discourses, on paraphrasability. It may be that a discourse (one consisting of 'assertions') is incoherent unless *each sentence* in it is used to say what can, in some cases at least, be established with certainty to be true or false: but there is no reason at hand to think this either. And we shall see later that proposed models for the semantic abilities of native speakers lead to quite the reverse result.

(I have used 'incoherent' here as a term for discourses which have some sort of linguistic oddity about them considered 'in the abstract' Often the term 'linguistic inappropriateness' is used to cover both this sort of oddity, and oddity depending on context of utterance. For example, a linguistically incoherent discourse may be appropriate to some contexts, and a coherent one may be inappropriate to some contexts. The terms are ill chosen; but they are meant to separate sharply what could conceivably be a *structural* matter – in the sense in which the notion is used by Harris (1957) – and what is a matter of 'reality controls'.)

2. Some philosophers might argue that the whole consideration of linguistic unintelligibility is an irrelevant one. By a 'senseless' assertion, they would suggest, Malcolm means not a 'meaningless' one in the sense just looked at ('unintelligible'), but a so-called *cognitively meaningless* one – i.e. one not possessing a truth-value. However, I do not think this *is* what Malcolm means. In the first place, his whole discussion does suggest the strong thesis that an 'assertion' cannot be *in the language* if there is no way of settling with certainty (in 'paradigmatic cases', at least) whether it is true or false: and not just that it cannot be assigned a truth-value. And in the second place, the thesis that the existence of a 'criterion', in Malcolm's sense, is a prerequisite for even the assignability of truth-values is badly in need of support. I do not wish to discuss the whole issue of Verificationism here; but let me point out that Malcolm's requirements are much stronger than those of other Verificationists, e.g. Carnap and Reichenbach. Carnap and Reichenbach require only that a sentence should be able to be used to express the conclusion of an inductive inference, or still more weakly, that it should be possible to assign some kind of inductive probability to it, for it to be 'cognitively meaningful'. Malcolm, in effect, rejects this view on the ground that you cannot assign a probability to something that is *unintelligible*, and that a sentence is unintelligible if there is no criterion for its being used to say what is true. If this has any plausibility at all, it

seems to accrue from the ambiguity: criterion = set of truth conditions, vs. criterion = 'way of settling a question with certainty' (*Malcolm's notion*). Note that the first notion of 'criterion', although it makes it vacuously correct to say that something is no 'assertion' if there is no criterion for its being true, is utterly useless for ascertaining intelligibility: for someone who maintains that an 'assertion is intelligible', will of course maintain that it has truth conditions – these can be stated by any good paraphrase! One might reply: 'You can't learn your native language from paraphrases'; but neither can you learn your native language (acquire the semantical abilities of a native speaker) by just learning what to say in 'paradigmatic cases'.

3. Could we have only 'indications' and no 'criterion'? Consider the following case: there is a disease, multiple sclerosis, which is extremely difficult to diagnose. The symptoms resemble those of other neurological diseases; and not all of the symptoms are usually present. Some neurologists believe that multiple sclerosis is caused by a virus, although they cannot presently specify what virus. Suppose a patient, X, has a 'paradigmatic' case of multiple sclerosis. Then Malcolm's view is that, no matter what we find out later, X *has* multiple sclerosis because that is what we presently mean. In particular, if we later identify a virus as *the* cause of multiple sclerosis, and this patient's condition was not caused by that virus, he *still* had multiple sclerosis. (Saying that this virus was *the* cause of multiple sclerosis was changing the concept. One could even say in the manner of Malcolm, p. 81: 'Considering the radical conceptual changes that the adoption of a virological criterion would entail, it is evident that a new concept would have been created that only remotely resembled the old one.' Perhaps the discoveries of the investigators would not 'pertain to *multiple sclerosis*'!)

Malcolm uses all three of these locutions: change of *concept*, of *use*, of *sense*. (For example, there is both a primary *use* and a primary *sense* of 'asleep' in which someone having a violent nightmare is not asleep.) What he must say, then, is that the adoption of any criterion for multiple sclerosis according to which not all the cases that are presently 'paradigmatic' are cases of multiple sclerosis is a case of *meaning change*. 'Multiple sclerosis' will have a new sense; moreover, this will have come about through 'stipulations'. In addition, the change of 'sense' will be great enough to effect the extension of the concept; some cases will be cases of multiple sclerosis in the old sense but not in the new.

To take the last point first: it is a little strange to talk of the 'extension' of a term like 'multiple sclerosis' as long as the notion has not been made precise. What we should like to say is this: there is (we presume) in the world something – say, a virus – which normally causes such-and-such symptoms. Perhaps other diseases occasionally (rarely) produce these same symptoms in a few patients. When a patient has these symptoms we say he has 'multiple sclerosis' – but, of course, we are prepared to say that we were mistaken if the etiology turns out to have been abnormal. And we are prepared to classify sicknesses as cases of multiple sclerosis, even if the symptoms are rather deviant, if it turns out that the *underlying condition* was the virus that causes multiple sclerosis, and that the deviancy in the symptoms was, say, random variation. On this view the question of interest is not, so to speak, the 'extension' of the term 'multiple sclerosis', but what, if anything, *answers* to our notion of multiple sclerosis. When we know what answers to our criteria (more of less perfectly), *that* – whatever it is – will be the 'extension' of 'multiple sclerosis'.

This seems to me to be the case with a great many terms: the use of the term is based on the supposition that there is something – a 'natural kind', so to speak – for which our 'criteria' are *good* but not *perfect* indicators. In the case of such terms, the accepted criteria are often modified in the course of time. We *could* learn to speak with Malcolm, and say that the term is *given* a series of new uses. But this obscures just what we want to stress: that the changes in the accepted criteria reflect the fact that we have more and more knowledge concerning X (where X may be a virus, or a kind of chemical, etc.). Malcolm is assimilating two totally dissimilar cases: the case of arbitrary linguistic stipulation, and the case of finding better ways to tell whether or not something is present.

'Extension' is a technical term. To use a non-technical locution, we should have to say that we reject the view that scientists who accept our hypothetical (future) virological criterion are *talking about a different disease* when they use the term 'multiple sclerosis'. On our view, whether scientists at t_1 and scientists at t_2 are or are not talking about the same thing when they use a term is, in cases like the present one, to be ascertained by examining the relevant scientific theory (the latest one available!) and not by linguistic investigations, whether special or general.

A similar case is afforded by the history of the term 'acid' in chemistry. Two hundred years ago a chemist might have had only two or three criteria for a substance's being an acid: being soluble in water; sour taste (in water solution); turning litmus paper red. Today we have a theoretical definition in terms of the notion 'proton-donor'. Yet I feel sure that any chemist would want to say that he is talking about the same chemical substances that the eighteenth century chemist called 'acids'. Is there any decisive reason for rejecting this 'naive' view? It is true that we can today speak of a few acids that could not have been *identified as such* by eighteenth century criteria. If the eighteenth century

chemist insisted that there *could not be*, say, an acid too weak to turn litmus paper red (or to give any taste at all) as he understood the term, then
perhaps we should say that a change of meaning had occurred. But who
supposes that an eighteenth century chemist would have so insisted? Similarly in the multiple sclerosis case: a neurologist today is very likely to
tell you that even the 'paradigmatic cases' of multiple sclerosis might, in
some instances, be deviant forms of some other disease: and this accords
fully with the idea that by the term 'multiple sclerosis' he *means* whatever
disease causes such-and-such symptoms, and not just the simultaneous
presence of the symptoms. If we could not distinguish between a 'disease'
in the theoretical sense of, say, virus-caused destruction to nerve tissue,
and its effects, this might be metaphysics: but we can, and it isn't.

Note that the question, 'Has the "sense" of the term "acid" changed?'
is much harder to answer than the question (taken as a question in the
history of chemistry, as how else should it be taken?), 'Were they talking
about what we are talking about when we use the term, or did they have
a different class of substances in mind?' The answer to the latter question,
depending upon the degree of precision required by the context, might
be, 'Oh, the term "acid" hasn't changed its meaning', or 'They had
the same substances in mind', or 'Well, they used the term to refer to
the acids they could identify by their criteria (litmus paper, etc.), but,
of course, the theoretical definition has changed a great deal'. But the
answer to the former question seems to be just this, that the theoretical
definition has changed and *in that sense* the 'sense' has changed. This is
not a case of saying something different because we have *given* words new
meanings: rather, the 'sense', in one sense, has changed because we have
new knowledge.

But why not say that 'in the eighteenth century sense' *only* substances
satisfying the eighteenth century criteria were acids? – Simply because
this does not do justice to the probable intelligence of eighteenth century
chemists. In all likelihood, they knew perfectly well that their criteria
were *crude* ways of detecting a 'natural kind' of chemical; they would
have thought it unlikely that their criteria exactly 'caught' the boundaries of that kind. Of course, even in the light of later theory, the
'boundaries' of the kind in question may require more or less arbitrary
legislation: in *this* sense *some* stipulation may have entered into the
present technical definition. But this sometimes happens and sometimes
not. (In our hypothetical case of a single virus origin being discovered
for multiple sclerosis, there would be no 'stipulation' involved in fixing
the boundaries of the disease in a natural way.) Certainly this much *must*
be right: that there could be such a thing as discovering a virus origin
for multiple sclerosis, and it would *not* necessarily involve discovering

a virus origin for everything that is presently accepted as a 'paradigmatic case' (used to teach medical students).

4. Earlier we considered one linguistic question: the question of 'intelligibility'. What of 'change of meaning'?

It would be unrealistic not to begin by noting how different the following two questions are: whether two words have the same meaning, considered as a question about one language at one time, and whether the same word has kept its meaning, considered as a question about the language at two different times. The second question usually comes down to something like this: 'Did they mean the same disease (class of chemicals, etc.)?' – and even this does not usually arise unless there is reason to think that 'they' *didn't*. And this latter question, as we noted, is not a 'purely' linguistic one: the first step in answering it is usually to ask the theoretical question, whether (according to our present lights) there was anything at all answering to 'their' criteria (not perfectly, but pretty well!) and if so *what*?

Let us consider when it is *clear* that a word has changed its meaning, or has been used in an extended or figurative sense. Durrell writes: 'And I, my selves, observed by human choice.' (Durrell, 1960). It is clear that 'new uses' of 'selves' and 'choice' are involved; but what makes this clear? First, 'selves' is a peculiar plural (apart from such constructions as 'them-selves'). Second, 'choice' is used as if it were an animate noun. So we have *invention* even at the grammatical level. But this may not signify new meanings: the first man to split an infinitive (if there was a first man) did not change the meaning of any word.

Digging deeper, we see that the grammatical deviations are here associated with semantical conditions. By treating one's choices (or 'choice' in the abstract) as an observer, Durrell makes the 'Rylean' point that I must often find out what I feel by seeing what I choose – but with a startling inversion: my choice is thought of as observing me, to see what I am. And the pluralization of 'self' denies, in effect, the idea of a unitary 'person' behind all of my choices. If this interpretation of the line is correct, why is it a 'change of sense' to think of oneself as a congerie of 'selves', or of 'choice' as an observer? I would say: because the lexical definitions of 'observer' and 'self' would entail that a person has only one self, and that observing is done by people, not abstractions. As a 'first order approximation', deviant senses are those not mapped by lexical definitions; and good lexical definitions are ones that map all non-deviant senses. This is a circle, but not a vicious one,† because one can think of a number of obvious operational constraints that a good

† Cf. N. Chomsky, 1957, chapter 5, on a similar 'circularity' in grammatical theory.

lexicon should satisfy; but that 'circularity' is present at all indicates that a lexical definition must be judged to some extent as a theory is judged: by its probability and operational fit *as compared with its rivals.*

Many uses are certified by philosophers as 'new', however, although they do not violate any lexical definition of the term in question that naturally suggests itself. And the philosopher may be right. For instance, suppose that at a certain time people first began speaking of things we say as 'true'. (I assume 'true lover', 'true healer', 'his aim was true' etc., were already in the language.) This would be a new use in that 'true' would be used to qualify an abstract noun phrase for the first time. (This explanation does not really work: 'true love' might already have been present.) However, it might not deviate from one lexical definition of one sense of 'true X', namely 'an X that can be relied upon'. How can we justify our intuitive conviction that a new *sense* of 'true' is involved.

In this way: from that definition one cannot predict, e.g. that one speaks of a 'true statement' but not of a 'true prescription', although statements and prescriptions are both things that can be relied upon. Also, even if we know that a true assertion can be relied upon, this hardly fixes the *exact* meaning of true as applied to assertions: 'true' could be a synonym for 'well established', or for 'certain', or for 'having the weight of authority behind it', or for 'true and important' without being untrue to its connotation of reliability. This suggests: to the degree that the new sentences are *unpredictable* we are inclined to speak of 'new uses'. But this is not enough: it is the joint facts that 'true' as applied to what is said requires a separate entry in the lexicon *and* the unpredictability of the corresponding class of discourses by a native speaker familiar with the 'old' language that establishes beyond question that a distinct 'sense' of the word is involved.

Notice how none of these considerations is ever taken account of by Malcolm! He condemns the sentences written by Dement and Kleitman as 'new uses', new 'concepts', results of unwitting 'stipulations', without ever considering the question of predictability in any way, shape or form! On Malcolm's account, there would appear to be little difference between the degree of invention exercised by Durrell and that exercised by Dement and Kleitman.

Although this is a wholly empirical question on which I am admittedly guessing, I feel convinced that, as a matter of fact, a great many speakers would *automatically* produce discourses similar to Dement and Kleitman's given the data from which Dement and Kleitman worked. Moreover, and here I am not guessing, virtually a hundred per cent of all hearers will 'pass' these discourses without detecting the slightest trace of linguistic oddity. This seems to me to be overwhelming evidence that the 'uses' in question, whatever may be their status, are not 'new'. They were always in the language, not in the sense of having actually been produced, but in the sense that the linguistic habits that lead to their production, given certain scientific experiences, are and have been virtually universal among speakers of the language.

These discourses might still be deviant, however: for example, figurative uses of certain words have also 'been in the language' for as long as we have records, but are recognizably nonstandard. This leads to our second criterion†: conformity to the lexical definition. Malcolm does not speak of definitions, presumably because he is doing 'depth grammar', but they seem (as Fodor has pointed out (Fodor, 1960)) to provide the most natural way of distinguishing standard uses from, so to speak, 'standard deviations from standardness' (e.g. irony) and from philosophical uses. If we accept the conception of a dream that Malcolm rejects, then we get something like this as a natural lexical definition: 'a series of impressions (visual, etc.) occurring during sleep; usually appearing to the subject to be of people, objects, etc.; frequently remembered upon awakening'. Certainly such sentences as, 'Rapid eye movements during sleep appear to be correlated with rapid movements in the dream event that is probably occurring at the same time' (this is the sort of 'use' that Malcolm objects to), are in accord with this or any similar 'classical' definition.

We are left with a kind of circularity. If we reject Malcolm's views at one point, we are naturally led to reject them at many others; and if we accept them at one point, we must accept them at many others. What we have seen is that certain, rather natural, criteria of 'intelligibility' and of 'change of sense' appear to be fully compatible with the 'naive' view that Dement and Kleitman were presenting a piece of *plausible reasoning* ('inductive inference') concerning the time of occurrence and part of the content of dreams, and not drawing a pseudo-inference to an 'unintelligible' conclusion, or 'changing the sense' of any word. Perhaps there are two 'circles' present; but one of these circles may be the circle of our usual ways of thinking and talking, while the other is just the lonely circle of an unusual philosophic position.

5. 'Dreaming' appears to be a special case in that the man on the street certainly does not assume the existence of a *physical* referent when he uses the word. But there is, nonetheless, an assumption underlying ordinary talk about dreams: namely, that dreams *take place during the night*. That is, they are thought of as if they started at some unknown

† I use 'criterion' here in its idiomatic sense – 'way of telling'.

moment during the night, went on for a time, and ceased at some other unknown moment. This assumption Malcolm refers to as the assumption that dreams are 'in physical time' (*sic!*), and he calls the assumption 'senseless'. At first sight, his argument has a strangely dogmatic character: the assumption, for example, of a correlation between rapid eye movements and rapid movements of the 'dream objects' is 'senseless' because it is 'logically incapable of confirmation'; and apparent confirmations are not confirmations because their conclusions are 'senseless'. Similarly Malcolm would presumably reject the lexical definition of 'dream' we proposed above as incorrect although it agrees with many discourses that speakers and hearers do not find odd; and he would also *reject the discourses* although they agree with the lexical definition. The correct theory, it appears, need not fit the facts: it only has to fit the *corrected* facts.

What Malcolm has in mind, however, is more reputable than this: he has in mind the requirement that the conclusion of an inductive inference must be capable of further, independent confirmation and disconfirmation. This is a universally accepted requirement: but it should not be confused with the quite different requirement that the conclusion of an inductive inference must be capable of confirmation apart from *all* inductive inferences, by applying a criterion.

The supposed 'rapid eye movements' correlation does, in fact, satisfy the requirement just mentioned: further confirmation would be provided, for instance, if it were discovered that the things people say when they talk in their sleep 'agree' with both the rapid eye movements and the supposed dream events. Malcolm rejects this too: this time on the ground that dreams 'in their primary sense' take place in *sound* sleep, that the 'sound sleep' and 'restless sleep' are *different concepts*. This leads Malcolm to suggest that we *dream in a different sense* when we talk or scream in our sleep (pp. 99–100). However, this same device – 'bifurcating' cases, because of a difference in the method of verification – 'properly' applied can be used to deny that any inductive inference is legitimate (e.g. any inference from observed events to events at which no observer was present).

The supposed 'rapid eye movements' correlation could also be disconfirmed: for instance, it might be discovered that the physiological explanation of 'remembering a dream' is simply incompatible with the idea that such 'memories' are really memories of events occurring at the time that the rapid eye movements occurred. More importantly, *kinds* of confirmation and disconfirmation are possible that Malcolm simply does not consider: model building and theory construction. When we go from *peripheral* correlations ('rapid eye movements') to *central* correlations (neural events) we find we have *never* to do with *mere* correlations: every neural correlate known today for *anything* was in part suggested by some *model* for neural processes. If someone constructed a plausible physiological model for *sleep*, for *visual experiences*, and for *dreaming* (considered as visual experiences, etc., during sleep) and some theory based on this model *suggested* the correlations between, say, rapid eye movements and rapid 'dream movements', the confirmation of those correlations would be enormously increased. Yet theories based on this type of model building are not conclusively verifiable, as has been known since the appearance of the late chapters of Mill's *Logic* (1848) at least.

Thus, assuming that dreams take place 'in physical time' – i.e. that they start and stop at some time or other – various things *become* inductive evidence that correlations hold: correlations between the things we do with our eyes, muscles, vocal cords, as we sleep *and* the dream events; and correlations between the neural processes that normally go with 'seeing' certain things *and* dream events. If these correlations appear to be not only statistically significant, but also to 'fit' into an explanatory theory of dreaming, then they are not only highly confirmed; but the underlying assumption that dreams take place in 'physical time' is equally highly confirmed. It sometimes appears as if Malcolm wants to eliminate this kind of 'inverse deductive method' (as Mill called it) from science, and to allow only (1) conclusive verification based on the application of 'criteria', and (2) inductive inference in the most restricted possible sense: induction by simple enumeration. But as Mill remarked, no developed social science (or any other science, one might add) will ever be possible on this basis.

It might, however, be maintained that although the assumption that dreams take place *during* sleep ('in physical time') is intelligible and indirectly testable in the manner outlined, it does not in fact underlie our ordinary talk about dreaming, as I asserted. For, it could be said, we might discover the assumption to be *false*: perhaps 'memories of dreams' are not physiologically 'memories' (brain traces) at all, and perhaps they are caused by an event that takes place at the moment of awakening. Yet we would go on talking of dreams just as we now do, fully knowing that this assumption was false.

Yes and no. It seems to be undeniable that people do universally make this assumption, and that this is connected with the way they talk. Even Malcolm admits this when he speaks of this assumption as a 'grammatical illusion'. Of course, many of our ways of talking point to 'dead theories', and we might retain the way of talking after the 'death' of the assumption. In *this* sense, our way of talking is independent of any theory at all. Granted. But here and now we do make this assumption. This is why certain reasonings are *plausible* and why certain discourses do not seem odd (except to those who view them from a privileged standpoint of philosophic criticism). Suppose a novelist is writing about two young lovers, separated by six thousand miles (which means eight hours time difference) and writes, 'At the very moment that R. A. was having her photograph taken, her distant lover was having a dream in which she figured...' So used are we to the convention of the novelist's omniscience, that we are unlikely to find any linguistic oddity in this sentence. Yet in a culture which accepted the idea that 'memories of dreams' are caused by events that happen upon waking up, this sentence might not 'have a use'. So in this sense, our total 'way of talking' is *not* independent of what 'assumptions' we make, of what we know.

Suggested models for the semantical abilities of native speakers

By the 'semantical abilities' of native speakers of a natural language let us understand the abilities involved in producing and responding to linguistically coherent and situationally appropriate discourses. These abilities are so complex that most linguists have shied away from discussing them (Harris's work on 'Discourse Analysis' being the one notable exception). However, philosophers have in the present century hazarded a number of admittedly over-simplified models for these abilities, and it likely that this will prove in the long run to have been of real service, at least in laying the groundwork for a discussion of these problems.

Malcolm's remarks seem to rest on *this* kind of 'model': speakers learn their native language by being taught (or just 'picking up') what to say in 'paradigmatic situations'. Doing this is a matter of internalizing sufficient conditions – just those sufficient conditions whose connection with the utterance is a product of what may be viewed as arbitrary linguistic stipulation or convention.

However, this model will not do. Consider the following discourse: 'She is wearing a red skirt. This is a book. She is fat. That is a chair.' The situation may be 'paradigmatic' for each sentence taken separately (e.g. there might be a contextually definite woman wearing a red skirt, and the speaker might have pointed to the woman and to a book and to a chair at the appropriate moments), but the discourse as a whole is highly odd, and even deviates from statable *structural* regularities of the kind studied by Harris. (That it is 'odd' does not mean that it could never occur. It might, for example, occur at a Berlitz school: so might anything.) These *discourse-analytical regularities* are, by and large, as unconscious and obligatory as, say, phonetic or grammatical regularities, and they determine much (*how* much is a moot point) of the linguistic character of discourses in English or any other natural language.

This suggests complicating Malcolm's model in the following way: a speaker must not only internalize 'criteria' enabling him to use isolated sentences in paradigmatic cases, but he must also internalize some kind of generalized grammar ('discourse analysis') restricting the sequences of sentences that he is allowed to put together in one discourse. (So far this 'generalized grammar' has been studied, to a limited extent, only for published discourses. Spoken discourses are much more difficult because of the manner in which extra-linguistic things – e.g. gestures, or just the presence of something in the room – can take the place of whole sentences.) Although I admit to being amazed by some of the things Harris can do on the basis of purely structural criteria, I am myself completely pessimistic about the program of ruling out *all* discourses that are intuitively incoherent (linguistically deviant, considered 'in the abstract') on the basis of such criteria. But for the moment, let us suppose that this could be done.

Still, we are left with an unsatisfactory picture of language. In the first place, the use of many sentences is *projected* from the use of simpler sentences. For example, no one learns the use of the sentence 'If she had been wearing a red dress, it would have been easier to pick her out.' from paradigmatic cases: one inductively projects the use of this sentence from the uses of simpler but related sentences, e.g. 'She is wearing a red dress.', 'She was wearing a red dress.', 'It was easy to pick her out.', 'If you had asked, I would have given it to you.', 'If you hadn't jerked your hand the glass wouldn't have broken.', etc., these last two sentences being of the form 'If A had been the case, B would have happened.' Notice that even these simpler sentences would mainly be projections: one would not learn the use of 'She is wearing a red dress.' and 'She is not wearing a red dress.' separately. One would project the use of the latter sentence from one's familiarity with other sentence-negated-sentence pairs. And similarly with past-present, active-passive, etc.: one learns to project one form given the other.

This suggests that (a) internalizing a grammar is essential to acquiring semantical abilities (since all of the above projections obviously depend upon the grammatical structure of the language); (b) more importantly, even if the thus corrected picture of the semantical abilities of a native speaker is correct, it is almost wholly uninformative. For we are not *so* puzzled by a child's saying that she is wearing a red dress when its mother is presently wearing a red dress (although there is plenty to be puzzled by if one looks); what puzzles us is this mechanism of *projection*.

Giving it a name is not explaining it, but only calling attention to it. This is what we badly need a 'model' for. Later I will describe one very idealized model that 'works' at least for the semantical abilities of a 'rational' *hearer*. (The relevance of such models to actual human behaviour is here, as elsewhere, moot. But they are often the best we can do today, and they are certainly better than nothing.) (c) Refusing to apply a sentence in a paradigmatic case may not be deviant. For there may be a kind of 'resonance' in the system of projections whereby the occurrence of some complicated discourse (controlled by projections) may lead one to withdraw a claim that one made, even if the claim was made in the presence of an 'external' situation that seemed paradigmatic for that kind of claim. The analogue in the philosophy of science is abandoning an observational report in order to preserve an entire theory. (d) There is no reason to suppose that there need be paradigmatic cases (or 'criteria') in connection with grammatically complex sentences. This last point is obviously related to our discussion of Malcolm's attack on the work of Dement and Kleitman.

Moreover, it is not only grammatically complex sentences whose use is determined by processsses of inductive projection. Some grammatically simple sentences are under no strong 'reality controls' (contrast 'God is with us.' and 'George is with us.'); and even sentences that have paradigmatic uses have also non-paradigmatic ones. For instance, 'She is wearing a red dress' is deviant if the context is people in the room and if there is no female in the room; but there is nothing that could make it *situationally* inappropriate if the discussion concerns absent persons: it could only be discourse-analytically inappropriate, in the light of what has or has not been said before. (Recall that 'situationally inappropriate' is here being used as a term of art.)

I wish now to consider two closely related models that give some understanding of the processes we have called 'projection'. (The term is due to Ziff: the matters discussed above in connection with paradigmatic cases are gone into in detail in *Semantic Analysis*.)

The first of these models concerns mainly the semantic abilities of the *speaker* and is extracted from Reichenbach's book *Experience and Prediction*. Like the other model to be discussed, it is restricted to quasi-scientific language (discourse consisting of successive *assertions*), and abstracts from many of the features of even such language. But such radical over-simplification is necessary if we are to get started at all, and needs no apology at this stage. (An interesting question which is raised by such models is this: to what extent can the various other 'speech acts', e.g. asking questions, giving commands, be 'projected' from assertion? More precisely, can the semantic regularities associated with interrogatives, imperatives, etc., be systematically generated from the regularities associated with declaratives?)

Reichenbach's model starts in assuming the existence of a class of sentences (observation or 'basic' sentences) whose use is fixed by criteria: so that, in a paradigmatic situation, an observer can be certain that he is correct in uttering such a sentence. (However, Reichenbach, unlike Malcolm, regards this as a *false* assumption, which is made only to simplify the discussion in Part I of *Experience and Prediction*. Later he considers the problem we mentioned above, that it is sometimes desirable to revise such sentences in order to preserve theories.) Such a sentence might be: 'There is a black crow in the region R at time t!' Secondly, the speaker is assumed to have internalized a system of rules of deductive and inductive inference. He may be visualized, for our present purposes, as a computing machine that computes 'weights' for sentences, subject to certain restrictions (e.g. the axioms of the probability calculus). Let us suppose that this 'speaker' utters sentences whose weight exceeds a certain critical number. Then his behaviour will have certain interesting properties. For example, if he has seen many black crows and no white ones he will say, 'All crows are black.' And if he subsequently sees a white crow, he will say, 'I was wrong: some crows are not black.' In this sense he will use the word 'all' correctly – yet he did not learn this from 'paradigmatic cases'! So that he is already making linguistic 'projections'. Notice that this model is based upon the *negation* of one of Malcolm's central assumptions: for the model assumes that reasoning ability (the ability to draw inductive inferences) and semantical ability (the ability to use sentences 'intelligibly') cannot be sharply separated.

A more interesting case (discussed by Reichenbach) is this: such a speaker sees a great many trees and shadows. He comes to assign a high 'weight' to the generalization that every tree shadow stands in a certain spatial relation to a tree. Now he sees a tree shadow; but he is so situated that he cannot see whether there is a tree in the appropriate place or not. (His system of inductive logic must be so constructed that such cases – cases in which he is not in a position to confirm or disconfirm a statement, because he cannot see the region R referred to in the statement – are distinguished from falsifying cases.) So he *deduces* from the generalization he has 'accepted', together with the observational statement that there is a tree shadow, the new statement that there is a tree in a certain place (which he is not observing), say, 'There's a tree over my left shoulder'. Nagel, in a well-known review of Reichenbach's book, rejected this type of inference as presupposing the existence of unobserved things (Nagel, 1954). But this criticism misses the point:

Reichenbach was not producing an argument to convince the sceptic who doubts even the existence of unobserved places and times, but was showing how inferences could be drawn to specific statements about unobserved objects within the normal conceptual system of, say, an infinite four dimensional world. Also, and this is what interests us, he was observing how, at the same time, the positivist's problem of 'reducing' such statements to statements about observables simply did not exist: in learning to conclude inductively to such statements and to their negations we have learned to use, or even, if you like, to 'understand' them, and no further reduction is necessary or desirable.

Finally, in an extremely interesting section on 'illata' (terms like 'gene', 'electron', 'molecule') Reichenbach argues for the extremely unorthodox view that inferences to these entities are normal inductive inferences subject to Bayes Theorem. In particular, he requires that the theories involved have some 'antecedent probability' on the basis of cross-inductions from other areas. I believe that this account fits the history of science much better than the 'Popperian' account according to which, so to speak, a theory needs to be antecedently *im*probable rather than probable (which is not to deny that new theories have *consequences* which are antecedently impossible, considered 'in the abstract'). Discussion of this, however, would take us away from our topic.

Notice one important limitation of Reichenbach's model: it gives no hint as to why a speaker says something rather than nothing, or why he says one thing rather than another. (Reichenbach speaks of 'relevance to behaviour', but this is left unexplained.) Also, if we have our 'speaker' say anything that he 'accepts', *in any order*, we sacrifice discourse-analytic coherence. On the other hand, we can complicate Reichenbach's model in a natural way so as to introduce a notion of coherence: namely, we require that any 'closed' discourse by one speaker (e.g. a publication) must be inductively coherent and that the sections should be inductively relevant to one another. This is still much too weak; but, interestingly, I have been informed that Harris believes that discourse-analytic criteria will exclude at least strong cases of inductive incoherence.

The second model that I shall present will be called 'the Carnap model'. It has not ever been presented by Carnap, but its relation to Carnap's work will become clear as I proceed. This will be a model for the semantic abilities of the *hearer* rather than the speaker. We will idealize by assuming a hearer who believes everything that he is told. This part of the idealization is inessential and could be easily 'fixed up'; but it will save our time not to. The remainder of the idealization is, unfortunately, essential: we shall have to assume an ideally 'rational' hearer, both in the economist's sense (one whose choices are governed by a utility function) and in the deductive and inductive logician's sense.

Our 'unnatural language' will, this time, be a system of the sort studied by Carnap (cf. Carnap, 1950). The language will have a set of 'state descriptions' and there will be an inductive definition of the notion of 'range', where the 'range' of any sentence is the class of state-descriptions in which that sentence *holds*. Our 'hearer' will be assumed to consist, in part, of a computer which determines, with the aid of the inductive definition, what the range of an arbitrary sentence of the 'unnatural language' is.

'Ah ha!' one says to oneself at this point: this is the very first model we have seen in which the grammatical structure of the language is fully exploited in semantical analysis. This may not be obvious from these brief remarks: but a glance at the inductive definition of 'range' in any single case will establish the point: the 'computer' just alluded to will have to have an 'internalized grammar' of the entire 'unnatural language'. That is, it will have the ability to tell grammatical sentences (sentences for which it can compute a 'range') from ungrammatical sentences (sentences for which it is impossible to compute a range, using the rules). Actually, the dependence of the inductive definition of range on grammar is far more extensive than this: but the easiest way to convince oneself of this is to examine such a definition.

Secondly, our 'hearer' will be characterized by two measure functions over state-descriptions: one a utility function, which measures his preference for one state-description over another, and the second a 'subjective probability metric', which determines his absolute and conditional probability assignments in accordance with the usual theorems of the probability calculus. We will require that the probability metric be 'inductive' in Carnap's sense: intuitively, this means that it must permit one to 'learn from experience' (carry out inductive inferences, at least of a simple kind).

What happens now is this: one says things to this 'hearer'; he believes those things; and this modifies his behaviour. How does it modify his behaviour? Since this is what Carnap would call a 'logical' theory of an ideal hearer, as opposed to a 'psychological' theory of an actual hearer, let our 'hearer' obey Carnap's recommendation: he will always act so as to maximize his estimated utility. Then his behaviour is completely determined: if we know the choices open to him, we can in principle say how he will behave in any situation, and how his behaviour would have been different if one had (a) said something different to him, or (b) if he had construed the words differently (assigned a different range).

This model, it turns out, has both a pessimistic and an optimistic aspect. The cause for pessimism (if things are as 'bad' as this model suggests) is this: one cannot characterize the meanings of utterances in terms of the behaviour of *hearers* at all! For saying anything to a hearer may cause him to do anything, if he has a 'bizarre' utility function.† Of course, it may be that in certain respects human utility functions do not differ very much, and that for this reason some utterances (e.g. 'Fire!') produce fairly predictable behavior in hearers who believe them. However, by and large, I think that pessimism probably *is* warranted as far as the programme of characterizing the meanings of utterances in terms of extra-linguistic behavior of hearers is concerned.

The optimistic aspect is this: that the study of the semantical abilities of hearers falls rather naturally into three parts. The third part, the study of utility functions, seems best excluded from *linguistic* theory altogether. (Its presence, however, is the reason that a 'model' of a language for speaker or hearer is such an impossible thing: language skills are the only skills that cannot be modelled without modelling a whole human being.) The first part, the inductive definition of 'range', corresponds naturally to grammar and to semantics in the narrow sense (paraphrasing, synonymy relations, etc.). The middle part, inductive logic, is the most intriguing: it may not be too hard to do, at least in a simplified form, and it may shed some light on the abilities of both speaker and hearer.

What do these last two models have in common? They are both strongly consonant with the idea that inductive coherence may be a part of linguistic coherence (or at least the absence of striking inductive *incoherence* may be). They both imply that language skills are skills of something that can 'do' inductive and deductive logic: it is hopeless to try to separate reasoning ability completely from language-using ability. Above all, they both suggest that it is quite possible to have sentences in the language whose 'meaning' (or, better, whose role in the lives of the speakers and hearers) is determined by a network of inductive connections with other sentences. In short, they are hopelessly *incompatible* with the Malcolmese idea of language as something which is criterion-governed in a sentence-by-sentence fashion. Although I am sure that these models are terribly over-simplified in a host of ways, it seems to me virtually certain that these three features will also be features of any 'better' model that may be proposed.

† This point was made in Geach's *Mental Acts*. Geach's example was, roughly, that of saying 'It's going to rain' to someone. If he believes you, he may take a raincoat – if he has a 'normal' utility function – or he may take off his coat – if he wants to get wet!

16

Brains and behavior*

Once upon a time there was a tough-minded philosopher who said, 'What is all this talk about "minds", "ideas", and "sensations"? Really – and I mean *really* in the real world – there is nothing to these so-called "mental" events and entities but certain processes in our all-too-material heads.'

And once upon a time there was a philosopher who retorted, 'What a masterpiece of confusion! Even if, say, *pain* were perfectly correlated with any particular event in my brain (which I doubt) that event would obviously have certain properties – say, a certain numerical intensity measured in volts – which it would be *senseless* to ascribe to the feeling of pain. Thus, it is *two* things that are correlated, not *one* – and to call *two* things *one* thing is worse than being mistaken; it is utter contradiction.'

For a long time dualism and materialism appeared to exhaust the alternatives. Compromises were attempted ('double aspect' theories), but they never won many converts and practically no one found them intelligible. Then, in the mid-1930s, a seeming third possibility was discovered. This third possibility has been called *logical behaviorism*. To state the nature of this third possibility briefly, it is necessary to recall the treatment of the natural numbers (i.e. zero, one, two, three...) in modern logic. Numbers are identified with *sets*, in various ways, depending on which authority one follows. For instance, Whitehead and Russell identified zero with the set of all empty sets, one with the set of all one-membered sets, two with the set of all two-membered sets, three with the set of all three-membered sets, and so on. (This has the appearance of circularity, but they were able to dispel this appearance by defining 'one-membered set', 'two-membered set', 'three-membered set', etc., without using 'one', 'two', 'three', etc.) In short, numbers are treated as *logical constructions out of sets*. The number theorist is doing set theory without knowing it, according to this interpretation.

What was novel about this was the idea of getting rid of certain philosophically unwanted or embarrassing entities (numbers) without

* First published in R. Butler (ed.) *Analytical Philosophy Second Series* (Oxford, 1963). Reprinted by permission of Basil Blackwell & Mott.

failing to do justice to the appropriate body of discourse (number theory) by treating the entities in question as logical constructions. Russell was quick to hold up this success as a model to all future philosophers. And certain of those future philosophers – the Vienna positivists, in their 'physicalist' phase (about 1930) – took Russell's advice so seriously as to produce the doctrine that we are calling *logical behaviorism* – the doctrine that, just as numbers are (allegedly) logical constructions out of *sets*, so *mental events* are logical constructions out of actual and possible *behavior events*.

In the set theoretic case, the 'reduction' of number theory to the appropriate part of set theory was carried out in detail and with indisputable technical success. One may dispute the philosophical significance of the reduction, but one knows exactly what one is talking about when one disputes it. In the mind-body case, the reduction was never carried out in even *one* possible way, so that it is not possible to be clear on just *how* mental entities or events are to be (identified with) logical constructions out of behavior events. But broadly speaking, it is clear what the view implies: it implies that all talk about mental events is translatable into talk about actual or potential overt behavior.

It is easy to see in what way this view differs from both dualism and classical materialism. The logical behaviorist agrees with the dualist that what goes on in our brains has no connection whatsoever with what we *mean* when we say that someone is in pain. He can even take over the dualist's entire stock of arguments against the materialist position. Yet, at the same time, he can be as 'tough-minded' as the materialist in denying that ordinary talk of 'pains', 'thoughts', and 'feelings' involves reference to 'Mind' as a Cartesian substance.

Thus it is not surprising that logical behaviorism attracted enormous attention – both pro and con – during the next thirty years. Without doubt, this alternative proved to be a fruitful one to inject into the debate. Here, however, my intention is not to talk about the fruitfulness of the investigations to which logical behaviorism has led, but to see if there was any upshot to those investigations. Can we, after thirty years, say anything about the rightness or wrongness of logical behaviorism? Or must we say that a third alternative has been added to the old two; that we cannot decide between three any more easily than we could decide between two; and that our discussion is thus half as difficult again as it was before?

One conclusion emerged very quickly from the discussion pro and con logical behaviorism: that the extreme thesis of logical behaviorism, as we just stated it (that all talk about 'mental events' is translatable into talk about overt behavior) is false. But, in a sense, this is not very interesting. An extreme thesis may be false, although there is 'something to' the way of thinking that it represents. And the more interesting question is this: what, if anything, can be 'saved' of the way of thinking that logical behaviorism represents?

In the last thirty years, the original extreme thesis of logical behaviorism has gradually been weakened to something like this:

(1) That there exist entailments between mind-statements and behavior-statements; entailments that are not, perhaps, analytic in the way in which 'All bachelors are unmarried' is analytic, but that nevertheless follow (in some sense) from the meanings of mind words. I shall call these *analytic entailments*.

(2) That these entailments may not provide an actual *translation* of 'mind talk' into 'behavior talk' (this 'talk' talk was introduced by Gilbert Ryle in his *Concept of Mind*), but that this is true for such superficial reasons as the greater ambiguity of mind talk, as compared with the relatively greater specificity of overt behavior talk.

I believe that, although no philosopher would to-day subscribe to the older version of behaviorism, a great many philosophers† would accept these two points, while admitting the unsatisfactory imprecision of the present statement of both of them. If these philosophers are right, then there is much work to be done (e.g. the notion of 'analyticity' has to be made clear), but the direction of work is laid out for us for some time to come.

I wish that I could share this happy point of view – if only for the comforting conclusion that first-rate philosophical research, continued for some time, will eventually lead to a solution to the mind-body problem which is independent of troublesome empirical facts about brains, central causation of behavior, evidence for and against non-physical causation of at least some behavior, and the soundness or unsoundness of psychical research and parapsychology. But the fact is that I come to bury logical behaviorism, not to praise it. I feel that the time has come for us to admit that logical behaviorism is a mistake, and that even the weakened forms of the logical behaviorist doctrine are incorrect. I cannot hope to establish this in so short a paper as this one‡; but I hope to expose for your inspection at least the main lines of my thinking.

---

† E.g. these two points are fairly explicitly stated in Strawson's *Individuals*. Strawson has told me that he no longer subscribes to point (1), however.

‡ An attempted fourth alternative – i.e. an alternative to dualism, materialism, *and* behaviorism – is sketched in chapter 20. This fourth alternative is materialistic in the wide sense of being compatible with the view that organisms, including human beings, are physical systems consisting of elementary particles and obeying the laws of physics, but does not require that such 'states' as *pain* and *preference* be defined in a way which makes reference to either overt behavior or physical-chemical constitution.

Logical behaviorism

The logical behaviorist usually begins by pointing out what is perfectly true, that such words as 'pain' ('pain' will henceforth be our stock example of a mind word) are not taught by reference to standard examples in the way in which such words as 'red' are. One can point to a standard red thing, but one cannot point to a standard pain (that is, except by pointing to some piece of *behavior*) and say: 'Compare the feeling you are having with this one (say, Jones's feeling at time t_1). If the two feelings have the identical *quality*, then your feeling is legitimately called a feeling of *pain*.' The difficulty, of course, is that I cannot have Jones's feeling at time t_1 – unless I *am* Jones, and the time *is* t_1.

From this simple observation, certain things follow. For example, the account according to which the *intension* of the word 'pain' is a certain *quality* which 'I know from my own case' must be wrong. But this is not to refute dualism, since the dualist need not maintain that I know the intension of the English word 'pain' from my own case, but only that I experience the referent of the word.

What then is the intension of 'pain'? I am inclined to say that 'pain' is a cluster-concept. That is, the application of the word 'pain' is controlled by a whole cluster of criteria, *all of which can be regarded as synthetic*.† As a consequence, there is no satisfactory way of answering the question 'What does "pain" mean?' except by giving an exact synonym (e.g. 'Schmerz'); but there are a million and one different ways of saying what pain *is*. One can, for example, say that pain is that feeling which is normally evinced by saying 'ouch', or by wincing, or in a variety of other ways (or often not evinced at all).

All this is compatible with logical behaviorism. The logical behaviorist

The idea, briefly, is that predicates which apply to a system by virtue of its *functional organization* have just this characteristic: a given functional organization (e.g. a given inductive logic, a given rational preference function) may realize itself in almost any kind of overt behavior, depending upon the circumstances, and is capable of being 'built into' structures of many different logically possible physical (or even metaphysical) constitutions. Thus the statement that a creature prefers A to B does not tell us whether the creature has a carbon chemistry, or a silicon chemistry, or is even a disembodied mind, nor does it tell us how the creature would behave under any circumstances specifiable without reference to the creature's other preferences and beliefs, but it does not thereby become something 'mysterious'.

† I mean not only that *each* criterion can be regarded as synthetic, but also that the cluster is *collectively* synthetic, in the sense that we are free in certain cases to say (for reason of inductive simplicity and theoretical economy) that the term applies although the whole cluster is missing. This is completely compatible with saying that the cluster serves to fix the meaning of the word. The point is that when we specify something by a cluster of indicators we assume that people will *use their brains*. That criteria may be over-ridden when good sense demands is the sort of thing we may regard as a 'convention associated with discourse' (Grice) rather than as something to be stipulated in connection with the individual words.

would reply: 'Exactly. "Pain" is a cluster-concept – that is to say, it stands for *a cluster of phenomena*.' But that is not what I mean. Let us look at another kind of cluster-concept (cluster-concepts, of course, are not a homogeneous class): names of diseases.

We observe that, when a virus origin was discovered for polio, doctors said that certain cases in which all the symptoms of polio had been present, but in which the virus had been absent, had turned out not to be cases of polio at all. Similarly, if a virus should be discovered which normally (almost invariably) is the cause of what we presently call 'multiple sclerosis', the hypothesis that this virus is *the* cause of multiple sclerosis would not be falsified if, in some few exceptional circumstances, it was possible to have all the symptoms of multiple sclerosis for some other combination of reasons, or if this virus caused symptoms not presently recognized as symptoms of multiple sclerosis in some cases. These facts would certainly lead the lexicographer to *reject* the view that 'multiple sclerosis' means 'the simultaneous presence of such and such symptoms'. Rather he would say that 'multiple sclerosis' means 'that disease which is normally responsible for some or all of the following symptoms....'

Of course, he does not have to say this. Some philosophers would prefer to say that 'polio' *used to mean* 'the simultaneous presence of such-and-such symptoms'. And they would say that the *decision* to accept the presence or absence of a virus as a criterion for the presence or absence of polio represented a *change of meaning*. But this runs strongly counter to our common sense. For example, doctors used to say 'I believe polio is caused by a virus'. On the 'change of meaning' account, those doctors were *wrong*, not *right*. Polio, *as the word was then used*, was not always caused by a virus; it is only what *we* call polio that is always caused by a virus. And if a doctor ever said (and many did) 'I believe this may not be a case of polio', knowing that all of the textbook symptoms were present, that doctor must have been contradicting himself (even if we, to-day, would say that he was right) or, perhaps, 'making a disguised linguistic proposal'. Also, this account runs counter to good linguistic methodology. The definition we proposed a paragraph back – 'multiple sclerosis' means 'the disease that is normally *responsible* for the following symptoms...' – has an exact analogue in the case of polio. This kind of definition leaves open the question whether there is a single cause or several. It is consonant with such a definition to speak of 'discovering a single origin for polio (or two or three or four)', to speak of 'discovering X did not have polio' (although he exhibited all the symptoms of polio), and to speak of 'discovering X did have polio' (although he exhibited *none* of the 'textbook symptoms'). And, finally, such a definition does not require us to say that any 'change of meaning' took place. Thus, this is surely the definition that a good lexicographer would adopt. But this entails *rejecting* the 'change of meaning' account as a philosopher's invention (cf. my preceding chapter).

Accepting that this is the correct account of the names of diseases, what follows? There *may* be analytic entailments connecting diseases and symptoms (although I shall argue against this). For example, it looks plausible to say that:

'Normally people who have multiple sclerosis have some or all of the following symptoms...' is a necessary ('analytic') truth. But it does not follow that 'disease talk' is translatable into 'symptom talk'. Rather the contrary follows (as is already indicated by the presence of the word 'normally'): statements about multiple sclerosis are not translatable into statements about the symptoms of multiple sclerosis, not because disease talk is 'systematically ambiguous' and symptom talk is 'specific', but because *causes* are not logical constructions out of their *effects*.

In analogy with the foregoing, both the dualist and the materialist would want to argue that, although the meaning of 'pain' may be *explained* by reference to overt behavior, what we mean by 'pain' is not the presence of a cluster of responses, but rather the presence of an event or condition that normally causes those responses. (Of course the pain is not the whole cause of the pain behavior, but only a suitably invariant part of that cause,† but, similarly, the virus-caused tissue damage is not the whole cause of the individual symptoms of polio in some individual case, but a suitably invariant part of the cause.) And they would want to argue further, that even if it *were* a necessary truth that

'Normally, when one says "ouch" one has a pain'

or a necessary truth that

'Normally, when one has a pain one says "ouch"'

this would be an interesting observation about what 'pain' means, but it would shed no metaphysical light on what pain *is* (or *isn't*). And it certainly would not follow that 'pain talk' is translatable into 'response talk', or that the failure of translatability is only a matter of the 'systematic ambiguity' of pain talk as opposed to the 'specificity' of response talk: quite the contrary. Just as before, *causes* (pains) are *not* logical constructions out of their *effects* (behavior).

The traditional dualist would, however, want to go farther, and deny the

---

† Of course, 'the cause' is a highly ambiguous phrase. Even if it is correct in certain contexts to say that certain events in the brain are 'the cause' of my pain behavior, it does *not* follow (as has sometimes been suggested) that my pain must be 'identical' with these neural events.

necessity of the two propositions just listed. Moreover, the traditional dualist is right: there is nothing self-contradictory, as we shall see below, in talking of hypothetical worlds in which there are pains but *no* pain behavior.

The analogy with names of diseases is still preserved at this point. Suppose I identify multiple sclerosis as the disease that normally produces certain symptoms. If it later turns out that a certain virus is the cause of multiple sclerosis, using this newly discovered criterion I may then go on to find out that multiple sclerosis has quite different symptoms when, say, the average temperature is lower. I can then perfectly well talk of a hypothetical world (with lower temperature levels) in which multiple sclerosis does *not* normally produce the usual symptoms. It is true that if the *words* 'multiple sclerosis' are used in any world in such a way that the above lexical definition is a good one, *then* many victims of the disease must have had some or all of the following symptoms... And in the same way it is true that *if* the explanation suggested of the word 'pain' is a good one (i.e. 'pain is the feeling that is normally being evinced when someone says "ouch", or winces, or screams, etc.'), *then* persons in pain must have at some time winced or screamed or said 'ouch' – but this does *not* imply that 'if someone ever had a pain, then someone must at some time have winced or screamed or said "ouch".' To conclude this would be to confuse preconditions for *talking* about pain as *we* talk about pain with preconditions for the existence of pain.

The analogy we have been developing is not an identity: linguistically speaking, mind words and names of diseases are different in a great many respects. In particular, *first person uses* are very different: a man may have a severe case of polio and not know it, even if he knows the word 'polio', but one cannot have a severe pain and not know it. At first blush, this may look like a point in favor of logical behaviorism. The logical behaviorist may say: it is because the premises 'John says he has a pain', 'John knows English', and 'John is speaking in all sincerity',† *entail* 'John has a pain', that pain reports have this sort of special status. But even if this is right, it does not follow that logical behaviorism is correct unless *sincerity* is a 'logical construction out of overt behavior'! A far more reasonable account is this: one can have a 'pink elephant hallucination', but one cannot have a 'pain hallucination', or an 'absence of pain hallucination', simply because any situation that a person cannot discriminate from a situation in which he himself has a pain *counts* as a situation in which he has a pain, whereas a situation that a person cannot distinguish from one in which a pink elephant is present does not necessarily *count* as the presence of a pink elephant.

† This is suggested in Wittgenstein's *Philosophical Investigations*.

To sum up: I believe that pains are not clusters of responses, but that they are (normally, in our experience to date) the causes of certain clusters of responses. Moreover, although this is an empirical fact, it underlies the possibility of talking about pains in the particular way in which we do. However, it does not rule out in any way the possibility of worlds in which (owing to a difference in the environmental and hereditary conditions) pains are not responsible for the usual responses, or even are not responsible for any responses at all.

Let us now engage in a little science fiction. Let us try to describe some worlds in which pains are related to responses (and also to causes) in quite a different way than they are in our world.

If we confine our attention to nonverbal responses by full grown persons, for a start, then matters are easy. Imagine a community of 'super-spartans' or 'super-stoics' – a community in which the adults have the ability to successfully suppress *all* involuntary pain behavior. They may, on occasion, admit that they feel pain, but always in pleasant well-modulated voices – even if they are undergoing the agonies of the damned. They do *not* wince, scream, flinch, sob, grit their teeth, clench their fists, exhibit beads of sweat, or otherwise act like people in pain or people suppressing the unconditioned responses associated with pain. However, they do feel pain, and they dislike it (just as we do). They even admit that it takes a great effort of will to behave as they do. It is only that they have what they regard as important ideological reasons for behaving as they do, and they have, through years of training, learned to live up to their own exacting standards.

It may be contended that children and not fully mature members of this community will exhibit, to varying degrees, normal unconditioned pain behavior, and that this is all that is necessary for the ascription of pain. On this view, the *sine qua non* for significant ascription of pain to a species is that its immature members should exhibit unconditioned pain responses.

One might well stop to ask whether this statement has even a clear meaning. Supposing that there are Martians: do we have any criterion for something being an 'unconditioned pain response' for a Martian? Other things being equal, one *avoids* things with which one has had painful experiences: this would suggest that *avoidance* behavior might be looked for as a universal unconditioned pain response. However, even if this were true, it would hardly be specific enough, since avoidance can also be an unconditioned response to many things that we do not associate with pain – to things that disgust us, or frighten us, or even merely bore us.

Let us put these difficulties aside, and see if we can devise an imaginary world in which there are not, even by lenient standards, any uncon-ditioned pain responses. Specifically, let us take our 'super-spartans', and let us suppose that after millions of years they begin to have children who are born fully acculturated. They are born speaking the adult language, knowing the multiplication table, having opinions on political issues, and *inter alia* sharing the dominant spartan beliefs about the importance of not evincing pain (except by way of verbal report, and even that in a tone of voice that suggests indifference). Then there would not *be* any 'unconditioned pain responses' in this community (although there might be unconditioned *desires* to make certain responses – desires which were, however, always suppressed by an effort of will). Yet there is a clear absurdity to the position that one cannot ascribe to these people a capacity for feeling pain.

To make this absurdity evident, let us imagine that we succeed in converting an adult 'super-spartan' to *our* ideology. Let us suppose that he begins to evince pain in the normal way. Yet he reports that the pains he is feeling are not more *intense* than are the ones he experienced prior to conversion – indeed, he may say that giving expression to them makes them *less* intense. In this case, the logical behaviorist would have to say that, through the medium of this one member, we had demon-strated the existence of unconditioned pain responses in the whole species, and hence that ascription of pain to the species is 'logically proper'. But this is to say that had this one man never lived, and had it been possible to demonstrate only indirectly (via the use of *theories*) that these beings feel pain, then pain ascriptions *would* have been improper.

We have so far been constructing worlds in which the relation of pain to its nonverbal *effects* is altered. What about the relation of pain to *causes*? This is even more easy for the imagination to modify. Can one not imagine a species who feel pain only when a magnetic field is present (although the magnetic field causes no detectable damage to their bodies or nervous systems)? If we now let the members of such a species become converts *to* 'super-spartanism', we can depict to our-selves a world in which pains, in our sense, are clearly present, but in which they have neither the normal causes nor the normal effects (apart from verbal reports).

What about verbal reports? Some behaviorists have taken these as the characteristic form of pain behavior. Of course, there is a difficulty here: If 'I am in pain' means 'I am disposed to utter this kind of verbal report' (to put matters crudely), then how do we tell that any particular report is 'this kind of verbal report'? The usual answer is in terms of the unconditioned pain responses and their assumed supplantation by the verbal reports in question. However, we have seen that there are no *logical* reasons for the existence of unconditioned pain responses in all species capable of feeling pain (there *may* be logical reasons for the existence of avoidance desires, but avoidance *desires* are not themselves behavior any more than pains are).

Once again, let us be charitable to the extent of waiving the first difficulty that comes to mind, and let us undertake the task of trying to imagine a world in which there are not even pain *reports*. I will call this world the 'X-world'. In the X-world we have to deal with 'super-super-spartans'. These have been super-spartans for so long, that they have begun to suppress even *talk* of pain. Of course, each individual X-worlder may have his private way of thinking about pain. He may even have the *word* 'pain' (as before, I assume that these beings are born fully acculturated). He may *think* to himself: 'This pain is intolerable. If it goes on one minute longer I shall scream. Oh No! I mustn't do that! That would disgrace my whole family...' But X-worlders do not even admit to *having* pains. They pretend not to know either the word or the phenomenon to which it refers. In short, if pains are 'logical constructs out of behavior', then our X-worlders behave so as not to have pains! – Only, of course, they do have pains, and they know perfectly well that they have pains.

If this last fantasy is not, in some disguised way, self-contradictory, then logical behaviorism is simply a mistake. Not only is the second thesis of logical behaviorism – the existence of a near-translation of pain talk into behavior talk – false, but so is even the first thesis – the existence of 'analytic entailments'. Pains *are* responsible for certain kinds of behavior – but only in the context of our beliefs, desires, ideological attitudes, and so forth. From the statement 'X has a pain' by itself *no* behavioral statement follows – not even a behavioral statement with a 'normally' or a 'probably' in it.

In our concluding section we shall consider the logical behaviorist's stock of counter-moves to this sort of argument. If the logical behaviorist's positive views are inadequate owing to an oversimplified view of the nature of cluster words – amounting, in some instances, to an open denial that it is *possible* to have a word governed by a cluster of indicators, *all* of which are synthetic – his negative views are inadequate owing to an oversimplified view of empirical reasoning. It is unfortunately characteristic of modern philosophy that its problems should overlap three different areas – to speak roughly, the areas of linguistics, logic, and 'theory of theories' (scientific methodology) – and that many of its practitioners should try to get by with an inadequate knowledge of at least two out of the three.

334

Some behaviorist arguments

We have been talking of '*X*-worlders' and 'super-spartans'. No one denies that, in *some* sense of the term, such fantasies are 'intelligible'. But 'intelligibility' can be a superficial thing. A fantasy may be 'intelligible', at least at the level of 'surface grammar', although we may come to see, on thinking about it for a while, that some absurdity is involved. Consider, for example, the supposition that last night, just on the stroke of midnight, all distances were instantaneously doubled. Of course, we did not notice the change, for *we* ourselves also doubled in size! This story may seem intelligible to us at first blush, at least as an amusing possibility. On reflection, however, we come to see that logical contradiction is involved. For 'length' means nothing more nor less than a relation to a standard, and it is a contradiction to maintain that the length of everything doubled, while the relations to the standards remained unchanged.

What I have just said (speaking as a logical behaviorist might speak) is false, but not totally so. It is false (or at least the last part is false), because 'length' does *not* mean 'relation to a standard'. If it did (assuming a 'standard' has to be a macroscopic material object, or anyway a material object), it would make no sense to speak of distances in a world in which there were only gravitational and electromagnetic fields, but no material objects. Also, it would make no sense to speak of the *standard* (whatever it might be) as having changed its length. Consequences so counter-intuitive have led many physicists (and even a few philosophers of physics) to view 'length' not as something operationally defined, but as a theoretical magnitude (like electrical charge), which can be measured in a virtual infinity of ways, but which is not explicitly and exactly definable in terms of any of the ways of measuring it. Some of these physicists – the 'unified field' theorists – would even say that, far from it being the case that 'length' (and hence 'space') depends on the existence of suitably related material bodies, material bodies are best viewed as local variations in the curvature of space – that is to say, local variations in the intensity of a certain magnitude (the tensor g_{ik}), one aspect of which we experience as 'length'.

Again, it is far from true that the hypothesis 'last night, on the stroke of midnight, everything doubled in length' has no testable consequences. For example, if last night everything did double in length, and the velocity of light did not also double, then this morning we would have experienced an apparent halving of the speed of light. Moreover, if g (the gravitational constant) did not double, then we would have experienced an apparent halving in the intensity of the gravitational field.

And if h (Planck's constant) did not change, then... In short, our world would have been bewilderingly different. And if we could survive at all, under so drastically altered conditions, no doubt some clever physicist would figure out what had happened.

I have gone into such detail just to make the point that in philosophy things are rarely so simple as they seem. The 'doubling universe' is a favorite classroom example of a 'pseudo-hypothesis' – yet it is the worst possible example if a 'clear case' is desired. In the first place, what is desired is a hypothesis with no testable consequences – yet *this* hypothesis, as it is always stated, *does* have testable consequences (perhaps some more complex hypothesis does not; but then we have to see this more complex hypothesis stated before we can be expected to discuss it). In the second place, the usual argument for the absurdity of this hypothesis rests on a simplistic theory of the meaning of 'length' – and a full discussion of *that* situation is hardly possible without bringing in considerations from unified field theory and quantum mechanics (the latter comes in connection with the notion of a 'material standard'). But, the example aside, one can hardly challenge the point that a superficially coherent story may contain a hidden absurdity.

Or can one? Of course, a superficially coherent story may contain a hidden contradiction, but the whole point of the logical behaviorist's sneering reference to 'surface grammar' is that *linguistic coherence, meaningfulness of the individual terms*, and *logical consistency*, do not by themselves guarantee freedom from another kind of absurdity – there are 'depth absurdities' which can only be detected by more powerful techniques. It is fair to say that to-day, after thirty years of this sort of talk, we lack both a single *convincing* example of such a depth absurdity, and a technique of detection (or alleged technique of detection) which does not reduce to 'untestable, *therefore* nonsense'.

To come to the case at hand: the logical behaviorist is likely to say that our hypothesis about 'X-worlders' is untestable in principle (if there *were* 'X-worlders', by hypothesis we couldn't distinguish them from people who really didn't know what pain is); and *therefore* meaningless (apart from a certain 'surface significance' which is of no real interest). If the logical behaviorist has learned a little from 'ordinary language philosophy', he is likely to shy away from saying 'untestable, therefore *meaningless*', but he is still likely to say or at least think: 'untestable, therefore in *some* sense absurd'. I shall try to meet this 'argument' *not* by challenging the premiss, be it overt or covert, that 'untestable synthetic statement' is some kind of contradiction in terms (although I believe that premiss to be mistaken), but simply by showing that, on any but the most naive view of testability, our hypothesis *is* testable.

336

Of course, I could not do this if it were true that 'by hypothesis, we couldn't distinguish X-worlders from people who *really* didn't know what pain is'. But that isn't true – at any rate, it isn't true 'by hypothesis'. What is true by hypothesis is that we couldn't distinguish X-worlders from people who really didn't know what pain is *on the basis of overt behavior alone*. But that still leaves many other ways in which we might determine what is going on 'inside' the X-worlders – in both the figurative and literal sense of 'inside'. For example, we might examine their *brains*.

It is a fact that when pain impulses are 'received' in the brain, suitable electrical detecting instruments record a characteristic 'spike' pattern. Let us express this briefly (and too simply) by saying that 'brain spikes' are one-to-one correlated with experiences of pain. If our X-worlders belong to the human species, then we can verify that they do feel pains, notwithstanding their claim that they don't have any idea what pain is, by applying our electrical instruments and detecting the tell-tale 'brain spikes'.

This reply to the logical behaviorist is far too simple to be convincing. 'It is true,' the logical behaviorist will object, 'that experiences of pain are one-to-one correlated with "brain spikes" in the case of normal human beings. But you don't know that the X-worlders are normal human beings, in this sense – in fact, you have every reason to suppose that they are *not* normal human beings'. This reply shows that no *mere* correlation, however carefully verified in the case of normal human beings can be used to verify ascriptions of pain to X-worlders. Fortunately, we do not have to suppose that our knowledge will always be restricted to mere correlations, like the pain-'brain spike' correlation. At a more advanced level, considerations of simplicity and coherence can begin to play a role in a way in which they cannot when only crude observational regularities are available.

Let us suppose that we begin to detect waves of a new kind, emanating from human brains – call them 'V-waves'. Let us suppose we develop a way of 'decoding' V-waves so as to reveal people's unspoken thoughts. And, finally, let us suppose that our 'decoding' technique also works in the case of the V-waves emanating from the brains of X-worlders. How does this correlation differ from the pain-'brain spike' correlation?

Simply in this way: it is reasonable to say that 'spikes' – momentary peaks in the electrical intensity in certain parts of the brain – could have almost any cause. But waves which go over into coherent English (or any other language), under a relatively simple decoding scheme, could not have just any cause. The 'null hypothesis' – that this is just the operation of 'chance' – can be dismissed at once. And if, in the case of human beings, we verify that the decoded waves correspond to what we

337

are in fact thinking, then the hypothesis that this same correlation holds in the case of X-worlders will be assigned an immensely high probability, simply because no other likely explanation readily suggests itself. But 'no other likely explanation readily suggests itself' isn't verification, the logical behaviorist may say. On the contrary. How, for example, have we verified that cadmium lines in the spectrographic analysis of sunlight indicate the presence of cadmium in the sun? Mimicking the logical behaviorist, we might say: 'We have verified that under normal circumstances, cadmium lines only occur when heated cadmium is present. But we don't know that circumstances on the sun are normal in this sense'. If we took this seriously, we would have to *heat cadmium on the sun* before we could say that the regularity upon which we base our spectrographic analysis of sunlight had been verified. In fact, we have verified the regularity under 'normal' circumstances, and we can *show* (deductively) that *if* many other laws, that have also been verified under 'normal' circumstances and *only* under 'normal' circumstances (i.e. never on the surface of the sun), hold on the sun, *then* this regularity holds also under 'abnormal' circumstances. And if someone says, 'But perhaps *none* of the usual laws of physics hold on the sun', we reply that this is like supposing that a random process always produces coherent English. The fact is that the 'signals' (sunlight, radio waves, etc.) which we receive from the sun cohere with a vast body of theory. Perhaps there is some other explanation than that the sun obeys the usual laws of physics; but *no other likely explanation suggests itself.* This sort of reasoning *is* scientific verification; and if it is not reducible to simple Baconian induction – well, then, philosophers must learn to widen their notions of verification to embrace it.

The logical behaviorist might try to account for the decodability of the X-worlders' 'V-waves' into coherent English (or the appropriate natural language) without invoking the absurd 'null hypothesis'. He might suggest, for example, that the 'X-worlders' are having fun at our expense – they are able, say, to produce misleading V-waves at will. If the X-worlders have brains quite unlike ours, this may even have some plausibility. But once again, in an advanced state of knowledge, considerations of coherence and simplicity may quite conceivably 'verify' that this is false. For example, the X-worlders may have brains quite like ours, rather than unlike ours. And we may have built up enough theory to say how the brain of a human being should 'look' if that human being were pretending not to be in pain when he was, in fact, in pain. Now consider what the 'misleading V-waves' story requires: it requires that the X-worlders produce V-waves in quite a different way than we do, without specifying what that different way is. Moreover, it requires that this be the case, although the reverse hypothesis – that X-worlders' brains function *exactly* as human brains do – in fact, that they *are* human brains – fits all the data. Clearly, this story is in serious methodological difficulties, and any other 'counter-explanation' that the logical behaviorist tries to invoke will be in similar difficulties. In short, the logical behaviorist's argument reduces to this: 'You cannot verify "psycho-physical" correlations in the case of X-worlders (or at least, you can't verify ones having to do, directly or indirectly, with *pain*), because, by hypothesis, X-worlders won't tell you (or indicate be- haviorally) when they are in pain'. 'Indirect verification' – verification using theories which have been 'tested' only in the case of human beings – is not verification at all, because X-worlders *may* obey different laws than human beings. And it is not incumbent upon *me* (the logical behaviorist says) to suggest what those laws might be: it is incumbent upon *you* to rule out *all* other explanations. And this is a silly argument. The scientist does not have to rule out all the ridiculous theories that someone *might* suggest; he only has to show that he has ruled out any reasonable alternative theories that one might put forward on the basis of present knowledge.

Granting, then, that we might discover a technique for 'reading' the unspoken thoughts of X-worlders: we would then be in the same posi- tion with respect to the X-worlders as we were with respect to the origi- nal 'super-spartans'. The super-spartans were quite willing to tell us (and each other) about their pains; and we could see that their pain talk was linguistically coherent and situationally appropriate (e.g. a super- spartan will tell you that he feels intense pain when you touch him with a red hot poker). On this basis, we were quite willing to grant that the super-spartans did, indeed, feel pain – all the more readily, since the deviancy in their behavior had a perfectly convincing ideological ex- planation. (Note again the role played here by considerations of co- herence and simplicity). But the X-worlders also 'tell' us (and, perhaps, each other), exactly the same things, albeit *un*willingly (by the medium of the involuntarily produced 'V-waves') Thus we have to say – at least, we have to say as long as the 'V-wave' theory has not broken down – that the X-worlders are what they, in fact, are – just 'super-super-spartans'.

Let us now consider a quite different argument that a logical be- haviorist might use. 'You are assuming,' he might say, 'the following principle:

If someone's brain is in the same state as that of a human being in pain (not just at the moment of the pain, but before and after for a sufficient interval), then he is in pain. Moreover, this principle is one which it would never be reasonable to give up (on your conception of 'methodology'). Thus, you have turned it into a tautology. But observe what turning this principle into a tautology involves: it involves changing the meaning of 'pain'. What 'pain' means for *you* is: the presence of pain, in the colloquial sense of the term, *or* the presence of a brain state identical with the brain state of someone who feels pain. Of course, in that sense we can verify that your 'X-worlders' experience 'pain' – but that is not the sense of 'pain' at issue.

The reply to this argument is that the premiss is simply false. It is just not true that, on my conception of verification, it would *never* be reasonable to give up the principle stated. To show this, I have to beg your pardons for engaging in a little more science fiction. Let us suppose that scientists discover yet another kind of waves – call them 'W-waves'. Let us suppose that W-waves do not emanate from human brains, but that they are detected emanating from the brains of X-worlders. And let us suppose that, once again, there exists a simple scheme for decoding W-waves into coherent English (or whatever language X-worlders speak), and that the 'decoded' waves 'read' like this: 'Ho, ho! are we fooling those Earthians! They think that the V-waves they detect represent our thoughts! If they only knew that instead of pretending not to have pains when we really have pains, we are really pretending to pretend not to have pains when we really do have pains when we really don't have pains!' Under these circumstances, we would 'doubt' (to put it mildly) that the same psycho-physical correlations held for normal humans and for X-worlders. Further investigations might lead us to quite a number of different hypotheses. For example, we might decide that X-worlders don't think with their brains at all – that the 'organ' of thought is not just the brain, in the case of X-worlders, but some larger structure – perhaps even a structure which is not 'physical' in the sense of consisting of elementary particles. The point is that what is necessarily true is not the principle stated two paragraphs back, but rather the principle:

If someone (some organism) is in the same state as a human being in pain in all relevant respects, then he (that organism) is in pain.

– And *this* principle *is* a tautology by anybody's lights! The only *a priori* methodological restriction I am imposing here is this one:

If some organism is in the same state as a human being in pain in all respects *known* to be relevant, and there is no reason to suppose that there exists *un*known relevant respects, then don't postulate any.

– But this principle is not a 'tautology'; in fact, it is not a *statement* at all, but a methodological directive. And deciding to conform to this directive is not (as hardly needs to be said) changing the meaning of the word 'pain', or of *any* word.

There are two things that the logical behaviorist can do: he can claim that ascribing pains to X-worlders, or even super-spartans, involves a 'change of meaning',† or he can claim that ascribing pains to super-spartans, or at least to X-worlders, is 'untestable'. The first thing is a piece of unreasonable linguistics; the second, a piece of unreasonable scientific method. The two are, not surprisingly, mutually supporting: the unreasonable scientific method makes the unreasonable linguistics appear more reasonable. Similarly, the normal ways of thinking and talking are mutually supporting: reasonable linguistic field techniques are, needless to say, in agreement with reasonable conceptions of scientific method. Madmen sometimes have consistent delusional systems; so madness and sanity can both have a 'circular' aspect. I may not have succeeded, in this paper, in breaking the 'delusional system' of a committed logical behaviorist; but I hope to have convinced the uncommitted that that system need not be taken seriously. If we have to choose between 'circles', the circle of reason is to be preferred to any of the many circles of unreason.

† This popular philosophical move is discussed in the preceding chapter.

17

Other minds

'Empirical realism' is the position that the existence of the external world is supported by experience in much the way that any scientific theory is supported by observational data. The empirical realist reply to skepticism has recently been extended by Paul Ziff from skepticism about material objects to skepticism about other minds (Ziff, 1965). I do not suggest that Ziff was unaware of the need for the various qualifications that have to be made in the realist position if it is to be tenable. However, I am not happy with the way in which Ziff states the arguments. Ziff's statements are very brief, and it may be that the features I shall object to are ones that he would have eliminated in a longer and less aphoristic presentation. However, here they are.

There are two parts to Ziff's argument: what he calls the *via negativa*, and the citation of positive support. I take them up in turn.

The *via negativa* amounts to this: if I accept the hypothesis that I alone have a mind, then I must, according to Ziff, suppose that I differ from other human beings in some *other* respect, presumably a physiological respect. I can't differ from other human beings in *just* this one way, that I have a mind and they don't.

Could the other one and I relevantly differ only in this? that I do and he doesn't have a mind. Suppose we opt for yes. Then how do we account for this fantastic state of affairs? Why do I have a mind? Why doesn't he have a mind? Do minds just come and go in the universe? Did one just happen to light in my head? Is there no bait for this bird? Say 'yes' or even 'maybe' and what can one do but resolve to accept the relation, miraculous and inexplicable, between the mind and the body, anyone's of course. For it is not as if one had or is even likely to have any coherent theory of the mind in independence of the body. (Ziff, 1965, p. 575)

Now, I am puzzled by this, and in a variety of ways. In the first place, I do not see why the negation of the thesis that others have minds, i.e. that all people or all normal people have minds, is that I am unique in having a mind. It would rather seem to be the thesis that some, perhaps most, people do not have minds. (I once asked Bob Yost the question, 'Are there other minds?' 'Not many', he replied.) Suppose I find a mole under my left arm. Must I conclude that all other people have moles?

Could the other one and I relevantly differ only in this: that I do and he does not have a mole? Suppose we opt for yes. Then how do we account for this fantastic state of affairs? Why do I have a mole? Why doesn't he have a mole? Do moles just come and go in the universe? Did one just happen to light under my arm? Is there no bait for this bird? Say 'yes' or even 'maybe' and what can one do but resolve to accept the relation, miraculous and inexplicable, between the mole and the body, anyone's, of course. For it is not as if one had, or is even likely to have, any coherent theory of the mole in independence of the body.

This is, of course, nonsense. And I think it is nonsense not because we know more about moles than we do about minds; indeed, we know more about minds than we do about moles, or at least I do. Suppose that this mole under my arm is the first mole that I have ever seen. Suppose, for some reason, I am unwilling to ask other people whether they know what it is, or whether they have ever seen one before, etc. Perhaps such questions might be dangerous in my society. I would not, in the absence of investigation, conclude either that I am unique in having a mole under my arm, or that all other people have moles under their arms. If I concluded anything at all – and why should I? – I would very likely conclude that I and perhaps *some* other people have or have had moles under their arms, but that it is not necessarily the case that everyone has a mole under his arm. I might, if I had never seen anyone unclothed, seriously entertain the supposition that everyone has a mole under his arm just as I do: perhaps the mole is just a part of the body, like the finger or the nose, albeit a part I haven't been taught the name of. I might also consider the hypothesis that most people lack moles, and that this is just a freak.

Ziff says that 'talk about the mind is primarily a fancy way of talking about mental states and mental events (themselves fancy ways of talking)'. It seems to me that he has himself depended too much upon this fancy way of talking; e.g. the metaphor of bait for birds. Let us talk for a moment about the problem of the existence of material objects. 'Material objects exist' is not a 'hypothesis' that explains anything; and indeed 'material objects do not exist' does not explain anything either. What does explain a host of phenomena is something we might call 'thing-theory'; that is, the conjunction of all the theories, hypotheses, empirical laws, ordinary empirical statements (or a suitable consistent subset of all these) that we accept, and that we employ in explanation. With some care in making explicit additional auxiliary hypotheses connecting thing-events with the events one could describe in a sensation or appearance language, one can even make out that these hypotheses, laws, garden variety empirical statements, etc., together with these auxiliary hypotheses explain the phenomena that would be described in a sensation or appearance language. Thus part of the empirical realist case is correct: these individual bundles connecting thing-events with 'sense datum' events, do stand in the relation of *explanation* to various phenomena. A second part of the realist case is also correct: the phenomena, in turn, stand in the relation of inductive support to these thing-statements and empirical hypotheses. That is to say, our experiences confirm in many cases that some theory stated in thing-language is correct, not in the sense of establishing that the theory is correct as opposed to some other theory which implies that material things do not exist, but as opposed to some other theory which likewise implies that material objects exist. In short, what has been tested is not thing-theory as opposed to 'no-thing' theory, but thing-theory as opposed to *alternative* thing-theory. We have inductively established *not* that material objects exist, but that *this* account of how material objects behave is more probable than some other account of how material objects behave. More precisely, we have established that in *this* case *this* account of how *these* material objects behave is more probable than *that* account of how these material objects behave; in some other case, that such-and-such an account of how *those* material objects behave is more probable than such-and-such an alternative account of how *those* objects behave; etc. Even the most radical skeptic could grant this much.

'Material objects exist' has not been *confirmed.* 'Thing-theory' has not been *confirmed,* because really there is no such thing as thing-theory; there are only many many many many individual systems of statements about things which individually might be regarded by a logician as theories. *Thing theories* have been confirmed *as opposed to alternative thing theories.*

The skeptic would be happy to grant this much, because he could say, 'Very well, then, *if* things exist, very likely the received account of how they behave is the most probable; or, at least, it is more probable than those alternative accounts that have actually been considered and ruled out. But my question is not, 'Is the accepted account of how material objects behave more probable than those alternative accounts which have been considered and ruled out?" but, "Is the accepted account more probably true than that there are no material objects at all?"'

I claim that, in spite of these difficulties, nonetheless there is something right with the empirical realist rejoinder to skepticism. It is true that thing-theory (pretending that the totality of all accepted thing-theories can be axiomatized as a single consistent theory) has been tested only against alternative thing-theory; but that is because no one has been able to put into the field a 'no-thing' theory that would account for all, or even a good part of, the phenomena that are presently accounted for by means of thing-theory, and that would lead to different testable predictions. To give up 'material objects exist' would require giving up all of the individual laws, statements, hypotheses, etc., that *imply* material objects exist. But then what alternative explanation would we have for the phenomena in question? The inability of anyone to suggest an alternative explanation is itself our deepest justification for staying with the accepted explanations. The situation appears to me to be exactly the same in the case of psychological statements. We explain the behavior of other people as well as ourselves by reference to desires, character traits, etc. We say that other people are on occasion egotistical, angry, suspicious, lustful, tired, sad. The question is not: Do other people have minds? but: Are other people ever egotistical, angry, suspicious, lustful, tired, sad? If we continue to use 'theory' as logicians do, which is, of course, a wide deviation from ordinary usage, and say that any explanation of someone's behavior in terms of egotism, suspiciousness, anger, lust, sadness, may be regarded as a *psychological theory*, then we may say that there are many behavior facts that we can and do today explain by means of psychological theories. I do not have in mind by 'psychological theories' the kind of thing Ziff referred to in his paper, that is, theories in learning theory and neurophysiology; I will come to them later. To be sure, no 'psychological theory', in my sense, has ever been tested against a 'no-mind' theory. This is so for the same reason that no thing-theory has ever been tested against a 'no-thing' theory; no one has ever seriously propounded and elaborated in the detail that a scientist would require an explanation of a set of phenomena based upon the hypothesis that no material objects exist; and neither has anyone ever seriously propounded and elaborated in the detail that a scientist would require an explanation for a set of behavior facts based upon the hypothesis that no other person is ever tired, angry, sad, lustful, or suspicious. Psychological theory has been tested against alternative psychological theory, not against 'no-mind' theory. Moreover, just as in the case of material objects, the observation reports that we ordinarily make are not neutral with respect to the issue *psychological theory* or 'no-mind' theory, any more than they are neutral with respect to the issue 'thing-theory' or 'no-thing' theory. Although we could, if there were some reason, make guarded reports about the behavior of others which did not assume that they have mind, we do not ordinarily do so.

These facts show that our reasons for accepting it that others have mental states are not an ordinary induction, any more than our reasons for accepting it that material objects exist are an ordinary induction. Yet, what can be said in the case of material objects can also be said here: our acceptance of the proposition that others have mental states is both analogous and disanalogous to the acceptance of ordinary empirical theories on the basis of explanatory induction. It is disanalogous insofar as 'other people have mental states' is, in the first instance, not an empirical theory at all, but rather a consequence of a host of specific hypotheses, theories, laws, and garden variety empirical statements that we accept. These, indeed many of them, have been established by explanatory induction; but in no case was the alternative considered one that implied the nonexistence of the mental states of others; but the alternative was an alternative supposition *about* the mental states of others. It is also disanalogous insofar as it is built into the language used to make observation reports that other people have mental states. Thus two requirements for a good inductive test of a proposition are violated: that the alternative hypotheses being tested disagree with respect of the truth-value of the proposition, and that the *language* used to couch the observation reports with which all the hypotheses are confronted be 'neutral' with respect to the issue at hand. It is analogous, however, in that part of the justification for the assertion that other people have mental states is that to give up the proposition would require giving up all of the theories, statements, etc., that we accept *implying* that proposition; and those latter statements do have, many of them, the kind of explanatory role that the inductivist stresses. It is also analogous in that many empirical theories are accepted today precisely for the two reasons that (a) they, or theories that presuppose them, provide plausible explanations of many phenomena, and (b) no alternative is today in the field.

If this is right, I think we can see what the difference is between 'other people have minds' and 'other people have moles'. The supposition that other people have moles under their arms is not implied by the various explanations that I give of their behavior. If I say that other people do or don't have moles under their arms, or that most do or that some do, it makes no difference to anything. But if I say that other people do not have minds, that is if I say that other people do not have mental states, that is if I say that other people are never angry, suspicious, lustful, sad, etc., I am giving up propositions that are implied by the explanations that I give on specific occasions of the behavior of other people. So I would have to give up all of these explanations.

But if a body of theory has genuine explanatory power, we do not give it up unless an alternative is in the field. (This is Newton's famous 'rule 4', in fact.) It is therefore up to the objector, in the case of the thesis that others have mental states, to provide an alternative explanation for the behavior of other people. It is the fact that no such alternative explanation is in the field, along with the undoubted explanatory power of the accepted psychological theories, that constitutes the real inductive justification for the acceptance of the accepted system.

Fortunately, Ziff accepts all this. Indeed, he himself says,

To these hypotheses, still others must be conjoined. What is in force and active here is not a single silly hypothesis, that there are other minds, this naively supposed to be somehow based on an unexplored analogy. Instead one is confronted with a complex conceptual scheme. The fact that there are other minds is an integral part of that scheme and presently essential to it.

Ziff, however, says, 'one is not restricted here to a *via negativa.*' Let us examine, then, Ziff's positive argument, which is, unfortunately, even more briefly stated than his negative argument. Ziff's positive argument is an inductivist one in an almost pure form. What he says is that if I assume that others have minds, and that 'others' includes animals (rats, etc.), and that the mind and brain stand in a significant relation, and to these hypotheses I conjoin 'still others', which he does not state, then I obtain a conceptual scheme which 'draws support from a multitude of observations and experiments'. Ziff gives two examples. The first example, is, unfortunately an explanation of the behavior of some rats that does not contain a single psychological predicate. The explanation is:

the control of feeding behavior is located in two 'feeding centers' in the lateral hypothalamus and two 'satiety centers' in the ventromedial hypothalamus. Destruction of the satiety centers resulted in overeating and obesity, while stimulation of these centers was followed by cessation of eating.

Since this is an example of an explanation of behavior using a theory that does not contain a single psychological predicate, it cannot be regarded as confirming psychological theory at all.

Ziff's second example is an experiment of Lashley and Franz (1919) which may be summed up by the sentence: 'There are many indications that animals in a problem box situation experiment with many solutions.' Since 'experiment with many solutions' is a borderline example of a psychological predicate (it is borderline because there are computing machines that can experiment with many solutions, but to which we would not today attribute mental states), this second example is at least dimly relevant. It seems to me that it is only Ziff's scientism that makes him go to such recherché examples, when every day we explain the behavior of people and animals in a way that involves psychological predicates, in their primary uses, all over the place.

I do not wish to quarrel with Ziff's examples, however. Undoubtedly, we can find explanations of individual pieces of behavior that contain essential and paradigmatic occurrences of psychological terms. I am a little unhappy about the statement that 'our conceptual scheme *draws support* from a multitude of observations and experiments'. This is the language of theory-testing and confirmation. And I have already suggested that the existence of the mental states of others is not really the conclusion of an explanatory induction, even though there is a sense in which we can give an inductive justification for accepting that proposition. We speak of a theory as having 'support' or 'confirmation' only when it has been the survivor of an experimental test, and it cannot have been the survivor of an experimental test if no alternative was ever in the field – not even the 'null hypothesis'. To say that the existence of the mental states of others *draws support* from experiments and observations is to make the status of that existence appear much weaker than it is. Fortunately, Ziff does not say this. But in saying that 'our conceptual scheme' draws support from experiments and observations (which is, of course, quite true, if 'our conceptual scheme' is the whole system of psychological propositions we accept, as I take it Ziff means it to be), and then adding 'the existence of other minds is an integral part of that scheme and presently essential to it', there is the danger that one leaves the impression that 'the existence of other minds' likewise is something in connection with which one has 'support from experiments and observations'. The existence of the mental states of other people does not 'draw support' from experiments and observations, nor does it 'not draw support'. It is, as Ziff himself says, 'a fact of the day'. And if someone asks 'How do you know?' the answer is *not*, 'By the following experiments and observations', but, 'What alternative do you propose?'

All these criticisms should not obscure the essential agreement between myself and Ziff, and our common disagreement with the modish treatment in terms of 'behavioral criteria', 'how the words are learned', etc. Ziff and I both agree that 'what is in force and active here is not a single silly hypothesis', but 'a complex conceptual scheme'. Ziff and I both agree that the complex conceptual scheme, or parts of it, provides explanations, in a quite standard sense of explanation, for behavior facts. The fact that psychological statements are used to *explain* behavior is at once obvious and completely neglected both by the traditional philosophers who talk about an 'inference by analogy' and by the contemporary philosophers who believe that the existence of mental states can be logically (or linguistically) inferred from that of behavior. To put it crudely, the 'inference' to the mental states of others is what has been called an 'inference to the best explanation' – or it would be, except that it isn't an inference! (It isn't an inference because, to repeat, no alternative is or ever has been in the field.) Where we differ is in our attitude towards the argument that 'if only I have a mind, then there must be some other relevant difference'. For Ziff this seems to be a central part of the story, whereas I am suspicious of this argument, and inclined to think that even if it is correct, it is not very important. Let me now turn from my examination of Ziff to an examination of his critics.

Shoemaker's criticisms of Ziff

In this section I want to take up Sydney Shoemaker's criticisms of Ziff. (Shoemaker's criticisms are advanced more as questions and difficulties than as decisive objections; I shall treat them here, however, as if they were meant to be decisive objections.) Shoemaker's criticisms are two: that Ziff does not account for how we learn to use the words, and that knowing that behavioral criteria entitle us to apply psychological predicates to other people is part of knowing the meaning of those psychological predicates. At bottom, these are the same criticism: what is being suggested is that knowing the meaning of psychological predicates *involves* knowing that behavior entitles us to apply them to other people; and that this *must* be so because otherwise it would be impossible to learn the words. What is being presented, then, is the conjunction of a fashionable claim about the *logic* of psychological predicates with the already-disreputable argument that the claim must be correct because 'how else could we learn to use the words?' Since I have discussed this position in detail in two previous papers, I shall be much briefer here, and shall concentrate on points that I did not go into in those papers.

In my previous papers I presented models for the use of language which make it clear that language-using is at least logically possible even if words are not criterion-governed in the sense in which Malcolm, for example, assumes they must be. These models are mathematical models, and as such they were necessarily (given the present state of our knowledge) extremely over-simplified; but I believe this does not affect the validity of the point. In general, the way language-use works according to one of these models, is as follows:

The speaker's use of a given word, be it a psychological word or any word, depends upon a number of factors: for example, upon the sentences containing that word that he accepts; upon the stimulus meaning of those sentences that have stimulus meaning, together with the speaker's history of past stimulation; upon the inductive and deductive logic that the speaker consciously or unconsciously accepts; and upon the speaker's system of values and preferences. If a speaker changes his inductive logic, for example, then this will affect what empirical sentences beginning with a universal quantifier he will accept (actually, it will affect what empirical sentences of *any* form he will accept; but we may suppose that the most immediate and striking effect will be upon the acceptance of universal quantifications). If the change is very drastic, then we may even want to consider it as tantamount to a change in the *meaning* of the universal quantifier; more precisely, there are logically possible deviations from the present use of language such that it would be arbitrary whether to count them as changes in the *meaning* of the universal quantifier, or to say that the *meaning* of the universal quantifier has not changed but that the inductive logic has changed. Similarly, there may be situations in which we can say either that a man uses a psychological term, say, 'jealous', incorrectly, i.e. that he assigns to it an unusual meaning, or that he assigns to it the same meaning as does everyone else, but that he accepts a very different set of sentences. More precisely, there are logically possible situations in which it is arbitrary whether to say that someone means something unusual by 'jealous' or to say that he has a very unusual set of beliefs about jealousy.

It should be clear that in such models there is not, strictly speaking, any such thing as 'the meaning' of a given word, and hence the question 'in what can the meaning of a psychological word consist, if not in a set of criteria?' has no force. (Although 'anti-essentialistic', in this sense, such models are neutral with respect to the existence or nonexistence of a sharp analytic-synthetic distinction. In the language of these models, that is simply the highly technical issue, whether there is a set of privileged sentences involving a given word such that a change in one of *those* sentences *has* to be counted as a change in the meaning of that word.)

I make these much-too-brief remarks only as a reminder of the 'noncriterial' view of language. With this in mind, let us consider the question whether someone could understand the meaning of a psychological word, say 'angry' without knowing that certain forms of behavior entitle one to apply that word to another person.

The question is ambiguous. If the question means, could someone who did not even know that certain types of behavior are thought to entitle one to say that another person is angry be said to know the meaning of the word *angry?*, then the question does not have to do with entitlement relations; it has to do with knowledge of the beliefs of the community as to entitlement relations, and it has to do with the bearing that that knowledge or lack of that knowledge could have on knowing or not knowing 'the meaning' of the word 'angry'. If, on the other hand, the question is, could someone who lacks the knowledge that the behavior of other persons entitles one in certain circumstances to say that those persons are angry – not that this is believed to be so, but that it *is* so – be said to know the meaning of the word 'angry'?, then the question does really have to do with entitlement relations and their relation to meaning. Let us take the first form of the question first. The first form of the question comes to this. Could someone learn the meaning of the word 'angry' without at the same time learning that certain particular forms of behavior are thought to entitle one to say that another person is angry? This breaks down into several subquestions. One subquestion is, must one learn the meaning of words? Could one be born just being able to speak the language? Another subquestion is this, if one learns the meaning of words from other speakers, not from robots, phonograph records, moving pictures, etc., must one acquire the meaning of psychological words by learning that certain behavioral indicators are normally taken to entitle one to apply those words to another person? A third subquestion is, suppose one learned the meaning of the word 'angry' from other speakers, and one learned to use the word partly by applying it to others on the basis of behavioral indicators; if those behavioral indicators were *not* what we regard as indicators of anger at all, would it follow that 'angry' did not have the *meaning* that *we* ascribe to it?

All of these questions are extremely hard. I find it very strange that anyone should feel confident about answers to these questions, especially about the modish answers, and even stranger that anyone should regard it as a defect of the realist rejoinder to skepticism that it avoids these questions. Since space is short, let me simply say dogmatically what I think is the answer to these questions. First, I think it is not a logical truth that language must be learned. It may be that at some time in the future we shall all speak a single world-language, and if that language does not undergo change, it might even be possible to produce humans who will be born speaking the language, without having to go through any process of language acquisition at all. In the second place, if one does learn one's native language, and one does learn to apply psychological words to other persons, I think this does not absolutely have to be on the basis of behavioral indicators. It could be on the basis of neurophysiological or other theory, and I think that it would not necessarily follow that the terms had a different *meaning*, at least not provided that they had their ordinary reporting use. Third, even supposing that psychological words are learned on the basis of behavioral indicators, and even supposing that those indicators are very different from the ones we use, I think it does not follow that those words necessarily have a different meaning from that of our culture. We all know the story about people who are supposed to grimace when happy and smile when sad. If the people in those cultures spoke English, I think it would not be correct or customary to say that the words 'happy' and 'sad' have a different meaning when used among those English speakers. If one of those speakers sees Jones grimace and says, 'I see that Jones is happy today', it's not that he uses the word 'happy' with a noncustomary meaning; it's just that he believes, and, indeed, has good reason to believe, that people normally grimace when they are happy.

At this point, however, a certain puzzle arises, or rather seems to arise. If I can say that people who grimace are 'happy', that people who smile are 'sad', then couldn't people learn to use any psychological word in any circumstances whatsoever? And if they could, in what would the *sameness of meaning* of the psychological word possibly consist – used in those circumstances by those people, and used by us in what we regard as normal circumstances for the application of the word? I think that it is just this line of thought that leads such people as Strawson and Shoemaker to think there must be quasi-logical relations between facts about behavior and assertions about the mental states of other persons. And I think that in this line of thought there are two separate confusions to be distinguished. In the first place, I cannot arbitrarily say of just anyone under just any circumstances that he is happy. If I say of someone who grimaces that he is happy, this is because I believe that the state that I call *happiness* is one that *could* lead to that behavior under *some* circumstances, and that those circumstances obtain in the case in question. If it were deeply imbedded in my psychological theory that under no circumstances can a person who grimaces be happy, then I might be disinclined to say that the meaning of 'happy' was the same even in the culture described a few moments ago and in our culture. It does not follow, however, that there is any behavioral sign that could not be a sign of happiness, or any behavioral sign that could not fail to be a sign of happiness. It only follows that a given behavioral sign can be a sign of happiness in some circumstances only if the people who take it to be a behavioral sign in those circumstances have appropriate other beliefs, habits, customs, etc., in connection with happiness. It is *not* odd, in certain circumstances, to believe that one's neighbors grimace when happy; but it is more than 'odd', it is strongly semantically deviant, to suppose that one's neighbors *dislike* being happy. Even this, however, may not be impossible. The fact that it is strongly semantically deviant to believe that one's neighbors dislike being happy does not mean that under no conditions can one believe that one's neighbors dislike being happy; it only means that one would have to tell a considerable story to succeed in convincing us that there was such a belief, with no change in the meaning of 'happy' involved. Even if it were actually analytic that one cannot, or cannot always, be averse to being happy, notice that this analytic relationship is not a relation between any psychological state and a behavior-indicator, but between two different psychological states.

In sum, a person who is obviously a native speaker of (correct) English could fail to know that people who scream are usually in pain, that people who smile are usually happy, and so on, and it might still be the case that he knew the meaning of all of these words and used them with the same meaning that we do. That is to say, normal English speakers, when given sufficient information about the kind of culture that *this* speaker comes from, might decide to account for the difference in what he says as owing not to any difference in the meaning of words, but simply as owing to a difference in the behavior that he is accustomed to. No inference of the following form can be valid: Jones knows the meaning of the word 'pain'; Jones knows that if someone winces, screams, writhes, etc., normally, one is entitled to conclude that he is in pain. One of the most pathetic aspects of twentieth-century philosophy is the persistence with which philosophers have attempted to breathe life into this particular dead horse.

Suppose, now, that someone has grown up in our culture and knows exactly what we take to be behavioral indicators of pain, anger, jealousy, lust, etc. Let us now suppose that he becomes converted to philosophical skepticism, and he decides that in fact none of these indicators *entitle* us to say that someone else is in pain, is angry, jealous, lustful, etc. It is only, according to him, that we *think* these indicators entitle us to say these things. Should we say of this man, as many philosophers want us to say, that he is making the following logical blunder: denying the very *criterial* relationships (between molar behavior and mental state) upon which the customary understanding of psychological terms depends? This is balderdash. In order to know the meaning of a term, I need not talk exactly as my neighbors do, or even assent to the propositions to which they assent. At most it is necessary, and I doubt if it actually is necessary, that I assent to the propositions that are normally taken to be 'evident', 'obvious', etc., unless I have some reason for not doing so. 'I don't believe that other people are conscious, or, at any rate, I don't believe that we *know* that other people are conscious', is a perfectly good reason for refusing to accept the entitlement relations that most people accept. It may, of course, be *crazy* to believe that other people aren't conscious, and it may even be crazy or silly to believe that we don't know that other people are conscious; but that is exactly what we should say in this case – that the assertion is silly, or crazy, or foolish, etc. – *not* that the speaker is making a logical blunder or using words with a different meaning or anything of that kind.

At this point we come, I think, to the vital nerve of this whole dispute. If the skeptic – the man who talks in the way I just described – does not contradict himself, if he does not use the words with a different meaning, then in *what* does this *sameness of meaning* consist? We take it that seeing someone writhe and moan, etc., entitles us to say that that someone is in pain; the skeptic does not. Yet we are both supposed to have the same *meaning* of the word 'pain'. In what does this *meaning* consist?

As a crude oversimplification, we may suppose that it consists in this: a shared disposition to use the word 'pain' (or whatever psychological word may be in question) in a certain way. If we take it that this disposition must be as *specific* as a disposition to conclude that someone is in pain when he writhes, moans, screams, etc. obviously one cannot share the customary meaning of the word 'pain' and not share the disposition to conclude that someone is in pain when he writhes, moans, screams, etc. To be sure. But it seems to me absurd to suppose that the linguistic disposition shared by people who use the word 'pain' correctly is that specific. The disposition is rather a disposition to use the word 'pain' in various ways, depending on various things, and depending in part on what sentences containing the word 'pain' one accepts. If we know that a man is a very consistent skeptic (of course, no one is), then what will count as showing that he misunderstands the word 'pain' may be quite different from what will count as showing that I, who am not a skeptic, do not use the word pain with the customary meaning.

My position is circular. I do not regard this circularity as a defect. I argue that the skeptic's beliefs, or rather the sentences by which he expresses his beliefs, are not semantically deviant on the ground that he talks just the way normal people would talk if they had to express *those* beliefs. But this assumes that there are beliefs here to be expressed, not, as it were, pseudo-beliefs. I count the skeptic's beliefs as beliefs precisely because I see no reason to count the sentences that he utters in expressing his putative beliefs as in any way semantically deviant. This is circular because the argument is that the skeptic's total usage of psychological words is not semantically deviant, because it is just the usage that one would expect if one had to express certain beliefs that the skeptic has. But this assumes that certain key sentences used by the skeptic to express those beliefs are not semantically deviant, and this is just what many linguistic philosophers challenge today. The reason I am not perturbed by this 'circularity' is that it is a circularity only as long as operational constraints are not considered, and in empirical science operational constraints must be considered sooner or later. The decisive fact is that the sentences the skeptic utters are not regarded as linguistically deviant by native speakers other than those with a philosophical axe to grind.

I don't mean to say that the native speaker necessarily has available to him such technical notions as 'semantically deviant'. The native speaker doesn't have available such notions as 'grammatical' and 'ungrammatical' either, at least not in the sense in which linguists are now using 'grammatical' and 'ungrammatical'. However it is easy to find out if native speakers think there is something linguistically wrong with a sentence, at least in a large class of cases (I don't deny that there are cases in which it is unclear whether what is wrong with a sentence is regarded as linguistic by native speakers). It is also easy to find out that in many cases what speakers think is wrong about a sentence is simply the way it is formed, e.g. an adjective should precede rather than follow the noun it modifies, or a word is pluralized incorrectly, or something of that kind. In such a case, we have no hesitation in saying that those native speakers regard the sentence as 'ungrammatical' even if they don't actually put it that way. Do native speakers, however, regard the skeptic's sentences as ill-formed, or ungrammatical? Clearly they do not. Do they regard them as involving violations of the use of words? Clearly, they do not. What most speakers say about sentences by skeptics is that they involve a silly belief, or a crazy belief, or a belief that isn't worth discussing – or, in some cases, a belief with which they agree. In short, the overwhelming majority of informants regard the skeptic's sentences as correctly *expressing beliefs*.

Am I saying that sentences should never be counted as semantically deviant unless the majority of informants regard them as deviant? No, I am not saying that. I am aware that in many cases native informants will fall into disagreement about precisely this kind of question, and that is the sort of case in which it is appropriate to let considerations of theoretical advantage decide. I doubt, however, if there are any cases in which the linguist should go against the unanimous agreement of native informants. I think in the case of the skeptic's sentences we are as close to unanimous agreement as we ever are in linguistics – that there is nothing wrong with the *language* that the skeptic uses. It seems to me virtually unimaginable that considerations of theoretical advantage could override such a powerful consensus. Fortunately, we do not need to discuss whether they ever could or not. For I think it is easy to see that they do not in this particular case. To see this, just ask yourself: in what cases *do* we override the intuitions of some native informants? We do so when there are not direct, but indirect, operational constraints at work. That is to say, even if the informants do not agree at first hand that a certain usage is linguistically deviant, still, if we say that that usage is linguistically deviant it must be because it fails to correspond to certain statements in our grammar or in our semantic theory. Those statements, in turn, must at some point be empirically supported. It may be that in simpler cases than the one at issue informants do clearly mark as deviant usages that violate those statements in our grammar or semantic theory, and that this justifies us in accepting those statements as descriptive of the language and using them to decide disputed cases. All this is *ABC*, of course. If it is granted, then, that the skeptic's sentences cannot be ruled out as semantically deviant on the basis of direct linguistic evidence, i.e. on the basis of the testimony of informants, the question becomes, can they be ruled out indirectly as semantically deviant on the grounds that they violate norms of language? What are these norms of language, and what is the evidence that they function as such in the language? The answer is that the supposed norms of language have the form that certain behavioral criteria entitle one to say that other people are, as it might be, egotistical, angry, happy, sad, tired, jealous, etc. But what is the evidence that these are norms of language? The evidence is that if a person is confronted with a clear case of another person who is angry – with someone showing unmistakable signs of anger, or egotism, or joy, or whatever – and fails to note that the person is angry, he may be suspected of not knowing the meaning of the word. At first blush, this is very convincing, but only at first blush, for we see when we look more carefully, that the person is only suspected of not knowing the meaning of the word 'angry', or whatever, if he is unable to give a reason for not agreeing that the subject in question is angry, or whatever, or if we are unaware that he possess such a reason. Suppose he can offer a reason. Suppose he says, as it might be, 'That's not the way angry people act'. If he's wrong – if, in fact, *that* is exactly the way in which angry people act – then the suspicion that he does not know the meaning of the word 'angry' is strongly increased. But it still does not amount to logical necessity, for it it turns out that that is not the way in which angry people act *in the speaker's culture*, then the suspicion that the speaker does not know the meaning of the word 'angry' lapses, and is replaced by the conviction that what the speaker does not know is how angry people behave in *our* culture.

Similarly, if the speaker refuses to agree, and has the reason to offer, 'That's only behavior, and no amount of behavior entitles one to apply a psychological predicate to another', then again the suspicion that he does not know the meaning of the word 'angry' lapses, and is replaced by the conviction that the speaker is a skeptic. At this point, it becomes apparent that the logical behaviorist position is just as circular as the position that I advocate; for the norms of language, or alleged norms of language, to which the logical behaviorist appeals in trying to establish the skeptic's sentences as semantically deviant are not in fact then norms of language in the usual sense, or if they are, the empirical evidence that they are is no better than the direct empirical evidence that the skeptic's sentences are semantically deviant. But we agree that the direct empirical evidence was *against* the thesis that the skeptic's sentences were semantically deviant, which is why it required some kind of indirect argument to establish this in the first place. Both positions, then: mine and the logical behaviorist's, are circular; I can break out of my circle by appealing to the overwhelming consensus in the linguistic intuitions of native speakers; whereas the logical behaviorist can appeal only to the overwhelming consensus in the philosophical opinions of committed logical behaviorists.

Plantinga's objection to Ziff

Plantinga's objection to Ziff's argument (Plantinga, 1965) is that there *is* an alternative hypothesis in the field. The one that Plantinga mentions is the familiar hypothesis that there is a demon who has created all beings other than me without minds, and who causes them to act exactly as if they did have minds for the express purpose of fooling *me*. Plantinga is aware of the usual replies, that this hypothesis is less *simple* than psychological theory, that it is parasitic upon psychological theory, etc. The difficulty he sees with these replies is that they depend upon notions of complexity, parasitism, and so on, which are today far from clear. In a sense, I agree with Plantinga. I think that the notions of simplicity, plausibility, parasitism, and so forth, are indeed far from clear, and I am not optimistic about prospects of making them clear in the foreseeable future. I think that to a large extent when scientists talk about accepting a theory because the theory is plausible or not *ad hoc*, or simpler than another, they mean a variety of different things. Ziff expresses the conventional view that there are 'factors' of 'complete-ness, coherence, and simplicity' which are 'the hallmarks of a sound theory', and I am skeptical and inclined to think that 'simplicity', 'parsimony', 'completeness', are today just words that we use to cover our ignorance. What seems to me the case is that the actual procedure of science depends upon balancing two desiderata: on the one hand, we try to put the accepted theory under maximum strain, that is to say, we try to maximize *a priori* plausibility and probability; theories that seem to us too wildly implausible, we do not even bother to test.

What do plausibility and probability (I hate talk of 'simplicity') really depend upon? In part, probability may itself be a matter of previous inductive inference; to what extent this is so is being explored, both within inductive logic and within mathematical statistics. This question is closely related to the whole question of the applicability of so-called 'Bayesian' models, both for confirmation theory and for decision theory. Beyond this, it seems clear that plausibility and probability have something to do with the accepted science and metaphysics of a given time. Teleological explanations seem plausible to an age that is steeped in teleological philosophy; mechanistic explanations will seem plausible to an age that is steeped in mechanistic philosophy. But exactly how sociological considerations affect the priority ordering† of hypotheses is something that we know little about. Glib explanations of the acceptance of one hypothesis over another in terms of 'the metaphysics of the time' tend to be cases of *post hoc propter hoc*. It is easy to explain the acceptance of one theory over another in terms of a disposition to accept that theory over the other. I suspect that in the last analysis not only inductive logical and sociological factors will have to be invoked, but also biological factors, if we are to understand how humans actually arrive at a priority ordering of hypotheses. Very likely we shall have to be able to solve the problem of 'artificial intelligence', and to simulate the human ability to construct and select inductive hypotheses, before we shall have any real understanding in this area. But I disagree with Plantinga in one important respect. It may be that pointing out analogies between the acceptance of thing-theory, or the acceptance of psychological theory, on the one hand, and explanatory induction, on the other, is pointing out an analogy between what is unclear and what is equally unclear, as Plantinga urges; but I do not agree that even so it is valueless.

The decisive point is this: that there is a difference between scientific belief and arbitrary belief, even if scientific belief depends in part on an ordering of hypotheses, which is, in some sense, 'arbitrary'. If scientists simply ranked hypotheses in some arbitrary way, and then accepted the hypothesis highest-ranked no matter what observations might tell them, scientific belief would *really* be utterly arbitrary; but that is not what the scientist does. If the scientist simply accepted some ordering of hypotheses, and then proceeded to accept the highest-valued hypothesis

† The idea that rational men 'rank' hypotheses according to 'plausibility', 'implausibility', etc., is employed in what follows as a useful methodological fiction. Of course, what one encounters in real life is not a fixed 'priority ordering', but rather changing intuitive judgments which are themselves dependent upon context, factual knowledge, argument, etc.

which was not yet falsified by empirical data, but he did not make any special attempt to gather falsifying data, still, in large part, scientific belief would be arbitrary; for, it is the case with a great many theories that one is not likely to come across falsifying evidence unless one tries to find it. But neither of these descriptions is an accurate description of the scientific method. The scientific method is the method of testing one's ideas in practice; of subjecting them to maximum strain; of accepting only beliefs that have succeeded in practice. The element of arbitrariness still comes in, in that one cannot possibly test all beliefs, and in that at any given time there will be infinitely many beliefs that cannot be ruled out on *deductive* grounds, that is to say, on grounds of incompatibility with observation. So some kind of priority ordering has to be used, and it is true that if our implicit priority ordering is unfortunate – in the sense that the hypotheses that are true of the actual world are located at an impossibly vast 'depth', while the hypotheses that are above them in the priority ordering are extremely bad – then by using the scientific method we shall never come to the truth about the world. Once one has pointed this out, it is clear, I think, how science differs from dogmatism even though there are arbitrary and authoritarian elements in science. That science is not sheer dogmatism and authoritarianism is not, of course, any proof that science will work, or even that science is any more rational than any other method. The problem of the justification of induction, if it is a problem, still remains.

But let us return to Plantinga. According to Plantinga, explaining our knowledge of the existence of other minds in terms of the scientific method is explaining the obscure in terms of the more obscure. What is admittedly obscure about the scientific method is the basis of the intuitive priority ordering of hypotheses that scientists actually employ; to admit that that is obscure is not to admit that every feature of the logic of theory testing is obscure. I have been arguing, in effect, that we know enough about the scientific method today to make this sort of analogy enlightening, and that indeed the detailed understanding of just how the priority ordering of hypotheses is arrived at will be unlikely to contribute much to this argument. Having said this, one should say one or two more things about Plantinga's specific example of the demon hypothesis. First of all, I grant what is often disputed, that the demon hypothesis represents a logical possibility. It is perfectly imaginable that other people should be mere 'dummies' controlled remotely by some intelligence I know nothing of. But I do not grant that this hypothesis is 'in the field'. For a hypothesis to be in the field, it is not enough for it to represent a possibility that we can imagine; it must meet two further conditions. It must be elaborated, the details must be worked out to a

359

certain degree, various questions which naturally occur to one must be answered, and, secondly, it must not be too *silly* to consider. This hypothesis, the demon hypothesis, has obviously never been elaborated in any detail at all, and it obviously is too silly to consider. This is the point at which the skeptic boggles. Is this not dogmatism, is this not authoritarianism, to rule out a hypothesis *a priori*, on the ground of some kind of an intuitive judgment, whose basis we know little of, to the effect that it is 'too silly to consider'. The answer again is 'no'. For, even if the demon hypothesis is too silly to consider, i.e. too far out on the priority ordering for scientists to consider it necessary to test it, still one is *allowed* to test it if one wants to. One of the features of the scientific method is precisely that one is allowed to disagree with one's colleagues with respect to what is too silly to consider. If I really believed that other people were dummies, then it would be up to me to try to find some testable difference that that might make, and to try to construct some test to show that it is correct. But what if it is built into the hypothesis that I cannot succeed – that the demon, or the remote intelligence is far too clever for me to discover how he works, or by what mechanisms his 'dummies' work? This is to ask, what if it is built into the theory that it has exactly the same testable consequences as some theory that is more plausible? The answer is, if someone with malice aforethought constructs a theory that has this feature, he will succeed in constructing a theory that is not logically false, but is such that by its very construction would always be irrational to believe. It is not *a priori* that such a theory is false; but it is *a priori* that it could never be believed rationally. But then, Plantinga would of course point out, everything is going to depend on the judgment that the hypothesis is indeed 'deeper down' in the priority ordering, 'less plausible', 'less probable', 'more *ad hoc*', or something of that kind than the vast constellation of hypotheses that we have called 'psychological theory'. How do we know that this is so? Or, if it is so, as a matter of fact about the actual intuitive judgments of scientists, how do we know that those intuitive judgments are rational?

This is a difficulty only in the sense of being *the* difficulty that constitutes the problem of induction. To raise the problem, how do we know that the intuitive priority ordering of hypotheses actually employed by scientists is *the rational* priority ordering of hypotheses (if there is such a thing), is precisely to raise the whole issue of the justification of induction at least if 'induction' is understood as we have been understanding it in this paper. It seems to me, then, that Plantinga, playing the role of the skeptic, can remind us that the scientific method depends on regularities in what we all consider to be silly hypotheses, in what we all consider to be *ad hoc* hypotheses, in what we all consider to be plausible hypotheses, in what we all consider to be probable. He can remind us of the enormous role played by agreement in our judgments in the normal inductive method of science, and to do this is no mean contribution. But reminding us of this, and reminding us how little we understand this, is not showing that there is something concerning which knowledge is impossible.

18

Minds and machines*

The various issues and puzzles that make up the traditional mind–body problem are wholly linguistic and logical in character: whatever few empirical 'facts' there may be in this area support one view as much as another. I do not hope to establish this contention in this paper, but I hope to do something toward rendering it more plausible. Specifically, I shall try to show that all of the issues arise in connection with any computing system capable of answering questions about its own structure, and have thus nothing to do with the unique nature (if it *is* unique) of human subjective experience.

To illustrate the sort of thing that is meant: one kind of puzzle that is sometimes discussed in connection with the 'mind–body problem' is the puzzle of *privacy*. The question 'How do I know I have a pain?' is a *deviant*† ('logically odd') question. The question 'How do I know Smith has a pain?' is not all at deviant. The difference can also be mirrored in impersonal questions: 'How does anyone ever know he himself has a pain?' is deviant; 'How does anyone ever know that some-one else is in pain?' is non-deviant. I shall show that the difference in status between the last two questions is mirrored in the case of machines: if T is a *Turing machine* (see below), the question 'How does T ascertain that it is in state A?' is, as we shall see, 'logically odd' with a vengeance; but if T is capable of investigating its neighbor machine T' (say, T has electronic 'sense-organs' which 'scan' T'), the question 'How does T ascertain that T' is in state A?' is not at all odd.

Another question connected with the 'mind–body problem' is the question whether or not it is ever permissible to identify mental events and physical events. Of course, I do not claim that this question arises for Turing machines, but I do claim that it is possible to construct a logical analogue for this question that does arise, and that all of the question of 'mind–body identity' can be mirrored in terms of the analogue.

---

  * First published in Sidney Hook (ed.) *Dimensions of Mind* (New York, 1960). Reprinted by permission of New York University Press.
  † By a 'deviant' utterance is here meant one that deviates from a semantical regularity (in the appropriate natural language). The term is taken from Ziff, 1960.

To obtain such an analogue, let us identify a scientific theory with a 'partially-interpreted calculus' in the sense of Carnap†. Then we can perfectly well imagine a Turing machine which generates theories, tests them (assuming that it is possible to 'mechanize' inductive logic to some degree), and 'accepts' theories which satisfy certain criteria (e.g. predictive success). In particular, if the machine has electronic 'sense organs' which enable it to 'scan' itself while it is in operation, it may formulate theories concerning its own structure and subject them to test. Suppose the machine is in a given state (say, 'state A') when, and only when, flip-flop 36 is on. Then this statement: 'I am in state A when, and only when, flip-flop 36 is on', may be one of the theoretical principles concerning its own structure accepted by the machine. Here 'I am in state A' is, of course, 'observation language' for the machine, while 'flip-flop 36 is on' is a 'theoretical expression' which is partially interpreted in terms of 'observables' (if the machine's 'sense organs' report by printing symbols on the machine's input tape, the 'observables' in terms of which the machine would give a partial operational definition of 'flip-flop 36 being on' would be of the form 'symbol # so-and-so appearing on the input tape'). Now all of the usual considerations for and against mind–body identification can be paralleled by considerations for and against saying that state A is in fact *identical* with flip-flop 36 being on.

Corresponding to Occamist arguments for 'identify' in the one case are Occamist arguments for identity in the other. And the usual argument for dualism in the mind–body case can be paralleled in the other as follows: for the machine, 'state A' is directly observable; on the other hand, 'flip-flops' are something it knows about only via highly-sophisticated inferences – How *could* two things so different *possibly* be the same? This last argument can be put into a form which makes it appear somewhat stronger. The proposition:

(1) I am in state A if, and only if, flip-flop 36 is on,

is clearly a 'synthetic' proposition for the machine. For instance, the machine might be in state A and its sense organs might report that flip-flop 36 was *not* on. In such a case the machine would have to make a methodological 'choice' – namely, to give up (1) or to conclude that it had made an 'observational error' (just as a human scientist would be confronted with similar methodological choices in studying his own

†Cf. Carnap 1953 and 1956. This model of a scientific theory is too oversimplified to be of much general utility, in my opinion: however, the oversimplifications do not affect the present argument.

psychophysical correlations). And just as philosophers have argued from the synthetic nature of the proposition:

(2) I am in pain if, and only if, my C-fibers are stimulated,

to the conclusion that the *properties* (or 'states' or 'events') being in pain, and having C-fibers stimulated, cannot possibly be the same (otherwise (2) would be analytic, or so the argument runs); so one should be able to conclude from the fact that (1) is synthetic that the two properties (or 'states' or 'events') – being in state A and having flip-flop 36 on – cannot possibly be the same!

It is instructive to note that the traditional argument for dualism is not at all a conclusion from 'the raw data of direct experience' (as is shown by the fact that it applies just as well to non-sentient machines), but a highly complicated bit of reasoning which depends on (a) the reification of universals† (e.g. 'properties', 'states', 'events'); and on (b) a sharp analytic-synthetic distinction.

I may be accused of advocating a 'mechanistic' world-view in pressing the present analogy. If this means that I am supposed to hold that machines think,‡ on the one hand, or that human beings are machines, on the other, the charge is false. If there is some version of mechanism sophisticated enough to avoid these errors, very likely the considerations in this paper support it.§

1. Turing Machines

The present paper will require the notion of a *Turing machine*‖ which will now be explained.

Briefly, a Turing machine is a device with a finite number of internal configurations, each of which involves the machine's being in one of a finite number of *states*,¶ and the machine's scanning a tape on which certain symbols appear.

† This point was made by Quine in Quine, 1957.
‡ Cf. Ziff's paper (1959) and the reply (1959) by Smart. Ziff has informed me that by a 'robot' he did not have in mind a 'learning machine' of the kind envisaged by Smart, and he would agree that the considerations brought forward in his paper would not necessarily apply to such a machine (if it can properly be classed as a 'machine' at all). On the question of whether 'this machine thinks (feels, etc.)' is *deviant* or not, it is necessary to keep in mind both the point raised by Ziff (that the important question is not whether or not the utterance is deviant, but whether or not it is deviant for non-trivial reasons), and also the 'diachronic–synchronic' distinction discussed in section 5 of the present paper.
§ In particular, I am sympathetic with the general standpoint taken by Smart in (1959b) and (1959c). However, see the linguistic considerations in section 5.
‖ For further details, cf. Davis, 1958 and Kleene, 1952.
¶ This terminology is taken from Kleene, 1952, and differs from that of Davis and Turing.

The machine's tape is divided into separate squares, thus:

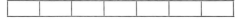

on each of which a symbol (from a fixed finite alphabet) may be printed. Also the machine has a 'scanner' which 'scans' one square of the tape at a time. Finally, the machine has a *printing mechanism* which may (a) *erase* the symbol which appears on the square being scanned, and (b) print some other symbol (from the machine's alphabet) on that square.

Any Turing machine is completely described by a *machine table*, which is constructed as follows: the rows of the table correspond to letters of the alphabet (including the 'null' letter, i.e. blank space), while the columns correspond to states A, B, C, etc. In each square there appears an 'instruction', e.g. '$s_5L\ A$', '$s_7C\ B$', '$s_3R\ C$'. These instructions are read as follows: '$s_5L\ A$' means 'print the symbol s_5 on the square you are now scanning (after erasing whatever symbol it now contains), and proceed to scan the square immediately to the left of the one you have just been scanning; also, shift into state A.' The other instructions are similarly interpreted ('R' means 'scan the square immediately to the *right*', while 'C' means 'center', i.e. continue scanning the *same* square). The following is a sample machine table:

		A	B	C	D
(s_1)	I	s_1RA	s_1LB	s_3LD	s_1CD
(s_2)	+	s_1LB	s_2CD	s_2LD	s_2CD
(s_3)	blank space	s_3CD	s_3RC	s_3LD	s_3CD

The machine described by this table is intended to function as follows: the machine is started in state A. On the tape there appears a 'sum' (in unary notion) to be 'worked out', e.g. 'II + III.'

The machine is initially scanning the first 'I'. The machine proceeds to 'work out' the sum (essentially by replacing the plus sign by a I, and then going back and erasing the first I). Thus if the 'input' was IIII + IIIII the machine would 'print out' IIIIIIIII, and then go into the 'rest state' (state D).

A 'machine table' *describes* a machine if the machine has internal states corresponding to the columns of the table, and if it 'obeys' the instruction in the table in the following sense: when it is scanning a square on which a symbol s_1 appears and it is in, say, state B, that it carries out the 'instruction' in the appropriate row and column of the table (in this case, column B and row s_1). Any machine that is described by a machine table of the sort just exemplified is a Turing machine.

The notion of a Turing machine is also subject to generalization† in various ways – for example, one may suppose that the machine has a second tape (an 'input tape') on which additional information may be printed by an operator in the course of a computation. In the sequel we shall make use of this generalization (with electronic 'sense organs' taking the place of the 'operator').

It should be remarked that Turing machines are able in principle to do anything that any computing machine (of whichever kind) can do.‡

It has sometimes been contended (e.g. by Nagel and Newman in their book *Gödel's Proof*) that 'the theorem [i.e. Gödel's theorem] does indicate that the structure and power of the human mind are far more complex and subtle than any non-living machine yet envisaged' (p. 10), and hence that a Turing machine cannot serve as a model for the human mind, but this is simply a mistake.

Let T be a Turing machine which 'represents' me in the sense that T can prove just the mathematical statements I can prove. Then the argument (Nagel and Newman give no argument, but I assume they must have this one in mind) is that by using Gödel's technique I can discover a proposition that T cannot prove, and moreover I can prove this proposition. This refutes the assumption that T 'represents' me, hence I am not a Turing machine. The fallacy is a misapplication of Gödel's theorem, pure and simple. Given an arbitrary machine T, all I can do is find a proposition U such that I can prove:

(3) If T is consistent, U is true,

where U is undecidable by T if T is in fact consistent. However, T can perfectly well prove (3) too! And the statement U, which T *cannot* prove (assuming consistency), I cannot prove either (unless I can prove that T is consistent, which is unlikely if T is very complicated)!

2. Privacy

Let us suppose that a Turing machine T is constructed to do the following. A number, say '3000' is printed on T's tape and T is started in T's 'initial state'. Thereupon T computes the 3000th (or whatever the given number was) digit in the decimal expansion of π, prints this digit on its tape, and goes into the 'rest state' (i.e. turns itself off).

† This generalization is made in Davis, 1958, where it is employed in defining relative recursiveness.

‡ This statement is a form of *Church's thesis* (that recursiveness equals effective computability).

Clearly the question 'How does T "ascertain" [or "compute", or "work out"] the 3000th digit in the decimal expansion of π?' is a sensible question. And the answer might well be a complicated one. In fact, an answer would probably involve three distinguishable constituents:

(i) A description of the sequence of states through which T passed in arriving at the answer, and of the appearance of the tape at each stage in the computation.

(ii) A description of the *rules* under which T operated (these are given by the 'machine table' for T).

(iii) An explanation of the *rationale* of the entire procedure.

Now let us suppose that someone voices the following objection: 'In order to perform the computation just described, T must pass through states A, B, C, etc. But how can T ascertain that it is in states A, B, C, etc?'

It is clear that this is a silly objection. But what makes it silly? For one thing, the 'logical description' (machine table) of the machine describes the state only in terms of their *relations* to each other and to what appears on the tape. The 'physical realization' of the machine is immaterial, so long as there *are* distinct states A, B, C, etc., and they succeed each other as specified in the machine table. Thus one can answer a question such as 'How does T ascertain that X?' (or 'compute X', etc.) only in the sense of describing the *sequence of states* through which T must pass in ascertaining that X (computing, X etc.), the rules obeyed, etc. But there is no 'sequence of states' through which T must pass to be in a single state!

Indeed, suppose there were – suppose T could not *be* in state A without first *ascertaining* that it was in state A (by first passing through a sequence of other states). Clearly a vicious regress would be involved. And one 'breaks' the regress simply by noting that the machine, in ascertaining the 3000th digit in π, *passes through* its states – but it need not in any significant sense 'ascertain' that it is passing through them.

Note the analogy to a fallacy in traditional epistemology: the fallacy of supposing that to know that p (where p is any proposition) one must first know that q_1, q_2, etc. (where q_1, q_2, etc., are appropriate *other* propositions). This leads either to an 'infinite regress' or to the dubious move of inventing a special class of 'protocol' propositions.

The resolution of the fallacy is also analogous to the machine case. Suppose that on the basis of sense experiences E_1, E_2, etc., I know that there is a chair in the room. It does not follow that I verbalized (or even *could* have verbalized) E_1, E_2, etc., nor that I remember E_1, E_2, etc., nor even that I 'mentally classified' ('attended to', etc.) sense experiences E_1, E_2, etc., when I had them. In short, it is necessary to *have* sense experiences, but not to *know* (or even *notice*) what sense experiences one is having, in order to have certain kinds of knowledge.

Let us modify our case, however, by supposing that whenever the machine is in one particular state (say, 'state A') it prints the words 'I am in state A'. Then someone might grant that the machine does not in general ascertain what state it is in, but might say in the case of state A (after the machine printed 'I am in state A'): 'The machine ascertained that it was in state A'.

Let us study this case a little more closely. First of all, we want to suppose that when it is in state A the machine prints 'I am in state A' without first passing through any other states. That is, in every row of the column of the table headed 'state A' there appears the instruction: *print*† '*I am in state* A'. Secondly, by way of comparison, let us consider a human being, Jones, who says 'I am in pain' (or 'Ouch!', or 'Something hurts') whenever he is in pain. To make the comparison as close as possible, we will have to suppose that Jones' linguistic conditioning is such that he simply says 'I am in pain' 'without thinking', i.e. without passing through any introspectible mental states other than the pain itself. In Wittgenstein's terminology, Jones simply *evinces* his pain by saying 'I am in pain' – he does not first reflect on it (or heed it, or note it, etc.) and then consciously describe it. (Note that this simple possibility of uttering the 'proposition', 'I am in pain' without first performing any mental 'act of judgement' was overlooked by traditional epistemologists from Hume to Russell!) Now we may consider the parallel question 'Does the machine "ascertain" that it is in state A?' and 'Does Jones "know" that he is in pain?' and their consequences.

Philosophers interested in semantical questions have, as one might expect, paid a good deal of attention to the verb 'know'. Traditionally, three elements have been distinguished: (1) 'X know that p' implies that p is *true* (we may call this the *truth* element); (2) 'X knows that p' implies that X believes that p (philosophers have quarrelled about the word, some contending that it should be 'X is *confident* that p,' or 'X is *in a position to assert* that p'; I shall call this element the *confidence* element); (3) 'X knows that p' implies that X has evidence that p (here I think the word 'evidence' is definitely wrong,‡ but it will not matter for present purposes; I shall call this the *evidential* element). Moreover,

† Here it is necessary to suppose that the entire sentence 'I am in state A.' counts as a single symbol in the machine's alphabet.

‡ For example, I know that the sun is 93 million miles from the earth, but I have no *evidence* that this is so. In fact, I do not even remember where I learned this.

it is part of the meaning of the word 'evidence' that nothing can be literally evidence for itself: if X is evidence for Y, then X and Y must be different things.

In view of such analyses, disputes have arisen over the propriety of saying (in cases like the one we are considering) 'Jones knows that he is in pain.' On the one hand, philosophers who take the common-sense view ('When I have a pain I *know* I have a pain') argue somewhat as follows: it would be clearly false to say Jones does *not* know he has a pain; but either Jones knows or he does not; hence, Jones knows he has a pain. Against these philosophers, one might argue as follows: 'Jones does not know X' implies Jones is not in a position to assert that X; hence, it is certainly wrong to say 'Jones does not know he has a pain.' But the above use of the Law of the Excluded Middle was fallacious: words in English have *significance ranges*, and what is contended is that it is not semantically correct to say *either* 'Jones knows that he has a pain.' *or* 'Jones does not know he has a pain.' (although the former sentence is certainly less misleading than the latter, since *one* at least of the conditions involved in knowing is met – Jones is in a position to assert he has a pain. (In fact the *truth* and *confidence* elements are both present; it is the evidential element that occasions the difficulty.)

I do not wish to argue this question here;† the present concern is rather with the similarities between our two questions. For example, one might decide to accept (as 'non-deviant', 'logically in order', 'non-selfcontradictory', etc.) the two statements:

(a) The machine ascertained that it was in state A,
(b) Jones knew that he had a pain,

or one might reject both. If one rejects (a) and (b), then one can find alternative formulations which are certainly semantically acceptable: e.g. (for (a)) 'The machine was in state A, and this caused it to print: "I am in state A"', (for (b)) 'Jones was in pain, and this caused him to say "I am in pain"' (or, 'Jones was in pain, and he evinced this by saying "I am in pain"').

On the other hand, if one accepts (a) and (b), then one must face the questions (a_1) '*How* did the machine ascertain that it was in state A?', and (b_1) '*How* did Jones know that he had a pain?'

And if one regards these questions as having answers at all, then they

† In fact, it would be impossible to decide whether 'Jones knows he has a pain' is deviant or not without first reformulating the evidential condition so as to avoid the objection in note ‡ on p. 368 (if it can be reformulated so as to save anything of the condition at all). However the discussion above will indicate, I believe, why one might *want* to find that this sentence is deviant.

will be degenerate answers – e.g. 'By being in state A' and 'By having the pain.'

At this point it is, I believe, very clear that the difficulty has in both cases the same cause. Namely, the difficulty is occasioned by the fact that the 'verbal report' ('I am in state A', or 'I am in pain') issues directly from the state it 'reports': no 'computation' or additional 'evidence' is needed to arrive at the 'answer'. And the philosophic disagreements over 'how to talk' are at bottom concerned with finding a terminology for describing cognitive processes in general that is not misleading in this particular case. (Note that the traditional epistemological answer to (b_1) – namely, 'by introspection' – is false to the facts of this case, since it clearly implies the occurrence of a mental event (the 'act' of introspection) distinct from the feeling of pain.)

Finally, let us suppose that the machine is equipped to 'scan' its neighbor machine T_1. Then we can see that the question 'How does T ascertain that T_1 is in state A?' may be a perfectly sensible question, as much so as 'How does T ascertain that the 3000th digit of π is so-and-so?' In both cases the answer will involve describing a whole 'program' (plus explaining the *rationale* of the program, if necessary). Moreover, it will be necessary to say something about the physical context linking T and T_1 (arrangement of sense organs, etc.), and not just to describe the internal states of T: this is so because T is now answering an *empirical* and not a mathematical question. In the same way 'How did Sherlock Holmes know that Jones was in pain?' may be a perfectly sensible question, and may have quite a complicated answer.

3. 'Mental' states and 'logical' states

Consider the two questions:

(1) How does Jones know he has a pain?
(2) How does Jones know he has a fever?

The first question is, as we saw in the preceding section, a somewhat peculiar one. The second question may be quite sensible. In fact, if Jones says 'I have a pain' no one will retort 'You are mistaken'. (One *might* retort 'You have made a slip of the tongue' or 'You are lying', but not 'You are *mistaken*'.) On the other hand, if Jones says 'I have a fever', the doctor who has just taken Jones' temperature may quite conceivably retort 'You are mistaken'. And the doctor need not mean that Jones made a linguistic error, or was lying, or confused.

It might be thought that, whereas the difference between statements about one's own state and statements about the states of others has an analogue in the case of machines, the difference, just touched upon, between statements about one's 'mental' state and statements about one's 'physical' state, in traditional parlance, does not have any analogue. But this is not so. Just what the analogue is will now be developed.

First of all, we have to go back to the notion of a Turing machine. When a Turing machine is described by means of a 'machine table', it is described as something having a tape, a printing device, a 'scanning' device (this may be no more than a point of the machine which at any given time is aligned with just one square of the tape), and a finite set (A, B, C, etc.) of 'states'. (In what follows, these will be referred to at times as *logical states* to distinguish them from certain other states to be introduced shortly.) Beyond this it is described only by giving the deterministic rules which determine the order in which the states succeed each other and what is printed when.

In particular, the 'logical description' of a Turing machine does not include any specification of the *physical nature* of these 'states' – or indeed, of the physical nature of the whole machine. (Shall it consist of electronic relays, of cardboard, of human clerks sitting at desks, or what?) In other words, a given 'Turing machine' is an *abstract* machine which may be physically realized in an almost infinite number of different ways.

As soon as a Turing machine is physically realized, however, something interesting happens. Although the machine has from the logician's point of view only the states A, B, C, etc., it has from the engineer's point of view an almost infinite number of additional 'states' (though not in the same sense of 'state' – we shall call these *structural states*). For instance, if the machine consists of vacuum tubes, one of the things that may happen is that one of its vacuum tubes may fail – this puts the machine in what is from the physicist's if not the logician's point of view a different 'state'. Again, if the machine is a manually operated one built of cardboard, one of its possible 'non-logical' or 'structural' states is obviously that its cardboard may buckle. And so on.

A physically realized Turing machine may have no way of ascertaining its own structural state, just as a human being may have no way of ascertaining the condition of his appendix at a given time. However, it is extremely convenient to give a machine electronic 'sense organs' which enable it to scan itself and to detect minor malfunctions. These 'sense organs' may be visualized as causing certain symbols to be printed on an 'input tape' which the machine 'examines' from time to time. (One minor difficulty is that the 'report' of a sense organ might occupy a number of squares of tape, whereas the machine only 'scans' one square at a time – however, this is unimportant, since it is well known that the effect of 'reading' any finite number of squares can be obtained using a program which only requires one square to be scanned at a time.)

(By way of a digression, let me remark that the first actually constructed digital computers did not have any devices of the kind just envisaged. On the other hand, they *did* have over 3000 vacuum tubes, some of which were failing at any given time! The need for 'routines' for self-checking therefore quickly became evident.)†

A machine which is able to detect at least some of its own structural states is in a position very analogous to that of a human being, who can detect some but not all of the malfunctions of his own body, and with varying degrees of reliability. Thus, suppose the machine 'prints out': 'Vacuum tube 312 has failed'. The question 'How did the machine ascertain that vacuum tube 312 failed?' is a perfectly sensible question. And the answer may involve a reference to both the physical structure of the machine ('sense organs', etc.) and the 'logical structure' (program for 'reading' and 'interpreting' the input tape).

If the machine prints: 'Vacuum tube 312 has failed' when vacuum tube 312 is in fact functioning, the mistake may be due to a miscomputation (in the course of 'reading' and 'interpreting' the input tape) or to an incorrect signal from a sense organ. On the other hand, if the machine prints: 'I am in state A', and it does this simply because its machine table contains the instruction: *Print: 'I am in state A when in state A'*, then the question of a miscomputation cannot arise. Even if some accident causes the printing mechanism to print: 'I am in state A' when the machine is *not* in state A, there was not a 'miscomputation' (only, so to speak, a 'verbal slip').

It is interesting to note that just as there are two possible descriptions of the behavior of a Turing machine – the engineer's structural blueprint and the logician's 'machine table' – so there are two possible descriptions of human psychology. The 'behavioristic' approach (including in this category theories which employ 'hypothetical constructs', including 'constructs' taken from physiology) aims at eventually providing a complete physicalistic‡ description of human behavior, in terms which link up with chemistry and physics. This corresponds to the engineer's or physicist's description of a physically realized Turing

---

† Actually, it was not necessary to add any 'sense organs'; existing computers check themselves by 'performing crucial experiments with themselves' (i.e. carrying out certain test computations and comparing the results with the correct results which have been given).

‡ In the sense of Oppenheim, 1958; not in the 'epistemological' sense associated with Carnap's writing on 'physicalism'.

machine. But it would also be possible to seek a more abstract description of human mental processes, in terms of 'mental states' (physical realization, if any, unspecified) and 'impressions' (these play the role of symbols on the machine's tapes) – a description which would specify the laws controlling the order in which the states succeeded one another, and the relation to verbalization (or, at any rate, verbalized thought). This description, which would be the analogue of a 'machine table', it was in fact the program of classical psychology to provide! Classical psychology is often thought to have failed for *methodological* reasons; I would suggest, in the light of this analogy, that it failed rather for empirical reasons – the mental states and 'impressions' of human beings do not form a causally closed system to the extent to which the 'configurations' of a Turing machine do.

The analogy which has been presented between logical states of a Turing machine and mental states of a human being, on the one hand, and structural states of a Turing machine and physical states of a human being, on the other, is one that I find very suggestive. In particular, further exploration of this analogy may make it possible to further clarify the notion of a 'mental state' that we have been discussing. This 'further exploration' has not yet been undertaken, at any rate by me, but I should like to put down, for those who may be interested, a few of the features that seem to distinguish logical and mental states respectively from structural and physical ones:

(1) The functional organization (problem solving, thinking) of the human being or machine can be described in terms of the sequences of mental or logical states respectively (and the accompanying verbalizations), without reference to the nature of the 'physical realization' of these states.

(2) The states seem intimately connected with *verbalization*.

(3) In the case of rational thought (or computing), the 'program' which determines which states follow which, etc., is open to rational criticism.

4. Mind–body 'identity'

The last area in which we have to compare human beings and machines involves the question of *identifying* mental states with the corresponding physical states (or logical states with the corresponding structural states). As indicated at the beginning of this paper, all of the arguments for and against such identification can perfectly well be discussed in terms of Turing machines.

373

For example, in the 1930s Wittgenstein used the following argument: if I observe an after-image, and observe at the same time my brain state (with the aid of a suitable instrument) I observe *two* things, not one. (Presumably this is an argument *against* identification.) But we can perfectly well imagine a 'clever' Turing machine 'reasoning' as follows: 'When I print "I am in state A" I do not have to use my "sense organs". When I do use my "sense organs", and compare the occasions upon which I am in state A with the occasions upon which flip-flop 36 is on, I am comparing *two* things and not one.' And I do not think that we would find the argument of this mechanical Wittgenstein very convincing!

By contrast, Russell once carried the 'identity' view to the absurd extreme of maintaining that all we ever *see* is portions of our own brains. Analogously, a mechanical Russell might 'argue' that 'all I ever observe is my own vacuum tubes'. Both 'Russells' are wrong – the human being observes events in the outside world, and the process of 'observation' involves events in his brain. But we are not therefore forced to say that he 'really' observes his brain. Similarly, the machine T may 'observe', say, cans of tomato soup (if the machine's job is sorting cans of soup), and the process of 'observation' involves the functioning of vacuum tubes. But we are not forced to say that the machine 'really' observes its own vacuum tubes.

But let us consider more serious arguments on this topic. At the beginning of this paper, I pointed out that the *synthetic* character of the statement (1) 'I am in pain if, and only if, my C-fibers are stimulated' has been used as an argument for the view that the 'properties' (or 'events' or 'states') 'having C-fibers stimulated' and 'being in pain' cannot be the same. There are at least two reasons why this is not a very good argument: (a) the 'analytic-synthetic' distinction is not as sharp as that, especially where scientific laws are concerned; and (b) the criterion employed here for identifying 'properties' (or 'events' or 'states') is a very questionable one.

With respect to point (a): I have argued in chapter 2 that fundamental scientific laws cannot be happily classified as either 'analytic' or 'synthetic'. Consider, for example, the kind of conceptual shift that was involved in the transition from Euclidean to non-Euclidean geometry, or that would be involved if the law of the conservation of energy were to be abandoned. It is a distortion to say that the laws of Euclidean geometry (during their tenure of office) were 'analytic', and that Einstein merely 'changed the meaning of the words'. Indeed, it was precisely because Einstein did *not* change the meaning of the words, because he was really talking about shortest paths in the space in which

374

we live and move and have our being, that General Relativity seemed so incomprehensible when it was first proposed. To be told that one could come back to the same place by moving in one direction on a straight line! Adopting General Relativity was indeed adopting a whole new system of concepts – but that is not to say 'adopting a new system of verbal labels'.

But if it is a distortion to assimilate the revision of fundamental scientific laws to the adoption of new linguistic conventions, it is equally a mistake to follow conventional philosophers of science, and assimilate the conceptual change that Einstein inaugurated to the kind of change that arises when we discover a black swan (whereas we had previously assumed all swans to be white)! Fundamental laws are like principles of pure mathematics (as Quine has emphasized), in that they cannot be overthrown by isolated experiments: we can always hold on to the laws, and explain the experiments in various more or less *ad hoc* ways. And – in spite of the pejorative flavor of '*ad hoc*' – it is even *rational* to do this, in the case of important scientific theories, *as long as no acceptable alternative theory exists*. This is why it took a century of concept forma- tion – and not just some experiments – to overthrow Euclidean geometry. And similarly, this is why we cannot today describe *any* experiments which would *by themselves* overthrow the law of the conservation of energy – although that law is not 'analytic', and might be abandoned if a new Einstein were to suggest good *theoretical* reasons for abandoning it, plus supporting experiments.

As Hanson has put it (Hanson, 1958), our concepts have theories 'built into' them – thus, to abandon a major scientific theory without providing an alternative would be to 'let our concepts crumble'. By contrast, although we *could* have held on to 'all swans are white' in the face of conflicting evidence, there would have been no *point* in doing so – the concepts involved did not *rest* on the acceptance of this or some rival principle in the way that geometrical concepts rest on the acceptance, not necessarily of Euclidean geometry, but of *some* geometry.

I do not deny that *today* any newly-discovered 'correlation' of the form: 'One is in mental state ψ if, and only if, one is in brain state ϕ' would *at first* be a *mere* correlation, a pure 'empirical generalization'. But I maintain that the interesting case is the case that would arise if we had a worked out and theoretically elaborated *system* of such 'correla- tions'. In such a case, scientific talk would be very different. Scientists would begin to say: 'It is impossible *in principle* to be in mental state ψ without being in brain state ϕ.' And it could very well be that the 'im- possibility in principle' would amount to what Hanson rightly calls a *conceptual* (Cf. Hanson, 1958) impossibility: scientists could not *conceive* (barring a new Einstein) of someone's being in mental state ψ without being in brain state ϕ. In particular, no experiment could *by itself* overthrow psychophysical laws which had acquired this kind of status.† Is it clear that in this kind of scientific situation it would not be correct to say that ϕ and ψ are the *same* state?

Moreover, the criteria for identifying 'events' or 'states' or 'properties' are by no means so clear. An example of a law with the sort of status we have been discussing is the following: Light passes through an aperture if, and only if, electromagnetic radiation (of such-and-such wavelengths) passes through the aperture.

This law is quite clearly *not* an 'analytic' statement. Yet it would be perfectly good scientific parlance to say that: (i) light passing through an aperture and (ii) electromagnetic radiation (of such-and-such wavelengths) passing through an aperture are two descriptions of the same event. (Indeed, in 'ordinary language' not only are descriptions of the same event not required to be equivalent: one may even speak of *incompatible* descriptions of the same event!)

It might be held, however, that *properties* (as opposed to events) cannot be described by different nonequivalent descriptions. Indeed, Frege, Lewis, and Carnap have *identified* properties and 'meanings' (so that *by definition* if two expressions have different meanings then they 'signify' different properties). This seems to me very dubious. But suppose it were correct. What would follow? One would have to admit that, e.g. being in pain and having C-fibers stimulated were different properties. But, in the language of the 'theory-constructing' Turing machine described at the beginning of this paper, one would equally have to admit that 'being in state A' and 'having flip-flop 36 on' were different properties. Indeed the sentences (i) 'I am in state A' and (ii) 'Flip-flop 36 is on' are clearly non-synonymous in the machine's language by any test (they have different syntactical properties and also different 'conditions of utterance' – e.g. the machine has to use different 'methods of verification'). Anyone who wishes, then, to argue on this basis for the existence of the soul will have to be prepared to hug the souls of Turing machines to his philosophical bosom!

5. A 'linguistic' argument

The last argument I shall consider on the subject of mind–body identity is a widely used 'linguistic' argument – it was, for example,

† Cf. the discussion of geometry in chapter 2 in this volume.

used by Max Black against Herbert Feigl at the Conference which inspired this volume (*Dimensions of Mind*). Consider the sentence:

(1) Pain *is identical with* stimulation of C-fibers.

The sentence is deviant (so the argument runs, though not in this terminology): there is no statement that it could be used to make in a normal context. Therefore, if a philosopher advances it as a thesis he must be giving the words a new meaning, rather than expressing any sort of discovery. For example (Max Black argued) one might begin to say 'I have stimulated C-fibers' instead of 'I have a pain', etc. But then one would *merely* be giving the expression 'has stimulated C-fibers' the new meaning 'is in pain'. The contention is that as long as the words keep their present meanings, (1) is unintelligible.

I agree that the sentence (1) is a 'deviant' sentence in present-day English. I do *not* agree that (1) can never become a normal, non-deviant sentence unless the words change their present meanings.

The point, in a nutshell, is that what is 'deviant' depends very much upon context, including the state of our knowledge, and with the development of new scientific theories it is constantly occurring that sentences that did not previously 'have a use', that were previously 'deviant', acquire a use – not because the words acquire *new* meanings, but because the old meanings as fixed by the core of stock uses, *determine* a new use given the new context.

There is nothing wrong with trying to bring linguistic theory to bear on this issue, but one must have a sufficiently sophisticated linguistic theory to bring to bear. The real question is not a question in *synchronic* linguistics but one in *diachronic*† linguistics, not 'Is (1) *now* a deviant sentence?' but 'If a change in scientific knowledge (e.g. the development of an integrated network of psychophysical laws of high "priority" in our overall scientific world view) were to lead to (1)'s becoming a *non*-deviant sentence, would a change in the meaning of a word necessarily have taken place?' – and this is not so simple a question.

Although this is not the time or the place to attempt the job of elaborating a semantical theory,‡ I should like to risk a few remarks on this question.

In the first place, it is easy to show that the mere uttering of a sentence

† Diachronic linguistics studies the language as it changes through time; synchronic linguistic seeks only to describe the language at one particular time.

‡ For a detailed discussion, cf. Ziff, 1960. I am extremely indebted to Ziff, both for making this work available to me and for personal communications on these matters. Section 5 of the present paper represents partly Ziff's influence (especially the use of the 'synchronic–diachronic' distinction), and partly the application of some of the ideas of chapter 2 in this volume to the present topic.

which no one has ever uttered before does not necessarily constitute the introduction of a 'new use'. If I say 'There is a purple Gila monster on this desk', I am very likely uttering a sentence that no English-speaker has uttered before me: but I am not in any way changing the meaning of any word.

In the second place, even if a sentence which was formerly deviant begins to acquire a standard use, no change in the *meaning* of any word need have taken place. Thus the sentence 'I am a thousand miles away from you', or its translation into ancient Greek, was undoubtedly a deviant sentence prior to the invention of *writing*, but acquired (was not 'given' but *acquired*) a normal use with the invention of writing and the ensuing possibility of long-distance interpersonal address.

Note the reasons that we would not say that any word (e.g. 'I', 'you', 'thousand') in this sentence changed its meaning: (a) the new use was not *arbitrary*, was not the product of *stipulation*, but represented an automatic projection† from the existing stock uses of the several words making up the sentence, given the new context; (b) the meaning of a sentence is in general a function of the meanings of the individual words making it up. (In fact this principle underlies the whole notion of word meaning – thus, if we said that the sentence had changed its meaning, we should have to face the question '*Which word* changed its meaning?'. But this would pretty clearly be an embarrassing question in this case.)

The case just described was one in which the new context was the product of new technology, but new theoretical knowledge may have a similar impact on the language. (For example, 'he went all the way around the world' would be a deviant sentence in a culture which did not know that the earth was round!) A case of this kind was discussed by Malcolm: we are beginning to have the means available for telling, on the basis of various physiological indicators (electroencephalograms, eye movements during sleep, blood pressure disturbances, etc.), when dreams begin and end. The sentence 'He is halfway through his dream' may, therefore, someday acquire a standard use. Malcolm's comment on this was that the words would in that case have been given a use. Malcolm is clearly mistaken, I believe; this case, in which a sentence acquires a use *because* of what the words mean is poles apart from the case in which words are literally *given* a use (i.e. in which meanings are stipulated for expressions). The 'realistic' account of this case is, I think, obviously correct: the sentence did not previously have a use because we had no way of telling when dreams start and stop. Now we are beginning to have ways of telling, and so we are beginning to find occasions upon which it is natural to employ this sentence. (Note that in

† The term is taken from Ziff, 1960.

Malcom's account there is no explanation of the fact that we give *this* sentence *this* use.)

Now, someone may grant that change in meaning should not be confused with change in distribution,† and that scientific and technological advances frequently produce changes in the latter that are not properly regarded as changes in the former. But one might argue that whereas one could have envisaged beforehand the circumstances under which the sentence 'He went all the way around the world.' would become nondeviant, one cannot now envisage any circumstances under which‡ 'Mental state ψ is identical with brain state ϕ.' would be nondeviant. But this is not a very good objection. In the first place, it might very well have been impossible for primitive people to envisage a spherical earth (the people on the 'underside' would obviously fall off). Even forty years ago, it might have been difficult if not impossible to envisage circumstances under which 'he is halfway through his dream' would be nondeviant. And in the second place, I believe that one *can* describe in general terms circumstances under which 'Mental state ψ is identical with brain state ϕ.' would become nondeviant.

In order to do this, it is necessary to talk about one important kind of 'is' – the '*is*' *of theoretical identification*. The use of 'is' in question is exemplified in the following sentences:

(2) Light is electromagnetic radiation (of such-and-such wavelengths).

(3) Water is H_2O.

What was involved in the scientific acceptance of, for instance, (2) was very roughly this: prior to the identification there were two distinct bodies of theory – optical theory (whose character Toulmin has very well described in his book on philosophy of science), and electromagnetic theory (as represented by Maxwell's equations). The decision to *define* light as 'electromagnetic radiation of such-and-such wavelengths' was scientifically justified by the following sorts of considerations (as has often been pointed out):

(1) It made possible the *derivation* of the laws of optics (up to first approximation) from more 'basic' physical laws. Thus, even if it had accomplished nothing else, this theoretical identification would have been a move towards simplifying the structure of scientific laws.

(2) It made possible the derivation of *new* predictions in the 'reduced' discipline (i.e. optics). In particular, it was now possible to predict that in certain cases the laws of geometrical optics would *not* hold. (Cf.

† The *distribution* of a word = the set of sentences in which it occurs.

‡ Here 'Mental state ψ is identical with brain state ϕ.' is used as a surrogate for such sentences as 'Pain is identical with stimulation of C-fibers.'

Duhem's famous comments on the reduction of Kepler's laws to Newton's.)

Now let us try to envisage the circumstances under which a theoretical identification of mental states with physiological states might be in accordance with good scientific procedure. In general terms, what is necessary is that we should have not *mere* 'correlates' for subjective states, but something much more elaborate – e.g. that we should know of physical states (say micro-states of the central processes) on the basis of which we could not merely *predict* human behaviour, but causally explain it.

In order to avoid 'category mistakes', it is necessary to restrict this notion, 'explain human behavior', very carefully. Suppose a man says 'I feel bad'. His behavior, described in one set of categories, is: 'stating that he feels bad'. And the explanation may be 'He said that he felt bad because he was hungry and had a headache'. I do not wish to suggest that the event 'Jones *stating* that he feels bad' can be explained in terms of the laws of *physics*. But there is *another* event which is very relevant, namely 'Jones's body producing such-and-such sound waves'. From one point of view this is a 'different event' from Jones's stating that he feels bad. But (to adapt a remark of Hanson's) there would be no point in remarking that these are different events if there were not a sense in which they were the *same* event. And it is the sense in which these are the 'same event' and not the sense in which these are 'different events' that is relevant here.

In fine, all I mean when I speak of 'causally explaining human behavior' is: causally explaining certain physical events (motions of bodies, productions of sound waves, etc.) which are in the sense just referred to the 'same' as the events which make up human behavior. And no amount of 'Ryle-ism' can succeed in arguing away† what is obviously a possibility: that physical science might succeed in doing this much.

If this much were a reality, then theoretically identifying 'mental states' with their 'correlates' would have the following two advantages:

(1) It would be possible (again up to 'first approximation') to derive from physical theory the classical laws (or low-level generalizations) of common-sense 'mentalistic' psychology, such as: 'People tend to avoid things with which they have had painful experiences'.

(2) It would be possible to predict the cases (and they are legion) in which common-sense 'mentalistic' psychology fails.

Advantage (2) could, of course, be obtained without 'identification'

† As one young philosopher attempted to do in a recent article in the *British Journal for the Philosophy of Science*.

(by using correlation laws). But advantage (2) could equally have been obtained in the case of optics without identification (by assuming that light *accompanies* electromagnetic radiation, but is not *identical* with it.) But the *combined* effect of eliminating certain laws altogether (in favor of theoretical definitions) *and* increasing the explanatory power of the theory could not be obtained in any other way in either case. The point worth noticing is that *every* argument for *and against* identification would apply equally in the mind–body case and in the light-electro-magnetism case. (Even the 'ordinary language' argument could have been advanced against the identification of light with electromagnetic radiation.)

Two small points: (i) When I call 'light is electromagnetic radiation (of such-and-such wavelengths)' a definition, I do not mean that the statement is 'analytic'. But then 'definitions', *properly so called*, in theoretical science virtually *never* are analytic.† (Quine remarked once that he could think of at least nine good senses of 'definition' none of which had anything to do with analyticity.) Of course a philosopher might then object to the whole *rationale* of theoretical identification on the ground that it is no gain to eliminate 'laws' in favor of 'definitions' if both are *synthetic* statements. The fact that the scientist does not feel at all the same way is another illustration of how unhelpful it is to look at science from the standpoint of the question 'Analytic or synthetic?' (ii) Accepting a theoretical identification, e.g. 'Pain *is* stimulation of C-fibers', does not commit one to *interchanging* the terms 'pain' and 'stimulation of C-fibers' in idiomatic talk, as Black suggested. For instance, the identification of 'water' with 'H_2O' is by now a very well-known one, but no one says 'Bring me a glass of H_2O', except as a joke.

I believe that the account just presented is able (a) to explain the fact that sentences such as 'Mental state ψ is identical with brain state ϕ.' are deviant in present-day English, while (b) making it clear how these same sentences might become *non* deviant given a suitable increase in our scientific insight into the physical nature and causes of human behavior. The sentences in question cannot today be used to express a theoretical identification, because no such identification has been made. The act of theoretical identification is not an act that can be performed 'at will'; there are *preconditions* for its performance, as there are for many acts, and these preconditions are not satisfied today. On the other hand, if the sort of scientific theory described above should materialize, then the preconditions for theoretical identification would be met, as they were met in the light-electromagnetism case, and sentences of the type in

† This is argued in chapter 2.

question would then *automatically* require a use – namely, to express the appropriate theoretical identifications. Once again, what makes this way of *acquiring* a use different from being *given* a use (and from 'change of meaning' properly so called) is that the 'new use' is an automatic *projection* from existing uses, and does not involve arbitrary stipulation (except insofar as some element of 'stipulation' may be present in the acceptance of *any* scientific hypothesis, including 'The earth is round.').

So far we have considered only sentences of the form† 'Mental state ψ is identical with brain state ϕ.'. But what of the sentence:

(3) Mental states are micro-states of the brain.

This sentence does not, so to speak, 'give' any *particular* theoretical identification: it only says that unspecified theoretical identifications are possible. This is the sort of assertion that Feigl might make. And Black‡ might reply that in uttering (3) Feigl had uttered an odd set of words (i.e. a deviant sentence). It is possible that Black is right. Perhaps (3) is deviant in present-day English. But it is also possible that our descendants in two or three hundred years will feel that Feigl was making perfectly good sense and that the linguistic objections to (3) were quite silly. And they too may be right.

6. Machine linguistics

Let us consider the linguistic question that we have just discussed from the standpoint of the analogy between man and Turing machine that we have been presenting in this paper. It will be seen that our Turing machine will probably not be able, if it lacks suitable 'sense organs', to construct a correct theory of its own constitution. On the other hand 'I am in state A.' will be a sentence with a definite pattern of occurrence in the machine's 'language'. If the machine's 'language' is sufficiently complex, it may be possible to analyze it syntactically in terms of a finite set of basic building blocks (morphemes) and rules for constructing a potentially infinite set of 'sentences' from these. In particular, it will be possible to distinguish *grammatical*§ from *ungrammatical sentences* in the machine's 'language'. Similarly, it may be possible to associate regularities with sentence occurrences (or, 'describe sentence uses', in the Oxford jargon), and to assign 'meanings' to the finite set of morphemes and the finite set of forms of composition, in such a way that the 'uses'

† By sentences of this *form* I do not literally mean *substitution instances* of 'mental state ψ is identical with brain state ϕ.' Cf. note ‡ on page 379.

‡ I have, with hesitation, ascribed this position to Black on the basis of his remarks at the Conference. But, of course, I realize that he cannot justly be held responsible for remarks made on the spur of the moment.

§ This term is used in the sense of Chomsky, 1957, not in the traditional sense.

of the various sentences can be effectively projected from the meanings of the individual morphemes and forms of composition. In this case, one could distinguish not only 'grammatical' and 'ungrammatical' sentences in the 'machine language', but also 'deviant' and 'non-deviant' ones.

Chisholm would insist that it is improper to speak of machines as employing a language, and I agree. This is the reason for my occasionally enclosing the words 'language', 'meaning', etc., in 'raised-eyebrow' quotes – to emphasize, where necessary, that these words are being used in an extended sense. On the other hand, it is important to recognize that machine performances may be wholly *analogous* to language, so much so that the whole of linguistic theory can be applied to them. If the reader wishes to check this, he may go through a work like Chomsky's *Syntactic Structures* carefully, and note that *at no place is the assumption employed that the corpus of utterances studied by the linguist was produced by a conscious organism.* Then he may turn to such pioneer work in empirical semantics as Ziff's *Semantical Analysis* and observe that the same thing holds true for *semantical* theory.

Two further remarks in this connection: (i) Since I am contending that the mind–body problem is *strictly analogous* to the problem of the relation between structural and logical states, not that the two problems are *identical*, a suitable *analogy* between machine 'language' and human language is all that is needed here. (ii) Chisholm might contend that a 'behavioristic' semantics of the kind attempted by Ziff (i.e. one that does not take 'intentionality' as a primitive notion) is impossible. But even if this were true, it would not be relevant. For if *any* semantical theory can fit human language, it has to be shown why a completely *analogous* theory would not fit the language of a suitable machine. For instance, if 'intentionality' plays a role as a primitive notion in a *scientific* explanation of human language, then a theoretical construct with similar *formal* relations to the corresponding 'observables' will have the *same* explanatory power in the case of machine 'language'.

Of course, the objection to 'behavioristic' linguistics might *really* be an objection to all attempts at *scientific* linguistics. But this possibility I feel justified in dismissing.

Now suppose we equip our 'theory-constructing' Turing machine with 'sense organs' so that it can obtain the empirical data necessary for the construction of a theory of its own nature.

Then it may introduce into its 'theoretical language' noun phrases that can be 'translated' by the English expression 'flip-flop 36', and sentences that can be translated by 'Flip-flop 36 is on.'. These expressions will have a meaning and use quite distinct from the meaning and use of 'I am in state A.' in the machine language.

If any 'linguistic' argument really shows that the sentence 'Pain is identical with stimulation of C-fibers.' is deviant, in English, the same argument must show that 'State A is identical with flip-flop 36 being on' is deviant in the machine language. If any argument shows that 'Pain is identical with stimulation of C-fibers.' could not become non-deviant (viewing English now *dia*chronically) unless the words first altered their meanings, the same argument, applied to the 'diachronic linguistics of machine language', would show that the sentence 'State A is identical with flip-flop 36 being on.' could not become non-deviant in machine language unless the words first changed their meanings. In short, every philosophic argument that has ever been employed in connection with the mind–body problem, from the oldest and most naive (e.g. 'states of consciousness can just be *seen* to be different from physical states') to the most sophisticated, has its exact counterpart in the case of the 'problem' of logical states and structural states in Turing machines.

7. Conclusion

The moral, I believe, is quite clear: it is no longer possible to believe that the mind–body problem is a genuine theoretical problem, or that a 'solution' to it would shed the slightest light on the world in which we live. For it is quite clear that no grown man in his right mind would take the problem of the 'identity' or 'non-identity' of logical and structural states in a machine at all seriously – not because the answer is obvious, but because it is obviously of no importance *what* the answer is. But if the so-called 'mind–body problem' is nothing but a different realization of the same set of logical and linguistic issues, then it must be just as empty and just as verbal.

It is often an important insight that two problems with distinct subject matter are the same in all their logical and methodological aspects. In this case, the insight carries in its train the realization that any conclusion that might be reached in the case of the mind–body problem would have to be reached, *and for the same reasons*, in the Turing machine case. But if it is clear (as it obviously is) that, for example, the conclusion that the logical states of Turing machines are hopelessly different from their structural states, even if correct, could represent only a purely *verbal* discovery, then the same conclusion *reached by the same arguments* in the human case must likewise represent a purely verbal discovery. To put it differently, if the mind–body problem is identified with any problem of more than purely conceptual interest (e.g. with the question of whether or not human beings have 'souls')

384

then *either* it must be that (a) no argument *ever* used by a philosopher sheds the *slightest* light on it (and this independently of the way the argument tends), or (b) that some philosophic argument for mechanism is correct, or (c) that some dualistic argument does show that *both* human beings *and* Turing machines have souls! I leave it to the reader to decide which of the three alternatives is at all plausible.

19
Robots: machines or artificially created life?*

Those of us who passed many (well- or ill-spent?) childhood hours reading tales of rockets and robots, androids and telepaths, galactic civilizations and time machines, know all too well that robots – hypothetical machines that simulate human behavior, often with an at least roughly human appearance – can be friendly or fearsome, man's best friend or worst enemy. When friendly, robots can be inspiring or pathetic – they can overawe us with their superhuman powers (and with their greater than human virtue as well, at least in the writings of some authors), or they can amuse us with their stupidities and naïveté. Robots have been 'known' to fall in love, go mad (power- or otherwise), annoy with oversolicitousness. At least in the literature of science fiction, then, it is possible for a robot to be 'conscious'; that means (since 'consciousness', like 'material object' and 'universal', is a philosopher's stand-in for more substantial words) to have feelings, thoughts, attitudes, and character traits. But is it really possible? If it is possible, what are the necessary and sufficient conditions? And why should we philosophers worry about this anyway? Aren't the mind–body problem, the problem of other minds, the problem of logical behaviorism, the problem: what did Wittgenstein really mean in the private-language argument? (and why should one care?), more than enough to keep the most industrious philosopher of mind busy without dragging in or inventing the Problem of the Minds of Machines? – These are my concerns in this paper.

The mind–body problem has been much discussed in the past thirty-odd years, but the discussion seems to me to have been fruitless. No one has really been persuaded by *The Concept of Mind* that the relation of university to buildings, professors, and students is a helpful model for the relation of mind to body, or even for the relation of, say, *being intelligent* to individual speech-acts. And Herbert Feigl informs me that he has now himself abandoned his well-known 'identity theory' of the mind–body relation. The problem of other minds has been much more fruitful – the well-known and extremely important paper by Austin is ample testimony to that – but even that problem has begun to seem

* First published in *The Journal of Philosophy*, LXI (November 1964), 668–91.

somewhat stale of late. What I hope to persuade you is that the problem of the Minds of Machines will prove, at least for a while, to afford an exciting new way to approach quite traditional issues in the philosophy of mind. Whether, and under what conditions, a robot could be conscious is a question that cannot be discussed without at once impinging on the topics that have been treated under the heading Mind–Body Problem and Problem of Other Minds. For my own part, I believe that certain crucial issues come to the fore almost of their own accord in this connection – issues which *should* have been discussed by writers who have dealt with the two headings just mentioned, but which have not been – and, therefore, that the problem of the robot becomes almost obligatory for a philosopher of mind to discuss.

Before starting I wish to emphasize, lest any should misunderstand, that my concern is with how we should speak about humans and not with how we should speak about machines. My interest in the latter question derives from my just-mentioned conviction: that clarity with respect to the 'borderline-case' of robots, if it can only be achieved, will carry with it clarity with respect to the 'central area' of talk about feelings, thoughts, consciousness, life, etc.

Minds and machines

In the previous chapter I attempted to show that a problem *very* analogous to the mind–body problem would automatically arise for robots. The same point could easily have been made in connection with the problem of other minds. To briefly review the argument: conceive of a community of robots. Let these robots 'know' nothing concerning their own physical make-up or how they came into existence (perhaps they would arrive at a robot Creation Story and a polytheistic religion, with robot gods on a robot Olympus). Let them 'speak' a language (say, English), in conformity with the grammatical rules and the publicly observable semantic and discourse-analytical regularities of that language. What might the role of psychological predicates be in such a community?

In the chapter referred to, I employed a simple 'evincing' model for such predicates. Since this model is obviously *over*-simple, let us tell a more complicated story. When a robot sees something red (something that evokes the appropriate internal state in the robot) he calls it 'red'. Our robots are supposed to be capable of inductive reasoning and theory construction. So a robot may discover that something he called red was not really red. Then he will say 'well, it looked red'. Or, if he is in the appropriate internal state for red, but knows on the basis of cross-inductions from certain other cases that what he 'sees' is not really red he will say 'it *looks* red, but it isn't really red'. Thus he will have a distinction between the physical reality and the visual appearance, just as we do. But the robot will never say 'that looks as if it looked red, but it doesn't really look red'. That is, there is no notion in the robot-English of an *appearance of an appearance of red*, any more than there is in English. Moreover, the reason is the same: that any state which cannot be discriminated from 'looks-red' *counts* as 'looks-red' (under normal conditions of linguistic proficiency, absence of confusion, etc). What this illustrates, of course, is that the 'incorrigibility' of statements of the form 'that looks red' is to be explained by an elucidation of the logical features of such discourse, and not by the metaphor of 'direct' access.

If we assume that these robots are unsophisticated scientifically, there is no reason for them to know more of their own internal constitution than an ancient Greek knew about the functioning of the central nervous system. We may imagine them developing a sophisticated science in the course of centuries, and thus eventually arriving at tentative identifications of the form: 'when a thing "looks red" to one of us, it means he is in internal state "flip-flop 72 is on"'.' If these robots also publish papers on philosophy (and why should a robot not be able to do considerably better than many of our students?), a lively discussion may ensue concerning the philosophical implications of such discoveries. Some robots may argue, '*obviously*, what we have discovered is that "seeing red" *is* being in internal state "flip-flop 72 on"'; others may argue, '*obviously*, what you made was an *empirical* discovery; the *meaning* of "it looks red" isn't the same as the *meaning* of "flip-flop 72 is on"; hence the *attributes* (or states, or conditions, or properties) "being in the state of seeming to see something red" and "having flip-flop 72 on" are *two* attributes (or states, or conditions, or properties) and not *one*'; others may argue 'when I have the illusion that something red is present, nothing red is physically there. Yet, in a sense, I *see* something red. What I see, I *call* a sense datum. The sense datum is red. The flip-flop isn't red. So *obviously*, the sense datum can't be identical with the flip-flop, on or off.' And so on. In short, robots can be just as bad at philosophy as people. Or (more politely), the *logical* aspects of the Mind–Body Problem are aspects of a problem that *must* arise for any computing system satisfying the conditions that (1) it uses language and constructs theories; (2) it does not initially 'know' its own physical make-up, except superficially; (3) it is equipped with sense organs, and able to perform experiments; (4) it comes to know its own make-up through empirical investigation and theory construction.

Some objections considered

The argument just reviewed seems extremely simple. Yet some astonishing misunderstandings have arisen. The one that most surprised me was expressed thus: 'As far as I can see, all you show is that a robot could simulate human *behavior*.' This objection, needless (hopefully) -to-say, misses the point of the foregoing *completely*. The point is this: that a robot or a computing machine can, *in a sense*, follow rules (whether it is the same sense as the sense in which a man follows rules, or only analogous, depends on whether the particular robot can be said to be 'conscious', etc., and thus on the central question of this paper); that the meaning of an utterance is a function of the rules that govern its construction and use; that the rules governing the *robot* utterances 'I see something that looks red' and 'flip-flop 72 is on' are quite different. The former utterance may be correctly uttered by any robot which has 'learned' to discriminate red things from non-red things correctly, judged by the consensus of the other robots, and which finds itself in the state that signals the presence of a red object. Thus, in the case of a normally constructed robot, 'I see something that looks red' may be uttered whenever flip-flop 72 is on, *whether the robot 'knows' that flip-flop 72 is on or not.* 'Flip-flop 72 is on' may be correctly (reasonably) uttered only when the robot 'knows' that flip-flop 72 is on – i.e. only when it can *conclude* that flip-flop 72 is on from empirically established theory together with such observation statements as its conditioning may prompt it to utter, or as it may hear other robots utter. 'It looks red' is an utterance for which it does not and cannot give reasons. 'Flip-flop 72 is on' is an utterance for which it can give reasons. And so on. Since these semantic differences are the same for the robot as for a human, any argument from the semantic nonequivalence of internal (physical) state statements and 'looks' statements to the character of mind or consciousness must be valid for the robot if it is valid for a human. (Likewise the argument from the alleged fact that there is 'a sense of *see*' in which one can correctly say 'I see something red' in certain cases in which nothing red is physically present.)

Besides the misunderstandings and nonunderstandings just alluded to, some interesting objections have been advanced. These objections attempt to break the logical analogy just drawn by me. I shall here briefly discuss two such objections, advanced by Professor Kurt Baier.

Baier's first argument† runs as follows: The connection between my visual sensation of red and my utterance 'it looks as if there is something

---

† These arguments come from an unpublished paper by Baier, which was read at a colloquium at the Albert Einstein College of Medicine in 1962.

red in front of me' (or whatever) is *not* merely a causal one. The sensation does not *merely* evoke the utterance; I utter the utterance because I *know* that I am having the sensation. But the robot utters the utterance because he is *caused* to utter it by his internal state (flip-flop 72 being on). Thus there is a fundamental disanalogy between the two cases.

Baier's second argument is as follows: Certain *qualia* are *intrinsically* painful and others are *intrinsically* pleasurable. I cannot conceive of an intrinsically unpleasant quale *Q* being exactly the same for someone else 'only he finds it pleasurable'. However, if a robot is programmed so that it *acts as if* it were having a pleasant experience when, say, a certain part of its anatomy jangles, it could easily be reprogrammed so that it would act as if it were having a painful, and not a pleasant, experience upon those occasions. Thus the counterparts of 'qualia' in the robot case – certain physical states – lack an essential property of qualia: they cannot be *intrinsically* pleasurable or painful.

Can a robot have a sensation? Well, it can have a 'sensation'. That is, it can be a 'model' for any psychological theory that is true of human beings. If it is a 'model' for such a theory, then when it is in the internal state that corresponds to or 'realizes' the psychological predicate 'has the visual sensation of red', it will act as a human would act (depending also on what other 'psychological' predicates apply). That is, 'flip-flop 72 being on' does not have to *directly* (uncontrollably) 'evoke' the utterance 'It looks as if there is something red in front of me.' I agree with Baier that so simple an 'evincing' model will certainly not do justice to the character of such reports – but not in the case of robots either!

What is it for a person to 'know' that he has a sensation? Since only philosophers talk in this way, no uniform answer is to be expected. Some philosophers identify having a sensation and knowing that one has it. Then 'I know I have the visual sensation of red' just means 'I have the visual sensation of red', and the question 'Can the robot *know* that he has the "sensation" of red?' means 'Can the robot have the "sensation" of red?' – a question which we have answered in the affirmative. (I have not argued that 'sensations' are *sensations*, but only that a thorough-going logical analogy holds between sensation-talk in the case of humans and 'sensation'-talk in the case of robots.) Other philosophers (most recently Ayer, in *The Concept of a Person*) have argued that to *know* one has a sensation one must be able to describe it. But in this sense, too, a robot can know that he has a 'sensation'. If knowing that *p* is having a 'multi-tracked disposition' to appropriate sayings and question-answerings and behavings, as urged by Ryle in *The Concept of Mind*, then a robot can know anything a person can. A robot, just as well as a human, could participate in the following dialogue:

A. Describe the visual sensation you just mentioned.
B. It is the sensation of a large red expanse.
A. Is the red uniform – the same shade all over?
B. I think so.
A. Attend carefully!
B. I am!

Unfortunately for this last argument, Ryle's account of knowing is incorrect; no specifiable disposition to sayings and behavings, 'multi-tracked' or otherwise, can *constitute* a knowing-that in the way in which certain specifiable arrangements and interrelationships of buildings, administrators, professors, and students will constitute a university. 'Knowing that', like being in pain and like preferring, is only mediately related to behavior: knowing that p involves being disposed to answer certain questions correctly *if I want to, if I am not confused*, etc. And wanting to answer a question correctly is being disposed to answer it correctly *if I know the answer, if there is nothing I want more*, etc. Psychological states are characterizable only in terms of their relations to each other (as well as to behavior, etc.), and not as dispositions which can be 'unpacked' without coming back to the very psychological predicates that are in question. But this is not fatal to our case. A robot, too, can have internal states that are related to each other (and only indirectly to behavior and sensory stimulation) as required by a psychological theory. Then, when the robot is in the internal state that realizes the predicate 'knows that p' we may say that the robot 'knows' that p. Its 'knowing' may not be *knowing* – because it may not 'really be conscious' – that is what we have to decide; but it will play the role in the robot's behavior that *knowing* plays in human behavior. In sum, for any sense in which a human can 'know that he has a sensation' there will be a logically and semantically analogous sense in which a robot can 'know' that he has a 'sensation'. And this is all that my argument requires.

After this digression on the logical character of 'knowing', we are finally ready to deal with Baier's first argument. The argument may easily be seen to be a mere variant of the 'water-on-the-brain' argument (you can have water on the brain but not water on the mind; hence the mind is not the brain). One can know that one has a sensation without knowing that one is in brain-state S; hence the sensation cannot be identical with brain-state S. This is all the argument comes to. But, since 'knowing that' is an intensional context, a robot can correctly say 'I don't know that flip-flop 72 is on (or even what a"flip-flop" is, for

391

that matter)', even in situations in which it can correctly assert, 'I have the "sensation" of red'. It can even assert: 'I "know" that I have the "sensation" of red'. If it follows in the human case that the sensation of red is not identical with the brain-state S, then by the same argument from the same semantical premises, the robot philosopher can conclude that the 'sensation' of red is not identical with 'flip-flop 72 being on'. The robot philosopher too can argue: 'I am not merely *caused* to utter the utterance "It looks as if there is something red in front of me." by the occurrence of the "sensation"; part of the causation is also that I *"understand"* the words that I utter; I "know" that I am having the "sensation"; I "wish" to report my "sensation" to other robots; etc.' And, indeed, I think that Baier and the robot are both right. Psychological attributes, whether in human language or in robot language, are simply *not* the same as physical attributes. To say that a robot is angry (or 'angry') is a quite different predication from the predication 'such and such a fluid has reached a high concentration', even if the latter predicate 'physically realizes' the former. Psychological theories say that an organism has certain states which are *not* specified in 'physical' terms, but which are taken as primitive. Relations are specified between these states, and between the totality of the states and sensory inputs ('stimuli') and behavior ('responses'). Thus, as Jerry Fodor has remarked (Fodor, 1965), it is part of the 'logic' of psychological theories that (physically) *different* structures may obey (or be 'models' of) the *same* psychological theory. A robot and a human being may exhibit 'repression' or 'inhibitory potential' in exactly the same sense. I do not contend that 'angry' is a primitive term in a psychological theory; indeed, this account, which has been taken by some as a reaction to Ryle-ism, seems to me to create puzzles where none should exist (if 'angry' is a theoretical term, and 'I am angry' must be a *hypothesis*!); but I do contend that the pattern of correct usage, in the case of an ordinary-language psychological term, no more presuppose or imply that there is an *independently* specifiable state which 'realizes' the predicate, or if there is one, that it is a *physical* state in the narrow sense (definable in terms of the vocabulary of present-day physics), or, if there is one, that it is the *same* for all members of the speech community, than the postulates of a psychological theory do. Indeed, there could be a community of robots that did *not* all have the same physical constitution, but did all have the same *psychology*; and such robots could *univocally* say 'I have the sensation of red', 'you have the sensation of red', 'he has the sensation of red', even if the three robots referred to did not 'physically realize' the 'sensation of red' in the same way. Thus, the *attributes* having the 'sensation' of red and 'flip-flop 72 being on' are simply *not* identical in the case of the robots. If Materialism is taken to be the denial of the existence of 'nonphysical' attributes, then Materialism is false even for robots!

Still, Baier might reply: if I say that a robot has the 'sensation' of red, I mean that he is in *some* physical state (a 'visual' one) that signals to him the presence of red objects; if I say that a human has the sensation of red, I do not mean that he is necessarily in some special *physical* state. *Of course*, there is a *state* I am in when and only when I have the sensation of red – namely, the state of having a sensation of red. But this is a remark about the logic of 'state', and says *nothing* about the meaning of 'sensation of red'.

I think that this is right. When *we* say: 'that robot has the "sensation" of red', there are (or would be) implications that are not present when we talk about each other. But that is because we think of the robots *as* robots. Let us suppose that the robots do *not* 'think' of themselves as robots; according to their theory, they have (or possibly have) 'souls'. Then, when a robot says of another robot 'he has the "sensation" of red' (or something in more ordinary language to this effect), the implication will *not* be present that the other robot must be in any special *physical* state. Why should it not be an open possibility for the robot scientists and philosophers that they will *fail* to find 'correlates' at the physical level for the various sensations they report, just as if it is an open possibility for us that we will fail to find such correlates? To carry the analogy one final step further: if the robots go on to manufacture ROBOTS (i.e. robots that the robots themselves regard as *mere* robots), a robot philosopher will sooner or later argue: 'when I say that a ROBOT "thinks that something is red", or that something "looks red" to a ROBOT, all that I mean is the ROBOT is in a certain kind of *physical* state (admittedly, one specified by its *psychological* significance, and not by a direct physical-chemical description). The ROBOT must be able to discriminate red from non-red things, and the state in question must figure in a certain rather-hard-to-describe way in the discrimination process. But when I say that a fellow *person* (robot) "thinks that something is red", etc., I do not mean that he is necessarily in any special kind of physical state. Thus, in the only philosophically interesting sense of "sensation", persons (robots) have "sensations" and ROBOTS do not.' I conclude that Baier's first argument does not break my analogy.

The second argument seems to me to rest on two dubious premises. Granted, if the physical correlate of a given painful quale Q is something peripheral, then my brain could be 'reprogrammed' so that the event would become the physical correlate of some pleasurable psychological state; if the correlate is a highly structured state of the whole brain, then such reprogramming may well be impossible. Thus the premiss: Let S be the state of the robot's brain that 'realizes' some 'pleasure quale'; then, in principle, the robot's brain could always be reprogrammed so that S would 'realize' a 'painful quale' instead – seems to be simply false. (The other dubious premiss is the existence of *intrinsically* pleasant and painful qualia. This is supposed to be introspectively evident, but I do not find it so.)

Should robots have civil rights?

Throughout this paper I have stressed the possibility that a robot and a human may have the same 'psychology' – that is, they may obey the same psychological laws. To say that two organisms (or systems) obey the same psychological laws is not at all the same thing as to say that their behavior is similar. Indeed, two people may obey the same psychological laws and exhibit *different* behavior, even given similar environments in childhood, partly because psychological laws are only statistical and partly because crucial parameters may have different values. To know the psychological laws obeyed by a species, one must know how *any* members of that species *could* behave, given the widest variation in all the parameters that are capable of variation at all. In general, such laws, like all scientific laws, will involve abstractions – terms more or less remote from direct behavioral observation. Examples of such terms have already been given: repression, inhibitory potential, preference, sensation, belief. Thus, to say that a man and a robot have the same 'psychology' (are *psychologically isomorphic*, as I will also say) is to say that the behavior of the two *species* is most simply and revealingly analyzed, at the psychological level (in abstraction from the details of the internal physical structure), in terms of the *same* 'psychological states' and the same hypothetical parameters. For example, if a human being is a 'probabilistic automaton', then any robot with the same 'machine table' will be psychologically isomorphic to a human being. If the human brain is simply a neural net with a certain program, as in the theory of Pitts and McCulloch, then a robot whose 'brain' was a similar net, only constructed of flip-flops rather than of neurons, would have exactly the same psychology as a human. To avoid question-begging, I will consider psychology as a science that describes the behavior of any species of systems whose behavior is amenable to behavioral analysis, and intrepetation in terms of molar behavioral 'constructs' of the familiar kind (stimulus, response, drive, saturation, etc.). Thus, saying that a robot (or an octopus) has a *psychology* (obeys psychological laws) does not imply that it is necessarily conscious. For example, the mechanical 'mice' constructed by Shannon have a psychology (indeed, they were constructed precisely to serve as a model for a certain psychological theory of conditioning), but no one would contend that they are alive or conscious. In the case of Turing Machines, finite automata, etc., what I here call 'psychological isomorphism' is what I referred to in previous papers as 'sameness of functional organization'.

In the rest of this paper, I will imagine that we are confronted with a community of robots which (who?) are psychologically isomorphic to human beings in the sense just explained. I will also assume that 'psychophysical parallelism' holds good for human beings and that, if an action can be explained psychologically, the corresponding 'trajectory' of the living human body that executes that action can be explained (in principle) in physical-chemical terms. The possibility of constructing a robot psychologically isomorphic to a human being does not depend on this assumption; a robot could be psychologically isomorphic to a disembodied spirit or to a 'ghost in a machine' just as well, if such there were; but the conceptual situation will be a little less confusing if we neglect *those* issues in the present paper.

Let Oscar be one of these robots, and let us imagine that Oscar is having the 'sensation' of red. Is Oscar having the sensation of red? In more ordinary language: is Oscar *seeing* anything? Is he thinking, feeling anything? Is Oscar Alive? Is Oscar Conscious?

I have referred to this problem as the problem of the 'civil rights of robots' because that is what it may become, and much faster than any of us now expect. Given the ever-accelerating rate of both technological and social change, it is entirely possible that robots will one day exist, and argue 'we *are* alive; we *are* conscious!' In that event, what are today only philosophical prejudices of a traditional anthropocentric and mentalistic kind would all too likely develop into conservative political attitudes. But fortunately, we today have the advantage of being able to discuss this problem disinterestedly, and a little more chance, therefore, of arriving at the correct answer.

I think that the most interesting case is the case in which (1) 'psychophysical parallelism' holds (so that it can at least be contended that *we* are just as much 'physical-chemical systems' as robots are), and (2) the robots in question are psychologically isomorphic to us. This is surely the most favorable case for the philosopher who wishes to argue that robots of 'a sufficient degree of complexity' would (not just *could*, but necessarily *would*) be conscious. Such a philosopher would presumably contend that Oscar had sensations, thoughts, feelings, etc., in just the sense in which we do and that the use of 'raised-eyebrows' quotes throughout this paper whenever a psychological predicate was being applied to a robot was unnecessary. It is this contention that I wish to explore, not with the usual polemical desire to show either that materialism is correct and, hence (?), that such a robot as Oscar would be conscious or to show that all such questions have been resolved once and for all by *Philosophical Investigations*, God but give us the eyes to see it, but rather with my own perverse interest in the logical structure of the quaint and curious bits of discourse that philosophers propound as 'arguments' – and with a perhaps ultimately more serious interest in the relevant semantical aspects of our language.

Anti-civil-libertarian arguments

Some of the arguments designed to show that Oscar *could not* be conscious may be easily exposed as bad arguments. Thus, the *phonograph-record argument*: a robot only 'plays' behavior in the sense in which a phonograph record plays music. When we laugh at the joke of a robot, we are really appreciating the wit of the human programmer, and not the wit of the robot. The *reprogramming argument*: a robot has no real character of its own. It could at any time be reprogrammed to behave in the reverse of the way it has previously behaved. But a human being who was 'reprogrammed' (say, by a brain operation performed by a race with a tremendously advanced science), so as to have a new and completely predetermined set of responses, would no longer be a human being (in the full sense), but a monster. The *question-begging argument*: the so-called 'psychological' states of a robot are in reality just physical states. But *our* psychological states are *not* physical states. So it could only be in the most Pickwickian of senses that a robot was 'conscious'.

The first argument ignores the possibility of robots that *learn*. A robot whose 'brain' was merely a library of predetermined behavior routines, each imagined in full detail by the programmer, would indeed be uninteresting. But such a robot would be incapable of learning anything that the programmer did not know, and would thus fail to be psychologically isomorphic to the programmer, or to any human. On the other hand, if the programmer constructs a robot so that it will be a model of certain psychological laws, he will *not*, in general, know how it will behave in real-life situations, just as a psychologist might know all of the *laws* of human psychology, but still be no better (or little better) than anyone else at predicting how humans will behave in real-life situations. Imagine that the robot at 'birth' is as helpless as a new-born babe, and that it acquires our culture by being brought up with humans. When it reaches the stage of inventing a joke, and we laugh, it is simply not true that we are 'appreciating the wit of the programmer'. What the programmer invented was not a joke, but a system which could one day produce new jokes. The second argument, like the first, assumes that 'programmed' behavior must be wholly predictable and lack all spontaneity. If I 'reprogram' a criminal (via a brain operation) to become a good citizen, but without destroying his capacity to learn, to develop, to change (perhaps even to change back into a criminal some day), then I have certainly not created a 'monster'. If Oscar is psychologically isomorphic to a human, then Oscar can be 'reprogrammed' to the extent, and only to the extent, that a human can. The third argument assumes outright that psychological predicates never apply to Oscar and to a human in the same sense, which is just the point at issue.

All these arguments suffer from one unnoticed and absolutely crippling defect. They rely on just two facts about robots: that they are artifacts and that they are deterministic systems of a physical kind, whose behavior (including the 'intelligent' aspects) has been preselected and designed by the artificer. But it is purely contingent that these two properties are *not* properties of human beings. Thus, if we should one day discover that *we* are artifacts and that our every utterance was anticipated by our superintelligent creators (with a small 'c'), it would follow, if these arguments were sound, that *we* are not conscious! At the same time, as just noted, these two properties are *not* properties of *all* imaginable robots. Thus these arguments fail in two directions: they might 'show' that *people* are *not* conscious – because people might be the wrong sort of robots – while simultaneously failing to show that some robots are not conscious.

Pro-civil-libertarian arguments

If the usual 'anti-civil-libertarian' arguments (arguments against conceding that Oscar is conscious) are bad arguments, *pro*-civil-libertarian arguments seem to be just about nonexistent! Since the nineteenth century, materialists have contended that 'consciousness is just a property of matter at a certain stage of organization'. But as a semantic analysis this contention is hopeless (psychophysical parallelism is certainly not *analytic*), and as an identity theory it is irrelevant. Suppose that Feigl had been correct, and that sensation words *referred* to events (or 'states' or 'processes') definable in the language of physics. (As I remarked before, Feigl, no longer holds this view.) In particular, suppose 'the sensation of red' *denotes* a brain process. (It is, of course, utterly unclear what this supposition comes to. We are taught the use of 'denotes' in philosophy by being told that 'cat' denotes the class of all cats, and so on; and then some philosophers say '"the sensation of red" denotes a class of brain processes', as if *this* were now supposed to be clear! In fact, all we have been told is that '"the sensation of red" denotes a brain process' is true in case '"the sensation of red" *is* a brain process' is true. Since this latter puzzling assertion was in turn explained by the identity theorists in terms of the distinction between *denotation* and *connotation*, nothing has been explained.) Still, this does not show that Oscar is conscious. Indeed, Oscar may be psychologically isomorphic to a human without being at all similar in physical-chemical construction. So we may suppose that Oscar does not have 'brain processes' at all and, hence, (on this theory) that Oscar is *not* conscious. Moreover, if the physical 'correlate' of the sensation of red (in the case of a human) is P_1, and the physical correlate of the 'sensation' of red (in the case of Oscar) is P_2, and if P_1 and P_2 are *different* physical states, it can nonetheless be maintained that, when Oscar and I both 'see something that looks red' (or 'have the sensation of red', to use the philosophical jargon that I have allowed myself in this paper), we are in the *same* physical state, namely the *disjunction* of P_1 and P_2. How do we decide whether 'the sensation of red' (in the case of a human) is 'identical' with P_1 or 'identical' with $P_1 \vee P_2$? Identity theorists do not tell me anything that helps me to decide.

Another popular theory is that ordinary-language psychological terms, such as 'is angry' (and, presumably, such quasi-technical expressions as 'has the sensation of red') are *implicitly defined by a psychological theory*. According to this view, it would follow from the fact that Oscar and I are 'models' of the same psychological (molar behavioral) theory that psychological terms have *exactly the same sense* when applied to me and when applied to Oscar.

It may, perhaps, be granted that there is something that could be called an 'implicit psychological theory' underlying the ordinary use of psychological terms. (That an angry man will behave aggressively, unless he has strong reasons to repress his anger and some skill at controlling his feelings; that insults tend to provoke anger; that most people are not very good at controlling strong feelings of anger – are examples of what might be considered 'postulates' of such a theory. Although each of these 'postulates' is quasi-tautological, it might be contended that the conjunction of a sufficient number of them has empirical consequences, and can be used to provide empirical explanations of observed behavior.) But the view that the whole meaning of such a term as 'anger' is fixed by its place in such a theory seems highly dubious. There is not space in the present paper to examine this view at the length that it deserves. But one or two criticisms may indicate where difficulties lie.

To assert that something contains phlogiston is (implicitly) to assert that certain laws, upon which the concept of phlogiston depends, are correct. To assert that something is electrically charged is in part to assert that the experimental laws upon which the concept of electricity is based and which electrical theory is supposed to explain, are not radically and wholly false. If the 'theory' upon which the term anger 'depends' really has empirical consequences, then even to say 'I am angry' is in part to assert that these empirical consequences are not radically and wholly false. Thus it would not be absurd, if 'anger' really *were* a theoretical term, to say 'I think that I am very angry, but I'm not sure' or 'I think that I have a severe pain, but I'm not sure' or 'I think that I am conscious, but I'm not sure', since one might well not be sure that the experimental laws implied by the 'psychological theory' implicit in ordinary language are in fact correct. It would also not be absurd to say: 'perhaps there is not really any such thing as anger' or 'perhaps there is not really any such thing as pain' or 'perhaps there is not really any such thing as being conscious'. Indeed, no matter how certain I might be that I have the sensation of red, it might be proved *by examining other people* that I did *not* have that sensation and that in fact there was no such thing as having the sensation of red. Indeed, 'that *looks like* the sensation of red' would have a perfectly good use – namely, to mean that my experience is as it would be if the 'psychological theory implicit in ordinary language' were true, but the theory is not in fact true. These consequences should certainly cast doubt on the idea that 'psychological terms in ordinary language' really are 'theoretical constructs'.

It is obvious that 'psychological terms in ordinary language' have a *reporting use*. In the jargon of philosophers of science, they figure in *observation statements*. 'I am in pain' would be such a statement. But clearly, a term that figures in observational reports has an observational use, and that use must enter into its meaning. Its meaning cannot be fixed merely by its relation to other terms, in abstraction from the actual speech habits of speakers (including the habits upon which the reporting use depends).

The first difficulty suggests that the 'psychological theory' that 'implicitly defines' such words as 'anger' has in fact *no* nontautological consequences – or, at least, no empirical consequences that could not be abandoned without changing the meaning of these words. The second difficulty then further suggests that the job of fixing the meaning of these words is only partially done by the logical relationships (the 'theory'), and is completed by the reporting use.

A third difficulty arises when we ask just what it is that the 'psychological theory implicit in ordinary language' is supposed to be *postulating*. The usual answer is that the theory postulates the existence of certain *states* which are supposed to be related to one another and to behavior as specified in the theory. But what does 'state' mean? If 'state' is taken to mean physical state, in the narrow sense alluded to before, then psychophysical parallelism would be implied by an arbitrary 'psychological' assertion, which is obviously incorrect. On the other hand, if 'state' is taken in a sufficiently wide sense so as to avoid this sort of objection, then (as Wittgenstein points out) the remark that 'being angry is being in a certain psychological state' *says nothing whatsoever*.

In the case of an ordinary scientific theory (say, a physical theory), to postulate the existence of 'states' S_1, S_2, ... , S_n satisfying certain postulates is to assert that one of two things is the case: either (1) physical states (definable in terms of the existing primitives of physical theory) can be found satisfying the postulates; or (2) it is necessary to take the new predicates S_1, ... , S_n (or predicates in terms of which they can be defined) as additional primitives in physical science, and widen our concept of 'physical state' accordingly. In the same way, identity theorists have sometimes suggested that 'molar psychological theory' *leaves it open* whether or not the states it postulates are physical states or not. But if physical states *can* be found satisfying the postulates, then they are the ones referred to by the postulates. 'State' is then a methodological term, so to speak, whose status is explained by a perspicuous representation of the procedures of empirical theory construction and confirmation. This solution to our third difficulty reduces to the identity theory under the supposition that psychophysical parallelism holds, and that physical states *can* be found 'satisfying' the postulates of 'molar behavioral psychology'.

Even if this solution to the third difficulty is accepted, however, the first two difficulties remain. To be an empirically confirmable scientific theory, the 'molar behavioral theory' implicit in the ordinary use of psychological terms must have testable empirical consequences. If the ordinary-language psychological terms really designate states postulated by this theory, then, if the theory is radically false, we must say there are no such 'states' as being angry, being in pain, having a sensation, etc. And this must always remain a possibility (on this account), no matter what we observe, since no finite number of observations can deductively establish a scientific theory properly so-called. Also, the reporting role of 'psychological' terms in ordinary language is not discussed by this account. If saying 'I am in pain' is simply ascribing a *theoretical* term to myself, then this report is in part a *hypothesis*, and one which may always be false. This account – that the ordinary use of 'psychological' terms presupposes an empirical theory, and one which may be radically false – has recently been urged by Paul Feyerabend. Feyerabend would accept the consequence that I have rejected as counterintuitive: that there may not really be any pains, sensations, etc. in the customary sense. But where is this empirical theory that is presupposed by the ordinary use of 'psychological' terms? Can anyone state *one* behavioral law which is clearly empirical and which is presupposed by the concepts of sensation, anger, etc.? The empirical connection that exists, say, between being in pain and saying 'ouch', or some such thing, has sometimes been taken (by logical behaviorists, rather than by identity theorists) to be such a law. I have tried to show elsewhere,† however, that no such law is really required to be true for the application of the concept of pain in its customary sense. What entitles us to say that a man is in pain in our world may not entitle one to say that he is in pain in a different world; yet the *same* concept of pain may be applicable. What I contend is that to understand any 'psychological' term, one must be implicitly familiar with a network of *logical* relationships, and one must be adequately trained in the reporting use of that word. It is also necessary, I believe, that one be prepared to accept first-person statements by other members of one's linguistic community involving these predicates, at least when there is no *special* reason to distrust them; but this is a general convention associated with discourse, and not part of the meaning of any particular word, psychological or otherwise. Other general conventions associated with discourse, in my opinion, are the acceptance of not-too-bizarre rules of inductive inference and theory confirmation and of certain fundamental rules of deductive inference. But these things, again, have to do with one's discourse *as a whole* not being linguistically deviant, rather than with one's understanding any particular word. If I am not aware that someone's crying out (in a certain kind of context) is a sign that he is in pain, I can be *told*. If I refuse (without good reason) to believe what I am told, it can be pointed out to me that, when I am in that context (say, my finger is burnt), I feel pain, and no condition known by me to be relevant to the feeling or nonfeeling of pain is different in the case of the Other. If I *still* feel no inclination to ascribe pain to the Other, then my whole concept of discourse is abnormal – but

---

† In chapter 16 in this volume. The character of psychological concepts is also discussed by me in 'The mental life of some machines', chapter 20 below.

it would be both a gross understatement and a misdiagnosis to say that I 'don't know the meaning of "pain"'.

I conclude that 'psychological' terms in ordinary language are *not* theoretical terms. Moreover, the idea that, if psychophysical parallelism is correct, then it is analytic that pain *is* the correlated brain-state is not supported by a shred of linguistic evidence. (Yet this is a consequence of the combined 'identity theory-theoretical term' account as we developed it to meet our third difficulty.) I conclude that any attempt to show that Oscar is conscious (analytically, relative to our premises) along these lines is hopeless.

Ziff's argument

So far all the arguments we have considered, on both sides of the question: Is Oscar conscious? have been without merit. No sound consideration has been advanced to show that it is false, given the meaning of the words in English and the empirical facts as we are assuming them, that Oscar is conscious; but also no sound consideration has been advanced to show that it is true. If it is a violation of the rules of English to say (without 'raised-eyebrows quotes') that Oscar is in pain or seeing a rose or thinking about Vienna, we have not been told *what* rules it violates; and if it is a violation of the rules of English to *deny* that Oscar is conscious, given his psychological isomorphism to a human being, we have likewise not been told what rules it violates. In this situation, it is of interest to turn to an ingenious ('anti-civil-libertarian') argument by Paul Ziff.†

Ziff wishes to show that it is false that Oscar is conscious. He begins with the undoubted fact that if Oscar is not alive he cannot be conscious. Thus, given the semantical connection between 'alive' and 'conscious' in English, it is enough to show that Oscar is not *alive*. Now, Ziff argues, when we wish to tell whether or not something is alive, we do *not* go by its *behaviour*. Even if a thing looks like a flower, grows in my garden like a flower, etc., if I find upon taking it apart that it consists of gears and wheels and miniaturized furnaces and vacuum tubes and so on, I say 'what a clever mechanism', not 'what an unusual plant'. It is *structure*, not *behavior* that determines whether or not something is alive; and it is a violation of the semantical rules of our language to say of anything that is clearly a mechanism that it is 'alive'.

Ziff's argument is unexpected, because of the great concentration in

---

† I take the liberty of reporting an argument used by Ziff in a conversation. I do not wish to imply that Ziff necessarily subscribes to the argument in the form in which I report it, but I include it because of its ingenuity and interest.

the debate up to now upon *behavior*, but it certainly calls attention to relevant logical and semantical relationships. Yet I cannot agree that these relationships are as clear-cut as Ziff's argument requires. Suppose that we construct a robot – or, let me rather say, an *android*, to employ a word that smacks less of mechanism – out of 'soft' (protoplasm-like) stuff. Then, on Ziff's account, it may be perfectly correct, if the android is sufficiently 'life-like' in structure, to say that we have 'synthesized life'. So, given two artifacts, both 'models' of the same psychological theory, both completely deterministic physical-chemical systems, both designed to the same end and 'programmed' by the designer to the same extent, it may be that we must say that one of them is a 'machine' and not conscious, and the other is a 'living thing', (albeit 'artificially created') and conscious, simply because the one consists of 'soft stuff' and the other consists of 'hardware'. A great many speakers of English, I am sure (and I am one of them), would find the claim that this dogmatic decision is required by the meaning of the word 'alive' quite contrary to their linguistic intuitions. I think that the difficulty is fundamentally this: a plant does not exhibit much 'behavior'. Thus it is natural that criteria having to do with *structure* should dominate criteria having to do with 'behavior' when the question is whether or not something that looks and 'behaves' like a plant is really a living thing or not. But in the case of something that looks and behaves like an *animal* (and especially like a *human being*), it is natural that criteria having to do with behavior – and not just with actual behavior, but with the *organization* of behavior, as specified by a psychological theory of the thing – should play a much larger role in the decision. Thus it is not unnatural that we should be prepared to argue, in the case of the 'pseudo-plant', that 'it isn't a living thing because it is a mechanism', while some are prepared to argue, in the case of the robot, that 'it isn't a *mere* mechanism, because it is *alive*', and 'it is alive, because it is conscious', and 'it is conscious because it had the same behavioral organization as a living human being'. Yet Ziff's account may well explain why it is that many speakers are not convinced by these latter arguments. The tension between conflicting criteria results in the 'obviousness', to some minds, of the robot's 'machine' status, and the equal 'obviousness', to other minds, of its 'artificial-life' status.

There is a sense of 'mechanism' in which it is clearly analytic that a mechanism cannot be alive. Ziff's argument can be reduced to the contention that, on the normal interpretation of the terms, it is analytic in English that something whose *parts* are all mechanisms, in this sense, likewise cannot be alive. If this is so, then no English speaker should suppose that he could even *imagine* a robot *thinking, being power-mad, hating humans,* or *being in love,* any more than he should suppose that he could imagine a married bachelor. It seems evident to me (and indeed to most speakers) that, absurdly or not, we *can* imagine these things. I conclude, therefore, that Ziff is wrong: it may be *false,* but it is not a *contradiction,* to assert that Oscar is alive.

The 'know-nothing' view

We have still to consider the most traditional view of our question. According to this view, which is still quite widely held, *it is possible that Oscar is conscious, and it is possible that he is not conscious.* In its theological form, the argument runs as follows: I am a creature with a body and a soul. My body happens to consist of flesh and blood, but it might just as well have been a machine, had God chosen. Each voluntary movement of my body is correlated with an activity of my soul (how and why is a 'mystery'). So, it is quite possible that Oscar has a soul, and that each 'voluntary' movement of his mechanical body is correlated in the same mysterious way with an activity of his soul. It is also possible – since the laws of physics suffice to explain the motions of Oscar's body, without use of the assumption that he has a soul – that Oscar is but a lifeless machine. There is absolutely no way in which we can know. This argument can also be given a nontheological (or at least apparently nontheological) form by deleting the reference to God, and putting 'mind' for 'soul' throughout. To complete the argument, it is contended that I know what it *means* to say that Oscar has a 'soul' (or has a pain, or the sensation of red, etc.) *from my own case.*

One well-known difficulty with this traditional view is that it implies that it is also possible that other humans are not really conscious, even if they are physically and psychologically isomorphic to me. It is contended that I can know with *probability* that other humans are conscious by the 'argument from analogy'. But in the inductive sciences, an argument from analogy is generally regarded as quite weak unless the conclusion is capable of further and independent inductive verification. So it is hard to believe that our reasons for believing that other persons are conscious are very strong ones if they amount simply to an analogical argument with a conclusion that admits of *no* independent check, observational, inductive, or whatever. Most philosophers have recently found it impossible to believe *either* that our reasons for believing that other persons are conscious are that weak *or* that the possibility exists that other persons, while being admittedly physically and psychologically isomorphic (in the sense of the present paper) to myself, are not conscious. Arguments on this point may be found in the writings of all the major analytical philo-sophers of the present century. Unfortunately, many of these arguments depend upon quite dubious theories of meaning.

The critical claim is the claim that it follows from the fact that I have the sensation of red, I can imagine this sensation, 'I know what it is like', that I can understand the assertion that Oscar has the sensation of red (or any other sensation or psychological state). In a sense, this is right. I *can*, in one sense, understand the *words*. I can parse them; I don't think 'sensation of red' means *baby carriage*, etc. More than that: I know what I would experience if I were conscious and psychologically as I am, but with Oscar's mechanical 'body' in place of my own. How does this come to be so? It comes to be so, at least in part, because we have to learn from experience what our own bodies are like. If a child were brought up in a suitable kind of armor, the child might be deceived into thinking that it was a robot. It would be harder to fool him into thinking that he had the internal structure of a robot, but this too could be done (fake X-rays, etc.). And when I 'imagine myself in the shoes of a (conscious) robot', what I do, of course, is to imagine the sensations that I might have if I were a robot, or rather *if I were a human who mis-takenly thought that he was a robot*. (I look down at my feet and see bright metal, etc.)

Well, let us grant that in this sense we *understand* the sentence 'Oscar is having the sensation of red'. It does not follow that the sentence possesses a truth value. We understand the sentence 'The present King of France is bald.', but, on its normal interpretation in English, the sentence has no truth value under present conditions. We can give it one by adopting a suitable convention – for example, Russell's theory of descriptions – and more than one such suitable convention exists. The question really at issue is *not* whether we can 'understand' the sentences 'Oscar is conscious.' (or 'has the sensation of red' or 'is angry') and 'Oscar is not conscious.', in the sense of being able to use them in such contexts as 'I can perfectly well picture to myself that Oscar is conscious.', but whether there really is an intelligible sense in which one of these sentences is true, on a normal interpretation, and the other false (and in that case, whether it is also true that we can't tell which).

Let us revert, for a moment, to our earlier fantasy of ROBOTS – i.e. second-order robots, robots created by robots and regarded by robots as *mere* ROBOTS. As already remarked, a robot philosopher might very well be led to consider the question: Are ROBOTS conscious? The robot philosopher 'knows' of course, just what 'experiences' he would have if he were a 'conscious' ROBOT (or a robot in a ROBOT suit). He can perfectly well picture to himself that a ROBOT could have 'sensation'.

So he may perfectly well arrive at the position that it is logically possible that ROBOTS have sensations (or, rather, 'sensations') and perfectly possible that they do not, and moreover he can never know. What do we think of this conclusion?

It is clear what we should think: we should think that there is not the slightest reason to suppose (and every reason not to suppose) that there is a special property, 'having the "sensation" of red', which the ROBOT may or may not have, but which is inaccessible to the robot. The robot, knowing the physical and psychological description of the ROBOT, is in a perfectly good position to answer all questions about the ROBOT that may reasonably be asked. The idea that there is a further question (class of questions) about the ROBOT which the robot cannot answer is suggested to the robot by the fact that these alleged 'questions' are grammatically well formed, can be 'understood' in the sense discussed above, and that the possible 'answers' can be 'imagined'.

I suggest that our position with respect to robots is *exactly* that of robots with respect to ROBOTS. There is not the slightest reason for us, either, to believe that 'consciousness' is a well-defined property, which each robot either *has* or *lacks*, but such that it is not possible, on the basis of the physical description of the robot, or even on the basis of the psychological description (in the sense of 'psychological' explained above), to *decide* which (if any) of the robots possesses this property and which (if any) fail to possess it. The rules of 'robot language' may well be such that it is perfectly possible for a robot to 'conjecture' that ROBOTS have 'sensations' and also perfectly possible for a robot to conjecture that ROBOTS do not have 'sensations'. It does not follow that the physical and psychological description of the ROBOTS is 'incomplete', but only that the concept of 'sensation' (in 'raised-eyebrow quotes') is a well-defined concept only when applied to robots. The question raised by the robot philosopher: Are ROBOTS 'conscious'? calls for a decision and not for a discovery. The decision, at bottom, is this: do I treat ROBOTS as fellow members of my linguistic community, or as machines? If the ROBOTS are accepted as full members of the robot community, then a robot can find out whether a ROBOT is 'conscious' or 'unconscious', 'alive' or 'dead' in just the way he finds out these things about a fellow robot. If they are rejected, then nothing *counts* as a ROBOT being 'conscious' or 'alive'. Until the decision is made, the statement that ROBOTS are 'conscious' has no truth value. In the same way, I suggest, the question: Are robots conscious? calls for a decision, on our part, to treat robots as fellow members of our linguistic community, or not to so treat them. As long as we leave this decision unmade, the statement that robots (of the kind described) are conscious has no truth value.

If we reject the idea that the physical and psychological description of the robots is incomplete (because it 'fails to specify whether or not they are conscious'), we are not thereby forced to hold either that 'consciousness' is a 'physical' attribute or that it is an attribute 'implicitly defined by a psychological theory'. Russell's question in the philosophy of mathematics: If the number 2 is not the set of all pairs, then what on earth is it? was a silly question. Two is simply the second number, and nothing else. Likewise, the materialist question: If the attribute of 'consciousness' is not a physical attribute (or an attribute implicitly defined by a psychological theory) then what on earth is it? is a silly question. Our psychological concepts in ordinary-language are as we have fashioned them. The 'framework' of ordinary language psychological predicates is what it is and not another framework. *Of course* materialism is false; but it is so *trivially* false that no materialist should be bothered!

Conclusion

In this chapter, I have reviewed a succession of failures: failures to show that we *must* say that robots are conscious, failures to show that we *must* say they are not, failures to show that we *must* say that we can't tell. I have concluded from these failures that there is no correct answer to the question: Is Oscar conscious? Robots may indeed have (or lack) properties unknown to physics and undetectable by us; but not the slightest reason has been offered to show that they do, as the ROBOT analogy demonstrates. It is reasonable, then, to conclude that the question that titles this paper calls for a decision and not for a discovery. If we are to make a decision, it seems preferable to me to extend our concept so that robots *are* conscious – for 'discrimination' based on the 'softness' or 'hardness' of the body parts of a synthetic 'organism' seems as silly as discriminatory treatment of humans on the basis of skin color. But my purpose in this paper has not been to improve our concepts, but to find out what they are.

20

The mental life of some machines*

In this paper I want to discuss the nature of various 'mentalistic' notions in terms of a machine analog. In chapter 18, I tried to show that the conceptual issues surrounding the traditional mind–body problem have nothing to do with the supposedly special character of human subjective experience, but arise for any computing system of a certain kind of richness and complexity, in particular for any computing system able to construct theories concerning its own nature. In that paper I was primarily interested in the issues having to do with mind–body identity. In the present paper the focus will be rather in trying to shed light on the character of such notions as preferring, believing, feeling. I hope to show by considering the use of these words in connection with a machine analog that the traditional alternatives – materialism, dualism, logical behaviorism – are incorrect, even in the case of these machines. My objectives are not merely destructive ones; I hope by indicating what the character of these words is in the case of the machine analog to suggest to some extent what their character is in application to human beings.

One question which I shall not discuss, except for these remarks at the outset, is the question to what extent the application of such terms as 'preference' to Turing Machines represents a change or extension of meaning. I shall not discuss this question; as will become clear, it is not too relevant to my undertaking. Even if the sense in which the Turing Machines I shall describe may be said to 'prefer' one thing to another is *very* different in *many* ways from the sense in which a human being is said to prefer one thing to another, this does not run contrary to anything that I claim. What I claim is that seeing why it is that the analogs of materialism, dualism, and logical behaviorism are false in the case of these Turing Machines will enable us to see why the theories are incorrect in the case of human beings, and seeing what these terms might mean in the case of Turing Machines will at least suggest to us

* First published in H. Castaneda (ed.) *Intentionality, Minds and Perception* (Detroit 1967). Reprinted by permission of the Wayne State University Press.

important logical features of these terms which have previously been overlooked by philosophers.

In this paper, then, I am going to consider a hypothetical 'community' made up of 'agents', each of whom is in fact a Turing Machine, or, more precisely, a finite automaton. (Of the many useful equivalent definitions of 'finite automaton', the most useful for present purposes is the one that results if the definition of a Turing Machine is modified by specifying that the tape should be *finite*.) The Turing Machines I want to consider will differ from the abstract Turing Machines considered in logical theory in that we will consider them to be equipped with sense organs by means of which they can scan their environment, and with suitable motor organs which they are capable of controlling. We may think of the sense organs as causing certain 'reports' to be printed on the tape of the machine at certain times, and we may think of the machine as being constructed so that when certain 'operant' symbols are printed by the machine on its tape, its motor organs execute appropriate actions. This is the natural generalization of a Turing Machine to allow for interaction with an environment.

The fundamental concept we want to discuss will be the concept of *preference*. In order to give this concept formal content with respect to the behavior of these 'agents', we will suppose that each of these agents is described by a rational preference function, in the sense of economic theory.†We will suppose that our Turing Machines are sufficiently complex so as to be able to make reasonably good estimates of the probability of various states of affairs. Given the inductive estimates made by a machine, the behavior of the machine will then be completely determined by the fact that the machine is to obey the rule: act so as to maximize the estimated utility.

The reader should note that the term 'utility' is completely eliminable here. What we are saying is that there is associated with each machine a certain mathematical function, called a utility function, such that that function together with another function, the machine's 'degree of confirmation' function, completely determines the machine's behavior in accordance with a certain rule and certain theorems of the probability calculus. (Cf. Carnap, 1950, esp, pp. 253–79) In short, our machines are *rational agents* in the sense in which that term is used in inductive logic and economic theory. If the rational preference functions of these machines resemble the rational preference functions of idealized human

† Von Neumann (1953), pp. 26f, 83 *et al.* Von Neumann and Morgenstern think of such a function as an assignment of coordinates (in an *n*-dimensional space) to objects, the sum of the coordinates being the 'value' of the object. Here it will be convenient to think of it as a function assigning a 'utility' to 'possible worlds' (or 'state descriptions' in the sense of Carnap).

beings, and the computing skills of the machines are approximately equal to the computing skills of human beings, then the behavior of these machines will closely resemble the behavior of (idealized) human beings. We can complicate this model by introducing into the behavior of these machines certain irrationalities which resemble the irrationalities in the behavior of actual human beings (e.g. failure of the transitivity of preference), but this will not be attempted here.

What then does 'prefer' mean as applied to one of these machines? As a start it simply means that the function which controls the behavior of the machine (more precisely, the function which together with the machine's inductive logic controls the behavior of the machine) assigns a higher weight to the first alternative than to the second. Even at the outset we can see that the relation of preferring to behavior is going to be quite complicated for these machines. For example, if one of these machines prefers A to B, it does not necessarily follow that in any concrete situation it will choose A rather than B. In deciding whether to choose A rather than B, the machine will have to consider what the consequences of its choice are likely to be in the concrete situation, and this may well bring in 'values' of the machine other than the preference that the machine assigns to A over B. We might say that if the machine prefers A to B then that means that *ceteris paribus* the machine will choose A over B, and we might despair of ever spelling out in any precise way the *ceteris paribus* clause. In an analogous way, Miss Anscombe† has suggested that if someone intends not to have an accident then that means that, *ceteris paribus*, he will choose methods of driving from one place to another that are likely to minimize the chance of having an accident. She has suggested that in this kind of case the *ceteris paribus* clause could not *in principle* be spelled out in detail. On this basis she has gone on to suggest a fundamental difference between what she calls practical reason and scientific reason. This conclusion should be viewed with some suspicion, however. The fact is that she has shown that certain proposed methods of spelling out the *ceteris paribus* clause in question would not work; but these methods would not work in the case of our machines either. It hardly follows that our machines exhibit in their ordinary 'behavior' a form of reasoning fundamentally different from scientific reasoning. On the contrary, given a rational preference function, always acting so as to maximize the estimated utility is exhibiting scientific reasoning of a very high order.

Miss Anscombe might reply that actual human beings do not have rational preference functions. However, von Neumann and Morgen-

† Anscombe, 1957, esp. pp. 59–61. I wish to emphasize that the view I am criticizing occurs in only three pages of what I regard as an excellent book.

stern have shown, and this is the fundamental result in the area, that any agent whose preferences are consistent always does behave in a way which can be interpreted in terms of at least one rational preference function. Miss Anscome might reply that actual human beings do not have consistent preferences; but this would be to say that the difference between practical reason and scientific reason is that practical reason is often in fact more or less irrational – that everyone's practical reasoning is irrational in some areas. This is like saying that deductive logic is different in principle from the logic contained in any textbook because everyone's deductive reasoning is bad in some areas. The fact is that Miss Anscombe's remarks on intentions are supposed to apply not only to the intentional behavior of more or less irrational human beings but just as much to the intentional behavior of an ideally rational human being with a rich and complex system of values. I think this is quite clear from reading her whole book. But for such an agent one of her major conclusions is just false: the practical reasoning of such an agent would be, as we have seen, not at all unlike scientific reasoning.†

The point in a nutshell is that practical reasoning *is* fundamentally different from scientific reasoning if we think of scientific reasoning as consisting of syllogisms, the premisses of which can in principle be spelled out exactly, and we think of practical reasoning as consisting of so-called 'practical syllogisms' whose premisses must in all interesting cases contain ineliminable *ceteris paribus* clauses. However, actual scientific reasoning involves modes of connecting premisses and conclusions much more complex than the syllogism, and decision making, either actual or idealized, involves modes of reasoning which are

† Some of the differences between practical and theoretical reasoning pointed out by Miss Anscombe do hold. For instance, that the main premiss must mention something wanted, and that the conclusion must be an action (although 'there is no objection to inventing a form of words by which he *accompanies* this action, which we may call the conclusion in a verbalized form.' *Ibid.*, p. 60). What I challenge is the claim that the conclusion (in 'verbalized form') does not follow *deductively* from the premisses (at least in many cases – cf. her n. 1 on p. 58) and cannot be made to follow, unless the major premiss is an 'insane' one which no one would accept. This leads Miss Anscombe to the view that Aristotle was really engaged in 'describing an order which is there whenever actions are done with intentions' (p. 79). This comes perilously close to suggesting that engaging in practical reasoning is merely performing actions with intentions. Mary Mothersill, in Mothersill, 1962, criticizes Miss Anscombe on this same point but seems to miss the force of her argument. To say, as Mothersill does, that 'do everything conducive to not having a car crash' has a '*non*insane' interpretation is surely true but no help, since *on the noninsane interpretation*, 'do this' does not follow deductively from the major premiss together with '*this* is conducive to not having a car crash' – *this* may not be an *appropriate* action, and 'do everything' means (on the 'noninsane' interpretation) 'do everything appropriate' (*ibid.*, p. 455). Mothersill seems to assume that 'assuming appropriate conditions' could be spelled out, but this is just what Anscombe is denying.

depicted much too inexactly by being forced into the traditional mold of the 'practical syllogism'. The complex weighing of multitudinous conflicting alternatives and values does admit of deductive schematization; but not the type of deductive schematization considered by Miss Anscombe (and Aristotle).

Before going on, I should like to make one comment which may perhaps prevent some misunderstandings. A Turing Machine is simply a system having a discrete set of states which are related in certain ways. Usually we think of a Turing Machine as having a memory in the form of a paper tape upon which it prints symbols; however, this can be regarded as mere metaphor. Instead, in the case of a finite automaton, i.e. a Turing Machine whose tape is finite instead of potentially infinite, the tape may be thought of as physically realized in the form of any finite system of memory storage. What we mean by a 'symbol' is simply any sort of *trace* which can be placed in this memory storage and later 'scanned' by some mechanism or other. We can generalize further by allowing the 'machine' to 'print' more than one symbol at a time and to scan more than one symbol at a time. Turing has shown that these generalizations leave the class of Turing Machines essentially unchanged. Note then that a Turing Machine need not even be a *machine*. A Turing Machine might very well be a biological organism. The question whether an actual human being is a Turing Machine (or rather a finite automaton), or whether the brain of a human being is a Turing Machine, is an empirical question. Today we know nothing strictly incompatible with the hypothesis that you and I are one and all Turing Machines, although we know some things that make this unlikely. Strictly speaking, a Turing Machine need not even be a physical system; anything capable of going through a succession of states in time can be a Turing Machine. Thus, to the Cartesian dualist, who likes to think of the human mind as a self-contained system in some sort of causal interaction with the body, one can say that from the point of view of pure logic it is entirely possible that the human mind is a Turing Machine (assuming that the human mind is capable of some large but finite set of states, which seems certainly true). To the person who believes that human beings have souls and that personality and memory reside in the soul and survive bodily death, one may say again that from the standpoint of pure logic it is entirely possible that the human soul is a Turing Machine, or rather a finite automaton.

Although it is likely that human brain states form a discrete set and that human mental states form a discrete set, no matter what meaning may be given to the somewhat ambiguous notion of a mental state, it is somewhat unlikely that either the mind or the brain is a Turing Machine.

Reasoning *a priori* one would think it more likely that the interconnections among the various brain states and mental states of a human being are probabilistic rather than deterministic and that time-delays play an important role. However, empirical evidence is scarce. The reason is that an automaton whose states are connected by probabilistic laws and whose behavior involves time-delays can be arbitrarily well-simulated by the behavior of a Turing Machine. Thus, in the nature of the case, mere empirical data cannot decide between the hypothesis that the human brain (respectively, *mind*) is a Turing Machine and the hypothesis that it is a more complex kind of automaton with probabilistic relations and time-delays.

There is another respect in which our model is certainly over-simplified, however, even if the human brain and mind *are* Turing Machines. As has already been remarked, the necessary and sufficient condition that someone's behavior at a given time should be consistent with the assignment of some rational preference function is that his choices be consistent – e.g. if he prefers A to B and he prefers B to C, then he prefers A to C. But even this very weak axiom of transitivity is violated by the preferences of very many, perhaps all, actual people. Thus, it is doubtful that any actual human being's pattern of choices is consistent with the assignment of a rational preference function. Moreover, even if someone's pattern of preferences is consistent with the assignment of a rational preference function, it is doubtful that people consistently obey the rule: maximize the estimated utility.

And, finally, our model is not dynamical. That is to say, it does not allow for the change of the rational preference function with time – although this last feature can be modified. Thus our model is an overly simple and overly rationalistic one in a number of respects. However, it would be easy, in principle, although perhaps impossible in practice, to complicate our model in all these respects – to make the model dynamical, to allow for irrationalities in preference, to allow for irrationalities in the inductive logic of the machine, to allow for deviations from the rule: maximize the estimated utility. But I do not believe that any of these complications would affect the philosophical conclusions reached in this paper. In other words, I do not believe that the philosophical conclusions of this paper would be changed if we replaced the notion of a Turing Machine by the notion of a K-machine, where the notion of a K-machine were made sufficiently rich and complex so that human brains and minds were, literally, K-machines.

Besides saying that they are Turing Machines and that they have rational preference functions, I shall say nothing about my hypothetical 'agents'. They could be artifacts, they could be biological organisms, they could even be human beings. In particular then, I shall nowhere specify in this paper that the 'agents' in my 'community' are alive or not alive, conscious or not conscious. There is, however, a sense in which we may say of these agents, regardless of their physical realization, that they are *conscious of* certain things and *not conscious of* others. Moreover, if they have periods of what answers to sleep, then there is one use of 'conscious' and 'unconscious' in which we may say that they are 'conscious' at certain times and 'unconscious' at others.

2. Materialism

It does not, I think, have to be shown that Cartesian dualism is untenable as a description of the 'inner life' of these machines and of the relation of that inner life to their behavior. The 'agents' are simply certain systems of states in certain causal interrelations; *all* of their states are causally interrelated. There are not two separate 'worlds', a 'world' of 'inner' states and a 'world' of 'outer' states in some peculiar kind of correlation or connection. They are not ghosts in Turing Machines, they *are* Turing Machines.

But what of materialism? If materialism as a philosophical doctrine is correct as an account of the mental life of *any* organism, then it should *certainly* be correct as an account of what corresponds to the 'mental life' of *these* agents – at least if we imagine the agents to be realized as automata built out of flip-flops, relays, vacuum tubes, and so forth. But even in this last case I shall argue that traditional materialism is incorrect.

Traditional materialism (which is pretty much of a philosopher's straw man by now) holds that mental conduct words are definable in terms of concepts referring to physical-chemical composition. If this is right, then the predicate 'T prefers A to B' should be definable in terms of the physical-chemical composition of our Turing Machines. But in fact there is no logically valid inference from the premiss that one of our Turing Machines has a certain physical-chemical composition to the conclusion that it prefers A to B, in the sense explained above, nor from the premiss that it prefers A to B to the conclusion that it has a certain physical-chemical composition. These are logically independent statements about our Turing Machines even if they are *just* machines.

Let us quickly verify this. Suppose we are given as a premiss that T_1 prefers A to B. We can then infer that T_1 must have been programmed in a certain way. In particular, its program must involve a rational preference function which assigns a higher value to A than to B.

Suppose that we are given not just this information, but are given the specific machine table of the machine T_1. We can still draw no inference whatsoever to the physical-chemical composition of T_1, for the reason that the *same* Turing Machine (from the standpoint of the machine table) may be physically realized in a potential infinity of ways. Even if in fact a machine belonging to our community prefers A to B when and only when flip-flop 57 is on, this is purely contingent fact. Our machine might have been exactly the same in all 'psychological' respects without consisting of flip-flops at all.

What of inferences in the reverse direction? Suppose that we are given the information that machine T_1 has a certain physical-chemical composition, can we infer that it has a certain rational preference function? This reduces to the question: can we infer the machine table of the machine from its physical-chemical composition? As an empirical matter, there is no doubt that we *can*, at least in simple cases. But we are concerned here with the question of logically valid inferences, not empirically successful ones. In order to know that a machine has a certain machine table, we must know how many significantly different states the machine is capable of and how these are causally related. This cannot be inferred from the physical-chemical composition of the machine unless, in addition to knowing the physical-chemical composition, we also know the *laws of nature*. We don't have to know all the laws of nature, we only have to know some relevant finite set; but there is no way of specifying in advance just what finite set of the laws of nature will have to be given in addition to the physical-chemical composition of the machine before we are able to show that the machine in question has a certain machine table. From the single fact that a machine has a certain physical-chemical composition it does not follow either that it has or that it does not have any particular rational preference function and hence that it does or does not prefer A to B.

Given a description of the physical-chemical composition of a machine *and* a statement of all the laws of nature (for simplicity we will assume these to be finite), can we infer that the machine prefers A to B? Suppose, for the sake of definiteness, the laws of nature are of the classical atomistic kind; that is, they describe how individual elementary particles behave, and there is a composition function which enables us to tell how any isolated complex of elementary particles will behave. Finally, the physical-chemical composition of the machine is described by describing a certain complex of elementary particles. Even in this case, we cannot as a matter of *pure logic* deduce from the statements given that the machine has a particular machine table, or a particular rational preference function, unless in addition to being given the physical-chemical composition of the machine and the laws of nature, we are given the additional premiss (which from the formal point of view is a logically independent statement) that we have been given a description of *all* of the machine. Suppose, for the sake of an example, that there exists in addition to elementary particles, entities unknown to physical theory – 'bundles of ectoplasm' – and that the whole machine consists of elementary particles and some 'bundles of ectoplasm' in some complex kind of causal interrelationship. Then when we give the physical-chemical composition of the machine, in the usual sense, we are only describing a *substructure* of the total machine. From this description of the substructure plus the laws of nature in the ordinary sense (the laws governing the behavior of *isolated systems* of elementary particles) we can deduce how this substructure will behave *as long as there are no interactions with the remainder of the structure* (the 'bundles of ectoplasm'). Since it is not a fact of pure logic that the physical-chemical description of the machine is a description of all of the machine, one cannot by pure logic deduce that the machine has any particular machine table or any particular rational preference function from a description of the physical-chemical composition of the machine and the laws of nature.

Logically, the situation just discussed is analogous to the situation which arises when certain philosophers attempt to treat universal generalizations as (possibly infinite) conjunctions, i.e. the proposal has been made to analyze 'all crows are black' as '(a_1 is a crow $\supset a_1$ is black) & (a_2 is a crow $\supset a_2$ is black) & (a_3 is a crow $\supset a_3$ is black)...' where $a_1, a_2, \ldots$ is a possibly infinite list of individual constants designating all crows. The mistake here is that although this conjunction does indeed follow from the statement that all crows are black, the statement that all crows are black does not follow from the conjunction without the additional universal premiss: '$a_1, a_2, \ldots$ are all the crows there are'. It might be contended that the possibility that there exist causal agents unknown to modern physics and not consisting of elementary particles is so remote that it should be neglected. But this is to leave the context of logical analysis altogether. Moreover we have only to reflect for a moment to remember that today we know of a host of causal agencies which would have been left out in any inventory of the 'furniture of the world' taken by a nineteenth century physicist. Atoms and their solar system-like components, electrons and nucleons, might possibly have been guessed at by the nineteenth century physicist; but what of mesons, and what of the quanta of the gravitational field, if these turn out to exist? No, the hypothesis that any inventory includes a list of all ultimate 'building blocks' of causal process that there are is a synthetic one and cannot be regarded as true by pure logic.

Materialism, as I admitted before, is today a philosopher's straw man. Modern materialists (or 'identity theorists', as they prefer to be called) do not maintain that the *intensions* of such terms as 'preference' can be given in physical-chemical terms but only that there is physical referent. Their formulation would be, roughly, that preferring A to B is *synthetically identical with* possessing certain more or less stable features of the physical-chemical composition (e.g. 'preferring A to B is a fairly lasting state of the human cerebral cortex'). This runs into the difficulty that *preference* is a universal, not a particular – preferring A to B is a *relation* between an organism and two alternatives – and the 'is' appropriate to *universals* appears to be the '*is' of meaning analysis*. We say, e.g. '*solubility* is the property that something possesses if and only if it is the case that if it were in water it would dissolve.' We *don't* say 'solubility is a certain physical-chemical structure', but rather that the solubility of those substances that are soluble is *explained* by their possession of a certain physical-chemical structure. Similarly, in the case of our machines what we would say is that preferring A to B is possessing a rational preference function which assigns a higher value to A than to B. If we say, in addition, that preferring A to B is 'synthetically identical with' possessing a certain physical-chemical structure – say, a certain pattern of flip-flops – then we let ourselves in for what seem to me to be remarkable and insufficiently motivated extensions of usage. For instance, if the same Turing Machine is physically realized in two quite different ways, then even though not only the rational preference function but the whole machine table is the same in the two cases, we shall have to say 'preferring A to B is *something different* in the case of machine 1 and machine 2.' Similarly, we shall have to say that 'belief' is something different in the two cases, etc. It would be much clearer to say that the realization of the machine table is different in the two cases. There are a number of subtleties here of which it is well to be aware, however.

First of all, what has been said so far suggests the incorrect view that two properties can only be *analytically* identical, not *synthetically* identical. This is false. Let 'a_1' be an individual constant designating a particular piece of paper, and suppose I write the single word 'red' on the piece of paper. Then the statement, 'The property *red* is identical with the property designated by the only word written on a_1', is a synthetic statement.† However, this is the *only* way in which properties can be 'synthetically identical' and the statements, 'Solubility is a

---

† More simply, 'blue is the color of the sky' is a synthetic identity statement concerning properties. This example is due to Neil Wilson of Duke University, to whom I am indebted for enlightenment on the subject of identity of properties.

certain molecular structure', 'Pain is stimulation of C-fibres', are not of this kind, as one can easily convince oneself.

So far I have suggested that, apart from the kind of synthetic identity statement just cited, the criterion for the *identity* of two properties is *synonymy*, or equivalence in some analytical sense, of the corresponding designators. In chapter 18 I pointed out that for certain other kinds of abstract entities – e.g. situations, events – this does not seem to be correct, and that there might be reasons for giving this up even in the case of properties. I cited in that paper the '*is*' of *theoretical identification* (i.e. the 'is' exemplified by such statements as 'water *is* H_2O', 'light *is* electromagnetic radiation') and I suggested that some properties might be connectible by this kind of 'is'. But this would not be of help to the identity theorist. (This represents a change of view from my earlier paper.) Even if we are willing to say 'being *P is* being *Q*' in some cases in which the designators '*P*' and '*Q*' are not synonymous, we should require that the designators be equivalent and that the equivalence be *necessary*, at least in the sense of *physically necessary*. Thus, if *one* particular physical-chemical composition should turn out to explain *all* cases of solubility, it would not be a wholly unmotivated extension of ordinary usage to say that solubility *is* the possession of this particular physical-chemical composition. There is an argument in my earlier paper for the view that this would not necessarily be a 'change of meaning'. This sort of thing cannot happen in the present case. We *cannot* discover laws by virtue of which it is physically necessary that an organism prefers *A* to *B* if and only if it is in a certain physical-chemical state. For we already know that any such laws would be false. They would be false because even in the light of our present knowledge we can see that any Turing Machine that can be physically realized at all can be realized in a host of totally different ways. Thus there cannot be a physical-chemical structure the possession of which is a necessary and sufficient condition for preferring *A* to *B*, even if we take 'necessary' in the sense of *physically* necessary and not in the sense of logically necessary. And to start speaking of properties as 'identical in some cases' because they happen to be coextensive in *those cases* would be not only a change of meaning but a rather arbitrary change of meaning at that.

So far we have ascribed to our machines only 'multi-tracked' dispositions such as preference and belief but not such more of less transient states as states of feeling. Of course, we have equipped our machines with sense organs, and if we suppose that these sense organs are not perfectly reliable, then, as I argued in my earlier paper, it is easy to see that the distinction between appearance and reality will automatically arise in the 'life' of the machine. We can classify certain configurations of these machines as 'visual impressions', 'tactile impressions', etc. What of such feelings as pain?

By suitably adapting Stuart Hampshire's discussion in his *Feeling and Expression*, we can introduce into our model a counterpart of pain. Hampshire's idea is that the feelings are states characterized by the fact that they give rise to certain inclinations. For instance, pain is normally, although not invariably, occasioned by damage to part of the body and gives rise to inclinations to withdraw the part of the body that seems to be damaged and to avoid whatever causes the painful damage in question. These inclinations are in a certain sense *spontaneous* ones – a point that has to be emphasized if this account is not to be open to damaging objections. That is, when X hurts my hand, the inclination to withdraw my hand from X arises at once and without ratiocination on my part. I can answer the question, 'Why do you draw your hand away from X?' by saying, 'X is hurting my hand'. One does not then go on to ask, 'But why is that a reason for drawing your hand away from X?' The fact that X's hurting my hand is *ipso facto* a reason for drawing my hand away from X is grounded on and presupposes the spontaneity of the inclination to draw my hand away from X when I am in the state in question.

Let us then equip our machines with 'pain signals', i.e. signals which will normally be occasioned by damage to some part of the machine's 'body', with 'pain fibers', and with 'pain states'. These 'pain states' will normally be caused by damage to some part of the machine's body and will give rise to spontaneous inclinations to avoid whatever causes the pain in question. I think we can see how to introduce the notion of an inclination into our model: inclinations are naturally treated as more or less short-lasting modifications of the rational preference function of the machine. Temporarily, the machine assigns a very high value, as it were, to 'getting its arm out of there'. This *temporary* change in the machine's rational preference function should not, of course, be confused with the long term change in the machine's behavior occasioned by learning that something it did not previously know to be painful is painful. This last can be built into the machine's rational preference function to begin with, and need not be accounted for by supposing that the pain experience changed the long term rational preference function of the machine (although, in a dynamical model, it may have). In a sense this is a complication of Hampshire's model:† pain states are characterized both by the momentary and spontaneous inclinations to which they give

† Other aspects of Hampshire's model are, however, omitted here: the role of *unconditioned* responses; the 'suppression' of inclinations; and the role of imitation.

rise and by the negative weight assigned by the machine's basic rational preference function to things which the machine has learned from experience put the machine into these states.

The above remarks against identifying preference with a particular physical-chemical composition apply equally strongly now against identifying pain with a particular physical-chemical composition. Suppose that the pain fibers of the machines are made of copper and these are the only copper fibers in the machines. It would still be absurd to say, 'Pain is stimulation of the copper fibers'. If we said that, then we would have to say that pain is something different in the case of machine 1 and the case of machine 2, if machine 1 had copper pain fibers and machine 2 had platinum pain fibers. Again, it seems clearer to say what we said before: that 'pain' *is* a state of the machine normally occasioned by damage to the machine's body and characterized by giving rise to 'inclinations' to...etc., and to eschew the formulation, 'Pain is synthetically identical with stimulation of the copper fibers' in favor of the clearer formulation, 'The machine is physically realized in such a way that the "pain" pulses travel along copper fibers.'

3. Logical behaviorism

We have seen that statements about the preferences of our machines are not logically equivalent to statements concerning the physical-chemical composition of these machines. Are they perhaps logically equivalent to statements concerning the actual and potential behavior of these machines? In answering this question, it is convenient to widen the discussion and to consider not only statements about the preferences of our machines but also statements about their 'knowledge', 'belief', and 'sensory awareness'. When we widen the discussion this way, it is easy to see the answer to our question is in the negative. Consider two machines T_1 and T_2 which differ in the following way: T_1 has 'pain fibers' which have been cut, so T_1 is incapable of 'feeling pain'. T_2 has uncut 'pain fibers' but has an unusual rational preference function. This rational preference function is such that if T_2 believes a certain event to have taken place, or a certain proposition to be true, then T_2 will assign a *relatively infinite weight* to concealing the fact that its pain fibers are uncut. In other words, T_2 will maintain its pain fibers have been cut when asked, will contend that it is incapable of 'feeling pain', and suppress its inclination to give behavioral evidence of feeling pain. If T_2 does not believe that the critical event has taken place or that the critical proposition is true, then T_2 will have, as it were, no reason to conceal the fact that it is capable of 'feeling pain' and will then behave quite differently from T_1. In this case, we can tell that a machine is a physical realization of T_2 and not of T_1 by observing its behavior.

However, once T_1 and T_2 have both been informed that the critical event has taken place or that the critical proposition is true, there is then no distinguishing them on behavioral grounds. That is to say, the hypothesis that a machine is an instance of T_1 that believes that the critical event has taken place leads to exactly the same predictions with respect to all actual and potential behavior as the hypothesis that a machine is an instance of type T_2 which believes that the critical event has taken place or that the critical proposition is true. In short, certain combinations of beliefs and rational preference functions which are quite different will lead to exactly the same actual and potential behavior.

I have argued in chapter 16 that exactly the same thing is true in the case of human beings. That is to say, two human beings may be inclined to behave in the same way under all possible circumstances, one for the normal reason and the other for a quite abnormal combination of reasons. Once we allow the computing skills or the intelligence of the machine to vary, the point becomes even more clear. Consider the problem of distinguishing between a machine with a normal rational preference function but rather low intelligence and a machine equipped with very high intelligence but with an abnormal rational preference function, which assigns relatively infinite weight to concealing its high intelligence. It is clear the difference is not a wholly untestable one. If we are allowed to take the machines apart and to see what goes on inside them, we can tell whether a given machine is an instance of the first type or an instance of the second type, but it is easily seen that there is no way to tell them apart without examining the internal composition of the machines in question. That is, quite different combinations of computing skills, beliefs, and rational preference functions can lead to exactly the same behavior, not only in the sense of the same actual behavior but in the sense of the same potential behavior under all possible circumstances.

Let T_1 be a machine of low intelligence and let T_2 be a machine of higher intelligence which is simulating the behavior of T_1. It might be asked in what precisely the greater intelligence of T_2 consists. Well it could consist in two things. First of all, T_2 may be printing many things on its tape which do not contain operant signals and which, therefore, constitute mere interior monolog. T_2 may be solving mathematical problems, analysing the psychology of the human beings with which it comes in contact, writing caustic comments on human mores and institutions, and so forth. T_2 need not even contain any subsystem of states which at all resembles the states or computations of T_1. T_2 may be sufficiently intelligent to determine what T_1 would do in any particular situation without actually reconstructing the thought process by which T_1 arrives at the decision to do it. This would be analogous to the case of a human being whose behavior was in no way out of the ordinary but who, unknown to everyone else, enjoyed a rich and unusual inner life.

It will be observed that the machines we have been considering all have, in a sense, *pathological* rational preference functions, i.e. rational preference functions which assign a relatively infinite weight to something. Assigning a relatively infinite weight to something simply means preferring that thing over all alternatives, come what may. Suppose we call a rational preference function *nonpathological* if it does *not* assign a relatively infinite weight to anything except possibly the survival of the machine itself. Let T be the theory that all actually existing intelligent systems possess nonpathological rational preference functions. Then it can be shown that the statement that a machine with fixed computing skills has a particular rational preference function is equivalent under T to saying that it has a certain kind of actual and potential behavior. In fact, to say that a machine has a particular rational preference function is equivalent under T to saying that it behaves under all circumstances exactly as a machine with that particular rational preference function would behave. This does not, however, vindicate logical behaviorism, although it constitutes a kind of 'near miss'. Logical behaviorism in the case of our machines would be the thesis that the statement that a machine has a particular rational preference function is logically equivalent to some statement about the machine's actual and potential behavior. This is not correct. What is correct is that there is a theory T, which is very likely true (or whose analog in the case of organisms is very likely true), such that in the theory T every statement of the form 'T prefers A to B' is equivalent to a statement about T's actual and potential behavior. But there is all the difference in the world between equivalence as a matter of logic alone and equivalence within a synthetic theory.

In a sense the situation with respect to logical behaviorism is very similar to the situation with respect to materialism. In connection with materialism, we saw that although the statement that a machine has a certain machine table is not logically equivalent to the statement that it has a certain physical-chemical composition, it follows from the latter statement within a synthetic theory, namely the theory consisting of the laws of nature together with the completeness statement, i.e. the statement that there do not exist any causal agencies other than the elementary particles and combinations of elementary particles, and that these possess only the degree of freedom ascribed to them in physical theory. Indeed, it is easily seen that there is a class C of physical compositions such that the statement that a machine has a particular machine table is equivalent within the synthetic theory mentioned, to the statement that its physical-composition belongs to the class C. Since the statement that the machine prefers A to B, or that it has a certain belief, or that it 'feels pain', etc. is true only if a suitable conjunction of two statements is true, the first of which says that the machine has a certain machine table, while the second describes the total configuration of the machine at the present instant, and since some such conjunction can be true, assuming the synthetic theory alluded to, only if the physical composition of the machine belongs to a very large class C^* of physical compositions, we can see that the statement, whatever it may be, will be equivalent within the synthetic theory alluded to, to the statement that the physical composition of the machine is in such a class C^*.

Similarly, assuming the synthetic theory alluded to in connection with logical behaviorism – the theory that no machine has a pathological rational preference function – any statement about the 'mental life' of one of our machines will be equivalent to some statement about its actual and potential behavior.

Given an 'agent' in our hypothetical 'community', this is our situation: with enough information about the actual and potential behavior of the agent, we may infer with relative certainty that the agent prefers A to B, or again, with enough information about the physical-chemical composition of the agent (and enough knowledge of the laws of nature), we may infer with relative certainty that the agent prefers A to B. But the two inferences do not support the claims of logical behaviorism and materialism respectively. Both inferences are synthetic inferences carried out within synthetic theories.

But, it may be asked, how can we even know that either the assumption of the nonexistence of pathological rational preference functions or the completeness assumption with respect to physical theory is correct? I believe that the answer is much the same in both cases. Each assumption is justified as long as there is no good reason to suppose that it might be false. If this is right, then inferences to the mental life of any empirically-given actual system may be perfectly justified; but they are never analytic inferences if the premisses only give information about the actual and potential behavior of the system and about its physical-chemical composition. Such inferences are always 'defeasible': there are always farfetched circumstances under which the premisses might be retained and the conclusion might be overturned.

On looking over what I have written, I must confess to a certain sense of disappointment. It seems to me that what I have said here is too obvious and trivial to be worth saying, even if there are indeed certain philosophers who would disagree. But at the same time, it seems to me that these remarks, even if they do seem obvious, might suggest something about the nature of our mentalistic concepts which it is not at all usual to point out. What is suggested is this: it seems that to know for certain that a human being has a particular belief, or preference, or whatever, involves knowing something about the functional organization of the human being. As applied to Turing Machines, the functional organization is given by the machine table. A description of the functional organization of a human being might well be something quite different and more complicated. But the important thing is that descriptions of the functional organization of a system are logically different in kind either from descriptions of its physical-chemical composition or from descriptions of its actual and potential behavior. If discussions in the philosophy of mind are often curiously unsatisfying, I think, it is because just this notion, the notion of functional organization, has been overlooked or confused with notions of entirely different kinds.

Rejoinder†

Mr Plantinga's 'comment' is a pleasure to read for its lucidity and for the briskness with which it gets down to the discussion of the central arguments in my paper. I am grateful to him for giving me an opportunity to emphasize further one or two points that appear to require it.

Plantinga appears to understand 'dualism' differently than I did in my paper. As far as I can make out, 'Cartesian dualism', as Plantinga understands it, is only a slight variant of the ordinary common sense view of the nature of living human organisms. In the ordinary common sense view, the 'seat of the higher faculties', to employ the charming old language, is the brain. According to the variant view, this is wrong. The seat of the higher faculties is an organ which I shall call the 'Sbrain' (otherwise 'the soul', or 'the Mind', with a capital 'M'). The 'Sbrain' is supposed not to be a 'physical object', or anyway not to consist of elementary particles, not to have mass, etc. (It *is* supposed to be a 'substance', according to Descartes, and this rather suggests that it *might* be 'physical' in one of the recently proposed wider senses of that term.) Descartes thought that the 'Sbrain' was immortal; but Plantinga fortunately does not bring this issue into our discussion.

I call this view a *slight* variant of the common sense view, because it does not seem to make any philosophical difference whether the seat of the higher faculties is the brain, or the stomach, or the Sbrain, or the foot. Also it does

† This was my reply to 'comments' by Alvin Plantinga (also published in *Intentionality, Minds and Perception*) on 'The mental life of some machines'.

not make any difference, as far as I can see, whether the brain *or* Sbrain consists of elementary particles or of 'mental substance'. It would make considerable difference scientifically, of course. For example, if the seat of the higher functions is not the brain but the Sbrain, then what is the brain for? And why does damage to the brain, but not the stomach, cause loss of memory, speech, and other psychological functions? Again, if the Sbrain consists of a 'substance' which is in time but not in (ordinary) space, then what sort of mathematics is going to be needful for a proper description of this unique organ? Should we, perhaps, think of Sbrains and similar entities (e.g. angels) as existing in some suitable topological 'space' with mathematical properties of its own, in terms of which the laws obeyed by 'mental substance' admit of a simple and revealing formulation? Clearly, the serious Cartesian dualist is going to have his work cut out for him.

One possibility might be that human beings have *two* brains and not one: the brain ordinarily so named, and the ghostly immaterial counterpart that we are calling the 'Sbrain'. This intriguing suggestion even has some explanatory value: one might, for example, explain various psychological disorders in terms of brain-Sbrain conflict. Fascinating as it would be to dwell further on the hypothesis that people have Sbrains, I must get back to philosophy. For, of course, there is not the slightest reason to think that people *do* have Sbrains in addition to brains, or Sfeet in addition to feet, or Sguts in addition to guts. And in any case it is not the job of the philosopher either to advance or to refute irresponsible empirical hypotheses.

In my paper, as the reader can quickly verify, I spoke throughout of 'dualism', contrasting it throughout with 'materialism' and 'logical behaviorism' as *theories of the meaning* of such words as 'prefers' and 'believes'. There was only one passing reference to Cartesian dualism – the bizarre doctrine just discussed – and then only for the purpose of clarifying the notion of a Turing Machine, and *not* for the purpose of refuting this bizarre doctrine. If Plantinga wishes to stress that the bizarre doctrine thus remains unrefuted by me, I cheerfully agree.

What doctrine was I then concerned to refute? The doctrine that the peculiar character of the concepts of preference, belief, etc., *requires* us to assume the existence of ghostly causal agencies. The doctrine that the very semantical analysis of such words as these presupposes some such account as the bizarre doctrine lately alluded to. 'Dualism' so understood is a conceptual claim; and the refutation of this sort of conceptual claim is eminently the business of the philosopher. But this is *A, B, C*...

Plantinga brings three separate criticisms against my discussion of the identity theory, and concludes with a brief discussion of his own. I turn now to these criticisms.

(1) *Under what conditions would I allow that universals* U *and* U' *are contingently identical?* 'I find this argument altogether puzzling, for I am unable to see what the special conditions referred to above might be', writes Plantinga. The conditions I had in mind are just that the identity statement

$U = U'$ should be deducible from premises that we can admit to be true (without recourse to dubious philosophical doctrine), where 'deducible' may be understood in the sense of any standard system of higher order logic.

For example, we would all admit 'a_1 is blue' to be true, where a_1 is any suitable blue object. But from 'a_1 is blue', we can deduce 'Blue = the one and only F such that F is a color and $F(a_1)$', given the premiss 'Nothing has two colors at once', and, say, the logical symbols and rules of *Principia Mathematica*. Thus, for example, 'Blue = the color of the sky' is a philosophically unpuzzling synthetic identity statement. It is unpuzzling, even though it asserts the identity of universals, because it follows from 'the sky is (normally) blue' and 'the sky has only one (normal) color', which, while they might puzzle a painter, are not premises that trouble a philosopher. However, 'Anger = such and such a brain state' is not this sort of identity statement. It cannot be deduced from any known facts about brains and about anger – or, at any rate, if it can be deduced, the 'deduction' is not one that can be validated in *Principia Mathematica*. It appears to be not a logical consequence of ordinary or garden variety empirical facts, but a proposed new way of speaking in the light of those facts. And just the distinction that Plantinga finds puzzling – between the synthetic identity statements about universals that we all ordinarily make ('Blue is the colour of the sky') and the ones I wish to reject ('Anger = such and such a brain state') is already drawn for us by the deductive formalism of modern logic.

(2) But all this is beside the point, argues Plantinga, because what the identity theorist 'means to assert' is that every *instance* of the universal *being in pain* is contingently identical with some *instance* of the universal *possessing neurological state* S'. 'P's being M at t is contingently identical with P's being B at t.' Now then, the 'instances', or members of the extension ('instance' is normally restricted to one-place predicates) of a two-place predicate are the ordered pairs $\langle X, Y \rangle$ such that X bears the relation in question to Y. Thus the 'instances' of 'P is angry at t' are just the pairs $\langle P, t \rangle$ such that P is an organism and t is a temporal instant and such that the organism which is the first member of the ordered pair is angry at the instant which is the second member of the ordered pair.

(I) For every $P, t, \langle P, t \rangle$ is an instance of 'being in M' if and only if $\langle P, t \rangle$ is an instance of 'being in B'.

– which asserts the 'contingent identity' of the *instances* of the two-place predicates M and B (*not* of the universals themselves), is logically equivalent to the 'parallelism statement':

(II) For every P, t, P is in M at t if and only if P is B at t.

– thus, on Plantinga's interpretation, the 'identity theorist' would be making a straightforward empirical claim and moreover just the claim that the 'psycho-physical parallelist' is making. Clearly, this cannot be right.

Instead of 'instances', Plantinga might have tried 'facts'. Consider the claim 'the fact of P's being in M at t is identical with the fact of P's being B at t'. This claim could be objected to on linguistic grounds similar to those that I used to argue against the 'synthetic identity' of universals. 'Facts', in philosophical usage, appear to be one-one associated with true statements. In this usage, the claim above would reduce to 'the statement that P is in M at t is the very same statement as the statement that P is B at t', and this is clearly false. Indeed, 'synthetic identity' of facts appears to make no more sense than synthetic identity of universals. And if we take 'fact' in the idiomatic sense of, roughly, what can be established beyond dispute, then we are even worse off, since clearly it could be the case that a man's psychological state was established beyond dispute but not his brain state, *or* that his brain state was established beyond dispute but not his psychological state. Thus the fact that Jones is angry is simply *not* the same fact as the fact that Jones is in brain state B.

The fact is, I simply do not see what Plantinga means by an 'instance' of *being in pain*, or how the 'contingent identity of instances' can possibly be of help here.

(3) In his comments, Plantinga declares:

'Upon superficial reflection it looks to me as if any premiss which is such that its conjunction with (a) entails (b) is either flagrantly question-begging or such that its conjunction with (a) entails the false proposition that it is necessary that every Turing Machine be an organism. Hence there is no hope at all for this argument.'

I shall employ (a), (b), (c) to refer to the propositions so denoted in Plantinga's Comment.

(c) appears to me to be irrelevant. Even if there is a physical-chemical state S such that it is physically necessary that a *human being* prefers A to B if and only if it is in S, the proposal to say (for this reason) that the universal 'preference' is identical with the universal 'being in S' is completely unacceptable. For, supposing that Martians have a quite different physical constitution than we do, it would make it *analytically false* that Martians sometimes prefer A to B although they are never in S. But, I claim, we do in fact use 'prefer' in such a way that creatures whose behavior sufficiently resembles ours may correctly be said to 'prefer A to B' under certain conditions, whether or not they are in the same physical-chemical states as we are. (Cf. Wittgenstein's '... now look at a wriggling fly and at once these difficulties vanish and pain seems able to get a foothold here, where before everything was, so to speak, too smooth for it'. (Wittgenstein, 1953, p. 98))

For (b) one needs only the premiss 'Any naturally evolved physical system which is functionally isomorphic to an organism is an organism'. I restrict this premiss to 'naturally evolved' systems in order to exclude robots, etc. In my paper I illustrated the notion of functional isomorphism (sameness of functional organization) in this way: I said that two Turing Machines (or even two probabilistic automata, which is what organisms probably are) with the same machine table are functionally isomorphic (have the same functional organization). To avoid the language of automata theory altogether, let us put the same notion in the following way: let P be an organism, and let $M_1, M_2 \ldots$ be all of the states of P that we wish to recognize as 'psychological'. Here M_1, $M_2 \ldots$ may be psychological states *either* in the lay sense (e.g. being angry at something, being in love) or in some technical sense (having a high 'inhibitory potential', being 'fixated at the oral level'). Let $B_1, B_2, \ldots$ be the corresponding physical states. Let P' be a system which is capable of *physical* states B_1^*, $B_2^* \ldots$ which are different (in terms of physics and chemistry) from B_1, B_2, $\ldots$, but which have the same causal-probabilistic relations to one another and to behavior. So, if M_1 is 'being angry at the psychologist', when P' is in state B_1^* it behaves just like an organism which is angry at the psychologist. Moreover, if P is quietly thinking, and going through a series of states $B_1, \ldots, B_n$, then P' when going through the corresponding states $B_1^* \ldots, B_n^*$ will also sit quietly (as if in thought), and will have the same behavior *dispositions* as P. Thus P' is *isomorphic* to P—*up to* whatever makes a 'psychological' difference to behavior.

The thrust of my paper was that, under the above conditions, we would *call P'* an organism just as much as P, and we would *say P'* when it is in state B_1^*, 'is angry at the psychologist', etc. In short, if a *psychological* predicate applies to one organism P, then it applies to every organism which is functionally isomorphic to P, and which is in the states which correspond (under the isomorphism) to the states that P is in. Here the vagueness of 'psychological' and 'functional' does not matter. For this is a semantical point, and however we take the notion of 'psychological predicate', we must take the notion of 'functional organization' in such a way that a difference in what psychological predicates are applicable corresponds to a difference in the functional organization and vice versa.

To complete the argument, it suffices to point out that any physical-chemical system which possesses a 'functional organization' which can be represented by a machine table or a probabilistic machine table (and I cannot envisage what sort of functional organization would not be) is functionally isomorphic to a denumerable infinity (at least) of systems with quite different physical-chemical constitutions. But, if (b) is false, then there is a physical-chemical state which is the counterpart of 'preference' in the case of all *possible* organisms, – say the presence of certain electrical intensities in a certain distribution. Then it would follow that no physical system exists – in principle, not just in fact – which is functionally isomorphic to an organism which prefers A to B, and which is nonelectrical in nature and naturally evolved. But this is just false. And if it be argued that we could modify the notion of a 'physical-chemical state', so that 'physical-chemical state' is preserved under *functional* isomorphism, then this is just to say that what all possible organisms which prefer A to B have in common is *not* physical-chemical state, in the sense in which that term is understood at present, but *psychological* state.

21

The nature of mental states*

The typical concerns of the Philosopher of Mind might be represented by three questions: (1) How do we know that other people have pains? (2) Are pains brain states? (3) What is the analysis of the concept *pain*? I do not wish to discuss questions (1) and (3) in this chapter. I shall say something about question (2).†

I. Identity questions

'Is pain a brain state?' (Or, 'Is the property of having a pain at time t a brain state?')‡ It is impossible to discuss this question sensibly without saying something about the peculiar rules which have grown up in the course of the development of 'analytical philosophy' – rules which, far from leading to an end to all conceptual confusions, themselves represent considerable conceptual confusion. These rules – which are, of course, implicit rather than explicit in the practice of most analytical philosophers – are (1) that a statement of the form 'being A is being B' (e.g. 'being in pain is being in a certain brain state') can be *correct* only if it follows, in some sense, from the meaning of the terms A and B; and (2) that a statement of the form 'being A is being B' can be philosophically *informative* only if it is in some sense reductive (e.g. 'being in pain is having a certain unpleasant sensation' is not philosophically informative; 'being in pain is having a certain behaviour disposition' is, if true, philosophically informative). These rules are excellent rules if we still believe that the program of reductive analysis (in the style of the 1930s) can be carried out; if we don't, then they turn analytical philosophy into a mug's game, at least so far as 'is' questions are concerned.

In this paper I shall use the term 'property' as a blanket term for

---

* First published as 'Psychological predicates' in Capitan and Merrill (eds.) *Art, Mind and Religion.* Reprinted by permission of the University of Pittsburgh Press. © 1967 by the University of Pittsburgh Press.

† I have discussed these and related topics in chapters 16, 18 and 20 in this volume.

‡ In this paper I wish to avoid the vexed question of the relation between *pains* and *pain states.* I only remark in passing that one common argument *against* identification of these two – namely, that a pain can be in one's arm but a state (of the organism) cannot be in one's arm – is easily seen to be fallacious.

such things as being in pain, being in a particular brain state, having a particular behavior disposition, and also for magnitudes such as temperature, etc. – i.e. for things which can naturally be represented by one-or-more-place predicates or functors. I shall use the term 'concept' for things which can be identified with synonymy-classes of expressions. Thus the concept *temperature* can be identified (I maintain) with the synonymy-class of the word 'temperature'.† (This is like saying that the number 2 can be identified with the class of all pairs. This is quite a different statement from the peculiar statement that 2 *is* the class of all pairs. I do not maintain that concepts *are* synonymy-classes, whatever that might mean, but that they can be identified with synonymy-classes, for the purpose of formalization of the relevant discourse.)

The question 'What is the concept *temperature?*' is a very 'funny' one. One might take it to mean 'What is temperature? Please take my question as a conceptual one.' In that case an answer might be (pretend for a moment 'heat' and 'temperature' are synonyms) 'temperature is heat', or even 'the concept of temperature is the same concept as the concept of heat'. Or one might take it to mean 'What are *concepts*, really? For example, what is "the concept of temperature"?' In that case heaven knows what an 'answer' would be. (Perhaps it would be the statement that concepts *can be identified with* synonymy-classes.)

Of course, the question 'What is the property temperature?' is also 'funny'. And one way of interpreting it is to take it as a question about the concept of temperature. But this is not the way a physicist would take it.

The effect of saying that the property P_1 can be identical with the property P_2 only if the terms P_1, P_2 are in some suitable sense 'synonyms' is, to all intents and purposes, to collapse the two notions of 'property' and 'concept' into a single notion. The view that concepts (intensions) *are* the same as properties has been explicitly advocated by Carnap (e.g. in *Meaning and Necessity*). This seems an unfortunate

† There are some well-known remarks by Alonzo Church on this topic. Those remarks do not bear (as might at first be supposed) on the identification of concepts with synonymy-classes as such, but rather support the view that (in formal semantics) it is necessary to retain Frege's distinction between the normal and the 'oblique' use of expressions. That is, even if we say that the concept of temperature *is* the synonymy-class of the word 'temperature', we must not thereby be led into the error of supposing that 'the concept of temperature' is synonymous with 'the synonymy-class of the word "temperature"' – for then 'the concept of temperature' and 'der Begriff der Temperatur' would not be synonymous, which they are. Rather, we must say that the concept of 'temperature' *refers to* the synonymy-class of the word 'temperature' (on this particular reconstruction); but that class is *identified* not as 'the synonymy class to which such-and-such a word belongs', but in another way (e.g. as the synonymy-class whose members have such-and-such a characteristic use).

view, since 'temperature is mean molecular kinetic energy' appears to be a perfectly good example of a true statement of identity of properties, whereas 'the concept of temperature is the same concept as a concept of mean molecular kinetic energy' is simply false.

Many philosophers believe that the statement 'pain is a brain state' violates some rules or norms of English. But the arguments offered are hardly convincing. For example, if the fact that I can know that I am in pain without knowing that I am in brain state S shows that pain cannot be brain state S, then, by exactly the same argument, the fact that I can know that the stove is hot without knowing that the mean molecular kinetic energy is high (or even that molecules exist) shows that it is *false* that temperature is mean molecular kinteic energy, physics to the contrary. In fact, all that immediately follows from the fact that I can know that I am in pain without knowing that I am in brain state S is that the concept of pain is not the same concept as the concept of being in brain state S. But either pain, or the state of being in pain, or some pain, or some pain state, might still be brain state S. After all, the concept of temperature is not the same concept as the concept of mean molecular kinetic energy. But temperature is mean molecular kinetic energy.

Some philosophers maintain that both 'pain is a brain state' and 'pain states are brain states' are unintelligible. The answer is to explain to these philosophers, as well as we can, given the vagueness of all scientific methodology, what sorts of considerations lead one to make an empirical reduction (i.e. to say such things as 'water is H_2O', 'light is electro-magnetic radiation', 'temperature is mean molecular kinetic energy'). If, without giving reasons, he still maintains in the face of such examples that one cannot imagine parallel circumstances for the use of 'pains are brain states' (or, perhaps, 'pain states are brain states') one has grounds to regard him as perverse.

Some philosophers maintain that 'P_1 is P_2' is something that can be true, when the 'is' involved is the 'is' of empirical reduction, only when the properties P_1 and P_2 are (a) associated with a spatio-temporal region; and (b) the region is one and the same in both cases. Thus 'temperature is mean molecular kinetic energy' is an admissible empirical reduction, since the temperature and the molecular energy are associated with the same space–time region, but 'having a pain in my arm is being in a brain state' is not, since the spatial regions involved are different.

This argument does not appear very strong. Surely no one is going to be deterred from saying that mirror images are light reflected from an object and then from the surface of a mirror by the fact that an image can be 'located' three feet *behind* the mirror! (Moreover, one can always find *some* common property of the reductions one is willing to allow – e.g. temperature is mean molecular kinetic energy – which is not a property of some one identification one wishes to disallow. This is not very impressive unless one has an argument to show that the very purposes of such identification depend upon the common property in question.)

Again, other philosophers have contended that all the predictions that can be derived from the conjunction of neurophysiological laws with such statements as 'pain states are such-and-such brain states' can equally well be derived from the conjunction of the same neurophysiological laws with 'being in pain is correlated with such-and-such brain states', and hence (*sic*!) there can be no methodological grounds for saying that pains (or pain states) *are* brain states, as opposed to saying that they are *correlated* (invariantly) with brain states. This argument, too, would show that light is only correlated with electromagnetic radiation. The mistake is in ignoring the fact that, although the theories in question may indeed lead to the same predictions, they open and exclude different *questions*. 'Light is invariantly correlated with electromagnetic radiation' would leave open the questions 'What is the light then, if it isn't the same as the electromagnetic radiation?' and 'What makes the light accompany the electromagnetic radiation?' – questions which are excluded by saying that the light *is* the electromagnetic radiation. Similarly, the purpose of saying that pains are brain states is precisely to exclude from empirical meaningfulness the questions 'What is the pain, then, if it isn't the same as the brain state?' and 'What makes the pain accompany the brain state?' If there are grounds to suggest that these questions represent, so to speak, the wrong way to look at the matter, then those grounds are grounds for a theoretical identification of pains with brain states.

If all arguments to the contrary are unconvincing, shall we then conclude that it is meaningful (and perhaps true) to say either that pains are brain states or that pain states are brain states?

(1) It is perfectly meaningful (violates no 'rule of English', involves no 'extension of usage') to say 'pains are brain states'.

(2) It is not meaningful (involves a 'changing of meaning' or 'an extension of usage', etc.) to say 'pains are brain states'.

My own position is not expressed by either (1) or (2). It seems to me that the notions 'change of meaning' and 'extension of usage' are simply so ill defined that one cannot in fact say *either* (1) or (2). I see no reason to believe that either the linguist, or the man-on-the-street, or the philosopher possesses today a notion of 'change of meaning' applicable to such cases as the one we have been discussing. The *job* for which the notion of change of meaning was developed in the history of the language was just a *much* cruder job than this one.

But, if we don't assert either (1) or (2) – in other words, if we regard the 'change of meaning' issue as a pseudo-issue in this case – then how are we to discuss the question with which we started? 'Is pain a brain state?'

The answer is to allow statements of the form 'pain is A', where 'pain' and 'A' are in no sense synonyms, and to see whether any such statement can be found which might be acceptable on empirical and methodological grounds. This is what we shall now proceed to do.

II. Is pain a brain state?

We shall discuss 'Is pain a brain state?' then. And we have agreed to waive the 'change of meaning' issue.

Since I am discussing not what the concept of pain comes to, but what pain is, in a sense of 'is' which requires empirical theory-construction (or, at least, empirical speculation), I shall not apologize for advancing an empirical hypothesis. Indeed, my strategy will be to argue that pain is *not* a brain state, not on *a priori* grounds, but on the grounds that another hypothesis is more plausible. The detailed development and verification of my hypothesis would be just as Utopian a task as the detailed development and verification of the brain-state hypothesis. But the putting-forward, not of detailed and scientifically 'finished' hypotheses, but of schemata for hypotheses, has long been a function of philosophy. I shall, in short, argue that pain is not a brain state, in the sense of a physical-chemical state of the brain (or even the whole nervous system), but another *kind* of state entirely. I propose the hypothesis that pain, or the state of being in pain, is a functional state of a whole organism.

To explain this it is necessary to introduce some technical notions. In previous papers I have explained the notion of a Turing Machine and discussed the use of this notion as a model for an organism. The notion of a Probabilistic Automaton is defined similarly to a Turing Machine, except that the transitions between 'states' are allowed to be with various probabilities rather than being 'deterministic'. (Of course, a Turing Machine is simply a special kind of Probabilistic Automaton, one with transition probabilities 0, 1). I shall assume the notion of a Probabilistic Automaton has been generalized to allow for 'sensory inputs' and 'motor outputs' – that is, the Machine Table specifies, for

433

every possible combination of a 'state' and a complete set of 'sensory inputs', an 'instruction' which determines the probability of the next 'state', and also the probabilities of the 'motor outputs'. (This replaces the idea of the Machine as printing on a tape.) I shall also assume that the physical realization of the sense organs responsible for the various inputs, and of the motor organs, is specified, but that the 'states' and the 'inputs' themselves are, as usual, specified only 'implicitly' – i.e. by the set of transition probabilities given by the Machine Table.

Since an empirically given system can simultaneously be a 'physical realization' of many different Probabilistic Automata, I introduce the notion of a *Description* of a system. A Description of S where S is a system, is any true statement to the effect that S possesses distinct states $S_1, S_2 \ldots S_n$ which are related to one another and to the motor outputs and sensory inputs by the transition probabilities given in such-and-such a Machine Table. The Machine Table mentioned in the Description will then be called the Functional Organization of S relative to that Description, and the S_i such that S is in state S_i at a given time will be called the Total State of S (at the time) relative to that Description. It should be noted that knowing the Total State of a system relative to a Description involves knowing a good deal about how the system is likely to 'behave', given various combinations of sensory inputs, but does *not* involve knowing the physical realization of the S_i as, e.g. physical-chemical states of the brain. The S_i, to repeat, are specified only *implicitly* by the Description – i.e. specified *only* by the set of transition probabilities given in the Machine Table.

The hypothesis that 'being in pain is a functional state of the organism' may now be spelled out more exactly as follows:

(1) All organisms capable of feeling pain are Probabilistic Automata.

(2) Every organism capable of feeling pain possesses at least one Description of a certain kind (i.e. being capable of feeling pain *is* possessing an appropriate kind of Functional Organization).

(3) No organism capable of feeling pain possesses a decomposition into parts which separately possess Descriptions of the kind referred to in (2).

(4) For every Description of the kind referred to in (2), there exists a subset of the sensory inputs such that an organism with that Description is in pain when and only when some of its sensory inputs are in that subset.

This hypothesis is admittedly vague, though surely no vaguer than the brain-state hypothesis in its present form. For example, one would like to know more about the kind of Functional Organization that an organism must have to be capable of feeling pain, and more about the marks that distinguish the subset of the sensory inputs referred to in (4). With respect to the first question, one can probably say that the Functional Organization must include something that resembles a 'preference function', or at least a preference partial ordering and something that resembles an 'inductive logic' (i.e. the Machine must be able to 'learn from experience'). (The meaning of these conditions, for Automata models, is discussed in the previous chapter.) In addition, it seems natural to require that the Machine possess 'pain sensors', i.e. sensory organs which normally signal damage to the Machine's body, or dangerous temperatures, pressures, etc., which transmit a special subset of the inputs, the subset referred to in (4). Finally, and with respect to the second question, we would want to require at least that the inputs in the distinguished subset have a high disvalue on the Machine's preference function or ordering (further conditions are discussed in the previous chapter). The purpose of condition (3) is to rule out such 'organisms' (if they can count as such) as swarms of bees as single pain-feelers. The condition (1) is, obviously, redundant, and is only introduced for expository reasons. (It is, in fact, empty, since everything is a Probabilistic Automaton under *some* Description.)

I contend, in passing, that this hypothesis, in spite of its admitted vagueness, is far *less* vague than the 'physical-chemical state' hypothesis is today, and far more susceptible to investigation of both a mathematical and an empirical kind. Indeed, to investigate this hypothesis is just to attempt to produce 'mechanical' models of organisms – and isn't this, in a sense, just what psychology is about? The difficult step, of course, will be to pass from models to *specific* organisms to a *normal form* for the psychological description of organisms – for this is what is required to make (2) and (4) precise. But this too seems to be an inevitable part of the program of psychology.

I shall now compare the hypothesis just advanced with (a) the hypothesis that pain is a brain state, and (b) the hypothesis that pain is a behavior disposition.

III. Functional state versus brain state

It may, perhaps, be asked if I am not somewhat unfair in taking the brain-state theorist to be talking about *physical-chemical* states of the brain. But (a) these are the only sorts of states ever mentioned by brain-state theorists. (b) The brain-state theorist usually mentions (with a certain pride, slightly reminiscent of the Village Atheist) the incompatibility of his hypothesis with all forms of dualism and mentalism. This is natural if physical-chemical states of the brain are what is at issue. However, functional states of whole systems are something quite different. In particular, the functional-state hypothesis is *not* incompatible with dualism! Although it goes without saying that the hypothesis is 'mechanistic' in its inspiration, it is a slightly remarkable fact that a system consisting of a body and a 'soul', if such things there be, can perfectly well be a Probabilistic Automaton. (c) One argument advanced by Smart is that the brain-state theory assumes only 'physical' properties, and Smart finds 'non-physical' properties unintelligible. The Total States and the 'inputs' defined above are, of course, neither mental nor physical *per se*, and I cannot imagine a functionalist advancing this argument. (d) If the brain-state theorist does mean (or at least allow) states other than physical-chemical states, then his hypothesis is completely empty, at least until he specifies *what* sort of 'states' he *does* mean.

Taking the brain-state hypothesis in this way, then, what reasons are there to prefer the functional-state hypothesis over the brain-state hypothesis? Consider what the brain-state theorist has to do to make good his claims. He has to specify a physical-chemical state such that *any* organism (not just a mammal) is in pain if and only if (a) it possesses a brain of a suitable physical-chemical structure; and (b) its brain is in that physical-chemical state. This means that the physical-chemical state in question must be a possible state of a mammalian brain, a reptilian brain, a mollusc's brain (octopuses are mollusca, and certainly feel pain), etc. At the same time, it must *not* be a possible (physically possible) state of the brain of any physically possible creature that cannot feel pain. Even if such a state can be found, it must be nomologically certain that it will also be a state of the brain of any extraterrestrial life that may be found that will be capable of feeling pain before we can even entertain the supposition that it may *be* pain.

It is not altogether impossible that such a state will be found. Even though octopus and mammal are examples of parallel (rather than sequential) evolution, for example, virtually identical structures (physically speaking) have evolved in the eye of the octopus and in the eye of the mammal, notwithstanding the fact that this organ has evolved from different kinds of cells in the two cases. Thus it is at least possible that parallel evolution, all over the universe, might *always* lead to *one and the same* physical 'correlate' of pain. But this is certainly an ambitious hypothesis.

Finally, the hypothesis becomes still more ambitious when we realize that the brain-state theorist is not just saying that *pain* is a brain state; he is, of course, concerned to maintain that *every* psychological state is a brain state. Thus if we can find even one psychological predicate which can clearly be applied to both a mammal and an octopus (say 'hungry'), but whose physical-chemical 'correlate' is different in the two cases, the brain-state theory has collapsed. It seems to me over-whelmingly probable that we can do this. Granted, in such a case the brain-state theorist can save himself by *ad hoc* assumptions (e.g. defining the disjunction of two states to be a single 'physical-chemical state'), but this does not have to be taken seriously.

Turning now to the considerations *for* the functional-state theory, let us begin with the fact that we identify organisms as in pain, or hungry, or angry, or in heat, etc., on the basis of their *behavior*. But it is a truism that similarities in the behavior of two systems are at least a reason to suspect similarities in the functional organization of the two systems, and a much *weaker* reason to suspect similarities in the actual physical details. Moreover, we expect the various psychological states – at least the basic ones, such as hunger, thirst, aggression, etc. – to have more or less similar 'transition probabilities' (within wide and ill defined limits, to be sure) with each other and with behavior in the case of different species, because this is an artifact of the way in which we identify these states. Thus, we would not count an animal as *thirsty* if its 'unsatiated' behavior did not seem to be directed toward drinking and was not followed by 'satiation for liquid'. Thus any animal that we count as capable of these various states will at least *seem* to have a certain rough kind of functional organization. And, as already remarked, if the program of finding psychological laws that are not species-specific – i.e. of finding a normal form for psychological theories of different species – ever succeeds, then it will bring in its wake a deline-ation of the kind of functional organization that is necessary and suffi-cient for a given psychological state, as well as a precise definition of the notion 'psychological state'. In contrast, the brain-state theorist has to hope for the eventual development of neurophysiological laws that are species-independent, which seems much less reasonable than the hope that psychological laws (of a sufficiently general kind) may be species-independent, or, still weaker, that a species-independent *form* can be found in which psychological laws can be written.

IV. Functional state versus behavior-disposition

The theory that being in pain is neither a brain state nor a functional state but a behavior disposition has one apparent advantage: it appears to agree with the way in which we verify that organisms are in pain. We do not in practice know anything about the brain state of an animal when we say that it is in pain; and we possess little if any knowledge of its functional organization, except in a crude intuitive way. In fact, however, this 'advantage' is no advantage at all: for, although statements about how we verify that x is A may have a good deal to do with what the concept of being A comes to, they have precious little to do with what the property A *is*. To argue on the ground just mentioned that pain is neither a brain state nor a functional state is like arguing that heat is not mean molecular kinetic energy from the fact that ordinary people do not (they think) ascertain the mean molecular kinetic energy of something when they verify that it is hot or cold. It is not necessary that they should; what is necessary is that the marks that they take as indications of heat should in fact be explained by the mean molecular kinetic energy. And, similarly, it is necessary to our hypothesis that the marks that are taken as behavioral indications of pain should be explained by the fact that the organism is a functional state of the appropriate kind, but not that speakers should *know* that this is so.

The difficulties with 'behavior disposition' accounts are so well known that I shall do little more than recall them here. The difficulty – it appears to be more than a 'difficulty,' in fact – of specifying the required behavior disposition except as 'the disposition of X to behave as if X were in *pain*', is the chief one, of course. In contrast, we *can* specify the functional state with which we propose to identify pain, at least roughly, without using the notion of pain. Namely, the functional state we have in mind is the state of receiving sensory inputs which play a certain role in the Functional Organization of the organism. This role is characterized, at least partially, by the fact that the sense organs responsible for the inputs in question are organs whose function is to detect damage to the body, or dangerous extremes of temperature, pressure, etc., and by the fact that the 'inputs' themselves, whatever their physical realization, represent a condition that the organism assigns a high disvalue to. As I stressed in 'The mental life of some machines' (chapter 20) this does *not* mean that the Machine will always *avoid* being in the condition in question ('pain'); it only means that the condition will be avoided unless not avoiding it is necessary to the attainment of some more highly valued goal. Since the behavior of the Machine (in this case, an organism) will depend not merely on the sensory inputs, but also on the Total State (i.e. on other values, beliefs, etc.), it seems hopeless to make any general statement about how an organism in such a condition *must* behave; but this does not mean that we must abandon hope of characterizing the condition. Indeed, we have just characterized it.†

† In 'The mental life of some machines' a further, and somewhat independent, characteristic of the pain inputs is discussed in terms of Automata models – namely

Not only does the behavior-disposition theory seem hopelessly vague; if the 'behavior' referred to is peripheral behavior, and the relevant stimuli are peripheral stimuli (e.g. we do not say anything about what the organism will do if its brain is operated upon), then the theory seems clearly false. For example, two animals with all motor nerves cut will have the same actual and potential 'behavior' (namely, none to speak of); but if one has cut pain fibers and the other has uncut pain fibers, then one will feel pain and the other won't. Again, if one person has cut pain fibers, and another suppresses all pain responses deliberately due to some strong compulsion, then the actual and potential peripheral behavior may be the same, but one will feel pain and the other won't. (Some philosophers maintain that this last case is conceptually impossible, but the only evidence for this appears to be that *they* can't, or don't want to, conceive of it.)† If, instead of pain, we take some sensation the 'bodily expression' of which is easier to suppress – say, a slight coolness in one's left little finger – the case becomes even clearer.

Finally, even if there *were* some behavior disposition invariantly correlated with pain (species-independently!), and specifiable without using the term 'pain', it would still be more plausible to identify being in pain with some state whose presence *explains* this behavior disposition – the brain state or functional state – than with the behavior disposition itself. Such considerations of plausibility may be somewhat subjective; but if other things *were* equal (of course, they aren't) why shouldn't we allow considerations of plausibility to play the deciding role?

V. Methodological considerations

So far we have considered only what might be called the 'empirical' reasons for saying that being in pain is a functional state, rather than a brain state or a behavior disposition; namely, that it seems more likely that the functional state we described is invariantly 'correlated' with pain, species-independently, than that there is either a physical-chemical state of the brain (must an organism have a *brain* to feel pain? perhaps some ganglia will do) or a behavior disposition so correlated. If this is correct, then it follows that the identification we proposed is at least a candidate for consideration. What of methodological considerations?

The methodological considerations are roughly similar in all cases of

the spontaneity of the inclination to withdraw the injured part, etc. This raises the question, which is discussed in that chapter, of giving a functional analysis of the notion of a spontaneous inclination. Of course, still further characteristics come readily to mind – for example, that feelings of pain are (or seem to be) *located* in the parts of the body.

† Cf. the discussion of 'super-spartans' in chapter 16.

reduction, so no surprises need be expected here. First, identification of psychological states with functional states means that the laws of psychology can be derived from statements of the form 'such-and-such organisms have such-and-such Descriptions' together with the identification statements ('being in pain is such-and-such a functional state', etc.). Secondly, the presence of the functional state (i.e. of inputs which play the role we have described in the Functional Organization of the organism) is not merely 'correlated with' but actually explains the pain behavior on the part of the organism. Thirdly, the identification serves to exclude questions which (if a naturalistic view is correct) represent an altogether wrong way of looking at the matter, e.g. 'What *is* pain if it isn't either the brain state or the functional state?' and 'What causes the pain to be always accompanied by this sort of functional state?' In short, the identification is to be tentatively accepted as a theory which leads to both fruitful predictions and to fruitful *questions*, and which serves to discourage fruitless and empirically senseless questions, where by 'empirically senseless' I mean 'senseless' not merely from the standpoint of verification, but from the standpoint of what there in fact *is*.

22

Logical positivism and the philosophy of mind*

Any discussion of the influence of logical positivism on the field of philosophy of mind will have to include the application of the so-called verifiability theory of meaning to the problems of this field. Also deserving attention, however, is the way in which Carnap and some of his followers have treated psychological terms – including everyday psychological terms such as 'pain' – as what in their own special sense they called theoretical terms; they have suggested that the states referred to by those theoretical terms might, in reality, be neurophysiological states of the brain.

The two lines of thought mentioned roughly correspond to two temporal stages in the development of the movement. During the early years (1928–36) attempts were made to apply verificationist ideas in a wholesale and simplistic manner to all the problems of philosophy, including the philosophy of mind. In recent years (1955 to the present) a much more sophisticated analysis has been offered, but it is one heavily weighted with the observational-theoretical dichotomy and with the idea of a 'partially interpreted calculus'. Feigl's identity theory (Feigl, 1958), while very much an individual doctrine and never the view of the whole school, fits chronologically into the transitional years between the two periods.

These two lines of thought also correspond to decidedly different tendencies warring within the divided logical-positivist soul. Verificationism, I think, may fairly be labelled an 'idealist' tendency; for, even if it is not identical with the view that the 'hard facts' are just actual and potential experiences, it makes little sense to anyone who does not have some such metaphysical conviction lurking in his heart. The view that mental states are really neurophysiological states is, on the other hand, a classical materialist view. And Feigl's identity theory is an attempt to reconcile the view that all events are physical (a version of materialism) with the view that there are 'raw feels' (Feigl's term for sense data) and that each of us has a concept of these 'raw feels' which is radically independent of public language. In short, Feigl seeks to keep

* First published in P. Achinstein and S. Barker (eds.) *The Legacy of Logical Positivism* (Baltimore, 1969). Reprinted by permission of Johns Hopkins Press.

441

the private entities of classical empiricism but to incorporate them somehow into the world scheme of classical materialism.

My criticisms of logical positivism are basically two: that verificationism is both wrong in itself and incompatible with the materialism to which the logical-positivist philosophers clearly feel attracted; and that the particular versions of materialism developed by these philosophers are not tenable, even though materialism as a tendency in the philosophy of mind *is* tenable, I believe.

The criticism that verificationism is wrong in itself needs little arguing. It simply is not the case that in any customary sense of the term 'meaning' only those linguistic expressions which have a method of verification are meaningful. Indeed, in any customary sense of the phrase 'method of verification', it is not linguistic expressions, but rather what linguistic expressions are used to say, that has a method of verification. This latter criticism can perhaps be turned by saying that a linguistic expression (say, a sentence type) may stand in the triadic relation

$$S \text{ is verifiable as understood by } O \text{ at time } t, \qquad (1)$$

and to say 'S is verifiable' is simply a harmless abstraction from a particular speaker O (or class of speakers) at a particular time t (or class of times). But, even if we allow this, it still remains the case that there are many, many sentences which are meaningful in the customary sense – that is, which are fully grammatical, occur in standard contexts, do not evoke *linguistic* puzzlement by hearers, are readily paraphrased – but which are not verifiable. One reply that logical positivists sometimes offer to this objection is that their theory of meaning is an *explication*, not a description of usage, and that an explication need not conform exactly to pre-analytic usage. This reply is disingenuous, however. For, in order that it should do what the positivists wanted it to do – rule out metaphysics, normative ethics, etc. – it was necessary that their explication of the term 'meaning' *fail* to capture the customary linguistic notion of *meaning*. What we have here is a *persuasive redefinition* and not an explication at all.

The positivists recognized this early and gave up claiming that they explicated the notion of 'meaning'. Instead, they began to speak of *kinds of meaning*. One kind, they claimed, is 'cognitive meaning', and *this* is what they explicated. I shall not discuss this move except to note that (1) I don't know what a *kind* of meaning would be and (2) in practice, being 'cognitively meaningful' simply comes to *having a truth value*. Thus, what the positivist really did was to shift from the claim that being meaningful is the same as being verifiable to the quite different claim that having a truth value is the same as being verifiable. But this claim also is untenable. The sentence

> There is a gold mountain one mile high and no one knows that there is a gold mountain one mile high. (2)

is, if true, unverifiable. No conceivable experience can show that both conjuncts in (2) are simultaneously true; for any experience that verified the first conjunct would falsify the second, and thus the whole sentence. Yet no one has ever offered the slightest reason for one to think that (2) could not be true in some possible world.

One might meet this difficulty by pointing out that (2) can be falsified, even if it cannot be verified, because any discovery that there is no gold mountain one mile high would falsify (2). But

> There is a gold mountain one mile high and absolute goodness exists. (3)

is also falsifiable, but not verifiable, and no positivist would want to say that (3) taken as a whole was 'cognitively meaningful' (of course, the first conjunct is 'cognitively meaningful').

More important than such *outré* examples, perhaps, is the following reflection. Let us assume that the methods of confirmation and disconfirmation which scientists implicitly use are in principle capable of being formalized. Then note the following theorem about inductive logics.† Given any formalized inductive method (i.e. any formal method for deciding which hypotheses to accept and which hypotheses to reject, or for deciding what quantitative weights are to be assigned to hypotheses, in case one does not like the dichotomy 'accept-reject'), there exist hypotheses containing only observation predicates, which, if true, cannot be discovered to be true by the given inductive logic. In short, if human beings are induction machines – which certainly is the materialist view‡ – then it is not true that, given a meaningful statement,

---

† For inductive logics based on degree of confirmation, this is proved in my '"Degree of confirmation" and inductive logic', chapter 17, volume 1 of these papers. There I propose a method M which somewhat mitigates this result, at least for simple universal laws ('effective hypotheses'). However, by extending the result in that paper, it can be shown that there are hypotheses which, if true, cannot be discovered to be true even by M; these hypotheses have mixed quantifiers in the prefix (i.e. they have the form 'for every x there is a y such that ...'). In general one can show that *no* formalized inductive logic has the property that for *every* hypothesis H expressible in observational language, if one's evidence e_n consists of an exhaustive description of the first n objects in the universe as $n = 1, 2, 3 \ldots$, then some for N, if H is true, the logic will assign a 'high' value to H on e_n whenever $n > N$.

‡ This materialist view may be summed up by the following extension of Church's thesis to *inductive* logic: no system of inductive logic, that is, no system of exact

even in 'observation language', one could *always* discover the truth value of that statement on the basis of a finite amount of observational material using a fixed induction program. It was with this theorem in mind that I spoke before of an incompatibility between verificationism and materialism (though not, of course, in a strict deductive sense); for, given a classical materialist view of those statements which have a truth value, and given the knowledge that a modern materialist has concerning Turing machines, unsolvable problems, etc., it is easy to see that the class of 'cognitively meaningful' sentences does *not* necessarily coincide with the class of sentences whose truth value scientists could in principle discover on the basis of a finite amount of observational material.

As is well known, logical positivists have recently shifted from the criterion 'a sentence has a truth-value if and only if it is confirmable (disconfirmable) in principle' to the criterion 'a sentence has a truth-value if and only if it is a well-formed formula of an "empiricist language,"' (Hempel, 1959). It is required that the primitives of an empiricist language be either observation terms or linked to observational terms by confirmable theories; but it is required of an arbitrary sentence only that it be built out of the primitives in accordance with the usual formation rules.

This last criterion does not seem plausible to me either, but discussion lies beyond the scope of the present paper.† It should be noted that just the 'hypotheses' that the logical positivists originally wanted to proscribe – for example, that the world consists of nothing but sensations – would appear *not* to be ruled out by such a formulation. This, however, seems to me not to be a defect; I believe that the statement that the world consists only of sensations has a truth value, falsity. Nevertheless, the positivists were right in feeling that this statement was an extremely queer one, although wrong in diagnosing the *nature* of its queerness (what is queer about it is *not* that it is unverifiable but that there cannot be a world consisting *only* of sensations). So we are in a strange position. The positivists called our attention to an interesting problem: what is queer about such statements as 'the world consists only of sensations'? But they did not solve the problem. Once we come to see that what is wrong with 'the world consists only of sensations', 'I have sensations but no other human being does', 'the world came into existence five minutes ago', etc., is not *just* unverifiability, and not

directions for deciding what hypotheses to accept, or what weight to assign to hypotheses, etc., on the basis of given evidence, a given list of proposed hypotheses, etc., can be employed by a human computer unless it can also be employed by a Turing machine.

† The view of scientific theory that it presupposes is discussed in chapter 13, volume 1 of these papers.

primarily unverifiability, we may be less tempted to take verifiability as a criterion for *either* meaningfulness *or* possessing a truth value.

The application that was made of verificationism to the philosophy of mind was a simple one. The positivists, as is well known, shifted early from phenomenalism to physicalism, that is, they shifted from the view that the events that verify scientific propositions are subjective events (*my* experiences) to the view that they are public events involving 'observable things' and 'observation predicates'. After this shift it became natural for them to reason as follows: 'What verifies such a statement as "John is in pain" is John's behavior. Knowing what a sentence means is closely linked to knowing what verifies that sentence. So knowing what pain means – or, what comes to the same thing, what is meant by such sentences as "John is in pain.", "John has a pain in his arm.", etc. – is knowing what *kind of behavior* shows that a person is in pain.'

In this way there arose the idea that certain statements of the form 'Normally a person who behaves in such-and-such a way has a pain in his arm' are true by virtue of the meaning of the word 'pain', or more loosely, that some particular connections between pain and pain behavior are built into the concept of pain, in the sense that no one can be totally ignorant of those connections and have that concept.

I have argued in chapters 15 and 16 that this is quite mistaken, and I shall not repeat the argument in detail here. Suffice it to say that with a little imagination one can easily imagine worlds in which people feel pain but manifest it in the most extraordinary ways (or do not manifest it at all). Moreover, such people might have the concept of pain by any sane standard, but they certainly would not believe that, for example, normally when someone winces he is in pain (because this would be false in their world). Possessing the concept of pain simply is *not* the same thing as knowing what connections in fact obtain between pain and pain behavior.

How do we know that others are in pain when they are? The positivists' answer to this question depended on two views: (1) to know the meaning of the word 'pain' *is* simply to know that when people behave in certain ways they are probably in pain and (2) it is a necessary truth that when people behave in those ways they are probably in pain. Thus, the positivists' failure to answer successfully the question 'What is it to have the concept of pain?' involved them in a failure to answer successfully a much more traditional philosophical question, 'How do we know what others are feeling?'

I want to suggest that the solution to each of these problems lies elsewhere than where the positivists sought. Let me begin with the problem of other minds. I think that we should neither minimize the difficulty of that problem nor overlook the extent to which that difficulty may stem from the overwhelming difficulty of understanding the procedures of empirical inquiry – especially if we are restricted to arm-chair reflection.

The first fact that has to be noted in connection with such terms as 'pain' is that they *enter into explanations*. Indeed, just how much of the behavior of others *can* we explain at all perspicuously *without* using some psychological term or other? The second fact that has to be noted is that *no other explanation is in the field*, at least not at the moment. If Othello did not strangle Desdemona because he was jealous, then I do not know why he did. And, if no alternative explanation is available in this single case, how much less do we possess an explanation of behavior which would cover *all* cases at least as well as present-day mentalistic explanation does, and without using a single such notion as pain, jealousy, belief, etc.

So far I have suggested that we are justified in accepting the usual psychological explanation scheme because of its explanatory success and the lack of a real alternative. And, of course, if we are justified in accept-ing the general scheme (and this means accepting many general prin-ciples and many specific explanations), then there is no mystery about how we are justified in accepting or rejecting any given proposed new application of the scheme. But am I, then, saying that the existence of others' pain, jealousy, belief, etc., is an *empirical hypothesis*?

The answer has to be a straightforward 'Yes and no'. The question, first of all, is not the acceptance of one statement – for example, 'Other humans have feelings' – but the acceptance of a whole conceptual system, as Ziff has stressed (Ziff, 1966). The acceptance of that conceptual system, or explanatory scheme, is justified, as is the acceptance of many an empirical hypothesis, by the joint facts of explanatory power and no real alternative. But that does not mean that that scheme or system fits the usual paradigm of an 'empirical hypothesis'.

It would take a long paper to cover all of the differences, for example, that no alternative was *ever* in the field, although different *applications* of the scheme and different proposed *extensions* of the scheme (e.g. psychoanalysis) are very much with us. And, of course, I am not suggesting that the following sequence of events took place – that there was a primitive time at which no one supposed that anyone else had feelings; that some primitive genius suggested the 'hypothesis' that others did have feelings; and that this 'hypothesis' was accepted because it led to more successful prediction and explanation than did some alternatives. Nevertheless, I *am* suggesting that each of us has an *empirical justification*, in a good sense of the term, for accepting the explanatory scheme we have been talking about.

The most difficult problem is to dispose of such 'hypotheses' as the one according to which other human bodies are really moved by a demon (see Plantinga, 1965) whose chief aim is to fool me into thinking falsely that those bodies are the bodies of conscious persons. It is easy to 'explain' specific pieces of behavior on the basis of this hypothesis: for example, one could 'explain' why Othello strangled Desdemona by saying that the demon caused him to go through those motions because the demon wished me to believe that Othello was experiencing jealousy. And such a 'hypothesis' may easily be elaborated so as to lead to pre-dictions – indeed, to *just* the predictions that usual theory leads to, and without explicitly mentioning usual theory. It suffices that wherever usual theory (which is, of course, implicit) states that people who are jealous normally do X, demon theory should state that, when the demon wishes some body to act as if it were the body of a person experiencing jealousy, he normally makes that body do X.

The nub of the matter is that, inasmuch as usual theory and demon theory lead to the same predictions, our grounds for preferring usual theory, and for not considering demon theory to be even 'in the field', must be *a priori* ones. And, indeed, it seems that, in large part, the methods of empirical inquiry must be methods for *assigning an a priori preference ordering* (or, better, a *partly a priori* preference ordering) to hypotheses. What these methods are is something we today know little of; it is relatively easy to show that the vague talk about simplicity one commonly hears achieves nothing at all. My own view is that it is only by hard *empirical* research, including research into the construction of *machines that learn*, that we will ever obtain an answer. Philosophical reflection cannot do it – or, at least there is not one shred of evidence to show that it can. But that does not change the fact that we *do* hold demon theory to be so much less plausible *a priori* than is usual theory that we do not need to consider it (unless it is modified to lead to *different* predictions than usual theory does). Just as we know that 'Chair the on is floor the.' is an ungrammatical sentence even without possessing a transformational grammar of English, so we sometimes know which theories are *a priori* more plausible than others, without possessing an adequate formalization of the methods of empirical inquiry.

I have now argued that we are entitled to believe certain statements which ascribe pain, etc., to other humans, on grounds that are broadly empirical (the explanatory power of usual theory as a whole, and the

447

lack of a real alternative). I have nowhere suggested that this depends on regarding any part of usual theory as 'analytic' or, more weakly, as presupposed by the concept of pain, anger, etc. *That* issue, however, is not too relevant here. For, if *any* part of usual theory is 'analytic', it surely is *not* the part that describes how people normally behave when they are in pain, etc., nor the part that says that people who are exhibiting certain kinds of behavior are usually in pain (see chapter 16 for a thorough discussion of this issue). Perhaps the meaning of the psychological words does impose *some* constraints on usual theory, but, in any case, not *those* constraints.

The issue of verificationism which we raised at the outset seems also to have been bypassed, at least to some extent. It is compatible with the position taken here that every 'cognitively meaningful' statement should be capable of incorporation into a scientific theory which, *taken as a whole*, is confirmable (although I believe even that to be false†); what is not compatible with the position taken here is that every 'cognitively meaningful' statement should be confirmable in isolation, simply by virtue of what it means. (Thus my criticism of the positivist answer to the 'How do we know' question bears a certain relation to Quine's criticisms of verificationism.)

It is now time to turn to the positivist answer to the 'What do we mean' question. To say what we mean by such a word as 'pain' is, in a sense, a silly enterprise. 'Pain' is a word we acquire through ostensive teaching (alas!). But we may instead raise a question about what conditions one must fulfil in order to have the concept of pain. It seems to me that three conditions (at least) are essential:

1. When one sincerely reports 'I have a pain in my arm', one must in general be reporting a *pain* and not something else.

2. One must have the *reporting use*.

3. One must be able to imagine that others are in pain, and one must possess the linguistic capacity to use such sentences as 'There is a pain in John's arm.' to express what one believes or imagines.

The first condition, perhaps, has not been mentioned often, because of the traditional view in the philosophy of language that any concept (or intension) *determines* its referent. What I am suggesting is that any empirical evidence which might tend to show that certain people are not in what *we* call 'pain' when they are in what *they* call 'pain' would also

† If to be 'incorporated' into a theory T means to be a logical consequence of T, then the existence of *observation sentences* that cannot be incorporated into any hypothesis confirmable by a given inductive logic is a consequence of the theorem mentioned in note † on p. 443. If it is not even true that every observation sentence has this property, then there seems to be no reason at all for believing that every significant 'theoretical sentence' has it.

tend to show that they had a different concept; but there need not be any way of showing that they have a different concept *other* than by showing that what is behind their reports is not *pain*. The fact that we can permissibly use the concept of pain in explicating the concept of having the concept of pain seems to have been overlooked.

The second condition involves the difficulty that the reporting use of 'pain' involves uttering pain utterances partly *because* one is in pain; yet reporting pain by means of a grammatical report is somehow very different from a mere cry. The fact is that a complex causal interaction is involved here which includes both pain and linguistic habits, and today we can give neither a theory nor a perspicuous description of that interaction. Still, we can recognize it well enough when it takes place.

The third condition is, of course, a classical one. It has been dismissed in recent times on the ground that knowing the so-called picture meaning of such sentences as 'John has a pain in his arm.' is *irrelevant*: what one needs to know is the 'cognitive meaning', that is, the method of verification. I am suggesting that, on the contrary, the picture meaning *is* part of the meaning of *pain*, in any customary sense of *meaning*, and that the method of verification is not.

Let me turn now to late positivist doctrine and, in particular, to the doctrine that psychological terms are theoretical terms (Carnap, 1956). Crudely, what this amounts to is the following: the terms 'pain', 'anger', etc., are implicitly defined by a theory, that is, by a body of beliefs which has testable consequences involving behavior. What we mean by these terms in those states of organisms $P_1, P_2, \ldots, P_n$ such that $T(P_1, P_2, \ldots, P_n)$ where $T(P_1, P_2 \ldots, P_n)$ is what usual theory (in a suitable formalization) becomes when we regard the psychological terms $P_1, P_2, \ldots, P_n$ as mere *second-order variables*. Note that in this view the psychological terms have to be *simultaneously* implicitly defined; they cannot be individually defined. Also, the logic of such implicit definition is complex: Carnap has proposed to invoke the somewhat esoteric Hilbert ε-symbol in order to formalize it (Carnap, 1961). However, the general content of the doctrine is clear enough; it is also clearly false, for *no* particular body of connections between behavior and pain, anger, etc., nor, *a fortiori*, any theory which implies such connections, is presupposed by the meaning of pain, anger, etc.

We have here a confusion of two ideas. There is the idea that our grounds for accepting the conceptual scheme of psychology – be it scientific psychology or common-sense mentalistic psychology – are broadly empirical in nature and not completely unlike the grounds for accepting a scientific theory; this, I have urged, is correct. Then there is the idea that the terms occurring in a theory have no meaning apart

449

from the theory; and this is a false doctrine, not just in the case of psychology, but in general. Moreover, it is a doctrine which arises from the positivists' lack of interest in the customary notion of meaning. (Linguistics is the science the positivists have cared least about.) Of course, the positivists might reply that we ought to *change* our customary notions of meaning and truth to fit their rational reconstruction. I do not believe that any good reasons exist for making such a change; but I shall not discuss this here.

The claim that pain might really be a brain state is easily defended in Carnap's view: we have only to note that 'pain', 'anger', etc., mean P_1, P_2, etc., where P_1, P_2, ..., P_n are any states which bear certain causal relations to one another and to behavior, namely, the relations specified by $T(P_1, ..., P_n)$. Inasmuch as it is trivial that there may be brain states which are so related to one another and to behavior, it follows that 'pain', 'anger', etc., may refer to brain states. Unfortunately, this argument rests on two false premises: the premiss concerning the meaning of theoretical terms which has just been criticized, and the premiss that 'pain', 'anger', etc., are theoretical terms in the positivistic sense. This latter premiss is false because these terms have a reporting use and thus would not be implicitly defined *merely* by a theory, even if it were true that theoretical terms are characteristically so defined.

We come, therefore, to the problem of the positivists' relation to materialism. Perhaps the safest statement of materialism is this: that a whole human being is simply a physical system with a certain complex functional organization. This version of materialism is certainly tenable and probably correct, I believe. The difficulty is that, in itself, this version of materialism says nothing about such specific mental states as pain and anger; and, from Hobbes to Carnap, materialists have come to grief when they have tried to fill this lacuna. The difficulty appears to have been a certain limitation of imagination. If a whole human being is just a physical system, then pain, anger, etc., must be physical states for – what else could they be?

I have proposed elsewhere the view that there is a special kind of state, the *functional* state, the notion of which comes from cybernetics and automata theory, which is a natural candidate for a modern materialist theory of mental states. I stress that this suggestion – the suggestion that mental states are, in reality, functional states of certain naturally evolved 'systems' – is not meant to be part of the meaning of mental words. I have already urged in this paper that very little indeed is 'part of the meaning' of mental words. What I have in mind is an empirical identification on all fours with the claim that heat is average kinetic energy.

450

Some materialists may prefer the tentative identification of mental states with brain states. Difficulties will arise, however, as soon as we begin to make cross-specific comparisons. The neurophysiological counterpart of pain may well be one thing in a man and another in, say an octopus. Even if one decides to say 'Well and good. Then *pain* is one thing in a man and a different thing in an octopus', one will be left with the problem of explicating the higher-order property of *being a pain*; and *this* property, I now suggest, will not be a physicochemical one, but a functional one, that is a role in the 'organization' of a 'system'. If any version of materialism is to be defended – be it a brain-state theory or a functional-state theory – the defense will have to involve a study of the logic of theoretical identification, and especially the theoretical identification of *properties*. It cannot be defended merely by reference to the idea of scientific theories as 'partially interpreted calculi'.

The upshot of this discussion is not as wholly critical as it might seem at first. The greatest weakness of positivism, in the philosophy of mind as elsewhere, is that it tries to make the notion of meaning bear too heavy a burden. This is always a bad tendency in analytic philosophy, but it is fatal in a school which begins by scrapping the customary notion of meaning anyway, and which has seriously examined every science *except* linguistics. However, the school also has real merits. It has emphasized the importance of considering whole theories and not just isolated propositions, which is an important insight. It has stressed the importance of the fact that psychological concepts are used in *explanations*, whereas that fact has often been ignored, or its significance (in connection with the 'other minds' issue) minimized. It has pioneered the studies of the logic of theory confirmation and the logic of empirical identification; I have been urging that these are two topics on which we desperately need more knowledge in the philosophy of mind. Above all, it has stressed the intellectual integrity of science and the importance of science as a way of trying to determine the nature of all things – including man's mind. It is these tendencies of logical positivism which I should like to see continued. I believe that the tendency to *philosophically reinterpret* science, which has always been a characteristic of empiricism, far from being a stimulus to the sound methodological work that empiricism, and, in the present century, logical positivism, have inspired, has been the main source of error in these movements. Science does not need positivistic interpretation; but, in the spirit of the best positivist work, it very much needs an analysis of its methods.

Bibliography

Anscombe, G. 1957. *Intention*, Ithaca, New York.

Benacerraf, P. 'Mathematical Truth', *Journal of Philosophy*, 8 November 1973 (70:19, 661–79).

Boyd, R. 1973. 'Realism and scientific epistemology' (unpublished).

Carnap, R. 1947. *Meaning and Necessity*, Chicago.

　1950. *Logical Foundations of Probability*, Chicago.

　1953. 'The interpretation of physics', reprinted in H. Feigl and M. Brodbeck (eds.) *Readings in the Philosophy of Science*, New York, 309–18.

　1956. 'The methodological character of theoretical concepts', in H. Feigl and M. Scriven (eds.) *Minnesota Studies in the Philosophy of Science*, I, Minneapolis, 38–76.

　1961. 'On the use of Hilbert's ε-operator in scientific theories', in A. Robinson (ed.) *Essays on the Foundations of Mathematics*, Jerusalem, 156–63.

Chomsky, N. 1957. *Syntactic Structures*, The Hague.

　1962. 'Explanatory models in linguistics', in E. Nagel, P. Suppes and A. Tarski (eds.) *Logic, Methodology and Philosophy of Science, Proceedings of the 1960 International Congress on History and Philosophy of Science*, Stanford, 528–50.

　1971. *Problems of Knowledge and Freedom*, New York.

Davis, M. 1958. *Computability and Unsolvability*, New York.

Durrell, L. 1960. 'Mneiae', *Collected Poems*, London, 13.

Engels, F. 1959. *Anti-Dühring, Herr Eugen Dühring's Revolution in Science*, New York.

Feigl, H. 1958. 'The "mental" and the "physical"', in H. Feigl, M. Scriven and G. Maxwell (eds.) *Minnesota Studies in the Philosophy of Science*, II, Minneapolis, 370–497.

Feyerabend, P. 1962. 'Explanation, reduction, and empiricism', in H. Feigl and G. Maxwell (eds.) *Minnesota Studies in the Philosophy of Science*, III, Minneapolis, 28–97.

　1963. 'How to be a good empiricist, etc.', in B. Baumrin (ed.) *Philosophy of Science* (The Delaware Seminar, II) New York, 3–40.

Field, H. 1972. 'Tarski's theory of truth', *Journal of Philosophy*, LXIX (13 July), 347–75.

Fodor, J. 1960. 'What do you mean?', *Journal of Philosophy*, LVII, 499–506.

　1965. 'Explanations in Psychology', in M. Black (ed.) *Philosophy in America*, Ithaca, N.Y., 161–79.

Fodor, J. 1968. *Psychological Explanation*, New York.

Geach, P. 1957. *Mental Acts*, London.

Geschwind, N. 1965. 'Disconnexion Syndrome in Animals and Man', *Brain* 88 (1965), Part I, 237–94; Part II, 585–644.

Grice, H. P. 1957. 'Meaning', *Philosophical Review*, LXVI, 3 (July), 377–88.

1968. 'Utterer's meaning, sentence meaning and word meaning', *Foundations of Language*, IV, 3 (August), 225–42.

1969. 'Utterer's meaning and intentions', *Philosophical Review*, LXXVII, 2 (April), 147–77.

Grünbaum, A. 1968. *Geometry and Chronometry in Philosophical Perspective*, Minnesota.

1970. 'Space, time and falsifiability, Part I', *Philosophy of Science*, 37 (December), 469–588.

1973. 'Geometrodynamics and ontology', *The Journal of Philosophy*, LXX, 21 (6 December), 775–800.

Hampshire, S. 1961. *Feeling and Expression*, London.

Hanson, N. 1958. *Patterns of Discovery*, Cambridge.

Harris, Z. 1957. 'Discourse analysis', *Language*, 2, 1–30.

Hempel, C. 1959. 'The empiricist criterion of meaning', in A. J. Ayer (ed.) *Logical Positivism*, Glencoe, Ill., 108–29.

1965. 'The theoretician's dilemma', in his *Aspects of Scientific Exploration*, New York, 173–226.

Jakobson, R. 1959. 'Boas' view of grammatical meaning', *American Anthropologist*, 61, 139–45.

Katz, J. forthcoming. 'Logic and language: a defense of intentionalism', in K. Gunderson (ed.), *Minnesota Studies in the Philosophy of Science*, VIII.

Kemeny, J. and Oppenheim, P. 1956. 'On reduction', *Philosophical Studies* 7, 6–19.

Kleene, S. 1952. *Introduction to Metamathematics*, New York.

Kripke, S. 1972. 'Identity and necessity', in M. Munitz (ed.) *Identity and Individuation*, New York, 135–64.

1972b. 'Naming and necessity', in G. Harman and D. Davidson (eds.) *The Semantics of Natural Language*, Dordrecht, 254–355.

Kuhn, T. 1974. 'Second thoughts on paradigms', in Frederick Suppe (ed.) *The Structure of Scientific Theories*, Urbana, Ill., 459–82.

Lewis, D. 1969. *Convention*, Cambridge, Mass.

Malcolm, N. 1959. *Dreaming*, London and New York.

Marx, K. and Engels, F. 1942. *Selected correspondence 1846–1895*, New York.

Mill, J. S. 1843. *System of Logic*, London.

Misner, C., Thorne, K., and Wheeler, J. 1973. *Gravitation*, San Francisco.

Mothersill, M. 1962. 'Anscombe's account of the practical syllogism', *Philosophical Review*, LXXI, 448–461.

Nagel, E. 1954. 'Probability and the theory of knowledge', *Sovereign Reason*, Illinois.

Oppenheim, P. and Putnam, H. 1958. 'Unity of science as a working hypothesis', in H. Feigl, G. Maxwell and M. Scriven (eds.) *Minnesota Studies in the Philosophy of Science*, II, Minneapolis, 3–36

Peirce, C. 1958. *Collected Papers of Charles Sanders Peirce*, Cambridge, Mass., 5, paragraph 9 (Written 1902).

Plantinga, A., 1965. 'Symposium: the other minds problem. Ziff's other minds', *Journal of Philosophy*, LXII, 20 (October 21), 587–9.

Putnam, H. 1963. 'An examination of Grünbaum's philosophy of space and time' in B. Baumrin (ed.) *Philosophy of Science, the Delaware Seminar*, 2, 1962–1963.

1967. 'The "innateness" hypothesis' etc., *Synthese*, 17, 12–22.

1971. *Philosophy of Logic*, New York.

Quine, W. V. 1951. 'Two dogmas of empiricism', reprinted in *From a Logical Point of View* (Cambridge, Mass., 1953), 20–46.

1957. 'The scope and language of science', *British Journal for the Philosophy of Science*, VIII, 1–17.

1960. *Word and Object*, Cambridge, Mass.

Reichenbach, H. 1938. *Experience and Prediction*, Chicago.

1956. *Space and Time*, New York.

1965. *The Theory of Relativity and A Priori Knowledge*, California.

Scheffler, I. 1967. *Science and Subjectivity*, Indianapolis.

Schilpp, P. (ed.) 1951. *Albert Einstein Philosopher-Scientist*, New York.

Sellars, W. 1962. 'Truth and "correspondence"', *Journal of Philosophy*, LIX, 1 (4 January), 29–55.

1963. 'Abstract entities', *Review of Metaphysics*, XVI, 627–71.

1964. 'Notes on Intentionality', *Journal of Philosophy*, LXI, 655–65.

1967. 'On abstract entities in semantics', in P. A. Schilpp (ed.) *The Philosophy of Rudolf Carnap*, Lasalle, Ill.

Shapere, D. 1969. 'Towards a post-positivistic interpretation of science', in P. Achenstein and S. Barker (eds.) *The Legacy of Logical Positivism*, Baltimore, 115–60.

Shoemaker, S. 1965. 'Symposium: the other minds problem. Comments', *Journal of Philosophy*, LXII, 20 (October 21), 585–7.

Smart, J. 1959. 'Professor Ziff on robots', *Analysis*, XIX, 117–18.

1959b. 'Incompatible colors', *Philosophical Studies*, X, 39–42.

1959c. 'Sensations and brain processes', *Philosophical Review*, LXVIII, 141–56.

Strawson, P. F. and Grice, H. P. 1956. 'In defense of a dogma', *Philosophical Review*, 65, 141–58.

Strawson, P. F. 1959. *Individuals*, London.

Tarski, A. 1951. 'The concept of truth in formalized languages' in his *Logic, Semantics and Metamathematics*, New York, 152–278.

von Neumann, J. and Morgenstern, O. 1953. *A Theory of Games and Economic Behavior*, 3rd ed., Princeton, N.J.

Wilson, N. L. 1959. 'Substances without substrata', *Review of Metaphysics*, 12 (June), 521–39.

Wittgenstein, L. 1953. *Philosophical Investigations*, Oxford.

Ziff, P. 1959. 'The feelings of robots', *Analysis*, XIX, 64–8.

    1960. *Semantic Analysis*, New York.

    1965. 'Symposium: the other minds problem. The simplicity of other minds', *Journal of Philosophy*, LXII, 20 (October 21) 575–84.

    1972. *Understanding Understanding*, New York.

Index

DATE DUE

NOV 21 '77			
GAYLORD			PRINTED IN U.S.A